The Origins of U.S. Po China Sea Islands Dispu

Ownership of the Senkaku Islands in the East China Sea is disputed between China and Japan, though historically the islands have been part of Okinawa, the southernmost islands of the Japanese archipelago. The dispute, which also involves Taiwan, has the potential to be a flashpoint between the two countries if relations become more strained, especially as the exploitation of gas reserves in the adjoining seabed is becoming an increasingly important issue. A key aspect of the dispute is the attitude of the United States, which, surprisingly, has so far refrained from committing itself to supporting the claims of one side or the other, despite its long-standing, strong alliance with Japan. This book charts the development of the Senkaku Islands dispute, and focuses in particular on the negotiations between the United States and Japan prior to the handing back to Japan in 1972 of Okinawa. The book shows how the detailed progress of these negotiations was critical in defining the United States' neutral attitude to the dispute and the problems this position presents.

Robert D. Eldridge is a former Associate Professor of U.S.-Japan Relations at the School of International Public Policy, Osaka University, and a visiting scholar at the Okinawa Institute for Law and Politics, Okinawa International University, both in Japan.

Routledge Security in Asia Series

The Origins of U.S. Policy in the East China Sea Islands Dispute

Okinawa's Reversion and the Senkaku Islands

Robert D. Eldridge

Routledge
Taylor & Francis Group

LONDON AND NEW YORK

First published 2014 by Routledge

2 Park Square, Milton Park, Abingdon, Oxon OX14 4RN

711 Third Avenue, New York, NY 10017, USA

Routledge is an imprint of the Taylor & Francis Group, an informa business

First issued in paperback 2016

British Library Cataloguing in Publication Data
A catalogue record for this book is available from the British Library

Library of Congress Cataloging in Publication Data
Eldridge, Robert D.
   The origins of U.S. policy in the East China Sea islands dispute : Okinawa's reversion and the Senkaku Islands / Robert D. Eldridge
      pages cm. -- (Routledge security in Asia series)
   Summary: "Ownership of the Senkaku Islands in the East China Sea is disputed between China and Japan, though historically the islands have been part of Okinawa, the southernmost islands of the Japanese archipelago. The dispute, which also involves Taiwan, has the potential to be a flashpoint between the two countries if relations become more strained, especially as the exploitation of gas reserves in the adjoining seabed is becoming an increasingly important issue. A key aspect of the dispute is the attitude of the United States, which, surprisingly, has so far refrained from committing itself to supporting the claims of one side or the other, despite its long-standing, strong alliance with Japan. This book charts the development of the Senkaku Islands dispute, and focuses in particular on the negotiations between the United States and Japan prior to the handing back to Japan in 1970 of Okinawa. The book shows how the detailed progress of these negotiations was critical in defining the United States' neutral attitude to the dispute" -- Provided by publisher.
   Includes bibliographical references and index.
   1. Senkaku Islands--International status. 2. Okinawa Island
(Japan)--International status. 3. United States--Foreign relations--Japan.
4. Japan--Foreign relations--United States. 5. United States--Foreign relations--China.
6. China--Foreign relations--United States. I. Title.
   KZ3881.S46E43 2014
   952'.29--dc23
                  2013024065

ISBN: 978-0-415-62926-3 (hbk)
ISBN: 978-1-138-20424-9 (pbk)

Typeset in Times New Roman
by Taylor & Francis Books

Contents

Illustrations

Figures

Tables

(Images in this book were sourced from Ishigaki City publications and the U.S. National Archives collections with their permission as well as from private donors and the author's collection.)

Preface

In the preface to my book on the Iwo Jima and the Bonin Islands I wrote, "this is a book I never planned to write."[1] If that feeling were true then for that work, it is especially applicable for this book on the Senkaku Islands.

I initially looked at the increasingly regular flare-ups of the Senkaku Islands dispute as essentially one between Japan and the People's Republic of China and the Republic of China (Taiwan), and not one that fit the paradigm of my "intra-alliance" studies of non-traditional "territorial disputes"—namely the retention of administrative control over another country's territory following a peace treaty—between Japan and my country, the United States—that my earlier books on Okinawa, the Amami Islands, and Iwo Jima and the Ogasawara Islands had examined in detail.[2]

And yet, as I delved into the history of the Senkakus more, particularly around the time of the reversion of administrative rights over Okinawa and the remainder of the Ryukyu Islands on May 15, 1972 after twenty-seven years of American occupation and administration, I realized how deeply involved the United States in fact was. True, the Senkaku Islands were not ones that the United States had large or significant bases on or seen as particularly strategically valuable to American interests *at the time* requiring the United States to retain absolute control over them, other than the two now-unused training ranges on Kuba Jima (otherwise known as Kobi Sho) and Taisho Jima (otherwise known as Sekibi Sho).[3]

While the American connection is much less strong today than it was in mid-1972, it is still significant in that a military attack on the Senkaku Islands *would* necessarily *invoke* Article 5 of the 1960 Treaty of Mutual Cooperation and Security between the United States and Japan, which obligates the United States to "act to meet the common danger" in the event of an "armed attack ... in the territories under the administration of Japan."[4] This issue—the obligations of the bilateral security treaty and some of the related problems emerging from the decision of the United States government at the time of Okinawa's reversion to Japan to adopt a "neutral" policy with regard to the sovereignty of the Senkakus—is discussed in the introductory and concluding chapters.

While there are many parallels to events today, this book is not about the contemporary aspects of the Senkaku Islands or East China Sea dispute, per se, which involve issues of sovereignty, security, oil and natural resource development, historical memory, and national pride, between Japan, China, and Taiwan, but instead about the negotiations over the handling of the status of the Senkaku Islands at the time of the reversion of Okinawa and the development of America's "neutrality" policy. The book focuses on the years 1969 to 1972 when the decision to return administrative rights over the Nansei Islands (of which the Ryukyu Islands are a part) south of twenty-nine degrees North Latitude,[5] including the Senkaku Islands, was made and how the negotiations over that return were conducted in the context of the Senkaku Islands. It explains in detail the spontaneous beginning and subsequent deepening of the Senkakus dispute during that period, the pressures placed on the U.S. government by the respective parties, such as official and non-official representatives of Japan, Okinawa, Taiwan, and China, and the calculations made by American leaders then as they re-considered America's long-strained relationship with the People's Republic of China and began to open up relations with the country it had long chosen not to recognize diplomatically. As a result of this leaning toward China, tensions rose in the relationship between Taiwan and the United States on the one hand and Taiwan and Japan on the other over Taiwan's concerns about American and Japanese intentions with regard to China. Similarly, stress existed in the relationship between the United States and Japan over their mutual interactions vis-à-vis China, trade friction, and Japan's role in the world.

This study also examines the situation locally in Okinawa and especially in Ishigaki Island, Miyako Island, and Yonaguni Island—collectively known as the Yaeyama Islands—an approach I have employed in previous books and articles by looking at how local movements affect national, bilateral, and international events, and vice-versa. It finds that while there was a large degree of agreement on the need to protect the Senkaku Islands as Okinawan, and therefore, Japanese, territory, Okinawans did not always view their economic and political interests as the same as those of mainland Japan. They were fearful of mainland companies exploiting the oil and other natural resources discovered to potentially lie in the area near the Senkakus at the expense of Okinawa, thus highlighting another aspect (feelings of neglect and victimization, for example) of the sometimes fractured relationship between Okinawa and mainland Japan.

Many of the issues in the Senkaku Islands dispute remain unresolved today and as such I introduce in the footnotes and elsewhere more recent discussions or other relevant points particularly as they affect the debate today and in the future. Tensions today, in 2013, forty years after the islands' reversion to Japan remain very high and the level of intensity and scale of repercussions grow with each iteration of clashes. I hope this book will be of reference in understanding the history and context of the dispute more, no matter what your interest is—legal, historical, diplomatic, military, or economic—or what your connection is—academic, media, political, government, or military. It goes without saying that the views in this book are my personal ones, and do not necessarily represent those of the U.S. Marine Corps, Department of Defense, or U.S. government. I began this book well before I assumed my current position, and being a historical study, I have not benefitted in any special way in writing it as a result of this position other than being significantly closer physically and psychologically to the center of the conflict than Osaka was.

Robert D. Eldridge
Okinawa Prefecture, Japan,
September 2013,
amid near daily intrusions by Chinese survey vessels and aircraft

Notes

1 Robert D. Eldridge, *Iwo Jima to Ogasawara o Meguru Nichibei Kankei* (Iwo Jima and the Ogasawara Islands in U.S.–Japan Relations) (Kagoshima City: Nanpo Shinsha, 2008). The English version is published as *Iwo Jima and the Bonin Islands in U.S.–Japan Relations: American Strategy, Japanese Territory, and the Islanders In-between* by Marine Corps University Press in 2013.
2 Those two other works were: Robert D. Eldridge, *The Origins of the Bilateral Okinawa Problem: Okinawa in Postwar U.S.-Japan Relations, 1945–1952* (New York: Routledge, 2001), and Robert D. Eldridge, *The Return of the Amami Islands: The Reversion Movement and U.S.-Japan Relations* (Lanham, MD: Lexington, 2004). Both are available in Japanese as well.
3 In U.S.–Japan official documents relating to the training ranges, such as those used in the Joint Committee (JC), United States Forces Japan (USFJ), and Department of the Navy (DON), the islands are curiously called by a Chinese-like name (Kobi Sho and Sekibi Sho) rather than their Japanese readings of Kuba Jima and Taisho Jima, a practice established during the U.S. administration of Okinawa and seemingly continued in the post-reversion period. The names of the islands themselves are prewar in origin.
4 Article 5 of the U.S.–Japan mutual security treaty states in full: "Each Party recognizes that an armed attack against either Party in the territories under the administration of Japan would be dangerous to its own peace and safety and declares that it would act to meet the common danger in accordance with its constitutional provisions and processes. Any such armed attack and all measures taken as a result thereof shall be immediately reported to the Security Council of the United Nations in accordance with the provisions of Article 51 of the Charter. Such measures shall be terminated when the Security Council has taken the measures necessary to restore and maintain international peace and security."
5 Those islands north of twenty-nine degrees North Latitude were returned in 1953. For a detailed study on that reversion process, see Eldridge, *The Return of the Amami Islands*. This date causes some confusion among some writers. For example, authors of Congressional Research Service reports on the Senkakus published in 1996 and 2012, respectively, both state that the U.S. administration for the Senkakus began in 1953, which is incorrect. See Larry A. Niksch, "Senkaku (Diaoyu) Islands Dispute: The U.S. Legal Relationship and Obligations," *CRS Report for Congress*, 96–798F, September 30, 1996, 2, and Mark E. Manyin, "Senkaku (Senkaku Diaoyu/Diaoyutai) Islands Dispute: U.S. Treaty Obligations," *CRS Report for Congress*, 7–5700, September 25, 2012, 3.

Acknowledgments

I have been helped by many people in writing this book and would like to acknowledge them here.

First, my heartfelt gratitude goes to my wife, Emiko, and children, Ami Mary and Kennan Thomas, for their love and encouragement. I did the initial work on this book before I left Osaka University where I was teaching at and the majority of the writing after we had moved to Okinawa. In particular, the family was very cooperative in supporting me in our transition to Okinawa, where I serve as the political and public diplomacy advisor to the Marine Corps, and in allowing me time to write as we balanced my daytime job, their schooling, and our many extracurricular activities

Second, I wish to thank the faculty and staff of both the Okinawa Institute of Law and Politics (*Okinawa Hosei Kenkyusho*) at Okinawa International University (*Okinawa Kokusai Daigaku*) in Ginowan City, Okinawa Prefecture, and the Okinawa International (*Okinawa Bunka Kenkyusho*) at Hosei University (*Hosei Daigaku*) in Tokyo for hosting me as a visiting scholar during the time I was writing this book. The collections at both institutes are truly first-rate, and the staff very kind and supportive.

Third, I wish to thank the many archivists out there who have assisted me: Nakamoto Kazuhiko and the staff of the Okinawa Prefectural Archives (*Okinawaken Kobunshokan*) in Haebaru Town, Okinawa Prefecture; the staff of the University of the Ryukyus Library (*Ryukyu Daigaku Shozoku Toshokan*) in Nishihara Town, Okinawa Prefecture; Kuniyoshi Masafuro and Kuniyoshi Makoma of the Senkaku Islands Materials Editorial Committee (*Senkaku Shoto Bunken Shiryohensankai*) located in Naha; the archivists and staff of National Archives II in College Park, Maryland, and those of the many Presidential libraries throughout the country; the staffs at the National Security Archives in Washington, D.C., especially Dr. Mary Curry, Public Service Coordinator and Research Associate; Stanford University, the staff at the Japanese Foreign Ministry's Diplomatic Records Office, and those at the library on Camp Foster in Okinawa Prefecture, especially Christi A. Bayha; the staff of the Okinawa Prefecture Assembly secretariat (*Okinawa Kengikai Jimukyoku*), and the mayors' secretariats in Ishigaki City and Yonaguni Town, both in Okinawa Prefecture. I also wish to thank several people who helped as research assistants, including Wang Huajia at Stanford University and Allison Hawkey at Georgetown University, who made trips to nearby archives to copy materials for me, and in the case of Huajia to translate the relative passages of Chinese text into English. I wish them the best of luck in their future careers. Similarly, Brian and Ivy Goldman came through with acquiring some materials from Ivy's native Taipei and kindly translated the related sections.

Fourth, I would like to acknowledge the work of those researchers who have gone before me, especially Okuhara Toshio, professor emeritus of international law at Kokushikan University, in Tokyo, who kindly met with me in June 2011 to discuss not only his research but also the individuals he came across as he advised the Japanese government around the time the territorial dispute was beginning. As the bibliography will show, Okuhara was the most prolific writer of the history of Senkaku Islands from a Japanese perspective, and he generously shared with me the full collection of his writings. Two other prolific well-published scholars, both of whom I was unfortunately able to meet due to illnesses, the scientist Dr. Takara Tetsuo (who visited the islands more than any other scholar prior to reversion), and Dr. Midorima Sakae, a Law of the Sea specialist at Okinawa International University, deserve our gratitude for their writings and efforts over the years to increase our understanding of the islands and their legal and historical dynamics. As always, I am also indebted to Dr. Higa Mikio, a retired scholar of Okinawan politics, for his insights into Okinawan views on the Senkakus issue, particularly sharing a perspective on the rather benign views of some of Okinawa's leaders today and in the past regarding China based on the long history of relations between the two. I also enjoyed a discussion on the Senkakus dispute and Taiwan's relationship with Japan I had with Taiwanese international law specialist, Dr. Dustin Kuan-Hsiung Wang, who is an associate professor at the National Taiwan Normal University in Taipei.

Fifth, I wish to thank officials from several countries whom I interviewed or otherwise received assistance from: Ambassador (ret.) Iguchi Takeo, who made the above meeting with Professor Okuhara possible through his introduction, for our many discussions about the work of the Treaties Division of the Ministry of Foreign Affairs (*Gaimusho Joyakukyoku*), at which he worked in the 1970s, and the views of the division with regard to the status of the Senkaku Islands both in the context of Japanese foreign policy as well as in international law; Ambassadors (ret.) Yoshino Bunroku and Numata Sadaaki for their insights into Japanese foreign policy then and now; Charles A. Schmitz, then with the Department of State, who was in charge of the legal aspects of the Okinawa Reversion Agreement, Howard M. McElroy, who was a key player on the Japan desk at the State Department at the time; Daniel C. Sneider, the son of Richard L. Sneider (who headed the U.S. Okinawa reversion negotiating team); the Honorable Philip Wang, a senior diplomat in the Ministry of Foreign Affairs, Republic of China, who provided insights into Taiwanese views on the territorial dispute and its diplomatic style as it relates to its relations with the United States, Japan, and the People's Republic of China.

Sixth, I would like to express my deep appreciation to Peter Sowden and Helen Hurd, both of Routledge, who worked closely with me during the preparation of this manuscript. I have had the opportunity to work with Peter before and have very impressed with his dedication to getting the study out there. Thank you for your confidence in this project as well!

I have had the opportunity to present the contents of the book at different academic meetings, including at the Society for the Historians of American Foreign Relations (SHAFR) in Washington, D.C. in June 2009, the Asiatic Society of Japan in Tokyo in June 2011, and the Fuji School of the Ground Self-Defense Force (*Rikujo Jieitai Fuji Gakko*) in Oyama Town, Shizuoka Prefecture, in June 2012. I also gave a presentation before a large room filled with Marine officers and senior civilians of III Marine Expeditionary Force in October 2010, shortly after the September 2010 flare-up when a Chinese captain of a trawler rammed two Japanese Coast Guard vessels, and a follow-up presentation in September 2012 after tensions had hit a new high before a similar audience. I would like to thank Richard B. Pellish and Major General Christopher S. Owens, commanding general of 1st Marine Air Wing, for arranging those respective opportunities. At each of these venues, I have been asked very good and thoughtful questions, the answers to some of them I hope I have been able to work into this story. Political parties in Japan asked me to present my findings as well, but I declined because of my official position at the time.

I am dedicating this book to Colonel Grant F. Newsham, United States Marine Corps, a long-time friend and mentor of things-Marine and United States–Japan relations, who has experienced with me many significant events and milestones, as well as challenges, over the past-decade plus. There is no one who takes the bilateral alliance more seriously and knows more about it and the issues facing the militaries of the two countries were a contingency to happen near the Senkaku Islands than he. If the leadership of both countries wish to move the United States–Japan bilateral relationship forward and put it on stronger footing politically, militarily, diplomatically, and even economically, his advice should be heeded much more.

Abbreviations

ADCC	Air Defense Command Center
ADIZ	Air Defense Identification Zone
AMOCO	American Oil Company
APEC	Asia-Pacific Economic Cooperation
ASDF	Air Self-Defense Force
CA	Civil Administrator
CCOP	Committee for Coordinating Joint Prospecting for Mineral Resources in Asian Offshore Areas
CGG	Company General de Geophysics
CGP	Clean Government Party
CHICOM	Chinese Communists, Communist China, People's Republic of China
CIA	Central Intelligence Agency
CIB	Central Intelligence Bulletin
CINCPAC	Commander-in-Chief, Pacific
CJOEP	Coordinated Joint Outline Emergency Plan
CNA	Central News Agency
COMUSJAPAN	Commander, United States Forces, Japan
COMUSTDC	Commander, United States Taiwan Defense Command
CONOCO	Continental Oil Company
CPC	Chinese Petroleum Corporation
CRS	Congressional Research Service
DA	Department of Army
DCM	Deputy Chief of Mission
DI	Director of Intelligence
DON	Department of Navy
DSP	Democratic Socialist Party of Japan
ECAFE	Economic Commission for Asia and the Far East
ESCAP	Economic and Social Commission for Asia and the Pacific
GOJ	Government of Japan
GRC	Government of the Republic of China
GRI	Government of the Ryukyu Islands
GSDF	Ground Self-Defense Force

HCRI	High Commissioner, Ryukyu Islands
HICOMRY	High Commissioner, Ryukyu Islands
HKG	Hong Kong Government
IA	International Affairs (U.S. Department of Army)
IBMND	Intelligence Bureau of the Ministry of National Defense
ICJ	International Court of Justice
IGY	International Geophysical Year
IIM	Interagency Intelligence Memorandum
ISA	International Security Affairs (Department of Defense)
JAPEX	Japan Petroleum Exploration Company
JC	Joint Committee
JCG	Japan Coast Guard
JCP	Japan Communist Party
JCS	Joint Chiefs of Staff
JDA	Japan Defense Agency
JFY	Japan Fiscal Year
JGOO	Japan Government Okinawa Office
JMA	Japan Meteorological (Observatory) Agency
JPDPC	Japan Petroleum Development Public Corporation
JSO	Joint Staff Office (Japan Self-Defense Forces)
JSP	Japan Socialist Party
KMT	Kuomintang (Nationalist Party)
LDP	Liberal Democratic Party
LN	Liaison Department, USCAR
MOD	Ministry of Defense
MOFA	Ministry of Foreign Affairs
MSA	Maritime Safety Agency
MSDF	Maritime Self-Defense Force
NCNA	New China News Agency
NPIC	National Photographic Information Center
NSC	National Security Council
OBGI	Office of Basic and Geographic Intelligence
OBONTA	Okinawa Bureau, Okinawa Northern Territories Agency
ODUSA	Office of the Deputy Under Secretary of the Army
OLDP	Okinawa Liberal Democratic Party
OSMP	Okinawa Social Masses Party
POLAD	Political Advisor
PRC	People's Republic of China
PrepCom	Preparatory Committee
PS	Public Safety Department, USCAR
RFY	Ryukyu Fiscal Year
RMA	Ryukyu Meteorological (Observatory) Agency
ROC	Republic of China
ROK	Republic of Korea
RPC	Ryukyu Property Custodian

SDF	Self-Defense Forces
TMG	Tokyo Metropolitan Government
UN	United Nations
UNCLOS	United Nations Convention on the Law of the Sea
UPI	United Press International
USA	United States Army
USAF	United States Air Force
USCAR	United States Civil Administration, Ryukyus
USFJ	United States Forces Japan
USG	United States Government
USGS	United States Geological Survey
USIB	United States Intelligence Board
USIS	United States Information Service
USMC	United States Marine Corps
USN	United States Navy

Introduction

In early 2010, a senior United States military commander on a visit to Japan sat down with a Japanese defense reporter for an on-the-record interview. One of the questions asked concerned the U.S. commitment to defend the Senkaku Islands, which are administered by Japan but also claimed by the China and Taiwan. The three-star general stumbled, a State Department-assigned Political Advisor (POLAD), who seemed unprepared to discuss the topic and a U.S. Embassy official gave incorrect and mixed advice, and the interview immediately went downhill.[1]

INTERVIEWER: … The final skepticism that I found out today is a lack of roles and missions to defend Japan. In case China invades the Senkakus, what would Third Marine Expeditionary Forces (III MEF) do?

U.S. GENERAL: I don't know. That is –

INTERVIEWER: That doesn't sound good, sir. You just said you don't know. It's going to be a headline. Seriously.

U.S. GENERAL: That, the issue of the Senkakus, is a government policy issue that's –

INTERVIEWER: It's the territory of Japan.

U.S. GENERAL: What's that?

INTERVIEWER: It's the territory of Japan.

U.S. GENERAL: Well, it's contentious or at least ambiguous in terms of the U.S. government.

INTERVIEWER: You say you don't defend the Senkakus?

U.S. GENERAL: I don't know. I don't know.

INTERVIEWER: Sir, that's really serious. If you say you don't know, it's going to be a headline. I'll give you a chance to rethink your answer. That's really bad.

U.S. GENERAL: The Senkaku issue is something that's unresolved at the government-to-government level, as far as I know.

INTERVIEWER: Okay, if you stay with that, I'll just go for that.

U.S. EMBASSY OFFICIAL: He's speaking of sovereignty.

INTERVIEWER: But he said he doesn't know.

U.S. EMBASSY OFFICIAL: No, what he said was that the Senkakus don't belong to Japan. From our point of view, they're under the administrative control, and I'm not being interviewed.

INTERVIEWER: Well, I'll just go with what he said, because you're not being interviewed.

U.S. STATE DEPARTMENT OFFICIAL: Can we go back? When he says he doesn't know ...

INTERVIEWER: I only have 20 minutes. You can tell me later.

U.S. EMBASSY OFFICIAL: We'll give you an extra three minutes. What he is saying is—and, sir, I don't mean to speak for you—

U.S. GENERAL: No, what I mean by "I don't know" is there is an ambiguity there at the government-to-government level that's above—it's above my role as an operational commander. I would need guidance for that from the national level. Based on that guidance, I would do what I was told.

INTERVIEWER: So, there is no plan to defend the Senkakus? Because, it's been so much talked about, that there is a possibility the Senkakus would be invaded by Japan. So, as you know, the Self-Defense Forces have a special unit established to defend the Senkakus, and you are saying the Marines in Okinawa don't know how to respond, for Japan?

U.S. GENERAL: No, I did not say that. I didn't say that. I said that if my government tells me to defend the Senkakus, I will be there with everything I got. And I—

INTERVIEWER: But there's no plan, not that you know of?

U.S. GENERAL: No, no, no, I didn't say that. I said if I'm told to do that, then everything I have will be focused on that.

INTERVIEWER: Okay, but you can't tell me exactly what kind of plan you have?

U.S. GENERAL: I cannot.

INTERVIEWER: You don't know whether III MEF will help the Self-Defense Forces to defend the Senkakus or not.

U.S. GENERAL: If I'm told to do that, absolutely they will.

The public reputation of that general and State Department officials, as well as of the bilateral assurance that the U.S. commitment to help defend the Senkakus, remained intact only because that part of the interview was not published through the intervention and pleading of U.S. officials and others who knew the reporter.[2]

It is difficult, however, to blame this one general for his ignorance of the Senkakus issue and inability to give a clearer picture of a U.S. response to a contingency affecting its ally. Indeed, Japanese leaders have made curious comments on the issue, too. For example, when asked by the then-nationalistic governor of Tokyo Ishihara Shintaro (who publicly called for purchasing the islands that were privately owned in an April 18, 2012 speech at the Heritage Foundation in Washington, D.C.[3]) if the Japan–U.S. security treaty would apply in the case of a violent clash between Japan and China over the islands at the *Zenkoku Chijikai* (National Governors Association) meeting on May 27, 2010, Prime Minister Hatoyama Yukio told the participants that he believed the treaty did in fact apply to the islands but that it "is necessary for the authorities of both Japan and China to discuss the sovereignty issue of the

Senkaku Islands."[4] Foreign Minister Okada Katsuya, preoccupied with the preparations for the joint statement on the Marine Corps Air Station Futenma relocation "decision" that same week, stated at his press conference the following day on May 28 that the prime minister's comments were "inappropriate ... There is no territorial problem, nor any room for discussion."[5] A few months later, a clash at sea between a Chinese fishing boat and a Japanese Coast Guard (*Kaijo Hoancho*) vessel, described below, led to a similarly inexplicable attempt to keep the video from the public as well as political pressure on the Japanese prosecutors, based in Okinawa's capital city of Naha, to release the ship's captain and send him back to China.

Even the Congressional Research Service of the Library of Congress, the publicly funded "think tank" of the United States Congress, got parts of the history of the Senkakus wrong including the description in its reports in 1996 and 2012—both at the height of tensions then over the islands. Writing "U.S. administration of the islands began in 1953 (*sic*) as a result of the 1951 Treaty of Peace with Japan," the reports seem to ignore the period from 1945 and almost everything that took place after that.[6]

The episode with the above commander, nevertheless, was emblematic of not only the nagging problem of general American ignorance of the region and the history of our involvement with it, but especially of the unnecessarily complicated policy of the United States with regard to the Senkaku Islands. (The complexity is demonstrated in the above episode with the interview. One could almost write a joke about it: Question—How many U.S. government officials does it take to explain its position on the Senkakus? Answer—three, but they still would have to get back to you with the answer later.)

In a nutshell (albeit a hard one to crack), the United States, as per the Okinawa Reversion Agreement of June 17, 1971 and the related Agreed Minutes (see Appendices 1 and 2), recognized the Senkaku Islands as part of the area for which the United States was returning administrative rights to Japan, but chose at the same time not to take a public position in the dispute between Japan, Taiwan, and China over the ultimate sovereignty of the islands other than to say it hoped the issue would be resolved peacefully between the claimants. This policy—the origins of which are the subject of this book—adopted, in other words, the stance that the islands fell under Japan's administrative control but that the sovereignty of the islands remain disputed. The evidence will show that this new neutrality policy went against previous positions and policies of the U.S. government, and even is inconsistent with the name, Japanese in origin, the United States used then and continues to use today almost exclusively for the islands, the Senkakus.

It goes without saying this stance endeared the United States to no one at the time. It is made worse by the fact that as per the 1960 Treaty of Mutual Security and Cooperation the United States is obligated to help defend territories under the administration of Japan. In other words, if the Senkaku Islands are attacked by a third party, a literal reading of the treaty would obligate the United States to "act to meet the common danger in accordance with its constitutional provisions and processes" even though the United States curiously does not publicly recognize Japan as having sovereignty over them.

The *Wall Street Journal*'s Pulitzer Prize-winning writer Nicholas D. Kristof alluded to this untenable situation immediately after the situation heated up following the September 2010 altercation between a Chinese fishing boat and a Japanese Coast Guard vessel when he wrote: "We're in the absurd position of being committed to help Japan fight a war over islands, even though we don't agree that they are necessarily Japanese."[7] Kristof, who in the above blog entitled "On the Ground," reintroduced his analysis from his 2000 book, *Thunder from the East*, co-authored with this goes on to argue that, "In reality, of course, there is zero chance that the United States will honor its treaty obligation over a few barren rocks. We're not going to risk a nuclear confrontation with China over some islands that may well be China's."[8]

Kristof has followed the issue since the 1980s and seems to have first written about it in an October 1996 *New York Times* thinkpiece entitled "Would You Fight for These Islands?"[9] He tends to believe the historical evidence supports China's arguments that it has sovereignty over the Senkakus and admits to being "sympathetic to China's position," posting an analysis by a Taiwanese research fellow, Han-yi Shaw, entitled "The Inconvenient Truth Behind the Diaoyu/Senkaku Islands."[10] In introducing it, Kristof, the son of political scientist originally from "a country that no longer exists, Austria-Hungary,"[11] stated that while the facts were not "100 percent clear ... I find the evidence for Chinese sovereignty quite compelling."[12] He wrote no such endorsement of a Japanese researcher's response when he simply posted it a couple of weeks later.[13]

As will be examined in this book, although I disagree with almost all of Kristof's description or understanding of the Senkakus dispute, especially his assertions that Japan's claim to the islands is "dubious" and that the Chinese claim is "probably stronger," he and his Chinese-American co-author (and spouse) do provide a valuable service (in addition to their great work in the humanitarian and education fields) by pointing out the above inconsistencies about the relationship to the 1960 U.S.–Japan security treaty for the informed American reader.[14] There are in fact many more inconsistencies with the United States' neutrality stance and the problems it creates vis-à-vis the security relationship with Japan, some of which will be explained in the historical discussion in the following pages and some others in the Conclusion itself.

As Kristof and others correctly point out, it may be unclear if the treaty commitment to Japan would be honored or not (although I think it would be), but what is quite apparent is that the U.S. government would be in a very difficult position vis-à-vis its own public and Congress over how to explain to the American people and their elected officials that the United States would be helping—and possibly dying on behalf of—an ally to defend territory that the U.S. government does not even recognize its ally as owning. Indeed, over the years, the United States has publicly wavered on whether it would help defend the islands. These vacillations and inconsistencies over the years, which some would call "strategic ambiguity," certainly do not inspire confidence and can easily lead to miscalculations by the different parties involved.

The possibility of a serious miscalculation did not become a big issue until 1996, when tensions rose to a high point, both in the Taiwan Strait as well as in the connection with the Senkaku Islands. In fact, over the years, there had been numerous frictions between Japan and China surrounding the Senkakus, such as the April 1978 dispatch of 200 fishing vessels to the Senkaku Islands and the competing claims by Japanese rightists that led to the landing on Uotsuri and building of a lighthouse by the Japan Youth Federation (*Nihon Seinensha*, or JYF[15]), and a fall 1990 attempt by Taiwanese activists to plant a torch on the island, among other issues. Following the U.S. withdrawal from the Philippines in November 1991 and China's declaration in February 1992 of the Law of the People's Republic of China on the territorial sea and the contiguous zone, which affirmed its sovereignty over all several archipelagos and islands, concern began to grow considerably over China's intentions, particularly in light of its crackdown at Tiananmen Square in 1989 and its rise as a new threat replacing the Soviet Union which had collapsed in 1991.

Beginning in 1995, China sent ocean surveillance ships and oil drilling rigs into the waters near the islands in an effort to tap the resources in the area.[16] In March 1996, China conducted missile tests near Taiwan, prompting the U.S. Seventh Fleet to dispatch its aircraft carrier to the area. In mid-July, a couple of days after Japan ratified the United Nations Convention on the Law of the Sea, the Japan Youth Federation built a second lighthouse in the Senkakus, this time on Kita Kojima, and later that month, the JYF applied for it to be recognized as an official lighthouse. The following month, the Senkaku Islands Defense Association (*Senkaku Shoto Boei Kyokai*), established in 1994 and headed by Megumi Chukyu, who was long involved in the Senkakus and other nationalistic issues, placed a Japanese flag next to the lighthouse on Uotsuri Island on August 18.[17] At that time, the six members of the team who went to Uotsuri also put up a sign in recognition of the existence of the village, and another sign honoring the victims of a sinking of two boats evacuating Ishigaki toward the end of World War II (discussed in Chapter 1).[18]

Later that month, Foreign Minister Ikeda Yukihiko, who was visiting Hong Kong prior to the territory's reversion to China after a century and a half under British control, commented that the Senkaku Islands have always been Japan's, and had effectively governed the islands so that a territorial problem did not exist. His remarks not only inflamed the Daioyu movement in Hong Kong, but also caused the Chinese government to issue a warning in an editorial in the *People's Daily*: "whoever expects the 1.2 billion Chinese people to give up even one inch of their territory is only daydreaming."[19] A Chinese Foreign Ministry spokesman offered to shelve the sovereignty dispute in favor of joint development of the resources in the area, but warned that China would not make any compromises on the sovereignty issue and cautioned against unilateral action that might lead to an escalation of the dispute.[20] On September 9, however, members of the JYF returned to Kita Kojima to repair the new lighthouse, which had been damaged by a typhoon, and reapplied for recognition of the lighthouse.

Questions began to be asked of the State Department about the American stance at this point and the U.S. government became once again publicly drawn into the dispute. On September 16 Kristof published a story which included comments by U.S. Ambassador to Japan Walter F. Mondale that the latter had said the USG "takes no position on who owns the islands and has said American forces would not be compelled by the treaty to intervene in a dispute over them."[21]

Kristof was referring to an interview he had done with Mondale in 1995 "before the issue became a hot topic and officials clammed up" when the ambassador "suggested what is common sense: that seizure of the islands would not automatically set off the security treaty and force American military intervention. In another interview early this year, [Mondale] expertly dodged the question but made an analogy to Taiwan, where the American policy is that the United States has no obligation to respond to a Chinese attack—but that it might anyway."[22] Mondale later regretted his remarks, confessing he "was misquoted but [it was] partly my fault. I should have realized earlier just how delicate an issue this was for Japan."[23] Mondale unfortunately does not discuss this issue in his memoirs, although he devoted a full chapter to his ambassadorship.[24]

Ishihara Shintaro, at the time a member of the member of the Lower House (since November 1972), exploded and publicly criticized Mondale as "unqualified as a diplomat (*gaikokan to shite wa futekikaku*)" in an early November commentary he wrote for a conservative newspaper,[25] and according to Ishihara later, "this forced the ambassador's recall" on December 16.[26] Obviously, the departure of the ambassador (probably long planned and in tradition with the end of a presidential administration term) is a misunderstanding or more likely an exaggeration on his part, and Mondale's deputy chief of mission, Rust M. Deming, described the assertion as "nonsense,"[27] but it reflected the anger and disappointment of many Japanese at the time with the American position. The U.S. stance on the Senkakus was (and is) seen as a "loyalty test": was the USG committed to helping Japan defend its territory or not?

During this 1996 crisis, and before, it was difficult to tell. The USG continued to reiterate its neutral position regarding the sovereignty issue while urging a peaceful resolution, which had been its policy over the previous two and half decades. On September 11, for example, career diplomat R. Nicholas Burns, spokesman of the Department of State and acting assisting secretary for Public Affairs since 1995, responded to reporters by stating that "The United States neither recognizes, nor supports the claim of any country to sovereignty over the *Diaoyu* Islands"[28] and urged that the various claimants settle their disputes "in an orderly and peaceful and stable manner."[46] Burns, who when asked if the United States would be obligated to assist Japan in a military conflict said "That would be a hypothetic situation, of course, and my policy is not to comment upon hypotheses ... I don't have the defense treaty in front of me ... I can't quote it,"[29] also said that the USG had no intention of serving as a mediator then and called for direct negotiations among the claimants.[30] Assistant Secretary of State for East Asia and the Pacific, Winston Lord, who briefly appears in Chapter 5 of this book in connection with his work on National Security Advisor Henry A. Kissinger in 1972, also could not or would not answer the question of whether Article 5 applied in the case of the Senkakus: "I will not comment on hypothetical situations."[31]

A couple of weeks later on September 23, 1996, Glyn Davies, who had been serving as Deputy Spokesman of the Department of State and Deputy Assistant Secretary for Public Affairs since October 1995, stated,

> We expect that the claimants to the islands will resolve their differences and do so peacefully. We urge all the claimants to exercise restraint as they move forward on this process ... We're not going to predict what's likely to happen. We're simply going to confine ourselves to calling on both sides to resist the temptation to provoke each other or raise tensions over those two islands. From a U.S. standpoint, though we understand it has a great emotional content, it's not the kind of issue that's worth elevating beyond a war of words, where we are not. So that is our position on it.[32]

Unfortunately, tensions rose quickly very dramatically a few days later when activists from the World Alliance of Chinese fishermen traveling on a freight vessel, the *Bao Yu*, were stopped by a Japanese patrol twelve nautical miles from the Senkakus and five of the passengers jumped overboard. One of the activists, David Chan Yuk Cheung, drowned, becoming the first known death in a Senkakus-related dispute since the attack by unidentified Taiwanese or Chinese more than forty years before in 1955 (see Chapter 2 for the *Daisan Seitoku Maru* Incident). News coverage was extensive, leading to a rise in anti-Japanese sentiment in Hong Kong, which was already "suffering from countdown anxiety," according to Asia-watcher Funabashi Yoichi.[33]

Foreign Ministry officials, especially Takeuchi Yukio, minister plenipotentiary at the Japanese Embassy in Washington, D.C., were concerned that Burns' comments represented a step backward in America's commitment to Japan, and "felt as if he had been slapped in the face" when he learned of what Burns had said: "This is so different from their former statements. It's terrible. We need to wake them up and fast!"[34] There was a difference of opinion within the Foreign Ministry at the time, about whether to directly confront the U.S. government or not. Fortunately, Takeuchi knew there were those who understood and sympathized with his position in the USG.

The Japan Desk at the State Department, for example, thought Burns "had blown it" but apparently Secretary of State Warren M. Christopher, who as deputy secretary of state, had had the unfortunate duty of telling the government of Taiwan about the establishment of official relations with China in

1979, "liked him" and so it was difficult for officials on the Japan Desk to ask Burns to correct it.[35] (In fairness to Christopher and the leadership of the State Department as well, their attention at the time was focused on the Dayton Accords, which brought an end to the Bosnian War.) "The initial reaction by the State Department," one official said,

> Was the wrong reaction, and it was done without being considered through. It was done in isolation, without thinking about the strategic alliance; it was done somewhat in isolation, from a legalistic point of view, without the right people intervening early on. And once that mistake had been made, it was defended for a few days too long before the more correct interpretation and decision was (sic) made. And I can only have a degree of sympathy for the frustration and irritation that *Gaimusho* [MOFA] had with regard to this.[36]

A generous interpretation of what happened at this time, provided by Funabashi, who was an editorial writer for the *Asahi Shimbun* at the time and authored what is now a classic and must-read on U.S.–Japan security relations called *Alliance Adrift*, was that the United States has poor institutional memory due to transitions in government. This is very true, as is its tendency to protect and sometimes, ironically, to reward poor performance, but a more cynical interpretation was that the U.S. government was attempting to safeguard its neutral stance.

According to Japan-watcher Michael J. Green, who subsequently became the director for Asian Affairs at the National Security Council (NSC), "Diplomatically, the administration was correct to remain neutral, but technically the United States is obligated under the U.S.-Japan Security Treaty to defend the Senkakus."[37] Green's description of this incident was in the context of his analysis of the consequences of the period in the late-1990s of the perception that the American policy toward its ally was one of "Japan passing," but he was probably being overly diplomatic himself in his critique of the State Department's incoherent and unconvincing stance.

Eventually, perhaps in part due to criticism in Tokyo about the U.S. stance or perhaps because of a relook at what U.S. commitments actually were, the USG, led by the Pentagon (which had increasingly asserted its control over U.S. policy-making toward Japan in the 1990s) declared that the islands were indeed covered by the bilateral security treaty. In late November, Secretary of Defense William J. Perry authorized Deputy Assistant Secretary of Defense for Asia and Pacific Affairs Kurt M. Campbell to reaffirm that "The United States has a very strong commitment to Japan under Article V of the security treaty. We abide by that commitment and its terms, requiring the United States to support Japan and its territories, are very clear."[38] Campbell, however, was careful to avoid making comments that supported the Japanese position on the Senkakus and distinguished the Senkaku Islands as simply those "under Japanese administration."

Much damage had been done already and great distrust emerged vis-à-vis the USG and particularly Democratic Party-led administrations at this point. For this reason, there was much attention on what would happen during a crisis under a Republican Party-led administration, which is traditionally seen by Japanese elites as being more "pro-Japan." Because of the nature of the Senkakus dispute—namely China's claims to the islands and continued incursions into the area—a new crisis was bound to emerge. It did in the spring of 2004.

Late the previous year, a "private" organization known as the Chinese Federation for Defending the Diaoyu Islands (*Zhongguo Minjian Baowei Diaoyutai Lianhehui*) was established in the city of Xiamen (or Amoy) in Fujian Province, across from Taiwan.[39] A few weeks later on January 15, the group sent two boats to the Senkakus, violating Japanese territorial waters in the process, and dropping about twenty stone markers in the area. Two months after that on March 24, seven activists from the group landed on Uotsuri Jima, the largest of the Senkaku Islands, and were subsequently apprehended by the Japan Coast Guard where they were charged with violating Japanese immigration laws by the Okinawa Prefectural Police (Okinawaken Keisatsu).

Attention immediately turned to Washington. That same day, J. Adam Ereli, deputy spokesman for the State Department, announced in clear, reassuring language that the bilateral security treaty applied to the Senkakus:

> The Senkaku Islands have been under the administrative control of Japan since having been returned as part of the reversion of Okinawa in 1972. Article 5 of the 1960 U.S.-Japan Treaty of Mutual Cooperation and Security states the treaty applies to the territories under the administration of Japan; thus, Article 5 of the Mutual Security Treaty applies to the Senkaku Islands. Sovereignty of the Senkakus is disputed. The U.S. does not take a position on the question of the ultimate sovereignty of the Senkaku Diaoyu Islands. This has been our longstanding view. We expect the claimants will resolve this issue through peaceful means and urge all claimants to exercise restraint.[40]

Although the U.S. government continued to maintain its neutrality in the dispute over sovereignty, this supportive stance in the defense of the islands, according to John J. Tkacik, Jr., a twenty-three year veteran of the State Department who had joined the Heritage Foundation as a research fellow in China Policy in its Asian Studies Center in 2001, became "affectionately known in Japan as the 'Armitage Doctrine'," after the strongly pro-Japan deputy secretary of State, Richard L. Armitage.[41] This stance also became the minimum bar by which American commitments to support Japan came to be judged.

Thus, there was much interest and concern when the Senkakus issue flared up again after a Democratic Party administration took office again in the

United States, and Hillary Rodham Clinton, the wife of former President William J. Clinton, became secretary of state as both were seen as pro-China. In early September 2010, a year after the Hatoyama administration, also seen as pro-China, had taken office in Japan ending nearly fifty-four years of rule by the Liberal Democratic Party (Jiyu Minshuto), a Chinese fishing boat rammed a Japanese Coast Guard vessel leading to the arrest of the Chinese captain.[42] Immediately, Japanese officials and reporters asked what the U.S. stance would be if a military clash occurred. The Barack H. Obama administration, in office since January 2009 and still preoccupied with the Futenma relocation issue, could not take a position less than that of the "Armitage Doctrine" or that of Campbell when he was deputy assistant secretary of defense as he was by then serving as assistant secretary of state for East Asia and Pacific affairs. Accordingly, a couple of weeks after the incident first began, Secretary Clinton in a September 23 meeting with Foreign Minister Maehara Seiji explained that the USG understood the actions the Japanese government was taking to deal with the incident and stressed that Article 5 of the security treaty did in fact apply to the Senkakus.[43]

With Secretary Clinton's affirmation, it could be said that the confusion caused in the previous Democratic administration was cleared up (although absolute trust remains low) and that the two American political parties had gotten in sync with regard to the U.S. national position on the Senkakus. Nevertheless, there are still huge gaps and many problems—discussed in the Conclusion—about what exactly "Article 5 applies to the Senkakus" means in reality, not to mention the basic question, raised time and time again by Kristof to American readers about the islands really being worth fighting for and expending national treasure (especially the lives of the young Marines based on the main island of Okinawa).

In the past, this was largely an academic exercise as China did not really have the capability nor, probably, the immediate and actual intention to launch an attack on the islands to seize them. However in recent years, Chinese military activity has been increasing to the point that it cannot be ignored despite the public talk over the years of a peaceful rise and cooperation in joint development of the area surrounding the islands believed to be the site of tens or even hundreds of billions of dollars of natural resources, especially oil.[44] China's behavior has been increasingly risky and outright dangerous as it seeks to probe Japanese (and U.S.) intentions and assert its claims. One anonymous writer in July 2012 even introduced a scenario which saw China launching a quick strike to create a *fait accompli* that September amid Japanese political and diplomatic chaos and military unpreparedness.[45] Tensions indeed rose uncomfortably high beginning the following month and continue in the fall of 2013.

In a move subsequently strongly criticized by China,[46] the U.S. Senate unanimously approved on November 30 a legislative amendment to the National Defense Authorization Act for Fiscal Year 2013 that stated that the U.S. government "acknowledges the administration of Japan over the Senkaku Islands" and also "reaffirms its commitment to the government of Japan under Article 5."[47] While the provision maintained the United States "takes no position on the ultimate sovereignty of the Senkaku Islands," it emphasized that "the unilateral actions of a third party will not affect" its acknowledgment of Japan's administration over the islands and noted that "the East China Sea is a vital part of the maritime commons of Asia." Less than two weeks after this amendment, a Chinese Oceanic Administration airplane intruded into Japanese airspace near Uotsuri Jima on December 13, causing the Japanese Air Self-Defense Force to scramble its old F-15 jets to the area and decry as "extremely deplorable" the intrusion.[48] Near-daily intrusions by Chinese survey and other vessels and planes occur at the time of this writing.

There is, in fact, a plethora of writings about potential for conflict. One of the more well known is *Showdown: Why China Wants War with the United States*. Written in 2006 by Jed Babbin, a former deputy undersecretary of defense in the George H. W. Bush administration, and Edward Timperlake, a retired U.S. Marine Corps fighter pilot, it includes several references to the Senkakus including an imagined telephone call from the prime minister of Japan to a new (female) U.S. president explaining the background of the dispute and new information that the Chinese and the Russian navies were conducting exercises close to the Senkakus. "They have never done that at the same time before. We fear," the prime minister informs Madame President, "they have reached a diplomatic and military agreement and will seize them at any moment." After expressing her gratitude for the phone call, she informs the prime minister that she would "give the matter serious consideration and talk with you again in a few days. I appreciate your concern." After hanging up, she tells her senior intelligence staff—the CIA director and the director of National Intelligence—"we have no problems with China. I'm sure they will act responsibly. And until then, I don't want to hear another word about this."[49] While the above dialogue is fictitious, for Japan it is probably a worst-case scenario.

Another book, this one by two Japanese commentators and entitled *Senkaku Senso* (The Senkakus War), was published in late 2010, shortly after tensions flared again between China and Japan over the repeated ramming of Japanese Coast Guard ships by a Chinese fishing vessel and the handling of the subsequent arrest of the captain and its crew. The bureaucrat, who was working for the JCG at the time and who released the video of the collision on Youtube (known as "Sengoku38" for his user name on the Internet), Chief Mate Isshiki Masaharu, subsequently published a book about the incident called, *Nani ka no Tame ni Sengoku38 no Kokuhaku* (Why I did it: Sengoku38's Report).[50] His later talk in Naha on October 1, 2011, attended by the author, drew a large and committed crowd.[51]

Other books published in Japan, such as *Senkaku ga Abunai* (The Senkakus Are in Danger) by a collection of retired Japanese Maritime, Ground, and Air Self-Defense Force officers in 2010, *Senkaku Shoto Oki Kaisen: Jieitai wa Chugokugun to Kono Yo ni Tatakau* (The Sea Battle Off the Senkaku Islands: This is How the Self-Defense Forces Will Fight the Chinese Military), written in 2011 by a former member of the Maritime Self-Defense Force now based in Perth, Australia, *Jieitai Vs. Chugokokugun* (The Self-Defense Forces Versus the Chinese Military), and *Senkaku o Tori ni Kuru Chugoku Kaigun no Jitsuryoku* (The Actual Strength of the Chinese Navy that is Coming to Take the Senkakus), *Senkaku Buryoku Shototsu: Nicchu Moshi Takawabu* (Japan, China, and a Military Conflict in the Senkakus), and a novel, *Senkaku Soshitsu* (Losing the Senkakus), by a prolific writer of fiction on war themes, all published in 2012, paint similarly grim pictures as the ones above about the potential for a clash.[52] Political scientist Sado Akihiro took the debate a step further (or back) by examining the related laws and budget of his country's military and warning that Japan was acutely unprepared to handle a contingency in the Senkakus.[53] Furthermore, Nakayama Yoshitaka, the young mayor of Ishigaki City, Okinawa Prefecture, which historically has administratively controlled the Senkaku Islands, has contributed a valuable local perspective to a national, bilateral, regional, and international issue in his recently published *Chugoku ga Mimi o Fusagu: Senkaku Shoto no Futsugo na Shinjitsu* (The Inconvenient Truth about the Senkaku Islands that China Does Not Want to Hear).[54]

American analysts and military officers are increasingly taking an interest in this issue as well and writing about it. Two articles, one published and one unpublished but widely circulated through e-mail, by two highly intellectual and effective officers both in the U.S. Marine Corps, are Lieutenant Colonel James R. Kendall's article in *Orbis* entitled "Deterrence by Presence to Effective Response,"[55] examining the Government of Japan's growing interest in the defense of the islands to the southwest, and Colonel Grant F. Newsham's thinkpiece entitled, "Defending Nansei Shoto: A Marine Officer's View."[56]

Both of these insightful writings, as well as the above books predicting a clash, are outside of the scope of this book, however, which deals with the historical aspects of the current dispute and in particular the origins of the U.S. policy of "neutrality," at least in the sovereignty issue.

In response to Chinese provocations and increasing encroachments, the Japanese side has been making plans to strengthen its defenses in the Nansei Island chain, developing what it calls a "Southwestern Islands Wall (*Nansei Shoto Boheki*)." The wall is hollow, however, and therefore fragile, leaving Japan vulnerable. Japan's Self-Defense Force (SDF, or *Jieitai*) is looking more and more to the United States to help plug the holes in the wall, thereby fortifying it. As the United States is Japan's only formal alliance partner, this desire of Japan is understandable, as are expectations by the Japanese public that America would help. (One conservative activist, quoted in the 1996 Kristof commentary above, said, "I think the U.S-Japan Security Treaty should function. If it doesn't, then I think Japan should abandon the treaty."[57]) It also highlights the possible need for the United States to do away with its somewhat ambiguous policy for deterrence to truly work and real planning to begin.

As was mentioned before, this book is about how the U.S. policy of neutrality with regard to the Senkakus developed—or *was* developed—at the time of the Okinawa Reversion Treaty, focusing on the period from 1969 to 1972. It is not a book about the Sino (including Taiwan)-Japanese territorial dispute per se—this issue has been written about in great detail and in some cases with much partisanship in numerous articles and books. This work, instead, is about the American angle and its efforts at the time to distance itself from a potential problem that, in fact and in retrospect, it would be unable to disengage completely from as long as it has an alliance with Japan and security interests in the region. Indeed, it is very much part of the problem.

Previous literature

The above books and articles are not the only ones about the East China Sea islands dispute. This section discusses the previous literature on the subject, and points out that in fact, there are surprisingly few full length manuscripts about the Senkaku Islands. Most of the writings are articles, and most of them date back to the early 1970s when the issue first flared up. This section will discuss the trend of the main previous literature.

While there were numerous studies done of the Senkaku Islands that focused on the natural sciences in the 1950s and 1960s (as well as in the prewar period), as discussed in Chapters 1 and 2, it was not until early 1970 that serious academic studies on the history and international relations of the islands began to emerge.

The first one was by Okuhara Toshio, then an assistant professor of international law at Kokushikan University (*Kokushikan Daigaku*) in Tokyo. Okuhara had been born in Dairen, Manchuria, following Japan's seizure of the area, and was repatriated with his family to Kumamoto in 1946, when he was thirteen. Interested in international problems, he ended up studying under the international law specialist, Ichimata Masao, at Waseda University.[58] After joining the faculty of Kokushikan in April 1965, Okuhara became interested in Okinawa as a research topic following a trip to Miyako in February 1968. He would work on issues related to the Senkaku Islands for the next decade, becoming Japan's most prolific writer and even personally correcting the editorial stance of *Asahi Shimbun* (Asahi Newspaper) in the early days of the dispute by providing documents that shed light on the history of Japan's administrative control and problems with Taiwanese and Chinese claims.[59]

"Senkaku Retto: Rekishi to Seiji no Aida (The Senkaku Islands, Between History and Politics)," was not only his first published article on the topic, but was the first time the subject had been covered in this way.[60] Okuhara worked closely with the Japanese government to both obtain access to documents as well as to share the fruits of his labor. He was later asked to join the Senkaku Islands Study Group (*Senkaku Retto Kenkyukai*), a semi-government body established in September 1970 and discussed in Chapter 2. He never published a book on the Senkakus, but wrote a couple of dozen articles about the issue, and wrote a fifty-four part series for a newspaper between 1972 and 1973 explaining the history of the dispute. Were these and the related footnotes and annotations combined into one book, they would easily be more than 125,000 Japanese characters, enough to make a solid and decisive academic book.

Some of Okuhara's writings on the Senkakus challenged those of a Japanese Marxist historian named Inoue Kiyoshi, who argued around the same time in the early 1970s that the Senkakus belonged to China. Inoue, a professor at Kyoto University who was strongly against the Emperor system, wrote several articles about the Senkakus, mostly in China-related publications and was later honored by the Chinese government. The two writers had a few heated exchanges in various journals, challenging one another's interpretations of documents. After correcting and elaborating on some of his previously published articles, Inoue combined them and speeches and other writings about discrimination against Okinawa and anti-militarism in a book published shortly after Okinawan's reversion.[61] While Inoue stopped writing about the Senkakus shortly by 1973, Okuhara would continue for years to come constantly digging and probing for more information and evidence of Japan's claims.[62] The conservative legal specialist, whose writings are the most methodical, evidence-based, and voluminous of any language, was frustrated dealing with the leftist historian. "Inoue's ideology was more like a religion," Okuhara told the author adding, "I don't mind if the conclusion is different; it is the process that is important."[63]

Another prolific writer on the Senkakus was Midorima Sakae, an Okinawan scholar of international law, who also approached the issue from a historical and international law perspective.[64] Trained by Irie Keishiro, a well-known international relations and law scholar introduced in Chapter 2, Midorima joined the faculty of the predecessor college to Okinawa International University in the early 1960s and stayed there until he retired in March 2001. His writings on the Senkakus, which began in the late 1970s, focused on the development of the waters around the islands and the Law of the Seas, leading to a book for the general reader still in print today simply titled, *Senkaku Retto* (Senkaku Islands), and fills most of a rack at a newsstand/giftshop near the gates at Naha International Airport.[65]

It would not be for another almost two decades before an academic book on the Senkakus appeared. Over the previous three decades until then, with the exception of the books described above and a book by a pro-China businessman, Takahashi Shogoro,[66] most of the writings about the Senkakus were either single academic articles or journalistic accounts. Several of the academic pieces focused on the ability to use international law to resolve the dispute using comparative perspectives, while others were either an analysis of a contemporary aspect of the problem or an examination of the respective claims. In some cases these latter works regurgitated commonly known views but did not add much to the historical discussion.

Suganuma Unryu's *Sovereign Rights and Territorial Space in Sino-Japan Relations* changed much of this by reaching deep back into history to examine both Japanese and Chinese claims to the islands, and introducing a whole host of previous unused primary materials using his rich linguistic ability to discuss irredentism, or the claim to a territory based on historical "rights."[67] Suganuma, who lived in China at one point but earned his bachelor's degree in Japan and his master's and doctoral degrees in the United States, had been interested in China's relations with the Ryukyu Islands, and this interest is reflected in the extensive discussion of his book on the tributary relationship that existed between the two and the existence of the Senkakus as a natural landmark when navigating between the two kingdoms.[68]

On the issue of U.S. involvement in the status of the Senkaku Islands, there is surprisingly little research in English or Japanese. One English-language article of more than a decade ago focused on the postwar involvement, primarily in the context of the administration of Okinawa, but dealt little with the status of the islands at the time of reversion and the development of the U.S. policy of neutrality.[69] A couple of articles written by Japanese scholars for a non-academic audience on the other hand focused primarily on the status of the islands in the connection of Article 5 of the security treaty.[70] Very recently, the topic has gotten some attention in the media, including a growing interest in the introduction of declassified documents, all of which are already used in this study. However, no such published, full academic study in English or Japanese has been attempted on this topic until now that I am aware of.

Significance of the book

In light of the above situation with the previous literature, the significance of this book is multi-fold. First, it is the first academic book in more than a decade focusing exclusively on the Senkakus issue and as such is able to make full use of the existing research, both books and articles, as well as postwar primary documents that are increasingly being declassified as well as memoirs and oral histories. Second, it is the first book that highlights and examines in detail the history of American involvement with this issue, and the origins of its neutrality policy, a topic that is only recently getting attention. Indeed, one might actually call it a "neutral-but-entrapped" policy. As such, the book identifies U.S. inconsistencies and suggests where the United States needs to make a more positive and unambiguous commitment to Japan both for deterrence to work and for our bilateral relationship. Third, it delves into unprecedented detail about Okinawa reversion process in the context of the issue of the Senkakus, bringing to light an unstudied aspect of not only the reversion agreement but also of the Senkakus historical record. Fourth, it examines the numerous actors on the Japanese side and the making of Japan's Senkaku policy, and serves as another case study of how Japanese foreign policy-making works. A fifth contribution of this book concerns its ability to highlight the views and actions of other official actors in the situation, namely Okinawa (then known as the Government of the Ryukyu Islands, or GRI), Taiwan, and China, as well as those of non-official players in civil society, the political world, and the business community. Through this, we gain a better appreciation of the domestic and international components of foreign policy-making. Sixth, this book sets the stage for further research on the post-reversion period to better understand the historical background affecting the East China Sea islands dispute in the hope that proper policies and responses will emerge based on this clearer understanding of the history. Related to this, while not the goal of the book, the above factual accounting in the end makes Japan's position in the dispute unassailable and hopefully this new information, combined with other measures such as appeals to the International Court of Justice and joint development of the natural resources in the area, as well as one proposal forty years ago to make the area a nature preserve,[71] will provide the other disputants a face-saving way to de-escalate the conflict making it a win-win situation if that is what they in fact desire. China's actions to date and over time, however, suggest otherwise.

This book makes extensive use of archival documents, declassified materials, and interviews with former policymakers in both Japan and the United States in an attempt to present a thorough and comprehensive accounting of the development of America's "neutrality" policy and its reception in Japan (and among its neighbors) in the early years of the Senkakus dispute. As with all my previous diplomatic histories, detailed footnotes will allow the reader to both appreciate the types of materials used and to follow up on her or his own research in a user-friendly manner.

Organization of the book

This book is at its heart a diplomatic and international history and as such is primarily organized in chronological order. At the same time the issues are extremely complex and interconnected, and thus the chapters are also very much intertwined. On several occasions the reader will be asked to look at other chapters to review or see how a particular issue developed or was handled. This is unavoidable as several related events were often occurring simultaneously in different capitals and parts of the world, often far away from the Senkaku Islands themselves.

The book is divided into seven chapters, including this Introduction and the Conclusion. Each chapter tells a different aspect of the story of the dispute and particularly of Japan's involvement, as well as of U.S. efforts later on to disengage itself from the conflict.

Chapter 1, entitled "A History of the Senkaku Islands," reviews the history of the islands. It is based on both primary and secondary materials. In particular, it focuses on the official and unofficial involvement of Japan with the islands, including the incorporation of the islands by the central government as a part of Okinawa Prefecture, and looks at the settlement and development of the islands by Koga Tatsushiro and his company, as well as at the surveys and other explorations of the islands conducted during the prewar period.

Chapter 2, "Okinawa and the Senkaku Islands under U.S. Occupation and Administration," provides an overview of the U.S. administration of the islands in conjunction with Okinawan authorities. It looks at the numerous official and non-official surveys of the islands by Japanese scholars and officials, the problems of incursions by Taiwanese fishermen and poachers, and the efforts of U.S. authorities to balance administering the islands without getting too drawn into the territorial dispute in the late 1960s and early 1970s. It is based on both primary and secondary sources.

"The ECAFE Survey and the Start of the East China Sea Islands Dispute," the title of Chapter 3, is based on primary and secondary sources and looks at the growing interest the countries in the region began to show upon the discovery of the potential for large oil and natural resources in the vicinity of the Senkakus. This chapter examines the race for concessions in the area between Okinawans and mainland Japanese as well as by Taiwan and U.S. companies. Similarly, it looks at the stance the U.S. government had to take among these competing claims and activities.

Chapter 4, "The Okinawa Reversion Negotiations and America's 'Neutrality' Policy," is based mostly on primary sources, including interviews, and to a lesser extent, secondary sources. It examines in detail the bilateral negotiations between Japan and the United States over the question of the inclusion of the Senkaku Islands in the Okinawa reversion treaty, the pressure by Taiwan to prevent that, and the efforts of the U.S. government to remain neutral in this territorial dispute among its two allies as well vis-à-vis China, which was becoming increasingly important to U.S. strategy in the region and worldwide, both toward ending the Vietnam War and changing the power balance with the Soviet Union. In addition, it looks at the attempts by the U.S. government to provide its good offices to promote a dialogue between Japan and Taiwan on the issue, and introduces a highly controversial attempt in the last days and weeks to possible withhold the Senkakus from the areas to be returned to pressure Japan to have this dialogue while using it to get Taiwan to acquiesce on the reversion agreement as well as to compromise on a textiles deal that was simultaneously being negotiated at the time.

Chapter 5, "Ratification of the Okinawa Reversion Agreement and Domestic and Regional Reactions," is based both on primary and some secondary sources, as well as interviews, and looks at the respective ratification processes, the positions of political parties and the media in Japan at the time, the official position of the Japanese government, continued tensions between Japan and Taiwan and their attempts to draw the U.S. government into the dispute, and China's views on the Senkakus, among other topics. It also looks at last-minute arrangements for the defense of the islands, including the establishment of the Air Defense Identification Zone and the continued use of training ranges in the post-reversion period.

Conclusion (Aftermath) is a short chapter that highlights some of the challenges and problems that existed at the time and with which we have to live today. Following the Conclusion, several appendices are included that provide relevant agreements and statements helpful to this study.

Since history is made by people, my approach to writing is to attempt to better understand the people that appear in the histories I work on and to introduce them and their decisions in these pages. Many of those appearing will be people the readers may have never heard of before, but they were significant in their own way to this story. Some had personal goals, some had political reasons, some had organizational concerns, some had financial motives, and some had national interests in mind. Some are still alive; others are deceased. I have done my best to interview as many as possible and introduce those who were involved in this, the Senkakus story.

I will discuss the naming of the islands in the following chapter, but I have elected to call the islands by their Japanese names for the most part as I believe the available evidence clearly and without a shadow of a doubt show them to be Japanese, at least for the last 118-plus years. Doing otherwise only confuses the issue and lends credence to the late-in-the-game claims by Taiwan and China. I realize this statement opens me up to accusations of bias, but I believe the dispassionate reader will come to the same conclusion as me by the end of the book.

Notes

1 A transcript of the interview, conducted on February 17, 2010, in Tokyo, Japan, was obtained by the author from someone indirectly associated with the interview. Since the interview was never published, the author has decided not to disclose the names of the interviewer, interviewee, and two State Department officials, one of whom was assigned to Tokyo and the other in Hawaii.

2 In an e-mail subsequently shared with the author, the reporter commented, "I was astonished. [The general] did not know the basic fact there is an agreement between GOJ and USG that Article 5 of the Japan-U.S. Security Treaty applies to the Senkakus. The United States has a treaty obligation to defend the Senkakus. He did not have knowledge of it. ... His lack of understanding of this crucial alliance issue left me with a profound disappointment and a deep concern."

3 Subsequently, a nation-wide fundraising drive was led by Ishihara and the Tokyo Metropolitan Government (*Tokyoto*) to purchase the islands during the spring and summer. In response, Prime Minister Noda Yoshihiko announced on July 7 that the central government intended to purchase them. (As explained in Chapter 1, of the five islands, four were privately owned, and three of those were available for sale. One, Kuba Jima, is currently leased from a member of the Kurihara family, Kurihara Kazuko, by the Japanese government for use as a U.S. Navy training range, which has remained dormant since the late 1970s.) Eventually, the central government and the owner of three of islands came to an understanding and signed an agreement on September 11, 2012. For more, see the memoirs of one of the family members of the owners involved in the sale, who serves as the family's spokesman, Kurihara Hiroyuki, *Senkaku Shoto Urimasu* (Senkaku Islands for Sale), (Tokyo: Kosaido Shuppan, 2012). According to Kurihara, who has known Ishihara for four decades, Ishihara had long called for the purchasing of the islands and often had those discussions with him. In addition to his book, see Kurihara Hiroyuki, "Senkaku Shoto 'Baikyaku' no Uchimaku (Behind the Scenes of the 'Purchase' of the Senkaku Islands)," *Shincho*, Vol. 31, No. 6 (June 2012), 22–25, and Ishihara Shintaro, "Senkaku Shoto to Iu Kokunan (The

National Problem That is the Senkaku Islands)," *Bungei Shunju*, Vol. 90, No. 10 (July 2012), 148–56. For movements on the central government side, including a May 18 (2012) meeting at which Noda "made up his mind to go ahead and purchase" the islands, as well as the September 4 meeting between Ishihara and former special adviser to the prime minister Nagashima Akihisa at which Ishihara agreed not to fight the central government over who would purchase the islands, see "Senkaku Snafu Laid to Broad Miscalculation," *Japan Times*, November 20, 2012. Although the central government purchased the islands, the use of more than one billion yen in donations collected by the TMG has not been finalized at the time of this writing. (See "1.4 Billion in Islet Funds in Limbo," *Japan Times*, November 1, 2012.) For recommendations on the possible use of these funds, see Robert D. Eldridge, "Option for Senkakus' Funds," *Japan Times*, November 18, 2012. A recent book by the young mayor of Ishigaki City, Nakayama Yoshitaka, provides details of his interaction with Ishihara to include the joint administration of the islands, as well as the limited contacts with the central government at the time. See Nakayama Yoshitaka, *Chugoku ga Mimi o Fusagu: Senkaku Shoto no Futsugo na Shinjitsu* (The Inconvenient Truth about the Senkaku Islands that China Does Not Want to Hear) (Tokyo: Wani Bukkusu, 2012), 3–9.

4 "Gaisho 'Shusho no Senkaku Hatsugen ha Futekisetsu' Ryodo Mondai wa Nai (Foreign Minister 'Prime Minister's Comments on Senkakus Inappropriate,' There is No Territorial Problem)," *Ryukyu Shimpo*, May 28, 2010. Ishihara, who has described the administration led by the Democratic Party of Japan (*Nihon Minshuto*), which took power in September 2009 but lost in the December 2012 general elections following Noda's dissolving of the Diet on November 16, as "incapable (*muno*)," wrote about this episode in an article in a national journal shortly after he announced he intended to purchase the privately owned islands. See Ishihara, "Senkaku Shoto to Iu Kokunan." His comment about the Hatoyama Administration is found on p. 155.

5 "Gaisho 'Shusho'."

6 Niksch, "Senkaku (Diaoyu) Islands Dispute: The U.S. Legal Relationship and Obligations," and Manyin, "Senkaku (Senkaku Diaoyu/Diaoyutai) Islands Dispute: U.S. Treaty Obligations." Manyin repeats verbatim, including several albeit minor factual mistakes, much of Niksch's study. An identical version of Niksch's late September 1996 report appeared five weeks later in *PACNET*, the newsletter of Pacific Forum, Center for Strategic and International Studies, based in Hawaii. See Larry A. Niksch, "Senkaku (Diaoyu) Islands Dispute: The U.S. Legal Relationship and Obligations," *PACNET*, No. 45, Pacific Forum CSIS, November 8, 1996. Some twenty years earlier, Niksch, an analyst in the Asian Affairs section, had also worked on another study of the islands for the Legislative Reference Service entitled "Competing Claims to the Senkaku Islands." The eleven-page paper was dated May 28, 1974, when another crisis was brewing over the islands between Japan, China, and Taiwan.

7 Nicholas D. Kristof, "Look Out for the Diaoyu Islands," *Wall Street Journal* "On the Ground" blog entry, September 10, 2010 (http://kristof.blogs.nytimes.com/tag/senkaku-islands/, accessed July 1, 2011). He followed up this commentary with a second, "More on the Senkaku/Diaoyu Islands," on September 20, 2010 (http://kristof.blogs.nytimes.com/2010/09/20/more-on-the-senkakudiaoyu-islands/, accessed July 11, 2011).

8 Kristof, "Look Out." Much of the blog is taken verbatim from his *Thunder from the East: Portrait of a Rising Asia*, coauthored with his wife, Sheryl Wu Dunn, and published by Alfred A. Knopf in 2000, particularly pages 256–57 and 262–63.

9 Nicholas D. Kristof, "Would You Fight for These Islands?" *New York Times*, October 20, 1996. An earlier article by him about the Sino-Japanese tensions over the Senkakus was factual and not simply commentary in nature. See Nicholas D.

Kristof, "An Asian Mini-Tempest Over Mini-Island Group," *New York Times*, September 16, 1996.

10 Han-yi Shaw, "The Inconvenient Truth behind the Diaoyu/Senkaku Islands," *Wall Street Journal* "On the Ground" blog entry, September 19, 2012 (http://kristof.blogs. nytimes.com/2012/09/19/the-inconvenient-truth-behind-the-diaoyusenkaku-islands/, accessed October 10, 2012).

11 Nicholas D. Kristof, "My Father's Gift to Me," *New York Times*, June 19, 2010. Kristof's interest in territorial issues may have been inspired by his father. See the article published the same year Nicholas was born—1959: Ladis K. D. Kristof, "The Nature of Frontiers and Boundaries," *Annals of the Association of American Geographers*, Vol. 49, No. 3 (September 1959), 269–82.

12 See untitled introductory remarks to Shaw's "The Inconvenient Truth." Kristof's comments appeared to have incurred the wrath of Japanese consulate in New York, and indirectly the Japanese Foreign Ministry. See "Consulate Rebuts N.Y. Times Senkakus Op-ed," *Japan Times*, October 5, 2012.

13 Takayuki Nishi, "The Diaoyu/Senkaku Islands: A Japanese Scholar Responds," *Wall Street Journal* "On the Ground" blog entry, October 4, 2012 (http://kristof.blogs. nytimes.com/2012/10/04/the-diaoyusenkaku-islands-a-japanese-scholar-responds/, accessed October 10, 2012). According to Nishi, he had several reasons for writing the article, including the concern that "Japanese experts were unlikely to have read Mr. Shaw's article, be capable of replying quickly in English, and bother to reply. Thus, Han-yi Shaw was likely to get the last word on Mr. Kristof's blog if I didn't reply," and the view that "American professors taught me that scholars have obligations toward society, so I felt I had a responsibility to point out facts to Mr. Kristof's readers." Author's interview with Nishi Takayuki, November 1, 2012, Shizuoka City, Japan (by e-mail).

14 Kristof and WuDunn, *Thunder from the East*, 256–57.

15 JYF is a rightist group formed in 1961 with ties to organized crime. For more on the JYF, see its website at: www.seinensya.org/ (accessed July 2012). Ishihara, who was the co-author of the nationalists' clarion call, *"No" to Ieru Nihon*, with Morita Akio of Sony Corporation. (The official English version, *The Japan That Can Say No: Why Japan Will Be First Among Equals*, published by Simon and Schuster in 1991, did not include Morita's chapters in it.) Ishihara, who was Minister of Transport (*Unyusho*) at the time, became governor of Tokyo in April 1999 but resigned in October 2012 to form a new national political party. For more on his connections to JYF, see Ishihara, "Senkaku Shoto to Iu Kokunan," 151, and his interview on the Fuji Television Network show, *Shin 2001 Hodo*, on September 2, 2012.

16 Niksch, "Senkaku (Diaoyu) Islands Dispute," 1.

17 This particular *Hinomaru*, made out of wood, measured three meters in length and two meters in height, and was set at a fifteen degree angle to be able to be seen from land, sea, and air. See Senkaku Shoto Boei Kyokai, ed., *Senkaku Shoto Uotsuri Jima*, 56.

18 Senkaku Shoto Boei Kyokai, ed., *Senkaku Shoto Uotsuri Jima*, 49–55.

19 "Japan, Do Not Do Foolish Things," Xinhua News Agency, August 30, 1996, cited in Erica Strecker Downs and Phillip C. Saunders, "Legitimacy and the Limits of Nationalism: China and the Diaoyu Islands," *International Security*, Vol. 23, No. 3 (Winter 1998–99), 133.

20 Downs and Saunders, "Legitimacy and the Limits of Nationalism," 133–34.

21 Kristof, "An Asian Mini-Tempest Over Mini-Island Group."

22 Kristof, "Would You Fight for These Islands?"

23 Funabashi Yoichi, *Alliance Adrift* (New York: Council on Foreign Relations Press, 1999), 405.

24 Walter F. Mondale, *The Good Fight: A Life in Liberal Politics* (New York: Scribner, 2010).

25 Ishihara Shintaro, "Opinionu Amerika e no Fumie, 'Senkaku' (Opinion Force the U.S. to Take a Loyalty Test on the 'Senkakus'), *Sankei Shimbun*, November 5, 1996.

26 Ishihara, "Senkaku Shoto to Iu Kokunan," 150.

27 Author's interview with Rust M. Deming, October 8, 2012, Washington, D.C. (by email).

28 Unryu Suganuma, *Sovereign Rights and Territorial Space in Sino-Japanese Relations: Irredentism and the Diaoyu/Senkaku Islands* (Honolulu: University of Hawaii Press, 2000), 135, and "U.S. backs no nation over Senkaku: Burns," Jiji Press Ticker Service, September 11, 1996.

29 Funabashi, *Alliance Adrift*, 401.

30 Vincent A. Pace, "The U.S.-Japan Security Alliance and the PRC: The Abandonment-Entrapment Dynamic, the Balance of Threat and National Identity in the Trilateral Relationship," Enosinian Honors Senior Thesis Program, Elliott School of International Affairs, George Washington University, May 3, 2003.

31 Funabashi, *Alliance Adrift*, 402.

32 Niksch, "Senkaku (Diaoyu) Islands Dispute: The U.S. Legal Relationship and Obligations."

33 Funabashi, *Alliance Adrift*, 402.

34 Funabashi, *Alliance Adrift*, 401, 403. Takeuchi had been in the Legal Affairs Division (*Hokika*) of MOFA in the late 1970s when the Senkakus issue flared up and had written a report on the Senkakus about the respective views of the countries involved in the dispute, and was thus familiar with the U.S. government's position.

35 Funabashi, *Alliance Adrift*, 406.

36 Funabashi, *Alliance Adrift*, 406.

37 Michael J. Green, "The Forgotten Player," *The National Interest*, No. 60 (Summer 2000), 47.

38 Akaza Koichi, "U.S. Confirms Security Treaty Covers Senkakus," *Daily Yomiuri*, November 29, 1996.

39 For more on this group and nationalism in China, see Sasajima Masahiko "Senkaku Joriku Jiken ni Miru Chugoku Nashonarizumu Seiji no Shuho (The Method of Chinese Nationalist Politics as Seen in the Landing on the Senkakus Incident)," *Chuo Koron*, Vol. 119, No. 6 (June 2004), 100–107.

40 Department of State Daily Press Briefing, Adam Ereli, Deputy Spokesman, March 24, 2004, cited in John Tkacik, Jr., "Japan's Islands and China's Illicit Claims," *Web Memo*, No. 723 (April 14, 2005), at www.heritage.org/research/reports/2005/04/japans-islands-and-chinas-illicit-claims (accessed June 2009).

41 John Tkacik, Jr., "China's New Challenge to the U.S.-Japan Alliance," *Web Memo*, No. 533 (July 13, 2004), at www.heritage.org/research/reports/2004/07/chinas-new-challenge-to-the-us-japan-alliance (accessed February 2009).

42 In a talk in Washington, D.C., in October 2010, a month after the clash at sea, Funabashi described the incident as "much larger than the Nixon Shock—Japan will never be the same." See "The United States and Japan at 50: Remarks by Yoichi Funabashi," Council on Foreign Relations, October 8, 2010 (www.cfr.org/japan/united-states-japan-50-remarks-yoichi-funabashi/p23148, accessed October 2012).

43 "Clinton: Senkakus Subject to Security Pact," *Japan Times*, September 25, 2010.

44 For a recent analysis of the Chinese Navy, see Toshi Yoshihara and James R. Holmes, *Red Star Over the Pacific: China's Rise and the Challenge to U.S. Maritime Strategy* (Annapolis: Naval Institute Press, 2010).

45 Name Withheld, Chatan, Okinawa Prefecture, "Beware a September Surprise," *Japan Times*, July 22, 2012.

46 "China Condemns Senkaku Amendment to U.S.-Japan Security Treaty," *Japan Times*, December 4, 2012.

47 "U.S. Reaffirms Senkaku Defense," *Daily Yomiuri*, December 2, 2012.

48 "Defiant Chinese Plane Intrudes Over Senkakus," *Japan Times*, December 14, 2012.

49 Jed Babbin and Edward Timperlake, *Showdown: Why China Wants War with the United States* (Washington, D.C.: Regenery Publishing, C., 2006), 76.

50 Isshiki Masaharu, *Nani ka no Tame ni Sengoku38 no Kokuhaku* (Why I Did It: Sengoku38's Report) (Tokyo: Asahi Shimbun Shuppan, 2011).

51 The lecture, which this author observed, was sponsored by the Okinawa Prefecture Chapter (*Okinawa Kenhonbu*) of the conservative Japan Conference, or *Nihon Kaigi*, of which former Governor Ishihara is a representative (*daihyo*).

52 Boei Shisutemu Kenkyusho, ed., *Senkaku Shoto ga Abunai* (The Senkaku Islands are in Danger) (Tokyo: Naigai Shuppansha, 2010); Tamogami Toshi, ed., *Tamogami Toshio no Jieitai Vs. Chugokugun: Jieitai ha Chugokugun to Ko Tataku* (Tamogami Toshi's Discussion of the Self-Defense Forces Versus the Chinese Military: This is How the SDF Would Fight the Chinese Military) (Tokyo: Takarajimasha, 2012); Kawamura Sumihiko, *Senkaku o Tori ni Kuru Chugoku Kaigun no Jitsuryoku: Jieitai ha Ikani Tachimukauka* (The Actual Strength of the Chinese Navy that is Coming to Take the Senkakus: How Should the Self-Defense Forces Stand Up [To This Threat]) (Tokyo: Shogakkan, 2012); Nakamura Hideki, *Senkaku Shoto Oki Kaisen: Jieitai wa Chugokugun to Kono Yo ni Tatakau* (The Sea Battle Off the Senkaku Islands: This is How the Self-Defense Forces Will Fight the Chinese Military) (Tokyo: Kojinsha, 2011); Inoue Kazuhiko, *Senkaku Buryoku Shototsu: Nicchu Moshi Takawabu* (Japan, China, and a Military Conflict in the Senkakus) (Tokyo: Asuka Shinsha, 2012), and Oishi Eiji, *Senkaku Soshitsu* (Losing the Senkakus) (Tokyo: Chuo Koron Shinsha, 2012).

53 Sado Akihiro, "Nihon no Boei Taisei ha Ryodo Yuji ni Kino Suru Ka (Will Japan's Defense Establishment Be Able to Respond in a Territorial Crisis?)," *Chuo Koron*, Vol. 127, No. 15 (November 2012), 118–26.

54 Nakayama, *Chugoku ga Mimi o Fusagu*.

55 James R. Kendall, "Deterrence by Presence to Effective Response: Japan's Shift Southward," *Orbis*, Vol. 54, No. 4 (Fall 2010), 603–14.

56 Newsham subsequently published a thought-provoking commentary, "U.S. Must Clearly Back Japan in Islands Dispute with China," *Christian Science Monitor*, October 25, 2012. www.csmonitor.com/Commentary/Opinion/2012/1025/US-must-clearly-back-Japan-in-islands-dispute-with-China-video (accessed October 26, 2012).

57 Kristof, "Would You Fight for These Islands?" The person quoted was Eto Toyohisa, the then-head of JYF.

58 Author's interview with Okuhara Toshio, June 21, 2011, Nagareyama City, Japan.

59 Author's interview with Okuhara.

60 Okuhara Toshio, "Senkaku Retto: Rekishi to Seiji no Aida (The Senkaku Islands, Between History and Politics)," *Nihon Oyobi Nihonjin,* January 1970, 54–63.

61 Inoue Kiyoshi, *"Senkaku" Retto: Tiaoyu Shoto no Shiteki Kaimei* (The "Senkaku" Islands: A Historical Clarification of the Diaoyu Islands) (Tokyo: Gendai Hyoronsha, 1972).

62 One of Okuhara's last Senkakus-related articles was his "Senkaku Retto to Nihon Ryoyuken (The Senkaku Islands and Japan's Territorial Rights: A Historical Look at the [Islands'] Becoming a Part of Japan)," *Sekai to Nihon*, No. 234 (April 15, 1979), 9–56.

63 Author's interview with Okuhara.

64 For more on Midorima, see his "Kaiyoho no Rekishi to Tenbo: Wagakuni o Meguru Konnichiteki Mondai (The History of Maritime Law and its Future Prospects: Today's Problems Surrounding Our Country)," *Okinawa Hogaku*, No. 30 (2001), 151–81.

65 Midorima Sakae, *Senkaku Retto* (Senkaku Islands), (Naha: Hirugisha, 1984).

66 Takahashi Shogoro, *Senkaku Retto Nooto* (Notes on the Senkaku Islands) (Tokyo: Seinen Shuppansha, 1979).

67 Suganuma, *Sovereign Rights*, 1.

68 Author's interview with Suganuma Unryu, October 27, 2012, Tokyo, Japan (by e-mail).

69 Jean-Marc F. Blanchard, "The U.S. Role in the Sino–Japanese Dispute over the Diaoyu (Senkaku) Islands, 1945–71," *China Quarterly*, No. 161 (March 2000), 95–123.

70 Toyoshita Narahiko, "'Senkaku Mondai' to Anpo Joyaku (The Senkakus Issue and the Japan-U.S. Security Treaty)," *Sekai*, No. 812 (January 2011), 37–48, and Shimada Yoichi, "Senkaku to Nichibei Kankei (Senkakus and Japan–U.S. Relations)," *Shin Nihongaku*, No. 19 (Winter 2011), 11–15. At least one study has been done in Chinese, as I provided my materials to an exchange graduate student from Wuhan University, who wrote his master's thesis on the topic of the U.S. neutrality policy from 1970–72. I would assume many students in China and Taiwan are similarly interested in the topic.

71 This proposal became known to U.S. officials in Taiwan in 1972 when Yu Hanting, a Taiwanese conservationist who attended a conference on national parks in Canada, reported a conversation he had with unidentified Japanese conservationists at the meeting about the possibility of declaring the Senkakus "an international wildlife preserve." (See "8. Senkakus," Folder: PET Senkaku Islands 1972, Box 14, Subject Files of the Office of China Affairs, 1951–75, RG 59.) According to Yu, the Japanese were "enthusiastic" but he doubted their enthusiasm would "extend beyond conservation circles." (Ibid.) Ryukyu University Professor Takara Tetsuo, the pre-eminent expert on the natural species of the islands (as well as their history), also proposed such an idea in the past.

1   A history of the Senkaku Islands

This chapter provides a brief overview of the islands and discusses the early history of the Senkaku Islands, including references to the islands in both Chinese and Japanese records. Although there are numerous references to the Senkaku Islands in Chinese materials, China did not demonstrate an actual administration over the islands. Thus, this chapter focuses on Japan's careful and cautious incorporation of the islands in the late 1800s and looks in detail at the development of the islands by a Japanese businessman after having been granted a lease to the islands following the incorporation of the islands into Japan. It also examines the various official and unofficial surveys of the islands in the prewar period.

An overview of the Senkaku Islands

The group of five volcanic islands and three groups of rocks that are at the center of regional tension and attention are situated about 106 miles (170 kilometers) north of Ishigaki Island in Okinawa Prefecture, Japan, 320 miles (420 kilometers) from Naha, the capital city of Okinawa Prefecture, and about 116 miles (186 km) northeast of Keelung, Taiwan. These islands and islets sit on the edge of the continental shelf of mainland Asia in the East China Sea and are separated from the Ryukyu Islands by the Okinawa Trough, a back-arc basin 1000 km in length and 100 km wide running from Western Kyushu in Japan to Taiwan. At its deepest point, the trough is 8912 feet (2716 meters). The Okinawa Trough, which should not be confused with the deeper Ryukyu Trench on the eastern side of Okinawa running the length from southern Japan to Taiwan, is still forming according to geologists. It also forms one of the frames of reference for discussion, particularly by international legal specialists regarding the continental shelf, as to who indeed owns the islands and mineral resources nearby. This point will be discussed later in the book.

The islands, known originally as the Sento Shosho and the Senkaku Shosho and later as the Senkaku Retto and the Senkaku Shoto in Japanese, the Daioyutai or Taioyutai in Chinese, and the Pinnacle Islands in English, are part of a larger group of islands known as the Sakishima Island Group (Sakishima Shoto), which also includes the Yaeyama Group (Yaeyama Retto) and the Miyako Group (Miyako Retto). Together, the total area of the five islands and three rocks is about seven square kilometers, or 2.7 square miles. The largest island is Uotsuri Jima. Uninhabited today, several photos from the early twentieth century show the ninety-nine dwellings and buildings of the some 248 Japanese (and Okinawan) inhabitants who began a fishing business there in the late nineteenth century which continued until the early 1940s.[1] The remnants of that village, called "Koga-son," after the name of the original owner, explorer, and developer, Koga Tatsushiro, are still there, and a map of the village's layout, circa the early 1900s, has been published in several books.[2]

With the exception of Taisho Jima, or Sekibi Sho, which is government-owned, four of the islands had been privately owned for decades but three were recently purchased by the Government of Japan in September 2012 (see fn 3 in the Introduction as well as Table 1.2). The islands are administered by Ishigaki City, Okinawa Prefecture, and each island has had a Japanese address for more than a century. As will be explained below, after being explored by Koga in 1884, the islands first came under Ishigaki's administration in 1895. Initially, Uotsuri Jima and Kuba Jima (or Kobi Sho) were placed under the jurisdiction of the Ministry of Agriculture and Commerce (*Noshomusho*) and Minami Kojima and Kita Kojima were placed under the authority of the Ministry of Internal Affairs (*Naimusho*). Because of its small surface area, Kume Aka Shima was not incorporated as national land until July 25, 1921, at which point its name was changed to Taisho Jima. Of the islands, Taisho Jima and the still privately owned Kuba Jima serve as U.S. Navy training ranges, although neither have been used since 1979 as alluded to earlier.[3] The area in and around the Senkaku Islands are also a popular fishing area for the fishing industries of all three countries, and especially the local fishermen in Okinawa.[4]

Tropical plants grow on five of the islands (Uotsuri, Kuba, Taisho, Minami Kojima, and Kita Kojima), and the remaining three rocks (Okino Kitaiwa, Okino Minamiiwa, and Tobise) of them are barren.[5] For the rare short-tailed Albatross (*Phoebastria albatrus*), Minami Kojima represents one of its few

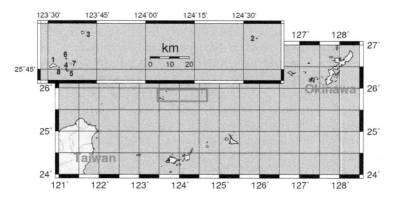

Figure 1.1 Map of the Senkaku Islands

Table 1.1 List of Island Names, Location, and Size

Island name (Japanese/Chinese)	Location	Size	Elevation
Uotsuri Jima/Diao Yu	25°44'39"N 123°28'26"E	1.7 sq miles (4.3 sq km)	1,275 ft (383 m)
Kuba Jima, Kobi Sho/ Huangwei Yu	25°55'23"N 123°40'59" E	0.4 sq miles (1.08 sq km)	384 ft (117 m)
Taisho Jima, Sekibisho/ Chiwei Yu	25°55'18"N 124°33'34"E	0.2 sq miles (0.61 sq km)	246 ft (75 m)
Minami Kojima/Nan Xiaodao	25°43'21"N 123°33'07"E	99 acres (0.40 sq km)	456 ft (139 m)
Kita Kojima/Bei Xiaodao	25°43'48"N 123°32'33 E	77 acres (0.31 sq km)	410 ft (125 m)
Okino Kita Iwa/Da Bei Xiaodao	25°46'47"N 123°32'32" E	N/a	N/a
Okino Minami Iwa/Da Nan Xiaodao	25°45'19"N 123°34'1' E	N/a	N/a
Tobise (Tobi Sho)/Yan Jiao Yan (Fei Jiao Yan, Yan Jiao Lai)	25°44'8"N 123°30'22"E	N/a	6.5 ft (2m)

breeding places. Similarly, Uotsuri Jima is home to a number of endemic species, such as the Senkaku mole (*Nesoscaptor uchidai*) and the *Okinawa Kuro Oari* giant ant.

The islands are believed to sit on or near large reserves of oil, natural gas, and other resources, which in large part drive the dispute between Japan, China, and Taiwan over the sovereignty claims over the islands which began to get seriously disputed in 1970. These competing claims over the Senkaku Islands will be discussed throughout this chapter, but first follows a brief international history of the islands.

The discovery and recording of the islands

The earliest known reference to the Diaoyu Islands appears in the manuscript *Yudi Jisheng* (History of Famous Geographical Locations in China), written in 1221 by Wang Xiangzhi.[6] As with much early history (that on the Bonin Islands is a prime example[7]), there is much confusion surrounding this reference. The biggest issue has to do with the fact that the location of the islands discussed in *Yudi Jisheng* is not the same as the currently disputed islands. Moreover, the manuscript was not widely used and it was not until the first half of the nineteenth century, or some six hundred years later, before the Chinese government (Qing Dynasty) actually referenced it.[8] Furthermore, there are no materials that verify the exact date when the Chinese government discovered and named the islands, although the Southern Song Dynasty may have been responsible for naming them.[9]

Table 1.2 List of Ishigaki City Addresses for Each Island and Ownership[5]

Island name	Ishigaki city address (year established)	Current and previous owner (residence)
Uotsuri Jima	2392 Tonoshiro, Ishigaki City, Okinawa Prefecture (1902)	Government of Japan (Ministry of Finance)
		Kurihara Kunikoshi (Saitama Prefecture)[6]
Minami Kojima	2391 Tonoshiro, Ishigaki City, Okinawa Prefecture (1902)	GOJ Ministry of Finance
		Kurihara Kunikoshi (Saitama Prefecture)
Kita Kojima	2390 Tonoshiro, Ishigaki City, Okinawa Prefecture (1902)	GOJ Ministry of Finance
		Kurihara Kunikoshi (Saitama Prefecture)
Kuba Jima (Kobi Sho)	2393 Tonoshiro, Ishigaki City, Okinawa Prefecture (1902)	Kurihara Kazuko (Saitama Prefecture)
		Koga Hanako (Okinawa Prefecture)
Taisho Jima (Sekibi Sho)	2394 Tonoshiro, Ishigaki City, Okinawa Prefecture (1921)	GOJ Ministry of Finance

With this said, the islands served for a long time as a navigational aid for vessels traveling between Japan, the Ryukyu Kingdom, and China. In 1372, China established a tributary relationship with Satto (also known as Chadu), the Chuzan chieftain based in present-day Urasoe City, who was told by a visiting Chinese delegate, Yang Zai, that it should come under the kingdom's influence.[10] This relationship would continue after 1429, when the various minor provinces in Okinawa were united into the Ryukyu Kingdom and the first Sho dynasty was established. It also continued following the invasion by forces from the Satsuma Domain, or *Satsuma Han*, in southern Kyushu in 1609, which sought, among other resources, to use Okinawa's trade, personal, and information connections to the outside world to better its position domestically. While the tributary relationship would come to an end with Japan annexing the Ryukyu Kingdom in the 1870s, for those five hundred years, the Senkaku Islands, whose highest point on Uotsuri Island was 383 meters, were like a lighthouse or beacon for sea traffic, lying as they do almost half-way between Naha and Fuzhou City in southeastern China.[11]

According to Okuhara Toshio, citing documents from the tributary missions and other interactions between China and the Ryukyu Islands including the *Chungshan Chuanhsin Lu* (Record of the Mission to the Royal Court of the Chung-shan) among other items, the islands were not known during those years as the Senkakus, but were recognized individually by the names Tsurigyodai, Kobi Sho, Sekibi Sho, which were probably used by Chinese navigators on the vessels used for tributary trade.[12] Locally and historically within Okinawa, the islands comprising what were later named the Senkakus at the end of the nineteenth century, such as Uotsuri Jima and Kobi Sho, were called Yukun and Kuba Jima, respectively.[13] "Yukun" means "fish island," and thus Uotsuri Island was likely recognized as a place good for fishing. It also had the name of Yokon and Haopinsan. Kuba Jima, on the other hand, is actually derived from Koba Jima, and likely acquired its name due to the heavy growth of *biro*, or Livingston Palm Tree, which was revered as a godly tree there. The island was also locally called Chausu Island. Furthermore, since Sekibi Sho is close to the island of Kume Jima, it was named "Kume Aka Shima" until the name officially changed in 1921. It was not only the Japanese who had variations for the names of the islands. The Chinese and those who relied on their navigators, did as well.

The islands as a group acquired the name of the Senkakus in a very roundabout way, and rather belatedly.[14] In January 1843 the British Navy ship, the H.M.S. *Samarang*, a vessel commanded by Sir Edward Belcher, departed England to survey the South China Seas after Britain's war with China, including the Philippines and the East Indies. In June 1845, the *Samarang* came upon Hoa-pin-san, the Chinese name for Diaoyu (Uotsuri) Island. After surveying the waters around Uotsuri, Belcher went on to describe the islands and area in the following way:

> On the morning following we were sufficiently near to Hoa-pin-san to secure a landing for the meridian distance ... Towards sunset the ship found anchorage on a bank to the eastward of Pinnacle Islands, and thus prevented her being drifted beyond our sight before the morning ... On the 16th [of June 1845], we endeavoured to obtain observations on Tia-usu [Huangwei Island]; a landing was effected, but the absence of sun prevented our obtaining satisfactory observations, and bad weather coming on hastened our departure. This group, comprehending Hoa-pin-san, Pinnacle rocks, and Tia-usu, form a triangle, of which the hypothenuse, or distance between Hoa-pin-san and Tia-usu, extends about fourteen miles, and that between Hoa-pin-san and the Southern Pinnacle, about two miles. Within this space lie several reefs; and although a safe channel exists between Hoa-pin-san and Pinnacle Islands, it ought not, (by reason of the strength of the tides destroying steerage) to be attempted if it can be avoided ... the extreme height of Hoa-pin-san was found to be 1181 feet, the island apparently cut away vertically at this elevation ... Traces of the wreck of Chinese or Japanese junks were noticed. The position of the south-east angle of this island was found to be in Latitude 25 degrees 47' 7" No., and Longitude 123 degrees 26' E. Pinnacle Group is connected by a reef and bank of soundings with Hoa-pin-san, allowing a channel of about twelve fathoms between it and Channel Rock ... some distressed beings had evidently visited this island, not Europeans, as their temporary beds were constructed of materials which belonged to canoes,

palmetto thatch & c [et cetera]. They had probably selected this cave as furnishing water by percolation from above, and were probably sustained by the bodies and eggs of the sea-birds which abound in the brush wood. In addition to the sea-birds noticed on Pinnacle Island, we found here the gigantic Petrel in all its stages ... We now sought Raleigh Rock [Chiwei Island], situated to the eastward, but were equally unfortunate in the want of sun ... I found landing practicable, and remained on the reef, upon which it rises, as long as any hope remained, either of seeing the sun, or obtaining the bearing of Tia-usu from it, but a heavy squall put an end to any further exercise of patience. Raleigh Rock rises abruptly from the reef to a height computed at ninety feet perpendicular on all sides, and covering an area of probably sixty feet, in diameter, appearing in the distance as a junk under sail.[15]

In the appendix of the above two-volume *Narrative*, Captain Belcher provides the geographical location and names of the islands. As seen above, Diaoyu Yu (Diao Island), located at 25 47' 7" and 123 25'44" E, is identified as "Hoa-pin-san." Huangwei Yu (Huangwei Island), at 25 57'13" N and 123 37'6" E, is named "Tia-usu." The small islets to the east of Diaoyu Island, are identified as the "Pinnacle Islands" and "Pinnacle Group" and are located at 29 51'48" and 129 48'12" E.[16] Chiwei Yu (Chiwei Island) is called "Raleigh Rock."[17]

Based on the *Narrative* of Captain Belcher, the *British Naval Waterway Record* introduced the Diaoyu Islands in the following way some forty years later in 1884: "*Haopinsu*, the south-western island of an isolated group about 90 miles northward of the west end of *Meiaco sima* [Miyako Jima], is 1,180 feet high with a steep cliff on the southern side of the summit, and a gradual slope on the eastern side. This island is barren and uninhabited; there are pools of fresh water, with fish in them, on the eastern slope."[18]

The Imperial Japanese Navy (*Dainippon Teikoku Kaigun*), established fifteen years before this account in July 1869 with British assistance, used the British navy's records to help it facilitate its own waterways studies when it published its waterway report (*Kanei Suiroshi*, or "Journal of the Waterways of the World"), including copying the names the British used for the Diaoyu Islands in the latter country's 1884 record.[19] Using Chinese characters and *katakana*, an alphabet designed to render foreign words into pronounceable Japanese, the naval authorities identified the Diaoyu Yu, Huangwei Yu, and Chiwei Yu as "Hoapin-san," "Tiau-su," and "Raleigh Rock," respectively.[20] It also identified the "Pinnacle Group," pointing out that the "huge rock in the Diaoyu Islands can be seen as a 'pinnacle' mountain when viewed from the sea."[21]

In its subsequent edition published in 1894, the Japanese Imperial Navy Record chose to eliminate the use of the Chinese characters and English alphabet and instead identified the islands in *katakana*. The 1908 edition of the record, however, used the Chinese characters and English alphabet again.[22]

It is Kuroiwa Hisashi, a physics teacher at the Okinawa Normal School (*Okinawa Shihan Gakko*), who is usually credited with naming the islands "Senkaku." He did so in an article appearing in 1900 in the Japanese journal, *Chigaku Zasshi* (Journal of Geography), published by the Tokyo Geographical Society (or *Tokyo Chigaku Kyokai*, founded in 1879). Kuroiwa writes that "the main island was formed by Chogyo Sho, Sento Shosho, and Kobi Sho. Because these islands do not have a single name to identify them, this has contributed to the difficulty of the geographical work. Therefore, these islands were given a single name, Senkaku Retto, to identify them as a whole."[23]

But Kuroiwa was simply referencing previous works, such as that by Sasamori Gisuke, in his *Nanto Tanken* (Southern Islands Exploration), published in 1884, and the 1886 Imperial Navy Record, which referred to the Pinnacle Islands.[24] Sento is a Japanese translation of "pinnacle," and Kuroiwa seems to have misread "Sento" as "Senkaku."

Growing awareness of the Senkaku Islands and their utilization by Japan

Japan's awareness of and interest in the so-called "Senkaku Islands" was initially weak. Even on the eve of the exploration and use of the islands by some entrepreneurial Japanese, maps and atlases produced by Japanese publishers did not include or name the Senkaku Islands by their Japanese reading.[25]

With this said, one person, Koga Tatsushiro, a businessman originally from Yamada Village in Yame County, Fukuoka Prefecture, became particularly interested in the possibilities the Senkaku Islands had to offer once he learned of their existence from local fishermen. The third son of Koga Monjiro,[26] Tatsushiro was known as a "Kiryu Shonin," or someone who went to Okinawa after the Meiji Restoration (1867) to establish a business there.[27] He arrived in Okinawa in 1879, at the age of 23,[28] and immediately set up his own shop (*Koga Shoten*) in Naha. He primarily dealt in tea but later got into ocean products, such as shells which would be used to make buttons, and sent them up to the family's main store (*Osaka Koga Shoten*) in Osaka, run by his two brothers, for sale to foreign companies. In 1882, his company had done well enough to set up a branch office on Ishigaki Jima known as Koga Shoten Yaeyama Shiten.[29] Locally, the store was called "Kuga Doun," the local pronunciation of "the Honorable Koga," which shows the deference Okinawans demonstrated to people from the mainland.[30]

In Ishigaki, Koga learned from fishermen and others about the uninhabited Senkaku Islands and the fact the islands were a nesting area for birds. That year (1884), Koga sent an exploratory party to the islands and learned that indeed the islands were a bird habitat and were rich in marine resources.[31] The following year, he sent some workers there to gather bird feathers and ocean products, and realizing that both supply and demand were promising, decided to make it a regular part of his business.[32] Over the next decade, he would send workers and fishermen there on a regular basis. Eventually, in 1894, Koga applied to the governor of Okinawa Prefecture, Nishimura Sutezo, for permission to allow him to develop Kuba Jima,[33] and he seems to have made the same request to the Japanese government, such as the Ministry of Home Affairs and Ministry of Agriculture and Commerce (about that same time). However, his request was denied due to the fact that the ownership of the islands was unclear.[34]

Koga would first visit the islands himself the following year in 1895, when he traveled on a small boat to Kuba Jima. He would describe the visit in the following way: "there were many trees growing, and an infinite number of birds on the island. So numerous in fact, that you could catch one in your hand. The nearby waters were also rich in fish and other marine items. It is a very promising place to develop."[35] After this trip, he went directly to Tokyo and met with Minister of Home Affairs Nomura Yasushi on June 10, 1895 to describe the investigation he had conducted and request to be allowed to lease the islands.[36] Since, as will be discussed below, the Japanese government had already approved earlier that year the inclusion of Uotsuri Jima and Kuba Jima as a part of Okinawa Prefecture (and thus a part of Japan), the situation was quite different from the previous year when Koga last applied for permission to lease the islands. Legally speaking, according to international law scholar Okuhara, there was now no problem in accepting the request. However, because the islands in question had not been officially designated "national land," or *kokuyuchi*, the minister decided to put off accepting Koga's request.

Some years before in 1885, Yamagata Aritomo, the Home Minister for the Meiji Government, requested for the first time of Okinawa Prefecture, which had been incorporated into Japan as a prefecture just six years before (in 1879), that it conduct a survey of Kume Aka Jima and the two other nearby islands. This was done as an internal order to Morimoto Nagayoshi, who was serving as the Okinawa Prefecture Supreme Secretary (*Okinawaken Daishokicho*) in Tokyo. Nishimura, the governor of Okinawa, learned more about the islands from Oshiro Eiko, a local official at Misatomagiri, through Ishizawa Hyogo, who worked in the 5th District (covering Yaeyama) of the prefecture government, and had the latter conduct a study on the possibility of developing the islands.[37]

The study, entitled *Kume Aka Jima Kuba Jima Uotsuri Jima no Santo Torishirabesho* (Report on the Three Islands of Kume Aka Jima, Kuba Jima, and Uotsuri Jima), was completed on September 21, and the following day (September 22, 1885), the governor forwarded it with a request to consider the possibility of erecting a national marker on the islands.[38] This was the first of three petitions that the governor of Okinawa would make to the central government on this issue.

In the meantime, Governor Nishimura, a native of Shimane Prefecture who served as the appointed governor of Okinawa from December 1883 to April 1886 after having been the head of the police division within the Home Ministry, dispatched several men, including Ishizawa and some other police officers, aboard the *Izumo Maru*, an Osaka Shipping Co. (*Osaka Shosen*) vessel, to the islands to conduct a study of the conditions of land and harbor areas for possible development. There were two reports that resulted from the trip, one (*Uotsuri Jima Hoka Futajima Junshi Torishirabe Gairyaku*, or "An Overview of the Investigation of Uotsuri Jima and Two Other Islands") written by Ishizawa, and the other (*Uotsuri, Kuba, Kume Aka Shima Kaiko Hokokusho*, or "A Report of the Maritime Journey to Uotsuri, Kuba, and Kume Aka Shima") written by the ship's captain, Hayashi Tsurumatsu.[39]

After studying the reports submitted by the *Izumo Maru* team, Nishimura followed up on his September 22 request, which had simply asked about the propriety of erecting national markers on the islands in light of the likely concerns with China, with a second request that actually asked about being allowed to construct the markers. This request, dated November 5, was joined by copies of the two reports of the survey mission.[40]

Yamagata was inclined to support the request. His ministry found no evidence that the islands ever actually belonged to China. Moreover, they were uninhabited islands close to the Miyako and Yaeyama Islands, both of which were administered as a part of Okinawa Prefecture. Yamagata worked on a memo for decision before the Council of State (*Daijokan Kaigi*).

At the same time, Yamagata discussed Nishimura's petition with Foreign Minister Inoue Kaoru, explaining that while the Chinese had used the islands as navigational aids on their way to and from the Ryukyu Kingdom, there was no indication that the islands in fact belonged to the Qing Dynasty. As such, he asked, if it was possible to build an administrative landmark on these islands.[41] The two men met on October 9 to discuss the issue, after Nishimura's first request had come in and well before the second one arrived.[42]

Inoue was worried about China's reaction and urged caution for the time being. In his written response dated October 21 he explained, "It has been found that these islands [the Diaoyu Islands] lie near the border area with the Qing," and continued, "Recently, there were articles in a Chinese newspaper saying we are occupying these offshore islands in the vicinity of Taiwan. If we erect the territorial landmark at this particular time, it would arouse Chinese suspicions. I would advise putting off establishment of the territorial landmark until a later time."[43]

Yamagata, who would travel early the next year to Okinawa, including Yaeyama and Miyako, studied the foreign minister's response carefully,[44] and requested the two meet to discuss a response to Governor Nishimura.[45] The two discussed the issue on December 4,[46] and the following day, with both ministers signing it, Yamagata sent his response to Nishimura, rejecting the request (for the time being) and insisting that the matter should not be revealed to the newspapers.[47] Nishimura would leave his post the following spring (approximately a month after Yamagata came to visit) and eventually go on to become governor of Osaka Prefecture, but his successors would continue to pursue the inclusion of the Senkaku Islands into Okinawa Prefecture and the construction of a territorial landmark there.

Having the administrative status of the islands clarified was in fact very important, not only for the central government, but also for the local governments. Several people began making visits to the islands, and it was easy to imagine conflicts arising over fishing, land, and other rights, not only between those within Okinawa, but between Okinawans and mainland Japanese, Japanese and Taiwanese, and Japanese and Chinese. (We would see this conflict emerge years later with the competition over fishing rights in the 1950s onward and still later mineral rights after the discovery of potential reserves of oil in the late 1960s.) As we saw earlier, Koga had already traveled there and brought some of his workers with him beginning in the mid-1880s. In 1891, Isawa Yakidai, of Kumamoto Prefecture, brought Okinawan fishermen with him to Uotsuri Jima and Kuba Jima, succeeding in gathering ocean-based items and bird feathers until the weather eventually forced them to return to Ishigaki. In addition, in 1893, two men named Nagai and Matsumoto from Kagoshima Prefecture, along with some Okinawan fisherman, went to Kuba Jima, but ran out of food and had to turn back. Subsequently, the same year, Isawa returned to Kuba Jima and succeeded again in his mission, but got blown off course on the way home, resulting in the death of nine crewmembers. Only one survived, making it to Fuzhou Province in China. Another individual, Noda Masaru, also of Kumamoto Prefecture, attempted to go to Uotsuri Jima and Kuba Jima, but were blown off course too, and failed to get there.[48]

In early 1890, the Yaeyama Island Office (*Yaeyama To Yakusho*) requested the governor to see to it that Kume Seki Jima and the other two islands be placed under the jurisdiction of Yaeyama. As a result, Maruoka Kanji, the seventh governor of Okinawa, wrote to Home Affairs minister Yamagata, who was by this point also serving as prime minister, on January 13, 1890.[49] Maruoka requested that Uotsuri and two other islands be placed under the jurisdiction of Yaeyama. Curiously, in the response that the governor received from Suematsu Kencho, the director of the Prefecture Administration Division (*Kenchikyoku*) of the Home Ministry, he was asked to forward a copy of the December 5, 1886 directive he had once received from Yamagata.[50] It is unclear whether Governor Maruoka eventually received a response, or even whether the issue was taken up with Foreign Minister Aoki Shuzo at the time. According to Senkaku Islands scholar Okuhara, it is likely that the foreign minister was opposed to it in any case due to international, namely Chinese, sensitivities.[51]

This does not mean the government was not interested, however, for it subsequently dispatched the *Kaimon*, an Imperial Japanese Navy a sail-and-steam corvette commissioned in March 1884 that would see service in the Sino–Japanese War, to survey the islands in August 1892.[52]

A third petition that was quite similar in contents to the 1890 one (in that it argued for the need for Okinawa Prefecture and Yaeyama Island in particular to be empowered to regulate fishing and other matters as well as constructing a national marker on the Senkakus) was presented on November 2, 1893 to Inoue Kaoru, now the interior minister, and Foreign Minister Mutsu Munemitsu.[53] On this occasion as well, permission was not immediately granted, but eventually it would be.

It was not until April 14, 1894 before the Meiji government took any action on the request. In a secret set of instructions to Okinawa governor Narahara Shigeru, an extremely powerful bureaucrat from Satsuma who served sixteen years as governor of Okinawa as he attempted to modernize it,[54] Inoue asked that Narahara provide answers to several questions regarding the islands: (1) the condition of harbors on the islands; (2) the likelihood of being able to develop the islands; (3) evidence that the islands belong to Japan; and (4) information about the historical relationship between the islands with Miyako and Yaeyama Islands.[55] After looking into their questions, Narahara discovered that no surveys had been carried out since the 1886 one by the *Izumo Maru*. As such, he responded that he could not answer with much certainty but that "there was no clear evidence or claims in older records that the islands in question belonged to our country. There are only the facts that Okinawan fishermen went to southern islands from Yaeyama to catch fish."[56]

With this response, it became clear that there was little evidence to show that the islands were in fact Japanese. This was no doubt worrisome to at least some officials in the government, for a few months later, hostilities broke out between Japan and China on August 1, 1894, in what has come to be known as the Sino–Japanese War of 1894–95. Wars occur due to a lot of different—and often overlapping—factors such as perceived slights on national honor, armed attacks, infringements on sovereignty, and territorial disputes, to list just a few. Changes in territory often result. The Senkakus were not directly related to this war or such changes in territorial status as a result of this war, but at the same time, the islands were not unrelated either.

In mid-December, when it was clear the Japanese side was winning the war (Port Arthur had fallen on November 21 and the city of Kaipeng fell on December 10), the Home Ministry prepared a document for submission to the Cabinet. Dated December 15, it gave three reasons why it was submitting it now: (1) the situation is very much changed from 1885 when it first raised the issue; (2) neither Uotsuri Jima nor Kuba Jima had been determined as yet to be any one country's territory; and (3) the islands should be recognized as part of Okinawa due to a better understanding of the geography.

Some ten days later on December 27, Home Minister Nomura met with Foreign Minister Mutsu to discuss the introduction of the position paper to the Cabinet for it to reach a Cabinet Decision (*Kakugi Kettei*) regarding the erection of administrative markers on Kuba Jima and Uotsuri Jima. In light of the likely victory of Japan over China, Nomura noted that the situation with regard to the Senkakus had changed. Munemitsu replied that he did not have any objection to erecting said markers, a view made more official when he responded in a confidential letter to Nomura dated January 11 (1895).[57] The following day, Prime Minister Ito Hirobumi called for his ministers to gather, which they did early the next week on January 14, 1895.[58] The matter was jointly submitted before the Cabinet and the request by the respective governors of

Okinawa Prefecture over the years to place on Kuba Jima and Uotsuri Jima national markers designating the islands as belonging to Japan, was approved.[59]

The following week, on January 21, the prime minister sent a draft order to the home minister to be used to inform the Okinawan governor, and the next day, January 22, that order was sent to the Foreign Ministry along with a request to discuss it.[60] Early the following month on February 2, the Foreign Ministry sent back a slightly revised or cleaned up version of the order, which was forwarded to the Okinawan governor on or sometime after February 3.[61] The order, which called on the governor to implement the decision within a week's time,[62] was signed by both the home minister and the foreign minister.

This latter point is instructive as the islands that came to be known as the Senkaku Islands were not only an interior issue but also a diplomatic issue as well from the very beginning for the Japanese government. Indeed, the timing of Japan's formal acquisition of the Senkakus was no doubt timed with the favorable turn in the direction of the war. Better said, the proponents of formally identifying the islands as Japan's, who had long pushed the view, used the new positive situation to push it again, this time successfully. However, this does not mean Japan "stole" the islands, for they were officially claimed by no one and thus were no one's to steal (an international legal concept known as *terra nullus*). Three months later, the Treaty of Shimonoseki between Japan and China, which, among other things, ceded Taiwan to Japan, was concluded on April 17.[63] The Senkakus were not identified one way or the other. This would become a part of the academic and political seventy-five years later when Taiwan and China claimed the Senkakus, as both of those countries argued that the Senkakus were part of Taiwan and thus paragraph b of Article 2, which referred to "The island of Formosa, together with all islands appertaining or belonging to the said island of Formosa," applied to the Senkakus, whereas Japan did not consider the Senkakus a part of Taiwan at that point when the treaty was signed, and thus the Senkakus were not "islands appertaining or belonging to the said island of Formosa."[64]

The following year on March 5, 1896, however, when the central government issued Imperial Edict No. 13 dividing Okinawa into five counties (*gun*), namely Shimajiri (southern part of the main island of Okinawa), Nakagami (central part), Kunigami (northern part), Miyako, and Yaeyama, with a description of what areas each county covered administratively. Two areas, Naha and Shuri, were not included in the above counties as they were scheduled to be counted as a separate district (*ku*).

The Senkakus were not specifically referred to in the edict, under the areas covered by Yaeyama, something which has caused an academic debate over its significance. One scholar, Suganuma, criticizes the "many pro-Japan irredentist scholars who claim that Imperial Edict No. 13 implemented the [January 14, 1895] decision of the Meiji government in 1896 … Nowhere in this edict are the names of the Diaoyu or Senkaku Islands mentioned in the Japanese, Chinese, or English language. Therefore, it is clear that this edict is irrelevant with respect to the sovereignty of the disputed Diaoyu Islands."[65] This is a technically correct, but somewhat illogical, counterintuitive, and counter factual argument and conclusion in light of the efforts of the Japanese government until then.

A more realistic answer is given by Okuhara. Until the early 1970s when the Senkakus dispute began in earnest, according to Okuhara, most people over the previous seventy-five years had considered Imperial Edict 13 as the time when the Senkaku Islands were joined with Japan, since Japanese law applied to them as part of Okinawa Prefecture and the islands had already been administratively included into Yaeyama the previous year.

In any case, the governor of Okinawa took measures to include the islands into Yaeyama County (following the going into force on April 1, 1896, of the Imperial Decree concerning the County System, or *gunsei*, of Okinawa Prefecture), and in December 1902, the islands were made part of Tonogusuku Village (Tonogusuku-son) of Ishigaki Island. Subsequently, they became part of Yaeyama Village (Yaeyama-son) again in 1908, only to become part of Ishigaki Village (Ishigaki-son) in 1914, Ishigaki Town (Ishigaki-cho), in 1926, and Ishigaki City (Ishigaki-shi) in 1947 (although by this point, the U.S. military was now in charge of the occupation of the Nansei Islands as explained in the next chapter).[66]

In the meantime Koga's request, entitled "Kanyuchi Haishaku Gogan," made to develop the islands, was officially approved at this juncture, in August 1896. Koga was allowed to use four of the islands—Uotsuri, Kobi Sho, Minami Kojima, and Kita Kojima—for thirty years free of charge. Afterwards, when the thirty-year gratuitous lease expired, the four islands were leased from the central government on an annual basis for 136.61 yen beginning in September 1925.[67] On March 31, 1932, at the solicitation of Koga's son, Zenji, who had assumed ownership of the family business after his father passed away in mid-August 1918, the government sold the four islands to him at the price of 1,824 yen for Uotsuri Jima, 247 yen for Kuba Jima, 47 yen for Minami Kojima, and 31.50 yen for Kita Kojima.[68] The transfer of property rights was conducted later that year—May 27 for Uotsuri Jima and Kuba Jima, and July 28 for Minami Kojima and Kita Kojima. Because the islands were now privately owned, they became subject to property taxes. On December 15, 1932, the insular rental valuation was fixed at 9.30 yen, and the land property tax was calculated on this basis for the next few years.[69] On June 1, 1936, the rental valuation was adjusted, and the tax for Koga's islands was lowered to 6.20 yen.[70]

Using two sea-going vessels that he had purchased and refurbished, Koga Tatsushiro started officially developing the islands in 1897. That year, in March and April respectively, he sent thirty-five workers from Ishigaki, with food, daily supplies, and other materials to the islands to set up operations there, and led another fifty the following year in 1898, using the Osaka Shosen's 1600-ton ship, the *Suma Maru*,[71] to make regular trips back and forth carrying supplies and returning with products for market.[72] This group in particular helped to build lodging, work stations, and a dock on Uotsuri and Kuba islands. Twenty-nine men followed in 1899 with supplies aboard both the *Suma Maru* and another 1600-ton vessel, the *Anping Maru,*[73] and thirteen men and nine women went to the island to work in 1900.

Unlike the first two years, in which workers stayed only temporarily, the group that traveled in 1899 stayed for a long time into the following year. One young scholar, Miyajima Mikinosuke, who traveled to the islands then with Koga, wrote about the good condition he found the workers in.[74] During this time, Koga's store in Yaeyama furnished the supplies for developing the islands. Creating reservoirs while carefully protecting the breeding grounds of the sea-birds, Koga was able to develop 147 acres of cultivated land for crops, vegetables and sweet potatoes, fruit trees, and lumber trees, as well as cattle-breeding. Koga had also engaged in collecting albatross plumage, shellfish, trepangs, shark fin, and turtlebacks, and after 1903, coral collecting, canning sea-birds, and stuffing birds. In 1905, he had three more ocean-going ships built on the mainland to expand his bonito business, and in 1906, had another five built. He also had several boats used for coral collecting. Eventually, the number of settlers grew to 248 people, or ninety-nine households by 1909. Earlier that same year, on January 22, Koga received the Order of Merit (*Ranju Hosho*) from the Emperor for his efforts to develop the islands and other deeds.

Koga seemed to be an inquisitive man, always seeking new opportunities. In May 1900, he traveled with the above young scientist, Miyajima (who would go on to become a professor of Keio University), and Kuroiwa Hisashi of the Okinawa Normal School to the islands aboard the *Yongkang Maru*, a 460-ton vessel Koga had chartered.[75] They first landed at Kuba Jima. The two scholars had come to do their own research, but Koga had also asked them to advise him on technical and scientific matters about the islands. Miyajima focused on Kuba Jima, and Kuroiwa traveled to Utosuri Jima, in addition to doing work on Kuba Jima. It was this same Kuroiwa who named (or misnamed) the group of islands.

Based on the recommendations of these two men, Koga created the following plan for his business and activities there: (1) limit intake of birds and fish and instead raise animals and crow crops for food; (2) build houses and other dwellings to permit settling; (3) build wells and other tanks to trap water for drinking and other needs; (4) build a docking area and make it low enough to be able to move supplies and goods easily; and (5) build roads and make the settlement as sanitary as possible.[76]

In May the following year (1901), Koga traveled with an engineer from the Okinawa Normal School, Kumakura Kyozo, seeking his advice on making improvements in the islands.[77] Based on these recommendations, Koga had numerous structures built (a total of thirty-five), continuing to import the materials from outside the islands for this construction. Some of the facilities built include: male and female dorms, offices, baths, warehouses, kitchens, etc.[78] This work would continue until the end of the first decade of the 20th century. During this time, he continued to purchase boats and ships on an annual basis for his ever-expanding business, including the 150-ton *Miura*

Figure 1.2 Uotsuri Village

Figure 1.3 Fishing Dock

Figure 1.4 Fish Caught Near Islands

Maru from the Japanese colonial administration in Taiwan known as the *Taiwan Sotokufu* (Japanese Governor-General). He renamed the boat the *Tatsujima Maru.*[79]

In 1907, hoping to expand his business enterprise into mining, he applied for mining concessions in the Senkakus area from the Fukuoka Office of Mining Affairs (*Fukuoka Kozan Kanshusho*) and his application was approved on August 19. Koga immediately began excavating guano, the excrement of cave-dwelling bats, seabirds, and seals, and continued this enterprise until 1925, when the price of shipping became too expensive to pursue his

Figure 1.5 Birds on Islands

enterprise profitably.[80] Koga Zenji continued managing his islands until the outbreak of World War II, when fuel rationing made it difficult to operate whatsoever from the islands.[81] The Yaeyama store closed in 1940, and Koga left Okinawa in late October 1944 as part of the evacuations on the eve of the Battle of Okinawa, after his store, goods, home, and belongings were destroyed in the October 10 air raids on Naha.[82] Although he and his wife, Hanako, who had nursing experience, wanted to stay and assist their neighbors, they had no place to live and temporarily moved to the mainland, staying in Nagano (his wife's hometown) and Tokyo. He and Hanako eventually returned to

Okinawa in 1961.[83] During that time, Koga still retained ownership of four islands with the related records held by Ishigaki City.[84]

The Koga business was not the only group to visit the islands during the latter years of the nineteenth century and first half of the twentieth. Prior to his coming, there were others who traveled there, as mentioned above. There were also many others who came while he had his business there.

In 1900, the mayor of Yaeyama, Nomura Doan, landed on the islands to conduct an administrative inspection.[85] Nomura traveled on the same ship that Koga and the two scholars he had enlisted to assist him had arrived on. While on Sekibi Sho, the men, along with Koga, erected a monument to their visit there in Japanese and English.[86]

The following year, in May 1901, Okinawa Prefecture conducted its first land survey of the islands in light of the new taxation system based on land productivity to be introduced from June 1, 1903 and which would abolish the old per capita taxation system.[87] The survey was conducted by its Provisional Bureau of Landed Property Coordination (*Rinji Okinawaken Tochi Seiri Jimukyoku*) and detailed scale maps of each of the islands were produced. In addition, Koga had asked that the prefecture include some technical specialists on the survey for planning and other purposes, and some engineers and others were brought along.[88]

In 1904, officials from Okinawa Prefecture and Yaeyama, including the police chief, made respective visits to the islands, and those visits were followed up by more police- and administrative-related visits in 1907.[89]

The following year, Iwai Jidama, a teacher from the Shimajiri Fishery School (*Okinawaken Shimajiri Suisan Gakko*), based in southern Okinawa, and one of his former students landed on the islands to teach some methods of making canned food, and another researcher disembarked there to do

Figure 1.6 Koga Tatsushiro

Figure 1.7 Koga Hanako

Figure 1.8 Koga Zenji

some analysis on local phosphates.[90] Other surveys followed over the years, including by the National Hydrographic Bureau (*Nihon Suirobu*) in 1915, the Imperial Japanese Navy's Bureau of Hydrography (*Kaigun Suirobu*) in 1917 and 1919, respectively, and by the Okinawa Forestry Office (*Okinawa Eirinsho*) in 1931. Another survey was conducted of the resources on the islands by the Ministry of Agriculture and Forestry (*Norinsho*[91]) in 1939. And in 1943, the staff of the Ishigaki Meteorological Station (*Ishigaki Sokkosho*) visited Uotsuri Jima as part of a preliminary survey to construct a meteorological station there.[92]

The islands saw other activities besides fishing and surveys. In 1940, a civilian airplane serving the Japan-Taiwan route for *Dai Nippon Koku Kabushiki Kaisha* (Imperial Japanese Airways Company, the forerunner to Japan Airlines) carrying thirteen passengers had to make a forced landing on Uotsuri Jima. They were all safe and were rescued by police from Yaeyama.[93]

There was another successful rescue of people some twenty years before that. In 1919, thirty-one fishermen from the province of Fuzhou, China were shipwrecked near Uotsuri Jima and rescued by Koga Zenji and his workers. They were transported to Ishigaki to be fed and sheltered and to have their medical concerns addressed. They were "taken care of very well," Koga remembered, "not just by me but by all the people of Ishigaki."[94] Eventually, after their ship was repaired, they were repatriated to China. For Koga's efforts, the Chinese Consulate in Nagasaki presented a certificate of gratitude to the then-mayor of Ishigaki, Toyokawa Yoshisuke, Koga, and two others. Interestingly, the certificate of appreciation, dated May 20, 1920, recognized the Senkaku Islands as belonging to Yaeyama County, Okinawa Prefecture, Japan.

Koga, who was the recipient of the letter and made it publicly available, found it odd, five decades later, that China would try to claim the islands since it had clearly recognized them as belonging to Japan as stated in the letter. "It was not a personal letter. It was a letter from the government of China. I still have it."[95]

Sadly, not all the shipwrecks ended happily. Just one week after the Battle of Okinawa was officially declared over on June 23, 1945, another tragedy affecting Okinawa began, this time with those residents who were being evacuated from Ishigaki and the neighboring islands to nearby Taiwan at the end of June/early July. It is all the more tragic because, although the war still continued, the actual Battle of Okinawa was already over. Such evacuations from outlying islands were somewhat common, but were more successful when they were done early in the war or well before a battle began—such as with the evacuation of Iwo Jima, Kita Iwo Jima, Haha Jima, and Chichi Jima in the summer of 1944.[96] The evacuations would not go well when they were done on the eve of a battle or in areas where the Allies already had established sea and air superiority. Evacuations from Okinawa were one such case where evacuees actually entered the battle grounds prematurely or unexpectedly. Some of the more famous incidents included the sinking of the *Tsushima Maru*[97] in August 1944 and the *Awa Maru*[98] in April 1945. The sinking of the vessels handling the evacuation of Ishigaki is less well known.

Although more than one week had elapsed since the Battle of Okinawa officially ended, there were still pockets of resistance. Indeed, Ishigaki and its neighboring islands were not yet under U.S. control. In the spring of 1945, in an effort to secure a route between Ishigaki and Taiwan, near which the United States had already established superiority, the 45th Independent Combined Division (*Dokuritsu Konsei Dai 45 Shidan*) built a small navy to help ship food, ammunition, and other supplies back and forth. The group of boats was comprised of three fishing vessels, the *Daiichi Senbaya Maru*, *Daisan Senbaya Maru*, and *Daigo Senbaya Maru*, which were commandeered by the navy for military use. Two of these vessels, the *Daiichi* (also known as *Yufuku Maru*) and the *Daigo* (also known as *Isshin Maru*), displaced about 150 tons. The ships' crews were made to work for the military.

In May, these ships made one trip to Taiwan and back safely using a route that took them near the Senkakus. On June 24, one day after organized resistance on Okinawa had ended, an announcement was made to evacuate women, children, and the elderly, and on June 30, the ships prepared to leave. The trip on June 30 was their second one, and they took the same route, in the hopes that the enemy's ships and planes would not be bold enough to attack them. It was an unfortunate miscalculation.

Because the *Daisan Senbaya Maru* had engine problems, it was not used for this second journey, and so it was on the *Daiichi* and *Daigo* that some 200 islanders had boarded.[99] As some officials had learned by this point, disbursing supplies and people aboard several vessels reduced the risk of everything being lost were it attacked. In other words two ships were better than one, but not the ideal. The vessels departed around 9:00 p.m., in a somewhat festive mood. Many were happy to be going to Taiwan where conditions were likely to be better and where friends and relatives had already been living to work or attend school. A smaller vessel carrying wounded and sick soldiers traveled with them but would break off partway through to go to Taiwan via Yonaguni, the southernmost island in the Ryukyu chain.

At 2 p.m. on July 3, the vessels were attacked by U.S. aircraft. The small ships sank and some of the survivors made it to Uotsuri Jima after a couple of days at sea. With no help coming after more than a month, the survivors made a small boat and few dedicated people left in the morning of August 12 making the journey by sea and arrived two days later at Kabira Bay in Ishigaki at 7 a.m. on the 14th. Help finally arrived on the 19th, but by then many had died of hunger on the island, having spent a total of forty-eight days there.[100]

Following the evacuation of the survivors, no one went to the islands for several years afterwards. Some of the survivors themselves would return in May 1969 for a ceremony on the island and the construction of a small memorial there.

Notes

1 See Nanpo Doho Engokai, ed., "Tokushu Senkaku Retto Dainishu (Second Special Issue for Senkaku Islands)," *Kikan Okinawa* (Quarterly Okinawa), No. 63 (December 1972), 4.
2 For more recent, detailed color photos, see Nakama Hitoshi, *Kiki Semaru Senkaku Shoto no Genjo* (The Dangerous Situation Today Facing the Senkaku Islands), (Tokyo: Adobansu Kikaku, 2002). For the map, see Megumi Tadahisa, *Senkaku Shoto, Uotsuri Jima Shashinshu Shiryoshu* (A Collection of Photographs and Documents about Uotsuri Jima in the Senkaku Islands), (Naha: Senkaku Shoto Boei Kyokai, 1996), 11–12.
3 The author has been unable to find any declassified document that specifically directed U.S. forces in Japan from discontinuing use of its ranges in the Senkaku Islands, but sources familiar with the use of the ranges have said it was the State

Department that decided not to allow use of the ranges for diplomatic reasons. Another possibility, although less likely, was that it was a request from the Ministry of Foreign Affairs in order not to aggravate Japan's relations with the People's Republic of China shortly after the two signed a peace treaty. In 2012, for example, the Foreign Ministry requested that a planned bilateral exercise to retake an island in Okinawa be cancelled. "Japan, U.S. Abandon Drill to 'Retake' Isle Joint Exercise Called Off Due to Fear of Backlash from China," *Japan Times*, October 21, 2012. Although the wire service story by *Jiji* did not shed further light on the situation, according to a U.S. official familiar with the situation, it was the leadership of the ruling party, the DPJ, that requested the cancellation.

4 For more on the types of fish caught there, and the times of year in which they are caught, see Senkaku Shoto Bunken Shiryo Hensankai, ed., *Senkaku Kenkyu Senkaku Shoto no Shizen Kaihatsu Riyo no Rekishi to Joho ni Kansuru Chosa Hokoku: Okinawaken ni Okeru Chiiki Shinko Shima Okoshi no Ichijo to Shite* (Senkaku Research Report on the History of Natural Use and Development of the Senkaku Islands and Related Data: Advice on Regional Promotion and Island Development in Okinawa), (Naha: Senkaku Shoto Bunken Shiryo Hensankai, 2011), 151–152.

5 The records for the addresses and ownership are on file at the Ishigaki Branch of the Naha Regional Justice Division (*Naha Chiho Homukyoku Ishigaki Shikyoku*). See Nakama Hitoshi, *Kiki Semaru Senkaku Shoto no Genjo* (The Dangerous Situation Today Facing the Senkaku Islands), (Tokyo: Adobansu Kikaku, 2002), 9. Originally, the islands were administered through Yaeyama Gun (Yaeyama County), but with the merger of Yaeyama with Ishigaki in 1914, they became part of Ishigaki's administrative district.

6 Kurihara Kunikoshi received the title to Uotsuri Island from Koga Hanako, the wife of Koga Zenji, in 1978. Kurihara had received the islands of Kita Kojima and Minami Kojima from Zenji, the son of the original developer, Koga Tatsushiro, in 1972. Kurihara Kazuko received Kuba Jima in 1985 from Hanako, three years prior to her passing in January 1988. The senior Koga, who hailed from Yame County in Fukuoka Prefecture, died in 1918 at the age of 62. The four islands he leased in the Senkakus passed to his son at this time. Zenji eventually purchased them in 1932. He and Hanako did not have children, and looked at Kunikoshi as almost like a son. Zenji died in March 1978 just before tensions rose over the Senkakus in April of that year. Hanako asked Kurihara to take Uotsuri off her hands when tensions rose. See Kurihara, *Senkaku Shoto Urimasu*, 44–48.

7 One Marine Corps helicopter pilot, previously in charge of 1st Marine Air Wing operations, noted to this author, "generally speaking, where there is vegetation, we can land."

8 Unryu, *Sovereign Rights*, 42.

9 For more, see Chapter 1 of Eldridge, *Iwo Jima to Ogasawara o Meguru Nichibei Kankei*.

10 Unryu, *Sovereign Rights*, 44.

11 Unryu, *Sovereign Rights*, 44.

12 For more on the start of the tributary relationship, see George H. Kerr, *Okinawa: The History of an Island People* (Boston: Tuttle Publishing, 1958), particularly Chapter 2. For more on China's relationships with tributary states like the Ryukyu Islands, see S. Y. Teng and John K. Fairbank, "On the Ch'ng Tributary System," *Harvard Journal for Asiatic Studies*, Vol. 1, No. 2 (June 1941), 135–246. Also see, Akamine Mamoru, *Ryukyu Okoku: Higashi Ajia no Koonaasutoon* (Ryukyu Kingdom: The Cornerstone of East Asia), (Tokyo: Kodansha, 2004), particularly Chapter 2.

13 Okuhara, "Senkaku Retto: Rekishi to Seiji no Aida," 54–55.

14 Okuhara, "Senkaku Retto: Rekishi to Seiji no Aida," 55.

15 Okuhara, "Senkaku Retto: Rekishi to Seiji no Aida," 55.

16 It should be pointed out that the naming of many other new areas and territories around the world also do have interesting and similar stories about their naming. Two examples include the Kazan Islands, which derived their name from being called the Volcano Islands, and the other one is the Ogasawara Islands, which is named after a mythical figure, and otherwise known as the Bonin Islands, which is a mistranslation of the word "Bunin," for uninhabited. For more, see Robert D. Eldridge, *Iwo Jima to Ogasawara o Meguru Nichibei Kankei*, Chapter 1.

17 Sir Edward Belcher, *Narrative of the Voyage of H.M.S. Samarang during the Years, 1843–1846, Vol 1* (London: Reeve, Benham, and Reeve, 1848), 315–320. Also see *Volume 2*, 572–574.

18 It is unclear if Belcher in fact named the islands "Pinnacle."

19 According to the *China Sea Directory*, Volume 4, Raleigh Rock was so named due its sighting by the H.M.S. *Raleigh* in July 1837.

20 Cited from the *Journal of the British Naval Waterway*, Vol. 4 (1884), as referenced in Okuhara Toshio, "Senkaku Retto no Ryoyuken to Meiho Ronbun (The Sovereignty Problem over the Senkaku Islands and the *Meiho* Article)," *Chugoku*, No. 91 (1971), 39.

21 Kaigunsho Suirokyoku, *Kanei Suiroshi* (Journal of the Waterways of the World), Vol. 1 (March 1884).

22 Kaigunsho Suirokyoku, *Kanei Suiroshi*.

23 Kuroiwa, "Senkaku Retto Tanken Kiji," 477, cited in Suganuma, *Sovereign Rights*, 91.

24 Suganuma, *Sovereign Rights*, 91–92.

25 Kuroiwa Hisashi, "Senkaku Retto Tanken Kiji (An Article about the Exploration of the Senkaku Islands)," in *Chigaku Zasshi*, Vol. 12, No. 8 (1900), 477, as translated by Suganuma, *Sovereign Rights*, 94. Kuroiwa was born in the Tosa Domain, now known as Kochi Prefecture, on the island of Shikoku. He moved to Okinawa in 1892 at the age of thirty–four to take up a teaching position at the Okinawa Normal School. In 1902, he became the first principal of the Kunigami Agricultural School (*Kunigamigun Kumiairitsu Nogakko*) in northern Okinawa. For more, see Arasato Kinbuku and Oshiro Tatsuyuki, *Kindai Okinawa no Hito-bito* (The People of Modern Okinawa), (Tokyo: Taiheiyo Shuppansha, 1972). Kuroiwa was chosen among the 104 people the editors did portraits on. Also see, Amano Tetsuo, "Kuroiwa Hisashi: Okinawa Shizenkai no Gakumonteki Kaitakusha (Kuroiwa Hisashi: The Academic Developer of Okinawa's Natural World)," *Shin Okinawa Bungaku*, No. 37 (December 1977), and Oshiro Masataka, ed., *Kuroiwa Hisashi Sensei Kensho Kinenshi* (Commemoration Publication of the Unveiling of Mr. Kuroiwa Hisashi's Statue), (Nago: Kuroiwa Hisashi Sensei Koseki Kenshokai, 1969).

26 Sasamori Gisuke, *Nanto Tanken* (Southern Islands Exploration), (Hirosaki: private publisher,1894).

27 Suganuma, *Sovereign Rights*, 99.

28 Makino Kiyoshi, "Senkaku Retto Koshi (A Short History of the Senkaku Islands)," in *Kikan Okinawa*, No. 56, 65.

29 For more about the Koga family and *Kiryu Shonin*, see Koga Zenji. "Senkaku Shoto no Aruji ha Watatshi (I am the Owner of the Senkaku Islands)," *Nihon Keizai Shimbun*, August 26, 1971, and the interview with his wife, Hanako, in Arasaki Moriteru, ed., *Okinawa Gendaishi he no Shogen* (Testimony about Modern Okinawan History), Vol. 2, (Naha: Okinawa Taimususha, 1982), 129–132.

30 It is usually written that Koga was twenty–four years old when he went to Okinawa. That number is based on differences between Western and traditional Japanese ways of counting one's age (i.e., Japanese babies were considered one year old upon birth).

31 The address of the new shop was No. 2, Ogawa–son, Yaeyama. See Makino, "Senkaku Retto Koshi," 65.

32 Makino, "Senkaku Retto Koshi," 65–66.

33 There are different dates used for when Koga went to the Senkakus and when he made some of his requests. I will use the ones I believe to most chronologically reliable.

34 Okuhara Toshio, "Senkaku Retto to Ryoyuken Mondai (The Senkaku Islands and the Territorial Problem)," *Sandei Okinawa*, No. 45, June 2, 1973.

35 Ozaki Shigeyoshi, "Senkaku Shoto no Kizoku ni Tsuite, Jo (Territorial Sovereignty of the Senkaku Islands, No. 3)," *Referensu* (Reference), No. 261 (October 1972), 43–44.

36 Okuhara, "Senkaku Retto to Ryoyuken Mondai," No. 45.

37 Okuhara, "Senkaku Retto to Ryoyuken Mondai," No. 45.

38 Okuhara, "Senkaku Retto to Ryoyuken Mondai," No. 45.

39 Okuhara Toshio, "Senkaku Retto to Ryoyuken Mondai (The Senkaku Islands and the Territorial Problem)," *Sandei Okinawa*, No. 39, April 14, 1973.

40 Okuhara, "Senkaku Retto to Ryoyuken Mondai," No. 39; "Kume Aka Shima Hoka Nito Torishirabe no Gi ni Tsuki Joshin (Request to Conduct Survey of Kume Aka Shima and Two Other Islands)," September 22, 1885, cited in Okuhara Toshio, "Senkaku Retto to Ryoyuken Mondai (The Senkaku Islands and the Territorial Problem)," *Sandei Okinawa*, No. 40, April 21, 1973.

41 Okuhara, "Senkaku Retto to Ryoyuken Mondai," No. 39. Both of these reports are included in Gaimusho Kokai Shiryo, *Teikokuban Zukankei Zakken* (Various Matters Relating to Imperial Version of Maps and Other Things).

42 "Uotsuri Jima Hoka Futajima Jicchi Torishirabe no Gi ni Fu Joshin (Report of the Survey Conducted on Uotsuri Jima and Two Other Islands)," Okuhara, "Senkaku Retto to Ryoyuken Mondai," No. 40.

43 Gaimusho (Ministry of Foreign Affairs), *Nihon Gaiko Monjo* (Documents on Japanese Foreign Relations), Vol. 18 (Tokyo: Nihon Kokusai Rengo Kyokai, 1951), 573–576. These documents were reprinted in Takahashi Shogoro, *Senkaku Retto Nooto* (Notes on the Senkaku Islands), (Tokyo: Seinen Shuppansha, 1979), 62–68, with the English found in Unryu, *Sovereign Rights*, 97.

44 Hamagawa, "Senkaku Shoto no Ryoyu o Meguru Ronten," 6.

45 *Ibid.*

46 "Meiji 18 Nen 11 Gatsu 27 Nichi Naimusho Kaigian (Plan for Interior Ministry Meeting, November 27, 1875)," cited in Okuhara Toshio, "Senkaku Retto to Ryoyuken Mondai (The Senkaku Islands and the Territorial Problem)," *Sandei Okinawa*, No. 41, April 28, 1973.

47 "Mujinto he Kokuhyo Kensetsu ni Kanshi Okinawa Kenrei he no Shireian Kyogi no Ken (Discussion of Directive to Okinawa Governor regarding Erecting National Marker on Uninhabited Islands)," cited in Okuhara, "Senkaku Retto to Ryoyuken Mondai," No. 41.

48 "Mujinto he Kokuhyo Kensetsu ni tsuki Okinawa Kenrei Yori Ukagaide ni taisuru Shirei ni Kanshi Kaito no Ken (Answer about Directive regarding Inquiry from Okinawa Governor on Erecting National Marker on Uninhabited Islands)," cited in Okuhara, "Senkaku Retto to Ryoyuken Mondai," No. 41.

49 Okuhara, "Senkaku Retto to Ryoyuken Mondai," No. 41.

50 Okuhara, "Senkaku Retto to Ryoyuken Mondai," No. 41.

51 Okuhara, "Senkaku Retto to Ryoyuken Mondai," No. 41.

52 Okuhara, "Senkaku Retto to Ryoyuken Mondai," No. 41.

53 Okuhara, "Senkaku Retto to Ryoyuken Mondai," No. 41.

54 Makino, "Iigun Kuba Jima Senkaku Retto Koshi," 66.

55 "Kuba Jima Uotsuri Jima e Honken Shokatsu Bogui Gi ni Tsuki Joshin (Request to Erect Marker Showing Okinawa Prefecture's Jurisdiction on Kuba Jima and

Uotsuri Jima)," cited in Okuhara Toshio, "Senkaku Retto to Ryoyuken Mondai (The Senkaku Islands and the Territorial Problem)," *Sandei Okinawa*, No. 42, May 5, 1973.

56 Narahara was powerful, but disliked by many Okinawans due to his apparent disregard for them as he implemented the modernization reforms. Nevertheless, due to his connection with the Senkakus, the mountain forming Uotsuri Island is named after him—Naraharadake (Narahara Peak).

57 "Naimusho Hibetsu Dai 34 Go (Classified Matters of the Home Ministry, No. 34)," cited in Okuhara, "Senkaku Retto to Ryoyuken Mondai," No. 42.

58 "Hi Dai 12 Go, no Naifuku Dai 153 Go (Classified Matter No. 153, within No. 12)," cited in Okuhara, "Senkaku Retto to Ryoyuken Mondai," No. 42.

59 "Shinten Daini Go, 1895.1.11," cited in Okuhara, "Senkaku Retto to Ryoyuken Mondai," No. 42.

60 Okuhara, "Senkaku Retto to Ryoyuken Mondai," No. 42.

61 Hamagawa, 6.

62 "Naimusho Hibetsu Dai 133 Go no Uchi 'Kuba Jima Uotsuri Jima e Honken Shokatsu Bogui Kensetsu no Ken (Classified Matter No. 133 about the Erection of a Marker Showing Okinawa Prefecture's Jurisdiction on Kuba Jima and Uotsuri Jima)," cited in Okuhara Toshio, "Senkaku Retto to Ryoyuken Mondai (The Senkaku Islands and the Territorial Problem)," *Sandei Okinawa*, No. 43, May 19, 1973.

63 Most writings attribute the order going to the Okinawa governor as having taken place on January 21, but that, according to Okuhara, who came across subsequent documents, was simply a draft. Okuhara revised his research and stated for the record in the series published in *Sandei Okinawa* (Sunday Okinawa) on May 19, 1973, that the order was likely sent on or after February 3, 1895. See Okuhara, "Senkaku Retto to Ryoyuken Mondai," No. 43.

64 Okuhara, "Senkaku Retto to Ryoyuken Mondai," No. 42.

65 The relevant text of the Treaty of Shimonoseki reads: "Article 2 China cedes to Japan in perpetuity and full sovereignty the following territories, together with all fortifications, arsenals, and public property thereon:....b) The island of Formosa, together with all islands appertaining or belonging to the said island of Formosa."

66 For more, see Irie Keishiro, Nisshin Kowa to Senkaku Retto no Chii (The Sino–Japanese Peace Treaty and the Status of the Senkaku Islands)," in Nanpo Doho Engokai, ed., "Tokushu Senkaku Retto Dainishu (Second Special Issue for Senkaku Islands)," *Kikan Okinawa*, 32–38.

67 See Suganuma, *Sovereign Rights*, 98–99.

68 For this early administrative history, see Toshio Okuhara, "The Territorial Sovereignty over the Senkaku Islands and Problems on the Surrounding Continental Shelf," *The Japanese Annual of International Law*, No. 15 (1971), 97–98. According to a Japanese specialist on the Senkakus, "for 75 years afterwards Japan had not heard any criticism of this from any country and had continuous control over the islands since then." See Okuhara Toshio, "Senkaku Shoto," in Serita Kentaro, ed., *Nihon no Ryodo* (Chuo Koron, 1990), 19. In fact, however, the U.S.–administered the islands since January 1946, so Okuhara's assertion of "75" years seems to be including the 25 years that the U.S. administered the islands on Japan's behalf.

69 The Senkaku Islands Study Group, "The Senkaku Islands and the Japan's Territorial Titles to Them," 23. The exchange rate in 1925 was 2.44 yen equaled one U.S. dollar.

70 The Senkaku Islands Study Group, "The Senkaku Islands and the Japan's Territorial Titles to Them," 23. In 1932, one U.S. dollar equaled 3.56 yen.

71 The Senkaku Islands Study Group, "The Senkaku Islands and the Japan's Territorial Titles to Them," 23.

72 The Senkaku Islands Study Group, "The Senkaku Islands and the Japan's Territorial Titles to Them," 23–24. In 1936, one U.S. dollar equaled 3.45 yen.

73 The *Suma Maru* was built by Mitsubishi Zosen (Mitsubishi Shipbuilding Co.) in Nagasaki in 1895.

74 Okuhara "Senkaku Retto to Ryoyuken Mondai," No. 45. For more on that trip, see the report by the captain of the *Suma Maru*: Okuma Shinji, "Zappo Taiwan no Hokuto ni Isuru Koritto (Various News: The Small Isolated Islands Located to the Northeast of Taiwan)," *Chigaku Zasshi*, Vol. 11, No. 10 (October 1900), 722–723.

75 The *Anping Maru* was built by Wigham Richardson & Co., Newcastle, England, in 1896.

76 Miyajima Mikinosuke, "Okinawa Kenka Mujinto Tankendan (A Story of Investigating the Uninhabited Islands of Okinawa Prefecture)," *Chigaku Zasshi*, Vol. 10, No. 9 (October 1900), 585–596.

77 Okuhara Toshio, "Senkaku Retto to Ryoyuken Mondai (The Senkaku Islands and the Territorial Problem)," *Sandei Okinawa*, No. 46, June 9, 1973.

78 Okuhara, "Senkaku Retto to Ryoyuken Mondai," No. 46.

79 Okuhara, "Senkaku Retto to Ryoyuken Mondai," No. 46.

80 Okuhara, "Senkaku Retto to Ryoyuken Mondai," No. 46.

81 Okuhara, "Senkaku Retto to Ryoyuken Mondai," No. 46.

82 The Senkaku Islands Study Group, "The Senkaku Islands and the Japan's Territorial Titles to Them," 22–23.

83 Hamagawa Kyoko, "Senkaku Shoto no Ryoyu o Meguru Ronten: Nicchu Ryokoku no Kenkai o Chushin Ni (The Debate over Ownership of the Senkaku Islands, with a Focus on the Views of Japan and China)," *Chosa to Joho*, No. 565 (February 28, 2007), 8.

84 Koga Zenji, "Senkaku Shoto no Aruji wa Watashi (I am the Owner of the Senkaku Islands)," *Nihon Keizai Shimbun*, August 26, 1970.

85 Koga, "Senkaku Shoto no Aruji."

86 Koga Zenji, "Mo San, Sato San Senkaku Retto wa Watashino 'Shoyuchi' Desu (Mr. Mao, Mr. Sato: I Own the Senkaku Islands)," *Gendai*, Vol. 6, No. 6 (June 1972), 144.

87 The Senkaku Islands Study Group, "The Senkaku Islands and the Japan's Territorial Titles to Them," 24.

88 The Senkaku Islands Study Group, "The Senkaku Islands and the Japan's Territorial Titles to Them," 24.

89 The Senkaku Islands Study Group, "The Senkaku Islands and the Japan's Territorial Titles to Them," 21–22.

90 The Senkaku Islands Study Group, "The Senkaku Islands and the Japan's Territorial Titles to Them," 24.

91 The Senkaku Islands Study Group, "The Senkaku Islands and the Japan's Territorial Titles to Them," 24.

92 The Senkaku Islands Study Group, "The Senkaku Islands and the Japan's Territorial Titles to Them," 24.

93 The ministry had been renamed the Ministry of Agriculture and Forestry in 1925, when the Ministry of Commerce was created and its functions removed from the Ministry of Agriculture and Commerce.

94 The Senkaku Islands Study Group, "The Senkaku Islands and the Japan's Territorial Titles to Them," 22–25. Japan was never successful in building one. It tried 30 years later while the island was under U.S. administration, but the U.S. government told the Japanese government to defer until after reversion. In the late 1970s, it reportedly considered building one but seems to have abandoned the plans. (See Kurihara, *Senkaku Shoto Urimasu*, 77–85.) It has not constructed one to date.

95 The Senkaku Islands Study Group, "The Senkaku Islands and the Japan's Territorial Titles to Them," 24–25.

96 Koga, "Mo San, Sato San," 145.

97 Koga, "Mo San, Sato San," 145.
98 For more on the Ogasawara Islands evacuations, see Robert D. Eldridge, *Iwo Jima to Ogasawara o Meguru Nichibei Kankei.*
99 Many books, comics, and animated movies have documented this incident, including: Kanezawa Kaichi, *Tsushima Maru no Sonan: Okinawa no Kodomotachi* (The Tragedy of the Tsushima Maru: The Children of Okinawa), (Tokyo: Asunaro Sosaku, 1972) and Oshiro Tachiyuki, *Tsushimamaru* (Tsushima Maru), (Tokyo: Rironsha, 1982). There is also a museum dedicated to remembering the victims called the *Tsushima Maru Kinenkan*, which opened in June 2001 in Naha.
100 For more on the *Awa Maru* incident see Roger Dingman, *Ghost of War: The Sinking of the Awa Maru and Japanese–American Relations,1945–1995* (Annapolis: Naval Institute Press, 1999).
101 Accounts vary as to how many evacuees were on the ships as passengers. See "Senkaku Shoto Sonan (1): Mujinto de Gashi Jigoku (The Senkaku Islands Shipwreck, 1: Hell of Starvation on an Uninhabited Island)," *Ryukyu Shimpo*, January 16, 2010. Also see Senkaku Retto Senji Sonan Shibotsu Ireino Kenritsu Jigyo Kiseikai, ed., *Chinmoku no Sakebi: Senkaku Retto Senji Sonan Jiken* (Screaming in Silence: The Senkaku Islands Wartime Shipwreck Incident), (Ishigaki City: Nanzansha, 2006).
102 The *Senkaku Retto Senji Sonansha Izokukai* (Senkaku Islands Wartime Shipwreck Bereaved Families Association) was later officially formed on December 18, 1978 for survivors and bereaved family members, although they had been meeting over the years since 1946. In July 2002, the *Izokukai* established a memorial in 2002 in the Arakawa district in the southwestern part of Ishigaki Island in honor of those who died, and published a book in 2006 of recollections of the tragedy. Previously, in May 1969, a memorial had been made and a ceremony held on Uotsuri. (See Senkaku Retto Senji Sonan Shibotsu Ireino Kenritsu Jigyo Kiseikai, ed., *Chinmoku no Sakebi*, for details.) In 2012, nationalist groups, such as the bipartisan *Nihon no Ryodo o Mamoru Tame Kodo Suru Giin Renmei* (Parliamentarians League to Take Action to Protect Japanese Territory, or *Ryodo Giren*), formed in 2004 and headed by Yamatani Eriko, a former reporter with ties to the *Sankei Shimbun* and an Upper House member of the Liberal Democratic Party (*Jiyu Minshuto*), asked Kedashiro Yotake, the chairman of the *Izokukai*, to sign a letter in support of the group's attempt to land on Uotsuri to conduct a memorial ceremony but according to news reports, he refused to sign, not wanting his organization's mandate of honoring those who died on Uotsuri to be used by the parliamentarians league's goal to pursue the territorial issue. (See "Senkaku Joriku: 'Ireisai Riyo Sareta' Izokukai, Shomei o Kyohi, Okinawa," *Mainichi Shimbun*, August 21, 2012.) The league's request made to the government to land on Uotsuri was also rejected (on August 13), and so the group conducted a memorial ceremony at sea (*yojo ireisai*). (Ishigaki City Mayor Nakayama describes some of the problems with the way the requests for landing on the island, of which he has made three— all of which have been rejected—are portrayed by the central government due to the way the documentation is written as being opposed by the landowners. See Nakayama, *Chugoku ga Mimi o Fusagu*, 54–57.) Following the ceremony, ten participants jumped ship and swam to Uotsuri and landed on it anyway on August 19. In contrast, activists from Hong Kong and Taiwan landed on Uotsuri on August 15, something that Prime Minister Noda Yoshihiko called "regrettable" in Diet testimony. In an accident or misfortune not directly related to 1945 tragedy, the father of Iramina Takayoshi, a former Speaker of the Prefectural Assembly (*Okinawa Kengikai*) from 2000 to 2002 and now a professional *samisen* player, died in September 1945 on Uotsuri. Professor Takara Tetsuo, a scientist who traveled to the islands many times in the postwar, found the remains of four people there during his second trip in 1952, and subsequently visited Iramina and

his family to tell them about it. Iramina himself later went in July 1977 to try to recover the remains of his father, bringing closure to a longtime dream of his to do so. See Iramina Takayoshi, "Chichi no Ikotsu Shushu ha, Jibun no Fune to Te de (Recovering My Father's Remains by My Own Hands and Boat)," Senkaku Shoto Bunken Shiryo Hensankai, ed., *Senkaku Kenkyu*, Vol. 1, 359–365.

2 Okinawa and the Senkaku Islands under U.S. occupation and administration

This chapter explores the history and status of the Senkaku Islands during the U.S. occupation (1945–52) and administration (1952–72) of the Nansei (or Ryukyu) Islands chain, following the start of the Battle of Okinawa until administrative rights over the remaining islands were returned to Japan on May 15, 1972. It focuses on the legal and geographical status of the Senkaku Islands, and discusses the use of the islands by the U.S. military and Okinawan fishermen, surveys of the islands by Japanese academics, scientists, and government officials, and intrusions and other illegal activities such as trespassing and poaching as well as physical violence against Okinawan fishermen on or near the Senkakus and neighboring islands by Taiwanese fishermen and unidentified vessels. It also looks at the U.S. side's handling of these and other issues involved in the administration of the Senkaku Islands exclusively or later in conjunction with Government of the Ryukyu Islands (GRI, or *Ryukyu Seifu*), whose executive, judicial, and legislative branches came into being on April 1, 1952.

The Senkaku Islands during the military occupation and early post-treaty years

The Senkaku Islands were not invaded or physically seized during the Battle of Okinawa, which officially began in late March 1945, partly because there were no known fortifications, airfields, or radio towers to impede or impact upon U.S. operations against Japan. However, being part of the Sakishima Island Group, U.S. aircraft, ships, and submarines regularly operated in the area in the last year of the Pacific War to disrupt shipping and troop movement and bomb targets ahead of the Battle of Okinawa (*Operation Iceberg*) and the future planned invasion of Kyushu (*Operation Olympic*), scheduled for September 1945.[1]

It is unclear if the Senkaku Islands themselves were ever bombed or strafed, as workers and other inhabitants on the islands had already been evacuated in 1940. However, there was one event that linked the islands to the Battle of Okinawa directly and tragically. This was the so-called *Senkaku Retto Senji Hinan Jiken*, or "Senkaku Islands Wartime Evacuation Incident," as discussed in the previous chapter, in which some eighty women, children, and older people died as a result of an attack at sea and subsequent starvation for those who were shipwrecked on Uotsuri, the largest of the Senkaku Islands.[2]

Although there was no battle per se involving the Senkaku Islands, they were considered part of the Ryukyu Islands group that the United States military occupied as a result of the signing of the local surrender agreement on September 7, 1945, which followed the September 2 official surrender of the Japanese military and the Government of Japan at Tokyo Bay, on what became known later as Kadena Air Base. The unconditional surrender document, written on U.S. Tenth Army letterhead, read in part:

> The undersigned Japanese commanders, in conformity with the general surrender executed by the Imperial Japanese Government, at Yokohama, on 2 September 1945, hereby formally render unconditional surrender of the islands in the Ryukyus within the following boundaries:
>
> 30°North 126" East, thence 24°North 122" East, thence 24°North 133" East, thence 29°North 131" East, thence 30°North 131" 30' East, thence to the point of origin.[3]

Lieutenant General Nomi Toshiro, Commander, Japanese Forces, Sakishima Gunto, as well as Major General Takada Toshisada, Commander, Japanese Army Forces, Amami Gunto, and Rear Admiral Kato Tadao, Commander Japanese Navy Forces, Amami Gunto, signed the document. It was accepted by General Joseph W. Stillwell, Commanding General of the Tenth Army. Of the ceremony "Vinegar Joe" Stillwell wrote "just cold, hard, business" in his diary.[4] Exactly a month later on October 7, Stilwell was inspecting Ishigaki, spending a couple of hours there. He found that eighty percent of the Japanese were sick with malaria.[5] Over the coming year, Ishigaki residents who had left the island for Taiwan for work or school (as Taiwan had been a Japanese colony) or had evacuated to Taiwan as a result of the war began

Figure 2.1 Surrender Ceremony on Okinawa, September 7, 1945

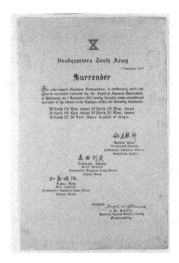

Figure 2.2 Surrender Document

returning, further complicating the situation there with the influx of unemployed people.[6] An earthquake in September 1947 off Ishigaki further added to their anxieties.

With this (and another surrender agreement for the Amami Islands), the United States came to occupy and administer the Nansei Islands chain, setting up operations in the Miyako Islands on December 8 and the Yaeyama Islands on December 28. The U.S. Military Government of the Ryukyu Islands, as it was formally known, also administered the Senkaku Islands, although no people were living on any of those islands at the time, other than fishermen and researchers who would occasionally visit there beginning in the late 1940s and early 1950s for very short stays of several hours, or overnight, or several days. As such, the military government did not establish a permanent physical presence on the Senkakus.

On January 29, 1946, this control, which had been conducted as part of the operations during the battle and subsequent military occupation, was further delineated through the issuance of SCAPIN (Supreme Commander for the Allied Powers Instruction) 677, which administratively separated certain outlying islands from Japanese control.[7] (This date is not insignificant—the month before, all Japanese Imperial Navy and Army forces had been demobilized and relocated back to the mainland by this point, and the disarmament of Japanese forces on the mainland had taken place in the early to mid-fall.) The instruction stated, "The Imperial Japanese Government is directed to cease exercising, or attempting to exercise, governmental or administrative authority over any area outside of Japan, or over any government officials and employees or any over persons within such areas," and defined Japanese territory "to include the four main islands of Japan (Hokkaido, Honshu,

Kyushu and Shikoku) and the approximately 1.000 smaller adjacent islands, including the Tsushima Islands and the Ryukyu (Nansei) Islands north of 30° North Latitude (excluding Kuchinoshima Island)." As such, the Japanese government lost administrative control over the Nansei Islands, including the Senkakus, and its near 800,000 people as part of the larger Allied Occupation of Japan. In this 1946 document, the Senkakus were called the Sento Shoto, and the islands specifically constituting the Sento Shoto were referred to as "Sekibi-jima," Koubi-jima," "Kita-jima," "Minami-jima," and "Uotsuri-jima."[8]

The U.S. military government for Okinawa underwent several changes in its composition over the first five years of the occupation of Okinawa and became the United States Civil Administration for the Ryukyu Islands (USCAR) on December 15, 1950. Just prior to this transformation on September 1 (1950), the Military Government announced Ordinance No. 22, which established regional governments within the islands. Article 1, Chapter 1, Paragraph D of the ordinance referred to the Yaeyama Islands, which included the Senkaku Islands based on the following geographical demarcation.

> d. Yaeyama Gunto—Comprising those islands and islets within the following boundaries:
>
> 27 degrees North Latitude, 124 degrees, 2 minutes East Longitude; thence
> 24 degrees North Latitude, 122 degrees East Longitude; thence
> 24 degrees North Latitude, 40 minutes East Longitude, thence to point of origin.[9]

Under Article 3 of the Treaty of Peace with Japan, signed a year later on September 8, 1951 by Japan and nearly fifty other countries in attendance at the peace conference in San Francisco, the United States was granted administrative rights over the Nansei Islands, including the Senkakus.[10] In other words, much of the same control the United States had over the Nansei Islands as per the 1946 SCAPIN document was reaffirmed in the peace treaty. Article 3 did not specifically mention the Senkaku Islands, but the islands were included in the Japanese territory covered by the article:

> Japan will concur in any proposal of the United States to the United Nations to place under its trusteeship system, with the United States as the sole administering authority, Nansei Shoto south of 29°north latitude (including the Ryukyu Islands and the Daito Islands), Nanpo Shoto south of Sofu Gan (including the Bonin Islands, Rosario Island and the Volcano Islands) and Parece Vela and Marcus Island. Pending the making of such a proposal and affirmative action thereon, the United States will have the right to exercise all and any powers of administration,

legislation and jurisdiction over the territory and inhabitants of these islands, including their territorial waters.[11]

It was at the San Francisco Peace Conference where the lead U.S. negotiator, John Foster Dulles, who served as special advisor to President Truman and Secretary of State Dean G. Acheson, announced that Japan had "residual sovereignty" over the Nansei and Nanpo Islands. It was unclear what exactly "residual sovereignty" meant, but the essence of it was that the United States would retain "all and any powers of administration, legislation and jurisdiction" over the islands while Japan retained ultimate, residual sovereignty. It was also unclear at the time when, or if, the island groups would be returned to Japan, but eventually they were gradually in three stages, over a twenty-year period. Japan had lobbied hard to be allowed to retain administrative rights (and thus sovereignty as well) over the islands, and lost, but importantly was able to retain "residual sovereignty." Legally speaking, one could make the argument that the fact that Japan was permitted to retain some form of sovereignty over the Nansei Islands, which includes the Senkaku Islands, meant by the U.S. government's own admission at the time in September 1951 that Japan in fact had sovereignty over the Senkakus as well.

Japan continued over the weeks, months, and years that followed to see all the islands returned quickly to Japan and it looked at one point that prior to the peace treaty going into effect on April 28, 1952, it might succeed. However, the supporting recommendations of the State Department and the Far Eastern Command were overruled by the Joint Chiefs of Staff and Article 3 of the Peace Treaty was implemented more or less as planned.[12]

In the meantime, before the peace treaty went into effect, the United States began refining its control over the Nansei Islands in preparation for that eventual day. Two months before, on February 29, 1952, the U.S. Civil Administration of the Ryukyu Islands published Ordinance Number 68, "Provisions of the Government of the Ryukyu Islands," which went into effect on April 1 that year. Section 1, Article 1 of this ordinance delineated the administrative jurisdiction of the GRI, over which sat USCAR:

> The area of political and geographical jurisdiction of the Government of the Ryukyu Islands shall constitute and include those islands and territorial waters within the following boundaries:
>
> 29°North Latitude, 125°22' East Longitude; thence
> 24°North Latitude, 122°East Longitude; thence
> 24°North Latitude, 133°East Longitude; thence
> 29°North Latitude, 131°East Longitude; thence to point of origin.[13]

The Senkakus were also included in the territorial definition of the Ryukyu Islands in Civil Administration Proclamation Number 27 of December 25, 1953, issued the same day administrative rights over the Amami Islands were reverted to Japan, which concerned the geographical boundaries of the Ryukyu Islands in light of the northern Ryukyus (Amami Gunto) being returned and no longer under USCAR or GRI control. Article 1 read:

> The territorial jurisdiction of the United States Civil Administration of the Ryukyu Islands, and the Government of the Ryukyu Islands are redesignated as all of those islands, islets, atolls and rocks and territorial waters within the following geographic boundaries:
>
> 28°North Latitude, 124°40' East Longitude; thence
> 24° North Latitude, 122° East Longitude; thence
> 24° North Latitude, 133° East Longitude; thence
> 27° North Latitude, 131°50' East Longitude; thence
> 27° North Latitude, 128°18' East Longitude; thence
> 28° North Latitude, 128°18' East Longitude; thence to the point of origin.[14]

Five weeks later on February 2, 1954, USCAR published Ordinance Number 125, which dealt with the control of entry and exit to and from the Ryukyu Islands. Titled "Control and Exit of Individuals Into and From the Ryukyu Islands," this ordinance went into force on February 15 that year. Section II, "Definitions," included the following description, the demarcation for which was verbatim to Proclamation 27 above:

> 6. Ryukyu Islands: Shall constitute and include those islands and territorial waters within the following boundaries:
>
> 28°North Latitude, 124°40' East Longitude; thence
> 24° North Latitude, 122° East Longitude; thence
> 24° North Latitude, 133° East Longitude; thence
> 27° North Latitude, 131°50' East Longitude; thence
> 27° North Latitude, 128°18' East Longitude; thence
> 28° North Latitude, 128°18' East Longitude; thence to the point of origin.[15]

The following year, on March 16, 1955, USCAR published Ordinance Number 144.[16] This ordinance was named "Codified Penal Law and Procedure" and was applied from April 9. It also delineated the Senkaku Islands as part of the Ryukyus, similar to previous published ordinances.

> 2.1.9 The "territorial jurisdiction of the whole of the Ryukyu Islands" as used herein shall include all land, rocks, reefs, shoals and waters within the following bounds:
>
> Beginning at 28 degrees North Latitude, 124 degrees 40 minutes East Longitude; thence to

24 degrees North Latitude, 122 degrees East Longitude; thence to
24 degrees North Latitude, 133degrees East Longitude; thence to
27 degrees North Latitude, 131 degrees 50 minutes East Longitude;
thence to
27 degrees North Latitude, 128 degrees18 minutes East Longitude;
thence to
28 degrees North Latitude, 128 degrees18 minutes East Longitude;
thence to the point of origin.[17]

In later years as is discussed in the second half of this chapter, USCAR and
the GRI would increasingly have difficulty enforcing these ordinances dealing
with illegal entry on a daily basis around the Senkakus and it would not be
until the late 1960s until strong measures began to be taken in conjunction
with the GRI and police, but even then these measures were sometimes found
to be inadequate.

Use of the Senkaku Islands by the U.S. Military for Target Practice

In light of tensions that were building in the region with the civil war in
China in the latter half of the 1940s, and the need for the U.S. military,
especially its pilots, to be trained and ready, Captain Millard O. Engen of the
U.S. Military Government of the Ryukyu Islands, a World War II veteran
who later served in Korea after North Korea launched its attack,[18]
announced on April 16, 1948, that Kobi Sho, or Kuba Jima, and the surrounding area would be used for target practice by the 1st Air Division of the
U.S. Air Force, which had replaced the 8th Army Air Force in early June
1946 and was at Kadena until early December 1948.[19] As such, Kobi Sho and
the vicinity around it would be designated as permanently dangerous areas
and fishing or other entry within the immediate vicinity was banned.

The following month, more details were released, namely that fishermen
and others were not to enter a five-nautical mile area around the island due to
the dangers associated with the bombing range.[20] These announcements,
however, apparently did not get fully relayed to the fishermen (or perhaps
were outright ignored by them) and the Air Force reported problems with the
bombing training due to fishermen and others being in the vicinity.[21] Major
Merle M. Glover, the military government officer of the Yaeyama Civil
Administration (which had been stood up in March 1947 after the Yaeyama
Provisional Government was disbanded) directed Yoshino Kozen, the governor of the Yaeyama Civil Government (*Yaeyama Gunto Seifu Chiji*), to
ensure the word got out to all of the fishermen through the newspapers and
public notices.[22]

To be on the safe side, early the next year, the military government dropped
notices to fishermen to inform them about avoiding the range at Kobi Sho
and not entering the five-nautical mile circumference area.[23] There was some
confusion around this time, however, as a second area (Tori Shima) had been

declared off-limits as well. Locally, Minami and Kita Kojima islands were known collectively as Tori Shima, but the actual training range was on another island named Tori Shima closer to Kume Jima (and is still used today). In order to clarify the areas, eventually the Air Force released on October 19, 1951, through the Okinawa Islands Government Economic Division (*Okinawa Gunto Keizaibu*) dates and specific latitudes and longitudes for when and where training would take place.[24] Afterwards, as well, prior to using the ranges, the U.S. military would inform the Government of the Ryukyu Islands that it was declaring the areas off-limits, and the GRI warned fishermen not to go near those waters through the *Yaeyama Chihocho* (Yaeyama Regional Office).[25]

Kobi Sho was used by the U.S. Air Force until 1955 for air-to-ground target practice, and then primarily by the U.S. Navy afterwards.[26] Beginning in mid-April 1956, the Navy also began using Sekibi Sho, or Taisho Jima. That same year, the military reduced its training area from five miles to 100 yards in radius for Kobi Sho, presumably to limit the scope of the impact on fishermen in the area. Indeed, requests had been made by local and GRI officials to ask the military to reduce the no-entry area based on the desires of local fishermen.[27] One such request was made in November 1955 by the GRI as the area around Kobi Sho was particularly good for the local fishing industry. This change was eventually agreed to. However, Sekibi Sho remained at five nautical miles as it does today.

It is unclear why the U.S. military chose to begin using Sekibi Sho as an additional range at this point in the mid-1950s. It may have been to offset the limited usage area at Kobi Sho. Or perhaps it had to with tensions in the Taiwan Strait, or even as a result of the violence at sea seen in the March 1955 *Daisan Seitoku Maru* Incident, events that may have been related in and of themselves, described below.

During the 1950s, the issue of the ranges was also taken up in prefectures in Kyushu that had boats going into the area, such as Nagasaki and Kagoshima Prefectures. In March 1954, a prefectural people's rally was held in Nagasaki against the training, and in September 1959, a similar rally was held in Kagoshima, both with large fishing communities. The issue of U.S. military training in the fishing areas was subsequently taken up in the Diet, or National Parliament, in the agriculture and fisheries committee (*Norin Suisan Iinkai*) of the House of Representatives, or *Shugiin*, in October and in the counterpart committee of the House of Councilors, or *Sangiin*, in November.[28] In the case of the House of Representatives (Lower House), the question had been raised by Akaji Tomozo, a Socialist Party (*Shakaito*) representative from Kagoshima Prefecture. At the time, the revision of the U.S.–Japan security treaty was also being discussed between the two governments and in the Diet, where the Socialists were critical of the treaty, attention was particularly high at the time.

While Sekibi Sho was state-owned,[29] Kobi Sho was privately owned land. According to its owner, Koga Zenji, the son of the entrepreneur who developed and owned four of the five main islands of the Senkakus introduced in Chapter 1, the U.S. military began paying rent on Kobi-Sho in 1950.[30] In July 1958, for reasons unclear, USCAR had the GRI act as its proxy in signing a lease with Koga.[31] According to the terms of the contract (Basic Lease, GRI, No. 183–1), USCAR paid Koga an annual rent of 5,763.92 U.S. dollars, which was raised to 10,567 dollars in 1963.[32] Koga began paying 400 dollars in taxes the following year to Ishigaki City, and for year 1971, he paid 450 dollars.[33] Koga, who was born in 1893, eventually died in 1978 at the age of eighty-four. But Kobi Sho as well as three other islands remained privately owned until recently when several of them were purchased by Japanese government in September 2012 as explained in the Introduction and Chapter 1.

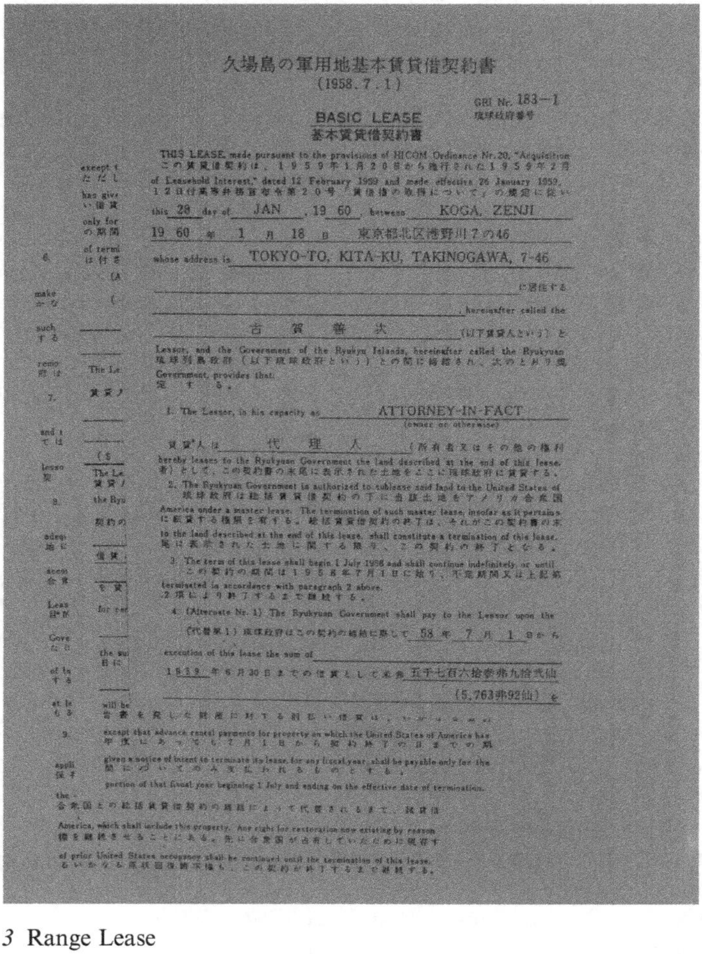

久場島の軍用地基本賃貸借契約書
(1958.7.1)

GRI Nr. 183−1

BASIC LEASE
基本賃貸借契約書

THIS LEASE, made pursuant to the provisions of HICOM Ordinance Nr. 20, "Acquisition of Leasehold Interest," dated 12 February 1959 and made effective 26 January 1959, this 28 day of JAN, 19 60, between KOGA, ZENJI

19 60 年 1 月 18 日 東京都北区滝野川7の46

whose address is TOKYO-TO, KITA-KU, TAKINOGAWA, 7-46

, hereinafter called the

古 賀 善 次

Lessor, and the Government of the Ryukyu Islands, hereinafter called the Ryukyuan Government, provides that:

1. The Lessor, in his capacity as ATTORNEY-IN-FACT (owner or otherwise)

代 理 人

hereby leases to the Ryukyuan Government the land described at the end of this lease.

2. The Ryukyuan Government is authorized to sublease said land to the United States of America under a master lease. The termination of such master lease, insofar as it pertains to the land described at the end of this lease, shall constitute a termination of this lease.

3. The term of this lease shall begin 1 July 1958 and shall continue indefinitely or until terminated in accordance with paragraph 2 above.

4. (Alternate Nr. 1) The Ryukyuan Government shall pay to the Lessor upon the execution of this lease the sum of

58 年 7 月 1 日から 1959 年6月30日までの賃貸として米貨 五千七百六拾参弗九拾弐仙 (5,763弗92仙) を

except that advance rental payments for property on which the United States of America has given a notice of intent to terminate its lease, for any fiscal year, shall be payable only for the portion of that fiscal year beginning 1 July and ending on the effective date of termination.

Figure 2.3 Range Lease

As part of the revised bilateral security treaty, signed in January 1960 and going into effect in June that year, as well as the related Status of Forces Agreement, the Japanese government continued to allow the United States Navy to use the ranges following Okinawa's reversion in May 1972. Kobi Sho Range was identified as W-175 (Facility No. 6084) and Sekibi Sho Range as W-182 (Facility No. 6085), but the ranges have not actually been used since 1979 due to the political sensitivity of the Senkaku Islands between Japan, China, and Taiwan.[34] Officials familiar with the issue state that this self-imposed restriction was at the behest of the State Department out of diplomatic considerations for China, which the United States had recently formally established full diplomatic relations with, and in light of the rise in tensions over the islands between Japan and China the year before.

Tensions in the Taiwan Strait and the *Daisan Seitoku Maru* Incident

In early September 1954, following a heavy build-up of troops on Quemoy and Matsu by the Republic of China and an exchange of words and warnings, the People's Republic began shelling Quemoy, 200 kilometers south of Fuzhou and directly across from the city of Xiamen. In November, People's Liberation Army planes bombed the Tachen Islands, near Fuzhou, forcing them to be evacuated. Pressure grew in the United States to bomb mainland China, and to possibly use nuclear weapons against it. Urged on by the pro-Taiwan Senator William F. Knowland, the United States signed a Mutual Defense Treaty with Taiwan on December 2, 1954. Although the treaty did not obligate the United States to defend islands along the mainland, the Formosa Resolution, which was passed by both houses of Congress on January 29, 1955, authorized the president to employ American forces to defend Taiwan and the Pescadores against armed attack, including such other territories as appropriate to defend them. After threats of the use of nuclear weapons in March, the Chinese proposed negotiations with Taiwan, and the shelling of Quemoy and Matsu stopped on May 1. The first Taiwan Strait Crisis came to an end.

According to one writer, Taiwanese troops retreating from Tachen Island during the Communist attacks on them in February reportedly garrisoned on the Senkakus and fired at approaching Japanese vessels.[35] It is unclear if the two situations are related but in the early afternoon on March 2, 1955, an Okinawan fishing boat, the *Daisan Seitoku Maru* (No. 3 Clean Virtues Vessel), a fifteen-ton boat crewed by eight, was fired on by two junks flying Republic of China flags in the waters near Uotsuri Jima. In that attack, three Okinawan crew members went missing, two of them having been shot. USCAR and Government of the Ryukyu Islands personnel conducted searches but the fishermen were not found and later presumed dead.

The related GRI officials immediately met the next day to discuss their response after reports of the attack came in. Their initial response was to advise fishermen and other vessels to avoid the area.[36] The Legislature of the Government of the Ryukyu Islands (*Ryukyu Seifu Rippoin*) passed a resolution on

Figure 2.4 Daisan Seitoku Maru Boat

March 5 calling on USCAR, the Government of Japan, and the United Nations to investigate the incident.[37] In May, the captain of the vessel and the bereaved families, among others, petitioned Higa Shuhei, Chief Executive (*Gyosei Shuseki*) of the GRI, who had been appointed by the military governor in April 1952, to pay compensation to the victims and families and "protect the life and property of the fisherman," among other demands.[38]

Working with the GRI and the police, USCAR conducted an investigation and queried the Government of the Republic of China (GRC) through the State Department. The GRC's response was negative, denying it did it or had any units in the area and suggesting it was mainland Chinese vessels that had attacked the Okinawan fishermen. "After a thorough investigation of the case based upon the information supplied by the American Embassy," a letter from the GRC to the U.S. Embassy in Tokyo states,

> the Government of the Republic of China wishes to state that the Chinese naval vessels and units had never operated in that part of the sea and therefore could not have attacked the crew of the Ryukyuan fishing vessel Daisan Seitoku Maru. The result of the investigation further makes it clear that the Chinese Navy did not have ships as were described. However, in view of the fact that the Chinese Communist motorboats based on Fukien or Chekiang Province are capable of operating in the specified

area, it was possible that the attack might have been made by the Communists for the purpose of disturbing the American-Ryukyuan friendly relations with the Republic of China.[39]

The case dragged on into the early 1960s with no closure. From the police perspective, there was nothing further it could do—it was an international or political/diplomatic matter. Lieutenant Colonel Kenneth S. Hitch, an administrative officer at USCAR, wrote to Chief Executive Ota Seisaku (a lawyer by training who served as a senior official in Taiwan during the war and returned to his native in Okinawa in the mid-1950s and was appointed to his new position by Lieutenant General Donald P. Booth, High Commissioner for the Ryukyu Islands, in November 1959[40]), to express his regret in being unable to establish "legal liability or responsibility for the incident based on the information and evidence available to him."[41] In the meantime, the GRI offered consolation payments ranging from 987.45 to 4,750.65 U.S. dollars to the families of the victims.[42] It also paid compensation to those who were unable to fish in the area due to the warnings about going there.

Not all the interaction between foreign vessels and Okinawan fishermen was bad however. In several cases, Okinawan fishing boats that had mechanical problems and were drifting or otherwise in trouble were aided by Taiwanese vessels (some of which had Okinawan crews on them). There were,

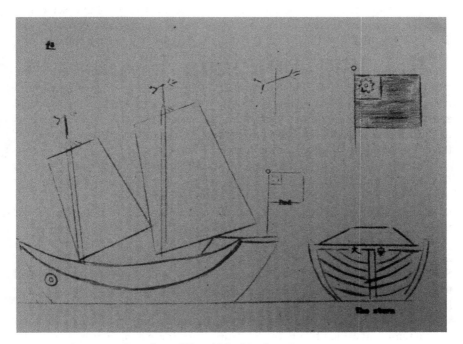

Figure 2.5 Statement Drawing of Vessel Used in Attack

nevertheless, incidents where the boats and crews eyed one another suspiciously, especially as fishermen of both areas viewed the waters surrounding the islands as prime for fishing for certain types of fish. As the incursions by Taiwanese boats, poachers, and salvage workers increased, so did the tensions between these two nominal friends and fellow allies of the United States who had long and sometimes very complicated relations among themselves.

Before we examine these incursions and frictions in more detail, it is necessary to look at the various investigations and activities in the area being conducted by Japanese scientific and academic groups, as there was a regular flow of researchers to the islands and quite often they were the ones to notice the various signs of illegal activity in the area and on the islands by fishermen and poachers.

Scientific surveys and studies by Okinawan and Japanese Academics

In addition to fishermen traveling to the Senkakus, scholars from Okinawa and mainland Japan regularly conducted scientific surveys there. These surveys had taken place not only in the prewar but also continued in the postwar during the years the United States controlled the islands as well as subsequently, albeit less so due to some problems, following their return to Japan.[43] The reports of these groups are preserved, and in the case of the missions by the University of the Ryukyus (*Ryukyu Daigaku*) professor Takara Tetsuo, have been bound and published in a two-volume set called *Senkaku Kenkyu: Takara Gakujutsu Chosadan Shiryoshu* (Research on the Senkaku Islands: The Papers of the Takara Scientific Investigation Group), along with some oral histories and other shorter reports of their experiences.[44] As is explained below, many of the surveys were purely academic in nature, related to the natural sciences, while others were more geological and resource-focused and thus had economic, political, diplomatic, and strategic connotations. Indeed, some of them were undertaken precisely for these reasons to prepare the way for Japanese governmental or commercial development of the area. Table 2.1 summarizes the respective surveys.

It was in 1950 that the first known scientific survey in the postwar was formally conducted. Some dozen and a half have been conducted in the interim but increasing tensions and restrictions placed on traveling to and landing on any of the Senkaku Islands seemed to have prevent a more robust frequency of visits in much of the latter post-reversion period.

In late March 1950, Takara, a former principal at the Yaeyama Agricultural High School (*Yaeyama Norin Koko*) who was called the "Pioneer of Senkaku Studies" and until hospitalized recently at the age of 100 continued to regularly meet with his students and those that participated in the near half-dozen survey trips he undertook, took off on his own to conduct biology studies on the island.[45] He traveled on the boat of Hatsuta Shigeharu, who had a temporary facility on the Uotsuri Jima for catching fish during the winter months, and spent several weeks there. Two reports, one entitled

Table 2.1 Scientific Surveys of the Senkaku Islands between 1950 and 1972

Dates (total no. of days on islands)	Leader (total no. in party)	Purpose
March 27–April 10, 1950 (15 days)	Takara Tetsuo (1)	Entomology
April 10–20, 1952 (10 days)	Takara (8), including team from Natural Resources Division, GRI	Natural Life and Resources
August 1–4, 1953 (4 days)	Takara (13)	Natural Life
May 15–18, 1963 (4 days)	Takara (8)	Birds, plants, and Maritime climate
July 7–9, 1968 (3 days)	Takaoka and Takara (Joint Survey) (14)	Sea-bed resources, water quality, sea birds, and plant life
May 30–July 18, 1969 (52 days)	Niino	Sea-bed geology
May 25–June 25, 1970 (31 days)	Niino	Sea-bed geology
September 28–30, 1970 (3 days*)	Ryukyu University	
November 29–December 12, 1970 (14 days)	Matsumoto (9) of Kyushu University and Nagasaki University	Geological, maritime life, sea birds
March 31–April 8, 1971 (9 days)	Ikehara (13) of Ryukyu University	Plant life, sea birds, geological

* Cut short due to bad weather

"Mujinto Tanpoki (A Record of Exploring Uninhabited Islands)," and "Senkaku Retto Homonki (A Record of Visiting the Senkaku Islands)," emerged from that trip, which Takara later published that year respectively in the *Nanryu Taimusu*, an Ishigaki-based newspaper, in ten installments between April 25 and May 22, and the *Uruma Shimpo*, the predecessor to the *Ryukyu Shimpo*, in two parts, September 15 and 16.[46]

Takara followed up this trip two years later in the middle of April 1952 with a longer and more extensive research expedition, involving a colleague and a handful of students from the newly established University of the Ryukyus (*Ryukyu Daigaku*). Importantly, a member of the GRI's Natural Resources Division (*Shigenkyoku Nokaika*) also participated, making it a joint Ryukyu

Figure 2.6 Dr. Takara Tetsuo

University-GRI study. Three reports also emerged from this trip, which lasted about ten days. The first of the reports, "Senkaku Retto Arekore (Various Things about the Senkaku Islands)," written by Takara, was published in eleven installments between May 8–29 that year.[47] The second of the reports, written by Tawada Shinjun, a technical official with the Ryukyu Forestry Experimental Station (*Ryukyu Ringyo Shikenjo*) and entitled "Senkaku Retto Saishuki (A Record of Collecting [Specimens] on the Senkaku Islands)," was published in seventeen installments in the *Ryukyu Shimpo* between June 29 and July 15.[48] A third report, written by one of the student participants, junior Matsumoto Akio from Amami Oshima, was published in three parts from June 2–4 in the *Ryukyu Shimpo* and was simply titled, "Senkaku Retto Chosa Hokoku (A Report on the Senkaku Islands Study Trip)."[49]

The third trip was conducted in the summer of 1953, this time with a much larger group (13 in total).[50] They were there from August 1–4, and for this trip, Inamine Ichiro, the president of the recently established *Ryukyu Sekiyu Kabushiki Kaisha* (and a future member of the Upper House who appears later in this book), donated the fuel.[51] Several reports, two of which were published at the time, emerged from the trip: "Senkaku Retto no Dobutsuso ni

Tsuite (Fauna of the Senkaku Islands, Ryukyus)," written by Takara, and Tawada's "Senkaku Retto no Shokubutsuso ni Tsuite (Flora of the Senkaku Islands, Ryukyus)."[52] Interestingly, Tawada warns in this article as he did in the earlier one, that regional tensions and the existence of pirates in the area made trips to the Senkakus dangerous and those going should be "on guard."[53]

It would be another ten years before Takara would visit the islands again. In the fall of 1959, Ryukyu University and Kagoshima University (*Kagoshima Daigaku*) were to combine their resources to conduct a joint survey but bad weather and an inability to secure a vessel at the time prevented it from occurring. Instead, the joint team focused on the immediate Yaeyama Islands group.[54] It was certainly a disappointment to the scientists of both schools not to have been able to go, but Takara's materials indicate that the respective presidents of Ryukyu University, a school built by U.S. military authorities in 1950 upon the request of the Okinawan people, were very supportive of the surveys.[55]

In May 1963, Takara led a six-person team to study the status of the albatross birds on the islands on behalf of the Cultural Assets Protection Committee of the GRI (*Ryukyu Seifu Bunkazai Hogo Iinkai*). In addition to the six members of the team, which included Niiro Yoshima (who ended up going a total of six times to the islands[56] and Ishimine Ashin from the Ryukyu Meteorological Agency (*Ryukyu Kishocho*)), four reporters from the local newspapers and broadcasting companies also traveled with the group to document the trip. This was the first time for someone from the Meteorological Agency to go, and Ishimine would travel to the islands a second time later in the decade. In addition to conducting their research, the group also came across Taiwanese poachers, who were taking bird eggs and other things from the islands, particularly on Minami Kojima.

Upon returning, Takara wrote a seven-part series in the local *Ryukyu Shimpo* about the history of the albatross on the islands and the challenges of preserving the natural habitat there.[57] His series was followed by one a week later written by two *Ryukyu Shimpo* journalists who traveled with the group, and focused on the problem of the extinction of the albatross on the islands, highlighting the environmental impact of intrusions by Taiwanese poachers and other problems on the Senkakus.[58] The *Okinawa Taimusu* reporter also ran a series in his newspaper toward the end of May entitled "Looking for the Albatross."[59]

The newspaper reports weren't the only articles to appear. The scholars on the trip each wrote a report for their professional journals as well. Ishimine's was entitled "Senkaku Retto Kaiyo Chosa Hokoku (A Report of the Maritime Survey of the Senkaku Islands)," and was published in the May 30, 1963 issue of *Ryuki Jiho*, a publication of the Ryukyu Meteorological Station (*Ryukyu Kishodai*).[60] Takara wrote an article for the March 1964 issue of *Minami to Kita* (South and North), a quarterly journal published by the Assistance Association for Okinawa and the Ogasawara Islands (*Nanpo Doho Engokai*, or *Nanen*), a quasi-governmental organization founded in 1956 to promote the interests of the people of Okinawa and Ogasawara, as well as of the Northern Islands, with the Japanese government as well as vis-à-vis the United States and Soviet Union.[61]

Niiro's article, "Senkaku Retto no Shokusei (Vegetation of the Senkaku Islands)," was published in the journal, *Ryukyu Daigaku Bunrigakubu Kiyo* (Bulletin of the Arts and Science Division of the University of the Ryukyus), in its May 1964 issue.[62]

There would be a gap of five years again before the next survey was conducted. That one occurred in August 1968 and was primarily a geological survey, as several more over the next few years would be. It would also be somewhat political in nature, as by this point it was becoming increasingly possible that the area surrounding the Senkakus possessed an abundance of oil and other natural resources following the release of some geological studies.

The political nature of the surveys was made clear when a member of the prime minister's consultative committee (Council on Okinawan and Other Problems, or *Okinawa Mondaito Kondankai*), Takaoka Daisuke, joined an already planned scientific survey of the islands scheduled for early July 1968, a few months before a survey was to be conducted by the United Nations Economic Commission for Asia and the Far East, or ECAFE. The dozen-man mission was comprised of scientists and academics from Ryukyu University and Ibaraki University (*Ibaraki Daigaku*), north of Tokyo, as well as officials from the GRI, Yaeyama District, and Ishigaki City, in addition to two armed police officers from Yaeyama and a photographer from a local newspaper, the *Ryukyu Shimpo*.[63] While surveying the islands, they encountered Taiwanese workers and fishermen there, incidents that are recounted later in this chapter.

Despite the somewhat political nature of this survey due to Takaoka's presence, there were several academic outputs from this trip as well. Takara was the first to have his published in the spring of the following year entitled "Senkaku Retto no Umidori ni Tsuite (Sea-fowls of the Senkaku Islands, Ryukyus)."[64] This was followed by an article in a journal produced by the *Nihon Kogyo Yosui Kyokai* (Japan Industrial Water Association), written by Kaneshima Kiyoshi, a native of Miyako, who after attending school in Taiwan and working for the colonial administration as a scientific researcher, became a member of the faculty at the University of the Ryukyus.[65] A third article, written by Takaoka, about the trip as a whole was published in a special issue on the Senkakus of *Nanen*'s quarterly, then called *Okinawa* at this point.[66] In addition, two participants, Ishimine and Masaki Jo, the latter who worked at the Yaeyama Meteorological Station (*Yaeyama Kishodai*), submitted a report to the GRI in June 1969 entitled "Kaiyogakuteki ni Mita Senkaku Retto (The Senkaku Islands Viewed from a Marine Science Perspective)."[67]

As discussed in the following chapter, upon his trip to the Senkakus Takaoka lobbied hard for more funding and official involvement in the surveys, particularly for those to begin looking at the geology of the area around the Senkakus in the hopes oil could be found. Following the release of the ECAFE report in May 1969, the Japanese Prime Minister's Office sponsored another survey of the islands for one month, from June 14 to July 13. Entitled "Scientific Survey on the Geological Quality of the Seabed in the Water Areas Near the Senkaku Islands (*Senkaku Retto Shuhen Kaiki no Kaitei Chishitsu ni*

Kansuru Gakujutsu Chosa)," and costing 9,435,000 yen, the survey was led by Niino Hiroshi, a professor formerly at the Tokyo University of Fisheries (*Tokyo Suisan Daigaku*) who was now with Tokai University (*Tokai Daigaku*) by this point. Niino's report was submitted on August 28.[68] It was shortly thereafter published in installments in the *Japan Petroleum Weekly*.[69] The first installment, which served as an outline to the report, appeared on September 29. It stated that "the recent survey ... has led us to believe the area is worth prospecting for oil resources."[70] This was a very important report as at the time Japan was already importing ninety-nine percent of its oil.

The Prime Minister's Office sponsored a second survey a year later on August 20, 1970. This one was led by Professor Hoshino Michihei of Tokai University— a school founded in 1942 and committed to science and engineering. Hoshino, who had served in the Maritime Safety Agency (*Kaijo Hoancho*) in the Waterways Bureau (*Suirobu*) from 1950 before joining the faculty of Tokai University in 1964, was a prolific writer on the earth's crust and ocean geology, and by the time he was asked to head the mission he had already published a half-dozen books including *Kaitei no Sekai* (The Underwater World) and more than two dozen academic papers.[71] Hoshino's survey confirmed that the area might contain one of the most prolific oil and gas reservoirs in the world.[72]

There were other survey missions to follow Hoshino's, comprised of teams from Ryukyu University and a joint mission by Kyushu University and Nagasaki University in late 1970. The group was comprised of nine people: four professors, one of whom, Matsumoto Yukio, headed the delegation, three professors and students from Nagasaki, and a reporter and cameraman from the Fukuoka Bureau of the *Mainichi Shimbun*. Their early findings, including the discovery of albatross on Kita Kojima for the first time in thirty years, were published in the local *Nagasaki Shimbun* in March 1971. A fuller report, approximately 150 pages in length, was completed in December 1973, and was comprised of three parts. While their one-month long trip was primarily scientific in nature, a long section at the end that included newspaper stories about the political and diplomatic tensions over the islands showed that the participants were certainly aware of the situation there.[73]

It should be pointed out that during the 1950s and 1960s, U.S. authorities in Okinawa were very cooperative with these surveys, approving almost all of those they were aware of. A survey the U.S. government did not approve, however, was one requested by a vice minister of defense, Noro Kyoichi, discussed in Chapter 5, a couple of months before reversion was to take place in March 1972, who desired to fly over the islands in a U.S. military aircraft. Political Advisor to the U.S. High Commissioner John F. Knowles felt that such a trip then would negatively affect an already internationally political sensitive issue and had the U.S. Embassy deny the request.

Another trip it had concerns with was that by a group from Tokai University which was hoping to visit the Senkakus area in late June or early July 1971. As the visit was similar to those that had been undertaken in 1969 and 1970, to which it had interposed no objection, USCAR informed the State

Department on June 2 it had no objections to the proposed visit, although it realized the "university-sponsored" survey might be viewed by the GRC as "attempt by GOJ to establish pattern of Japanese activity in Senkakus in years just prior to reversion rather than for the stated purpose to conduct 'seismic research'."[74] The State Department subsequently told the Embassy in Tokyo that it thought the visit should be postponed. The Embassy subsequently suggested to the GOJ that the visit be postponed, which it did. (The Embassy was later informed that the university decided to conduct a survey well north of the Senkakus, which neither the Embassy nor USCAR had a problem with.[75])

Nevertheless, throughout the years, U.S. military authorities had historically encouraged the GRI to be more involved in administering the Senkakus. The military, for example, proposed to build a weather station on Uotsuri Jima in the early 1950s, which would help detect and monitor typhoons and other weather behavior, but it appears officials in the GRI and Ryukyu Meteorological Station felt it would be too difficult to staff and maintain, and the idea was dropped.[76] On the other hand, when the islands became the subject of international political attention in the early 1970s, the U.S. government became reluctant to permit one to be built in the Senkakus before reversion, and in fact, no weather station has been built in the post-reversion years either.

In 1968, it encouraged, too, the GRI to put up a sign in English, Chinese, and Japanese on the islands but it took another couple of years before that became a reality (discussed later in this chapter). Moreover, it blessed or at least did not prevent local surveys, conducted by Ishigaki City, as well as those trips conducted to highlight or enforce Ishigaki's administration over the islands.

Ishigaki City, under which the Senkaku Islands have historically administratively fallen, conducted some administrative surveys as well in the 1960s. The first one in the postwar done on April 11, 1961 was of a fiscal nature, in order to assess the real land values. The survey was initiated as a result of the recently passed Act for Land Rental Stabilization (*Tochi Chintai Anteiho*).[77]

A more politically motivated trip to the islands was conducted on behalf of Mayor Ishigaki Kiko of Ishigaki City by Arakaki Senei, a member of the city assembly, in May 1969.[78] The city planned to install administrative signs on each of the islands, as well as to erect a small memorial to the victims of the July 1945 attack on the boats evacuating from Ishigaki, as discussed earlier. After conducting a memorial ceremony in the afternoon of the 9th at Torinji, a temple first built in 1611 (but damaged in the 1771 earthquake and tsunami), Arakaki and the others in the two vessels (*Daisan Kyoei Maru* and *Daisan Sumiyoshi Maru*) departed Ishigaki at 5:00 and 5:20 p.m. respectively, reaching the Senkaku Islands early the next morning. The group spent two days in the Senkakus, visiting each of the five main islands and erecting administrative landmarks on them.[79] On Uotsuri Jima, the largest of the islands, the city also erected a concrete sign listing the eight islands and rock formations comprising the Senkaku Islands group.

Arakaki was also joined by representatives of the bereaved families, who witnessed the erection of a small memorial on Uotsuri on May 10. The message

Figure 2.7 Uosturi Marker

engraved on the back described what happened the summer of 1945 and explained that the memorial was made to soothe the spirits of those who died.

Illegal activities in the vicinity of the Senkaku Islands, the U.S. response, and Japanese interest

As mentioned above, during the course of the surveys, examples of the results of poaching and other illegal activities on the islands were seen afterwards or in some cases, the intrusions were witnessed in person. Of course, these

Figure 2.8 Senkaku Victims Memorial

weren't the only illegal activities and frictions that existed; there were many more, which this section describes.

In the latter part of the 1950s, the number of Taiwanese boats fishing in the area of the Senkakus grew dramatically. From about the early to mid-1960s, there were some 3000 fishing vessels a year operating around the Senkakus, and fishing cooperatives in Yonaguni and Ishigaki were reporting various troubles that they were having not only in the vicinity of the Senkakus but actually near their own immediate islands as well.[80]

As mentioned above, Taiwanese vessels were observed around the Senkaku Islands by Okinawan fishermen as well as the participants in the survey missions—the most well-known interaction being that when the Taiwanese were found on islands during an inspection by the Senkaku Retto Survey Team, co-led by Takaoka Daisuke a former member of the Diet and a member of the Prime Minister's personal advisory body called the Council on Okinawa and Other Problems (*Okinawa Mondaito Kondankai*), who visited the islands between July 7–10, 1968. Two armed police officers, Taira Shigeharu, who had lived in Taiwan and left there when he was in the 4th grade,[81] and Iraha Sachio, who had only days before he finished the police academy and was just twenty-one years old,[82] from the Yaeyama Police Station accompanied the team.

The survey team found three Taiwanese vessels anchored approximately 150 meters north of Uotsuri Jima on the morning of July 8, as the team's ship, the *Tonan Maru*, was arriving. The police ordered the three vessels to leave the area and they complied. However, when the *Tonan Maru* arrived at Kita Kojima, some miles due east of Uotsuri, they found seventeen Taiwanese vessels, which then fled toward Kobi Sho, farther to the northeast.

In the early afternoon of the next day (July 9), seventeen Taiwanese vessels, which appeared to be the same ones as the day before (only nine in total were identified), approached Minami Kojima and dropped anchor. Some of the fishermen boarded rafts and went ashore. The policemen followed them and learned that six fishermen had collected approximately 400 bird eggs. Taira ordered the fishermen to leave the islands without the eggs, which they did.

While on Minami Kojima, the police learned that some sixty Taiwanese laborers were staying on the island, living in tents, and engaged in salvaging a 10,000-ton vessel that had grounded and wrecked nearby. In the tents, the police found ten boxes of dynamite, each containing twenty-five kilograms of explosives. There was also a lot of food there, as a cargo vessel, the *Tai Ya-Ho*, had just dropped anchor that morning and was delivering food for the laborers. The police did not arrest anyone, but instead told the Taiwanese to leave the island as soon as possible and come back with the proper entry clearance.[83]

The report, filed by Taira when he returned to Ishigaki, was in turn sent to the chief of police of the GRI on July 13 who forwarded it to Ralph C. Anderson, the director of the Public Safety Department of USCAR, on July 26.[84] In the meantime, USCAR received a copy of the July 14 edition of the *Yaeyama Mainichi Shimbun*, established in March 1950 and known as "Japan's southernmost newspaper," which criticized the Taiwanese landing on the islands and poaching eggs at will and lamenting the fact that the GRI has "no diplomatic control over the matter."[85]

Lieutenant Colonel George E. Suzuki, chief of the Yaeyama Civil Affairs Team, who shared this story with USCAR, added that not only have the Taiwanese poached eggs on the Senkakus and other outer islands, but were fishing in the area as well as occasionally coming ashore illegally to replenish their food supply. "Although this situation has not as yet become overt 'political grist' for the opposition in the forthcoming elections," Suzuki observed, "there is fear among certain conservatives that this can be used to embarrass the ineptitude of GRI and even the U.S. in their impotency to achieve positive results. This will also be, according to the same conservatives, added fuel for the cause of early reversion, implying that GOJ will be able to cope with the matter, if not the U.S."[86]

Suzuki's pointing out of Taiwanese coming ashore to replenish their food supply not only had to do with the Senkakus but was also seen on Ishigaki proper as well. On July 6, for example, a Taiwanese fishing vessel, the *Chin Chen Hsing* (14.7 tons) entered Ishigaki waters at Yoshihara, a district on the central western side of the island, and the captain and mate were subsequently arrested while on shore for illegal entry and non-payment of a taxi-fare. (The cab driver for Mitsuboshi Taxi Company in Ishigaki had alerted police when the two did not pay for their fare back to Yoshihara[87.]) Police took into custody six others, all juveniles, for illegal entry although the charge was later *nolle prossed* by the prosecutor who received the cases on July 10. Eventually, two of the older men were tried in an Ishigaki Summary Court, sentenced to eight and six months imprisonment, respectively, and compulsory repatriation (deportation) at their own expense, although imprisonment was suspended with a stay of execution for two years upon deportation. The captain and his crew departed Ishigaki on their own vessel in the morning of July 30 and were escorted by a GRI police patrol boat to the southern edge of the territorial jurisdiction of the Ryukyus towards Taiwan. Yara Chokei, chief of the Ishigaki Branch, Naha District Procurator's Office, in announcing the disposition of the Taiwanese crew later that morning, advised local police that if any craft comes within three nautical miles of island, to warn them away, and if any person illegally set foot on land (without proper permission, as per CA Ordinance 144/55, Chapter 2.2.27.1), to apprehend them. The procurator also admitted that with only one small patrol boat in Yaeyama, "constant surveillance of all of the islands and atolls is virtually impossible."[88]

At USCAR, the Liaison Department contacted the U.S. embassies in Tokyo and Taipei to make sure information got out to the official counterparts concerned with the matter. In particular, it wanted to confirm GRC authorities had been informed of the arrest, sentencing, and deportation. The U.S. Embassy in Taipei was also to take appropriate action with the GRC to "attempt to preclude these entries in the future" as "illegal entry of Taiwanese fishing vessels continues to be a problem."[89]

A week before the above incident, another one had occurred in which a thirty-nine year old man (Higa Yasumasa) was fishing about 500 meters off Hateruma Island when a 10-ton Taiwanese vessel with a crew of seven or eight approached Higa's boat with grappling hooks. Some of the Taiwanese boarded Higa's boat, threatened him with knives, blamed him for stealing their fishing net and ropes, and searched his boat. Nothing reportedly was taken from Higa, but he was badly shaken by the experience.[90]

Suzuki had been worried about the situation for a couple of reasons. First, he felt local fisherman and residents might take the law (with its diplomatic repercussions) into their own hands. Suzuki wrote, "because of these bolder incursions and the incident of intimidation, there is a potential fear that local fishermen may take matters into their own hands, since the United States and GRI have failed thus far to settle the matter with the Republic of China. No tangible evidence of this exists at present; however, with these incidents occurring each year without any action on the part of GRI and U.S., local exasperation may turn to something more than words of dissatisfaction."[91] As an example of this local tension, Suzuki cited the *Yaeyama Mainichi Shimbun* headline from July 9, "Yaeyama Fisherman Intimidated by Taiwanese Vessel," stating that this recurring problem had been discussed several times during the years but to no avail. It was, as Suzuki noted out of his second concern—relations between Okinawa and the United States—an indirect criticism of the United States "for not achieving a solution to the problem."[92]

The criticism was not far off, and probably was partly shared by Suzuki. There was a great difference in opinion within the U.S. government, between the American embassies in Taipei and Tokyo, and even within USCAR about the seriousness of the situation, and a tendency to downplay GOJ entreaties to address the problem of Taiwanese incursions, treating them in some cases like innocent mistakes.

At the same time, USCAR began to acknowledge by the mid-summer of 1968 that the issue of illegal entry into the Senkakus "was heating up."[93] The intrusions were particularly worrisome for the GOJ: "They may some day inherit Chinese squatters unless they press us to eject them and secure GRC cooperation to keep them out ... there are various indications here as well of growing GRI preoccupation with this problem."[94] For example, a couple of months earlier, Yamano Kokichi, the director of the Special Areas Liaison Bureau, raised the matter of incursions into the Senkakus when he visited Okinawa with a survey mission from May 27 to June 3, and USCAR officials learned that a Naha-based reporter for the *Asahi Shimbun* intended to travel to the Senkaku Islands to do a story about the intruders. "In view of recent press interest in Taiwan Chinese illegal entry incidents," Foreign Service Officer Ronald A. Gaiduk, who was serving in Okinawa a second time and in this case as the deputy director of the Liaison Office of USCAR, warned, "considerable undesirable publicity can be expected in Japan as well as here, exacerbating the situation and embarrassing GOJ/GRI/USG relations."[95]

Perhaps for this reason, but seemingly counterintuitive at the same time, USCAR demonstrated an unwillingness to accept a request by the Japanese Government Okinawa Office (*Nihon Seifu Okinawa Jimusho*, or JGOO) to conduct a fact-finding survey, either by the GOJ and GRI, or jointly with USCAR: "we do not intend to go along with JGOO joint survey proposal and will try to discourage JGOO from unilateral actions as inappropriate at this time."[96] USCAR believed this request was a follow-up to an expression of interest by Yamano, whom U.S. officials once described after he had been named to be the director of the Special Areas Liaison Bureau in late 1964, as "an energetic man with a good sense of humor," in the incursions problem.[97] If it was not going to allow the Japanese government to conduct a fact-finding survey, USCAR would have to conduct one itself or in conjunction with the GRI.[98] As such, Gaiduk stated that the Senkakus were "too remote for the GRI to police. We are planning to arrange for GRI investigation, not only to learn the facts for any further action including possible further State [Department] demarche to GRC, but also to forestall unilateral visit by JGOO (which we cannot very well prohibit) and Japanese press play to effect USG not properly looking after Ryukyuan real estate for which it responsible."[99]

This exchange became the immediate impetus for a trip the following week to the Senkakus by Gaiduk and a USCAR colleague in the Public Safety Department, Ronald M. Ota, with officials from the Yaeyama police and immigration offices. However, the rise in incursions and their visibility, particularly during Takaoka's survey mission, made it a high political priority to ensure the situation was being properly taken care of.

On August 12, 1968, the *Chitose*, carrying Yaeyama Immigration Division (*Shutsunyu Kanricho Yaeyama Shucchosho*) Chief Shiroma Shobun, the two USCAR observers (Gaiduk and Ota), an assistant GRI police inspector (Tokeshi

Kenzo), and two police officers (Taira, who had traveled to the Senkakus the previous month, and Kudaka Shinobu), arrived at Minami Kojima after hearing reports of there being Taiwanese in the area. While they did not see any Taiwanese vessels nearby, when the six-person boarding party landed, which was in itself "extremely difficult" and presumably dangerous due to the pre-typhoon high seas, they found forty-five Taiwanese salvage workers still at work on the island.[100]

The salvage workers were employed with a Taiwanese company based in Kaoshing City called Hsing-nan Salvage (Iron Works) Company which had purchased salvage rights for $18,000 to a Panamanian freighter that had been irreparably damaged in a storm. The papers attesting to salvage rights were apparently in order, Gaiduk later reported, adding USCAR and local officials were unaware of anyone contesting the salvage rights: "Illegal entry is evidently the only issue."[101] According to the leader of the workers, company officials had consulted with U.S. consular officials in Taiwan but were told they did not need any special permission to enter the islands or conduct their salvage operations. The immigration official registered all forty-five men, admonished them to obtain entry permits before entering Ryukyus territory in the future, explained the procedures for doing so, and ordered them to leave on the first available Taiwanese vessel.

Due to an approaching typhoon (the deadly Tropical Storm "Polly" or Typhoon No. 7 that killed at least 112 people in Japan), the police craft was forced to return to Ishigaki the following day, arriving in the afternoon. The USCAR observers returned to Naha the next day (14th) and reported their findings. Ota had made copious notes, which included the comment: "After on-the-spot observation, PS [Public Safety Department] feels that the salvage crew, when they undertook the salvage operation, were acting in good faith and were not cognizant of the applicable immigration laws and procedures concerning entry into the uninhabited Senkaku Retto Islands."[102] As such, Ota recommended that the U.S. Embassy in Taipei notify the GRC of all entry requirements into the Ryukyu Islands.[103]

When the typhoon passed, the police vessel returned to the Senkakus on August 18 to check on compliance and found the Taiwanese salvage workers still on Minami Kojima. Two Taiwanese vessels were also there, the *Fuyingwan* and the *Senlonghao*. The first one had just loaded scrap, the police subsequently learned, and departed for Taiwan without taking any salvage workers with it. The police then ordered the workers to board the second, 150-ton vessel and depart the island. The workers, however, said the vessel could only carry twenty passengers and told the police that the first ship, after unloading the scrap, would be coming back to pick them all up by August 23 and return them to Taiwan. Another approaching typhoon forced the *Chitose*, a 130-ton vessel that was built in 1963 initially for rescue operations and the prevention of smuggling activities which was often employed in these missions, to return to Ishigaki again the following morning.[104] Weather permitting, they planned to return on the 24th to see if in fact the Taiwanese workers had left and "to enforce the expulsion order if necessary."[105]

In a subsequent report, USCAR stated that while the Taiwanese were "tardy in compliance with order to leave" having been warned twice (in July and again on August 12), they had cooperated with GRI immigration registration, were apparently aware they were on Ryukyuan territory, and did not question GRI jurisdiction over the Senkaku Islands.[106] The only reason the Taiwanese were reluctant to depart, Gaiduk commented, was that almost half the salvaging remained to be done on the wrecked hull.

U.S. officials met with the Taiwanese Ministry of Foreign Affairs at the end of August to explain the entry procedures—which were really "quite simple"—on August 27.[107] Acting political counselor, Leo J. Moser, a veteran Foreign Service Officer who later served as Ambassador to Laos, called on Tang Wu, director of North American Affairs, to also tell him about the problems encountered in July and August and share photos that a reporter from the *Ryukyu Shimpo* had taken in July. After expressing his appreciation for the information, Tang told Moser that the Fisheries Bureau of the Taiwan Provincial Government had been directed to "bring an end to the illegal visits of Taiwanese fishermen to the Senkaku Islands" and that the same bureau had recently set up a "series of penalties that would apply to any persons caught trespassing."[108]

While the GRC and Tang himself appeared accommodating on the above issue, when Moser mentioned the GOJ's interest in this issue, Tang's tone and demeanor changed. Japan is "not entitled to say anything" about the status of the Ryukyus, he asserted, arguing that "in the view of the GRC the United States government is administering the islands not in the name of Japan but in the name of all the Allied Powers victorious over Japan in World War II. Until there is a final multilateral treaty providing for the future of the islands, Japan has no right to express its views on the administration of the Ryukyus."[109] Expressing "great concern," Tang added, "for Japan to have done so was 'too aggressive' and the U.S. should have rejected the note sent it by the GOJ."[110]

Moser reminded Tang that the USG recognizes "residual Japanese sovereignty" in the Ryukyus and that "to his knowledge the GRC is the only country that does not agree with this view."[111] Moser noted as well the connection of the Senkaku Islands issue with Japanese public opinion and domestic politics, but Tang retorted, correctly, that "Japan was not the only country that had internal political problems. Every country had them."[112] Tang told Moser there were many legislators in the Legislative Yuan who were causing problems for MOFA and "for himself personally" on the status of the Ryukyus, and having had to testify before their committees, had been "subjected to their chastisement."[113] Legislators questioned MOFA about the need to recognize Japanese passports issued to the inhabitants of the Ryukyus or Ryukyuan ships flying the Japanese flag with a special pennant above it. MOFA officials were doing "all that is possible to quiet agitation" by these legislators for a "stronger GRC policy" toward the status of the Ryukyus, Tang added.[114] Tang also repeated an earlier request for GRC consular representation in Naha, saying that if there were a consulate it could investigate on the spot such reports of intrusion, but Moser noted that "GRC unwillingness to recognize Japanese residual sovereignty in the Ryukyus" would "prove an obstacle."[115]

Following Takaoka's visit to the Senkakus where the survey team found Taiwanese workers in the area, the Japanese Ministry of Foreign Affairs submitted a *note verbale* to U.S. officials informing them that the GOJ is "seriously interested in the cases of trespassing into the territorial waters and illegal landing by fishermen of the Republic of China, which have been occurring frequently from some time ago, in the Senkaku Islands area, which form a part of the Nansei Islands, which are the territory of Japan," and requesting that the USG take "necessary and effective measures to control the trespassers and to prevent the recurrence of such cases of trespassing in the future."[116] The MOFA official included a three-page annex to the *note verbale*, which provided details of the July 8–9 sightings and interactions by the research vessel, *Tonan Maru*, which had on board Takaoka from the prime minister's advisory body and the survey team.

The U.S. Embassy responded at the end of September. In its own *note verbale*, it informed the Ministry of Foreign Affairs that U.S. "authorities in the Ryukyus, in cooperation with the Government of the Ryukyu Islands, had removed unauthorized entrants from the Senkaku Islets," adding that the "United States has also reviewed the general problem of trespassing in the Senkaku Islets and has taken the necessary actions."[117] Speaking with GRC officials at the end of August had been one of those actions.

It is likely that the GOJ was not entirely satisfied with the response. Later that fall, it forwarded to the U.S. Embassy a report prepared by JGOO, which had received its information from the Fisheries Division (*Suisanka*) of the GRI. The Fisheries Division had been aware of the issue of illegal intrusions by Taiwanese fishermen, and the problems they caused, for a while. For example, as early as 1965, the Fisheries Division had been informed by the *Tonan Maru*, which regularly operated in the area, that it had found "many fishing vessels" from Taiwan in the area around the Senkakus, and that Taiwanese crew members were found on the islands gathering sea bird eggs. The crew of the *Tonan Maru* provided a similar report in 1966.

In April 1967, Nakatake Hiroshi, president of the Yonaguni Fisheries Cooperative (*Yonaguni-cho Gyogyo Kyodo Kumiai*), went further to request the Fisheries Division to take appropriate countermeasures, and the following month, the mayor of Yonaguni Town (Yonaguni-cho), Irinaka Seizo, and the speaker of the Yonaguni Town Assembly (*Yonaguni-cho Gikai*), Kuga Hisashi, expressed concerns about the Taiwanese invasion of the fishing grounds and "security" issues caused by Taiwanese landing and visiting private homes.[118] Their concerns about fishing, poaching, stealing medicinal plants, and the safety of the residents were primarily local in nature but also resembled the problems Ishigaki was having and were of course closely related to them. JGOO's report, summarizing these incursions and requests by the leadership of Yonaguni, concluded that the "livelihood [of the people of Yaeyama] is

Figure 2.9 Poachers

Figure 2.10 Salvage Workers

being jeopardized. Such being the case, it is requested that the United States as the administering authority establish their fundamental attitude to protect the properties and livelihood of the Okinawan people and protest without delay to the Government of Taiwan against such illegal activities and strongly negotiate with it to assure no recurrence of such undesirable events in the future."[119]

In early 1969, the U.S. Embassy referenced the report in a talking paper. Coordinating with USCAR officials, the Embassy provided the following coordinated comments in January 4 talking paper in response to the points raised in the report.

> Taiwanese intrusions into the territorial limits of the outlying islands of the Ryukyuan chain have been a seasonal, chronic problem for a long time. However, in our judgment the problem has never exceeded minor and manageable proportions. We see no need to increase the GRI patrol and enforcement measures now in effect. Moreover, since the GRI's measures to contain this problem are well within the GRI's police competence and are entirely adequate, the United States Civil Administration of the Ryukyu Islands does not see any justification for intervention in a matter of routine local police and immigration control. We do not regard these intrusions as a threat to the territorial integrity of the Ryukyu Islands. In the only case where there might conceivably have been a question of Ryukyuan territorial integrity, that of the Senkaku Gunto, the United States Civil Administration took the step of directly observing GRI police measures, which proved to be entirely competent. The Civil Administration's observations also failed to establish any basis for concern about the prospect of territorial questions arising from the incidents in question.[120]

As late as the end of 1968, however, U.S. authorities in Okinawa had not seen a need for action, and tended to downplay the Senkakus situation. In a December 26 telegram to other American officials in Tokyo, Hawaii, and D. C., Gaiduk described Taiwanese intrusions as a "seasonal, chronic problem for a long time" which has "also been of minor and manageable proportions, clearly within capabilities and jurisdiction of Ryukyuan law enforcement establishment."[121] Gaiduk was basing this view on his personal assessment, as an observer on the survey that went to the Senkaku Islands in August, where he gathered a favorable impression of GRI Police ability to handle the situation: "GRI's measures to contain this problem [are] well within GRI competence and entirely adequate."[122] Gaiduk went so far as to say that "we do not regard this to be a threat to territorial integrity of Ryukyu Islands ... [and] see no need to increase or modify present GRI patrol and enforcement measures now in effect ... USCAR would not see any justification in interfering in routine local police and immigration control matter."[123]

Gaiduk was responding to a U.S. Embassy telegram sharing the contents of a GOJ report on Taiwanese intrusions, which was called the "Nagato Report." Within USCAR, Gaiduk's views were shared by others. For example, Ralph C. Anderson, the director of the Public Safety Department, concurred in Gaiduk's reply writing, "This appears to be another case of our Japanese friends tweaking the nose of the U.S. over a *minor* problem."[124] Anderson explained the problems he saw in the report in the following ways:

> Throughout the Nagato Report it is implied that Taiwanese fishing vessels are "intruding into Ryukyuan waters" when they are within the geographical boundaries of the Ryukyu Islands. (CA Proclamation No. 27, December 25, 1953.) This is contrary to the generally accepted three-mile limit. Certain countries claim a 12-mile limit or more but the generally accepted limit is three miles.
>
> Historically, the natives of Taiwan and the natives of the Yaeyama group have had relatively friendly relations for hundreds of years. As an example of this friendship, when the eight Taiwanese fishermen were arrested and held in the Ishigaki jail in July 1968, residents of Ishigaki brought food to the Taiwanese throughout their incarceration.
>
> The number of "intrusions" alleged in the Nagato report gives a distorted picture. Exact numbers, as reported by GRI, are not available, however it is known that the same vessel was counted daily until the vessel departed. Thus the implication in the Nagato report that as many as 5,000 vessels intrude per year is incorrect.
>
> GRI police patrol vessel conducted 53 separate patrols during 1967. The number of 1968 patrols is not available but will exceed the 1967 total. Another patrol vessel for this area is programmed for purchase in FY 70, using ARIA funds.[125]

While the information presented by him is factual, it seems Anderson was more interested in pointing out the problems with the report than in addressing the concerns raised in it.

With this said, however, there were others who had been concerned with the issue of intrusions, in part facilitated by Okinawan officials with intimate knowledge of the area, such as Shinjo Tetsutaro, a native of Ishigaki who was the chief of the Foreign Liaison Section of the General Affairs Bureau (*Somukyoku Shogaika*) of the GRI. Shinjo was one of the participants in the July trip to the islands with Takaoka and worked hard to get the views of the GRI and Japanese government across to his counterparts in USCAR.[126] Perhaps as a result of this, some in USCAR wanted to take a more proactive role.

In early September (1968), USCAR got word that the Taiwanese salvage workers who were "illegally" on Minami Kojima had dismantled their gear and left the islands, due in part to the recent patrols by the GRI Police vessel *Chitose*.[127] In a letter to Chief Executive Matsuoka Seiho, Stanley S. Carpenter, a Foreign Service Officer who was serving as the civil administrator for USCAR under the High Commissioner[128] since July 1967, proposed "an occasional military overflight" over the Senkaku Islands as part of a "system of spot checks at irregular intervals," and requested that the GRI Police also patrol the islands "from time to time" in order to "help discourage illegal entry in this area in the future."[129] Carpenter also encouraged that the organizations conducting the respective patrols keep the other informed at the working level.

A few days before Carpenter sent this letter, Gaiduk had met with a representative of CINCPAC, Colonel Vincent A. Abrignani, on August 29 about the military overflights at the "earliest practicable opportunity to provide a final check" as to whether the Taiwanese have departed from Minami Kojima.[130] Gaiduk also requested "monthly overflights of Senkaku Gunto for three months" which would be reduced "to a quarterly basis" if "no unusual activity is observed."[131]

In addition to the two proposals for patrolling, Carpenter also recommended that the GRI put up "relatively permanent" signs on each of the islands in Japanese, Chinese, and English "at various vantage points located in likely landing areas" to help avoid misunderstandings about the territorial status.[132] The reason Carpenter said he was suggesting it was because he believed that some of the Taiwanese fishermen going into the area around the Senkakus "were not sure either of their exact location because of navigational imprecision or are not sure of the territorial status of the island group. In other words," he continued, "they are often honestly unaware that they require an entry permit to land on Senkaku and that they are in fact trespassing."[133] Carpenter, adding that emergency entry due to storms or other mechanical or safety concerns should be considered, asked Matsuoka, who had been serving as chief executive since October 1964,[134] his reactions to the proposals "which represent an effort to minimize further illegal intrusions into Ryukyus territory."[135]

Chief Executive Matsuoka, who had studied in the United States in the 1910s and 20s and later founded Matsuoka Construction (*Matsuoka Kensetsu*) and Matsuoka Power Distribution Company (*Matsuoka Haiden*), the latter the predecessor to Okinawa Power and Electric Company (*Okinawa Denryoku*), agreed with Carpenter, writing he found his proposals "most useful and appropriate" and giving his concurrence "in principle" on October 21.[136] Matsuoka "strongly desire[d] that the occasional military overflight ... be put into practice" in close coordination with the Ryukyu Police patrols, but mentioned that the other two suggestions—increased police patrols and the installment of no trespassing signs on the islands would require financial assistance from USCAR.[137]

Shortly after receipt of Carpenter's letter, the related departments of the GRI immediately set to work to develop estimates of the cost involved in erecting the signs. By the end of March 1969, the Immigration Agency (*Shutsunyu Kanricho*) of the GRI submitted several documents to USCAR's Public Safety Department, including drawings and the expected costs ($7,549) for the seven signs.[138] USCAR subsequently came up with its own estimates for the project, which turned out to be slightly lower, at $6,815. Curiously, even though the signs were suggested by USCAR, no action was immediately taken on allocating the money, perhaps as a result of the slow wheels of the bureaucracy and budgeting.[139]

USCAR realized that the posting of signs "would not completely solve this problem" but believed it "would serve as a warning to those who may unknowingly or illegally enter these waters, or land on the islands under U.S. administration."[140] Over the summer, however, it began to be concerned that the United States might be going too far by having proposed the signs.

As we know, during the spring and summer 1969, interest in the potential for oil and other natural resources grew among a variety of countries and commercial interests. By the early fall—one year since the proposal was originally made—the situation had gotten serious enough for USCAR to reevaluate U.S. involvement in the erection of the signs. "Since the project was initially conceived," the director of the Public Safety Department of USCAR, Harriman N. Simmons, wrote,

> there has been a growing international interest in the waters around the Senkakus due to the suspected existence of extensive oil reserves under the continental shelf. In addition, USCAR is aware that the GRC officially opposes the reversion to Japan of sovereignty over the Ryukyu Islands, including the Senkakus. USCAR is not aware of the U.S. Government's views toward the GRC position outlined above, nor whether there are any other international issues possibly involving the Senkakus. However, USCAR is anxious to avoid taking any action which could be construed as prejudicial to U.S. interests, and USCAR funding for the warning signs might conceivably be regarded as de facto recognition of the merits of certain claims as opposed to others.[141]

Simmons ended his memorandum to John F. Knowles, who had been assigned to Okinawa in December 1968 as the new political adviser to the High Commissioner and who would serve until reversion in 1972, with a request for his opinion and advice as to whether USCAR should participate further in the warning sign project.

Knowles' response was not immediately forthcoming, but in the meantime, Richard E. Snyder, a Foreign Service Officer who served as director of the Liaison Office from 1967 to 1969 (having succeeded John C. Monjo[142]), quickly answered Simmons' request for information with a detailed and carefully argued two-page response on September 27. Snyder (not to be confused with Richard L. Sneider who would later come to Tokyo to negotiate the Okinawa Reversion Agreement) began by stating that "The U.S. policy toward the Senkaku Retto is clear: The United States has consistently asserted that the Senkaku Retto is a part of the Ryukyu Islands under the control of the United States and under the jurisdiction of the GRI."[143] After explaining some of the examples of the "consistent exercise of this claim" and "other practices and usage over the years," which Snyder said was not meant to be an inclusive or exhaustive list, he stated, "USCAR's contemplated action in defraying the costs of erecting permanent territory marker signs on the Senkaku Islands is entirely consistent with the above policy position," and added for good measure that "the recent heightened interest in the Senkaku Islands in connection with the oil explorations on the North East Asia continental shelf does not alter this finding. It does increase the need for the posting of these markers without delay."[144] Snyder recommended the Legal Department's advice be sought on the exact wording but felt that in any case, "defray[ing] part or all of the expense of posting these signs ... is entirely consistent with our interest and with the initiating role which USCAR has played, including assurances given the GOJ, in the matter of territory posting of Senkaku."[145]

With this advice, the Public Safety Department wrote to the High Commissioner the following week on October 2 to recommend that the Ryukyu Property Custodian be authorized to pay the GRI $6,815 to erect multi-language "no trespassing" signs on each of the Senkaku Islands.[146] It is unclear when Lieutenant General James B. Lampert, the High Commissioner since January 1969, gave his approval, but his political advisor wrote to him on November 28 to express his concurrence in USCAR's proposed course of action.

It seems that Knowles took some time prior to responding to the mid-September request for his opinion in order to study the Liaison Department's "fat file" on the Senkakus issue.[147] Knowles had been worried that "others might attempt to construe U.S. (sic) putting up signs on Senkaku (which we have nowhere else) as evidence of U.S. support for Japanese claims vs. GRC over offshore waters and oil resources," but discovered in the above file memoranda indicating "State and [U.S. embassies at] Taipei as well as Tokyo consider it in U.S. interest to do everything possible to show U.S. support for Japanese sovereignty over Senkakus and to avoid any GRC or CHICOM [Communist China] claim."[148] Knowles asked that the High Commissioner, in any case, inform the Department of Army, Department of State, and the Tokyo and Taipei embassies once action was taken.

This was done, and with the exception of a minor budget justification challenge on the Department of Army side and a suggestion for minor revision of the wording on the State side, there were no serious problems.[149] Subsequently, the Japanese Ministry of Foreign Affairs also made a minor request to change the wording, and this was accommodated.[150] Based on communication with the Legal Affairs Department of GRI, USCAR learned the signs were to be finished in May and erected in June. USCAR asked to be advised when the project was completed.

As it turns out, it was not until July before the GRI workers were dispatched to erect the signs. In June, six Taiwanese fishermen landed on the islands and were arrested, and tensions rose. It is unclear if this was in fact the reason for the delay in the dispatch, but it is certainly possible. It does suggest yet an additional urgency in getting the signs posted. This need became all the more apparent as the team dispatched to erect the signs came across a total of fourteen Taiwanese who were discovered on Kuba Jima, salvaging sunken ships. Their situation was similar to the one above. Their work permits identified their place of work by longitude and latitude but did not specify the name of the country.[151] They were ordered to leave immediately.[152]

The team, headed by Security Section (*Keibika*) Chief Higa Kenji, a forty-four-year old official with the Immigration Agency of the GRI (*Ryukyu Seifu Shutsunyu Kanricho*), departed Ishigaki port late in the evening of July 8, 1970.[153] Higa and his team arrived the next day off the southern side of Uotsuri and began their work. One thing that surprised Higa in particular was the number of "illegal intrusions" by Taiwanese they witnessed while they were there.[154] While on Uotsuri, Higa came across nine Taiwanese using an outdoor natural bathing area and afterwards showed them the signs to confirm that the Chinese writing on the signs was recognizable and that they understood they were violating USCAR ordinances by being on the island. "That in itself was quite an accomplishment," Higa later said.[155] When his team traveled to their sixth destination, Kuba Jima, they found fourteen Taiwanese workers on the island and a freighter moored offshore. After speaking with the leader of the group and conducting further investigations, Higa learned that they did not have the proper permissions from USCAR to be there. Apparently, their work permits identified their place of work by longitude and latitude but did not specify the name of the country.[156] They were thus in violation of the 1968 reaffirmation (discussed below) with Taiwanese officials of Ordinance 125 (that had been effect in the Ryukyu Islands since February 1954) and Higa advised them to leave the area immediately.

On July 13, the team completed the erection of the signs on all the islands in three languages—Chinese, English, and Japanese—warning against

Figure 2.11 Officials Putting Up Sign

trespassing. The signs read: "Entry into any of the Ryukyu Islands, including this Island, or their territorial waters other than innocent passage, by persons other than the residents of the Ryukyu Islands, is subject to criminal prosecution except as authorized by the U.S. High Commissioner. By Order of the High Commissioner of the Ryukyu Islands." According to one of the workers who placed "no entry" signs on the islands, the fact that USCAR paid for the signs implies that the USG was not only administering the islands but that it also recognized Japanese sovereignty.[157]

GRC request for temporary shelter

Around this time, the GRC made a request with regard to temporary shelters for its fishermen. This request was made on May 18, 1970, when Frederick Chien, who was serving as the acting director of the North American Affairs Bureau of Taiwan's MOFA, called in Moser, the political counselor at the U.S. Embassy in Taipei, and presented him with the GRC case for a "temporary shelter" for Taiwanese fishermen in the Senkaku Islands area.[158] According to Chien, Taiwanese fishing vessels often had to seek emergency haven in the area during stormy weather but were not sure about U.S. military training grounds, firing ranges, etc., there. As such, the Ministry of Economic Affairs asked MOFA, through the Executive Yuan, to request that the USG designate an island in the Senkaku group that would serve as a "temporary shelter" and give advance permission to Taiwanese fishing vessels for their use under emergency conditions. It is unclear what response the political counselor at the time gave, but the same day, the Embassy queried the State Department for advice.

The State Department in turn informed the High Commissioner that because international law "generally recognizes right to seek shelter in territorial or internal waters in legitimate emergencies caused by weather or other force majeure—and only under such circumstances," the USG supports this right with respect to the Ryukyu Islands and "will continue to do so for period of U.S. administration."[159] A balance would obviously have to be struck if this right was abused or excuses made, particularly if there was an increase in incursions deemed illegal in the first place. In retrospect, it seems that if the GRC request had been adopted literally (and to an extreme), Taiwan might have been able to develop a semi-permanent presence and thus gradually get control over at least one island in the group. This certainly had to be the intention of at least a few officials in the GRC.

On at least one occasion afterward, the GRC tried to use the "temporary shelter" argument. On April 11–12, 1972, a month before reversion, GRI Police patrols near the Senkakus area intercepted two Taiwanese fishing vessels which were ordered to leave the area. Chien, who read about the incident through a Kyodo News Agency report appearing in the April 13 edition of the English language newspaper *China Post,*[160] made a representation to the U.S. Embassy in Taipei to protest this action against the fishermen stating that they were seeking refuge at the time and pointing out that the Taiwanese had been fishing in the area for years. The GRC, according to Chien, considered the action of the Okinawan police "provocative and uncalled for" and requested the USG "prevail on Okinawan police to exercise restraint in such activities in order to keep tensions down."[161] The U.S. Embassy official replied that while he had not seen the stories, he would report Chien's request to the Department and ask U.S. authorities in Okinawa for any available information. He also reminded Chien that Taiwanese vessels had been asked to leave several times in the past few years and hoped that the GRC would try to minimize the possibility of incidents "particularly in last few days" of U.S. administration of the Ryukyus.[162]

Assignment of an MSA vessel and training crew

In the middle of tensions in July and August 1970 over the granting of exploration concessions near the Senkakus by the GRC to an American oil company (discussed in detail in the next chapter), the Japanese government assigned two members of the Maritime Safety Agency, Mori Meisaburo and Imai Tsunekatsu, to the GRI Police, a move that seemingly caught both the GRI and USCAR off guard. The two men, who would serve as captain and chief engineer, respectively, showed up at GRI Police headquarters "unannounced" and explained that they were there to prepare the police for the arrival of a new patrol vessel, the *Okinawa*, whose construction was scheduled to be completed that fall.[163] Neither USCAR nor GRI knew, however, of any personnel exchange agreements or of any specific one that provided the officers to the GRI. In addition, no preparations had been made on the local side for the training of a yet-to-be-chosen Okinawan crew.

This did not prevent the local newspapers from getting ahead of the story. The August 21st edition of the *Okinawa Times* reported their arrival, and Mori was quoted as saying that although specific instructions on the vessel's operations had not been received, he thought the overall operations plan might include patrolling, for example, the waters in the vicinity of the Senkakus Islands.

The High Commissioner requested the Embassy in Tokyo to look into the matter and clarify "any misunderstanding" within the GOJ regarding the role of MSA officers.[164] "In the absence of a U.S.-GOJ agreement delineating GOJ operational role over GRI Police," the High Commissioner's office wrote, "we do not think two GOJ officers should serve in any capacity in operation of the vessel except for training of Okinawan crew."[165]

It should be pointed out that the new patrol boat itself was not unknown to the USG. In 1968, the GOJ had proposed to make available to the GRI police a 346-ton police patrol vessel under the Ryukyu Fiscal Year (RFY) 1970 GOJ aid program. However, both USCAR and GRI objected to the proposal because the funds were not available to maintain and operate the twenty-six-man vessel. The following year, the GOJ offered to make such funds available and to start training an Okinawan crew well in advance. The funds—$555,555—were then included in the 1969 budget for the vessel, and the JFY 71 budget included $185,000 for reimbursement to the GRI for salaries of the crew and its maintenance and operation.[166]

After the vessel was completed and delivered, the USG was very excited. With this said, however, the assignment of the two MSA personnel to the GRI Police patrol vessel was done without proper clearance, and the U.S. Embassy in Tokyo agreed with the High Commissioner's office that if allowed, it would "set an undesirable precedent."[167] The Embassy told Sato Yoshiyasu of the Foreign Ministry that the two MSA officers should not be allowed to perform their duties on "Okinawa" until a bilateral U.S.–Japan memorandum on personnel exchange (a draft of which was submitted by the Foreign Ministry on September 21[168]) was worked out or other formal approval by the U.S. government had been given.[169] The Okinawa Bureau, Okinawa Northern Territories Agency (*Okinawa Jimushoku, Okinawa Hoppo Taisakucho*) of the Government of Japan in Okinawa, or OBONTA, was subsequently instructed to make an immediate approach to USCAR to make the formal request for approval of their assignment and to provide more details on the two officers.

Eventually, construction on the 309-ton *Okinawa* patrol ship was completed in October 1970, and the vessel was given to the GRI which stood up the Ryukyu Maritime Safety Agency (*Ryukyu Kaijo Hoancho*[170]) in September 1971. In late April 1972, on the eve of reversion, the GOJ assigned it to the Maritime Safety Agency to conduct, among other activities, patrols near the Senkaku Islands.[171] The *Okinawa* stayed in service in Okinawa Prefecture until 1987 before it was transferred to Kure and renamed as the *Misasa*.

New guidance for handling intrusions

In the meantime, on March 9, 1971, Ishikawa Hoko, chief of the Yaeyama Police Station (*Yaeyama Keisatsu Kyoku*), wrote to his superiors at GRI Police Headquarters (*Ryukyu Keisatsu Honbu*) to ask for guidance on control and future enforcement of illegal entry into the Senkaku Islands. Noting that actions to date have been taken on the basis of CA Ordinance Number 125 of February 1954, Ishikawa asked for instructions on the following situations:

1. Heretofore, upon finding a vessel (chiefly Formosan fishing boats) which has illegally entered into the territorial waters of Ryukyu Islands, the police issued verbal warning and ordered the vessel to leave the waters, without arresting the offenders. Should we continue to operate on the same policy?
2. What action should we take against a vessel which defies police warning? It will be difficult to make an arrest when there are more than two illegally entered vessels.
3. What are the sources of action to follow when there is a foreign naval vessel or patrol boat in the waters or when personnel of such vessel landed on the islands (on the assumption of conducting a survey or construction)?

The GRI Police in turn requested a meeting with USCAR officials about the guidance it should give to its Yaeyama counterparts. USCAR took this request seriously, and seems to have appreciated the request for the meeting and further guidance. "During the past two years," an internal memo starts,

> The Senkaku Retto's (sic) have been a volatile and critical international issue. ... Incidents arising from excessive GRI police action will no doubt occur without the establishment of a coordinated U.S. policy; otherwise it could develop into far-reaching ramifications in relationships between GRC, GOJ, ROK, and the U.S. During the coming fishing season, commencing on/about 1 May 1971, past experience indicates many illegal entries and infringements of fishing rights, mostly by GRC vessels, have occurred and are foreseen for this year, unless advance agreements are reached.[172]

At the request of the GRI Police, USCAR held a meeting on March 24, attended by GRI Police Chief Arakaki Tokusuke and the directors of the USCAR Public Safety and Legal Departments. The police wished to get the guidance of USCAR on establishing a policy to control Taiwanese fishing vessels found poaching in the waters off Yonaguni and the Senkakus. This was a particularly pressing issue, not only in light of past violations to date and the fact that reversion was approaching, but due to the fact as alluded to above that the new fishing season would start on May 1 and the GRI Police anticipated an increase in incidents involving Taiwanese vessels.[173]

Arakaki, who started his tenure as police chief in August 1968 (and would serve until December 1971), began by explaining that the police would continue to warn illegal fishermen that they were in GRI territorial waters and order them to leave the area, and for persons found on shore, they would be arrested as in past years. The problem was—and the reason for the request for guidance and hence the meeting—was an uncertainty as to what action should be taken if foreign fishing vessels refused to depart the area despite the police warnings, or more worrisome, in the event a foreign patrol ship was found in the area.

USCAR officials agreed that the GRI police should continue past practices as described above. With regard to a potential problem with foreign vessels not leaving the area, it was agreed that the police would report "all available information" such as identity and description of vessel, as well as the number of crew members observed, to USCAR, which would then undertake "initial action ... through diplomatic channels and therefore any confrontation should be avoided and publicity on such incidents withheld" until the proper coordination between USCAR and GRI had been conducted.[174]

Arakaki stated that a draft operational order would be prepared for the chief of the Yaeyama Police reflecting this policy which would be cleared by USCAR before being sent. Arakaki urged that all of this be completed before the fishing season began in order to better control the intrusion by the

Taiwanese fishermen. USCAR, in summarizing the meeting in its telegram to the Department of the Army, noted that there might be value in having the embassies in Tokyo and Taipei advise the GOJ and GRC respectively of the steps being taken locally to avoid confrontation during the coming months.

By March 26, Arakaki had his draft ready, and USCAR officials appeared happy with its contents after doing a translation and circulating it internally, noting it "meets guidelines set forth in USCAR/GRI meeting."[175] On April 9, answers were provided to Ishikawa's original set of questions.

1. Answer: It should continue to be the principle, in cases involving fishing boats, that the police issue a warning as in the past, and have the boats leave the territorial waters immediately.
2. Answer: When a vessel does not leave the territorial waters in spite of warnings issued by the police, but personnel of such a vessel do not land on the islands, information as to type of vessel, purpose of visit, and other pertinent information should be reported promptly. USCAR is to give concrete instructions in each case. Special care should be taken to prevent discharge of police firearms that might provoke the other parties.
3. Answer: When a foreign naval vessel or patrol boat illegally enters the waters, or when personnel of such a vessel land on the island, detailed information of the circumstances should be reported and police should act in accordance with instruction given under answer to b above. When personnel of other vessels (chiefly fishing boats) illegally land on the islands they may be arrested for violation of CA Ordinance 125, Articles 14 and 29.

The draft was sent to Washington on April 9 and final approval was given to GRI on April 20.[176] By then, new tensions had begun to flare with a statement made by the press spokesman for the State Department with regard to the USG's cautious stance on oil concessions in the area discouraging them as ownership of the islands was disputed and about its position on the larger territorial dispute (discussed in Chapters 3 and 4). Fortunately, there does not appear to have been any serious incidents with fishing vessels in the spring of 1971 as the stage for confrontations had shifted to the political capitals and major cities of Japan, Taiwan, and the United States, as well as a few other countries and territories.

However, incidents began occurring later that summer. For example, about three weeks after the signing of the Okinawa Reversion Agreement, on the morning of July 5, 1971, a Taiwanese vessel in the waters off of Ishigaki Island's Shiraho Village raised a red flag and motioned to two canoes with Okinawan fishermen in them. When the canoes approached the men, a Taiwanese crew member raised a harpoon and waved it as if he were going to throw it at the canoes. The fishermen immediately left the area and reported the incident to police. Later that morning, Chief Ishikawa contacted the GRI Police Head-quarters to request instructions about what sort of action should be taken against the vessel, mentioning that if the vessel were still in the territorial waters the Yaeyama Police Station would like to make an arrest. In forwarding the request to USCAR, GRI Police Chief Arakaki added,

> The Senkaku Island problems may have some connections, however, recently there has been a number of Taiwanese fishing vessels fishing within the waters of the Ryukyu Islands as if they are fishing within their own territorial waters. The intimidating action against the local fishermen cannot be overlooked. Furthermore, the safety of the lives of the local fishermen may be in danger and, therefore, in order to enforce an effective control over these acts by the Taiwanese fishermen it is recommended that arrest action be taken against these offenders.[177]

Simmons subsequently responded that the provisions in Arakaki's letter to the Yaeyama police chief that spring, namely "Control of Incidents Involving Illegal Entry into Senkaku Retto," should be followed in dealing with foreign vessels in Ryukyuan waters, and any unusual occurrences or apparent violations should be promptly dealt with and reported to the GRI Police Headquarters and USCAR. Simmons agreed that "criminal acts or threats of violence against Ryukyuans by crew members or others aboard foreign vessels illegally or legally in Ryukyuan waters should not be condoned," but pointed out that "physical violence, including use of fire arms, should be avoided if possible in accordance with current policy."[178]

The day after the above incident took place, the *Chitose* during its patrol discovered the eighteen-ton Taiwanese fishing vessel, *Chin Chen Lu*, with six crew members, anchored near Minami Kojima. Inspecting the boat, they discovered approximately 600 bird eggs on it and were told by the crew members that the eggs had been collected on the island. Photographs were taken and the boat and crew were allowed to depart after being issued a warning that anyone found on the island without a permit would be subject to criminal prosecution.[179] In a bit of irony, the police while there also ascertained that the warning signs in Chinese, English, and Japanese were "still in good condition," and sent along some photos showing the eggs (since boiled, either to preserve them or protect them from cracking) and the signs, the same ones that were supposed to warn against intrusions in the first place.[180]

The United States would continue to monitor the situation but actually try to stay out of it as much as possible. Tensions would continue after the reversion of Okinawa as well, as they do today.

Attempts to construct a weather station

One of those tensions still around today concerns building any type of structure on the Senkakus, such as a weather station. As mentioned earlier, USCAR had initially but eventually unsuccessfully tried to encourage the GRI to build a weather station on the islands in the early 1950s. As reversion approached, however, the USG was less interested in pursuing the idea.

In early January 1971, the Japanese government informed the United States of its plans to construct a weather observatory in the Senkakus on Uotsuri Jima for the purpose of expanding the existing GRI's weather forecasting network and to support future oil exploration activities in the vicinity of the Senkaku Islands.[181] A representative from OBONTA explained to USCAR officials that the GOJ proposed to use $105,422 of reserve funds under the JFY 1970 GOJ Aid Program for Okinawa for the construction and travel expenses for Japanese Meteorological Agency (*Kishocho*) personnel. The proposal was "routinely submitted" to USCAR for approval and notification to GRI under the established technical committee.[182] The High Commissioner's office, however, felt this request could be problematic "in view of sensitivity any actions pertaining to Senkakus" and requested the comments of the Embassy in Tokyo, and if it was "inadvisable" for the USG to approve it, asked for "suggestions as to substance and method of handling disapproval."[183]

Early the next week the U.S. Embassy in Tokyo responded, stating it believed that it would be "preferable" the Japanese government not construct the observatory as it would be noticed in Taiwan and would probably be attributed to an attempt by the Japanese government, with America's assistance, to improve the Japanese claim to Senkakus by physical occupation.[184] Nevertheless, the Embassy found it hard to justify a denial of the request to both the GOJ and the GRI, noting that the Japanese government had intended to use aid funds for the construction and had properly made the request to the High Commissioner's office. Moreover, because the U.S. position "respecting at least present administration of Senkakus was already matter of record," it would be difficult, the Embassy pointed out, "to disapprove the project on grounds of uncertainty of Senkakus status."[185]

The telegram mentioned that the Foreign Ministry was aware that the PRC might also be "unhappy" with the construction of a weather station on the Senkakus but that MOFA had "already discounted Chinese reaction" in light of the lack of normal relations between the two countries.[186] With no other reasons to disapprove the construction, the Embassy in Tokyo explained it had no choice but to recommend a "quiet pro forma approval" of the project.[187] In response, the U.S. Embassy in Taipei "doubted the wisdom of U.S. discounting Chinese reaction" to construction of the weather station even if the Japanese government had done so, and argued that in light of the "almost certain strong negative reaction against us as well as Japan in both Taipei and Peking, it would seem desirable for construction of the weather station to be delayed at least until reversion of Okinawa to Japan."[188] It urged that the State Department inform the GOJ that it did not wish to become "further embroiled" in the dispute and that it felt approving the construction of the weather station at the present time would have exactly that effect.[189] The Taipei Embassy added that it believed "this action, which is without prejudice to our basic position on Senkakus sovereignty, is justifiable on general policy and expediency grounds and is consistent with our effort to discourage actions which would exacerbate the problem."[190]

In light of the potential for the construction of the weather station to impact other Chinese communities, David L. Osborn, the Chinese-speaking Consul General in Hong Kong, chimed in by stating that he "fully support[ed]" the views of the Embassy in Taipei that the PRC's "reaction should not be dismissed out of hand and that the U.S. should do whatever it appropriately can, on political rather than legal grounds, to delay installation of a Japanese weather station on the Senkakus at least until after Okinawa reversion."[191] Osborn, who had been serving as the consul general since the previous year after he left his position as the deputy chief of mission in Tokyo, continued:

> The establishment of a weather station even after reversion will no doubt be troublesome to the Chinese, but that is an issue which Peking, Taipei, and Tokyo must work out for themselves. Regardless of the legal technicalities, for permanent installation to be constructed on the Senkakus while the U.S. still maintains administrative control would be to place us squarely in the center of the dispute and, aside from complicating our relations with Taipei, likely to evoke substantial Chinese communist suspicion and hostility.[192]

Back in Washington, the Department of the Army, which was charged with the administration of Okinawa, reviewed the GOJ request and the exchanges between the U.S. embassies in Tokyo and Taipei as well as Osborn's comments, and examined a draft telegram co-written by Howard M. McElroy and Mary E. McDonnell of the State Department's Office of East Asian Affairs, who were on the Japan and Taiwan desks, respectively. The Army made some editorial as well as substantive corrections to the draft, to include a comment that if the decision was made to reluctantly support the GOJ's plans, which the USG was not willing to do (at least not until after reversion), that such approval be given only after the embassies in Tokyo and Taipei and the High Commissioner had another chance to consider it and had "perceived no objection to this approach."[193]

On January 25, the State Department informed the Embassy in Tokyo that it, with the concurrence of the Defense Department, viewed the construction of the weather station as "undesirable," and instructed it to make the following points with the Foreign Ministry: (1) the project is undesirable and should be postponed until after reversion; (2) U.S. position on the matter was without prejudice to its position that Japan has residual sovereignty over islands administered by USG under Article 3 of the Peace Treaty; (3) USG believes it was already taking adequate measures to discharge responsibilities as administering authority over Ryukyus; (4) U.S. position was based on desire to avoid a needless increase in tension—construction of weather station would be interpreted by both Taipei and Peking as raising stakes in dispute; (5) weather station was not needed at this time; and (6) USG concerned that GOJ had advanced this proposal on sensitive issue through relatively open OBONTA channel without opportunity to discuss in diplomatic channels.[194]

On January 26, an officer from the Embassy met with his counterpart at the Foreign Ministry, Sato, to inform him of the Department decision along the lines of the above instructions.[195] Sato subsequently phoned the embassy officer and asked that the Department reconsider on the grounds that the disapproval would become public knowledge and could be embarrassing. At the end of the week, Richard E. Sneider and an embassy officer met with Yoshino Bunroku, who had just succeeded Togo Fumihiko as director general of the American Affairs Bureau. Sneider reiterated the points made to Sato and suggested that "now is not the time to create new problems" with Taiwan by constructing the station on the islands. Instead, he suggested that it might be preferable "tactically" to postpone plans for construction of the station until next year "on the grounds other 'projects' now more urgent."[196]

Yoshino, who admitted that there were "strong and emotional views" within his ministry, chose not to respond directly, but instead said that his efforts to hold off construction of the weather station would be made easier if the U.S. government "could find a way to include mention of the Senkakus in the reversion agreement," an issue discussed in detail in Chapter 4.[197] The embassy officer told the Japanese side that they would be prepared to transmit to the State Department any additional information for U.S. consideration, and informed the department in its telegram regarding the conversation that Yoshino's remark indicated that "at least part of GOJ consideration" in proposing construction of the weather station on Uotsuri was to ease concerns over the reliability of the USG position regarding Senkakus.[198] The Embassy concluded the telegram by asking for suggestions for alternate references to the Senkakus in the Okinawa Reversion Agreement being discussed at the time (see Chapter 4) as they could be helpful both to the Embassy as well as to Yoshino in convincing GOJ to postpone construction plans.

In early April, the GRC asked Walter P. McConaughy, a veteran diplomat who had been serving as U.S. ambassador to the Republic of China since 1966, about the status of the GOJ's plans to build a weather station. According to a telegram prepared for McConaughy to use in a reply to the acting foreign minister, he was to inform the Taiwanese government of the above and also to explain that it was never contemplated that a "Japanese" station be built on the Senkakus but rather the GOJ had offered funds to the GRI for construction of a "GRI" weather station.[199] The ambassador was to add that none of the information could be released to the public as if it was publicized, the GOJ would "undoubtedly face, and probably have to give into, popular pressure to commit itself to construct a station."[200] In a private note to the ambassador, the Department told McConaughy that if it became public not only would the above happen, but "our ability to influence the situation short of outright public veto which could adverse results on Okinawa and in reversion negotiations."[201] The Department also noted that the GRI could probably circumvent the entire situation by funding the project on its own, suggesting it was not completely against it or doubtful of its need. However, political sensitivities overrode the scientific or practical needs.

As the countdown to reversion happened, other issues of concern would arise as well with requests for university surveys and overflights by officials, as well as fears over unauthorized, politically motivated landings by activists from both Japan and Taiwan. These issues are discussed in Chapters 4 and 5.

Notes

1 In what became known as the "Ishigaki Jima Jiken," or Ishigaki Island Incident, an American Navy pilot and two crewmembers parachuted out of their Avenger, which had been hit by anti-aircraft fire, and landed on the shore of Ishigaki Island on the morning of April 15, 1945. They were immediately captured. That night two were beheaded, and one was shot. Many Imperial Japanese Army forces were involved, and their war crime was discovered and tried later. Requests for leniency were granted to some of those who had participated. See "Ishigaki Jima Jiken," in Okinawa Daihyaka Jiten Kanko Jimukyoku, ed., *Okinawa Daihyakka Jiten Jokan* (Okinawa Encyclopedia, Vol. 1), (Naha: Okinawa Times, 1983), 166–67.

2 Even in less violent times, journeys between Taiwan and the southern islands of Okinawa sometimes ended in tragedy. For example, in early November 1945, a ship carrying back evacuees and others who were then living in Taiwan, was shipwrecked or capsized, and more than 100 people died. The exact figure varies, according to the author of a book about the Okinawans in Taiwan. See Matsuda Yoshitaka, *Taiwan Sokai: 'Ryukyu Nanmin' no Ichinen Juikkagetsu* (Evacuation to Taiwan: The One Year and Eleven Months of the 'Ryukyu Refugees'), (Ishigaki City: Nanzansha, 2010), 169.

3 "Instrument of Surrender, 7 September 1945," copy courtesy of Okinawa Prefectural Archives.

4 Simon Bolivar Buckner, Jr., and Joseph W. Stilwell (edited by Nicholas Evan Sarantakes), *Seven Stars: The Okinawa Battle Diaries of Simon Bolivar Buckner, Jr. and Joseph Stillwell* (College Station, TX: Texas A & M University, 2004), 114.

5 Buckner and Stilwell, *Seven Stars*, 124.

6 For more on the lives of these residents, particularly those who had safely evacuated, see Matsuda, *Taiwan Sokai*. Also see Ota Shizuo, "Yaeyama After WWII," in Okinawa: The 50 Years of the Postwar Era Committee, ed., *Okinawa: The 50 Years of the Postwar Era* (Naha: Okinawa Prefecture, 1995), 436–37. For more on Okinawa's relations with Taiwan, see Okinawaken Bunka Shinkokai, ed., *Okinawa Kenshi Bijuaruban 6 Kindai 1: Okinawa to Taiwan* (Okinawa and Taiwan) (Itoman: Okinawaken Kyoiku Iinkai, 2000).

7 "AG 091, Memorandum for Imperial Japanese Government on Governmental and Administrative Separation of Certain Outlying Areas from Japan (January 29, 1946)," in Fukunaga Fumio, ed., *GHQ Minseikyoku Shiryo, Vol. 2 Senryo Kaikaku-Senkyoho-Seiji Shikin Kiseiho* (GHQ Government Section, GHQ Materials, Vol. 2 Occupation Reforms: Election Law and Political Funds Law), (Tokyo: Maruzen, 1997), 141–42.

8 The Senkaku Islands Study Group, "The Senkaku Islands and the Japan's Territorial Titles," 26.

9 Headquarters, Military Government of the Ryukyu Islands, "MG Ordinance, Number 22, The Law Concerning the Organization of the Gunto Governments, 4 August 1950," in Gekkan Okinawasha, ed., *Laws and Regulations During the U. S. Administration of Okinawa, 1945–1972* (Naha: Ikemiya Shokai, 1983), 489.

10 In other areas, including Okinawa and the Senkakus, some twenty-five years later, the State Department, in a briefing book prepared for the Senate hearings on the

Okinawa Reversion Treaty, explained the basis for including the Senkakus under Article 3 of the Peace Treaty with Japan in the following way: "World War II Japanese and American maps showed the Senkakus in the area then administered by Japan as part of the Ryukyus. The Japanese surrendered the Senkakus as part of their surrender of the Ryukyus." See "Memorandum from Howard M. McElroy to Mr. Sheats and others on Okinawa Reversion, July 13, 1971," Folder: Questions/Answers Index Senate Hearings on Okinawa Reversion, Box 26, History of Civil Administration, Records of the Office of the Chief Military History, RG 319, Records of the Army Staff, National Archives, College Park.

11 For more on the making of Article 3, see Eldridge, *The Origins of the Bilateral Okinawa Problem*, chapter 7.

12 For more on these efforts to return Okinawa and the remaining islands in 1952, see Eldridge, *The Origins of the Bilateral Okinawa Problem*, 363–72.

13 United States Civil Administration of the Ryukyu Islands, Office of the Deputy Governor, "CA Ordinance Number 68, Provisions of the Government of the Ryukyu Islands, 29 February 1952," in Gekkan Okinawasha, ed., *Laws and Regulations*, Vol. 1, 1003.

14 United States Civil Administration of the Ryukyu Islands, Office of the Deputy Governor, "CA Proclamation Number 27, Geographical Boundaries of the Ryukyu Islands, 25 December 1953," in Gekkan Okinawasha, ed., *Laws and Regulations*, 850.

15 United States Civil Administration of the Ryukyu Islands, Office of the Deputy Governor, "CA Ordinance Number 125, Control and Exit of Individuals Into and From the Ryukyu Islands, 11 February 1954," in Gekkan Okinawasha, ed., *Laws and Regulations*, Vol. 2, 200.

16 United States Civil Administration of the Ryukyu Islands, Office of the Deputy Governor, "CA Ordinance Number 144, Code of Penal Law and Procedure, 16 March 1955," in Gekkan Okinawasha, ed., *Laws and Regulations*, Vol. 2, 319–20.

17 "CA Ordinance Number 144."

18 See "Oral History with Millard Engen," Cactus Hills Arizona Heritage Project (www.azhp.org/index-3.html, accessed June 2012).

19 Miyako Minseifu, ed., "Kokyu Kiken Kuiki (Permanent Danger Area)," *Koho "Shin Miyako"* (Public Announcement, "New Miyako"), No. 3 (May 6, 1948), cited in Senkaku Shoto Bunken Shiryo Hensankai, ed., *Senkaku Kenkyu Senkaku Shoto Kaiiki no Gyogyo ni Kansuru Chosa Hokoku: Okinawaken ni Okeru Senzen-Nihon Fukki (1972) no Ugoki* (Senkakus Research A Report on Fishing in the Vicinity of the Senkaku Islands Focusing on the Prewar and Pre-Reversion (1972) Period in Okinawa Prefecture), (Naha: Senkaku Shoto Bunken Shiryo Hensankai, 2010), 215.

20 Rinji Hokubu Nansei Shoto Seicho, ed., "Tokubetsu Kokuji Daiichigo (Ryukyugun Sakusen Yoko Dainigo) (Special Proclamation No. 1 [Ryukyu Military Operations Order No. 2)," *Rinji Hokubu Nansei Shoto Seicho Koho*, No. 35 (May 5, 1948).

21 Senkaku Shoto Bunken Shiryo Hensankai, ed., *Senkaku Kenkyu Senkaku Shoto Kaiiki no Gyogyo ni Kansuru Chosa Hokoku*, 215.

22 "Senkaku Retto Kobi Sho wa, Eikyu Kiken Chiiki (Senkaku Shoto's Kobi Sho, Permanent Danger Zone)," *Nansei Shimpo*, November 3, 1948. The *Nansei Shimpo* was a small newspaper that began operations on September 6, 1945 and continued until December 28, 1951.

23 "Senkaku Retto ni Chikayoru Na Beikokugun ga Keikoku (Do Not Go Near the Senkaku Islands, U.S. Air Force Warns)," *Miyako Minyu*, January 14, 1949. The *Miyako Minyu Shimbun* ran from July 10, 1946 to February 24, 1950.

24 Senkaku Shoto Bunken Shiryo Hensankai, ed., *Senkaku Kenkyu Senkaku Shoto Kaiiki no Gyogyo ni Kansuru Chosa Hokoku*, 217–18. Also Ozaki Shigeyoshi, "Senkaku Shoto no Kizoku ni Tsuite, Chu," *Refarensu*, No. 261 (October 1972),

58, citing *Ryukyu Shiryo, 1945–1955*, Vol. 8 (Naha: Ryukyu Seifu Bunkyokyoku, 1958), 59.

25 An example of the announcement and copies of the leases can be found in *Kikan Okinawa*, No. 56, 141–54, cited in Ozaki, "Senkaku Shoto no Kizoku ni Tsuite, Chu," 58. According to Fung Hu-hsiang, "Evidence beyond Dispute: Tiaoyutai (Diaoyutai) is Chinese Territory!" www.skycitygallery.com/japan/evidence.html (accessed January 2011), the U.S. military applied each time to the ROC government for authorization to use the islands for bombing practice, "confirming again that Tiaoyutai is ROC territory." Fung is a former legislator in Taiwan and a professor of philosophy at National Central University in Taipei. This explanation is highly unlikely, however.

26 The Senkaku Islands Study Group, ed., "The Senkaku Islands and the Japan's Territorial Titles to Them," *Kikan Okinawa*, No. 63, 27.

27 "'Arasareru Kobijima Gyoba' Bakugeki Enshu Kuiki Henko Uttaeru (Demanding a Change in the Bombing Practice Zone that is "Tearing Up the Kobi Island Fishing Area)," *Miyako Mainichi Shimbun*, November 10, 1955.

28 See Senkaku Shoto Bunken Shiryo Hensankai, ed., *Senkaku Kenkyu Senkaku Shoto no Shizen Kaihatsu Riyo*, 145.

29 During this time, the Yaeyama Regional Office (*Yaeyama Chihocho*) discovered the administrative responsibility for Sekibi Sho was unclear and requested an internal investigation. In some regulations and descriptions, the island appeared to fall under the jurisdiction of the Miyako Islands Regional Office (*Miyakoto Chihocho*), but officials later found prewar Okinawa Prefecture records that found Taisho Jima had been recorded as a part of Ishigaki City in 1921 (or the 10th Year of Taisho). See "'Sekibijima' no Ishigakishi no Shokan, Taisho 10 Nen ni Taishojima to Shite Toroku ('Sekibi Jima' Falls Under Ishigaki City, Registered in 10th Year of Taisho as Taisho Island)," *Ryukyu Shimpo*, March 16, 1956. A month later, the U.S. Navy announced it was using the island for target practice. Senkaku Shoto Bunken Shiryo Hensankai, ed., *Senkaku Kenkyu Senkaku Shoto Kaiiki no Gyogyo ni Kansuru Chosa Hokoku*, 231–32.

30 Koga, "Mo San, Sato San," 145.

31 Ozaki, "Senkaku Shoto," 58–59.

32 The Senkaku Islands Study Group, "The Senkaku Islands and the Japan's Territorial Titles," 27. Also see "Kuba Jima no Gunyochi Kihon Chintai Keiyakusho (Basic Lease for Military Land on Kuba Jima), in *Kikan Okinawa*, No. 56, 142–49. See Okuhara, "The Territorial Sovereignty over the Senkaku Islands," 101. For some reason, an influential politician from Kyushu, who would have a long association with Okinawa, states in his memoirs that the landowner was paid only 340 dollars per year for use of the island. See Yamanaka Sadanori, *Kaerimite Kui Nashi: Watashi no Rirekisho* (I Have No Regrets Looking Back: My Life Story), (Tokyo: Nihon Keizai Shimbunsha, 2002), 233.

33 Koga, "Mo San, Sato San," 145.

34 It is unclear why the Chinese reading of the islands' names, rather than the Japanese—Kuba Jima and Taisho Jima, were used in the documents exchanged at the time of Joint Committee meeting on May 15, 1972, when the use of the continued ranges was agreed to and signed for.

35 Fung, "Evidence beyond Dispute."

36 Senkaku Shoto Bunken Shiryo Hensankai, ed., *Senkaku Kenkyu Senkaku Shoto Kaiiki no Gyogyo ni Kansuru Chosa Hokoku*, 225–26.

37 The Senkaku Islands Study Group, "The Senkaku Islands and the Japan's Territorial Titles," 28.

38 "Petition to Chief Executive, GRI, May 1955," Folder: 10, Policy and Precedent Files, Daisan Seitoku Maru Case, Box 92, Record Group 260, Records of the United States Occupation Headquarters, World War II, Records of the U.S. Civil

Administration of the Ryukyu Islands (USCAR), Okinawa Prefectural Archives (hereafter, Daisan Seitoku Maru Files).

39 "Letter from Major Harry Apple, on behalf of Deputy Governor (Major General James E. Moore), to Chief Executive (Higa Shuhei), regarding the Case of the Dai San Seitoku Maru, January 4, 1956," Daisan Seitoku Maru Files.

40 Author's interview with Ota Seisaku, June 10, 1997, Ogikubo, Tokyo, Japan. None of Ota's four books discuss the Daisan Seitoku Maru or the Senkakus issue, unfortunately.

41 "Letter from Major Harry Apple to Chief Executive (Higa Shuhei), January 4, 1956."

42 "Letter from Major Harry Apple to Chief Executive (Higa Shuhei), January 4, 1956."

43 Two problems identified have been the central government's reluctance to allow visitors to the islands (both to preserve the natural setting as well as to keep the islands from becoming a political or diplomatic issue), and the demands of their subsequent owner to require permission before landing on them. Previously, when the islands were owned by Koga Zenji, he did not mind if people visited them, as a letter dated July 2, 1968, and sent to the Government of the Ryukyu Islands suggests. See "Jinushi ni Taishi, Wazawaza Joriku Chosa Shodakusho o Moto-meru Kore ga Yabuhebi to Nari, Chimeiteki Akuhei no Ichiin to Naru (Asking Permission of the Land Owner to Land on the Islands Ends Up Waking a Sleeping Dog and Becomes a Fatal Problem Afterwards)," in Senkaku Shoto Bunken Shiryo Hensankai, ed., *Senkaku Kenkyu: Takara Gakujutsu Chosadan Shiryoshu*, Vol. 2, 134.

44 Senkaku Shoto Bunken Shiryo Hensankai, ed., *Senkaku Kenkyu: Takara Gakujutsu Chosadan Shiryoshu.*

45 The editorial committee for the Takara collection organized separate roundtables with approximately a dozen participants of the second and third survey trips (1952 and 1953) and the fourth and fifth survey trips (1963 and 1968) on February 14, 2006 and November 11, 2005 respectively. The proceedings are published in Sen-kaku Shoto Bunken Shiryo Hensankai, ed., *Senkaku Kenkyu: Takara Gakujutsu Chosadan Shiryoshu*, Vol. 1, 251–86, and Vol. 2, 315–28.

46 Senkaku Shoto Bunken Shiryo Hensankai, ed., *Senkaku Kenkyu: Takara Gakujutsu Chosadan Shiryoshu*, Vol. 1, 3–5, 11–14, 46–64.

47 Senkaku Shoto Bunken Shiryo Hensankai, ed., *Senkaku Kenkyu: Takara Gakujutsu Chosadan Shiryoshu*, Vol. 1, 65–74.

48 Senkaku Shoto Bunken Shiryo Hensankai, ed., *Senkaku Kenkyu: Takara Gakujutsu Chosadan Shiryoshu*, Vol. 1, 75–100.

49 Senkaku Shoto Bunken Shiryo Hensankai, ed., *Senkaku Kenkyu: Takara Gakujutsu Chosadan Shiryoshu*, Vol. 1, 103–9.

50 Senkaku Shoto Bunken Shiryo Hensankai, ed., *Senkaku Kenkyu: Takara Gakujutsu Chosadan Shiryoshu*, Vol. 1, 103–9.

51 Inamine, who was the father of future Governor Inamine Keiichi (who had served as president and chairman of the company as well), had formed a partnership in September 1950 with the American oil company Caltech (now Chevron) which controlled the distribution of oil in Okinawa.

52 They were both published in the *Ryukyu Daigaku Nogakubu Gakujutsu Hokoku* (Science Bulletin of the Faculty of Agriculture of the University of the Ryukyus), No. 1 (April 1954), which are included in Senkaku Shoto Bunken Shiryo Hensan-kai, ed., *Senkaku Kenkyu: Takara Gakujutsu Chosadan Shiryoshu*, Vol. 1, 113–46. One of the participants, Morita Tadayoshi, a student from Amami, subsequently wrote a report in 2006 about the trip entitled, "Senkaku Retto Seibutsu Chosa ni Sanka Shite (Participating in the Research Trip on Living Creatures to the Senkaku Islands)," which was included in the Takara collection (Ibid., 149–58).

53 Tawada, "Senkaku Retto Seibutsu," 88 in the original article (p. 144 in the Takara collection, Vol. 1). This point was stressed by the editors of the Takara collection,

particularly in light of an incident the following year in which several Okinawan fishermen were killed by unknown assailants, believed to be from Taiwan (see below).

54 "Maboshi ni Owatta Senkaku Retto Kyodo Gakujutsu Chosa: Kadai, 'Rainen Soso, Saichosa' to Katatte Ita Ga (Joint Scientific Survey That Never Happened: Kagoshima University Said It Would Try Again Early the Next Year, But)," in Senkaku Shoto Bunken Shiryo Hensankai, ed., *Senkaku Kenkyu: Takara Gakujutsu Chosadan Shiryoshu*, Vol. 2, 109.

55 "Kaigakuji Kara Jimoto Daigaku no Judai na Shimei, Kagaku Hatten ni Kiyo to Zengakutekina Bakkuappu: San Gakucho ga Senkaku Chosa ni Jinryoku (University's Full Support Given to Fulfill its Important Mission as a Local University and Contributor to the Development of Science from the Beginning: Three Presidents Made Efforts on Behalf of Senkaku Surveys)," in Senkaku Shoto Bunken Shiryo Hensankai, ed., *Senkaku Kenkyu: Takara Gakujutsu Chosadan Shiryoshu*, Vol. 2, 110.

56 Niiro Yoshima, "Hakkan no Igi o Sanaete (Endorsing the Significance of This Publication)," in Senkaku Shoto Bunken Shiryo Hensankai, ed., *Senkaku Kenkyu: Takara Gakujutsu Chosadan Shiryoshu*, Vol. 2, 1.

57 Takara Tetsuo, "Horobiyuku Ahodori: Senkaku Retto no Genchi Chosa Kara (The Dying Off of the Albatross: A Report from the Senkaku Islands)," *Ryukyu Shimpo*, May 3–12, 1963 (seven installments).

58 Tazumi Tomokichiro and Moriguchi Katsu, "Mujinto ha Ikiteiru (The Uninhabited Islands are Alive)," *Ryukyu Shimpo*, May 19–26, 1963 (seven installments). Also see Moriguchi Katsu, "Hiyaase Hyakato no 'Maborishi no Daisukuupu'(A Big Scoop that Turned Out Not to Be Had That Made Me Very Nervous)," in Senkaku Shoto Bunken Shiryo Hensankai, ed., *Senkaku Kenkyu: Takara Gakujutsu Chosadan Shiryoshu*, Vol. 2, 363–64.

59 Aguni Yasuo, "Ahodori o Motomete (Looking for the Albatross)," *Okinawa Taimusu*, May 20–24, 1963 (5 installments). Also see Aguni Yasuo, "Ofureko de Chosa Zokko (Continuing Surveys Off-record [in the Senkakus," in Senkaku Shoto Bunken Shiryo Hensankai, ed., *Senkaku Kenkyu: Takara Gakujutsu Chosadan Shiryoshu*, Vol. 2, 361–62.

60 Ishimine Ashin, "Senkaku Retto Kaiyo Chosa Hokoku (A Report of the Maritime Survey of the Senkaku Islands)," *Ryuki Jiho*, No. 7 (May 30, 1963), 28–36.

61 Takara Tetsuo, "Senkaku no Ahodori o Saguru (Looking for the Albatross on the Senkaku Islands)," *Minami to Kita*, No. 26 (March 1964).

62 Niiro Yoshima, "Senkaku Retto no Shokusei (Vegetation of the Senkaku Islands)," *Ryukyu Daigaku Bunrigakubu Kiyo* (Bulletin of the Arts and Science Division of the University of the Ryukyus), No. 7 (May 1964), 71–93.

63 Takaoka Daisuke, "Senkaku Retto Shuhen Kaiiki no Gakujutsu Chosa ni Sanka Shite (Participating in the Academic Surveys in the Waters Around the Senkaku Islands)," *Kikan Okinawa*, No. 56 (March 1971), 42–64.

64 Takara Tetsuo, "Senkaku Retto no Umidori ni Tsuite (Sea-fowls of the Senkaku Islands, Ryukyus)," *Ryukyu Daigaku Nogakubu Gakujutsu Hokoku*, No. 16 (October 1969), 1–12.

65 Kaneshima Kiyoshi, "Senkaku Retto no Suishitsu (Chemical Survey of Waters in the Senkaku Islands)," *Kogyo Yosui*, No. 128 (1969), 42–45.

66 Takaoka, "Senkaku Retto Shuhen."

67 Senkaku Shoto Bunken Shiryo Hensankai, ed., *Senkaku Kenkyu: Takara Gakujutsu Chosadan Shiryoshu*, Vol. 1, 9–10, 241–50.

68 Takahashi, *Senkaku Retto Nooto*, 18.

69 "Professor Niino's Report on Submarine Geology near Senkaku Islands," *Japan Petroleum Weekly*, September 29, 1969 (outline); October 6, 1969 (topography); October 13 and October 20, 1969 (geology); October 27, 1969 (magnetic survey); December 1, 1969 (summary).

70 "Professor Niino's Report on Submarine Geology near Senkaku Islands," *Japan Petroleum Weekly*, September 29, 1969, 2.

71 Hoshino Michihei, *Kaitei no Sekai* (The Underwater World) (Tokyo: Tokai Daigaku Shuppankai, 1966). In light of his work, he was also made a foreign emeritus professor of Qingdao Oceanological University of China in 1989.

72 Takahashi, *Senkaku Retto Nooto*, 19.

73 Kyushu Daigaku Nagasaki Daigaku Godo Senkaku Retto Gakujutsu Chosatai, ed., *Higashi Shinakai no Tanima Senkaku Retto: Kyushu Daigaku Nagasaki Daigaku Godo Senkaku Retto Gakujutsu Chosatai Hokoku* (The Senkaku Islands in the Valley of the East China Sea: The Report of the Scientific Exploration Party to the Senkaku Islands by the Exploration Clubs of Kyushu and Nagasaki Universities) (Fukuoka: Kyushu Daigaku Seikyo, 1973).

74 "Telegram 020630 from HICOM Okinawa to State Department, June 2, 1971," Folder 4, Box 20, History of USCAR, RG 319.

75 "Telegram 160200Z on Senkakus-GOJ Survey Request, June 16, 1971," Folder 4, Box 20, History of USCAR, RG 319.

76 "Taifu no Zenshochiten, Uotsuri Jima to Rasa Jima ni Sokkojo, Gun ga Keikaku (Typhoon Outpost, Military Plans Weather Station on Uotsuri and Rasa Islands)," *Ryukyu Shimpo*, March 20, 1953, and Okinawa Kishodai, ed., *Okinawa Kishodai Hyakunenshi* (A 100-Year History of the Okinawa Weather Bureau) (Naha: Okinawa Kishodai, 1990), 272, cited in Senkaku Shoto Bunken Shiryo Hensankai, ed., *Senkaku Kenkyu: Senkaku Shoto Kaiiki no Gyogyo ni Kansuru Chosa Hokoku*, 228.

77 The Senkaku Islands Study Group, "The Senkaku Islands and the Japan's Territorial Titles," 28.

78 Mayor Ishigaki of the conservative Democratic Party (*Minshuto*) had been in office since the spring of 1966, having been elected in a very controversial election on March 20 that year. Supporters of the opposing candidate, Miyara Chogi of the Okinawa Social Masses Party (*Okinawa Shakai Taishuto*) violently challenged the results when they were announced late the following day decrying irregularities. The Ishigaki City Election Committee was forced to announce in the middle of the night on the 22nd that the election was invalid. However, later that same day, the head of the committee rescinded the declaration and then fled to the Yaeyama Police Station to protect himself. Miyara's supporters surrounded the police station, demanding that the chairman be turned over to the protestors. Some 130 extra police were flown to Ishigaki by U.S. military aircraft to quell the riot. See Okinawa Daihyaka Jiten Kanko Jimukyoku, ed., *Okinawa Daihyakka Jiten Jokan* (Okinawa Encyclopedia, Vol. 1) (Naha: Okinawa Times, 1983), 77.

79 The Senkaku Islands Study Group, "The Senkaku Islands and the Japan's Territorial Titles to Them,", 28, and Ishigaki City Office, Report on the Erection of Landmark on the Senkaku Islands, May 15, 1969, cited in Okuhara, "The Territorial Sovereignty Over the Senkaku Islands," 101.

80 Okuhara Toshio, "Senkaku Retto no Ryoyuken Mondai (The Problem of the Ownership of the Senkaku Islands)," *Kikan Okinawa*, No. 56, 86.

81 Taira Shigenao, "Senkaku Retto Keigo Dokoki (A Record of the Police Escort to the Senkaku Islands)," in Senkaku Shoto Bunken Shiryo Hensankai, ed., *Senkaku Kenkyu: Takara Gakujutsu Chosadan Shiryoshu*, Vol. 2, 349–54.

82 Iraha Sachio, "'Umidori no Tamago ha Piitan no Genryo' ni Kyogaku (Surprised That Sea Bird Eggs Are Used As Century Eggs)," in Senkaku Shoto Bunken Shiryo Hensankai, ed., *Senkaku Kenkyu: Takara Gakujutsu Chosadan Shiryoshu*, Vol. 2, 371–72.

83 "Memo from Miyazawa Kaoru, Superintendent Yaeyama Police Station, to Chief of Police, GRI, on Formosan Activities on Sengaku (sic) Retto, July 13, 1968," Folder 5 (Emigration and Immigration Files, 1968: Entry and Exit Control Files,

Illegal Entry and Deportations), Box 10, Records of the Operation Division, Public Safety Department, RG 260.

84 "Memo from Kochi Chokei, Director, Police Department, to Director, Public Safety Department, on Formosan Activities in Sengaku (sic) Retto, July 26, 1968," Folder 5 (Emigration and Immigration Files, 1968: Entry and Exit Control Files, Illegal Entry and Deportations), Box 10, Records of the Operation Division, Public Safety Department, RG 260.

85 "Memo from George E. Suzuki, Chief, Yaeyama Civil Affairs Team, to Public Safety Department, USCAR, on Taiwanese Fishermen, July 15, 1968," Folder 5 (Emigration and Immigration Files, 1968: Entry and Exit Control Files, Illegal Entry and Deportations), Box 10, Records of the Operation Division, Public Safety Department, RG 260.

86 "Memo from George E. Suzuki, Chief, Yaeyama Civil Affairs Team, to Public Safety Department, USCAR, on Taiwanese Fishermen, July 15, 1968."

87 Mitsuboshi Takushii, which began operations in the early postwar years, is still in service today. The author used the company some years back during a research trip there.

88 "Memo from George E. Suzuki, Chief, Yaeyama Civil Affairs Team, to Deputy Civil Administrator, USCAR, on Taiwanese Fishermen, August 1, 1968," Folder 5 (Emigration and Immigration Files, 1968: Entry and Exit Control Files, Illegal Entry and Deportations), Box 10, Records of the Operation Division, Public Safety Department, RG 260.

89 "Background for Talking Points, Taiwanese Illegal Entrants, HICOM Meeting with CA, August 6, 1968," Folder 5 (Emigration and Immigration Files, 1968: Entry and Exit Control Files, Illegal Entry and Deportations), Box 10, Records of the Operation Division, Public Safety Department, Record Group 260. Interestingly, it was not only Taiwanese fishermen causing problems—Okinawan fishermen occasionally were arrested and vessels seized off the waters of Indonesia. One such arrest occurred on the morning of August 7 of the No. 3 *Koryo Maru*, a forty-nine ton vessel owned by Kinjo Shukin. See "Telegram HC-LN 823508 from D. R. Holmes to DA, August 9, 1968," Folder 5 (Emigration and Immigration Files, 1968: Entry and Exit Control Files, Illegal Entry and Deportations), Box 10, Records of the Operation Division, Public Safety Department, RG 260.

90 "Memo from George E. Suzuki, Chief, Yaeyama Civil Affairs Team, to Deputy Civil Administrator, USCAR, on Taiwanese Fishermen, July 11, 1968," Folder 5 (Emigration and Immigration Files, 1968: Entry and Exit Control Files, Illegal Entry and Deportations), Box 10, Records of the Operation Division, Public Safety Department, Record Group 260.

91 "Memo from Suzuki to Deputy Civil Administrator on Taiwanese Fishermen, July 11, 1968."

92 "Memo from Suzuki to Deputy Civil Administrator on Taiwanese Fishermen, July 11, 1968."

93 "Telegram HC-LN 822011 from Gaiduk to DA, August 7, 1968," Folder 5 (Emigration and Immigration Files, 1968: Entry and Exit Control Files, Illegal Entry and Deportations), Box 10, Records of the Operation Division, Public Safety Department, RG 260.

94 "Telegram HC-LN 822011 from Gaiduk to DA, August 7, 1968."

95 "Telegram HC-LN 822011 from Gaiduk to DA, August 7, 1968." Author's interview with Mrs. Ronald A. Gaiduk, June 8, 2000, Washington, D.C. Gaiduk had been born in the Soviet Union in 1921, naturalized, and served in the U.S. Army during World War II before joining the Foreign Service in the 1950s. Previously, he had worked as a junior official in the consulate a decade before.

96 "Telegram HC-LN 822011 from Gaiduk to DA, August 7, 1968."

97 "Airgram 758 on Biographic Information: Kokichi Yamano, Director of the Special Areas Liaison Bureau, Prime Minister's Office, December 7, 1964," POL 15–1 Japan, RG 59.

98 "Telegram HC-LN 822011 from Gaiduk to DA, August 7, 1968."

99 "Telegram HC-LN 822011 from Gaiduk to DA, August 7, 1968."

100 "Telegram HC-LN 823509 from Gaiduk to DA, August 21, 1968," Folder 5 (Emigration and Immigration Files, 1968: Entry and Exit Control Files, Illegal Entry and Deportations), Box 10, Records of the Operation Division, Public Safety Department, RG 260.

101 "Telegram HC-LN 823509 from Gaiduk to DA, August 21, 1968." According to an undated note in USCAR files, a study was done looking into the disabled ship and the salvaging operations. It read: "The Silver Peak grounded at Uotsuri Shima on 12 April 1967. The vessel was *en route* from Yahata, Fukuoka to Hong Kong. Lloyds Agent from Australia visited the vessel after she was abandoned and discovered vessel burned out completely (this makes salvage simpler) and considered the vessel a total loss and therefore no salvage was made. In other words the Chinese salvaging the vessel now is illegal." See "Silver Peak, undated," *Ibid.*

102 "Memo from Ronald M. Ota, Public Safety Department, USCAR, to Civil Administrator on Report on 'Chitose' Voyage to Senkaku Retto (Uotsuri Island), August 14, 1968," Folder 5 (Emigration and Immigration Files, 1968: Entry and Exit Control Files, Illegal Entry and Deportations), Box 10, Records of the Operation Division, Public Safety Department, RG 260.

103 "Disposition Form from Public Safety Department to Civil Administrator on Intrusion into Ryukyuan Waters by Taiwanese, August 16, 1968," Folder 5 (Emigration and Immigration Files, 1968: Entry and Exit Control Files, Illegal Entry and Deportations), Box 10, Records of the Operation Division, Public Safety Department, RG 260. Subsequently, a special consideration was made for the Taiwanese who possessed proper permission that they would not need to go all the way to Ishigaki but could instead go directly to the Senkakus to operate or work.

104 The *Chitose* was under the Ryukyu Police (*Ryukyu Keisatsu*) until reversion in 1972. After that, it was attached to the Maritime Safety Agency and renamed the *Nobaru*.

105 "Telegram HC-LN 823502 from Gaiduk to DA, August 21, 1968," Folder 5 (Emigration and Immigration Files, 1968: Entry and Exit Control Files, Illegal Entry and Deportations), Box 10, Records of the Operation Division, Public Safety Department, RG 260.

106 "Telegram HC-LN 823502 from Gaiduk to DA, August 21, 1968."

107 "Telegram HC-LN 823502 from Gaiduk to DA, August 21, 1968." Specifically, according to the same telegram, they were: "Applicant brings passport to Consular Section of Embassy, which forwards request to USCAR. USCAR, after coordinating with GRI Immigration and interested departments (Public Works in salvage case) wires or telephones clearance or decision to Consular Section, which then issues or denies permit. In Senkaku case, where trip from Taipei to Naha, Ryukyu's only port of entry, would constitute hardship, special permission can be granted to go direct Taiwan to Senkaku for salvage operation without going through Naha." On August 28, 1968, Li Ching Chang, a representative of Hsing Nan Salvage Works, called at the U.S. Embassy in Taipei and submitted a letter requesting permission for 50 workers to conduct operations in the area, together with a list of vessels and the actual workers. Slightly more than three-fifths of the workers were also from Kaoshiung. Consul Paul M. Miller advised the company that it would be necessary to obtain work permits from the Ryukyuan Bureau of Labor, and forwarded the letter and lists to the High Commissioner the following day. USCAR granted permission for 50 of them, working from three ships, to

re-enter the area beginning on August 30, 1968, until October 31, 1969. See "Letter from Paul M. Miller, American Consul, to High Commissioner, USCAR, August 29, 1968," Folder 5 (Emigration and Immigration Files, 1968: Entry and Exit Control Files, Illegal Entry and Deportations), Box 10, Records of the Operation Division, Public Safety Department, RG 260. That number was subsequently raised to 78 on April 21, 1969. See the Senkaku Islands Study Group, "The Senkaku Islands and the Japan's Territorial Titles to Them," 29.

108 "Telegram 4265 from Embassy Taipei to State Department, August 27, 1968," Folder 5 (Emigration and Immigration Files, 1968: Entry and Exit Control Files, Illegal Entry and Deportations), Box 10, Records of the Operation Division, Public Safety Department, RG 260.

109 "Telegram 4265."

110 "Telegram 4265."

111 "Telegram 4265."

112 "Telegram 4265."

113 "Telegram 4265."

114 "Telegram 4265."

115 "Telegram 4265."

116 K. Hori, Ministry of Foreign Affairs, "Bei Hoku No. 257, Note Verbale, August 3, 1968," Senkaku Retto (Senkaku Shosho) (Tia Yu Tai) Folder, Okinawa Prefectural Archives. A *note verbale* is a type of diplomatic communication which is more formal than a note, but less formal than an aide-mémoire, prepared in the third person but unsigned.

117 U.S. Embassy, "No. 1305, Note Verbale, September 25, 1968," Senkaku Retto (Senkaku Shosho) (Tia Yu Tai) Folder, Okinawa Prefectural Archives.

118 "Illegal Invasions of the Waters around Yonaguni-Jima by Fishing Vessels of Taiwan," undated, unsigned report (likely prepared by Fisheries Division, GRI)," Senkaku Retto (Senkaku Shosho) (Tia Yu Tai) Folder, Okinawa Prefectural Archives.

119 "Illegal Invasions of the Waters around Yonaguni-Jima by Fishing Vessels of Taiwan."

120 Embassy of the United States of America, Tokyo, Japan, "Talking Paper, January 4, 1969," Senkaku Retto (Senkaku Shosho) (Tia Yu Tai) Folder, Okinawa Prefectural Archives.

121 "Telegram HC-LN 836205 from Gaiduk to Embassy Tokyo, December 26, 1968," Folder 5 (Emigration and Immigration Files, 1968: Entry and Exit Control Files, Illegal Entry and Deportations), Box 10, Records of the Operation Division, Public Safety Department, RG 260.

122 "Telegram HC-LN 836205."

123 "Telegram HC-LN 836205."

124 "Memo from Ralph C. Anderson to Liaison Department on Alleged Taiwanese Intrusions into Ryukyu Territory, December 26, 1968," Folder 5 (Emigration and Immigration Files, 1968: Entry and Exit Control Files, Illegal Entry and Deportations), Box 10, Records of the Operation Division, Public Safety Department, Record Group 260, Records of the U.S. Civil Administration of the Ryukyu Islands (USCAR), National Archives, College Park, Maryland. Italics by author.

125 "Memo from Ralph C. Anderson to Liaison Department on Alleged Taiwanese Intrusions into Ryukyu Territory, December 26, 1968."

126 Shinjo Tetsutaro, "Beikaigun Kansen ha Sakusenka de Shika Ugokasenai (U.S. Navy Ships Can Only be Employed in Operations)," in Senkaku Shoto Bunken Shiryo Hensankai, ed., *Senkaku Kenkyu: Takara Gakujutsu Chosadan Shiryoshu*, Vol. 2, 369–70.

127 "Letter from Stanley S. Carpenter to Matsuoka Seiho, September 3, 1968," Folder 5 (Emigration and Immigration Files, 1968: Entry and Exit Control Files,

Illegal Entry and Deportations), Box 10, Records of the Operation Division, Public Safety Department, RG 260. Carpenter had learned from GRI Police and Immigration officials in late August that the Chinese salvage workers had left the Senkakus, "presumably for Taiwan." See "Telegram from Gaiduk to Department of Army on Senkaku Gunto: Illegal Entry by Taiwanese, August 31, 1968," *Ibid.*

128 Lieutenant General Ferdinand T. Unger was serving as high commissioner at the time, since November 1966. He was succeeded by Lieutenant General James B. Lampert in late January 1969, and would be in office until May 1972.

129 "Letter from Stanley S. Carpenter to Matsuoka Seiho, September 3, 1968."

130 "Memorandum for Col Abrignani, CINCPACREPSEC on Senkaku Gunto: Overflight, September 3, 1968," Folder 5 (Emigration and Immigration Files, 1968: Entry and Exit Control Files, Illegal Entry and Deportations), Box 10, Records of the Operation Division, Public Safety Department, RG 260.

131 "Memorandum for Col Abrignani, CINCPACREPSEC on Senkaku Gunto: Overflight, September 3, 1968."

132 "Letter from Carpenter to Matsuoka, September 3, 1968."

133 "Letter from Carpenter to Matsuoka, September 3, 1968."

134 Matsuoka would finish in November (1968) as chief executive, as he had chosen not to run in the first public election for the position that fall.

135 "Letter from Carpenter to Matsuoka, September 3, 1968."

136 "Letter from Matsuoka Seiho, Chief Executive, to Stanley S. Carpenter, on Immigration Control at Senkaku Retto, October 21, 1968," Folder 6 (Civic Action Project Files, 1971: Senkaku Retto), Box 37, Records of the Operation Division, Public Safety Department, RG 260.

137 "Letter from Matsuoka to Carpenter, October 21, 1968."

138 "Letter from Superintendent, Immigration Agency, GRI, to Director, Public Safety Department, USCAR, on Erection of Warning Signs on Senkaku Retto, March 28, 1969," Folder 6 (Civic Action Project Files, 1971: Senkaku Retto), Box 37, Records of the Operation Division, Public Safety Department, RG 260.

139 "Cost Estimate of Erecting 7 Warning Signs on Sengaku (sic) Islands, May 19, 1969," Folder 6 (Civic Action Project Files, 1971: Senkaku Retto), Box 37, Records of the Operation Division, Public Safety Department, RG 260.

140 "Cost Estimate of Erecting 7 Warning Signs."

141 "Memorandum from Harriman N. Simmons, Director, Public Safety Department, USCAR, to POLAD on Erection of No Trespassing Warning Signs at Vantage Points in Senkaku Retto, September 15, 1969," Folder 6 (Civic Action Project Files, 1971: Senkaku Retto), Box 37, Records of the Operation Division, Public Safety Department, RG 260.

142 Monjo had succeeded Edward O. Freimuth, who had served in Okinawa since 1946. Freimuth's papers were donated to the Okinawa Prefectural Archives by his children upon his passing in late 2001. The papers include a rich collection of Senkaku-related materials that he collected well into the 1990s.

143 "Memorandum from Richard E. Snyder, Liaison Department, to Public Safety Department, USCAR, on Erection of No Trespassing Warning Signs at Vantage Points in Senkaku Retto, September 27, 1969," Folder 6 (Civic Action Project Files, 1971: Senkaku Retto), Box 37, Records of the Operation Division, Public Safety Department, RG 260.

144 "Memorandum from Snyder to Public Safety Department, September 27, 1969."

145 "Memorandum from Snyder to Public Safety Department, September 27, 1969." Lieutenant Colonel Richard K. McNealy, Director of the Legal Department, chimed in a couple of days later with the comment that the last line of the sign should include, "By Order of the U.S. High Commissioner of the Ryukyu Islands." See "Memorandum from Richard K. McNealy, to Public Safety

Department, USCAR, September 29, 1969," Folder 6 (Civic Action Project Files, 1971: Senkaku Retto), Box 37, Records of the Operation Division, Public Safety Department, RG 260.

146 "Memorandum from Harriman N. Simmons, Director, Public Safety Department, USCAR, to HICOM on Erection of No Trespassing Warning Signs at Vantage Points in Senkaku Retto, October 2, 1969," Folder 6 (Civic Action Project Files, 1971: Senkaku Retto), Box 37, Records of the Operation Division, Public Safety Department, RG 260.

147 "Confidential Memorandum from Political Adviser to SA/HICOM, November 28, 1969," Folder 6 (Civic Action Project Files, 1971: Senkaku Retto), Box 37, Records of the Operation Division, Public Safety Department, RG 260.

148 "Confidential Memorandum from Political Adviser to SA/HICOM, November 28, 1969."

149 "Memorandum from Ralph C. Anderson, Acting Director, Public Safety Department, USCAR, to HICOM on Erection of No Trespass Signs at Vantage Points in Senkaku Retto, January 9, 1970," Folder 6 (Civic Action Project Files, 1971: Senkaku Retto), Box 37, Records of the Operation Division, Public Safety Department, RG 260.

150 "Memorandum from H. L. Conner, Chief of Administration, to Chief Executive, GRI, on Transmittal of Funds, April 28, 1970," Folder 6 (Civic Action Project Files, 1971: Senkaku Retto), Box 37, Records of the Operation Division, Public Safety Department, RG 260.

151 Matsui, "Law of Territorial Acquisition," 30.

152 The Senkaku Islands Study Group, "The Senkaku Islands and the Japan's Territorial Titles to Them," 29. Matsui, "International Law," 30; Okuhara, "The Territorial Sovereignty Over the Senkaku Islands," 101–2.

153 Higa Kenji, "Keikoku Ita Secchi no Omoide (Recollections on Setting Up the Warning Signs)," in Senkaku Shoto Bunken Shiryo Hensankai, ed., *Senkaku Kenkyu: Takara Gakujutsu Chosadan Shiryoshu*, Vol. 2, 285.

154 Higa, "Keikoku Ita Secchi no Omoide," 286–87.

155 Higa, "Keikoku Ita Secchi no Omoide," 287.

156 Matsui, "Law of Territorial Acquisition," 30.

157 Higa Kenji, "'Keikoku Ita' Secchi no Omoide (Recollections on Placing the 'Warning Sign')," *Yaeyama Mainichi Shimbun*, August 25, 2009.

158 "Telegram 2197 from Taipei Embassy to State Department, May 18, 1970," POL 19 Ryu Is, RG 59.

159 "Telegram 086030 from State Department to HICOMRY on Senkaku Islands, June 4, 1970," POL 19 Ryu Is, RG 59.

160 The *China Post* was founded in 1952, as a pro-KMT newspaper and rival to the *China Times* (now *Taiwan Times*) that had been established in 1949.

161 "Telegram 1854 from Embassy Taipei to State Department on Senkakus, April 14, 1972," POL 19 32–36 Senkaku Is, RG 59.

162 "Telegram 1854."

163 "Telegram from HICOMRY to Embassy Tokyo on Assignment of Two Maritime Safety Agency Officers, August 22, 1970," Folder: Message Traffic Concerning the Senkaku Islands, 1971–72, Box 11, James B. Lampert Papers (hereafter, Lampert Papers), Military History Institute, Carlisle Barracks, Carlisle, Pennsylvania.

164 "Telegram from HICOMRY to Embassy Tokyo on Assignment, August 22, 1970."

165 "Telegram from HICOMRY to Embassy Tokyo on Assignment, August 22, 1970."

166 "Telegram from HICOMRY to Embassy Tokyo on Assignment, August 22, 1970."

167 "Telegram 7751 from Embassy Tokyo to HICOMRY on Assignment, September 30, 1970," POL 19 Ryu Is, RG 59.
168 The full draft text, to be signed by the Director, General Affairs Division, Okinawa-Northern Territories Agency, Government of Japan, and the Director, General Affairs Department, GRI, and concurred to by the High Commissioner, was provided in a subsequent telegram. (See "Telegram 8023 from Embassy Tokyo to Secretary of State on Okinawa Reversion: GOJ-GRI Personnel Exchange Memorandum, October 7, 1970," POL 19 Ryu Is, RG 59.) The request for exchange personnel was first discussed in the spring of 1970. The Embassy made some suggested corrections and comments to the above draft, to which the High Commissioner concurred the same day, October 7. (See "Telegram 8022 from Embassy Tokyo to State Department on Okinawa Reversion: GOJ-GRI Personnel Exchange Memorandum, October 7, 1970," POL 19 Ryu Is, RG 59.) The suggestions were worked into a U.S. counter draft, submitted on October 12, and after some discussions the GOJ responded with some word changes later in October. (See "Telegram 8470 from Embassy Tokyo to State Department on Okinawa Reversion: GOJ-GRI Personnel Exchange Memorandum, October 20, 1970," POL 19 Ryu Is, RG 59.) The Embassy was happy with changes as the memorandum would "allow constructive GOJ involvement in GRI" and "prevent, or at least inhibit, unwarranted GOJ interference." (See "Telegram 8470.")
169 "Telegram 7751."
170 Upon reversion on May 15, 1972, the agency became the 11th Regional Coast Guard Headquarters (*Dai Juichi Kanku Kaijo Hoan Honbu*) under the Japan Maritime Safety Agency, which is now the Japan Coast Guard, whose vessels and personnel are often seen in the news dealing with intrusions by vessels from China, Taiwan, and Hong Kong.
171 "Japanese Patrol Boat to Be Sent to Senkaku Area," *Nihon Keizai Shimbun*, April 25, 1972, evening edition.
172 "Memorandum from Harriman N. Simmons, Director, Public Safety Department, on Meeting Concerning Control of Illegal Entry into Senkaku Retto, March 19, 1971," Folder 6 (Civic Action Project Files, 1971: Senkaku Retto), Box 37, Records of the Operation Division, Public Safety Department, RG 260.
173 "Telegram from HICOMRY to Department of Army on Control of Illegal Entry into Senkakus, March 27, 1971," Folder 4, Box 20, History of USCAR, RG 319.
174 "Telegram from HICOMRY to DA on Control of Illegal Entry into Senkakus, March 27, 1971."
175 "Telegram from HICOMRY to Department of Army on Control of Illegal Entry into Senkakus, April 9, 1971," Folder 4, Box 20, History of USCAR, RG 319.
176 "Memorandum from Harriman N. Simmons, Director, Public Safety Department, to Chief of Police, GRI, on Control of Illegal Entry into Senkaku Retto, March 19, 1971," Folder 6 (Civic Action Project Files, 1971: Senkaku Retto), Box 37, Records of the Operation Division, Public Safety Department, RG 260.
177 "Letter from Arakaki Tokusuke, Chief of Police, GRI, to Director, Public Safety Department, USCAR on Request Instruction on Control of Taiwanese Fishing Vessels, undated (circa July 1971)," Folder 6 (Civic Action Project Files, 1971: Senkaku Retto), Box 37, Records of the Operation Division, Public Safety Department, RG 260.
178 "Letter from Harriman N. Simmons, Director, Public Safety Department, USCAR, to Arakaki Tokusuke, Chief of Police, GRI, on Control of Taiwanese Fishing Vessels, July 13, 1971," Folder 6 (Civic Action Project Files, 1971: Senkaku Retto), Box 37, Records of the Operation Division, Public Safety Department, RG 260.
179 "Letter from Arakaki Tokusuke, Chief of Police, GRI, to Director, Public Safety Department, USCAR on Suspected Trespassing and Illegal Landing on Senkaku

Islands by Formosan Fishing Vessel, July 31, 1971," Folder 6 (Civic Action Project Files, 1971: Senkaku Retto), Box 37, Records of the Operation Division, Public Safety Department, RG 260.

180 "Letter from Arakaki."

181 "Telegram from HICOMRY to Embassy Tokyo, January 8, 1971," Folder 4, Box 20, History of USCAR, RG 319.

182 "Telegram from HICOMRY to Embassy Tokyo, January 8, 1971."

183 "Telegram from HICOMRY to Embassy Tokyo, January 8, 1971."

184 "Telegram 266 from Embassy Tokyo to State Department on Weather Observatory for the Senkaku Island, January 11, 1971," POL 19 Ryu Is, RG 59.

185 "Telegram 266."

186 "Telegram 266."

187 "Telegram 266."

188 "Telegram 162 from Embassy Taipei to State Department on Weather Observatory for the Senkaku Island, January 13, 1971," POL 19 Ryu Is, RG 59.

189 "Telegram 162."

190 "Telegram 162."

191 "Telegram 264 from AmConsul Hong Kong to State Department on Weather Observatory for the Senkaku Islands, January 15, 1971," POL 32–36 Senkaku Is, RG 59. For more on Osborn, see "Interview with David L. Osborn, January 16, 1989," Association for Diplomatic Studies and Training Foreign Affairs Oral History Project.

192 "Telegram 264."

193 "Cover Sheet, Weather Observatory for Senkaku Islands, January 18, 1971," Folder 4, Box 20, History of USCAR, RG 319.

194 "Telegram 12669 from State Department to Tokyo Embassy on Weather Observatory for Senkaku Islands, January 25, 1971," POL 32–36 Senkaku Is, RG 59. The telegram also included a concern that the State Department had about the manner in which the proposal on a "sensitive issue" was made through the "relatively open [Obonta] channel without the opportunity to discuss in diplomatic channels." See "Draft Telegram on Weather Observatory for Senkaku Islands, January 15, 1971," Folder 4, Box 20, History of USCAR, RG 319.

195 "Telegram 86, from Tokyo Embassy to State Department Senkakus Weather Station, January 29, 1971," POL 32–36 Senkaku Is, RG 59.

196 "Telegram 868."

197 "Telegram 868."

198 "Telegram 868."

199 "Telegram 057191 from State Department to Embassy Taipei on Senkaku Islands Dispute, April 6, 1971," Folder 4, Box 20, History of USCAR, RG 319.

200 "Telegram 057191."

201 "Telegram 057191."

3 The United Nations Economic Commission for Asia and the Far East (ECAFE) Survey and the origins of the East China Sea Islands dispute

This chapter examines the growth of the geological and economic interest in the East China Sea, particularly the area around the Senkaku Islands in the 1960s and early 1970s. Specifically, it introduces an international study published in 1969 by the United Nations Economic Commission for Asia and the Far East (ECAFE[1]) and the race for mining and oil concessions that report produced. It also discusses the tensions that developed between Japan and the Republic of China (ROC), as well as Okinawa and the ROC, and even looks at the frictions that emerged between Okinawa and Japan itself over the question of local prosperity versus national needs.

The ECAFE Survey

The origins of the Senkaku Islands dispute, according to one author, began not in 1971 when Taiwan and the People's Republic of China (PRC) formally laid claims to the islands, but a decade before that. "The problem began," Takahashi Shogoro matter-of-factly declares in his book, *Senkaku Retto Nooto* (Notes on the Senkaku Islands), "when Niino Hiroshi, a professor of geology at Tokyo University of Fisheries [*Tokyo Suisan Daigaku*],[2] published his paper, 'Sediment of Shallow Portions of East China Sea and South China Sea',"[3] in 1961. As a result of Niino's paper, co-authored with Kenneth O. Emery[4] of the Woods Hole Oceanographic Institution, a private research organization incorporated in 1930 and based in Massachusetts in the United States, "the world's geologists and international majors (oil companies) began to take notice" because it pointed to the possibility of large reserves of oil and natural gas in the continental shelf/seabed.[5]

It is unclear at this point who took the lead in preparing the above study. Emory had visited Japan shortly after the end of World War II and may have met Niino then. According to an essay written about Emory at the time of his death in 1998, "K.O. loved to engage younger colleagues in discussion to test out his ideas in addition to stimulating their thought. He never hesitated to open such discussions, of great benefit to the geologists of occupied Japan when he visited there just after the war. His influence had impact on the later development of Japanese marine geology. Wherever he went, he was a mentor and left his influence."[6] Emory's knowledge of the ocean floor dated back to his work conducting sea-bottom studies for the U.S. Navy's anti-submarine operations at the Division of War Research at the University of California, San Diego, from 1943 to 1945. By the time the two of them collaborated on their study, Niino who was born in 1905 and was thus nine years Emory's senior, had already published several books including one on the geology of the sea and another on the resources of the sea.[7] Niino was able to use Japanese war-time sea-bottom studies and postwar Japanese oceanographic surveys when co-writing their paper.[8] They would collaborate later in the decade, too, and their work would become controversial with oil companies who felt their analysis complicated their business dealings and legal negotiations with countries issuing concessions.

One person who challenged Niino's and Emory's work on scientific grounds was a leading Chinese oceanographer, Ch'in Yun-shan, who published a paper in 1963 that stressed a different interpretation of the accumulation of sedimentary deposits.[9] He did not dispute the belief that there were significant deposits of offshore oil. However, he stressed the different stages at which interior and exterior sediments were deposited, calling it "intensive accumulation." That paper was part of a series Ch'in had been working on. A couple of years before the Niino and Emory study, Ch'in had published the results of the first marine geological surveys of the East China Sea and other areas close to China and had contributed in his own way to raising expectations that there was oil out there, off shore.[10] The challenge for China, technologically behind, was how to get it, and ironically in retrospect, it was often Japanese technology that the Chinese relied on.[11]

Five years following the Niino and Emory study, the Committee for the Coordination of Joint Prospecting for Mineral Resources in Asian Offshore Areas (CCOP) was established in 1966 to support the sharing of information for exploration, including conducting surveys of continental shelf/seabed minerals on the Eastern Coast of Asia. The CCOP was originally the idea of C. Y. Li, a geologist from mainland China who had fled to Taiwan in the late 1940s. He had joined ECAFE at its inception and was serving as the deputy director of its Division of Industry and Mineral Resources when he launched the CCOP idea in 1965.[12] He not only believed in the petroleum prospects in the area, but was a talented and ambitious bureaucrat who saw the need for a larger regional organization.

The ROC and South Korea, both relatively small and backward, immediately recognized the importance of a regional organization. Later, the more advanced Japan came to appreciate the value of such an organization, as well. The original members of CCOP thus included Japan, South Korea, Taiwan, and the Philippines. The United States, United Kingdom, France, and West Germany later served as advisors or cooperating countries, although the United States and United Kingdom were initially cool to the idea of a regional structure, believing instead it should be left to private enterprise.[13] In addition, Thailand, South Vietnam, Cambodia, Malaysia, and Indonesia joined shortly after.[14]

In June the following year (1967), Emery and Niino published the results of a follow-on second study, which took into account further sea-bottom samplings and the published findings of Soviet oceanographers who had surveyed areas off of China prior to the Sino–Soviet split.[15] The two authors described the East China Sea as "one of the potentially most favorable but little investigated regions" of the world and noted that "by comparison with other continental shelves, one can predict that the chances of successes are likely to be good after a well-managed program of geophysical and geological exploration has been completed in the East China Sea."[16] They noted as well that "the most favorable province for future submarine oil and gas fields is a wide belt along the outer part of the continental shelf" west of the Ryukyu Islands, but pointed out that it would be "risky" to base predictions on only the "few rocks that have so far been drilled from the sea floor."[17]

Because their study was not conclusive, Emery organized with CCOP officials a "more ambitious" survey in the fall of 1968 with the cooperation of the U.S. Naval Oceanographic Office and geologists sent by the governments of Japan, South Korea, and the ROC.[18] The CCOP team worked aboard the U.S. Navy ship, *R. V. Hunt*, which was under the command of the U.S. Seventh Fleet and based out of Yokosuka, Japan, where the U.S. has had an important naval base since the end of World War II. The scientists spent five weeks aboard the *R. V. Hunt* from October 20 to November 29.[19] Having conducted seismic and geomagnetic profiles over some 7,450 miles, the team's report, released in Bangkok in May 1969, attracted much interest when it concluded that there is a "high probability ... that the continental shelf between Taiwan and Japan may be one of the most prolific oil and gas reservoirs in the world."[20] It also noted, in a foreshadowing of tensions to come, that "It is also one of the few large continental shelves of the world that has remained untested by the drill, owing to military and political factors."[21]

The scientific nature of the report and its conclusion regarding the offshore potential caused "most oil companies ... to share a positive appraisal" of it, but, as alluded to above, those same companies, which had already quietly begun preliminary surveys of their own in 1967, felt the report complicated their negotiations for offshore concessions with the countries involved due to the excitement generated over the report.[22] Emery was subsequently removed from his position as principal American representative at the CCOP meetings as a result, in part, of these company pressures as well as bureaucratic rivalries within the United States Geological Survey (USGS), an American government agency first established in 1879 and headquartered in Virginia.[23] Emery would live for another thirty years, but it appears that he did not conduct (or at least publish) anything else about the Senkakus afterwards. Niino, who was in poor health and would die a premature death in 1973, continued to be involved in the issue having assumed a consulting position with the Kyushu Oil Development Company (*Kyushu Sekiyu Kaihatsu Kabushiki Kaisha*).

In retrospect, there was another reason the oil companies, such as Gulf and Amoco, were not happy about the report. According to Selig S. Harrison, an

Asia specialist and former *Washington Post* Bureau Chief in Northeast Asia who worked on a study for the Carnegie Endowment for International Peace in the mid-1970s entitled *China, Oil, and Asia: Conflict Ahead?*, the reaction to the "report reflect[ed] in part their coolness toward the very idea of a regional intergovernment agency conducting public oil survey operations."[24]

The race for concessions—Japan and Okinawa

In 1969, the year the ECAFE report came out, Japan's annual oil consumption amounted to 150 million tons, and according to an article written in early 1971, Japan's annual consumption was expected to increase to 400 million tons by 1980. "400 million tons," the article noted, "is the equivalent of having a line of 100,000-ton oil tankers stretching at five-kilometer intervals between the Persian Gulf and Japan."[25] Japan was already spending one billion dollars a year to meet its fuel needs. A near-treble increase in demand would not only drive up the price of oil and increase costs across the board, but also cause competition among companies and countries to grow exponentially.

For this reason, the discovery of a huge oil deposit—perhaps one of the ten largest in the world, and some believed the largest in the world—was seen as a "boon" for Japan then in a period of rapid economic growth with average annual growth of ten percent in the 1960s.[26] A *New York Times* article from 1969 mentioned that the potential reserves in the Senkaku area amounted to more than one trillion dollars. One trillion dollars, another article pointed out, was the "equivalent of the annual budget of the Government of the Ryukyu Islands for the next 5000 years."[27]

In light of the above surveys and the expectation that there were potential reserves of oil and other resources, private individuals and mainland Japanese oil companies began applying for mining concessions in the areas near the Senkaku Islands at a quicker pace.[28] As will be seen in this chapter, "There is an expression," one story about this time points out, "'economic animals [is a phrase used to describe Japanese],' but Okinawans are without doubt 'political animals'."[29]

The first and most well-known person to apply for concessions was Omija Tsunehisa, an Okinawan native, in early February that year (1969).[30] His applications, submitted on February 5, 1969, were for mining concessions covering 5,527 sea-bed sections, and were officially accepted by the Government of the Ryukyu Islands' Trade and Industry Division (*Tsusankyoku*) on March 10.[31] (This was actually his third set of applications, having previously submitted applications between 1963 and 1966.)

Omija was born in 1928 in Osaka and having experienced much discrimination as someone of Okinawan descent in mainland Japan moved to his family's home-town of Kunigami in northern Okinawa after the war in 1946 as part of the larger "repatriation" efforts.[32] Seeing the devastation that had befallen Okinawa, he began to think about international affairs, why the war happened, and how Okinawa got caught up in the war. "Okinawa was brought into World War II due to Japan's search for raw materials, such as oil," he recalled thinking, and asking how and where oil could be found.[33] Referring to old documents and using some self-possessed knowledge of coal and other rock formations, he immediately realized oil might be found near Yaeyama. Over the course of nineteen years, he made some 200 trips to Yaeyama and the Senkakus, taking samplings. His confidence that there was oil and other valuable minerals grew each time he went to the islands.

In the meantime, Omija had found employment working for the U.S. military as an equipment operator, and stayed in the employ of the military until about 1960. He then opened a clothing store in Naha followed by a gift shop and jewelry and precious stones shop on International Street (*Kokusai Dori*). All of his savings and profits from his business went toward his geology research. As a descendent of the fifth king, Sho Gen, of the second Sho Dynasty of the Ryukyu Kingdom, Omija felt a calling to help Okinawa. People thought him crazy, however, and had hoped that after getting married in 1956, he would forget about looking for oil. He did not.

In 1963, Omija drew up plans for how he would apply for exploration concessions. He divided up the region he was focused on exploring into five parts. He would apply for rights in areas he labeled A and B, which were within three nautical miles of Okinawa and gradually expand into areas C, D, and E on the continental shelf out to sea when he had enough money to do so (the application fee for each section initially was fourteen dollars, rising to twenty-one dollars later). In 1966, he applied to the Government of the Ryukyu Islands, which was authorized to conditionally issue concessions as per a 1960 USCAR ordinance, for mineral rights to 308 sections, followed by his later request in 1969. Area B, which included the Senkaku Islands and the areas around it, were included in the 1966 request, and Area C, which he applied for in 1969, was just to the north.

Suggestive of the confidence he felt, Omija wrote up three reports and made them publicly available. The first one was entitled "Report on Oil and Natural Gas Deposits in Yaeyama Taketomi Island (*Yaeyama Taketomi Jima o Chushin to Suru Sekiyu, Tennen Gasu Kosho Chosa Hokokusho*)," dated March 1966, and the other two were "Report on Oil in Sakishima (to include the Senkaku Islands *Sakishima (Senkaku Retto o Fukumu) Sekiyu Chosa Hokokusho*)," dated March 1969, and "Explanatory Documents on Oil Deposits in the Continental Shelf under the Water Areas Near the Senkaku Islands (*Senkaku Retto Shuhen Kaiiki Tairikudana ni okeru Sekiyu Kosho Setsumeisho*)," dated December 1969. Omija would also write up two more in 1970 that provided a narrative and record of his efforts to secure the concessions based on the above work.[34]

The announcement of the ECAFE report greatly complicated his methodical approach to these concessions, however, as an "oil war" had begun as a result, according to Omija.[35] Shortly after submitting his application to the GRI in early February 1969, Omija was approached by the Japan Petroleum Development Public Corporation (*Nihon Sekiyu Kaihatsu Kodan*), which had

Figure 3.1 Chart Produced by Omija Tsunehisa

been established in 1967 under the auspices of the powerful Ministry of International Trade and Industry (*Tsusho Sangyosho*).[36] Officials from JPDPC promised him "all sorts of things, but to someone who had become crazy about oil," as he told an interviewer later, "I could not simply turn over my rights to someone else, so I eventually refused their offers."[37] He was even offered the directorship of any future company or consortium that would be created to drill in the area.[38]

Initially, Omija tried to hold them off and avoid making any commitments. He even agreed to hold off on releasing the studies he had done to date on the area when officials from the JPDPC visited him. However, on February 17, the JPDPC applied for 7,611 sections using the name of one of its Okinawa-born employees, Furugen Soko (technically, he worked for the Okinawa Development Public Corporation, or *Okinawa Kaihatsu Kodan*, rather than the JPDPC directly), as a clause in the local 1905 mining law (*Kogyoho*) required that the applicants be from Okinawa.[39] Omija was particularly bothered by JPDPC's high-handedness as its funds were all from the central government rather than truly from the private sector and important players on the mainland believed it violated the spirit of the law that the development of the resources around Okinawa be exclusively for Okinawa's prosperity and the welfare of its people. He became especially concerned when there were subsequent suggestions that the law would be revised after reversion which would lead to the exploitation of the area by non-Okinawans.

Omija was also bothered by the fact that the JPDPC had applied for sections that he had been intending to apply for when he had enough money to submit the next batch of applications, based on his earlier plans. At the time, it was costing close to twenty dollars to apply for each section, and the average worker's monthly pay was $60.[40] Omija's application, including the creation of the attached maps, came to more than $200,000–a lot of money in those days for one person.[41]

Because he did not cooperate with JPDPC, he was subjected to a vicious rumor campaign against him according to Omija, saying that foreign companies were backing him and that he was linked to rightwing groups and organized crime. He was also called a "traitor," ready to "sell out the country."[42] He added, "It was I who had refused foreign offers. It was the mainland Japanese companies that were taking money from the foreign companies. I was really ticked off."[43] Some of his business partners, including one mainland oil company, were also pressured into not doing business with him any longer, and it became difficult for him to raise funds.[44]

In the middle of this, a third person, Shinzato Keiichi, applied for 11,726 sections and reportedly was supported by American financiers, in April 1969.[45] Considering the costs involved, it was clear that Shinzato was doing so with someone else's money, especially since he was not well known in the business community in Okinawa and probably did not have much money on his own. According to Omijia, Shinzato, who was said to have been close to Vice Chief Executive Chinen Choko,[46] who was serving as under Yara since December 1968, had once approached him about working together on behalf of American companies.[47] When he refused, Shinzato went ahead and made an identical application, taking advantage of some mistakes Omija had made in his application. It appears that Omija's diagrams of the area had been leaked, something entirely likely in light of the potential riches involved and the variety of people involved in processing or reviewing the claims at the GRI.[48] Shinzato, along with the above applicant, applied for what were Areas D and E in Omija's maps.

In September 1970, Shinzato published his own report, a fourteen-page mimeographed document calling on the GRI to process his applications and those of Omija and Furugen, and justifying why his application was more proper than that of Omija.[49] Three months later on December 20, 1970, Shinzato created the Ryukyu Mining Development Limited Liability Stock Company (*Ryukyu Kogyo Kaihatsu Kabushiki Kaisha*).[50]

In addition to the personal and economic investment Omija had made over the previous two decades, he was concerned about foreign and even mainland companies (as well, the Japanese government to which, he seems to have harbored a grudge over years of discrimination) scooping up Okinawa's resources and potential profits. In a brochure he published in July 1970 to call on Okinawans to help protect their resources, Omija explained his desire to help Okinawa: "Over the past nineteen years, through the development of Okinawa's underground resources, I have sought to help Okinawa leave once and for all its poor situation that it has found itself in since the dissolution of the Ryukyu Kingdom and to bring prosperity and social welfare to the people of the prefecture."[51] He added that as someone who has spent much time studying these issues, to the point of being called "crazy," he felt that the development of the oil resources around the Senkaku Islands was the "only true way to make the economy self-reliant and to bring prosperity to Okinawa."[52] Later that year, the Okinawa Prefecture Senkaku Islands Oil and Natural Resources Development Promotion Council (*Okinawaken Senkaku Retto Sekiyu Shigento Kaihatsu Sokushin Kyogikai*), chaired by Naha City Mayor Taira Ryosho, was formed from almost fifty organizations within Okinawa centered around the Okinawa teacher's union (*Okinawa Kyoshokuinkai*), in large part it seems to support the efforts of Omija.[53]

By 1972, however, Omija still had seen no progress in his claims. "What's worse," he told an interviewer, "I heard that the mineral rights he received were in turn passed to America in October last year (1971)."[54] Omija, who had already formed the Persia Resource Development Limited Liability Stock Company (*Perushia Shigen Kaihatsu Kabishiki Kaisha*), went on to form a partnership with East Seas Development Limited Liability Stock Company (*Toyo Sekiyu Kaihatsu Kabushiki Kaisha*) in October 1973, around the time of the Yom Kippur War which triggered the first oil crisis. The company they created was called Uruma Resources Development (*Uruma Shigen Kaihatsu Kabushiki Kaisha*).[55] In a March 1975 article in a major Japanese monthly magazine, *Gendai*, Omija, ever the optimist, explained his efforts over the years, his views that Okinawa's resources should be for Okinawans, and how he hoped to see the profits from these resources used to better Okinawa in the future.[56]

Omija seems to have been the only true applicant from Okinawa—the other two represented mainland Japanese and foreign interests respectively—and for this reason he would have his supporters in Okinawa. In the end, he was not successful, however, in part due to the lack of funds and moratoriums placed on drilling. He died in 1986 without having his dream realized, and his claims were passed on to his son.

In the meantime, as alluded to above, applications by both Japanese and foreign companies started to pour in. In mainland Japan, four companies— Japan Petroleum Exploration Co., Ltd (*Sekiyu Shigen Kaihatsu Kabushiki Kaisha*), Teikoku, or Imperial, Oil (*Teikoku Sekiyu*), working with Gulf, Nippon Oil (*Nihon Sekiyu*), working with Texaco, and West Japan Oil (*Nishinihon Sekiyu*), working with Shell, all applied for mining rights during 1969 for areas west and south of Kyushu along the Nansei Island chain.[57] For the area around the Senkakus, which Japan designated as concession area J-1, it was JPDPC that had applied.

Interest had been growing in Japan for some time among not only oil companies but also in government and political circles. During his trip to Okinawa in July 1968, Takaoka met with Omija, perhaps to learn more about the potential for oil in the area or simply to learn about the political issue of the islands, and after returning to Tokyo, Takaoka gave a presentation at the end of August about his fact-finding mission. Originally an Indian specialist who had led the Lower House delegation to Southeast Asia in April 1955 to attend the Bandung Conference and traveled with Prime Minister Kishi Nobusuke during the latter's official trip to the region in late May 1957, Takaoka had also been interested in Okinawa issues over the years and had become involved with the prime minister's consultative committee.

Takaoka had decided to call a meeting of those interested in Senkaku issues to help raise awareness of the problem of poaching in the area and develop policies to counteract it. The meeting began at 1 p.m. on the afternoon of August 30 and was attended by more than a dozen officials and members of the *Nanen*, which was closely aligned with the Prime Minister's consultative committee on Okinawa. Takaoka had asked Professor Takara and the others who had participated in the mission to send the reports up to him by mail, and he brought those papers, his own notes, and some samples of different objects from the islands with him to the meeting. Ohama Nobumoto, the chairman of *Nanen* and a native of Ishigaki City who had worked closely behind the scenes and publicly to promote Okinawa's return to Japan, chaired the meeting.[58] Following Takaoka's talk, Professor Niino was asked to comment, and the floor was opened to questions. The meeting ended at 4:30 p.m.

One of the conclusions reached from the discussions was that the Japanese government should conduct an official survey of the islands the following year. However, funds did not seem available. A Cabinet reshuffle on November 30 brought in Tokonami Tokuji, long a supporter of Okinawa-related issues from Kagoshima Prefecture, as the new director general of the prime minister's office (*Sorifu Somu Chokan*). He would help secure those funds.

In the meantime, the ECAFE survey went ahead as planned. In September that year, the United States, Japan, South Korea, and Taiwan undertook a joint survey using the *Tenyo Maru*, a vessel belonging to the Japanese National Fisheries University, located in Yamaguchi Prefecture. The survey was led by a team from Woods Hole, with Japan sending technicians from the JPDPC, which had the goal to ensure that Japan secure on its own thirty percent of its consumption by autonomous development by 1985.[59] Their report, mentioned in the previous chapter, was released in May 1969.

During this time in the fall of 1968 Yoshida Shien, who had long been involved in trying to resolve Japan's territorial issues as an official in the Ministry of Foreign Affairs and Prime Minister's Office (*Sorifu*) and was then serving as a director of the *Nanen*, met with Takaoka and Niino. Both men were worried about the ECAFE survey and what that meant for the regional competition for the resources in the area. Niino in particular stressed that his "research to date had shown there to be very valuable stores of natural resources on the sea-bead, including a large supply of oil."[60]

Yoshida brought Takaoka, Niino, and Ohama to meet with Tokonami on December 4, the week after he assumed his new position, to request his support for a scientific mission to the Senkaku Islands.[61] Tokonami without delay expressed his support and promised that the Prime Minister's Office would make such a budget request with the Ministry of Finance (*Okurasho*).

Ohama immediately called a meeting at the offices of the *Nanpo Doho Engokai*, asking Niino and Yoshida Shien to attend, along with Sakurai Tsuyoshi, an official within the Prime Minister's Office, to draw up a draft budget request right then and there.[62] Later on December 17 in the basement conference room of the Prime Minister's Office, Takaoka and Niino met with officials from the respective ministries to impress upon them the importance of this budget request.[63] By this point, the government's budget had already been formulated, and the coordination had already been done with the various ministries on their respective budget requests. In effect, this meant no new requests were being entertained. However, in light of the seriousness of the situation and the fact that the results of the ECAFE survey would likely be publicized the following spring, it was important that Japan have its own study prepared and that it be proactive in the Senkaku resources issue.

As a result of this realization, the Cabinet supported the request and Takaoka received word from the Prime Minister's Office's Special Areas Liaison Bureau (*Tokubetsu Chiiki Renrakukyoku*) on January 8, 1969, that a budget of 9,435,000 yen had been approved.[64] Takaoka immediately called on Tokonami to express his gratitude. Tokonami told him it obviously was not enough and that he would work to get more, and indeed, more money came for the survey the following year, and for an additional survey for the year after that.[65]

Because Tokai University was the only school with a Maritime Department, the Prime Minister's Office decided to commission it to conduct the survey.[66] Professor Niino, who was hospitalized at this point, was asked to coordinate the project with Tokai University, where he was now teaching at.[67] On January 31, Takaoka met with two professors of Tokai University, Hoshino Michihei and Iwashita Mitsuo, in the chairman's room within *Nanen*'s office to enlist their support. As mentioned in Chapter 2, the Prime Minister's Office sponsored another survey of the islands from June 14 to July 13, shortly after the ECAFE report had come out.

Race for concessions—Taiwan

A couple of months after the ECAFE report came out (and Ishigaki City signs had been erected on all of the islands making up the Senkakus), the Executive Yuan of the GRC announced a statement on July 17, 1969 that it "could exercise its sovereign right over all natural resources in the sea floor and its subsoil in the vicinity of the coast of the ROC and beyond its territorial waters."[68] This blanket statement included the problematic Senkakus area, and was likely made in preparation for the issuance of future mining or other concessions. According to a brief analysis by the U.S. Embassy in Taipei requested by the U.S. Embassy in Tokyo,

> [It is] very likely the GRC July 17 statement was made in response to reports of Japanese surveys in order to keep alive GRC hopes of participation in exploitation of the Senkaku Islands ... The July 17 statement, by raising possibility GRC may regard certain Ryukyuan waters as belonging within China's continental shelf, may be calculated to make GOJ think twice about plunging ahead in assigning oil exploration concessions around the Senkakus.[69]

For some reason, the media was slow to pick up on the GRC's statement, but in late August, the *New York Times* published a front page story entitled "Japanese Oil Find Poses Title Problem," and other newspapers, such as the *Nihon Keizai Shimbun* and *Japan Times*, also began to report on it.[70] Greater attention began to be given to the issue, which triggered the request for information, but it did not seem to dominate the news at the time.

Despite the relatively low key media attention, there apparently was great tension emerging within the GRC over the issue. Since at least that spring, the GRC was aware of the "potential economic significance" of the islands, and some elements within the GRC, especially Ministry of Economic Affairs Mining Department Director Wu Po-Chen, who was also serving as the Ministry of Economic Affairs member on the ad-hoc committee created to consider the problem, were pressing for an outright GRC claim to sovereignty over the Senkakus Islands as part of the continent shelf.[71] In contrast, Taiwan's Foreign Ministry believed the GRC should be more cautious in pressing such claims.

Taiwan was particularly interested in exploiting its rights under the 1958 Continental Shelf Convention, to which it was a signatory. However, it had not yet ratified the convention. In early September 1969, Che Yin-Shou, director of the International Organizations Bureau of the Taiwan Ministry of Foreign Affairs, informed the U.S. Embassy that the convention would be sent to the Legislative Yuan for ratification during the next session. Che told chargé d'affaires Vance I. Armstrong at their September 4 meeting that MOFA hoped for ratification during October that year so that the "legal groundwork would be ready for negotiations with the Japanese."[72] Indeed, this was just one of several steps Taiwan was pursuing to seek internationally legally recognized legitimacy for its claims.[73]

In the meantime, the GRC, through the state-owned China Petroleum Corporation, or CPC, signed a preliminary agreement with American Oil Company, or Amoco, permitting it to begin some slope drilling along the west coast of the northern half of Taiwan (centered on 24–30 degrees North latitude). Amoco, then a division of Standard Oil of Indiana, had been the first foreign oil company to take a "serious interest" in Taiwan, providing a "letter of interest" to Taiwan as early as mid-1967 about conducting studies prior to negotiations.[74] Both Amoco and Taiwan had various motives in working together at this time, according to Harrison whose *China, Oil, and Asia* was "the first book to focus on the profound political consequences of China's ambitious effort to develop offshore petroleum."[75] For Amoco, one of them was the political stability Taiwan represented. Former associate general counsel of Amoco, Thomas Caffey, recalled in 1975, "the future of Taiwan at that time wasn't as questionable as it is now ... No one ever thought the U.S. would turn around and do what we did in 1972."[76] Taiwan on the other hand wanted to anchor American companies, and thus the U.S. government, to Taiwan's future, both its economic prosperity and political stability. The Embassy suggested if Amoco was encouraged by this test drilling, which had already begun, it might end up applying to the GRC for a formal concession agreement.

Similarly, discussions were proceeding with Pacific Gulf Co., a U.S. oil company subsidiary based out of Tokyo, whose concession area would be adjacent to Okinawan waters but had not reached a preliminary agreement.[77] Indeed Gulf's preliminary negotiations had begun in 1968 and its *Gulfrex* survey vessel entered the Taiwan Strait in the fall of 1968 just as the *R.V. Hunt*, conducting the survey on behalf of ECAFE, was leaving. Pacific Gulf was subsequently granted concessions by South Korea in areas closer to the peninsula in April 1969 (and eventually to waters near the Senkakus).

In addition to the above commercial negotiations, the Embassy in Taipei learned that the Institute of Oceanography, a new center established within the National Taiwan University's College of Science in 1968, would shortly send its research vessel, the *Kiu Lien*, to begin certain petroleum-oriented investigations in the "Taiwan Basin," which was defined in a September 1969 GRC National Science publication as "located on continental shelf in East China Sea and extending north-northeast from northern coast of Taiwan up to latitude 31 degrees north."[78]

By the following summer (1970), Taiwan and the above companies were ready to finalize their negotiations. Japan had gotten word of it by this point, and on July 20, a year after the GRC had announced its sovereign right over all natural resources in the seafloor and subsoil, the GOJ sent a note stating that any unilateral claim over the Senkaku Islands or the continental shelf was invalid under international law and that such claims did not affect the rights of Japan to the continental shelf.[79]

Nevertheless, the GRC went ahead the following week with the first of several contracts that its government-owned CPC signed with foreign companies for joint exploration and exploitation of the continental shelf. The first one was with Amoco (for Block 1) on July 27. This was followed by contracts with Pacific Gulf (for Block 2) on July 28, Oceanic Exploration Company (for Block 3) on August 13, and Clinton International (for Block 4) on September 22.[80]

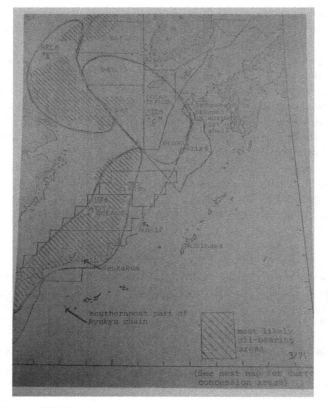

Figure 3.2 Map of Oil Concessions

The Senkaku Islands were located in Gulf's concession area, known as Block II, which gave the American company (whose headquarters in Asia was ironically located in Tokyo) the right to explore and exploit resources around the islands and on the continental shelf.[81] The contract for exploration and exploitation of the area was signed between Pacific Gulf and the state-owned CPC. Two days later, the Executive Yuan in Taiwan had approved on July 30 a draft statute governing the exploration and drilling of oil and gas in China's territorial waters and the adjacent continental shelf, chalking off an area covering 69,000 square miles for undersea oil prospecting.[82]

Chiang Kai-shek began writing in his diary from around this time in the middle of August about the Senkakus and Japan. Interestingly he used the Japanese name, "Senkakus," rather than the Chinese name for the islands despite his view that they were not Japan's territory. With this said, Chiang seemed to think that since Taiwan and an America company signed an oil and mineral exploration agreement, "Japan shall not dare to raise the issue again."[83] If anything Taiwan's actions ended up inflaming the problem, increasingly galvanizing the Japanese government, Diet, and media to pay more attention to the problem.

Over the course of a week, Chiang wrote almost daily in his diary about the islands, personally editing on the morning of August 18 a statement being prepared to give to Japan. His thinking on the issue can be seen in his August 16 entry:

> Regarding the issue of sovereignty of the Senkaku Islands, not only has my country never given up the sovereignty of the islands, but also, indeed, even the sovereignty of the Ryukyus has never been acknowledged to Japan by any government throughout history and politics. And, when Japan at the [end of] World War II, it was already confirmed that the outer islands had all been given up. Only because the government of my country, based on the principle of peace and harmony, did not raise the issue of sovereignty, lest the friendly atmosphere be harmed by the controversy over such a tiny island county. However, the Chinese government, based on 400 years' history, will never see these islands as under the sovereignty of Japan, nor do we see any documented agreement regarding this.[84]

On August 20, the GRC Cabinet had reportedly approved in principle a statement refuting Japan's claims and reaffirming GRC sovereignty over the Senkakus. The statement, drafted in the Taiwanese Foreign Ministry, reportedly gave the historical and geographic relation of the Senkakus to Taiwan and was to be released after examination by a special panel.[85] It is likely this statement that Chiang had personally edited. The next day on August 21, Taiwan conditionally ratified the above Convention.

Taiwan's ratification included the following reservations: "With regard to the determination of the boundary of the continental shelf as provided in Paragraphs 1 and 2 of Article 6 of the Convention, the Government of the ROC considers: (1) that the boundary of the continental shelf appertaining to two or more States whose coast are adjacent to and/or opposite each other shall be determined in accordance with the principle of the natural prolongation of their land territories; and (2) that in determining the boundary of the continental shelf of the ROC, exposed rocks and islets shall not be taken into account."[86] While the Senkaku Islands were not specifically mentioned here, Deputy Foreign Minister Ru Jian Gang subsequently informed the Legislature on September 25 that the "exposed rocks and islets" in the above sentence did indeed mean the Senkakus.[87]

According to a comment by a member of the Foreign Relations Committee of the Legislative Yuan, the reservations were based on the "principle of natural prolongation of the land," which was established in a decision of the International Court of Justice in the North Sea Continental Shelf Case given in February 1969, and which stated that exposed rocks and islets were part of the continental shelf itself and therefore no separate right could be asserted over the continental shelf areas adjacent thereto. In summarizing the GRC's position, the State Department noted the GRC, while claiming the continental shelf as an extension of the land mass of the mainland, over which it had declared itself to be the legitimate government, it had never defined either the northern or southernmost limits of the China shelf or the limits of its claim to that shelf.[88]

Unfortunately, Taiwan's granting of the concession to the area around the Senkakus, which overlapped with competing claims by the above Okinawans and Japanese entitled, the Senkakus issue had become "international" at this point, and would grow increasingly complex over the coming weeks, months, and years. The GRC's granting of this concession became, in the words of Takahashi, who wrote about the Senkaku Islands and was a businessman active in mainland China–Japanese trade, the official start of the dispute between Japan and Taiwan.[89]

It is ironic that only the week before Taiwan signed the related contracts, representatives of that country had attended the 15th General Meeting of the Japan-Taiwan Cooperation Committee (*Nikka Kyoryoku Iinkai*) and had even, on July 7, 1970, agreed at its Political Subcommittee to create a Japan–Korea–Taiwan Liaison Committee to discuss cooperating on developing the continental shelf.[90] Although this was a private body, there were direct connections with the governments of each country in all three cases. In the case of Japan, Kishi Nobusuke, a former prime minister and the brother of the current premier, Sato Eisaku, was the lead on the Japanese side. The issue was to quickly become politicized in light of the competing Okinawa, Japanese, and Taiwanese (and soon to be heard Chinese) claims, not to mention the implications for other countries, such as Korea and the United States. And perhaps for this reason, the body did not seem to play a leading role although it is possible that it worked behind the scenes to try to lower the temperature.

On August 22, Foreign Minister Wei reported to the Executive Yuan that the GRC had informed Japan, in part in response to the GOJ's July 1970 note to the GRC, that the ROC had the right to prospect and develop the continental shelf north of Taiwan in accordance with the principles of international law and the Convention on the Continental Shelf.[91] And on September 3, the day after personnel and media from a Taiwanese vessel landed on the Senkakus and planted a flag (apparently unbeknownst to the GRC), President Chiang promulgated new regulations governing the exploration and exploitation of undersea oil resources, the statute for which had been in the works since July when it was conditionally approved.

Japan's response to Taiwan's moves and Taiwanese counter-reactions

On July 20, 1970, a week before Gulf's formal signing with CPC, the GOJ made an official representation to the GRC regarding the continental shelf between Kyushu and Taiwan in order to make clear to the GRC that the GOJ was concerned about the former's claims to oil development areas around the Senkakus. According to Okawara Yoshio, the deputy director of MOFA's

North American Affairs Bureau, the GOJ told the GRC that it did not consider any unilateral claim by the GRC to the area designated for oil development as "effective under international law" and that such claims did "not affect the rights of the GOJ to the continental shelf."[92] Sneider, summarizing their meeting, told the department that it could expect the Japanese Embassy in Washington to approach it in the near future as both the GOJ and GRC realized that the "continental shelf matter would have to be resolved sooner or later."[93]

Taiwan's decision to grant concessions during the summer of 1970 to Pacific Gulf was taken up in the Special Committee on Okinawa and the Northern Territories (*Okinawa Oyobi Hoppo Mondai ni Kansuru Tokubetsu Iinkai*) of the Upper House of the Japanese Parliament that summer. On August 10, Aichi Kiichi, a member of Prime Minister Sato Eisaku's faction who had become foreign minister in November 1968, criticized the GRC move, denouncing it as a unilateral act having no effect in international law, and disclosed the fact that he had filed a protest to that effect against Taiwan.[94]

In response to Aichi's statement before the Upper House, the spokesman for the ROC's Foreign Affairs Department published a comment the same day which stated that the Taiwanese government had already informed the Japanese government of its position and that "the Government of the Republic of China has the right to explore for and exploit natural resources on the continental shelf extending north of Taiwan, in accordance with the principles of international law as well as the Continental Shelf Convention of 1958."[95] In the middle of August, newspaper reports hinted that the GRC planned to issue a statement at a Cabinet meeting on the Japanese protest. It finally did so on August 19 in a note to the Japanese government rejecting the Japanese claim to the Senkakus and Japan's rights to the "Chinese continental shelf."[96] Interestingly, the note, which was shown to a U.S. Embassy official in Taipei by Muto Takeshi, the Japanese chargé d'affaires in Taiwan, "specifically denied existence of a Chinese claim" to the Senkakus.[97]

Two days later, on August 21, the GRC conditionally ratified the Convention, as described above, with reservations that applied to the Senkakus. Nervous about what was going on, the Legislature of the Government of the Ryukyu Islands passed a resolution at the end of the month (described later this chapter), and caught in the heat of the moment, members of the media and personnel of a vessel belonging to the Taiwanese Fisheries Experiment Center, landed on the Senkakus raised the Taiwanese flag on Uotsuri Jima. Tensions would flare dramatically at this point, and heavily involve the United States. It would also propel Japan and Taiwan into a direct dialog on the Senkakus issue, with neither one of them willing to give in.

This dynamic was apparent in a couple of episodes that month in the respective parliaments. In Japan, Foreign Minister Aichi was asked about the problem of ownership of the Senkakus in deliberations before the Foreign Affairs Committee (*Gaimu Iinkai*) of the Lower House. In response, he answered that the issue was not up for discussion with any country and that the islands were clearly Japanese territory.[98] Aichi continued with the same view in his testimony two days later on September 12 before the Lower House's Special Committee on Okinawa and the Northern Territories.[99]

And in Taiwan, following a series of discussions on the Senkakus, the Taiwan Provincial Assembly passed a resolution on September 30, 1970, "join [ing]," in the words of the recently arrived political officer, L. Desaix Anderson, "the news media, national legislators, and the public generally, in appealing to the central government to protect China's legitimate rights over the Tiao Yu Tai (Senkaku) Islands."[100]

Before we look at the U.S. position on concessions and the Okinawan reaction to Taiwanese moves, it is necessary to look at the flag-planting problem and how it was handled.

The Taiwan flag-planting issue

On September 2, 1970 Republic of China nationalists traveling on a ROC Marine Research Laboratory vessel landed on Uotsuri Island and planted a Chinese Nationalist flag, the so-called Blue Sky, White Sun, and a Wholly Red Earth. In addition, they painted several rocks at the base of flag pole with "Long Live Chiang Kai-shek" and other pro-Taiwan statements. A photo caption appearing on September 4 in the independent *Chung Kuo Shih Pao* (China Times) identified the group as one composed of journalists from the newspaper and members of the ship's crew.[101] By the morning of the 5th, most Japanese newspapers were carrying wire service reports of the landing.[102]

The Japanese Embassy in Taipei asked the ROC's Ministry of Foreign Affairs about it but the representative said if a flag was flown, it "was not done at the direction of the [government]."[103] Muto, the chargé, reported this reply to Tokyo and awaited further instructions. In the meantime, back in Tokyo, Sato of the Japanese Ministry of Foreign Affairs, who was "speaking under instructions," asked on September 5 that American authorities in Okinawa investigate the situation and take the necessary actions.[104]

The issue had the potential to become very serious, quickly. So much so that the Directorate of Intelligence at the Central Intelligence Agency included a fairly long report on the "heating up" of "a dispute over oil rights" between Japan and the Republic of China in its daily *Central Intelligence Bulletin*. The September 4, 1970 *Bulletin* mentioned that the issue might "be solved through diplomatic channels" but also correctly pointed out that the "dispute could be complicated later by Communist China ... [although] Peking's position in the controversy has not been made clear."[105]

On September 5, USCAR issued instructions to the GRI Police assigning it as the "appropriate action agency" to look into the ROC flag issue.[106] The police did not initially take action, however, and in its place the director of the GRI Trade and Industry Bureau, Sunakawa, had been assigned responsibility. According to an internal memo in USCAR, the Public Safety

Department believed that GRI "considers USCAR as the action agency and consequently [did] not wish to become involved."[107] Another interpretation is that Sunakawa's office, which was in charge of mining concessions and thus handled the Senkaku Islands territorial issue, was carefully watching the flag dispute in the context not only of an illegal intrusion but also for what it meant for the larger Senkakus issue as a whole and thus was cautious and uncertain about how to proceed.

During the middle of the dispute, the High Commissioner's office learned through the U.S. Preparatory Committee element that a member of the GOJ PrepCom staff in Okinawa, plus two additional GOJ and three GRI officials, were planning a two-day trip to Yonaguni on September 7. Ostensibly, the purpose of the trip was to investigate: 1) immigration control; 2) smuggling; 3) the relationship of Yonaguni to the Senkaku Islands; 4) agricultural development; and 5) possible problems of national defense and public order. A member of the Japanese group asked if someone from the U.S. side could go, thus making it a GOJ-GRI-USG undertaking, but a U.S. official declined, "pleading the press of business."[108] Unofficially, however, the U.S. official was told that the trip was seen by the GOJ as "showing the flag on Yonaguni" and "lending support in the Senkakus dispute," as well as of course to serve as a "data collection expedition to support GOJ claim to the Senkakus."[109] U.S. officials also learned later that week that GRI legislators were preparing to travel to Tokyo to present their resolution on the Senkakus and to visit the U.S. Embassy, and so informed the State Department.[110]

By September 11, the GRI Police still had not confirmed the presence of the flag on Uotsuri. "Poor weather conditions and budget limitations" were given as reasons for not sending the *Chitose* from Naha to investigate, but the High Commissioner's office tended to believe that the delay in the GRI investigation was due to the desire of both the GRI and GOJ to have the USG take the lead in investigating the matter, dispose of the flag if found, and protest to the GRC, thereby taking the lead against the GRC.[111] Nevertheless, GRI Police Chief Arakaki Tokusuke eventually instructed Yaeyama Police Chief Tamamura Yakichi, who had primary responsibility for the Senkakus, to investigate the situation and a senior police official from Naha was being sent to Ishigaki that day (11th) to coordinate the local investigation.

When it became clear that that the USG was not going to commit American personnel and equipment to remove the flag, the GRI Police agreed to do so after discussions with USCAR. It dispatched the *Chitose* from Naha on the evening of the 13th, stopping on route at Ishigaki to allow two newsmen to come on board for the trip to the Senkakus.

Arriving at Uotsuri Island at six a.m. the morning of the 15th, the police found the Taiwanese flag, 1.2 m long by 70 cm wide, attached to a seven-meter pole. The pole was imbedded one meter into the ground, with its base buttressed by rocks. They also found Chinese writing the rocks that read, "Banzai (10,000 Lives, or Long Live) Chiang Kai-Shek," "*Chung Kuo Shih Pao* (China Times)," "Marine Experimental Station," as well as some family names.[112] Four

Taiwanese vessels were near the island, too, within the three-mile limit. Police warned the vessels to leave the area and took "appropriate pictures."[113] The police reported its findings to USCAR at 10:30 that morning.

The police stated they had no orders from USCAR or the Okinawa Bureau of the Okinawa Northern Territories Agency, otherwise known as OBONTA, but had requested instructions from the latter. They added that OBONTA had previously recommended the flag be removed. The police told USCAR that they would have to leave around 11:00 due to tide conditions near the island. (They actually stayed until after noon.) After conferring by telephone with the U.S. Embassy in Tokyo, which concurred, USCAR suggested at 11:45 to the GRI police (in the absence of Chief Executive Yara and Deputy Chief Executive Chinen) that the flag be removed "with care and respect extended to any foreign flags" and the Chinese characters painted on the rocks be painted over "with care and neatness."[114] USCAR emphasized to the police officials that their actions should be carried out with "dignity" and in a manner to avoid possible charges of desecration of a national symbol.[115]

By 12:30, the flag was on board the GRI police vessel and the "Banzai" message on the rock had been painted over. The *Chitose* departed at 12:40 for Ishigaki to get more paint, with the intention to return the next day and finish painting over the rocks. At 1:15 p.m., it reported to USCAR that it had departed Uotsuri.[116]

The *Chitose* reached Ishigaki at 9:30 p.m. that night (15th), and was instructed to return to Uotsuri the following day. The police were provided with fifteen gallons of paint by the chief of the Yaeyama Civil Affairs Team, Lieutenant Colonel Harry K. Fukuhara, to paint over the remaining Chinese lettering. That same day, September 16, the flag was flown from Ishigaki to Naha and shown to Chief Executive Yara at his request.[117]

While on Ishigaki, the policemen gave a report to Chief Tamamura, who informed Lieutenant Colonel Fukuhara that the police had found the attitude of the Taiwanese fishermen around Uotsuri Jima "very belligerent" when the *Chitose* approached them and warned them to leave the territorial waters of the Ryukyu Islands.[118] The "initial response by the Taiwanese crews," according to a telegram prepared by the High Commissioner's office, "was to point to the GRC flag, stilling flying on Uotsuri at that time, and state they were in GRC waters."[119] When contradicted by the police, who said the island was not the ROC's and that they would have to move at least three miles away from the island, they replied that they would not leave until they caught a "sufficient amount of fish."[120] The police noted that the "attitude of fishermen contrasted with past reactions of Taiwanese fishermen who have cleared the area with only minor grumbling when requested to do so."[121] After some more exchanges, the fishermen said they would leave when the wind shifted, but they were still there when the *Chitose* departed Uotsuri shortly past noon. Tamamura told Lieutenant Colonel Fukuhara that he wished to "avoid an international incident," and that if the *Chitose* returned, "anything [might] happen ... The police on the *Chitose* are armed to protect themselves."

Expecting the Taiwanese fishermen to be there when they returned, the police were probably surprised not to find them there the next day initially. Arriving at 6 a.m. on the morning of the 17th, the police landed to finish painting over the rocks (which they completed at 7:40 a.m.). When the *Chitose* prepared to leave at 10:00 a.m., however, the police discovered nine Taiwanese vessels within one kilometer of Uotsuri Jima. The fishing boats were warned off and they departed the area without incident.[122]

Despite the fact there were no incidents, the USG was concerned for a couple of reasons. First, it wanted to "minimize possibility of confrontations in sensitive Senkakus area" and had the Embassy Taipei call on the GRC, describe the situation, and request its urgent intervention to ensure that ROC vessels leave the area immediately.[123] The USG also advised the GRI police to refrain from the use of force against the fishing vessels.

Another concern had to do with the flag. Removing it actually placed the USG in a "difficult position," in part because the question then arose about who—USCAR or GRI—should retain custody of it.[124] When GRI Police Chief Arakaki brought the flag to USCAR officials on September 17, they told him that they had no "appropriate storage facilities" (a rather strange and unconvincing excuse for a military organization) and that the flag should be retained by the GRI. (It was shown to Yara that same day too.[125]) Arakaki may have decided to provide GRI and USCAR a face-saving solution. After the flag's arrival in Naha, he told U.S. officials that he "thought the flag should be kept by the police as 'evidence' inasmuch as unidentified person or persons had illegally entered the Ryukyu Islands and with intentions to claim ownership."[126] Further study was to have been done by the police on the final disposition of the flag, but in any case, it ended up in the custody of GRI Police headquarters in Naha afterwards.

In the meantime, the State Department wrote to the U.S. Embassy in Taipei requesting it to bring the matter before the ROC Foreign Ministry and request that appropriate action be taken to ensure the immediate departure of the Taiwanese vessels in the area and prevent future "illegal incursions" into the territorial waters subject to U.S. administration.[127] It reminded the Embassy that the U.S. government viewed that any dispute over the sovereignty of the Senkakus should be resolved by the parties concerned, and that the USG had full administrative responsibility over the islands and would act accordingly. It emphasized there would be stronger actions taken if the vessels did not depart immediately.

Subsequently, there were at least two requests by the GRC for the flag's return.[128] The USG had been placed in a "difficult position" because of the issue—both the planting of the flag by the Taiwanese and its seizure by the GRI police—and the High Commissioner's office proposed two solutions: leaving it at the GRI Police Headquarters and ensuring the GRC that its "national emblem is being properly safeguarded and will at all times be treated in courteous and appropriate manner" or to request GRI turn the flag over to U.S. authorities for return to the GRC "thus terminating in dignified fashion matter of illegal implantation of flag in Ryukyuan territory."[129] Eventually, in light of the growing tensions between Taiwan and Japan, as well as Taiwanese public dissatisfaction with the United States in April, the Embassy in Taipei asked the State Department on April 22 to instruct the High Commissioner to request the GRI to hand the flag over to U.S. authorities in order to return it to the GRI.[130] The Embassy said on returning the flag to the GRC it would ask the Foreign Ministry either to retain it or hand it over in a way that would not "create further difficulties."[131]

The request was made through the Department of the Army the same day and the USCAR Public Safety director subsequently personally received it from Arakaki, who was told only that the "GRC had requested return of flag and USG wished to comply with request."[132] The flag was sent by a USCAR courier, who departed Naha on April 25 to deliver it to the American Embassy in Taipei. After arriving in Taipei, the flag was then delivered to the Ministry of Foreign Affairs by the political counselor at the U.S. Embassy, who handed it to Ellen Woo, the deputy director for North American Affairs, on April 27. William W. Thomas told Woo that the flag had been obtained from the GRI in a "low-key manner" and said he hoped the ROC would also handle the matter in a way which would "avoid publicity, since newspaper wars like that of last September were in the interest neither of [ROC] nor of U.S."[133] Woo, who "has yet to make a substantive comment to U.S. on any issue since assuming her present position," told the political counselor the "[ROC] appreciated the return of the flag" and that she would report the request about no publicity to her superiors.[134] During a meeting a couple of days later on another subject on April 28, Chien expressed his appreciation to Ambassador McConaughy for the U.S. efforts to obtain the return of the ROC flag from the GRI and told him that the Foreign Ministry would retain the flag and avoid publicity on the matter.[135]

In the four decades since, there have been several attempts by Taiwan to replant the flag in the Senkakus as well as at least two efforts to do it simultaneously with the Chinese flag, most recently in August 2012.

The U.S. position on concessions

A central theme of this book, as described by several writers and observers in the past, is that the dispute between Japan, Taiwan, and China over the Senkakus derives from the fact that there was a great deal of interest in the possibility of large oil reserves being in the immediate area. Survey and other concessions were an issue that the U.S. government followed very closely. This attention was found both at the local level in Okinawa as well as regionally, not only because of the territorial implications but also because U.S. companies tended to be a direct or indirect part of the discussions due to the high level of technology and economic interests involved.

As early as June 1969, for example, several officials from Gulf Pittsburgh, including its chief geologist, Joseph Carter, and attorney, Robert Rees, called on the State Department to inquire about the boundary between Taiwan and the Ryukyus and to discuss the question of offshore oil. Gulf had been discussing with the Republic of China, specifically its CPC, joint exploration of the seabed north and northeast of Taiwan, but had been informed that the sea boundary between the ROC and the Ryukyus was unsettled, although Japan has residual sovereignty over the Ryukyus. Carter explained that Gulf had also heard that a Japanese firm had obtained concessions from the GRI around the Senkaku Islands, which "lie within the contemplated Gulf concession area."[136]

Robert W. Barnett, a China specialist serving as the deputy assistant secretary of state for East Asia since January 1964, replied he had not heard that any concession had been granted by the GRI, noting that "international law is murky, that the U.S. adheres to the Continental Shelf Convention but that other countries, including the ROC and Japan, do not."[137] The Shanghai-born Barnett explained as well that the "settlement of the Ryukyu-Taiwan boundary question would require that the U.S. act for Japan in negotiations with the ROC, since the U.S. administers the Ryukyus but recognizes that residual sovereignty rests with Japan, but that the U.S. is reluctant to get involved with Japan on this matter at this time with the return of the Ryukyus under active discussion with the Japanese."[138]

Carter asked then if Gulf, celebrating almost seventy years in business, could apply to the GRI for concessions. Barnett replied that the USG considered it a "Japanese affair," and that "Japanese residual sovereignty was recognized by everyone but its exercise has still to be worked out. And in this 'Ryukyus year' [i.e., the decision to return administrative rights over Okinawa to Japan] we are not willing to inject this question into more basic matters."

The Washington representative of Gulf, Stuart Nelson, asked if the status of the "Sento" Island was in dispute. Charles A. Schmitz, who would later be in charge of drafting the reversion treaty on exactly this matter, replied that the islands were including within the lines of USCAR a proclaimed area and therefore the "Sentos" were within the Ryukyu Islands. He added that both the United States and the ROC "behaved" as if they were.[139] When Nelson asked for specific ROC examples to this effect, Lynn H. Olson, the country officer for the Republic of China within the East Asia Bureau, referred to the case of the Taiwanese fishermen and ship salvage operations which Japan protested against and the ROC "acted to get the squatters off."[140]

The discussion then turned to the ROC and Communist China, and later on Barnett stated that while the Taiwan Strait is "not an area of constant combat ... there is mutual harassment [between the two Chinas] at a low tactical level and there could certainly be no sense of great security."[141] Barnett then proceeded to read the following statement with regard to Gulf's question about the Taiwan-Ryukyuan territorial jurisdiction.

The proposed concessional area includes: (1) Ryukyuan territory, specifically the Senkaku (or Sento) Islands and (2) Ryukyu continental shelf areas, the precise extent of which could only be determined in negotiations with the ROC; and that we do not feel that we have the authority to negotiate a dividing line between the Republic of China and the Ryukyu Islands and are reluctant to raise this issue with the Japanese at this time. We feel that the ROC would be on tenuous legal and political grounds if it were to assert a legal right to grant this extensive a concession, particularly including the southeastern portion, to Gulf. The legal situation is not clear, and the United States has not yet taken a position regarding the extent to which it considers coastal states should exercise jurisdiction over seabed natural resources or regarding the stance it should take when other governments assert claims of jurisdiction which the United States determines to be unsupported by international law. We are sure that Communist China will not accept the legality of such concessions and are unable to assess whether they might take military action against installations particularly if the concessions and the existence of installations on the shelf within 50 miles from Communist China were to become a public issue. We could not give Gulf any commitment to protect such concessions.[142]

Barnett ended the meeting by telling the Gulf representatives the USG remained interested in the above matter and his own personal willingness to meet again if they had any further questions.[143]

Later that summer in August, the Washington representative and attorney for a different company, Union Carbide, a U.S. petrochemical company founded in 1917, called on the State Department to explain its interest in filing an application for an oil exploration concession in an area off-shore the Senkakus, and to seek clarification of several points.

Richard B. Finn, the country director for Japan since January that year,[144] explained that the United States considered the Senkaku Islands to be part of the Ryukyu Islands, that this was the understanding of the GOJ and that the GRC has not challenged this position but that it might advance a claim that the islands were part of China. When asked by Joseph E. Goeghan, Union Carbide's attorney, about the GRI's claims to the continental shelf adjacent to the Senkaku Islands, Finn, who had spent most of his career in the State Department involved in Japan-related work, replied (using a similar phrase as that prepared for Barnett by Schmitz[145]) that "international law was murky on this issue; that there was a Ryukyuan shelf, the precise extent of which would probably have to be determined by negotiations between the interested parties; and that we do not feel that we have the right to grant a concession in this area or make determinations affecting the continental shelf boundaries without the concurrence of Japan."[146]

Finn's colleague, Bernard H. Oxman, a specialist on international law and the Law of the Sea who served as a legal advisor in the State Department, chimed in pointing out that mainland China might eventually exert a claim over the area of the continental shelf in question, and that this could cause political as well as legal problems. Geoghan stated he was very much concerned with that, as well as getting caught in the middle were Japan to negotiate with the PRC and thus place Union Carbide at odds with U.S. law and policy (of not trading or interacting with the PRC, which the USG still did not recognize). Goeghan went on to explain that Union Carbide had encountered difficulties in filing applications with the GRI for exploratory concessions. He said first, the Japanese company with which it was associated had been advised by the Ministry of International Trade and Industry (*Tsusansho*) "not to proceed with the application."[147] Second, he was told in Tokyo that the GRI was "strongly anti-American and would not accept an application by a Ryukyuan in behalf of an American company."[148] Finn stated that he did not consider the GRI anti-American but that "the GRI in situations like this might be receiving unofficial guidance from MITI," and that Union Carbide should "consult closely with both MITI and the GRI" with reversion being a "distinct possibility within a few years, it would be essential to have an understanding with MITI."[149] Oxman, who later became a professor of international law, concluded the meeting by saying that it was a "mistake to automatically interpret a desire to maintain domestic control of continental shelf resources as anti-American. Many countries, including the U.S., have similar policies, which makes it awkward for the U.S. to press the case for concessions to U.S. private interests abroad."[150]

Around this time in Okinawa, the staff at USCAR was also watching the issue of mining concessions and came up with "very similar conclusions. It is recognized that far-reaching international law precedents are anything but clear."[151] A mid-November 1969 USCAR memo for the Department of the Army also pointed out that it was "interesting to note that the Government of the Ryukyu Islands also seems sensitive to these same implications and is moving exceedingly slowly on adopting any sort of official position."[152]

With this said, USCAR was in the process of forming the basis of a local policy vis-à-vis GRI on the issue of concessions, which it shared with GRI after receiving an additional oil exploration and mining request from the New York-based mining company, Alaska-Canada Minerals, Inc., dated September 12. The essence of its decision, which was misunderstood (or misportrayed) in the local press, was that offshore waters were to be considered to be under the control of the Ryukyuan Property Custodian, an office similar to ones created in different theaters to handle the property of former enemies, which required the prior approval of the civil administrator before the GRI could grant any permit or license.

The thinking behind this policy was as follows. Under usual circumstances, the granting of mining and prospecting rights, including the development of oil resources, would be a matter of exclusive concern for the GRI under the provisions of HICOM Ordinance No. 33 of June 24, 1960, which transferred such authority and responsibility to the GRI.[153] This ordinance, according to USCAR's lawyers, was applicable to oil exploration, regardless of whether done on land or at sea. However, a subsequent decision in November 1968 limited the territorial waters to three miles, and as such, the Custodian "possesses paramount rights in, and full dominion and power over such property," in the areas beyond that.[154] "It is thus our opinion," the USCAR memo states, "that oil prospecting and exploitation in off-shore waters require the prior approval of the civil administrator. This does not, in our view, restrict the GRI from receiving and processing any and all applications which are submitted. The essential point taken by USCAR is that before actual prospecting and/or exploitation shall begin, the CA must issue a specific approval or disapproval in each case."[155]

The next issue USCAR had to decide was whether in the above case it actually had any authority to approve exploration or mining in the seabed in those areas outside the three-mile territorial waters. The applications submitted to date showed the tracts to be explored went beyond the three-mile territorial waters. Civil Administration Ordinance No. 68, of February 28, 1952, which established the geographic jurisdiction as introduced in Chapter 2, tended to be quite limited and not providing any greater U.S. or GRI territorial claim than that of existing islands, islets, atolls, rocks, "and territorial waters" which are within the specified longitudes or latitudes. "Any extension of U.S. interests to off-shore waters will thus," USCAR concluded, "have to be predicated on international law precedents rather than reliance upon USCAR or GRI legislation."[156]

USCAR's position, introduced in the local media in the context of the application from Alaska-Canada Minerals, Inc., apparently caused some people in Okinawa to view the United States as attempting to "appropriate the possible oil resources for its own use" and intervening to prevent the GRI from processing the applications.[157] In fact, this was not the case—merely USCAR was concerned about the "international implications in any off-shore exploration" and "its responsibilities in the international field."[158] USCAR officials, as they told higher headquarters, intended to "monitor" the GRI review of applications, but not "interfere" with it.[159]

Indeed, USCAR officials did not feel that the GRI was "interested in a priority review of the applications that are now pending in its hands."[160] Some GRI staff members even said unofficially that it might be several years before the GRI would be able to make recommendations to the civil administrator on the applications. The reasons it felt this were explained in a meeting the following year, one which was called by USCAR, to have the GRI provide an "informal update" on the processing of the mining applications for the Senkakus area.[161] At the outset, GRI officials explained that three applicants had filed for exploration and/or exploitation mining concessions in the area of the Senkakus. A total of 24,841 separate applications were involved due to the particular requirements of the mining law. This mass of submissions thoroughly taxed the limited manpower resources of the GRI Mining Section (*Kozanka*). Despite the use of extra and part-time employees, there was still a considerable lag in the completion of even the initial screening of the many applications.

The GRI representatives further explained that the mining law provided that applications are entertained on a first-come, first-served basis and that when mining rights are subsequently recommended, they would follow the priority of their original filing. That was, of course, subject to the application being from an appropriate person or entity and otherwise being in accordance with local law. Nakamura Shoichi, chief of the Mining Section, Trade and Industry Department, GRI, commented that he did not think they would be in a position to make any recommendations on the until the middle of 1971, although they said they were making every effort to shorten the time.

Lieutenant Colonel Richard K. McNealy, Director, Legal Affairs Department, reminded Nakamura that the GRI mining law required approval of the civil administrator for any prospecting or any exploration within the areas under the control or administration of the USG and this would apply to offshore Senkakus areas. Both USCAR and GRI officials then agreed that it would be useful to maintain close coordination on the Senkaku mining situation with a view to facilitating these necessary clearances at the appropriate time.

Kina Akira, chief of the Commerce and Industry Division, Trade and Industry Department, followed up by stating that GRI was interested in preserving the GRI administration over the Senkaku Islands and requested USCAR assistance in protecting these GRI interests. McNealy answered that he was aware of its concerns, but apparently did not commit USCAR any further.

USCAR continued to watch the situation, however, and in some cases be drawn into the problem. That same month, the High Commissioner received a petition entitled "An Opinion for a Meeting to Protect Okinawa Senkaku Islands," presumably from either the Legislature of the Government of the Ryukyu Islands or one of the local groups that came into being during August and September to protect the resources of the Senkakus. There was clearly some sympathy on the part of USCAR, but there was also some frustration seen as well.

In an internal memo recommending how to respond to the petition, McNealy told the Liaison Department, "while sympathetic to the very legitimate desire to have Okinawans share in the profits of a Senkaku oil strike, it's rather tiresome to see that [the petition] is flavored with anti-foreign sentiments, particularly citing the designs of American big business."[162] He went on to write, as the EC Department "accurately points out, the GRI is, and has been, holding up granting of mining rights by its own bureaucratic implementation of an awkward GRI mining law. Some effort is being made to speed up the processing, but the end of 1970 is still considered earliest date GRI will be in a position to seek CA approval for recommended exploration or exploitation rights."[163]

Bureaucratic procedures were one explanation for this delay. According to a subsequent internal memo from the EC Director, Edgar E. Hoppe, GRI had been "urged [by MITI for a long time] to go slow on processing the applications" which had been filed for oil exploration in the vicinity of the Senkaku Islands.[164] Moreover, in Japan, where a similar licensing system is used, one trained person could only process approximately about eighty applications per year, and as a result, GRI Trade and Industry staff said, contrary to what was discussed at the meeting on September 18, they did not expect much progress on the 25,000 applications prior to reversion, especially considering they had processed only 1500 between 1966 and October 1970.

The following week the *Ryukyu Shimpo* reported that MITI was planning to dispatch in the near future to speed up the process, however. The October 7 story, translated by the Public Affairs Department of USCAR in its daily "Okinawa News Highlights," generated much attention within USCAR, and the deputy civil administrator asked for more information.[165] Hoppe reported back the next day that MITI's policy had taken a "180-degree turn" after Taiwan's China Petroleum Corporation signed contracts on July 28, 1970 with U.S. firms Gulf and Amoco for joint surveys and exploration in the area.[166] At MITI's urging, the GRI increased on October 1 the number of staff responsible for processing mining applications from five to seven plus four temporary employees. GRI in turn asked MIT to assist them by sending seven additional people to work on the applications, and told the EC that they expected perhaps five or six of the seven would be sent.[167] According to the newspaper story, a date was not given when the personnel would be sent, if at all, but in the meantime, MITI had announced a few officials from the Okinawa-Northern Territories Agency would be sent to study the GRI's ability to handle the mining applications.[168]

About half a year later, USCAR requested a following up meeting with the GRI Trade and Industry Department mining/prospecting representatives, who met with the EC and Legal (LE) staff on February 12, 1971 on the current status of the processing of off-shore applications. GRI representatives reported they were still reviewing the "acceptability" of the applications, with special attention being accorded to 14–15,000 applications that are within the sea areas more proximate to the Ryukyus.[169] The preliminary screening was to be completed in March, and the second stage of the decision-making process, to determine which applicant filed first, would commence in April. GRI officials said the work was "still very complex" and that they were hoping to be in a position to make awards before reversion.[170] GOJ assistance had been useful in the past in expediting their work and would probably be requested again. USCAR officials reminded the GRI representatives again at this meeting as well that there was a requirement for CA approval prior to awarding any such rights. They understood, and stated they wished to work closely with USCAR.

At the end of the meeting, there was a discussion about the GRI plan to ask all three applicants to join together to form a single corporation rather than compete against one another. The GRI representatives seemed much in favor of this idea, asserting it would actually be less expensive in taxes, etc., for the three candidates, and that would also offer the best chance to direct the general benefits of the petroleum industry development towards the whole of the Ryukyuan people. It appeared that Omija, who many considered to have had the best chance for the choice locations, was resisting this consortium initiative, according to the GRI representatives' explanation.

McNealy wrote to Edward O. Freimuth, the former chief liaison officer for USCAR who had served in Okinawa consistently from 1946 to 1966 until he moved to Washington, D.C., to become the special assistant to the deputy undersecretary of the army for international affairs, to provide him an update on the issue of the mining/oil concessions. McNealy acknowledged that it was "still some months before HICOMRY [was] directly involved, but that date is approaching," with McNealy estimating that the GRI might reach the awards stage "by fall 1971."[171] The director of the Legal Affairs Department reminded Freimuth that USCAR reminded GRI officials that any final decision on mining applications could not be made without prior approval by the civil administrator, he admitted "it is always hard to predict what the GRI will do or say at the critical time," and warned that "even if they follow our instructions and pass the proposed awards to USCAR, we find ourselves in the avoidable position of approving GRI recommendations—and antagonizing Taiwan—or turning down the GRI nominee, so incurring the wrath of the prefectural people."[172] McNealy further hinted at problems with Japan:

> Where the GOJ will line up is also an interesting speculation, but I suspect the USG can't expect too much aid and comfort from that or any other foreign source. We will be damned if we do and damned if we don't. We could attempt to stall our decision, but I judge the Ryukyuans will 'demand' an answer almost at once to preclude the whole matter passing to GOJ control after reversion. As an old Okinawa veteran, I know you will appreciate the typical 'dilemma' aspect of this problem, which all too frequently characterizes U.S. options over here.[173]

McNealy ended his letter to Freimuth, which included copies of each of the above memos and summaries of the two meetings with GRI officials, noted that it would likely be the State Department that would "most probably have to work out the U.S. position," but he knew the Department of the Army would be interested in these questions and wanted to ensure Freimuth was aware of the status.[174]

Upon receipt of the letter, Freimuth spoke with his assistant, Edward O'Flaherty, who had been carefully following the issue and preserving records, and requested that a DOA policy be confirmed and guidance prepared.[175] Guidance recommendations were subsequently ready for the deputy under secretary of the army for international affairs in early May.

Brigadier General Clarke T. Baldwin, Jr., director, International and Civil Affairs at the Department of the Army, provided three possible courses of action, and laid out the pros and cons of each one:

1. One course of action would be to withdraw authority from the GRI for granting offshore exploration and exploitation licenses. However, this action would be highly critical in the Ryukyus as a retrogression of Ryukyuan autonomy. USCAR could probably bear the political heat generated

locally by such a step only if it were prepared to approve all requests for grants which favor Ryukyuan interests, to the probable detriment of U.S.– Taiwan relations. This course of action would thus compound the adverse aspects of the dilemma without achieving any compensating benefit.

2. However, if, as is recommended in the preceding paragraph, the authority to grant such licenses be left with the GRI, we feel that action should be taken immediately to ensure that the GRI will not fail to refer all proposed awards to USCAR for approval. One way of doing this would be for USCAR to develop a memorandum of understanding with the GRI, specifying the required approval procedures for processing the applications. One of the required steps, of course, would be that the GRI must refer its proposed action on each such application to USCAR for approval. This would effectively ensure that the GRI will not unilaterally grant licenses in controversial situations.

3. When the GRI submits to USCAR any recommended award for approve, one theoretical course of action which USCAR might take would be to make no final decision thereon before reversion, thus leaving these applications for the GOJ to handle. However, since the GRI apparently plans to submit its recommendations to USCAR this coming fall, USCAR could not appropriately defer its decision thereon for such a long time. This therefore was not regarded as a promising course of action.[176]

Baldwin recommended then that the "best guidance" would be for USCAR to "carefully review" all GRI-recommended awards to ensure that they meet the "usual legal and other requirements, that they involve no serious international complications, and that any adverse impact on U.S. interests [be] precluded or minimized," adding that "if a serious problem [were] seen to exist (such as a conflict of local laws or international boundary complications), USCAR will then be in a position to inform the GRI that the recommended award [be] disapproved."[177]

These issues, however, were the crux of the problem—honoring the spirit of local and national laws, particularly between GRI and GOJ, and the challenges of the regional dispute with Taiwan. It appears the above memorandum and recommendations provided no real or further guidance at all for USCAR officials, only a means to buy more time. Time, however, they did not have unless they were trying to hold out until the final buzzer rang in 1972 when the islands were to be returned. Time became shorter when tensions began to rise or unilateral actions by Japan, Okinawa, Taiwan, and China made the waters rockier.

The Okinawan response

As Taiwan, Japan, and the United States made comments and decisions on the concessions that affected the interests and future of Okinawa, the recently elected mayor of Ishigaki City, Tobaru Yoei, stated in August 1970 it was time for Okinawa to move away from being a poor, backwater place and instead become a "Petroleum Paradise (*Sekiyu Tenkoku*)," and called for the creation of a group to both protect and develop Okinawa's petroleum resources.[178] The inaugural meeting of the Development Council for Petroleum near the Senkaku Islands (*Senkaku Shoto Shuhen no Sekiyu Shigen Kaihatsu Sokushin Kyogikai*) was held in the meeting hall of the Yaeyama Branch Office of the Bank of Okinawa (*Okinawa Ginko*) on August 8. Nearly sixty individuals attended, including the heads of various organizations in the community, members of the Ishigaki City Assembly, and some other community leaders. Following the explanation of the purpose of the group by Tobaru and deliberations on the rules and scope of the organization, the participants voted to choose Tobaru chairman of the council. He was joined by several others who served as vice-chairmen and another twenty-nine in different capacities.

The council met again on August 19 to decide on its budget and plans, including raising awareness of the need to protect the petroleum and other natural resources near the Senkakus, leading to the creation of an Okinawa-wide organization, and to call on the Ryukyu Legislature and Ryukyu Government, as well as the U.S. government, to help protect the Senkakus and to promote their development "by the people of Okinawa for the people of Okinawa."[179] The council also agreed to send the following signed petition to the nine city mayors comprising the Okinawa Mayors' Association (*Okinawa Shichokai*), of which Tobaru was also a member.[180]

Petition to the Okinawa City Mayors' Association for the Promotion of the Development of Petroleum Resources near the Senkaku Islands

Much attention is surrounding the development of petroleum resources near the Senkaku Islands and mineral rights are becoming an international issue.

Whether the people of Okinawa are able to develop Okinawa's resources by themselves, or whether these resources are developed by companies from mainland Japan or worse, foreign countries, while we stand by and do nothing is a serious, Okinawa-wide crisis for the people.

In particular, we believe it is important to clarify the significance of this situation prior to reversion, thereby contributing to the development of Okinawa's industry, and think that the time has come to make a decision without remorse and take action.

Because of these reasons, we formed the Association for the Promotion of the Development of Petroleum Resources near the Senkaku Islands on August 8, 1970, in the Yaeyama area with the goal of taking action based on the autonomy of local authorities to positively promote the democratic development for the benefit of the people of Okinawa Prefecture.

Moreover, in order to see our efforts to protect the prefecture people's interests with regard to the petroleum resources and to provide for Okinawa a new era based on self-reliance, autonomy, and prosperity develop into a strong prefecture-wide movement, we decided to call on all the cities, towns, and villages as well as numerous organizations to participate.

We would like to ask your esteemed association to endorse the objectives of our activities and to give us special consideration.

1. We would like to see our activities develop into a strong centralized organization comprising all of the cities, towns, and villages, and regions.
2. We would like you to appeal to the Government of the Ryukyu Islands and other related organizations.

Upon receiving the petition, the Okinawa Mayors' Association met early the following week on August 24 to discuss the letter. Tobaru traveled from Ishigaki to Naha to attend the meeting, and personally explained its contents and the history of Japan's administration of the islands. Tobaru further explained his hope that the council created on Ishigaki would grow into an Okinawa-wide organization. After asking some questions, the Okinawa Mayors' Association passed a unanimous resolution agreeing to the request to support the council's work.[181]

Exactly one week later on August 31, the Legislature of the Government of the Ryukyu Islands passed its own resolution relating to the Senkaku Islands addressed to the President of the United States, Secretary of State, and High Commissioner.[182] It was titled, "Resolution Requesting Defense of Territorial Rights over Senkaku Islands," and read:

Resolution Requesting Defense of Territorial Rights over Senkaku Islands

At the moment that oil resources of Senkaku Islands have gained world attention and the prefectural people have come to place great expectations on their development, the Government of Republic of China awarded oil exploration rights to Gulf Oil Corporation of United States. Not only this, the Government of Republic of China is claiming territorial rights over the Senkaku Islands. The prefectural people are appalled by reports of these developments. The Senkaku Islands have, from the beginning, come under administrative jurisdiction of Aza Tonoshiro, Ishigaki City, Yaeyama. Before the war, the Koga Company of Ishigaki City carried out lumbering and fishery activities in those islands. In consequence, there is no room for any doubt regarding ownership of those islands. The Legislature of the Government of the Ryukyu Islands, therefore, protests the erroneous claim of Government of Republic of China, and requests that measures to bring about abandonment of such claim be undertaken on an urgent basis.

Resolved as above. 31 August 1970. GRI Legislature.

According to Knowles, the political advisor to the High Commissioner who would later serve as the first post-reversion U.S. consul general in Okinawa,[183] the resolution came about rather suddenly and was driven in part by local

Okinawa and domestic Japanese political considerations. Namely, the resolution was the result of "impulsive action" on the part of the conservatives within Okinawa, led by the Okinawa Liberal Democratic Party,[184] to "steal the march on the reformists" by introducing the resolution on the last day of the legislative session.[185] The OLDP apparently had sought to enhance its position on this "growing issue" in the upcoming September municipal elections and November 15 Diet elections (when Okinawan representatives would be chosen for the first time in the postwar in the national elections), and in light of reformists in Yaeyama having won the mayoral contest in March that year and taken the lead in establishing the above council to protect the petroleum and other natural resources in the Senkaku Islands from outside encroachment.[186] Despite the politics behind the resolution's submission and the suddenness of the action, it was adopted "without debate and without opposition," according to the reporting officer, because the resolution "reflects the sentiments of Okinawans in general, who believe the Senkakus should be staked out for primary benefit of Okinawa."[187]

The passage of the resolution was aided by the twin facts that the conservatives held a majority of the seats, having won eighteen of the thirty-two seats in the 8th legislative elections conducted on November 10, 1968,[188] and that the speaker of the legislature, Hoshi Katsu, was a member of the OLDP. Indeed, Hoshi himself was well versed in the Senkakus issue, having been born and raised in Ishigaki, teaching school at Shiraho Primary School (*Shiraha Jinji Koto Shogakko*), and later, in the postwar period serving as the deputy mayor and then mayor of Ohama-cho (now a part of Ishigaki City) followed by serving as an assembly member in the Yaeyama Gunto Assembly (*Yaeyama Gunto Kaigi*) before becoming a member of the legislature in March 1954.

Locally, the Ishigaki-based council held an emergency meeting on September 8 to call on the GRI, GOJ, and USCAR to make clear to Taiwan that the Senkakus belonged to Japan, and to strongly protest the illegal entries into the water areas and landings onto the Senkakus.[189] In addition, the council called on the Okinawa City Mayors Association, Okinawa Town and Village Mayors Association (*Okinawa Chosonchokai*), Okinawa City Assembly Speakers Association (*Okinawa Shigikaichokai*), and Okinawa Town and Village Speakers Association (*Okinawa Choson Gikai Chokai*) to petition the GRI, GOJ, and USCAR to protest as well.[190]

Two days later on September 10, Tobaru, on behalf of both the council and Ishigaki City, sent the following petition to Chief Executive Yara, the GOJ, and USCAR. Tobaru was close with Yara—both men had gone to teachers' school together (Yara was a couple of years his senior), worked on education issues together (Tobaru as chairman of the Yaeyama Teachers Association [*Yaeyama Kyoshoku Iinkai*] and Yara as the head of the Okinawa Teachers Association [*Okinawa Kyoshoku Iinkai*]), and were both center-left politically. Moreover, Yara had written the foreword to Tobaru's first book, *Yaeyama no Minshuka no Tame ni* (For Yaeyama's Democratization).[191] (The petition was several pages long, too long to print here, but it repeated some of the previous arguments.)

That same day, September 10, a meeting of the heads of the different bureaus within the GRI known as the *kyokucho kaigi* was held at which the directors agreed that indeed, the Senkakus were an integral part of the Ryukyu Islands.[192] The morning meeting was personally attended by Chief Executive Yara, Vice Chief Executive Chinen Choko,[193] and approximately a dozen others in Yara's own office on the third floor of the GRI building. The problem of the Senkaku Islands—both the issue of ownership as well as the development of the resources in the area—was the fourth and last issue to be discussed during their three-hour meeting.

Sunagawa led the discussions about the Senkakus. He was joined by Nakamura Shoichi, who was in charge of the Mining Division within the bureau. Sunagawa, who continued in that position through the summer of 1971 and was one of the longest serving directors, began with the conclusion of his office—that the Senkaku Islands belonged to Okinawa and that as such Okinawa had the right to develop the resources near the continental shelf. He gave four overall reasons for his office's view, all of which have been introduced so far and are abbreviated here. Sunagawa's fellow directors, including the four who were represented by their deputies, supported his office's recommendations and these in turn were agreed to by Yara and Chinen. As such, the directors' meeting came to the unanimous conclusion that the Senkakus were part of Okinawa. The Government of the Ryukyu Islands' statement, approved at the above directors' meeting and titled "Claim Concerning Territorial Rights and Continental Shelf Development Rights on Senkaku Islands," was released the same day and read,

> The Senkaku Islands are situated between 25 degrees 40 minutes and 26 degrees north and between 123 degrees 20 minutes and 123 degrees 45 minutes east. It is clear beyond any doubt that these islands belong to the Ryukyu Islands and are included in the area to be returned to Japan in 1972 for the following well-known reasons:
>
> A. The islands were discovered by Higa Tatsushiro in 1884 (native of Fukuoka Prefecture). From then until about 1917, Koga gathered feathers, turtle shells, shellfish and guano, and established a bonito processing plant on the island. The surrounding waters have been used as fishing groups by Okinawan fishermen.
>
> B. On the basis of a Japanese cabinet decision on 14 January 1895, and Imperial Order No. 13 of April 1, 1896, the islands were recognized as Japanese territory under Ishigaki-son, Yaeyama-gun, Okinawa Prefecture.
>
> C. Following the separation of Okinawa Prefecture from Japan upon the effectuation of Japanese peace treaty, this treaty and the U.S.–Japan agreement on the Amami Islands provided the basis for USCAR Proclamation No. 27, "Geographical Boundaries of the Ryukyu Islands." Article 1 of this proclamation defined an area in which the Senkaku Islands are

situated. Therefore, with regard to the continental shelf lying between the Senkaku Islands and China, we are able to exercise sovereignty-like rights of exploration and development of coastal and continental shelf mineral resources, based upon the concepts of the Convention on Continental Shelves, which has already become customary international law. In other words, according to this convention, delimitation of the continental shelf shall be determined by agreement among these nations. Where there is no agreement, insofar as no other just delimitation can be made on the basis of special circumstances, the convention provides that the delimitation shall be fixed at midway.

In the foregoing manner, our claim respects international law, and points to the human ideal of international cooperation. Our claim is sufficiently grounded in these respects.[194]

This was in fact the already-held view of the chief executive. The previous month, Yara stated at a press conference on August 18 his opinion, although it may have taken time in forming, that the Senkaku Islands were Japanese territory belonging to Ishigaki City, and that he wanted to announce the official position of the Government of the Ryukyu Islands as soon as possible following further study.[195] The September meetings gave him that chance.

The discussion at the directors' meeting was undoubtedly aided by the nine-part series of commentaries in the *Okinawa Taimusu* newspaper by the international legal scholar, Okuhara Toshio, an associate professor at Kokushikan University in Tokyo.[196] Okuhara had already published two articles earlier that spring about the history and legal status of the Senkaku Islands.[197] He was also working closely with *Nanen*, the semi-official organization formed in 1956 to work on behalf of Okinawa-related issues, that had published one of his articles in the March 1970 issue of its quarterly publication, *Kikan Okinawa*.

Beginning in April (1970), *Nanen* began gathering administrative and historical documents relating to the Senkaku Islands, and on September 14, it established the Senkaku Islands Study Group (*Senkaku Retto Kenkyukai*).[198] The study group was headed by *Nanen*'s chairman, Ohama Nobumoto, former president of Waseda University who served as Prime Minister Sato's advisor on Okinawan affairs and was born and raised on Ishigaki Island himself, and included former parliamentarian Takaoka Daisuke, who had already visited the Senkakus several times, Irie Keishiro, a prewar reporter raised in Shanghai and postwar international relations and law specialist who was serving as a visiting scholar at Waseda University, Hoshino Michihei, professor of geology at Tokai University, and Okuhara, as well as some officials from the Foreign Ministry, Ministry of International Trade and Industry, and the Tokyo office of the Government of the Ryukyu Islands. The Study Group continued to gather materials and analyze them from an international law and historical perspective, particularly as it concerned effective/actual control over the islands.[199] They were not unbiased—they saw as their mission to show that the Senkakus belonged to Japan.

Eventually, the Study Group published what would become the first of two edited volumes, entitled *Tokushu: Senkaku Retto* (Special Issue: Senkaku Islands), in quarterly journal about Okinawa called *Kikan Okinawa* sponsored by *Nanen* in March 1971.[200] The first volume, published in Japanese, was more than 260 pages long, and was "a solid work comprised of contents that could easily stand up to claims on the islands by Taiwan and China."[201] The chapters included: "On the Publication of the Special Issue on Senkaku Islands," an introductory chapter written by Ohama; "The Senkaku Islands and Japan's Territorial Titles to Them," written collectively in the name of the group; "The Legal Foundation of the Development of the Senkaku Islands Seabed," by Irie (who is also the father of the equally famous Harvard University historian, Iriye Akira); a dialog with several officials and scholars, including Hoshino and Sakurai Tsuyoshi, an official with the Okinawa Northern Territories Agency, on the development of the oil resources in the area; a personal account of the 1968 trip to the Senkakus by Takaoka; a short history of the Senkaku Islands by Makino Kiyoshi, a former deputy mayor of Ishigaki and well-known local historian; and an article by Okuhara entitled, "The Senkaku Islands and the Territorial Status Problem." Yoshida Shien, an official in the *Nanen* who had forebodings about the potential for the Senkakus and other outlying islands to be vulnerable to claims by other countries some two decades before that, wrote that he was "quite proud of the results."[202]

Because the issue did not go away, the study group continued its research and document-collecting. Late in 1972, following Okinawa's reversion in what would be the *Nanen*'s last research project, the Study Group released a follow-up volume, *Tokushu: Senkaku Retto Daini Shu* (Special Issue: Senkaku Islands, Volume 2).[203] Many of the authors were the same contributors to the first volume, but their chapters slightly differed, including the publishing in English of the earlier chapter written collectively. (It is clear they were trying to raise international awareness to Japan's claims, an approach *Nanen* had taken in the past vis-à-vis the United States in an attempt to influence American public thinking and policy makers.) Irie wrote on the Treaty of Shimonoseki and the status of the Senkaku Islands about the end of the Sino–Japanese War in 1895; Okuhara discussed the legal status of the islands during the Ming and Qing Dynasties, Ryukyu University Associate Professor of Japanese History Kishaba Kazutaka discussed the Senkaku Islands in the records of the tributary relations between the Ryukyu Kingdom and China; Makino wrote a detailed rebuttal to arguments that supported China's claims by Inoue Kiyoshi, a history professor at Kyoto University; and Hoshino published a short article on the continental shelf in the East China Sea. Despite the different chapters, the arguments were the same: the Senkaku Islands were Japanese territory.

Shortly before the study group was officially formed, Takaoka visited Okinawa again in June 1970 for his third trip to the Senkakus as an advisor to the Tokai University mission. While there, he met with Kuwae Choko, an Okinawa Liberal Democratic Party member of the Ryukyu legislature who had been serving as the chairman of the legislature's Special Committee on Reversion Countermeasures (*Fukki Taisaku Tokubetsu Iinkai*). Takaoka, who knew Kuwae through the latter's work as the chairman of the Association of Military Use Landowners (*Gunyochi Jinushi Rengokai*), told Kuwae that the central government was very interested in developing the Senkakus:

> The prime minister's office, the Mining Division of the Ministry of International Trade and Industry (*Tsusansho Kozankyoku*), and the JPDPC were all working hard to develop the oil resources in the Senkaku Island. However, because the islands are under U.S. administration, they can not be touched right now. It is very important the Government of the Ryukyu Islands create as soon as possible a special corporation, affiliated with the government (*tokushu hojin*) and begin to develop the resources. The government and the JPDPC have promised to provide their full and complete support. Chief Executive Yara Chobyo, Vice Chief Executive Chinen Choko, and Director of the Trade and Industry Division Sunagawa Keisho have been told about this and their support strongly requested. The cooperation of the Ryukyu Legislature and its encouragement to the GRI are needed at this time.[204]

Kuwae promised to raise the issue in the Legislature after learning more about the oil development problem. He gathered materials from the one of the oil companies about development prospects in the region, and about establishing a company of this magnitude, later working closely with Sunagawa from the GRI.

On June 29, during the party representatives' question time, Kuwae grilled Chief Executive Yara on his policy regarding the Senkakus, stating:

> I believe the development of the oil resources near the Senkakus will lead to the protection of permanent interests and thus the autonomous development by the people of the prefecture should be pursued. However, the newspapers are reporting that "Processing the Mining Claims is Being Delayed," the "Government of the Ryukyu Islands is Weak-kneed," and "Mainland Japan Will Scoop Up All the Profits, Bypassing Okinawa." I want to hear what the Chief Executive has to say about this. Also, I want to know that the Chief Executive's basic policy is about the development of the oil resources in the Senkaku Islands for the preservation of the long-term interests of Okinawa."[205] In response, Yara stood up and answered, "As I have stated in my message, I will continue with investigations in the Senkaku Islands and when it comes time to develop the islands, will move forward with creating an enterprise relating to natural

gas. I look at this—just one of our ethnic resources (*minzoku shigen*)—as a big plus for Okinawa's economic development, and will continue to study it."[206]

Kuwae was happy to get this promise from the chief executive and decided to follow up in the budget committee (*Yosan Iinkai*) of the Legislature. Kuwae continued as well to study on his own, and could not stop thinking about the possibilities of the development of the islands. "I could probably be accused of counting the chickens before they hatched," he admitted in his memoirs.[207]

In the meantime, Takaoka visited Okinawa again in August 1970 with Ikebe Yutaka of the Japan Petroleum Exploration Company (*Sekiyu Shigen Kaihatsu Kabushiki Kaisha*) and met with Vice Chief Executive Chinen to request the support of the GRI in creating the above special corporation.[208]

In light of all these and other movements in August and September 1970, in addition to the various resolutions, official statements, and rallies, Sunagawa Keisho, director of the GRI's Trade and Industry Bureau since December 1968, announced on September 26 its intent to create a Senkaku Oil Fields Development Corporation (*Senkaku Yuden Kaihatsu Kabushiki Kaisha*), which would pull together the efforts of the different players and stakeholders, including the three men who owned the concession rights, the government and other private individuals.[209] In addition, Sunakawa announced the corporation would handle the concession rights and examinations, but the development phase would include participation from mainland Japan was well. Moreover, he stated that five or six experts from the mainland would come to assist in processing the applications for concessions.

With this announcement, Ikebe traveled again to Okinawa in October, where he met with Chinen reportedly at the latter's request. They discussed the idea of establishing the special corporation, and Ikebe "promised his full support" for what he said was the GRI's idea.[210] In a for-publication discussion the following month with officials and others interested in the Senkaku problem that was included in the first Senkakus special edition of *Kikan Okinawa* mentioned above, Ikebe explained the concept of the special corporation.

The GRI would take the lead in creating the special corporation, according to Ikebe, which would be in charge of development. The funds necessary for this development, however, would be huge and thus the GRI alone could not cover it all. A certain degree of the rights to the area would be given to mainland companies who would do some of the work. The companies would not be paid in money for their work, but instead would be reimbursed when what they discovered was developed or turned into a final product for sale. In other words, costs would be reimbursed to the companies only when something was discovered and developed.[211]

After the moderator of the published discussion, Yoshida Shien, asked Ikebe who would be paying for the development costs prior to the finding of and production of the natural resources, Ikebe responded,

It is the same as if a Japanese group went to another country to do work as part of a contract. The mainland companies will work with the company that [a future] Okinawa Prefecture creates. The mainland companies could be given a fifty percent stake in the company in exchange for doing tens of hundreds of million yen projects, and the mainland companies would then receive fifty percent of the profits. In this way, the development could proceed. This is, in my opinion, the best way.[212]

Yoshida interjected that he thought that if this was the case, Okinawa would likely support the idea, and added:

Here is an example where the prefecture's interests and natural interests are one in the same. If the prefecture's interests aren't protected, the natural interest is harmed, and vice versa, the prefecture will not do well if the national interests aren't served. It is important to find that point where the interests truly converge. This is very much like the way the Japanese economic structure is right now. The government cooperates to help the companies. It will be a problem if Okinawa does not proactively participate in this arrangement.[213]

The above discussion took place on November 21, in Tokyo. One week before, November 15, 1970, elections were held to choose representatives to the Upper and Lower Houses of the Diet for the first time in the postwar period. In the Upper House contest, a close ally of Yara, Kyan Shinei, was elected from the reformist camp, and Inamine Ichiro, the owner of *Ryukyu Sekiyu* (Ryukyu Oil) and a strong proponent of development of the Senkaku Islands, was chosen by the conservatives. For the House of Representatives, Nishime Junji and Kokuba Kosho, were chosen from the LDP, while the three reformists were elected from three different leftist parties.

   Immediately following the GRI's announcement of its views with regard to the Senkakus, the Okinawa Prefecture Senkaku Islands Oil and Natural Resources Development Promotion Council, introduced above, was established on September 18, comprising forty-six organizations within Okinawa from the business, welfare, and private sectors. Taira Ryosho, the mayor of Naha City elected from the Okinawa Social Masses Party (*Okinawa Shakai Taishuto*), was chosen as the chairman.[214] The general purpose of the council was to be able to respond to the increased interest in the Senkaku Islands shown by the central government and mainland oil companies.[215] Specifically, it set out several goals for itself: (1) protect the oil resources near the Senkaku Islands and natural resources of all of Okinawa, and promote the democratic development of natural resources based on the principle of local autonomy and contribution to the interests and development of the people of Okinawa, and (2) gather materials on natural resources and development and conduct research, undertake public information campaigns to educate the people of the prefecture, develop a consensus of the will of the people and undertake efforts on their behalf.[216] It does not appear to have been too active, however, and Taira does not even refer to the Council in his memoirs.[217] Without further documentation, the cynical observer might even conclude it was simply a political ploy prior to the Diet elections for the reformists, although Omija had possibly placed strong hopes in it to help him.

With the elections behind them, Sunakawa and his team continued to work on the concept for a local corporation to develop the Senkakus. By early February 1971, the GRI was in the final stages of preparing a bill to submit on March 1 for the Legislature to consider that would promote development on the premise of Okinawa being the primary benefactor (*keneki daiichi shugi*).[218] According to the GRI, the legislation would cover requests for development of the Senkakus and other areas within the geographical delineations of the Ryukyu Islands. Requests for areas outside of this would be accepted but a final decision would be subject to discussions with the related countries in the future based on the principles of the Treaty on Continental Shelves. Sunakawa of the GRI also stated that the respective stakeholders have agreed in principle, but the details need to be worked out and would be done so parallel to the deliberations on the legislation.

By March 10, the GRI had received a total of 24,864 applications for mining rights from the three individuals (Omija, Furugen, and Shinzato) previously named. According to the Trade and Industry Division, there were forty stages to the process to check and grant approval to the applicants, and it explained it expected to be able to complete its work by October (1971) and give its approval to the applicants.[219]

Progress was hindered on that process as well as the creation of a corporation that spring, however. A series of scandals rocked the Yara administration in the early part of 1971, causing problems not only with the opposition conservatives but within the progressive camp as well. Moreover, Yara's more practical approach to reversion (focus on reversion first, and the base problems later) angered the more extreme elements of his progressive supporters. As tensions within the progressive camp deepened, Yara offered to resign, but his offers were rejected.[220]

Kuwae raised the issue of the corporation and the applications again on June 21, 1971, four days after the Okinawa reversion agreement was signed, during his question time of the chief executive in the legislature. After explaining the new information Kuwae had about the possibilities of the oil fields and the requests made to the GRI by the central government, he then asked what the status was of the applications made by Omija and the others more than two years before, and what the GRI's intentions were to create the special corporation. In response, a representative from the GRI stated, "We have already decided to recommend to the legislature that the special corporation be created. We also will deal with the issue of the mining rights before the end of the year."[221]

By early July 1971, it was becoming clear that the GRI would be unable to submit the bill. In addition to the differences with the central government on it, the GRI was having trouble reaching agreement with the three concession applicants from Okinawa.[222] The situation was desperate by early August, and the GRI decided to hold off on submitting the bill.[223] The death nail may have been when Omjia announced on August 6 he would not participate in the project.[224]

The situation worsened, Kuwae writes, when there was a change in the leadership at the GRI. Tensions within the progressive supporters of the Yara administration had apparently not calmed by his offers to resign. Eventually, some of the senior members of the administration tendered their resignations in the summer of 1971, including Chinen and Sunakawa, both of whom, Kuwae writes "did their best to help with the Senkakus issue."[225] Their replacements, Miyazato Matsusho and Kikukawa Hiroshi, "did nothing, and lacked an understanding of the importance of the Senkaku Islands," according to Kuwae, whose statue adorns a park in his old electoral district of Okinawa City, formerly known as Koza.[226] As an example of this, when Kuwae asked again about the status of the mining rights applications and the overall plans for the development of the Senkaku oil resources in his April 21, 1972 questioning in the legislature, the deputy director of the GRI's Trade and Industry Division, Kinjo Sakuichi, responded, "all of the applications will be handled by the central government at the time of reversion through a special measures law."[227]

Kuwae was livid, thinking about all the times he had been told by the GRI in questioning that it was handling the issue. He wrote in his memoirs that it was "extremely regrettable" the way it was handled, and noted that in the end, $3,182,361 was spent on application fees with nothing to show for it.[228] Kuwae accused Yara of mismanaging the issue. "As proof of your botching Okinawa's future, and this has to be told to future generations, the people of Okinawa could become the richest in Japan if the oil resources of the Senkaku Islands were developed. Instead, you let this slip out of your hands, and you will go down in history as having badly mishandled it."[229] We continue to see examples of how Okinawa Prefecture misses the boat again and again due to poor and delayed decisions today as well.

Notes

1 ECAFE was renamed ESCAP (Economic and Social Commission for Asia and the Pacific) in 1975, becoming the forerunner for APEC (Asia Pacific Economic Cooperation).
2 Niino is often introduced as a professor at Tokai University, but prior to his moving there, he was a professor at *Tokyo Suisan Daigaku*. He was a professor at the latter school when he wrote his 1961 paper. Tokyo University of Fisheries merged with another school in 2003 to become the Tokyo University of Marine Science and Technology, or *Tokyo Kaiyo Daigaku*.
3 Takahashi, *Senkaku Retto Nooto*, 9–10; Niino, H., Emery, K.O., "Sediment of Shallow Portions of East China Sea and South China Sea," *The Geological Society of America Bulletin*, Vol. 72 (1971), 731–62. Takahashi served as a standing board member of the pro-China trade council, *Nihon Kokusai Boei*

Sokushin Kyokai (Japan Association for the Promotion of International Trade, or JAPIT), which was established in 1954 to promote trade and economic relations with the People's Republic of China. Takahashi, who was the president of his own company, himself visited China on a regular basis, including in 1965 where he learned about China's growing interest in offshore oil development. In addition to the above book, Takahashi wrote at least one article about the Senkakus("Iwayuru Senkaku Retto wa Nihon no Mono Ka (Are the Senkaku Islands Japan's?)," *Asahi Ajia Rebyuu*, No. 10 (Summer 1972), 26–31), and co-authored with Tanaka Shujiro a book explaining how to trade with China (*Nicchu Boeki Kyoshitsu* [Learning About Japanese–Sino Trade], Tokyo: Seinen Shuppansha, 1968).

4 Emery, who went by "K.O.", was born in 1914 in Canada but studied in the United States under Francis P. Shepard, considered by many the "father" of marine geology. In 1962, K.O. joined Woods Hole, and in 1963 he was given the position of "senior scientist." See "In Memoriam: Kenneth O. Emery, April 14, 1998," Woods Hole Oceanographic Institution Media Relations Office. The author would like to thank the Information Office at WHOI for providing this article to me.

5 Takahashi, *Senkaku Retto Nooto*, 9.

6 "In Memoriam: Kenneth O. Emery, April 14, 1998."

7 Niino Hiroshi, *Umi no Chigaku* (The Earth Science of the Sea), (Tokyo: Tenzensha, 1944), and *Umi to Sono Shigen* (The Sea and its Resources), (Tokyo: Sanseido, 1951).

8 Harrison, *China, Oil, and Asia*, 45.

9 Ch'in Yun-shan, "Initial Study of the Relief and Bottom Sediment of the Continental Shelf of the East China Sea," *Hai-yan Yu Hu-chao* (Ocean and Lakes), No. 5 (1963), cited in Harrison, *China, Oil, and Asia*, 60, 279. Ch'in continued to work on this topic over the years. See Qin Yunshan, *Geology of the East China Sea* (Beijing: Science Press, 1997).

10 Ch'in Yun-shan and Hsu Shan-min, "Preliminary Study of Submarine Geology of China's East Sea and the Southern Yellow Sea," *Translations on Communist China*, No. 97, Joint Publication Research Service 50252, 7 April 1970, 12–36, translation from the original in *Hai-yang Yu Hu-chao*, No. 2 (1959), 82–84, cited in Selig S. Harrison, *China, Oil, and Asia: Conflict Ahead?* (New York: Columbia University Press, 1977), 58, 278. It is interesting to note that this work was translated in 1970, as much attention was being given to the area by this point.

11 Harrison speculates that when the head of the Italian state oil enterprise, Ente Nazionale Idrocarburi (ENI), concluded a controversial $200 million trade deal with China for refineries and related equipment, there "is reason to believe that other equipment related to onshore and offshore oil exploration was included in ENI transactions at this early stage." Harrison, *China, Oil, and Asia*, 60. Romania and France were also cooperating with China in oil development in the early 1960s as well, according to Harrison.

12 Harrison, *China, Oil, and Asia*, 90–91.

13 Harrison, *China, Oil, and Asia*, 91.

14 Takahashi, *Senkaku Retto Nooto*, 10.

15 Harrison, *China, Oil, and Asia*, 45–46. One of the Soviet studies referenced was M.V. Klenova, "Sediment Maps," *Oceanologia et Limnologia Sinica*, Vol. 1, No. 2 (1958), 243–54.

16 Emery, K.O., Niino H., "Stratigraphy and Petroleum PXX Prospects of Korea Strait and the East China Sea," *Report of Geophysical Exploration*, Vol. 1, No. 1 (1967), reprinted in the Geological Survey of Korea (June 1971) and in the *CCOP Technical Bulletin*, Vol. 1, United Nations ECAFE (Bangkok, June 1968).

17 *Ibid.* Niino published the Japanese version of the article in the journal *Nihon no Kagaku to Gijutsu* (Japanese Chemistry and Technology) in September 1967,

attracting much attention in Japan. See Kuwae Choko, *Tochi ga Aru, Ashita ga Aru* (When You Have Land, You Have a Tomorrow), (Naha: Okinawa Times, 1991), 175.

18 Harrison, *China, Oil, and Asia*, 46.

19 Takahashi, *Senkaku Retto Nooto*, 11–13.

20 K.O. Emery, et al., "Geological Structure and Some Water Characteristics of the East China Sea and the Yellow Sea," *CCOP Technical Bulletin*, Vol. 2, United Nations ECAFE (Bangkok, May 1969).

21 *Ibid.*

22 Harrison, *China, Oil, and Asia*, 50.

23 Harrison, *China, Oil, and Asia*, 50.

24 Harrison, *China, Oil, and Asia*, 50.

25 Inabuchi Shozo, "Senkaku Retto Meguru Senjin Arasoi: Hondo Fukki Mokuzen ni Shite, Taiwan, Chukyo, Kankoku mo Nanori (The Competition Over the Senkakus: Taiwan, China, and Korea are Throwing Their Names in the Hat on the Eve of Reversion to Japan)," *Zaikai*, February 15, 1971, 86.

26 "Japanese Oil Find Poses Title Problem: Japan Reports Huge Oil Find in Sea near Taiwan," *New York Times*, August 28, 1969.

27 Cited in "Senkaku Retto no Kaitei Daiyuden o Nerau Nichiryubeitai (The Large Seabed Oil Reserves near the Senkaku Islands Sought by Japan, Okinawa, the U.S., and Taiwan)," *Shukan Asahi*, Fall 1970, 135.

28 Park, "Oil Under Troubled Waters," 220.

29 Inabuchi, "Senkaku Retto Meguru Senjin Arasoi," 87. (Those still following Okinawa or working with its representatives would argue they have become even more politically active since then as well.)

30 Omija's first name can also be pronounced "Koju." Writings about him use both readings of his name. On at least one of his articles he wrote out the pronunciation to his name as "Tsunehisa" so I have chosen to use that one. See Omija Tsunehisa, "Okinawa Kaitei Dai-yuden ha Waga Te no Naka ni Ari (Okinawa's Big Undersea Oil Fields Are in My Hands)," *Gendai*, Vol. 9 No. 3 (March 1975), 358–63.

31 Park, "Oil under Troubled Waters," 221; "Senkaku Shigen no Shikutsuken (Mining Rights for Senkaku Resources)," *Kikan Okinawa*, No. 56 (1971), 39.

32 Koga, "Mo San, Sato San," 146, and Omija, "Okinawa Kaitei," 359. The family of the current governor of Okinawa, Nakaima Hirokazu, born in Osaka, was one of those who chose to "repatriate" to Okinawa in 1946, bringing him with them at the time.

33 "Senkaku Retto no Kaitei Daiyuden o Nerau Nichiryubeitai," 136.

34 Omija Tsunehisa, *Senkaku Yuden no Kaihatsu to Shinso: Sono Futatsu no Sokumen* (The Development of the Senkaku Oil Fields and the Truth: Those Two Aspects). Self-published report, May 15, 1970, and "Shuisho Senkaku Yuden ni Tsuite no Shinso o Akiraka ni Shi, Shikisha no Minasama no Gorikai to Go Kyoryoku o Uttaeru (Prospectus: Introducing the Truth about the Senkaku Oil Fields and Appealing for the Understanding and Cooperation of Well-Informed, Thinking People)," Self-published report, July 1970.

35 Koga, "Mo San, Sato San," 147.

36 Takahashi, *Senkaku Retto Nooto*, 9; "Insaido Repooto (Inside Report)," *Shukan Toyo Keizai*, July 26, 1971. An expert on trade with China, Takahashi felt the establishment of the JPDPC was a little late and that other countries already had the jump on Japan with offshore oil development. For more on the ministry, see Chalmers Johnson, *MITI and the Japanese Miracle: The Growth of Industrial Policy, 1925–1975* (Palo Alto, CA: Stanford University Press, 1982).

37 Koga, "Mo San, Sato San," 146–47.

38 "Senkaku Retto no Kaitei Daiyuden," 136.

39 Omija, *Senkaku Yuden no Kaihatsu to Shinso*, 12. Also see Omija, "Okinawa Kaitei," 147. The JPDPC was created in October 1967.

40 Oshiro Moritoshi, "Senkaku Retto Kobutsu Shigen Yobi Chosa ni Sanka Shite (Participating in the Preparatory Investigation of Mineral Resources in the Senkaku Islands)," in Senkaku Shoto Bunken Shiryo Hensankai, ed., *Senkaku Kenkyu: Takara Gakujutsu Chosadan Shiryoshu*, Vol. 2, 348

41 "Senkaku Retto no Kaitei Daiyuden o Nerau Nichiryubeitai," 136.

42 Koga, "Mo San, Sato San," 147.

43 Koga, "Mo San, Sato San," 147.

44 "Senkaku Retto no Kaitei Daiyuden o Nerau Nichiryubeitai," 136.

45 "Senkaku Shigen no Shikutsuken."

46 Inabuchi, "Senkaku Retto Meguru Senjin Arasoi," 89.

47 Koga, "Mo San, Sato San," 147.

48 "Senkaku Retto no Kaitei Daiyuden o Nerau Nichiryubeitai," 136.

49 Shinzato Keiichi, *Senkaku Retto no Yuden Kaihatsu ni Tsuite* (Regarding the Development of the Senkaku Islands Oil Fields), Self-published report, September 1970.

50 Inabuchi, "Senkaku Retto Meguru Senjin Arasoi," 89.

51 Omija Koju, *Shuisho: Senkaku Yuden ni Tsuite no Shinso o Akkirakani Shi, Shikisha no Minasama no Gorikai to Gokyoryoku o Uttaeru* (Prospectus: Clarifying the Truth about the Oil Fields near the Senkakus and Calling Upon Opinion Leaders for Their Understanding and Support), Self-published report, July 1970, 3.

52 Omija, *Shuisho*, 3.

53 See an interview with Taira and a member of the teacher's union, Fukuchi Hiroaki, in "Senkaku Retto no Kaitei Daiyuden o Nerau Nichiryubeitai," 138.

54 Koga, "Mo San, Sato San," 147.

55 Omija, "Okinawa Kaitei," 362, and "Uruma Resources Development Starts Prospecting Islands Off Okinawa; One of Few Promising Virgin Areas," *Nikkan Kogyo*, July 1, 1974. The company was established with 500 million yen in capital, and its president was Wakisaka Yasuhiko, executive director of Maruzen Oil. See "Seabottom Oil Fields to be Developed Around Okinawa; Toyo Oil Development to Begin Prospecting Areas around Miyakojima Island and Yaeyama Islands; Attracting Attention of Industry Concerned as a Clue to Developing 'Senkaku'," *Sankei Shimbun*, December 23, 1973. Today, the Uruma Resources still exists, with a capitalization of 100 million yen. Sojitz Corporation (*Sojitsu Kabushiki Kaisha*), the successor to Nissho Iwai, retains 72.3%, Cosmo Oil Company, Limited (*Cosmo Sekiyu Kabushiki Kaisha*, successor since 1986 to Maruzen Petroleum, or *Maruzen Sekiyu Kabushiki Kaisha*) owns 21.9%, Arabian Oil Company, Limited (*Arabia Sekiyu Kabushiki Kaisha*) 5.3%, and Osaka Gas (*Osaka Gasu Kabushiki Kaisha*) 0.5%.

56 Omija, "Okinawa Kaitei."

57 Park, "Oil Under Troubled Waters," 219.

58 For more on Ohama, see Robert D. Eldridge, "'Mr. Okinawa': Ohama Nobumoto, the Reversion of Okinawa, and an Inner History of U.S.–Japan Relations," *Doshisha Amerika Kenkyu*, No. 39 (March 2003), 61–80.

59 Takahashi, *Senkaku Retto Nooto*, 11. Takahashi introduced a different name for the ship, but the correct one seems to have been *Tenyo Maru*. Regarding the JPDPC, see Ikebe Yutaka, Sakurai Tsuyoshi, Takahashi Tatsunao, Hoshino Michihei, and Yoshida Shien, "Kaihatsu o Matsu Senkaku Retto no Sekiyu Shigen (Waiting to Develop the Oil Resources of the Senkaku Islands)," *Kikan Okinawa*, No. 56 (1971), 30.

60 Yoshida Shien, *Chiisana Tataki no Hibi: Okinawa Fukki no Urabanashi* (The Days of Many Small Struggles: Behind the Scenes of the Reversion of Okinawa) (Tokyo: Bunkyo Shoji, 1976), 220.

61 There are some discrepancies in the dates provided in the accounts by Takaoka and Yoshida. Since Takaoka's was written closer to the events, and is thus presumed to be more reliable, I am using his.

62 For more their work at this time, see Sakurai Tsuyoshi, "Kokueki to ha Nanika: Senkaku Retto ni Yoseta Yoshida Senpai no Jonetsu (What is National Interest: The Passion Our Superior, Mr. Yoshida, Showed toward the Senkaku Islands)," in Yoshida Shien Tsuito Bunshu Kanko Iinkai Henshubu, ed., *Kaiso Yoshida Shien* (Remembering Yoshida Shien) (Tokyo: Yoshida Shien Tsuito Bunshu Kanko Iinkai, 1990), 240–42. Also see Sakurai Tsuyoshi, *Okinawa Sokoku Fukki Monogatari* (The Story of the Reversion of Okinawa to the Homeland), (Tokyo: Okurasho Insatsukyoku, 1999).

63 Takaoka, "Senkaku Retto Shuhen," 55.

64 Takaoka, "Senkaku Retto Shuhen," 56. *Tokurenkyoku*, as it was commonly called, was established on May 15, 1958 within the Prime Minister's Office to handle issues concerning Okinawa, Ogasawara, and the Northern Territories. It combined previously existing offices into one bureau. It was replaced on May 1, 1970 by the Okinawa Northern Territories Agency (*Okinawa Hoppo Taisakucho*).

65 Takaoka, "Senkaku Retto Shuhen," 56, and Sakurai, "Kokueki to wa Nanika," 241.

66 Sakurai, "Kokueki to ha Nanika," 241.

67 Takaoka, "Senkaku Retto Shuhen," 56.

68 "Telegram 7122 from Embassy Tokyo to Embassy Taipei on Press Reports to GRC Claims Senkaku Shoto, August 30, 1969," Folder 4, Box 20, History of USCAR, RG 319.

69 "Telegram 3517 from Embassy Taipei to Embassy Tokyo on GRC Claims Senkaku Shoto, September 10, 1969," Folder 4, Box 20, History of USCAR, RG 319.

70 Philip Shabecoff, "Japanese Oil Find Poses Title Problem," *New York Times*, August 28, 1969.

71 "Telegram 3517."

72 "Telegram 3517."

73 Park, "Oil Under Troubled Waters," 224–25.

74 Harrison, *China, Oil, and Asia*, 91.

75 Harrison, *China, Oil, and Asia*, inside cover description.

76 Harrison, *China, Oil, and Asia*, 93.

77 "Telegram 3517."

78 "Telegram 3517."

79 "Telegram 6967 from Embassy Tokyo to State Department on Japanese Note, July 21, 1970," cited in "Chronology of Events, October 12, 1970," Folder: Senkaku Retto (Sento Shosho) (Tia Yu Tai), Okinawa Prefectural Archives.

80 "Chronology of Events, October 12, 1970," Folder: Senkaku Retto (Sento Shosho) (Tia Yu Tai), Okinawa Prefectural Archives.

81 Various dates are used in the respective documents and secondary research. See Park, "Oil under Troubled Waters," 224 (fn 37), as well as "Telegram 4174 from Embassy Taipei to State Department, September 24, 1970," Lampert Papers. The chairman of the board for Clinton was Robert B. Anderson, the former secretary of the treasury, who often tried to meet with Sato. Sato eventually pushed him off on to Tanaka Kakuei, his minister for international trade and industry. See diary entry for February 28, 1972, *Sato Eisaku Nikki*, Vol. 5, 54.

82 Suganuma, *Sovereign Rights*, 131.

83 Diary entry for August 14, 1970, Diary of Chiang Kai-shek, Hoover Institution, CA: Stanford University. Translation by Huajia Wang.

84 Diary Entry for Friday, August 16, 1970, Diary of Chiang Kai-shek. Translation by Huajia Wang.

85 "Chronology of Events, October 12, 1970," Folder: Senkaku Retto (Sento Shosho) (Tia Yu Tai), Okinawa Prefectural Archives. As of mid-October, the

statement had not been released, although one was released ten months later on June 11, 1971 on the eve of the signing of the reversion agreement.

86 Okuhara, "The Territorial Sovereignty," 103–4.

87 Okuhara, "The Territorial Sovereignty," 104, fn 30, citing the Chung Yan Newspaper (*Chung Yan Ry Bau*), September 26, 1970.

88 "Memorandum from Mary E. McDonnell to Thomas P. Shoesmith on Rival Claims of the GRC and Its Neighbors to the China Shelf, October 12, 1970," Folder 4, Box 20, RG 319.

89 Takahashi, *Senkaku Retto Nooto*, 22.

90 Takahashi, *Senkaku Retto Nooto*, 21.

91 "Telegram 3530 from Embassy Taipei to Secretary of State on Japanese Note, August 22, 1970," Folder: Senkaku Retto (Sento Shosho) (Tia Yu Tai), Okinawa Prefectural Archives.

92 "Telegram 5524 from Embassy Tokyo to State Department on Senkaku Oil Development, July 21, 1970," Pol 32–36 Senkaku Is, RG 59.

93 "Telegram 5524."

94 Okuhara, "The Territorial Sovereignty," 103, citing Sangiin (House of Councillors), *Okinawa Oyobi Hoppo Mondai ni Kansuru Tokubetsu Iinkai Gijiroku* (Official Record of the Special Committee on Okinawa and the Northern Territorial Problems), No. 3 (August 10, 1970), available at: http://kokkai.ndl.go.jp/cgi-bin/KENSAKU/swk_list.cgi?SESSION=27376&SAVED_RID=4&mode=1&dtotal=1&dmy=23439 (accessed September 2012). Also see, Takahashi, *Senkaku Retto Nooto*, 22.

95 Cited in Okuhara, "The Territorial Sovereignty," 103. Although Taiwan was about to ratify the convention, Japan still had not done so and has not to date.

96 "Telegram 3913 from Embassy Taipei to State Department on Senkaku Islands, September 9, 1970," Pol 32–36 Senkaku Is, RG 59.

97 "Telegram 3913."

98 Takahashi, *Senkaku Retto Nooto*, 24.

99 Takahashi, *Senkaku Retto Nooto*, 24.

100 "Telegram from Embassy Taipei to Secretary of State on Taiwan Provincial Assembly Resolution on Senkakus, October 29, 1970," Folder: Senkaku Retto (Sento Shosho) (Tia Yu Tai), Okinawa Prefectural Archives. The resolution gave the following reasons: (1) The Tiao Yu Tai Islands are part of the territory of the Republic of China. The Japanese government has no right to claim these islands; (2) According to historical documents from the Japanese occupation of Taiwan (period), the Tiao Yu Tai Islands were under the jurisdiction of Taipei County; (3) the Tiao Yu Tai Islands have been an important fishing area for Taiwanese fishermen in past decades. No country ever bothered their operations.

101 "Telegram 3872 from Embassy Taipei to State Department on Senkaku Islands, September 5, 1970," Pol 32–36 Senkaku Is, RG 59.

102 "Telegram 6988 from Embassy Tokyo to State Department on Senkaku Islands, September 5, 1970," Pol 32–36 Senkaku Is, RG 59.

103 "Telegram 6988." A later telegram reported that the Japanese Embassy in Taiwan had learned from the ROC Foreign Ministry that the ship visit to the Senkakus was "arranged" by the *China Times* and that the ROC had "nothing to do with it." See "Telegram 3913." This report was separately confirmed by the U.S. Embassy in Taipei. See "Telegram 3477 from Embassy Taipei to State Department, October 8, 1970," Pol 32–36 Senkaku Is, RG 59.

104 "Telegram 6988."

105 Directorate of Intelligence, *Central Intelligence Bulletin*, No. 0212/70 (September 4, 1970), 3. For more on the history of the CIB, which began as "Current Intelligence Bulletin" in 1951, see the declassified internal report, C. Fred Albrecht, Office of Current Intelligence "A History of the Central Intelligence Bulletin (SC No. 12416/68, May 12, 1967)," available at: http://www.gwu.edu/~nsarchiv/NSAEBB/

NSAEBB116/albrecht.pdf (accessed August 2012). Also see Ray S. Cline, *Secrets, Spies, and Scholars: Blueprint of the Essential CIA* (Washington, DC: Acropolis Books, 1976). Cline served in Taiwan as the CIA station chief from 1957 to 1962. In that capacity, he had a close relationship with the son of Chiang Kai-Shek, Chiang Ching-kuo, and was a strong supporter of Taiwan. Cline wrote about the younger Chiang and Taiwan after his passing in 1988. See Ray S. Cline, *Chiang Ching-Kuo Remembered: The Man and His Political Legacy* (Washington, DC: Global Strategic Council, 1989).

106 "Memorandum for Executive Assistant from Harriman M. Simmons, Director, Public Safety Department, on PS Staff Topics, September 10, 1970," Folder 6 (Civic Action Project Files, 1971: Senkaku Retto), Box 37, Records of the Operation Division, Public Safety Department, RG 260.

107 "Memorandum for Executive Assistant from Harriman M. Simmons, Director, Public Safety Department, on PS Staff Topics, September 10, 1970," Folder 6 (Civic Action Project Files, 1971: Senkaku Retto), Box 37, Records of the Operation Division, Public Safety Department, RG 260.

108 "Telegram from HICOMRY to State Department, September 6, 1971," Folder: Senkaku Retto (Senkaku Shosho) (Tia Yu Tai), Okinawa Prefectural Archives.

109 "Telegram from HICOMRY to State Department, September 6, 1971."

110 "Telegram from HICOMRY to State Department, September 11, 1971."

111 "Telegram from HICOMRY to State Department, September 11, 1971," Folder: Senkaku Retto (Senkaku Shosho) (Tia Yu Tai), Okinawa Prefectural Archives.

112 "Telegram from HICOMRY to DA, September 15, 1971," Folder: Senkaku Retto (Senkaku Shosho) (Tia Yu Tai), Okinawa Prefectural Archives.

113 "PS Note, Staff Meeting—17 September," Folder 6 (Civic Action Project Files, 1971: Senkaku Retto), Box 37, Records of the Operation Division, Public Safety Department, RG 260.

114 "PS Note, Staff Meeting—17 September."

115 "Telegram from HICOMRY to Secretary of State, September 15, 1971." USCAR reported that the handling of the matter was complicated by the fact that the GOJ PrepCom Counselor (Kaya) had initially told the police on September 12 that he thought the flag should not be removed. He modified this view by saying on the morning of September 14 that it could be removed but not at USCAR discretion, and finally later that day at noon, he "fell into step" saying that the GOJ desired the flag to be removed "with care." (Ibid.)

116 For more on the efforts of the Ryukyu Police to remove the Taiwanese flag, see the article by a member of the Yaeyama Police Department who traveled to Uotsuri twice in 1969, Nakamoto Masakazu, "Senkaku Shoto ha Nihon no Ryodo: Uotsuri Jima to Seitenhaku Nikki (The Senkaku Islands are Japanese Territory: Uotsuri Island and the Taiwanese Flag)," *Ryukyu Shimpo*, November 6, 2010. One of the boats the police used was the *Hayakaze*, a relatively small vessel that was not much larger than a typical fishing boat. A photo of the *Hayakaze*, docked next to a slightly larger U.S. vessel in Ishigaki, appears in the October 25, 1970, edition of the *Mainichi Gurafu*, a photo-news magazine of the *Mainichi Shimbun*. See "Namidakai Senkaku Retto o Yuku (Going to the Senkaku Islands, with Their High Waves)," *Mainichi Gurafu*, Vol. 23, No. 46 (October 25, 1970), 20. According to the story focusing on the Senkakus (written by Ono Katsunori) in the *Mainichi Gurafu*, the order to remove the flag was given by the U.S. Civil Administration for the Ryukyus.

117 "PS Note, Staff Meeting—17 September."

118 "Memorandum from John M. Ohira to Director, Public Safety Department, USCAR on Senkaku Island Report, September 16, 1970," Folder 6 (Civic Action Project Files, 1971: Senkaku Retto), Box 37, Records of the Operation Division, Public Safety Department, RG 260.

119 "Telegram from HICOMRY to DA, September 16, 1971," Folder: Senkaku Retto (Senkaku Shosho) (Tia Yu Tai), Okinawa Prefectural Archives.
120 "Memorandum from John M. Ohira to Director, Public Safety Department, USCAR on Senkaku Island Report, September 16, 1970." According to report, the police told Fukuhara that the fishermen were there to catch marlin and tuna, as that was the season for them then, and that the fishermen would probably remain there four to five days until they ran into a school of fish.
121 "Telegram from HICOMRY to DA, September 16, 1971," Folder: Senkaku Retto (Senkaku Shosho) (Tia Yu Tai), Okinawa Prefectural Archives.
122 "Telegram from HICOMRY to Embassy Taipei, September 16, 1971," Folder: Senkaku Retto (Senkaku Shosho) (Tia Yu Tai), Okinawa Prefectural Archives.
123 "Telegram from HICOMRY to DA, September 16, 1971," Folder: Senkaku Retto (Senkaku Shosho) (Tia Yu Tai), Okinawa Prefectural Archives.
124 "Telegram from HICOM Okinawa RYIS to DA, April 19, 1971," Folder 4, Box 20, History of USCAR, RG 319.
125 "Flag Taken From Senkakus Brought to Naha by Police," *Japan Times*, September 17, 1971.
126 "PS Note, Staff Meeting—17 September (Revised)," Folder 6 (Civic Action Project Files, 1971: Senkaku Retto), Box 37, Records of the Operation Division, Public Safety Department, RG 260.
127 "Telegram 152136 from State Department to Embassy Taipei on Senkaku Islands, September 16, 1970," Pol 32–36 Senkaku Is, RG 59.
128 "Telegram from HICOM Okinawa RYIS to DA, April 19, 1971."
129 "Telegram from HICOM Okinawa RYIS to DA, April 19, 1971."
130 "Telegram 1868 from Embassy Taipei to Secretary of State, April 22, 1971," Folder 4, Box 20, History of USCAR, RG 319.
131 "Telegram 1868."
132 "Telegram from Department of Army to HICOM Okinawa RYIS, April 22, 1971," Folder 4, Box 20, History of USCAR, RG 319. (This telegram is cited as a reference to "Telegram from HICOM Okinawa RYIS to DA, April 24, 1971," Folder 4, Box 20, History of USCAR, RG 319.)
133 "Telegram 1962 from Embassy Taipei to State Department on Senkakus: Return of GRC Flag, April 27, 1971," POL 32–36 Senkaku Is, RG 59.
134 "Telegram 1962."
135 "Telegram 2004 from Embassy Taipei to State Department on Return of GRC Flag, April 30, 1971," POL 32–36 Senkaku Is, RG 59.
136 "Memorandum of Conversation on Offshore Oil: Taiwan-Ryukyus Boundary and Related Matters, June 6, 1969," Folder 4, Box 20, History of USCAR, RG 319.
137 "Memorandum of Conversation on Offshore Oil."
138 "Memorandum of Conversation on Offshore Oil." For more on his involvement with China, see Robert W. Barnett, *Wandering Knights: China Legacies, Lived, and Recalled* (New York: M. E. Sharpe, 1990).
139 "Memorandum of Conversation on Offshore Oil."
140 "Memorandum of Conversation on Offshore Oil."
141 "Memorandum of Conversation on Offshore Oil."
142 "Memorandum of Conversation on Offshore Oil."
143 Several years later, Barnett, who had retired from the State Department and was serving as the director of the Washington Center of Asia Society, an organization founded in 1956 by John D. Rockefeller, III, to promote greater understanding of Asia in the United States, wrote in an op-ed suggesting ways the USG could "continue to respect the declared and implied One China commitments of the [February 1972] Shanghai Communique" in the following manner: "Washington could tell American oil companies we will be disposed to recognize Peking's assertion of sovereign claim to the entire shelf area of the Taiwan Straits,

including Taiwan, as being 'China,' with the practical consequences of this declaration to be worked out among all shelf claimants in East Asia within the context of law of the sea negotiations." See Robert W. Barnett, "Taiwan and the Peking Summit," *Washington Post*, November 21, 1975.

144 Author's interviews with Richard B. Finn, August, September, November 1997 and June 1998, Bethesda, Maryland.

145 "Memorandum to Robert W. Barnett, April 24, 1969 on Gulf Oil Company Request for Guidance in its Application for Concessions from the Republic of China for Oil Exploration Concessions from the Seabeds Around Taiwan—Possible Talking Points for Your Meeting, April 24, 1969," Folder: PET 10–12 Senkakus 1969, Box 4, Office of the Country Director for Japan, Records Relating to Japanese Political Affairs, 1960–75, RG 59.

146 "Memorandum of Conversation on Ryukyu Islands: Offshore Exploration Rights, August 21, 1969," Folder: PET 11–12 RYU IS, RG 59.

147 "Memorandum of Conversation on Ryukyu Islands: Offshore Exploration Rights."

148 "Memorandum of Conversation on Ryukyu Islands: Offshore Exploration Rights."

149 "Memorandum of Conversation on Ryukyu Islands: Offshore Exploration Rights."

150 "Memorandum of Conversation on Ryukyu Islands: Offshore Exploration Rights."

151 "Memorandum from H. L. Conner to Deputy Chief of Staff for Military Operations on Senkaku Oil Exploration, November 17, 1969," Folder 4, Box 20, History of USCAR, RG 319.

152 "Memorandum from Conner to Deputy Chief of Staff, November 17, 1969."

153 "HICOM Ordinance Number 33, Administration of Mining and Prospecting Rights, June 24, 1960," Folder: Senkaku Islands US, 1969.

154 "Letter from HCRI-LE to GRI, November 25, 1968," cited in "Memorandum from H.L. Conner to Deputy Chief of Staff for Military Operations on Senkaku Oil Exploration, November 17, 1969."

155 "Memorandum from Conner to Deputy Chief of Staff, November 17, 1969."

156 "Memorandum from Conner to Deputy Chief of Staff, November 17, 1969."

157 "Memorandum from Conner to Deputy Chief of Staff, November 17, 1969."

158 "Memorandum from Conner to Deputy Chief of Staff, November 17, 1969."

159 "Memorandum from Conner to Deputy Chief of Staff, November 17, 1969."

160 "Memorandum from Conner to Deputy Chief of Staff, November 17, 1969."

161 "Memorandum for the Record on Briefing at USCAR by GRI Staff Involved with Mining Rights in Senkaku, September 23, 1970," Folder 4, Box 20, History of USCAR, RG 319.

162 "Memorandum from LE to LN on Transmittal of a Request—Promotion for Developing Petroleum Resources in and around the Senkaku Islands, October 2, 1970," Folder 2, Basic Resource Control Files, 1970, Box 161, RG 260.

163 "Memorandum from LE to LN on Transmittal of a Request."

164 "Memorandum from EC to DCA on Mining Applications in the Senkaku Islands, October 8, 1970," Folder 2, Basic Resource Control Files, 1970, Box 161, RG 260.

165 "Note from Deputy Civil Administrator to Mr. Hoppe, EC, October 7, 1970," Folder 2, Basic Resource Control Files, 1970, Box 161, RG 260.

166 "Memorandum from EC to DCA on Mining Applications in the Senkaku Islands, October 8, 1970."

167 "Memorandum from EC to DCA on Mining Applications, October 8, 1970."

168 "MITI Officials to Assist Handling of Applications for Senkaku Mining Rights," *Okinawa News Highlights*, October 7, 1970 evening edition.

169 "Memorandum for the Civil Administrator on GRI Processing of Off-shore Mining Applications, February 16, 1971," Folder 4, Box 20, History of USCAR, RG 319.

170 "Memorandum for the Civil Administrator on GRI Processing of Off-shore Mining Applications, February 16, 1971," Folder 4, Box 20, History of USCAR, RG 319.

171 "Letter from Richard K. McNealy to Edward O. Freimuth, April 9, 1971," Folder 4, Box 20, History of USCAR, RG 319.
172 "Letter from McNealy to Freimuth, April 9, 1971."
173 "Letter from McNealy to Freimuth, April 9, 1971."
174 "Letter from McNealy to Freimuth, April 9, 1971."
175 "Memorandum from E. O. Freimuth to Edward O'Flaherty on Mining Rights in Senkaku, April 19, 1971," Folder 4, Box 20, History of USCAR, RG 319.
176 "Memorandum from Clark T. Baldwin, Jr., to Deputy Under Secretary of the Army for International Affairs on Mining Rights in the Senkakus, May 5, 1971," Folder 4, Box 20, History of USCAR, RG 319.
177 "Memorandum from Baldwin to Deputy Under Secretary, May 5, 1971."
178 Tobaru Yoei, *Sengo no Yaeyama Rekishi* (A History of Postwar Yaeyama), (Ishigaki: Tobaru Yoei, 1986), 502–3. Tobaru was a newspaper reporter and an educator who became mayor in 1970. In addition to this book on postwar Yaeyama, he authored two other works on Yaeyama, one on the eve of being elected about his life and times and the other about the Yaeyama reversion movement in the context of the overall larger Okinawan reversion movement. According to a later analysis by the High Commissioner's office, the association was partly created by reformists as a political maneuver vis-à-vis the conservatives. Also see Takahashi, *Senkaku Retto Nooto*, 22. Takahashi used the following name for the group: Association to Protect Petroleum in the Senkaku Islands (*Senkaku Retto no Sekiyu o Mamoru Kai*). The previous election in 1966 of a conservative candidate, Mayor Ishigaki, had been particularly controversial as discussed in the previous chapter.
179 Tobaru, *Sengo no Yaeyama Rekishi*, 505.
180 Tobaru, *Sengo no Yaeyama Rekishi*, 505–6.
181 Tobaru, *Sengo no Yaeyama Rekishi*, 506.
182 "Telegram from HICOMRY to DA on Resolution on Senkakus, September 2, 1970," Folder: Message Traffic Concerning the Senkaku Islands 1971–72, Box 11, Lampert Papers.
183 Author's interview with John F. Knowles, March 26, 2001, Alexandria, Virginia.
184 The OLDP, which had seen its internal divisions and splits, and was known as the *Okinawa Jiyu Minshuto* until March 1970, changed its name to *Jiyu Minshuto Okinawaken Shibu Rengokai* (League of Okinawa Prefectural Chapters of the Liberal Democratic Party) in an effort to further align itself with the LDP on the mainland of Japan in preparation for the upcoming elections to the Diet and reversion afterwards. It was headed at the time by former chief executive of the Ryukyu Islands, Ota Seisaku, who served from November 1959 to October 1964.
185 "Telegram from HICOMRY to DA on Resolution on Senkakus, September 2, 1970."
186 "Telegram from HICOMRY to DA on Resolution on Senkakus, September 2, 1970."
187 "Telegram from HICOMRY to DA on Resolution on Senkakus, September 2, 1970."
188 This election was called the "Sandai Senkyo" because there were three elections conducted at the same time: the election for the legislature, one for the mayor of Naha City, and one for the Chief Executive (governor) of Okinawa.
189 Tobaru, *Sengo no Yaeyama Rekishi*, 507.
190 Tobaru, *Sengo no Yaeyama Rekishi*, 507.
191 Tobaru Yoei, *Yaeyama no Minshuka no Tame ni* (For Yaeyama's Democratization) (Ishigaki: Tobaru San o Hagemasukai Akarui Ishigakishi o Tsukurukai, 1970).
192 Tobaru, *Sengo no Yaeyama Rekishi*, 509.
193 Chinen and Yara, both progressives, had long worked together, and even headed their own divisions (legal and education respectively) in the short-lived Okinawa Gunto Government under then-governor Taira Tatsuo from 1950–51. See Toyama Masaki, *Seiji no Butaiura: Okinawa Sengoshi, Seito Seijihen* (Behind the Scenes in Politics: Political Parties and Politics in Postwar Okinawa History), (Ginowan: Okinawa Aki Shobo, 1987).

194 "Telegram from HICOMRY to Department of Army on GRI Statement on Senkakus, September 12, 1970," Folder: Message Traffic Concerning the Senkaku Islands, 1971–72, Lampert Papers.

195 Takahashi, *Senkaku Retto Nooto*, 22.

196 Okuhara Toshio, "Senkaku Retto: Sono Hoteki Chii (The Senkaku Islands: Their Legal Status)," *Okinawa Taimusu*, September 2–9, 1970. Author's interview with Okuhara.

197 Okuhara, "Senkaku Retto: Rekishi to Seiji no Aida," 54–63, and Okuhara Toshio, "Senkaku Retto no Hoteki Chii (The Legal Status of the Senkaku Islands)," *Kikan Okinawa*, No. 52 (March 1970), 1–12.

198 Yoshida, *Chiisana Tatakai no Hibi*, 221. Also see Ohama's chapter, "Senkaku Retto no Kaitei Shigen to Jimoto no Keneki The Seabed Resources near the Senkaku Islands and Benefits to the Local Community," in his memoirs, *Henkan Hishi: Watashi no Okinawa Sengoshi* (The Secret History of the Reversion: My Post-war History of Okinawa), (Tokyo: Konshu no Nihon, 1971), 132–35. In it, he also discusses the issue of development of the resources including the efforts of Omija.

199 Yoshida, *Chiisana Tatakai no Hibi*, 221.

200 Nanpo Doho Engokai, ed., *Kikan Okinawa Tokushu Senkaku Retto*, No. 56 (March 1971).

201 Yoshida, *Chiisana Tatakai no Hibi*, 222.

202 Yoshida, *Chiisana Tatakai no Hibi*, 222.

203 Yoshida, *Chiisana Tatakai no Hibi*, 222, and Nanpo Doho Engokai, ed., *Kikan Okinawa Tokushu Senkaku Retto Dainishu* (Second Special Issue for Senkaku Islands), which was a special edition of *Kikan Okinawa* (Quarterly Okinawa), No. 63 (December 1972).

204 Kuwae, *Tochi ga Aru*, 176–77.

205 Kuwae, *Tochi ga Aru*, 177.

206 Kuwae, *Tochi ga Aru*, 177.

207 Kuwae, *Tochi ga Aru*, 177.

208 Kuwae, *Tochi ga Aru*, 178.

209 "Senkaku Yuden Kaihatsu KK no Setsuritsu e Kaihatsu, Hondo no Sanka de, Seifu, Kogyokensha, Minkan ga Shusshi (Toward the Establishment of a Senkaku Oil Fields Development Corporation, Mainland Participation, Government, Concession Rights Owners, Private Individuals to Contribute Funds)," *Okinawa Taimusu*, September 27, 1970.

210 Ikebe, et al., "Kaihatsu o Matsu," 36.

211 Ikebe, et al., "Kaihatsu o Matsu," 36.

212 Ikebe, et al., "Kaihatsu o Matsu," 36.

213 Ikebe, et al., "Kaihatsu o Matsu," 36–37.

214 Takahashi, *Senkaku Retto Nooto*, 24.

215 "Okinawa ni Senkaku Retto Kaihatsu Sokushinkyo ga Hossoku (Senkaku Islands Development Promotion Council Begun in Okinawa)," in *Kikan Okinawa*, No. 56, 78.

216 "Okinawa ni Senkaku Retto Kaihatsu Sokushinkyo ga Hossoku."

217 Taira Ryosho, *Taira Ryosho Kaikoroku: Kakushin Shisei 16 Nen* (The Memoirs Taira Ryosho: 16 Years of Reformist City Administration) (Naha: Okinawa Taimususha, 1987).

218 "Keneki Daiichi Shugi de Kaihatsu: Okinawa Sekiyu Shigen Kaihatsu KK Hoan Raigetsu Tsuitachi ni Rippo Kankoku (Prefecture Primary Benefactor of Development: Okinawa Oil Resources Development Corporation, Legislation to be Submitted on First of Next Month)," *Ryukyu Shimpo*, February 5, 1971.

219 "Senkaku Shigen no Shikutsuken," *Kikan Okinawa*, No. 56, 39.

220 For a concise summary of events during this time, see Sakurazawa Makoto, "Sengo Okinawa ni Okeru '68 Nen Taisei' no Seiritsu: Fukki Undo ni Okeru Okinawa Kyoshokuinkai no Doko o Chushin ni (The Establishment of the 1968

System in Postwar Okinawa with a Focus on the Trend of the Okinawa Teachers Association in Postwar Okinawa)," *Ritsumeikan Daigaku Jinbun Kagaku Kenkyusho Kiyo*, No. 82 (December 2003), 175.
221 Kuwae, *Tochi ga Aru,* 178.
222 "Chu ni Uku Rippoan Senkaku Kaihatsu KK Hondo Sochi Mitoshi Tatatazu (Senkaku Development Corporation Bill Still Upon in Air, Mainland Japan Measures Not Decided)," *Okinawa Taimusu*, July 4, 1971.
223 Senkaku Shoto Bunken Shiryo Hensankai, ed., *Senkaku Kenkyu: Senkaku Shoto Kaiki*, 331–33.
224 "Senkaku Shigen Kaikatsu KK Koso wa Zasetsu: Omijashi ga Fusanka (Frustration with the Senkaku Resources Development Cooperation Concept: Mr. Omija is Not Participating)," *Okinawa Taimusu*, August 7, 1971.
225 Kuwae, *Tochi ga Aru,* 178.
226 Kuwae, *Tochi ga Aru,* 178–79.
227 Kuwae, *Tochi ga Aru,* 180.
228 Kuwae, *Tochi ga Aru,* 180.
229 Kuwae, *Tochi ga Aru,* 180.

4 The Okinawa reversion negotiations and America's "neutrality policy"

Japanese concerns, Taiwanese pressure, and a looming China

Introduction

This chapter explores the negotiations over the Okinawa Reversion Treaty, which officially began in 1970 and was concluded in June 1971. It first reviews the decision to return the Ryukyu Islands before examining in detail the afore-mentioned negotiations as they related to the Senkaku Islands. It focuses on how the United States government assessed and handled the respective claims, counterclaims, and other pressures placed on it by the governments of its two allies, Japan and the Republic of China (ROC), with regard to the status of the Senkakus against the backdrop of the eventual (yet still-then secret) intention of the Richard M. Nixon administration to normalize relations with the People's Republic of China (PRC). It also looks at GOJ–ROC discussion on the issue and the eventual unsuccessful efforts by the USG to promote a dialogue between those two disputants in the hopes that a resolution would be found.

Background to the decision to return Okinawa

The United States came to occupy Okinawa in the spring of 1945 when it landed forces there as part of its larger wartime strategy to invade the main islands of Japan in the fall of 1945 and the spring of 1946. Although the war with Japan ended sooner than expected, the occupation and administration of Okinawa and the remainder of the Nansei Shoto, or Ryukyu Islands, would continue over the next twenty-seven years.

Pressure for the return or reversion of Okinawa actually began well before the 1951 Allied Treaty of Peace with Japan and impacted the U.S. decision-making process. Future Ambassador to Japan (1953–56) John M. Allison, who served as the deputy to John Foster Dulles, special envoy in charge of Japanese peace treaty, described it in the following way: "We were deeply impressed by the Japanese plea for the restoration of the Ryukyus and Bonin Islands. While we could not grant their wishes at the time, I believe it was then that Dulles conceived the idea, which he later announced at the San Francisco Peace Conference, that Japan should retain residual sovereignty over the islands but that they should administered by the United States."[1]

Although, as I discuss in detail in *The Origins of the Bilateral Okinawa Problem: Okinawa in Postwar U.S.-Japan Relations, 1945–1952*, it appeared that Japan might even be allowed to retain Okinawa at the time of the peace treaty through "practicable arrangements" in which, for example, the United States would maintain bases in Okinawa and Japan would be allowed to retain not only sovereignty but also administrative rights as well, that was not to be due to the strong opposition of the Joint Chiefs of Staff who wanted to retain control of the Nansei and Nanpo Islands indefinitely.[2] In December 1953, however, the Amami Islands, north of Okinawa were returned to Japan, and fifteen years later in June 1968, the Nanpo Islands, which include Iwo Jima and the Ogasawara (or Bonin) islands, were reverted without much difficulty.[3] These returns would become proof to Japan (and to the international community) that the United States did not harbor territorial ambitions which would have been in violation of the Atlantic Charter of war aims announced by President Franklin D. Roosevelt and British Prime Minister Winston Churchill in August 1941, and would each become preludes or models for the future reversion of Okinawa.

It was not until 1967, when the USG announced it was returning the Ogasawara Islands that it also formally committed to the reversion of Okinawa. At the summit meeting between President Lyndon B. Johnson and Japanese Prime Minister Sato Eisaku on November 14–15, the Japanese leader "emphasized the strong desire of the Government and people of Japan for the return of administrative rights over the Ryukyu Islands to Japan and expressed his belief that an adequate solution should promptly be sought on the basis of mutual understanding and trust between the governments and peoples of the two countries," and "further emphasized that an agreement should be reached between the two governments within a few years on a date satisfactory to them for the reversion of these islands."[4] Johnson "stated that he fully underst [ood] the desire of the Japanese people for the reversion of these islands," and the two leaders agreed to "keep under joint and continuous review the status of the Ryukyu Islands, guided by the aim of returning administrative rights over these islands to Japan in the light of these discussions."[5]

The understanding at this point thus essentially was a two-stage formula to realize the reversion of the islands: the USG agreed to decide within two or three years on a specific date for the return of Okinawa. This decision on the date was announced, after much preparatory work, by the next president, Nixon, who came into office on January 20, 1969, during a meeting with Sato on November 21 that year in Washington, D.C. There, the two agreed that "the mutual security interests of the United States and Japan could be accommodated within arrangements for the return of the administrative rights over Okinawa to Japan" and thus the two governments "would immediately enter into consultations regarding specific arrangements for accomplishing the early reversion of Okinawa without detriment to the security of the Far East including Japan. They further agreed to expedite the consultations with a view to accomplishing the reversion during 1972 subject to the conclusion of these specific arrangements with the necessary legislative support."[6]

The negotiating teams and framework for negotiations

Official negotiations began the following year over the return of the islands. U.S. Ambassador Armin H. Meyer, who had arrived in Tokyo in late June 1969 with an impressive diplomatic career but no Japan experience,[7] and Foreign Minister Aichi Kiichi, a veteran politician and key member of Prime Minister's faction,[8] were the chief negotiators, and would meet once or twice a month to "ratify the handiwork" of the American and Japanese negotiating teams.[9] The U.S. team was headed by Deputy Chief of Mission Richard L. Sneider, and comprised Howard Meyers, Charles A. Schmitz, Larry Dutton, and Dalton V. Killion with a handful of military representatives as well led by Vice Admiral Walter L. Curtis, Jr.[10] The Japanese counterparts included: Togo Fumihiko, Director of the Foreign Ministry's North American Affairs Bureau (*Hokubeikyoku*), Okawara Yoshio, and Chiba Kazuo, among others.[11] Nakajima Toshijiro participated as well as the chief of the Treaties Section, Treaties Bureau (*Joyakukyoku*) of the Foreign Ministry as did Kuriyama Tadakazu Chief of the Legal Affairs Section (*Hokika*) of the same bureau.[12] Yoshino Bunroku later joined when he succeeded Togo as head of the North American Affairs Bureau, having been brought back by Aichi who knew him from a previous assignment (although Ambassador Ushiba Nobuhiko had not wanted to lose him).[13] According to Kuriyama, the directors of the bureaus leading the negotiations—namely the North American Affairs Bureau and Treaties Bureau—were those who had been involved in the negotiations leading up to the revision of the security treaty in 1960. "There was a conscious effort to have our best members in charge," Kuriyama told an interviewer later.[14]

Sneider, who was a "Type A plus ... with sharp teeth and sharp elbows" according to one of the members of the U.S. team, had been on the Japan Desk at the State Department before joining the National Security Council under Dr. Henry A. Kissinger, the national security adviser to President Nixon.[15] However, Sneider had a falling out with Kissinger and went to Japan to head the negotiations. "He was a man who was very effective in getting his way and obviously often bruised people in the process," said Schmitz, who was brought to Japan by Sneider.[16] Sneider was a veteran of Japan affairs, having served in the Army as a Japanese linguist and helped in the interrogation of Japanese prisoners in the Battle of Okinawa and the deciphering of captured documents.[17] He later served in Japan from 1954 to 1958, when agitation was growing over the security treaty, and then became the first director of the Japan desk at the State Department afterwards where he worked closely with his Japanese counterparts, such as Togo, on the revised security treaty, signed in January 1960 and known as the Treaty of Mutual Cooperation and Security between the United States and Japan, which is still in effect today. From 1965, he was tasked by Assistant Secretary of State William B. Bundy to head an intragovernmental working group to prepare the way for the eventual return of Okinawa. Few, if any, in the U.S.

government knew the Okinawa reversion issue and U.S.–Japan security relations better than Sneider.

Shortly after everyone had arrived and the team assembled, Sneider was made the deputy chief of mission, and Schmitz effectively became the chief of staff of the negotiating team. Sneider continued to watch over the negotiations and do the "heavy lifting on the interagency concurrences and initial work on Congressional approval of the treaty," and Schmitz handled the "day-to-day job of finding solutions to the issues."[18] Schmitz in particular took the lead with the legal/political aspects of the treaty, and was primarily responsible for the agreed minutes (see below), including that regarding Article I defining the territorial delineation of the reversion agreement.[19] The talks would finish with the signing of the reversion treaty on June 17, 1971, and the remaining islands under Article 3 of the peace treaty, including the Senkakus, were actually reverted just eleven months later on May 15, 1972, becoming one of the first examples of territory, after the return of Iwo Jima, taken in war being returned peacefully.

Unlike the reversion processes for the Amami Islands and the Ogasawara Islands which were handled through bilateral executive agreements, the Okinawa reversion process was done through a formal treaty. This was an issue that Sneider and Schmitz, who had attended Yale College and Yale Law School and joined the State Department in July 1964 working in the office of the Legal Advisor, strongly disagreed on. Sneider thought it should be done through an executive agreement as he did not wish to have to "fool with Congress," but Schmitz, who had come to the conclusion that "Okinawa was a different kettle of fish qualitatively" and that returning Okinawa "was a matter of policy for the country," argued the State Department could not win the legal argument that the Iwo Jima precedent would apply and thus they would have to go to the Senate for ratification.[20] Schmitz turned out to be correct, and the treaty route was pursued.

In retrospect, it was the correct decision from the State's perspective. Even Sneider admitted he was wrong, Schmitz noted in an oral history twenty years after the treaty was signed. "The reason he did that was because had he won, we would have lost in the negotiations because we had on our side in the negotiations a very powerful argument for nearly every one of these delicate issues and that was, 'you might be able to persuade us, but how the hell are we going to persuade the Senate of the United States'," Schmitz explained, describing the "irrational partner" model, adding, "So the effect was to benefit Sneider, benefit the Embassy, and benefit the State Department because this was a very important negotiation."[21]

According to Schmitz, "there were about a thousand issues that had to be resolved government to government in that negotiation."[22] With the big policy decision made, namely that to return administrative rights over the Ryukyu Islands to Japan, the issues became technical in nature, but many of them, like the Senkaku Islands, had big policy implications in turn. The Department of State vetted the big policy implications internally within the Department and within the USG between the State Department, High

Commissioner's Office, White House, Department of Defense, and other interested agencies. At State, it was initially Richard B. Finn, a long-time Japan specialist, who had been handling Japan and Okinawa matters at the Country Director for Japan at the State Department since January 1969.[23] He was succeeded in September 1970 by Richard A. Ericson, Jr., a diplomat with long experience in Northeast Asia who had just returned from the Tokyo Embassy where he was serving as the political counselor initially under U. Alexis Johnson. Ericson was there for the majority of the time for the difficult negotiations and coordination on the Senkakus issue.

According to the Northeast Asia correspondent Don Oberdorfer, Ericson was "not a typical suave, striped-pants diplomatic type."[24] His very frank oral history with its blunt assessments of policy and people shows why. For example, Ericson found Ambassador Meyer, a Middle East expert who had succeeded Johnson, "never at ease in Japan. He was very uncomfortable with Japan specialists, too."[25] Ericson attributed Meyer's being uncomfortable to the fact that the ambassador had an inflated but undeserved ego, and that there were many senior members of his staff who were Jewish, including Sneider, which apparently bothered the Arab specialist. With Sneider "a very aggressive, hard charging kind of guy ... the two of them did not pull terribly well in harness ... So, we had a very uneasy ambassador on our hands," Ericson reminisced.[26]

The same could probably be said of Nixon and Kissinger. Neither paid much attention to Japan, at least initially. "Particularly Kissinger," Ericson recalled,

> who paid much less attention to Japan than Japan warranted. There was also the fact that when they did pay attention to Japan, when did have something they wanted done, they did not use the embassy to do it. ... [they] never felt secure working with career specialists. They seemed to feel that these people, especially the State Department, were out to do them in ... When Kissinger did want to accomplish something in Japan, he worked through his own emissaries and used CIA communications. The Embassy did not see the messages that went back and forth between his people when they were in Tokyo and we were not consulted on what the hell it was he was doing ... Kissinger and Nixon shared the conviction that in virtually any country you could get things done by getting to the one politician who had the power, and that there was such an individual. All you had to do was find him and pull his lever. That was the way to do it and you could safely ignore the bureaucracies, etc. Well, maybe you could safely ignore the bureaucracies in the United States, but you can't do it in Japan. But they were convinced that this was the case. Whether they were successful or not, I really don't know. Did they irritate the Embassy? Yes![27]

With this said, Ericson was able to give praise where it was due. The "decision to revert Okinawa ... something that Alex [Johnson] has to be given enormous credit for ... was probably one of the finest accomplishments of American diplomacy anywhere, anytime, anyhow. A peaceful return of territory to a defeated enemy negotiated in friendship and peace and done with great smoothness."[28]

Above Ericson was Winthrop G. Brown, who "handled Okinawa," according to one member of the staff, as the deputy assistant secretary of State for East Asia and the Pacific, where he had been serving since 1968. Brown, who replaced Robert W. Barnett, had never served in Japan, China, or Taiwan, but had held a variety of posts in the larger Asia-Pacific region, including as deputy chief of mission in New Delhi, and ambassador to both Laos and later South Korea.

Brown's immediate boss was Assistant Secretary of State Marshall Green, a veteran Foreign Service Official who served in pre-war Japan as an aide to Ambassador Joseph C. Grew and was an East Asian regional policy planner in the 1950s under Secretary of State John Foster Dulles. Above Green was U. Alexis Johnson as undersecretary for Political Affairs whom Ericson had also known when he served in Yokohama in the early postwar period and Johnson was consul general as well as more recently when Johnson was ambassador to Japan (1967–69). Although one member of the staff said they avoided bothering Green, who "had Vietnam on his plate," and instead worked with Brown, there were instances where the assistant secretary was directly involved particularly in the last few highly charged weeks before the signing of the Okinawa Reversion Treaty.[29]

Heading the State Department at the time was Secretary of State William P. Rogers, a lawyer and close friend of Nixon who was overshadowed in foreign affairs by Kissinger. Once Kissinger and the White House had worked out the overall Okinawa reversion deal, including agreeing to the Japanese principles of "reversion by 1972, without nuclear weapons, on par with the mainland," the details of the reversion agreement were left to Foggy Bottom, the nickname for the State Department, and specifically the team working in Tokyo at the Embassy and being supported by the Japan Desk back in D.C. with input from military, Department of the Army, and State Department officials in Okinawa working for USCAR and the High Commissioner's Office.

Although the Japan Desk was one of the largest in the State Department at the time with about seven officers and three secretaries Ericson had only one person, Howard M. McElroy, working on the Okinawa reversion negotiations, who "did an absolutely superb job."[30] In Ericson's view, "[the desk] worked quite well in the sense that Marshall Green ... did funnel everything that came to EA involving Japan to us. We worked very closely with and through him."[31] Ericson continued,

> The negotiations themselves with the Japanese took place in Tokyo and were done primarily through Dick Sneider and his operation. Our role was the formulation of the instructions to Sneider and his team, receipt of his reports of their meetings with the Japanese, consultations with the

Defense Department, consultations within the State Department, referral where necessary to the NSC and the White House, and then the sending of approved instructions back to Sneider and his time to agree or disagree or to get this point or not to get that point. It was a very busy time.[32]

In addition, both Ericson and Schmitz had high praise for the Japanese team negotiating the reversion treaty. There were "a great bunch of people at the Foreign Office at that time," Ericson said in a 1995 oral history.[33]

The two politicians that were the Foreign Minister and the Vice Minister were absolutely superb. The director of the North American Bureau, Togo Fumihiko, who later became ambassador in Washington, was probably the best friend the United States ever had in Japan ... He was neither [articulate in foreign languages nor possessed an outgoing personality]. Even in conversations with us in his office about Okinawa, he would open with a hesitantly delivered, brief statement and then turn the discussion over to his deputy, Okawara, who was also [later] ambassador here, or to the American Desk chief, Chiba Kazuo, and let them do all the talking in English. Then Togo would wrap it up at the end. But there was never any question of who was in control on their side. He just couldn't articulate in English. He had the same kind of difficulty in Japanese, although they tell me he was a holy terror sometimes when crossed or displeased. But right down to the junior desk officers they had great personnel, and they accorded Togo great respect.[34]

On the Japanese side, Kuriyama highly praised the Americans: "The American side was very reasonable in its dealings with us. We said what had to be said ... and were able to realize these hopes ... for the most part, we got what we wanted."[35] Yoshino, who interacted with senior officials on the U.S. side as North American Affairs director general and prior to his returning to Tokyo had been at the Japanese Embassy in Washington, D.C., similarly had high praise for the U.S. side, feeling Sneider, for example, "listened carefully" to what he said and was certainly not abrasive with his Japanese counterparts; an attitude presumably held exclusively by his American colleagues.[36]

The eventual return of Okinawa was hailed by both governments as "epoch-making," but domestically, especially in Japan, and regionally there was much criticism at the time (a topic discussed in the next chapter). One of the most controversial issues had to do with the uncertain status internationally of the Senkakus. As this chapter will introduce, while the United States had announced the Senkakus were included in the treaty area as part of the Ryukyu Islands to be returned and was aware there was a dispute between Japan and the Taiwan (and eventually the PRC) on the islands, it took no position on the claims to the Senkaku Islands. The Japanese side, on the other hand, desired to see the United States publicly (and in writing in the reversion treaty) recognize Japan's *full* and questionable sovereignty over the Senkakus and had to settle for somewhat less, although it remains in administrative control of the islands today. The ROC, in the meantime, was successful in asserting its claims enough to raise attention to the dispute, discourage the United States from automatically "recognizing" sovereignty over the Senkaku Islands to Japan, and pressuring Japan (both bilaterally and through the United States) to talk about the issue, albeit with limited success (as of the time of this writing, 2013, the 41st anniversary of the reversion of Okinawa, Japan still denies there is a territorial dispute between it and China and Taiwan but is willing to discuss joint development of the continental shelf). The ROC was unsuccessful in getting the United States to recognize ROC sovereignty over the Senkakus or even giving it any positive control in the administration of the islands. It was also unsuccessful in preventing the reversion of the Senkaku Islands to Japan as it had demanded. In the meantime, the very existence regionally of the PRC, which was not recognized by the United States, Japan, or of course the ROC, nevertheless became a player in the dispute indirectly through its statements and increasingly pushed Taiwan out of, or at least co-held, its role of defender of Chinese national interests.

Before we look at the negotiations over the status of the Senkakus in the reversion agreement, it is necessary to look at how a rise in tensions over the Senkakus during the summer and early fall impacted the reversion negotiations.

Intrusion of the Senkakus Issue: Summer-Fall 1970

As discussed in the previous chapter, the countries in the region, Japan and Taiwan especially, as well as Okinawa (known as the Government of the Ryukyu Islands at the time), expressed a growing interest in the possibilities for development or exploitation of its resources that the Senkaku Islands possessed following the announcement of the results of the ECAFE study in May 1969. Numerous applications for concessions began to be filed in Okinawa and Taiwan, and Japan was sending regular study missions to the islands. In July 1970, the ROC granted a U.S. oil company, Pacific Gulf, the right to explore and exploit the resources near the Senkakus. Later that month, it prepared legislation concerning the exploration and drilling for oil and gas and the following month rejected Japanese claims to the Senkakus. Japan and Taiwan, both allies of the United States, began a war of words which saw an escalation in the diplomatic and political maneuvering vis-à-vis each other, their domestic constituents, and the United States.

The U.S. government did not watch the rise in tensions between its two allies with indifference. However, it is clear that it intended to maintain a neutral policy despite regular and sometimes enormous pressure from both the Japanese and Taiwanese sides described later. This desire was first articulated in a February 27, 1970, letter from McElroy, a former Marine who had served in Japan, to Schmitz, in which the comments of the Japan Desk were provided to a draft general agreement: "Article 1; we would prefer to stick to the description used in Art. III of the Peace Treaty, avoiding the Senkaku problem."[37]

This desire was apparent in a telegram the State Department sent to the American Embassy in Taipei on August 11, 1970, in the middle of the above dispute. It noted that the Japanese Embassy (in Washington, D.C.) "had not [yet] asked for a definition of the term 'Nansei Shoto'," but as the treaty negotiations were about to start that if it did, the U.S. government would take the following position:

> Term as used in Article III of Japanese Peace Treaty was intended to include Senkaku Shoto (Senkaku Gunto). Nansei Shoto, as used in Treaty, refers to all islands south of 29 degrees north latitude, under Japanese administration at end of Second World War, that were not otherwise specifically referred to in the Treaty.
>
> Under the Treaty, the USG administers the Senkaku Islands as part of the Ryukyu Islands, but considers that residual sovereignty over the Ryukyus remains with Japan. Administration of Ryukyus, it is anticipated, will revert to Japan in 1972.
>
> The USG considers that any conflicting claims to Senkakus and continental shelf areas adjacent to them are a matter for resolution by the claimants.[38]

The State Department clarified its position in a follow-up telegram on August 19 by explaining paragraph c in the August 11 telegram was "not intended to cast doubt on Japan's sovereignty over these islands but merely to indicate that, in the event of a sovereignty dispute over Senkaku Islands should arise, neither Peace Treaty nor Reversion agreement would be dispositive of claim which would have to be resolved by claimants or, if they choose, through third party adjudication" such as by the International Court of Justice.[39]

Around that time on August 20, Chiba, the director of the First North American Division in the Foreign Ministry, met with Sneider and his staff to brief them on the debate within Japan on the Senkakus, and the discussions between Japan and the ROC. In response to a question in the Lower House Committee on Commerce and Industry (*Shoko Iinkai*), Counselor Kanazawa Masao of the Foreign Ministry's Asia Division (*Ajia Kyoku*) had expressed the government's opinion that unilateral statements by the ROC did not determine the merits of the issue (particularly in the context of the continental shelf), and added that the issue should be settled by international law between the parties, as the Government of the Republic of China was aware of the GOJ's position. Moreover, he noted that the GRC had not accepted the Japanese government's request to negotiate the matter.[40]

Chiba continued, explaining that the GOJ "had never understood" that the GRC had "significant doubts as to the status of the Senkakus," and noted the concern, which was also shared by the U.S. Embassy and State Department, that the two issues of the status of the Senkaku Islands and the question of the continental shelf surrounding the Senkakus were being blurred, especially by the media in Taiwan.[41] Embassy officers stated their agreement that "it would seem to be in everyone's interest to avoid blurring this important distinction."[42]

Chiba, who as a young member of the Imperial Japanese Navy had participated in the planning for the Battle of Okinawa,[43] stated that while the GOJ did not consider any action by the USG, as administrator of the islands, was necessary at the moment, there were those within the Japanese government who felt American "involvement" was "desirable."[44] He also mentioned that if the territorial issue of the Senkakus was raised, the GOJ planned to use the absence of any objections by the GRC to the delimitation of the Ryukyu Islands by Proclamation 27 of December 1953, or any of the earlier ones as evidence of GRI acquiescence.

While not raised at this point, there have been many other examples of Taiwanese and Chinese officials and official publications describing the Senkaku Islands as part of Japan over the years which the USG was surely aware of. These are discussed in more detail in Chapter 5.

It does not appear that Chiba or other officials discussed these matters at this time with the U.S. Embassy, but in any case, Sneider was worried about Japanese desires to see the United States involved, and responded that the USG was "not at all anxious to become caught in middle between GRC and GOJ on this issue," and his staff added that the High Commissioner in Okinawa had directed the posting of signs in three languages to "forestall possible GRC claims based on occasional visits by Chinese fishermen."[45] They could not answer if the signs were still there when Chiba asked them, stating that the U.S. government had "no recent information since the Senkakus were not easily accessible from Okinawa."[46] Info'ing the telegram to the High Commissioner's office, the Embassy suggested "it might be helpful if we could assure from time to time that Senkaku Islands remain posted."[47]

One of the most insightful parts of the conversation came however when Chiba discussed the "developing polarization" in the Japanese government on the issue of the Senkakus. He said that the "hawks" on the issue were centered around Yamanaka Sadanori (of the Nakasone Yasuhiro faction[48]), the director general of the Prime Minister's Office, and Yamano Kokichi,[49] the head of the Okinawa-Northern Territories Agency (*Okinawa-Hoppo Taisakucho*), which had come into being on May 1 that year as an external agency of the Prime Minister's Office to prepare for the return of Okinawa, on one side, and the "doves," primarily the lawyers in the Treaties Bureau of the Foreign Ministry who seemed uncertain about some of the legal arguments. Eventually the lawyers came to strongly support the government's case due to a combination of the need for unity, internal political pressure, or more likely some merits of the case.

Sneider urged "restraint" by the GOJ at least until the position of the GRC became clearer.[50] In addition to pointing out the complex legal and political difficulties involved in the issue, Sneider presciently warned that "Peking might decide that action on its part is necessary."[51] Indeed, that is what happened, and what also partly motivated the government of the ROC—its fear that Peking would seek to replace Taipei as the defender of Chinese national interests.

About ten days after this discussion, Foreign Minister Aichi raised the Senkaku issue with Ambassador Meyer at their meeting on August 31, and expressed the hope that the USG would not object to a GOJ statement to the effect that the United States had in the past stated in proclamations that the Senkakus are part of the Ryukyus. The Japanese government, he added, might make "an explicit reference to establishing area containing Ryukyu Islands and to indicate specifically that the Senkakus were within that area."[52] Meyer responded that indeed the USG administered the Senkakus "as part of the Ryukyus" and that U.S. proclamations so indicate, but explained (on instructions from the State Department) that it was concerned "not to be caught in the middle of dispute" involving Japan and Taiwan.[53] Meyer added his country believed the "dispute should be between claimants to territory and should not involve the USG."[54]

That same day the Foreign Ministry had instructed its embassy in Taipei to inform the GRC that the Japanese government took the position that "there is no doubt whatsoever about sovereignty of Senkaku Islands," and that whatever action the GRC might take on the continental shelf, the GOJ position on the continental shelf in the area of the Senkaku Islands "cannot be affected."[55] The U.S. Embassy in Tokyo, which had read press reports that the GOJ was going to approach the GRC on this issue, inquired about the media stories to the Foreign Ministry, and was told in confidence by Sato of the North American Affairs Bureau of MOFA on September 4, that such instructions had been given but that it had received no confirmation that the approach had been made nor had they received any indication as to the GRC reaction.

In the meantime, tensions flared and the United States was more directly brought into the dispute when on September 2, the crew of a GRC Marine Research Laboratory vessel, along with some journalists from the *China Times*, planted a Taiwanese flag on Uostsuri Island, a fact that become known on the 4th. The flag-planting became a direct matter for the USG not only locally as administrator in coordinating with GRI Police, as explained in Chapter 3, but bilaterally as well as with its embassies in Taipei and Tokyo getting involved.[56] It became linked to the status of the Senkaku Islands in the reversion agreement when early the following week in Washington, Japanese Embassy official Kiuchi Akitane called on Japan Country Director Ericson to inform him that the Japanese public was increasingly concerned about the incident and the GRC's attitudes toward the Senkakus.[57] Kiuchi stated that the GOJ position in Diet interpellations scheduled that week would be "eased" by a public statement by the U.S. Government on Japanese residual sovereignty over the Senkakus.[58] Ericson explained that the USG would have no objection to the Japanese government referencing that position, but opined that the USG was unlikely to release such a public statement itself.

Likely coordinated ahead of time, around same day in Taipei, Charge d'affaires Muto Takeshi showed an official at the U.S. Embassy a copy of a note from the GRC, dated August 19, in which the GRC rejected the Japanese claim to the Senkakus and Japan's rights to the "Chinese continental shelf."[59] In response, the Japanese government reportedly later replied that the Senkakus are in part an "integral part of [the] Ryukyus."[60]

Meanwhile in Tokyo on September 8, Togo met with Sneider and informed him that his government was considering asking for a "formal" statement from the USG to the effect that the Senkaku Islands were part of the Ryukyus and would be included with the Ryukyus at the time of reversion.[61] Sneider echoing Meyer's comments the week before—prior to the flag-raising issue—cautioned that the USG still "[did] not wish to make a formal statement or get involved in the dispute," but offered that if the question were raised at a daily press briefing, the State Department spokesman might be prepared to respond.[62] In reporting the meeting, the Embassy informed the State Department it should expect the question to be raised at one of the press briefings.

This exchange would become the basis for the statement by Robert McCloskey at a noon press briefing on September 10. McCloskey, who had served as the Department spokesman during both the Johnson and Nixon administrations, was asked by an unidentified Japanese reporter what the U.S. position was with regard to the future disposition of the Senkakus. McCloskey responded,

> Under Article III of the Peace Treaty with Japan, the U.S. has administrative rights over the "Nansei Shoto." This term, as used in that treaty, refers to all islands south of 29 degrees north latitude, under Japanese administration at the end of the Second World War, that were not otherwise specifically referred to in the treaty. The term, as used in the treaty, was intended to include the Senkaku Islands. Under the treaty, the U.S. Government administers the Senkaku Islands as a part of the Ryukyu Islands, but considers that residual sovereignty remains with Japan. As a result of an agreement reached by President Nixon and Prime Minister Sato in November 1969, it is anticipated that administration of the Ryukyus will revert to Japan in 1972.[63]

McCloskey was next asked what the U.S. position would be, therefore, if a conflict arose over the sovereignty of the Senkakus. He responded that "with respect to any conflicting claims, we consider this would be a matter for by the parties concerned."[64] In other words, the United States would remain neutral.[65] It is unclear here if "conflict" meant political, legal, or military. The USG answered it as if it were a legal or territorial claim but there were also political and especially military implications that it would face—how could it be neutral in a territorial dispute of an ally? It is unclear how much it had thought these questions out at the time.

While America's neutral stance would end up angering the more hardliners in the Japanese government as time went on, MOFA's Sato, who later served as Japan's Ambassador to China from 1995 to 1998, "indicated satisfaction" with McCloskey's response, and in general the State Department comment "received a warm welcome in Japan," according to Embassy reporting.[66] This appears in retrospect to have been wishful thinking as the media and political leaders took an even stronger position on the issue.

For example, the press stories in the afternoon newspapers (of September 11, due to the time difference) gave "important coverage" to the U.S. statement, but the Embassy noted, "Japanese concern regarding the Senkaku issue continues to increase and news coverage is increasingly flamboyant."[67] This sort of press reporting in turn would gradually inflame domestic public opinion, create new political pressures, and play into the hands of the nationalists within Japan, as it would in Okinawa and Taiwan.

One example of the pressure the GOJ was receiving was from the Diet. Aichi, a veteran politician himself, had been questioned about the Senkakus issue in the Lower House's Foreign Affairs Committee around this time. In response to a question on September 10 from Tokano Satoko, a foreign policy specialist within the Socialist Party, Aichi stated the Senkaku issue was not a territorial problem, in the opinion of the government, as it was of the "firm conviction" that the Senkakus were part of the Ryukyus.[68] He referred to USCAR ordinances which, he explained, confirmed the Japanese position and announced that the Japanese government had approached the USG to take appropriate actions to insure protection of the Japanese claim to the Senkakus, as well as having made a "strong representation" to the GRC about the much publicized intrusion by Taiwanese that month.[69] Aichi's comments received prominent play in the press the following morning, September 11.

MOFA made sure U.S. Embassy officials were aware that the Japanese government was under "strong pressure" to assure the public that the USG was in fact taking "strong action" to preserve Japan's claims to the Senkakus.[70] As a result, the Foreign Ministry was to send instructions to its Embassy in Washington, D.C., to officially request the USG take measures to keep the Taiwanese off the Senkakus through the constant patrolling in the area and the removal of the Taiwanese flag and messages written on the rocks. "Otherwise," he added, "the Japanese public would not appreciate that the USG was doing everything it [could] to preserve Japanese rights" to the islands.[71] The unidentified U.S. official responded that he believed USG–GOJ "purposes regarding the Senkakus are identical," noting that the Japanese claim was intact and that that the USG was taking "whatever action is appropriate" to carry out that purpose.[72] The problem was, however, he noted, that it is "not readily apparent that melodramatic actions by USG or GRI involving constant patrolling of Senkakus and exciting encounters with [Taiwanese] adventurers sponsored by [Taiwanese] newspapers necessarily would be appropriate action."[73] Sato appeared somewhat bothered by this argument, responding, in the "absence of such energetic actions by USG, [Taiwanese] might be encouraged by apparent USG acquiescence" in their seizure of control over Senkakus, and noting that the incident of the flag raising had no real "legal effect on state of possibly conflicting claims to Senkakus" but was more an issue of concern in the "public affairs area."[74]

In contrast, while its response was subdued, the GRC was clearly unhappy that the statement had been made at all. The acting foreign minister, James

(Chang-huan) Shen, who would later become the last ROC ambassador to the United States before recognition was switched to the PRC in 1979,[75] called in Ambassador McConaughy on September 15 and stated that while he would not "protest" the position the U.S. government had taken in the press conference and actually could "understand why the USG felt it had to take this position," the GRC nevertheless did not agree with the U.S. interpretation and expressed the hope the USG would not make more statements on the subject.[76] McConaughy promised to report Shen's views to the Department, and referring to the Department statement on the Senkakus, asked Shen if the GRC agreed that the dispute should be settled by the two parties "without active U.S. government involvement." Shen, who called the islands by their Chinese name (Diaoyutai) throughout the meeting, concurred.

For clarification purposes, the ambassador asked if his understanding of the GRC's position was correct—namely, that the GRC rejected the GOJ claim of sovereignty over the Senkakus but that the GRC did not officially make a counter-claim of sovereignty although it felt that it had the grounds to do so. Shen agreed that that was the GRC position at the current time. McConaughy then asked if the reservations made by the GRC when it ratified the continental shelf convention during the summer were meant to say that even if Japan had sovereignty over the Senkakus it would not affect GRC rights arising from the principle of the continental shelf. Shen acknowledged that while it was not spelt out that was the implication.

Shen explained that the GRC had told the Japanese government that it did not accept the Japanese claim to sovereignty over the Senkakus, but had not officially refuted the arguments on which the Japanese government based it claims. He then handed the ambassador the text of an oral statement, which was meant for a future release. He believed at this point, however, it was necessary to officially inform the U.S. government of the dispute that existed between the ROC and Japan.

The oral statement was three pages in length, and essentially divided into three parts: an explanation as to why the ROC had not to date challenged the arrangements for the Ryukyu Islands after World War II, the refutation of Japanese claims, and the expression of the hope that the USG would "take full notice of the Chinese government's views and position on this question" and promise to keep the USG informed of any further developments.[77]

A few days prior to this meeting, the U.S. Embassy in Taipei had asked the State Department "for our own edification, to help us understand GRC and GOJ maneuvering" its opinion on the extent of Japan's residual sovereignty over the Senkakus and how that affected the offshore oil rights in the area, which the GRC was claiming.[78] This request was likely due to the USG having been notified of the exchanges between the ROC Foreign Ministry and the Japanese Embassy in Taipei mentioned above. According points 1 and 3, the relevant parts of the State Department's response, which was drafted and sent on September 14.

1. The U.S. recognizes residual sovereignty of Japan over Nansei Shoto, including Senkakus, which U.S. administers pursuant to Article III of Japanese Peace Treaty. It is U.S. position, however, that treaty alone is not necessarily final determinant of sovereignty issue. In U.S. view, any dispute that might arise regarding sovereignty over Senkakus or continental shelf around them should be resolved among claimants or through third party adjudication, for example, International Court of Justice (ICJ).
2. [Not included here]
3. There appear two possibilities for determination of extent of continental shelf for Senkakus, both deriving from fact that Senkakus alone among Ryukyus are located on shelf, separated from remainder of Ryukyus by trench:

   a. Sovereignty over Senkakus would extend to territorial waters and underlying area, that is, to no more than three miles from islands; or
   b. Sovereignty over Senkakus could be basis for claim to sovereignty over an adjacent portion of the continental shelf.

   We do not, however, wish to take a position as to which would apply in case of Senkakus.
4. [Not included here.]
5. [Not included here.][79]

Over the coming weeks, U.S. and Taiwanese officials met often over the Senkakus issue. On September 16, Ambassador Chow Shu-kai called on Assistant Secretary Green about another matter, but ended up making representations of GRC views on the Senkakus. Chow mentioned the "strategic" position of the islands, being closer to Taiwan than to most of the other islands in the Ryukyu Islands chain, and the fact that Foreign Minister Wei Tao-ming had been exposed to "intense grilling" by the Legislative Yuan and press.[80] Chow asked that the USG give "serious consideration" to GRC views and handle the Senkakus problem "with utmost care" as the GRC had avoided its "reservations" on the Okinawa reversion agreement publicly "out of concern for friendly relations" with the United States, but the Senkakus issue was the "last straw."[81] Chow also added that he hoped official statements by the USG would not appear to support GOJ claims to the Senkakus. Green informed Chow of the U.S. position, and assured him that the USG had taken note of the GRC's concerns.

Chow's meeting with Green was followed by one with Thomas P. Shoesmith, the desk officer for ROC Affairs at the State Department, in which the American diplomat said that the Senkakus issue was "difficult to handle" for the USG.[82]

In mid-September, ROC Ambassador to Japan Peng Meng-chi called on Vice Minister of Foreign Affairs Mori Haruki regarding the Senkakus.

According to Chiba, who met with Sneider and U.S. Embassy officials on September 21, Peng seemed anxious to see the Senkakus issue resolved quickly, and felt that it was important to let the press in both countries "cool off" and to ensure any "governmental contacts be kept confidential."[83] Peng, who was a former commander of the Taiwan Provincial Garrison Command which had been accused of oppressive tactics, said that the GRC was "clamping a lid" on the press in Taiwan and asked that the GOJ take "similar actions" with the Japanese press.[84] Apparently, there had been media reports in Tokyo that 100 Taiwanese or Chinese ships were entering the Senkakus, and reports in Taipei that two SDF "warships" were in the area.[85] According to Chiba, Mori told Peng the GOJ "could not yield on territorial issue" of the Senkakus but was "completely willing to enter discussions" on the continental shelf.[86]

Subsequently, on September 23, Frederick Chien, Director of North American Affairs Bureau at the Taiwanese Ministry of Foreign Affairs, called in Moser, the political counselor at the U.S. Embassy in Taipei, to give him, on instructions from the acting foreign minister, an oral statement about the GRC's "basic position" on the islands. The essence of the message was that the "GRC does not accept or consent to recent action by the Government of the Ryukyu Islands in interfering, with concurrence of USG, with normal visits of Chinese fishing vessels to Senkakus."[87] Chien told Moser that a Taiwanese vessel, *Chien Sui-wan*, "fishing in waters surrounding the Senkakus" was boarded by GRI police and its flag "hauled down" from the mast and taken away (before it was returned the next day), an incident neither he nor anyone on the U.S. side had heard before.[88]

Moser said he would report it but also stressed that the GRI had on numerous occasions acted to prevent violations of the territory and its territorial waters by Taiwanese fishermen. Chien said that in these instances the GRC had "merely taken note" of USCAR's support of the GRI, but that this did not "denote acquiescence" as the issue was that of "rice bowl" for Chinese nationals.[89] Chien warned that the actions by the GRI Police, "with the concurrence of the U.S. ... are considered provocative, and have had an irritating impact" on the GRC.[90] "At a future date," Chien explained, he intended to "take exception to the current U.S. administration of the Senkakus" but was not "prepared at present to do so."[91]

Moser picked up on Chien's last comment and noted in his telegram to D.C. that Chien might be preparing to "take a more aggressive line" on the Senkakus, and would probably argue that the "GRC has never recognized U.S. administration of the islands, even tacitly," which is "patently not the case."[92] Moser recommended that if the GRC tried to take exception to the U.S. administration of the Senkakus that the negotiating record of the mutual defense treaty of 1954 be explored for any references of Chinese acceptance of U.S. administration.[93]

The U.S. Embassy in Tokyo chimed in after this to point out that a GRC attempt to state it does not recognize U.S. jurisdiction over the Senkakus and that visits by Taiwanese vessels were normal practice would be a position that differed from what it had taken the last time intrusions were discussed in 1968. Namely, the GRC "accepted legitimacy and representation" by the USG in a number of interactions, to include an early August 1968 meeting at which U.S. officials were told the Taiwan Defense Command "would continue to pursue the matter," a mid-August 1968 meeting that U.S. officials were told the GRC "definitely wanted to get the situation under control" and that the crew and owners of the fishing vessel "convicted of intrusion in the Ryukyus had been penalized" by the Kaosiung Fishermen's Association, and were solicited for "suggestions for more effectively controlling intruders and tracing offenders," and a late August 1968 meeting where U.S. officials were informed that the fisheries bureau of the Taiwan Provincial Government had been instructed to stop intrusions and had established penalties for violators.[94]

By the end of September 1970 the Embassy in Tokyo was quite "concerned" with the "escalation" of the unsettled Senkaku issue.[95] It warned that under "present circumstances additional incidents that could be extremely detrimental to U.S. interests in the Western Pacific seem to us almost certain to occur"[96] and that the PRC would find satisfaction in the dispute between the GOJ and GRC over the Senkaku Islands particularly because of the likelihood the USG "will find itself caught in a difficult position between its two allies."[97] As a result, the Tokyo Embassy recommended that representations should be made to "both sides that actions and positions must be tempered, and especially the GRC should not be left in doubt about U.S. position or resolve in this matter."[98] "Impartiality," it concluded, "may be better served in this case by activity rather than passivity."[99]

Specifically, Ambassador Meyer and his staff warned that the "extreme position" of the GRC regarding the Senkakus and its apparent lack of "intention to restrain" its fishermen and eggpoachers from entering the Senkakus would likely result in increased pressure from the GOJ for "more assertive measures" in this regard, and "despite our wish to the contrary," the USG might be "caught squarely in the middle of the territorial issue" as well as in the "complicated continental shelf issue."[100] As such, the USG had "no option other than to show" the GOJ that it was continuing "effective administration" over the Senkakus, including the "vigorous" implementation of "Ryukyuan laws respecting illegal entry."[101] If the USG, the telegram continued, did anything to "appear to retreat from firm stand it took ... in 1968, the GOJ and GRC might conclude that the USG had developed new views on substance of issues between them and shifted ground accordingly."[102] Put succinctly, "the best hope of avoiding exacerbation of the existing problem," the ambassador noted, "would lie in making clear that USG has no alternative to taking firm stand on Chinese incursions."[103]

The Embassy suggested that any representations the USG government made might include a statement to both the GRC and GOJ that the United

States, "of course, has no post-reversion interest in the ultimate outcome of claims to the Senkakus or adjacent continental shelf among the rival parties and would accept whatever decision as to sovereignty and other rights eventuate from a negotiated settlement. As a good friend of both parties, our main concern is to promote the desire of two trusted allies amicably to settle this matter."[104] Ironically, this may not have been what the GOJ and GRC wanted: they would have preferred that the United States took a side, namely its side.

The State Department agreed with the Tokyo Embassy, sharing its concern about the escalation of the issue and the need to prevent a GOJ–GRC confrontation "particularly since we would likely be caught in the middle."[105] John N. Irwin, II, the undersecretary of state who had previously served as the deputy assistant secretary of defense (International Security Affairs) during the Dwight D. Eisenhower administration, authorized its Tokyo and Taipei embassies to make representations to both sides and emphasize the "importance we attach to avoidance of an acrimonious dispute between our two close allies."[106] It included a request to U.S. officials in Taipei to do an assessment of the GRC's intentions and attitudes.

After a series of exchanges between the American Embassy in Taipei and GRC representatives, as well as between GRC and GOJ representatives, the U.S. Embassy in Taipei answered the mail by doing a long analysis of the Senkaku problem and America's involvement. It noted that the U.S. government was involved for three reasons: first, Japan and Taiwan were "our allies and we want them to maintain amicable relations."[107] More directly, however, were the inter-related facts that the U.S. government had taken the position that the Japanese government has residual sovereignty over the Senkakus and that the U.S. government was the current administering authority. The Embassy therefore urged that the U.S. government "avoid problems" on the last point in order to be in a "better position to regain impartiality on sovereignty issue ... and ... on continental shelf issue."[108] Further, the Embassy suggested that the State Department make the following representation to the foreign ministers of both the ROC and Japan. First, the U.S. government should tell the GRC that it would be "most unfortunate—and not in [ROC] interests—to challenge" the USG administering authority over the Senkakus and that it welcomed the efforts of the GRC to prevent fishing and other intrusions into the Senkakus and hoped it would continue those efforts.[109] Moreover, the USG, the telegram continues, should tell the GRC that the United States would accept for the period it is the administering power any fishing arrangement the Japanese and Taiwanese governments agreed to and that the USG was urging the GOJ to discuss "all aspects [of the] Senkaku problem" with Taipei. To the Japanese government, the telegram suggests, the United States should tell the Japanese government what it is saying to the GRC and urge it to "start talking ASAP [as soon as possible]" to the GRC "so an amicable solution" can be found.[110] The Embassy also expressed its assumption that the USG would not "give any support to apparent GOJ position that it is unwilling to discuss issue of sovereignty over Senkakus" as "prospects for amicable solution will be poor if GOJ were to insist upon [GRC] conceding sovereignty as a precondition of any talks."[111]

The passage by the Taiwan Provincial Assembly of a resolution on September 30 appealing to the central government to protect "China's legitimate rights" over the islands and criticizing Japanese interference with Taiwanese fishing vessels caused the Senkakus to continue to be in the news and probably did not ease U.S. anxiety.[112] On October 5 in Taipei, the deputy chiefs of mission from the U.S. Embassy and the Japanese Embassy had the chance to talk about the Senkakus, including the problem of Ambassador Itagaki Osamu's return to Taipei without instructions about the Senkakus.[113] During the conversation Ito Hiromichi volunteered his "personal" belief that the problem of intrusions by Taiwanese fishing boats into the waters around the Senkakus could be resolved "fairly easily" as in his understanding, they have been fishing around the Senkakus for "25 years" and that Okinawans "do not (*sic*) fish those waters."[114] According to Deputy Chief of Mission Vance I. Armstrong, Ito's "somewhat surprising" proposal seemed to be saying that the "GOJ and presumably GRI would have no major problem" with fishing in the area by Taiwanese boats "if the GRC were willing to disassociate this matter from issue of sovereignty over the Senkakus."[115]

The U.S. Embassy in Tokyo, which had been info'd on the account of the meeting, took this suggestion up the next day at a regularly scheduled meeting between Sneider and Togo on October 6. Sneider raised the question of an *ad hoc* arrangement whereby Japan might consent to Taiwanese fishing in territorial waters near the Senkakus on the basis of "custom without prejudice to question of sovereignty," to which Togo responded it would have to be on the "basis of a negotiated fisheries agreement ... [that] would explicitly confirm Japanese sovereignty."[116] Kuriyama followed up by mentioning that the Treaties Bureau was considering, despite problems pointed out by Ambassador Togo, a possible arrangement to defuse the illegal fishing problem, along the lines of an idea floated by Ito in Taipei. The Embassy reminded Kuriyama that, in any accommodation, the GRI, and thus the USG, would be involved.

Toward the end of that first week of October, McConaughy noted that the Taiwanese government seemed to have mellowed a bit. "Recent actions by the government of the Republic of China," he wrote, "lead us to believe that it has not only cooled off somewhat on the Senkakus but has taken actions to restrain its more enthusiastic nationals."[117] The ambassador acknowledged that the media and the legislature were still likely to remain sensational on the Senkakus issue, but stated he believed that violations of territorial waters by Taiwan in the near future were less likely. He added that while he agreed with the Tokyo Embassy's suggestion that the GRC needed to be cautioned against provocative intrusions into the waters near the Senkakus, he believed the USG's main effort should be directed at getting the GOJ and GRC to "start talking about all aspects of the problems."[118]

McConaughy observed that the Senkakus issue was divided into three separate problems that had become entangled—violations of territory and water of Senkakus, more basic problems of sovereignty over the Senkakus, and the rights to the continental shelf.[119] With regard to the two approaches that the GRC has taken, the ambassador observed that the GRC has taken a "fairly hard line" with the USG in diplomatic conversations with the press taking a "tougher line" with Japan, while making "unpublicized efforts" to put a stop to further incidents.[120] Specifically, with regard to the measures the GRC had taken to stop the escalation, McConaughy reported that the Taiwanese Foreign Ministry had given the *China Times* a "severe dressing down" for its involvement in the "unauthorized" flag-raising, that Chien had sent someone from his office during the week of September 23 to meet with the fishermen's group, presumably in light of a subsequent complaint against the Foreign Ministry that it was interfering in their livelihoods, to tell them to stop their activities in the vicinity of the Senkakus, and that the leadership of the KMT had "discouraged" organizers of a rally scheduled for October 2 at National Taiwan University from conducting demonstrations over the Senkakus issue.[121] In addition, the vice minister for foreign affairs, Tsai Wei-Ping, explained before a committee in the Legislative Yuan that since the Senkakus were under U.S. administration, the GRC should discuss the issue with the USG, but that it would not refuse to hold "informal talks" with the Japanese government on the issue since the two countries were on friendly terms.[122]

The ambassador pointed out that the USG was involved due to three reasons: (1) the GRC and GOJ are U.S. allies and the USG wanted them to maintain "amicable relations"; (2) the U.S. position is that Japan has residual sovereignty over Senkakus; and (3) U.S. responsibilities as administering authority.[123] "If we can avoid problems arising from third point," McConaughy noted, "we will be in a better position to regain impartiality on sovereignty issue ... and remain impartial on continental shelf issue."[124] The ambassador was encouraged by recent GRC actions, which he thought suggested it wanted to avoid a confrontation with the USG over intrusions into the Senkakus, and suggested that if the GRC and GOJ could work out an arrangement for fishing in the area, the immediate problem most involving the USG would be resolved. Furthermore, he noted, that the GRC "has left the door open to concede GOJ sovereignty eventually" by not claiming sovereignty over the Senkakus, and that because the "principal GRC interest" was in undersea rights, the GRC might be planning to use the sovereignty issue as a bargaining chip on their rights.[125]

McConaughy was worried, however, that while the GRC was prepared to talk with the GOJ, the latter so far had not been. He thus recommended that representations be made to the foreign ministers of both the GRC and GOJ. To the GRC, the USG should say that "it would be most unfortunate—and not in GRC interests—to challenge USG administering authority over Senkakus; that we welcome recent GRC efforts to prevent fishing and any other intrusions and hope it will continue these efforts; that we will accept for period we are administering power, any fishing arrangement GOJ and GRC agree to; and that we are urging GOJ to discuss all aspects of Senkaku problem with GRC."[126] To the GOJ, the ambassador suggested, the USG should inform it of what the USG was saying to the GRC and "urge the GOJ to start talking as soon as possible to GRC so an amicable solution can be found to all three aspects of problem. We assume we will not give any support to apparent GOJ position that it is unwilling to discuss issue of sovereignty over Senkakus. Certainly prospects for amicable solution will be poor if GOJ were to insist upon GRC conceding sovereignty as precondition for any talks."[127]

Before the Tokyo Embassy had a chance to weigh in, Ericson wrote he was "gratif[ied]" with Taiwan's effort to control the illegal incursions, but expressed concern that it still did not appear the two parties were actually moving toward resolving the impasse and recommended to the respective embassies in Taipei and Tokyo to stress to their counterparts the "importance the U.S. government attaches to an amicable resolution of the Senkakus issue" between the GOJ and GRC.

With regard to Taiwan, Ericson said that in addition to the above message, the Embassy should inform the GRC that the United States welcomed recent efforts to prevent fishing and other incursions and that it hoped these efforts would continue, that it would be "unfortunate—and not in GRC interests—" to challenge the United States in its administrative responsibilities for the Ryukyu islands, that the U.S. government intends to carry out those responsibilities, that as part of these responsibilities, authorities in Okinawa will soon have improved patrolling capability, and that the USG is urging the GOJ to discuss all aspects of the Senkakus problem with the GRC.[128]

For Tokyo, Ericson told the Embassy to inform the GOJ of the substance of the message to Taipei and urge GOJ discussions with the GRC to reach an "amicable resolution on all aspects of Senkakus problem."[129] Ericson also told the Embassy that "if appropriate" it should express the hope that the GOJ would avoid "preconditions" which might prevent the initiation of discussions with the GRC, i.e., refusal to discuss the sovereignty of the Senkakus.[130]

The State Department, Ericson pointed out, believed that some form of agreement providing Taiwanese access to the Senkakus fishing area would remove one source of friction and possible future confrontation with both the GOJ and the U.S. authorities, such as during the spring when the fishing season picked up again. Ericson suggested the agreements could either be made between the governments or even between fishery associations in Taiwan and Okinawa. "In either case," he noted, "success would depend in large part in Okinawan acceptance."[131] Before pursuing the matter, however, Ericson asked for the High Commissioner's views on the prospects for Okinawan acceptance.

Another issue Ericson asked the High Commissioner about was the possibility of delaying the GRI's approval of applications for offshore exploration concessions, which, as was discussed in the previous chapter, overlapped with concessions already granted by the GRC and which would extend well beyond the Senkaku territorial waters. The GRI granting of such concessions, Ericson warned, would force the USG to choose among "acquiescence, veto, or prolonged delay, the latter of which might be the least palatable from the USG view. USG delay or veto would however appear likely to embarrass GOJ."[132] Ericson felt it would likely be less embarrassing for the U.S. and Japanese governments if the GRI action on the applications could be delayed until reversion "or until the GOJ and GRC work the problem out."[133]

William Clark, Jr., a Foreign Service Officer serving in Okinawa who headed the Liaison Office, responded on behalf of the High Commissioner, explaining the difficulties of a government-to-government agreement on fisheries, as the USG had held the position that it was responsible for Okinawa's foreign relations.[134] While an agreement on fishing had been worked out with Australia in cooperation with the GOJ, the GRI itself did not engage in direct diplomatic negotiations nor was it staffed to be able to do so. Clark did not say it, but he may have been implying that since Japan was a party in the dispute with Taiwan, it might have been seen as not having been able to broker an arrangement on behalf of Okinawa. An agreement between fishing associations, similarly, would be difficult. Clark pointed out that no such association existed for Okinawan fishermen in the area as many fishermen from different areas operated there: "Unlike many fishing areas around the larger islands in the Ryukyus, the Senkaku area has not been granted to one particular fishing association. Thus there is no local fishing association particularly responsible for the area."[135] Clark continued to explain that Okinawan fishing around the Senkakus was "sporadic" and that it was "possible that more [Taiwanese] fishing boats visit area in course of a year than do Okinawan boats."[136] The California native then noted that the fishing in the area included three main types, including "netting" where the net is pulled up onto the shore, and that according to local sources, the "best fishing" is found within the territorial limit.[137] Thus, it would be difficult to separate fishing from penetration of territorial waters and landing. Clark, who stated that "we have encouraged and supported the GRI in its exercise of sovereignty over Senkakus as has GOJ," noted that in order for a fishing agreement to work, the GRC would have to recognize the GRI's claim to the Senkakus: "[it] appears doubtful ... that GRC would be willing to accord sovereignty to the GRI in return for fishing rights."[138] Of course, recognizing GRI sovereignty meant recognizing that of the GOJ.

On the issue of offshore exploration concessions, Clark noted the "special Okinawan overtones," in that not only was there concern in Okinawa, shared by the GOJ, that active exploration in the GRC concessions, GRI officials were concerned, as discussed in detail in the previous chapter, over the possible loss to Okinawa of benefits of any oil discoveries if the decision on mining concessions were delayed until after the post-reversion period, particularly as the three applicants were all Okinawan (although two were backed by mainland Japan interests).[139] In light of the GRI having increased its staff screening the applications, Clark was told that the applications could be approved as early as the spring of 1971. "Given the Okinawan parochial concerns on this matter," he pointed out, "it is unlikely that GRI would be receptive to U.S. efforts to delay granting of offshore concessions, even if this position were supported by the GOJ."[140]

As the aforementioned cable from the State Department suggests, the United States was very much concerned about the lack of dialogue between the GOJ and the GRC. During the critical month of September, Ambassador to the ROC Itagaki had returned to Tokyo for consultations. The acting foreign minister for Taiwan, Shen, told the U.S. Embassy in Taipei he was expecting Itagaki to return to Taipei with instructions. However, Japan's ambassador returned without them, explaining that the GOJ regarded the issue of Japanese sovereignty over the Senkakus as non-negotiable and that while it was willing to discuss questions of the continental shelf with the GRC, the GOJ had not yet defined its position on the shelf issue. According to a summary, it appeared that the Japanese were "trying to resolve internal differences regarding geographic and legal relationships of the Senkakus with other Ryukyu Islands."[141] A State Department cable to the Tokyo Embassy asked it to determine from appropriate GOJ officials whether the Japanese postponement of discussions with the GRC had any other meaning than that described above, and if not, when were they likely to be prepared to talk and on what issues. It also asked for information on Japan's intentions and thinking, in order to assist the department to determine the "tenor of representations" that the United States might make to the GOJ and GRC.[142]

The Embassy in Tokyo did its homework, meeting with various GOJ officials concerned with the Senkakus issue. Reporting back on October 15, it informed the State Department it had confirmed with Kuriyama that Ambassador Itagaki had indeed returned to Taipei without instructions because the GOJ position that the territorial issue was not negotiable had already been conveyed to the GRC and because the GOJ was still studying the continental shelf issue. Namely, according to Kuriyama, whose office was considered being like a "goal keeper" to protect Japan from other countries "scoring" on it,[143] the "principal difficulty" of the continental shelf issue was to determine the proper legal position respecting the amount of influence exerted by the uninhabited island group.[144] Consideration of the issue was complicated, he continued, by the fact that the Japan–Korea continental demarcation discussions would also involve uninhabited islands. According to the Embassy, Kuriyama, who twenty years later would become the Japanese ambassador to the United States from March 1992 to December 1995, did not indicate that there were any internal difficulties, as suggested by Taipei, regarding the geographic and legal relationship between the Senkakus and the other Ryukyu Islands. In fact, it appeared that the GOJ regarded the GRC position on the territorial issue as "one adopted by the GRC only for negotiating purposes on the continental shelf."[145]

In writing their report, the Embassy had several conversations with MOFA officials that week. On October 13, the political counselor had met with

Treaties Bureau Director General Ikawa Katsuichi who remarked that the GOJ could not make a formal agreement with the GRC lest it stimulate the PRC to interject itself in the dispute and possibly claim the entire shelf under the natural prolongation theory. Ikawa seemed to accept the inevitability that the PRC would become involved in the issue, but he felt the position the PRC would take would depend on the timing it decided to become involved. In contrast, he indicated a preference for an informal agreement with the GRC on rights to oil deposits in the continental shelf but was unsure what form it might take. He remarked that the Foreign Ministry was coming under pressure from Japanese oil companies and "Okinawan nationalists to take an early, firm stand" on the Senkakus question.[146]

The same day, an Embassy officer had lunch with Hanaoka Sosuke, director of the Mine and Coal Bureau Development Division (*Sekitankyoku Sekiyu Kaihatsuka*) of MITI, who expressed the view that the Senkakus and the rest of the Ryukyu Islands "deserved full weight in drawing any boundary line" between Japan and China on the continental shelf and thus, demarcation, "should be equidistant" between the Senkakus and Taiwan and between the Ryukyus and China along the "entire length of Chinese coast."[147] Although the Embassy did not have a chance to speak with the Fisheries Agency (*Suisancho*), it assumed the latter organization was following the matter "with some interest and some concern for repercussions" as it was scheduled to renew a fishery cooperatives agreement in June 1972.[148]

As such, the Embassy had the impression that while the GOJ might be willing to hear the GRC representations on the territorial issue informally, it would only be prepared to respond substantially to the continental shelf issue, and then only after at least several weeks as it established its position. In summary, the embassy concluded, it considered the GOJ was "moving as fast as it can" to devise a negotiating position with the GRC over the Senkakus issue.[149]

On the afternoon of October 23, Watanabe Koji, deputy director of the China Affairs office at MOFA who was visiting Taipei at the time, called at the U.S. Embassy there, furnishing after some questioning an outline of the emerging GOJ position on the continental shelf. The GOJ believed that a formal demarcation of a boundary on the continental shelf with China would require a treaty, but it was reluctant to conclude a treaty with the GRC because of the PRC's possible reaction, and thus the GOJ wanted an informal "modus vivendi" for the time being pending a formal resolution to the problem.[150] Watanabe said the GOJ was not willing to discuss sovereignty over the Senkakus, but in return for the GRC ceasing to dispute Japan's claim, the GOJ would agree to permit Taiwanese fishermen to fish in the waters around the Senkakus on the "basis of custom and comity."[151]

With regard to the continental shelf, the position the GOJ developed was to draw a median line between Kyushu, the Ryukyus, and the Senkakus on the East and the China mainland and Taiwan on the west. While the GOJ had no interest in the area to the west of the median, it wanted to ensure that all exploration and exploitation east of the median be subject to mutual agreement. Watanabe noted that although the Ryukyus were used in computing the base line for the *modus vivendi*, it did not mean the islands would necessarily be used in the formal demarcation of the continental shelf. Complicating this GOJ position, an irritated Watanabe said, was the publication on October 15 by the GRC of new boundaries for GRC claims on the shelf, "a move that upset carefully negotiated clearances within the GOJ and forced a re-examination of the problem, which resulted in stiffer instructions to Taipei from Tokyo."[152] Watanabe added that he had been "impressed" by the PRC's complete silence on the Senkakus and continental shelf issue, frankly admitting that although the GOJ was "ostensibly" negotiating with Taipei on the continental shelf, it was a "one-China" proposal "carefully developed with Peking's reaction in mind."[153]

Watanabe felt that the positions between the GOJ and GRC were "too far apart for an early compromise," which explained the GRC's "cool" reaction to a presentation Ambassador Itagaki had given upon his return to Taipei.[154] Meeting with Deputy Foreign Minister Tsai to express the hopes of the GOJ that the issue of the continental shelf could be solved by "quiet bilateral discussions," Itagaki had noted that the "extensive GRC exploration zones" all the way to northern Kyushu, announced the previous week, were "unacceptable" and requested "flexibility in delimitation of such zones to allow for possible compromise."[155] Itagaki also informed Tsai, who had studied at the University of Illinois in the prewar period and later headed the Coordination Council for North American Affairs (a "non-embassy, non-consulate, non-liaison office"[156] established in February 1979 after the USG ended diplomatic relations with Taiwan), that the GOJ was "not prepared" to discuss GRC claims to the Senkakus since, from the GOJ perspective, there were "no questions" regarding "Senkakus ownership" as the Senkakus were "not covered" under Article 2 of the Allied Peace Treaty with Japan.[157] In response, the deputy foreign minister argued that the Senkakus were indeed included under Article 2 since the Senkakus were acquired by the Japanese as a result (*sic*) of the Sino–Japanese war of 1894–95, but that with regard to a GOJ claim on the continental shelf, while he was not in a position to outright reject it and would have to check with the minister, the continental shelf was a prolongation of the Chinese mainland and that the deep ocean trench between the shelf and the Ryukyu Islands "clearly establishes that Japan would have no claim to any part of the shelf."[158] Itagaki was not instructed to table any specific formulas for apportioning the shelf at that time.

Back in Tokyo Kuriyama, in relaying the results of the meeting to Sneider, was not optimistic about the future, having found the GRC as "unduly rigid" and showing "no indications [it was] attempting to defuse possibility of confrontations on Senkakus."[159] Watanabe, still in Taipei, similarly felt that an "impasse" had already been reached.[160]

This view was apparently prevalent on most other matters as well among Japanese diplomats assigned to Taiwan, even before the Senkakus issue arose.

In the spring the year before, U.S. diplomat Charles T. Sylvester dined with Kuroiwa Shuroku, first secretary at the Japanese Embassy in Taipei who was scheduled to become chargé for part of the summer until Ambassador Itagaki arrived from Ottawa. Kuroiwa was both "happy" and "nervous" about it—"who knows, the Gimo might die while I am in charge"—he said using the nickname for Generalissimo Chiang Kai-shek.[161] One thing Kuroiwa and his Japanese colleagues were not happy about, however, apparently was serving in Taiwan:

> This is a difficult post to serve in for Japanese officers ... and few people want to come to Taipei. It is an uncomfortable post from a professional point of view. Those Chinese whom we should know well are very cool to us; those we don't need are all too friendly. Besides, many officers fear that drastic changes in Japan's China policy could occur during their tour here which would make it even more difficult to work in Taipei. In the long run, he said, a tour on Taiwan could be prejudicial to a hypothetical, but much more interesting, tour on the mainland. Not only is it difficult to contact leading Chinese figures, but also day-to-day working relations with GRC officialdom are excruciating ... Negotiations on the simplest matters drag on forever and are conducted with great suspicion and niggling attention to detail.[162]

By the middle of November, it had become even more clear that the GOJ and GRC were unable to come to an understanding on the Senkakus, and in a meeting between U.S. Embassy officers and both Kuriyama and Watanabe, the U.S. official re-introduced the idea of a *modus vivendi* which "would prevent occurrence of additional incidents that might increase public pressures on either side" in light of the inability of Japan and Taiwan to agree on larger issues.[163] Both Kuriyama and Watanabe agreed such a *modus vivendi* would be important to limit the tensions and facilitate larger negotiations, but noted there were several problems. First, the idea of a *modus vivendi* for fishermen would be easier to accept for the GOJ if it applied not only to fishing but also to those who went ashore to collect bird eggs, as the danger to those bird colonies had been one of the factors motivating Japan's intervention. Moreover, a *modus vivendi* would only be workable they pointed out if the GRC concessionaires stayed away from areas in their concessions close to the Ryukyus. They doubted too whether any delays in processing concessions that the negotiations might cause would be acceptable on the GOJ side. Nevertheless, Kuriyama and Watanabe agreed to conduct "discreet soundings" within the government to "test receptivity" to the idea of a *modus vivendi*.[164]

U.S. officials were increasingly worried about the ability to resolve the issue, no doubt. A couple of weeks before the impasse between the GOJ and GRC became clear, Shoesmith, who was visiting Taiwan at the time, had called on Chien, meeting with him for 80 minutes to discuss the islands. According to Chien's memoirs, published in 2005, he told him that it was "very clear" that the ROC had the sovereignty over the Diaoyutai Islands and that it had strong opinions on the issues related to the islands, and that it hoped the U.S. Government would resolve the issue "without favoring Japan."[165] Chien also pointed out that because the GRC valued the relationship between the United States and Taiwan, and also the security in this area, the GRC had not objected to the actions of the U.S. military government in charge of the islands. "However," he continued, "it does not mean that we agree with those actions. When the mission of the military government is completed in Okinawa, the U.S. should return these islands back to the ROC."[166] This certainly was not what the USG wanted to hear.

Japan's suggested text for the Okinawa Reversion Treaty

As the GOJ–GRC interactions over fishing rights and the division of the continental shelf were continuing, the Japanese and the U.S. governments were discussing a possible paragraph or other description of the Senkakus for the Okinawa reversion agreement. On October 8, 1970, the Foreign Ministry provided its counterproposal text to the preamble and articles I and II of the U.S. draft originally shared on August 31.[167] With regard to the article/paragraph concerning the territorial scope of the Ryukyu Islands, the drafts were essentially identical, except that an additional sentence, in italics below, was added. Paragraph 2, Article I, stated:

> For the purpose of this Agreement, the term "the Ryukyu Islands and the Daito Islands" means all the territories and their territorial waters with respect to which the right to exercise all and any powers of administration, legislation and jurisdiction was accorded to the United States of America under Article 3 of the Treaty of Peace with Japan other than those with respect to which such right has already been returned to Japan in accordance with the Agreement concerning the Amami Islands and the Agreement concerning Nanpo Shoto and Other Islands signed between Japan and the United States of America, respectively on December 24, 1953 and April 5, 1968. *The territories defined in this paragraph are indicated in the annex.*[168]

The annex added read:

> The territories defined in Paragraph 2 of Article I are all of those islands, islets, atolls, and rocks situated in an area bounded by the straight lines connecting the following coordinates in the listed order:
>
> 28 degrees North Latitude, 124 degrees 40 minutes East Longitude;
> 24 degrees North Latitude, 122 degrees East Longitude;
> 24 degrees North Latitude, 133 degrees East Longitude;
> 27 degrees North Latitude, 131 degrees 50 minutes East Longitude;

27 degrees North Latitude, 128 degrees 18 minutes East Longitude;
28 degrees North Latitude, 128 degrees 18 minutes East Longitude;
28 degrees North Latitude, 124 degrees 40 minutes East Longitude.

The Japanese draft, particularly as it related to the description of territories, caused some consternation on the U.S. side. The following week on October 12, members of the U.S. team met with Nakajima of the Foreign Ministry to discuss the Japanese counterproposal. Nakajima explained that the GOJ felt the narrative description in its draft "emphasized more than the U.S. proposal did the attractive political fact that the Ryukyu reversion terminates Article III rights," and that the "stated purpose" of the metes and bounds territorial description "is to add precision."[169] Sensing an ulterior motive, the Embassy officers probed some more. Nakajima confirmed that the GOJ government did in fact consider the Senkaku issue when it drafted the metes and bounds description. In other words, the Japanese side wanted to ensure that the USG would include the Senkakus in the islands to be returned.

The Embassy officers pointed out that the U.S. government preferred to "stay out of the middle" of the Senkakus issue as the reversion agreement was probably not the "proper place to refer even indirectly" to the Senkakus dispute.[170] They also explained that Article 3 of the Peace Treaty with Japan did not contain such a metes and bounds description and that an annex was "essentially redundant."[171] They emphasized that "redundancy should be avoided as a matter of principle in solemn international documents as reference in agreement to same thing in two different ways can give rise to later misunderstandings."[172] Nakajima, who would later serve as an ambassador to China and Australia as well as a member of Japan's Supreme Court, expressed his sympathy to each of the points, but said the Senkakus issue "may be extremely important to the Government of Japan in 1972."[173]

Nakajima lived until late 2011, so he saw that the unsettled status of the islands continued to be a problem for Japan for decades to come. According to one American participant in the negotiations who visited Japan later for the 20th anniversary of the reversion of Okinawa, Nakajima was still bitter twenty years later about the way the Senkakus were handled by the United States.[174] In addition to an essay he penned around the time of the above anniversary ceremony, Nakajima fortunately conducted an oral history with Japanese diplomatic historians shortly before his passing that was published posthumously. In it, he says,

the [issue of the] Senkakus belonging to Japan became one of the most important topics that we discussed ... To be sure, we should not have even had to discuss it as it was clear that the Senkakus were part of the areas that the United States continued to occupy due to Japan's recognizing America's administrative rights [over the Nansei Islands] as per Article 3 of the Treaty of Peace with Japan. Despite this, Taiwan and

China raised some problems. Making it clear that the Senkakus, which naturally were areas to be reverted, indeed fell within the scope of the administrative rights areas that were to be returned became the main purpose of the negotiations on this matter [in the Okinawa Reversion Treaty]. The U.S. side did not question this whatsoever. Certainly Schmitz did not. It was apparent that both Taiwan and China began to make these claims in light of oil interests, but the [sovereignty over the Senkakus] was so clear it just became a matter for us of ensuring the language of the treaty ensured that the Senkakus were included. The U.S. side did not object at all. However, Taiwan was whining and complaining so much that the U.S. side wanted to avoid language that glaringly made it clear [that the islands were being reverted to Japan]. In this sense, we took into consideration the U.S. side's concern and thought about how to phrase it in a way that from a Japanese perspective left no doubt. Initially, I think we proposed something that was very straightforward. The U.S. side did not have any problem with it per se, but taking into consideration the international reaction, it said it did not want to be too straightforward in it. We further took U.S. desires into consideration and continued to discuss how to phrase it in the agreement. The U.S. side had no problem with formulating Agreed Minutes, although it took some time between us and Schmitz to get the right phrasing.[175]

On October 23, the State Department wrote back with comments on the Embassy's telegram describing the above Japanese counterproposal. State agreed with the Embassy's comments to Nakajima, and stated that the "reversion description should follow Art[icle] III language as closely as possible."[176] Embassy officers shared these comments with their Japanese Foreign Ministry counterparts on October 30.[177]

The Foreign Ministry continued with its studies on the reversion agreement while dealing with related challenges vis-à-vis Taiwan (and then China, as it became more vocal with the publication of an article on December 4 by the official New China News Agency siding with Taiwan and accusing Japan of aggression against China in the Senkakus issue[178]) about the Senkakus and the continental shelf.[179] By December 16, the Embassy was able to report that the Japanese government had "moved in the U.S. direction" on several remaining differences but that the "major outstanding issue" was how to address the Senkakus problem.[180]

Embassy officials had met the week before on December 11 with Nakajima to discuss the treaty and specifically the handling of the Senkaku issue. Nakajima stated that the GOJ-proposed annex establishing the metes and bounds description of the territories had been reconsidered "at the highest levels" in the Foreign Ministry and, despite the arguments presented by the Embassy to the GOJ against the idea of an annex in mid-October, it still wished to stick to its proposal. Nakajima explained that the government's concern with the Senkakus issues has only grown since the PRC indicated its support, on December 4, for the GRC claim of sovereignty over the Senkakus.[181] The essential purpose of the annex remained, he continued, was "to make it clear that the Senkakus are included in the territories being returned by United States."[182] But, he admitted, his government would be willing to consider "other means to clearly establish this point."[183]

An unidentified Embassy official referred to earlier conversations in which the U.S. government preference to "maintain distance from the Senkakus territorial issue" and view that the reversion agreement "was not the proper place to refer to the Senkakus dispute" was mentioned, but reaffirmed that the U.S. government did consider the Senkakus "well within the area defined as the Ryukyu Islands" and that it was the "intention" of the U.S. government to revert administrative control of the Senkakus to the Japanese government upon reversion.[184]

Nakajima asked at this point that the USG consider other means by which recognition of the Senkakus in the Ryukyu reversion could be clearly established in the documentation if not included in the territorial annex. It is unclear if he was acting on instructions or not, but the Embassy official suggested that the U.S. and Japanese governments might consider: including the Senkakus as "a footnote or agreed minute to Article 1," issuing an official map of the territories to be reverted, making clear references to the Senkakus in future joint communiqués, press releases, reversion white papers, etc.[185] Nakajima agreed to have the Japanese side consider such alternate forms of reference for the Senkakus, and asked that the U.S. side do so as well.

In reporting on the meeting, the Embassy requested the Department's consideration of alternate references, and added the following comment: "Regarding the Article I problem, we consider that GOJ will be amenable to any suggestions for handling Senkaku issue that will make it clear in some fashion that Senkakus are being returned to Japan along with Ryukyus."[186]

Before the two sides had the opportunity to finalize their draft on the territorial scope of the treaty, another related issue appeared which would impact the discussions. This issue concerned the construction of a weather station on the Senkakus, discussed in Chapter 2, and one could argue that the timing of the request was probably meant, in part, to force concessions on the U.S. side with regard to an annex or actual reference to the Senkakus in the reversion agreement. The USG eventually decided to not permit the construction of the weather station at the time.

A U.S. statement on the Senkakus (agreed minute)

The Embassy's request to the Department for suggestions on alternate references bore fruit. A week after the above January 26 meeting, Foreign Minister Aichi, Yoshino, Deputy Director General Okawara Yoshio, his successor Deputy Director General (designate) Tachibana Masatada, and Chiba met with Ambassador Meyer and Sneider at the New Otani Hotel on the evening of

February 1 to review the status of the overall negotiations. As the Senkakus remained an important issue, both regionally and in the context of the reversion treaty, the issue was the first one raised after the question of timing of the agreement.

Aichi asked that an "explicit statement" be included that the Senkaku Islands were being reverted as part of the Ryukyus. "Setting aside the unmanned weather station," he continued, "there was the problem of relations with Taiwan, and future relations with Communist China, and the Government of Japan wished to have an explicit statement in the Agreement on the Senkakus."[187] Responding at Meyer's request, Sneider said he knew the Japanese side was "unhappy with our handling" of the definition of the territory and the Senkakus in the draft agreement.[188] The DCM went on to say that they had asked the Japanese side for a draft formulation for Washington's consideration, including perhaps a footnote or an attached map, and to mention that the U.S. side was thinking of a statement to the effect that the USG was returning the territory defined in Article III of the Peace Treaty and felt that no specific definition of the Senkakus was necessary. Sneider emphasized that the United States would be pleased to consider a Japanese suggestion in any case.

The foreign minister did not seem satisfied, and responded that "the U.S. draft of Article III language would leave the status of the Senkakus unclear. There were many ways to clarify it, such as giving the latitudes and longitudes as in the Bonins and Amami reversion agreements. But, without such an explicit statement, their status would remain unclear."[189]

In early March, officials from the Embassy and High Commissioner's office met as the OCC, or Okinawa Coordinating Committee, to take an "inventory of outstanding issues" on the reversion negotiations.[190] The status of the Senkakus remained one of those issues.

In light of the lack of remaining time, the U.S. government eventually accepted Japan's arguments. While it did not specifically include the name of the Senkaku Islands in the agreement, it did express its willingness in early March to include the following verbiage in an agreed minute to the general reversion agreement:

The territories defined in paragraph 2 of Article one of the Agreement between the United States of America and Japan Concerning the Ryukyu Islands and the Daito Islands are understood to mean all of those islands, islets, atolls and rocks, and their territorial waters, situated in an area bounded by the straight lines connecting the following geographic coordinates in the listed order:

28 degrees North Latitude, 124 degrees 40 minutes East Longitude;
24 degrees North Latitude, 122 degrees East Longitude;
24 degrees North Latitude, 133 degrees East Longitude;
27 degrees North Latitude, 131 degrees 50 minutes East Longitude;

27 degrees North Latitude, 128 degrees 18 minutes East Longitude;
28 degrees North Latitude, 128 degrees 18 minutes East Longitude.[191]

According to McElroy, who drafted the document, and Ericson, who approved it, "this formula: (1) meets basic GOJ concern; (2) clearly delineates area now administered by US and over which USG has agreed to relinquish administrative rights; (3) permits agreement itself to follow Article 3 language more closely; and (4) does not involve USG in question of ultimate sovereignty."[192] Fortunately for the Japanese side, a couple of weeks later the State Department informed the Tokyo Embassy that it was authorized to propose at an "appropriate stage in the negotiations" the following agreed minute (as opposed to an annex, as originally suggested by the Japanese side the year before) to the general reversion agreement.[193]

The territories defined in paragraph 2 of Article I of the Agreement between the United States of America and Japan Concerning the Ryukyu Islands and the Daito Islands are understood to include all territories which the United States of America now administers under Article 3 of the Treaty of Peace with Japan. These territories are designated under the Civil Administration Proclamation No. 27 of December 25, 1953, all of those islands, islets, atolls and rocks within the following geographic boundaries:

28 degrees North Latitude, 124 degrees 40 minutes East Longitude;
24 degrees North Latitude, 122 degrees East Longitude;
24 degrees North Latitude, 133 degrees East Longitude;
27 degrees North Latitude, 131 degrees 50 minutes East Longitude;
27 degrees North Latitude, 128 degrees 18 minutes East Longitude;
28 degrees North Latitude, 128 degrees 18 minutes East Longitude;
28 degrees North Latitude, 124 degrees 40 minutes East Longitude.

The U.S. government proposal was accepted in principle by the Japanese government, which came back with another draft with simplified wording on April 28. The revised draft was presented by Nakajima's senior, Director General of the Treaties Bureau Ikawa.[194] The Embassy was happy with it and saw "no reason to reject the GOJ proposal for short form," particularly as the changes were found to reduce redundancy and were "helpful to U.S. government as recitations of authority for [its] elaboration of metes and bounds," and recommended to the State Department in a telegram the following day that it accept the GOJ draft.[195]

In response, Undersecretary Irwin noted that it was "essential to limit meets and bounds to context of description of area U.S. now administering. GOJ proposal ... could be misunderstood as U.S.–GOJ agreement on proper boundaries of Nansei Shoto or Ryukyus and lead to USG involvement in sovereignty issue. Accordingly we prefer original USG proposal."[196]

The latest USG counterproposal was transmitted to the Foreign Ministry on May 10, and on May 11, Ambassador Meyer discussed the American and Japanese proposals with Aichi. Prior to this, on May 6, Sneider met with Yoshino and Ikawa to discuss the treaty. Sneider had just returned from a trip to Taipei, which he talked about at the beginning of the meeting. He described the Senkakus issue as having become "emotional" within Taiwan, with the PRC "skillfully exploiting" the dispute.[197] Sneider told Yoshino that he did not engage in a debate with GRC officials on this matter, that it was "Japan's problem" to deal with, and recommended that a dialog be begun with Taiwan on it.[198] It is unclear if Yoshino or Ikawa, knowing how difficult it would be, responded at all to the suggestion.

At their meeting on the 11th, Foreign Minister Aichi described the GOJ proposal as "simpler and more straightforward" than the American proposal and requested the U.S. side to reconsider, with Meyer explaining that the USG had proposed language it thought would be "helpful" to the GOJ and "wishes only to make clear that we are returning to Japan the area that we administer and are attempting not to appear to adjudicate respective claims to Senkakus."[199] According to the Japanese version of the memorandum of conversation, Aichi felt the U.S. proposal was a "repetition of past wordings" and that the one the Japanese side presented was the better of the two, but agreed to reconsider it.[200] In either case, Aichi said the GOJ "fully understood the USG position, that there were no basic disagreements between the two governments, and that the GOJ merely prefers more straightforward description of territories."[201] The two representatives decided to leave the work up to the experts, and the following day, May 12, the Foreign Ministry presented a compromise agreed minute, which read:

> The territories defined in paragraph 2 of Article I; namely the territories which are under the administration of the United States of America under Article 3 of the Treaty of Peace with Japan, are, as designated under the Civil Administration Proclamation No. 27 of December 25, 1953, all of those islands, islets, atolls and rocks within the following geographic boundaries:
>
> 28 degrees North Latitude, 124 degrees 40 minutes East Longitude;
> 24 degrees North Latitude, 122 degrees East Longitude;
> 24 degrees North Latitude, 133 degrees East Longitude;
> 27 degrees North Latitude, 131 degrees 50 minutes East Longitude;
> 27 degrees North Latitude, 128 degrees 18 minutes East Longitude;
> 28 degrees North Latitude, 128 degrees 18 minutes East Longitude;
> 28 degrees North Latitude, 124 degrees 40 minutes East Longitude.[202]

While there were some problems with the language, the Embassy believed the proposed agreed minute and the present Article 1 would not be misunderstood to involve the USG in the sovereignty issue, and it recommended that the Embassy be instructed to accept the GOJ proposed agreed minute to Article 1.

U. Alexis Johnson, who had negotiated the Ogasawara reversion agreement, was unhappy with it, however, firing back the next day (May 17) that the Japanese proposal was not acceptable: "The operative language remains 'territories are.' Fact that it refers to Article 1, Paragraph 2 which begins 'For purpose of this agreement' does not necessarily limit meaning of agreed minute. Nor do descriptive phrases in minute (i.e., 'namely' and 'as designated') necessarily limit operative language."[203] Johnson wrote that he believed the earlier U.S. government proposals were straightforward and met the basic GOJ desire for inclusion of metes and bounds. They also met, in his view, the essential USG requirement that metes and bounds formula must stay within the context of the description of territories that the United States was administering. Johnson ended by proposing a compromise. The "slight revision of the Japanese proposal," he noted, "would make it acceptable: The territories defined in paragraph 2 of Article I are the territories which are under the administration of the United States of America under Article III of the Treaty of Peace with Japan, namely, as designated under the Civil Administration Proclamation No. 27 of December 25, 1953, all of those islands, etc."[204]

The Embassy shared these concerns with the Foreign Ministry and on May 18, the Embassy reported to Washington that the GOJ proposed a revised minute, which Ikawa darkly characterized as a "complete GOJ surrender."[205] The GOJ proposal by this point was identical to the U.S. draft, with a few minor changes. The Embassy said the GOJ draft seemed "satisfactory" and recommended acceptance of the draft.[206] The final version of the agreed minute, which was included in the reversion treaty signed on June 17, is included in this study as Appendix 2.

Later that month, the U.S. side officially informed the GRC of its decision to include the Senkakus in the area to be returned to Japan. Before we look at the USG's transmittal of that decision, it is necessary to look at the pressure the GRC was placing on the USG with regard to the Senkakus, as well as the actions and reactions of Taiwanese and Chinese students.

ROC pressures on U.S. government

During the late winter and spring of 1971, the ROC had dramatically raised the stakes, attempting to bring the United States ever more into its dispute with Japan.[207] These efforts would continue until the eve of the signing of the Okinawa Reversion Treaty and in some cases afterward as well until the islands were returned to Japan on May 15, 1972.

As described in Chapter 3, amid the increased tensions between Japan and Taiwan over the Senkakus, the GRC publicly and for the first time ever asserted its own claim to the islands on February 23, 1971, moving beyond simply rejecting Japan's claims. While it had previously denied Japan's claims to the islands, the GRC had not publicly stated that Taiwan owned them. However, this statement fundamentally changed the paradigm, and Taiwan crossed the figurative Rubicon.

Frustration apparently had been building for some time, and the news that the Japanese government was planning to build a weather station on the Senkakus caused Taiwan to consider countermeasures, according to a UPI story in early February. Namely, GRC sources told a UPI reporter that if the GOJ went ahead with those plans, it would encourage Taiwanese businessmen to do "less business" with Japan, which would increase the number of firms Taiwan did not do business with (as some Japanese firms did business with China, and were thus blacklisted by the GRC).[208]

It was during a response to questioning at the opening of the 47th Session of the Legislative Yuan on February 23 when Foreign Minister Wei Tao-Ming claimed publicly for the first time that the ROC had sovereignty over the Senkakus:

> Regarding sovereign rights on Tiao Yu Tai Islets, we disagree with Japanese government in latter's claim that they are part of Japanese Nansei Gunto. Our disagreement is based on ground that from historical, geographical and usage viewpoints, these islets should belong to Taiwan. Our views and position on this issue have been repeatedly communicated to Japanese government. What is involved in case of the Tiao-Yu-Tai Islets is sovereign rights and we shall not yield even inch of land or piece of rock. Government will not waver in its determination on this matter. As to exploration and exploitation of the continental shelf, according to existing principles of international law and convention on continental shelf, should be Okinawa trough. Any exposed islets or rocks within this area cannot be used as a baseline for establishing rights of exploration. We, therefore, have full and unrestricted rights in exploration and exploitation of continental shelf in this area.[209]

The Foreign Ministry Treaty Department deputy director, Kuo Kang, told a U.S. Embassy officer in Taipei that the GRC claim to the Senkakus was a "long-standing position," and that the claim had been made known to the GOJ but that Wei's statement was the first time the GRC had made the claim publicly.[210] Curiously, the director of the North American Affairs Bureau, Chien, was caught unawares and was "uninformed" on the new GRC position.[211]

Two days later on February 25 in Taipei, Japanese Embassy Counselor Muto and Second Secretary Yoshida Shigenobu shared with the U.S. Embassy a copy of a note the ROC Ministry of Foreign Affairs had delivered on February 20 in response to the Japanese note given to the GRC in October at the time of Watanabe's trip to Taipei. The text read:

> The GRC shares the GOJ's view that friendly relations existing between the two countries should not in any way be jeopardized on account of the

continental shelf issue. The GRC disagrees with the GOJ claim that Tiao Yu Tai Islands belong to Japan. From history, geography, and usage, Tiao Yu Tai Islands appertain to and belong to Taiwan. Furthermore, in demarcation of boundaries of continental shelf any exposed rocks and islands should not be taken into account. GRC, therefore, regrets that it is unable to accept GOJ's proposed modus vivendi of using the Tiao Yu Tai Islands as Japanese boundary (sic) in applying principle of median line equidistant between territory of Japan and China.[212]

Muto and Yoshida both confirmed that the GRC had challenged the GOJ claim in informal conversations since October but that this written communication went beyond previous comments to actually claim sovereignty on the Senkaku Islands. They admitted they were surprised by Foreign Minister Wei's public statement, but that their ambassador had interpreted the change in GRC policy was the result of: (1) the PRC's claim to the Senkakus; (2) legislative interpellations on the subject; and (3) student demonstrations in the United States. (Ambassador McConaughy, in his report to Washington, agreed with Itagaki's assessment and added that press attention was also a factor.[213]) Muto told a U.S. official that his embassy had not received any instructions yet from Tokyo on how to deal with the new situation but that the Japanese position would be that its sovereignty over the Senkakus was "non-negotiable."[214] The GRC position appears to have been delivered on March 5 in Washington.

In a subsequent move, ROC Ambassador to the United States Chow Shu-kai presented Assistant Secretary Green with a *note verbale* on March 17 concerning the GRC claim to sovereignty over the Senkakus and to request that the Senkaku Islands be excluded from the rest of the Ryukyu Islands reverting to Japan. As this suggests, the meeting, while cordial, was not about pleasant subjects; in addition to this presentation, Chow was there to protest the recent USG decision to lift restrictions on travel to the mainland, which the GRC correctly saw as another step in the calculated moves by the United States in expanding its relations with the PRC at the eventual expense of the GRC.[215]

The *note verbale* summarized the historical, geographical, geological, and legal basis of the GRC claim to the Senkakus, as introduced in other interactions previously, and noted that the GRC "failure to challenge the inclusion of Senkakus in the U.S. military occupation of the Ryukyus should not be construed as acquiescence on its part of Tiaoyutai islets being considered as part of Ryukyu Islands."[216] The note also asserted that the Senkakus "should be treated as appertaining or belonging to Taiwan" and requested that the sovereign rights of the ROC over the islets should be respected and that they be restored to the GRC when the "aforesaid termination of the U.S. occupation of the Ryukyu Islands should take place."[217] Chow placed the note in the context of student demonstrations (described below) in the United States and Hong Kong over the Senkaku issue, and the GRC desire to handle the matter in a way that did not exacerbate relations with the United States and

Japan, mentioning efforts (albeit without "much success") by the government to moderate student movement and keeping it from taking an anti-U.S. and anti-Japan stance.[218] Chow also raised the GRC's efforts to "minimize negative publicity" on this issue, such as not publicizing Japanese plans to construct a weather station, and noted that his government did not intend to announce the delivery of the note.[219] However, he mentioned that the government might feel compelled at a later date to make both actions public.

In response, Green, after telling the ambassador that he would bring the GRC note to the attention of those within the Department concerned with the matter, reviewed the U.S. position on the question of sovereignty, noting that the USG did not consider that the reversion of the Senkakus to Japanese administration as part of the Ryukyus "necessarily was determinant of question of sovereignty," which the USG believed should be resolved between the claimants or through third party arbitration.[220] Acknowledging the difficult position the GRC was in domestically with the student demonstrators and the PRC's claim, Green expressed appreciation for Taiwan's efforts to prevent the issue from disrupting "US–GRC–GOJ solidarity."[221] The assistant secretary suggested that the best course for the GRC would possibly be to take the position that the government was pursuing the matter with the countries concerned as it was a legal problem to be resolved through diplomatic processes—"in this way, GRC can make clear that it was making its case with other governments concerned, at same time minimizing irritation by handling issue quietly."[222] To this, Chow agreed that the challenge for his government is to "assure its people that it is exercising the proper concern for national interests without stirring up reaction in Japan."[223] Toward the end of their discussion, Green noted that the USG had been under pressure to return the Ryukyus quickly, as if it had delayed any longer in reaching an agreement with the GOJ on reversion, "it might not have been possible to obtain agreement to the continued U.S. use of and access to those bases in a way which is helpful to GRC," a point Chow acknowledged.[224]

Later that week, Vice Foreign Minister Shen followed up on Chow's meeting with Green by calling in Ambassador McConaughy to make a strong presentation about the GRC's claim to the Senkakus and to "deprecate" Japan's claims.[225] Shen said that his government was increasingly concerned about demonstrations on U.S. campuses by Chinese students and reported that some distinguished scholars of Chinese descent in the United States were also getting involved. It had learned that sizeable demonstrations were planned for April 9 and 10 (which indeed occurred), and in an effort to calm the Chinese academic community there, Presidential Secretary General Chang Chun had written a letter the week before setting forth the "firm claim of the GRC to the Senkakus."[226] Shen talked at length, sometimes sarcastically sometimes forcefully, about Japan's "uncompromising posture" about the Senkakus, and stated the GRC was "troubled by the rigidity shown by the Japanese in calling their claim to the Senkakus 'non-negotiable'."[227] After some "rather sarcastic" remarks about Japanese efforts to "document a long-standing claim to the Senkakus," Shen stated the GRC position on the Senkakus was that ROC sovereignty over the Senkakus should be recognized and that the Senkakus should be turned over to the GRC "upon termination of the U.S. occupation," adding that the GRC saw no requirement upon U.S. to deliver them to Japanese administration."[228] He emphasized, "Since the Senkakus were not a part of the Ryukyus they did not have to be handled in the same manner as the Ryukyus at the time of reversion."[229]

Although Shen did not explain the reason for the GRC's claims to the islands during his near monolog, he admitted the GRC position as to the Senkakus had become more "positive" in recent weeks, "going beyond the mere denial of Japanese claims to sovereignty, to the active assertion of GRC sovereign rights," implying that the GRC decision to do so was influenced by the PRC public entry into the "fray" and by the Chinese student disturbances.[230] Shen ended by asking that the USG not permit the Japanese construction of a meteorological station while the USG still had administrative powers, not turn the administration of the Senkakus over to Japan at the time of reversion of the Ryukyus, and to respect the GRC claim to sovereignty over the Senkakus by restoring the administration of the Senkakus to the GRC when the termination of the "Ryukyuan occupation" terminated.[231]

McConaughy responded by telling Shen that the USG was not taking any position as to sovereignty over the Senkakus then or at the time of reversion. He urged that the GRC do "all it could to prevent this issue from becoming abrasive at a time when GOJ cooperation and goodwill were greatly needed in connection with important pending issues."[232] Shen agreed with the latter point, and said he had already suggested to the GOJ that two governments "damp down publicity" on the Senkakus issue, and that while the GRC was following this policy "carefully" and thought the GOJ was trying to do the same, some of the Japanese press had been continuing "to fan the issue to some extent."[233]

These efforts by the GRC to push its views with the USG obviously placed the USG in a very difficult position vis-à-vis its two allies who were now embroiled in a territorial dispute that did not become more heated at this time only because the United States was still administering the islands. That difficult position became very clear in the first half of April when ROC Ambassador to the United States Chow Shu-kai made farewell calls on President Nixon and National Security Advisor Kissinger, and raised the Senkakus issue directly with them.

Prior to his meeting in the Oval Office on April 12, Chow, who was returning to Taiwan to become the foreign minister, called on Assistant Secretary of State Green on April 9. Chow raised the Senkakus issue with Green, who in turn prepared a detailed memo for Kissinger and the president.

On April 12, Chow visited Nixon and National Security Advisor Kissinger, who had prior warning from Green in the form of a detailed memorandum of the ambassador's intention to raise the Senkakus issue during the farewell call.[234] Ambassador Chow reviewed the GRC's position at President Nixon's suggestion with Kissinger, but as a subsequent summary of the conversation states, the national security advisor listened without comment.[235] The same afternoon Chow met again with Kissinger and Holdridge to further discuss the Senkakus issue. According to Chow, he explained that many influential Chinese scholars regarded the outcome of the Senkakus issue as a "test whether the GRC has the will and the ability to stand firm for a Chinese national position" where the United States is involved.[236]

These meetings took place amid demonstrations by Taiwanese and Chinese students around the world, and shortly after a State Department press briefing that took place at noon on April 9 that was seen by GRC authorities as pouring fuel on the fire.

In response to questions, press secretary Charles W. Bray, III, who had succeeded McCloskey earlier in the year, stated that "the term used in the treaty [of peace with Japan] was intended to include the Senkaku Islands," repeated part of the statement the previous year in September.[237] While it was not necessarily news, and was meant to prevent U.S. oil companies from contributing to a race for oil or rise in tensions, it also had the effect of suggesting to Taiwan that its demands were not being heard or accepted.

This press conference came one day before a large "Senkakus demonstration" was to be held by Chinese students and others in D.C. as part of a worldwide effort to raise awareness of the issue. Demonstrations had been going on in New York, Los Angeles, San Francisco, Honolulu, and even in Montreal, not to mention Hong Kong and Taiwan, for some time. The media exchange and Bray's response poured fuel on the fire.

Student demonstrations had been actually occurring for a while. In late January 1971, approximately 1000 Chinese students rallied near the United Nations headquarters as well as the Japanese mission to the UN to protest Japan's claim to the Senkakus. The students, from Princeton, Harvard, Yale, Columbia, and other schools on the East Coast, raised signs saying "Smash U.S.–Japanese Conspiracy" and "Remember Pearl Harbor."[238] Another 1000 reportedly gathered in Chicago, San Francisco, Los Angeles, and Honolulu to protest.

On February 20, 1971, about 100 students staged a protest in front of the Japanese Cultural Center and Consulate General in Hong Kong against the GOJ's stand on the Senkaku Islands and denouncing Japanese militarism, U.S. imperialism, and United States–Japan collusion on the Senkakus.[239] The demonstration, according to David Dean, the internal relations officer who wrote the report and who had spent most of his professional life on Chinese affairs and previously served in Hong Kong a decade before, was "apparently organized by local students in response to similar demonstrations held in America."[240] The demonstration was organized by a student journal, *70's Bi-Weekly*, which according to one of the "anti-colonial" activists who helped publish it, Mok Chiu-Yu, had a readership of "more than 10,000."[241] (The Consulate described it, however, as a "noisy and sometimes controversial publication with leftist sympathies and little influence," but noted that the most recent issue had devoted two full pages to the Senkaku Islands issue, urging protection of Chinese claim to the Senkakus but without making reference to either Taipei or Peking.[242]) While the demonstration was peaceful and a local source said there was "no information to suggest Communists were involved," earlier reports had indicated that the demonstrators were planning to burn a Japanese flag and effigy of Prime Minister Sato in front of the Japanese consulate.[243]

There was some newspaper coverage of the event. The Communist newspaper, *Ta Kung Pao* (Public News), which is the oldest Chinese language newspaper in Hong Kong and funded by the PRC since 1949, reported on the demonstrations estimating the crowd at 200 in its February 21 edition, while the pro-KMT newspaper, the *Sing Tao Jih Pao* (Sing Tao Daily), in its February 23 editorial announced its support of the protests in Hong Kong and the United States, blaming the USG in part for encouraging Japanese ambitions toward the Senkakus since it agreed to turn the Ryukyus over to Japan without the consent of the GRC.

Around the same time, Taiwan Foreign Minister Wei met with Ambassador McConaughy on February 20 and during the course of their discussions Wei mentioned the demonstrations that had taken place in the United States. He said that his government, having carefully investigated, was convinced that the demonstrations had been caused by "small cells of Communists motivated by a desire to undermine GRC-U.S. and GRC-GOJ relations."[244] Although most of the participants were non-Communist students "who thought they were taking part in a purely patriotic exercise ... they had been cleverly duped by a small number of Communist organizers."[245] Wei added that the GRC disapproved of the demonstrations, and was concerned at the "apparent malleability" of the participating students.[246]

Within Taiwan, too, student demonstrations continued in the spring, and the GRC would eventually decide to meet with the protestors on their own turf. This decision was in part forced on it by it seems the growth and intensity of the "Defend the Diaoyutai" movement, criticism of U.S. and Japanese policy, and the feeling that the GRC was not doing enough. While the GRC continued to blame the protests on the Communists, it became clear that explanation alone was not sufficient.

In mid-March 1971, some 500 professors, scholars, and students at over fifty American universities and institutes sent a letter to President Chiang Kai-shek emphasizing that the Senkakus were Chinese territory and urging the government to "firmly thwart Japan's new attempt at aggression."[247] Their letter was supported by an editorial in the March 18 edition of the privately owned *Chung Kuo Shih Pao* (China Times), a newspaper with a circulation then of about 220,000 with close ties to the KMT and which had planted the flag on Uotsuri Jima six months before, noted that "there was not a shred of evidence historically or in Japanese administrative records to support contention that Senkakus do not belong to Taiwan," and stated that the "question of sovereignty should be separated from the question of underwater exploration for crude oil," urged the GRC "not to let efforts at regional cooperation interfere with the preservation of sovereignty" and to "make a clear explanation of its stand."[248]

The names on the letter included senior scholars and scientists at some of the best known universities. In light of their prestige in Chinese society, and perhaps the growing media interest, Chiang was obligated to provide an answer. This was done by an old friend of Chiang, Presidential Secretary General Chang, who said the GRC would "take a firm stand, would defend its rights on continental shelf, and would do everything possible to protect even an inch of land or a piece of rock" in the disputed Senkakus.[249] The U.S. Embassy noted that the "escalation of the issue to the presidential office is evidence of the seriousness with which the GRC views the problem," and observed that the "GRC is caught between a desire to defuse the issue in difficult Chirep [Chinese representation in United Nations] year and substantial popular and press support for hard line toward Japan. GRC probably feels unable to take softer line than Peking."[250]

Indeed, for some time, Chiang had viewed with concern the PRC's influence in the dispute in several ways: the ability of the "Communist gangsters," according to a December 7, 1970 entry in his diary, to divide Taiwan, Japan, and the United States on the Senkaku issue;[251] to make itself appear as the defender of China's interests; and the success it was having in stirring up the students not only in Taiwan but abroad, such as in the United States. According to a January 31, 1971 entry, Chiang noted that "The Communist gangsters organized the 'Righteous Harmonious Fist' and 'Red Guards' in the United States to launch rally and protest in the name of the Senkaku Islands. These are simply aimed to exploit this issue only to destroy relations among the ROC, Japan, and the United States. Unfortunately, the United States is not taking any action for it, not sensing the slightest of danger of how disastrous this could become in the future!"[252]

In early April, Acting Foreign Minister Yang Hsi-kun called McConaughy in to discuss the Senkakus, expressing the GRC concern at the success the Chinese Communists had in stirring up demonstrations in the United States and elsewhere over the Senkakus issue. In particular, the GRC was concerned about the protests scheduled for April 10, as "rather elaborate arrangements" were being made for demonstrations in several cities, including Washington, D.C.[253] "The Chicom hand behind the scene in organizing demonstrations was becoming more evident," Yang stated, and while "most of the prospective demonstrators are innocent dupes ... a small core of demonstrators are probably subversive and knowingly acting for Chicoms."[254] Yang explained that within Taiwan, legislators, top KMT party members, and senior advisors to President Chiang were all bothered and felt that a "record of active GRC efforts to counter Japanese claims and maneuvers had to be established in face of Chicom propaganda assertions: when the Chinese Communists endeavor to preempt a Chinese national issue involving territorial matters, the GRC [could] not afford to seem indifferent."[255] Yang also told McConaughy that Ambassador Chow was delaying his departure from Washington due in part to the student demonstrations scheduled the following week, and that Chow intended to meet with a small delegation of demonstration leaders then. Yang ended the meeting by requesting the help of the USG in "refraining from taking any actions which would put the GRC in a poor light as the defender of a Chinese national position" and in further helping to deal with the "very troublesome Chicom propaganda blasts of December 3 and December 29 which improperly tied the Senkaku issue with the Chicom offshore oil and territorial claims," and asked for assurances that the "Japanese would not be permitted" to build a weather station on the Senkakus during the remaining period of U.S. administration.[256] He added that he hoped the U.S. position against construction of the weather station would be regarded as unclassified so that Ambassador Chow could use it in his meeting with demonstration leaders.

To the latter request, the American ambassador stated that he felt "reasonably sure the Japanese were aware of our definite opposition to construction" of a meteorological station on the Senkakus while the United States remained responsible for the administration, and "did not anticipate that the issue would arise in any acute form during the remaining period of our responsibility."[257] McConaughy added, however, that the information must be considered classified "at this time and in view of the general sensitivity of the subject" doubted whether the State Department would feel that the information could be used in the way the GRC intended to use it.[258] The ambassador promised to check with the Department, which he did, and he received the guidance about how to respond to Yang, as described in an earlier section.[259]

Around the same time in Canada student demonstrations were held on April 3 by the China Students' Union of Canada, having formed a "Special Committee on Tiao Yu Tai Incident." Organizers contacted the Japanese Consulate in Montreal ahead of time and requested a meeting to deliver a protest letter to Prime Minister Sato stating that the group would "defend Chinese sovereignty" over the islands, "oppose the revival of Japanese militarism," and "protest against any conspiracy against Chinese territorial sovereignty over the islands."[260] The 200 demonstrators gathered at McGill University, and then proceeded to the Japanese Consulate on Dorchester Street, before ending up at the U.S. Consulate on McGregor Street. The march was, according to a newspaper account, "spirited and extremely orderly."[261] Nevertheless, some of the signs the students carried said, "Smash Japanese–US Conspiracy" and "Fight for TiaoYu Tai."[262]

It was amid this atmosphere and the day before a series of protests in Washington, D.C., and other cities in the United States as well as Hong Kong when an April 9 noon press briefing at the State Department touched a nerve with the Taiwanese authorities and protestors, and ended up escalating tensions. The briefing by Bray, referenced above, was done primarily to inform American oil companies that the USG was concerned about their conducting surveys in the disputed areas, including near the Senkakus, and was calling for a moratorium on exploration.[263] The guidance given to these companies (see Appendix 3) stated in part, "The United States Government strongly recommends that American firms suspend all exploration and exploitation activities in areas around the Yellow and East China Seas and the Taiwan Straits subject to two or more claims until the claimants reach agreement regarding the limits to their rights to these areas."[264] The reasoning for this statement was given in preceding paragraphs, two of which stated that the USG "does not have the authority to determine the national boundaries of the continental shelf of East Asia," and that the USG "is determined not to permit itself to be drawn into the dispute over conflicting claims of the People's Republic of China, the Republic of China, Japan, the Republic of Korea, and the Democratic Republic of Korea or into contention with any of the disputants over the merits of their claims."[265]

An Associated Press story from Washington about Bray's comments was immediately sent around the world, and in response, the GRC issued its own statement on the evening of Saturday, April 10. The Foreign Ministry spokesmen announced that:

> Tiao-Yu Tai Islets are part of the Republic of China's territory. The Government of the Republic of China has made repeated representations through diplomatic channels calling on the Government of the United States to respect Chinese sovereignty over these islets and to return them to the Republic of China upon the termination of the occupation of these islets. The Chinese Government has found it difficult to understand why the State Department has made such a statement even before it has given a reply to the Chinese Government's representations and hence takes strong exceptions to it. As soon as the Ministry of Foreign Affairs learned of this statement, it made another strong representation to the U.S. Government.[266]

Prior to the issuance of the foreign minister's statement, Yang had telephoned the deputy chief of mission at the U.S. Embassy in Taipei that same evening to express his "grave concern" over the comments at the press briefing.[267] Yang went on to say he "found it impossible to understand why statement was made at this time," fearing it would "pour oil on the fire" of the problem being caused by the demonstrations in the United States (and in Hong Kong and Taiwan, among other places).[268] Yang referred as well as to his recent discussion of this problem including the GRC concern over the PRC's "manipulation and exploitation of these demonstrations," and requested further information on the Department's press briefing.[269]

In the response that subsequently came, the State Department noted that the comments to the press "had been the USG position for some time," and pointed out for the benefit of the Embassy that:

> the United States has tried to avoid public statements of its position on Senkakus partly out of regard for problems which this issue poses for

GRC. When, however, as in present instance, we [were] pressed for statement of USG position, we cannot say less than already on public record or appear to be drawing back from our agreement with Japan on reversion. We are sure the GRC appreciates the importance to our mutual security interests of smooth implementation of that agreement.[270]

The State Department telegram also included a summary of U.S.–GRC interactions on the question of the status of the Senkakus, which it instructed the Embassy to "recall for" the acting foreign minister—diplomatic speak for the GRC's case being weak and their target of frustration misplaced:

Department spokesman's statement of September 10, 1970 and Q and A subsequently made available to press for attribution. In this connection, we note that in meeting with Ambassador on September 15, 1970, Acting Foreign Minister Shen did not protest U.S. position—i.e., that Senkakus regarded as part of Ryukyus and that residual sovereignty rests with Japan—and could understand why USG felt it had to take that position, although Shen noted GRC disagreement with USG interpretation. Also relevant in this connection are Ambassador Chow's representation to Assistant Secretary Green on September 14, 1970 and Green's response along lines of Para 1, State 150567. Finally, on occasion Chow's presentation of GRC *note verbale* March 17, 1971, Green again pointed out that USG considers Senkakus to be part of Nansei Shoto and that these islands will therefore be turned back to Japanese administration under reversion agreement. Green pointed out, however, that USG does not consider that reversion of Senkakus to Japanese administration as part of Ryukyus necessarily is determinant of question of sovereignty, which we believe should be resolved between claimants or through third party arbitration.[271]

Whether this reply and its subsequent relaying to MOFA had any positive effect is unclear, as the response at the press briefing generated a great deal of attention. This attention, in turn, did indeed add fuel to the fire of previously scheduled protests and may have acted to stimulate new ones too.

According to the *Washington Post* the demonstrations in Washington, D.C., on April 10 were attended by some 1000 people who marched to the State Department and the Embassies of Japan and the ROC.[272] Student protestors from Taiwan or of Chinese descent came from all around the country, including the University of Alabama at Auburn, Los Angles, San Francisco, Seattle, Chicago, Houston, and Honolulu.[273] A three-person delegation, led by Frank Chu, a member of the Action Committee for the Defense of Tiao Yu Tai, met with Shoesmith of the State Department's Office of China Affairs to read a protest over Japan's claims, while speeches continued outside. A letter of protest was also delivered to the Japanese Embassy, and another demand was made to the ROC embassy to oppose the return of the islands to Japan. In addition, according to the *New York Times*, some 2000 Chinese protested around the country, which the article pointed out, if the size of the Chinese community in the United States was taken into account would be the proportional equivalent of one million Americans participating in a rally.[274]

Not only were protests held in the United States by students from Taiwan and Hong Kong or of Chinese descent, but students in Hong Kong continued to protest and even students in Taiwan, still under martial law, began to get more active.

Several hundred students gathered at National Cheng Chi University in Taipei on April 16, for example, and decided to march on KMT party head-quarters. KMT Secretary-General Chang Pao-shu told the students he would address them at City Hall, which he did, followed by the KMT First Section Chief, Chen Chien-chung. Both men expressed sympathy with the student views, but tried to get students to avoid further demonstrations and allow the government to negotiate.

This request apparently did not mollify the students (who were apparently upset in part at the KMT's refusal to permit the press to carry photographs of previous demonstrations), and perhaps even aroused them to carry on their demonstration by marching on the American Embassy to deliver a protest to the ambassador. Approximately 200 students appeared in front of the gate that afternoon, carrying slogans and banners similar to those used in earlier demonstrations. In the ambassador's absence, the political counselor received a student delegation but it refused to deliver the protest message to anyone but the ambassador. Eventually the students were urged to disperse by police forces and when McConaughy returned, the ambassador met with two student representatives, one of whom "was excited and impolite," who read aloud the following strong protest note on behalf of the Federation of Student Associations, National Cheng Chi University.[275]

> Your excellency, your government violated international treaties and dis-regarded international morality when it made the statement on April 9 on the future of the Tiaoyutai Islands. This has violated our territorial sovereignty. The students of this university are all angered by this state-ment and hope that you will rein in at the precipice and withdraw this statement. If not, your government will have to be held responsible for the grave consequences arising from this issue.[276]

When leaving, the students stated that their protests would continue until a response was received.

That evening, McConaughy met with Chiang Ching-kuo, otherwise known as "CCK," and told the son of President Chiang who was serving as vice premier, that Embassy officials were willing to receive peaceful petitioners on the Senkakus issue but hoped efforts would be made to avoid situations that disrupted the normal operations of the Embassy. Yet, the ambassador was probably not hopeful, as he concluded his observations in a telegram to the

State Department with the warning, "Students are now apparently feeling their oats and future demonstrations may occur."[277]

Indeed, earlier that day in the morning, another student delegation—including the president of the National Taiwan Student Council and the head of NTU's "News Agency"—called on the ambassador to present a protest petition on the Senkakus signed by 2000 students. The ten-person delegation was polite and well dressed. McConaughy informed them he would forward their petition to the USG, and let them know that the USG took "no position on sovereignty over Senkakus. In other words, we have not recognized Japanese or other sovereignty. The U.S. is non-committed on this issue, and hopes that the claimants can resolve it between themselves."[278]

The ambassador repeated a similar message when he met with a delegation of ten faculty members and students from National Tsinghua University, formed in 1955 by scientists and scholars from Tsinghua University who had fled mainland China, on the morning of April 19. One professor and two students presented a protest message on the Senkakus issue.[279] (Others, such as an eleven-person delegation from Fu Jen University, then thirty students from National Normal School, and a group of faculty members from National Cheng Chi University, were expected in the afternoon but had not shown up by the end of the day.)

In reviewing the current situation, the Embassy reported in a subsequent telegram that students at "various universities" began holding meetings on April 10 "in response to the Department spokesman's April 9 statement at the press briefing."[280] "Their activism" was encouraged by the media attention given to the demonstrations in the United States, and the "initiative," in the Embassy's eyes, "appears to have come more from the students than from the government [although] latter has probably given tacit approval because of its reluctance to oppose patriotic outpouring of youth. Dissatisfaction over U.S.–China policy and oil exploration moratorium are other factors influencing government's tacit approval."[281] The Embassy noted that authorities have attempted to keep the demonstrators under "tight control," kept the Embassy informed of plans and movements, been on the scene "inconspicuously but in great strength," and "otherwise effectively" prevented demonstrations from getting out of hand at U.S. and Japanese embassies.[282] Nevertheless, the students apparently felt emboldened, as it knew the GRC was vulnerable on a whole range of issues, and thus sensed the government was giving them tacit approval.

The GRC, on the other hand, went out of the way to show that they were not behind the demonstrations in the United States. Chinese Embassy officials in Washington, for example, told their counterparts in the State Department that the GRC was not involved and that the "prime movers" were "outside, i.e., Chinese Communist, elements."[283] The State Department admitted in an internal communication that the USG had been "unable to pinpoint who [was] behind the demonstrations" but noted that Hong Kong refugees and students with a mainland background had been "quite active."[284] It informed the Embassy in Taipei that it "tentatively estimate[d] that the movement was spontaneously derived from frustrated nationalism felt by young Chinese in U.S. and [drew] on organizational skills which have become quite developed on U.S. campuses and among minority groups. It probably reflects some of the same spirit which has led to the growth of 'Boxers (I Kor Yuen)' in New York and Hua Hsing in San Francisco."[285]

By the second half of April, the Embassy reported that there were "indications" that the GRC had begun to act to halt mass demonstrations in Taipei, at least near the American Embassy, despite the continued delivery of petitions.[286] One example the Embassy cited was the fact that the new minister of education, Lo Yun-ping, issued a statement that, while expressing appreciation for the "patriotic sentiment" of the students, noted that the "issue was complex and would take time to solve" and declared that the government's stance was "firm."[287] Lo added that if the students wanted to make their opinions and recommendations known, they should do it in writing to the appropriate government authorities.

Perhaps seizing on this moment, Ambassador McConaughy gave an interview about the Senkakus dispute with Li Wan-lai, a reporter with the Central News Agency, a government-supported organization which was founded in 1924 in southern China. In the interview, printed in the April 21 editions of Taiwanese newspapers, the ambassador explained that the USG was not endorsing the Japanese or Taiwanese claims to the islands, and that the "determination of sovereignty" over the islands was not "the responsibility of the United States."[288] He went on to say "the students are mistaken when they think the United States is taking sides with Japan ... we are non-committal on the issue."[289] McConaughy re-emphasized his open-mindedness in hearing opinions from the students, adding that the "people to people contact will contribute to mutual understanding" and that the seven petitions he had received to date and been sent to the USG for consideration, although the position of the USG was already known.[290]

The media seems to have responded to the clues, and gave only "low-key" coverage of the demonstrations.[291] The press wrote calming editorials, including one "expressing relief that the students have listened to their elders and returned to campuses and studies ... as demonstrations would likely lead to misunderstandings and precedents of dubious value."[292] As a result, the Embassy was confident enough to write that in light of the "past few days of student behavior," it appeared that the government had "reined in the students, and will possibly try to limit them to small, peaceful delegations carrying protest to ambassador."[293] Certainly, the GRC did not want to see large-scale demonstrations or things getting out of hand.

However, it was touch and go for a while. One day, the Embassy would happily report, "No demonstrations or delegations today at Embassy, and we have heard of none elsewhere,"[294] and another it would point out, "Senkakus is hot political issue here. Several thousand students have already demonstrated at their schools and elsewhere over Senkakus question, and at least some meetings had demanded that the flag [still being held in Okinawa as of April] be returned."[295]

The demonstrations were for the most part orderly, but there were times when things got out of hand. According to a story by United Press International, two panes of glass at the U.S. Information Service office in Taichung were broken on the morning of April 20 by people protesting the U.S. position on the islands.[296] Normally, this might have been dismissed as not important in the larger scheme of things, but because a riot had seriously damaged the American Embassy and USIS Headquarters in Taipei fourteen years before in an incident called "Black Friday" following an apparently unjust verdict in a court case, it had to be taken seriously by those with a long involvement in United States–Taiwan relations.[297]

The press, too, was divided. The Independence Evening Post (*Zili Wanbao*), an independent newspaper with a circulation of 40,000 that occasionally had critical articles about the government (and thus was heavily monitored and often censored), for example, issued an editorial on April 19, 1971, supporting the "Patriotic Solidarity Movement" of the students and criticized the U.S. and Japanese governments.[298] The editorial went on to link the Senkakus issue with other problems in the Sino–U.S. relationship:

> Some Americans are even engaging in alienation movement, promoting two-China theory and flirting with Chicoms. Series of unpleasant incidents all have contributed to Chinese losing confidence in U.S. In addition to Japan's unjustifiable claim to Tiaoyutai Islands, U.S. has announced plans to return islands to Japan together with Ryukyus. State Department went even further on eve of demonstrations by Chinese students in U.S. April 8 and reiterated U.S. support for Japanese sovereignty over Tiaoyutai. College students in Taiwan, indignant at unwise U.S. decision, have staged protests on campus and delivered protests to American Embassy ... Let all Chinese unite together and expand patriotic movement to safeguard Tiaoyutai, UN representation, and Chinese culture. We warmly support patriotic movement.[299]

The *China Times* also chimed in about the demonstrations, praising the students' patriotic spirit while noting that normal diplomatic channels were the proper means to resolve the sovereignty issue: "Students by their actions showed they only intended to express voice of the Chinese people and have never doubted the government's efforts to safeguard sovereignty."[300] Obviously the staunchly pro-KMT daily wanted to ensure it had control of the public perception of the movement and counter criticism of its dealings with Japan and the United States.

Even the PRC's New China (*Hsinhua*) News Agency noted the demonstrations in the United States against attempts by the United States and Japan, "in collusion with the Chiang Kai-shek bandit gang," to annex "China's territory the Tiaoyu and other islands" and to plunder China's seabed and subsoil resources.[301] The April 23 article, according to a summary, denounced as "bumptious" the State Department position that the Senkakus would be returned to Japan as part of the Okinawa reversion, although the story did not report that the USG took no stand on the Sino–Japanese dispute over the sovereignty of the islands.[302] While it was first "PRC media attention" to any of the recent demonstrations on the Senkakus issue, the article did not, interestingly, mention any of the protests on Taiwan. According to the American Consulate in Hong Kong, which was charged with watching news and people coming out of China and reading the tea leaves, "Thus far, the PRC's treatment of the issue seems largely designed to keep its claims in view and does not amount to a major propaganda offensive. For the time being at least, Peking seems content to let the matter fester as a dispute between the GOJ, GRC, and USG."[303] Subsequently, in the May Day issue of the *People's Daily* on May 1, the PRC warned the Japanese government on the islands, describing the Tiaoyutai Islands as Chinese territory.[304] Radio Peking read the commentary on its broadcast the next day. It "us[ed] language that made the Taiwanese sound moderate by comparison," one U.S. official wrote about the broadcast.[305]

The demonstrations in Taiwan continued against this background. In an effort to be more proactive, Chow Shu-kai, now back from D.C. as foreign minister, and Chien addressed approximately 2000 students at National Taiwan University, a school founded in 1928 during the Japanese colonial years and considered Taiwan's most prestigious university, and answered questions from the floor.[306] The demonstrations had been going on for days by that point. Chow spoke for ten minutes, saying that "his views were the same as theirs" and that they had "no corner on patriotism" but that the "best way to get the Senkakus back" was to support the government's diplomatic efforts.[307] Chien echoed this latter theme, after giving a historical, legal, and geographic view of the Senkakus issue. He encouraged the students to support the government in its negotiations and to "take no action" that could damage the government's negotiating position.[308] According to the Foreign Office, the students were generally "receptive" but "groaned and hissed" when Chien suggested they could best help the government by giving up their demonstrations and go back to their studies.[309] The two men received a total of fifty-four questions from the audience in writing, forty-nine of which he answered. Five were about the demonstrations. The questions were "pointed."[310]

According to Chien, who did not want the information shared with the GOJ, Chow apparently had used his personal background to appeal to the students, stating that "none of the students could have a better claim to hate the Japanese than he" and explaining that "his father was the son of a poor and illiterate peasant who saved enough money to teach his son how to read. His father was thus able to become a low-ranking army officer and to send [Chow] through college ... his father did not have enough money to purchase clothes, so that Chow wore hand-me-downs throughout his college years ... his father had been starved to death by the Japanese."[311]

The above explanation had been provided by Chien to the political coun-selor at the U.S. Embassy in Taipei, William W. Thomas, who took advantage of the conversation to ask Chien what steps the GRC was taking to discuss the Senkakus issue with the Japanese government. Chien explained that his government had made no demarche to Japan since Vice Minister Shen had replied to a Japanese request for a *modus vivendi* over a month before that. Thomas asked if the GRC's reluctance to raise the issue had to do with the "mere fact of raising it would concede that the GOJ had a case for sover-eignty over the Senkakus," and expressed his hope that the two countries could have a discussion on the Senkakus problem.[312] Chien asked for U.S. assistance, and reiterated three grievances on the issue: (1) ROC was excluded from San Francisco Peace Treaty Conference of 1951; (2) it was not consulted on the Nixon-Sato communiqué (of 1969); and (3) it was not consulted on the Bray statement of April 9. Thomas responded that the GRC had not claimed the Senkakus until 1971, and reminded Chien there was no reaction from the GRC on the September 1970 State Department statement. Chien did not respond to this point, it seems, which in part probably explains student agitation on the issue—the GRC's belated handling of the issue.

Of note, the protests were not limited to Taiwan. In Hong Kong on the afternoon of April 10, students demonstrated in front of the Japanese Cultural Office against the GOJ claims. The demonstration, which was organized by an ad hoc group of students and youth who called themselves the "Protect Tiaoyutai Islands Action Group of Hong Kong" and members of the staff of *70's Bi-Weekly*, had not been permitted by the police, however, and had so informed the students ahead of time.[313] When students refused a police order to disperse and a scuffle ensued, 21 students were arrested and taken to a nearby police station. The rally ended at this point, and protestors gave up on their plan to proceed to the U.S. Consulate General to present a petition there.

Although they had not been in charge of organizing the demonstration, two student federations called a meeting that evening to complain of "police brutality" and to chart the future of the protests, including the possible boy-cott of Japanese and American products.[314] Student leaders that evening and the next day in press interviews stressed that the demonstration was not directed at the Hong Kong Government and that the demonstrations on the Senkakus issue had "no political implications" and instead came from "patriotic considerations alone."[315]

The political adviser for the Hong Kong Government said it was "not much concerned" over the demonstration, agreeing that "young students are always looking for popular causes, and Senkaku is a good one."[316] "Chinese of all political coloration resist Japanese," he continued, with the "chief danger of young student demonstrators [being] that they might be taken over by more experienced people with more sinister motives, but there was no evidence so far that this had happened."[317] The political adviser felt that the Japanese consul general in Hong Kong was always "most sensitive to any suggestion of anti-Japanese sentiment" and as he always asked for police protection when any demonstration was likely, this may have "prompted an extra-firm police reaction to the demonstration."[318] David L. Osborn observed that overall, the "publicity-hungry students appear[ed] to have been the moving influence behind the demonstration" and that there was "little significant political backing" and "no indication of Communists' involvement."[319] Osborn noted that more protests were scheduled for the coming weekend and that while "further disorder is still possible ... nothing serious anticipated."[320]

Osborn was correct. That weekend on April 17 some 1500 youths and students in Hong Kong organized by the Hong Kong Federation of Students gathered at different schools in the colony displaying banners critical of Japan's "ambitions to the sovereignty of the Senkakus."[321] Some students also criticized "U.S.–Japan connivance," and called for a Hong Kong-wide boycott of Japanese and American goods. Still others called for a protest march into the central district of the city. The next day (April 18), a smaller group of students met, and a professor called on the assembled crowd to boycott Japanese goods as a student took his Japanese-made watch and smashed it to the cheers of the crowd who apparently vowed not to buy Japanese products. Editorials in the local press, the Embassy report stated, were generally supportive of the students' interest in protecting Chinese rights in the Senkakus but urged that there be no disorderliness or lawlessness.

Student protests in Hong Kong continued over the following weeks. On May 4, for example, some fifty to seventy-five students wearing "Protect Senkaku Islands" armbands and chanting various slogans and displaying banners that read: "Senkakus are China's Sacred Soil," "Oppose U.S.–Japanese Collusion on Senkakus," and "U.S. Has No Right to Dispose of Senkakus," peacefully demonstrated in front of the U.S. Consulate General in the latter afternoon.[322] Prior to showing up there, about 200 demonstrators had gathered at the Queen's Pier Concourse to protest Japanese claims to the Senkakus. Twelve of the demonstrators, including the editor *70's Bi-Weekly*, were arrested by police as the gathering was not approved. Osborn noted that some of the students had planned to court arrest to get publicity for their cause. Police warned the remaining protestors to disperse, which they did, heading to the U.S. Consulate.

A couple of weeks later on May 16, a subsequent demonstration was held in front of the Consulate by "64 generally docile and disciplined Chinese teenagers, outnumbered by onlooking newsmen, Hong Kong Police, and spectators."[323] Slogans denouncing "U.S. Imperialism" and "Japanese militarism" were displayed and sung, as was one that said "Both Tiao Yu Tai and Hong Kong are Chinese Territories." The demonstrators asked the Consulate if they could burn a Japanese flag but were denied permission, so they proceeded to trample on and tear a small, homemade flag depicting a rising sun.

On May 23, 1971, an "Open Letter to President Nixon and Members of Congress" costing 10,000 dollars was published in the *New York Times*, which had been signed and financed by over 700 professors, scholars, professional people, and students opposed to "turn[ing] the Tiao Yu Tai islands over to Japan" as part of the Okinawa Reversion Agreement.[324] The letter noted that the USG's allowing the islands to be reverted to Japan "contradicted the principle of neutrality" established by the State Department in its September 10, 1970 statement, and it asked the president and Congress to "reconsider" the U.S. position on the return of the islands.[325] It ended with "an appeal to you to use your initiative and moral authority to assure that the legitimate rights of the Chinese People will not be sacrificed as an expedient to international politics. Your just action in this matter will improve the prospects for peace in the Pacific area."[326]

These government-to-government exchanges only highlighted the tensions that had been growing in the ROC–United States relationship in the past couple of months and the degree of the Taiwanese public's anxieties over these issues. A telegram in early April from the U.S. Embassy in Taipei noted that "there has been an upsurge of Chinese nationalist feeling on [the Senkakus] issue in Taiwan and among overseas Chinese, evidenced by a heated reaction to the Bray statement of April 9. This wave of feeling in Taipei has led to public criticism of the ROC's management of the affair and strong feeling against the ROC's two strongest friends," the United States and Japan.[327] The Embassy recommended either it be allowed to urge the ROC to request bilateral discussions with the Japanese (and the United States endorse those talks), or that a statement be made by the United States that the 1952 Sino–Japanese Peace Treaty provides a "mechanism" for dealing with the dispute.[328] It further emphasized that "the anti-American feeling generated in April was a new development here which we must make every effort to counter. There is an urgent need to consider this and other ways to remove the U.S. from a dispute which basically does not involve the U.S. and which seems to augur greater difficulties for the future unless we can get the GOJ to the conference table where it belongs with the GRC."[329]

During this time, rumors had been circulating that the Senkakus had been occupied by "Okinawan troops" who were firing on ROC fishing boats from Ilan County. Chien followed up with Thomas about these rumors.[330] The political counselor responded that he knew of no such troops nor of anyone "occupying" the Senkakus, but offered to check on the rumor and subsequently contacted the High Commissioner's office to inquire. In response, the High Commissioner's office the next day responded that a local check confirmed the Senkakus remained "uninhabited" and "unoccupied" and that the only recent activity in the Senkakus area had been a Ryukyu University survey team in late March-early April and a GRI Police patrol boat responding to a distress call by a GRC vessel and conducting a search in the Sekibi Sho area on April 5–6.[331] As such, the High Commissioner's office responded, the "rumor appears [to be] without foundation."[332]

Later the next month (June), after the signing of reversion agreement, Chien was informed of a photography operation to be conducted by a private company, Lyon Associates, on behalf of the GRI, which would complete a contract signed between the two parties a year and a half before. "It would have no effect," the political counselor of the U.S. Embassy in Taipei assured the director, "on the GRC position with regard to the Senkakus."[333] Chien responded that he appreciated being informed and expressed the hope that nothing would be released, such as a map which would indicate that the U.S. government treated the Senkakus as part of the Ryukyu Islands. The political counselor reiterated the above position.

The Embassy in Taipei had initially been reluctant to allow the photography project to go ahead in the first place. "From our point of view," it noted, "the timing clearly is not propitious" and urged that this "minor project" be delayed until time when "GRC or the Japanese can do it without reference to us."[334] The Embassy was particularly concerned that if the GRC learned of the survey, particularly through the press, it would find it "both embarrassing and objectionable."[335] The likelihood of finding out was high because ROC fishing vessels would probably be in the area and could see the low-flying Piper Aztec plane of the Lyon Associates.

The High Commissioner, on the other hand, while acknowledging the dispute over the Senkakus, and that indeed the Senkakus' air space bordered the Taiwan ADIZ (but was not within it, although it was controlled from Taiwan and thus pilots had to notify it upon entry into air space over Senkakus) felt that in light of Lyon's long-standing contract with the GRI the proposed flight should go through or else some difficulties would be caused both in Okinawa and Japan.[336] Indeed, the survey had begun in April 1970, and the aircraft being used was in Miyako at the time photographing the southern islands. The contract was set to expire at the end of the month.

Perhaps due to the High Commissioner's recommendation, the Department responded that it appreciated the concerns mentioned by the Embassy in Taipei but did not think the USG should intervene at this point to stop the survey in light of the possible costs and "likely reaction on Okinawa."[337] It suggested that while it did not think that the operation would get too much attention, the Embassy was welcome to inform the GRC about it.

There was one survey, however, that the State Department was reluctant to permit: a petroleum-related study by Tokai University, which was scheduled to leave in late June or early July. Although the High Commissioner's office had no objections to it, the State Department thought it to "inopportune" to be done at that time in light of the "timing ... of the reversion agreement" and "political sensitivity" of the Senkakus issue to the GRC, and noted that the visit "would surely raise strong feelings" among Chinese academic community in Taiwan, United States, and elsewhere.[338]

As will be made clear later, the inclusion of the Senkaku Islands in the reversion Okinawa to Japan—in other words, the reversion of administrative rights over the Senkaku Islands, too—was not, in the U.S. government's opinion, "necessarily determinant of [the] question of sovereignty, which we believe should be resolved between claimants or through third party arbitration."[339]

The statement by Bray had been in fact the U.S. position for some time, but it had tried to avoid public statements on the Senkakus, the State

Department told the Embassy in Taipei, "partly out of regard for problems which this issue poses" for the ROC.[340] However, as the Department was pressed for a statement of the government's position in the briefing, "we cannot say less than already on public record or appear to be drawing back from our agreement with Japan on reversion."[341]

The statement represented, perhaps, the type of public announcement that the Embassy in Tokyo had offered to make to ease Japanese concerns about the territorial definition of the islands to be returned. It probably was not enough for the Japanese side, who wanted a more permanent record rather than an oral statement in a press briefing, however.

On the other hand, it was too much for the GRC. As mentioned above, the State Department officially informed the GRC on May 26 that the United States intended to turn the Senkakus over to Japan,[342] and the following week on May 31, Foreign Minister Chow,[343] on the instructions of President Chiang Kai-Shek and his son and vice premier Chiang Ching-kuo, met with Ambassador McConaughy to discuss the Senkakus and other matters, "Senkakus Islands issue [being the] most urgent."[344] Chow noted that he had seen press stories that the signing of the reversion agreement might be as early as June 15 and that Nakasone Yasuhiro, director general of the Japan Defense Agency, had stated to the effect that Japanese forces would defend the Senkaku Islands and station troops there. The GRC, Chow told the ambassador, was under attack in some of the Chinese-language media and if the agreement were signed as planned, and the Japanese press played it up "which is likely," the GRC would find it "very embarrassing and be under severe pressure" even though the islands are "intrinsically unimportant; just a few rocks in the ocean, but they are of great symbolic significance to the Chinese, and have been made into an issue of real significance by Chinese intellectuals in the U.S."[345]

Having requested the USG to consider excluding the Senkakus from the Okinawa Reversion Treaty in his farewell call on President Nixon, Chow told McConaughy that he had now been instructed to make a formal follow-up request to the USG to exclude the disputed area from the agreement and kept under U.S. control pending the outcome of negotiations between the GRC and the GOJ as to their conflicting sovereignty claims. "Turning over control to the Japanese," he argued, "would be bound to prejudice the prospect for constructive negotiations."[346] McConaughy promised to convey the request to the State Department, explained that it would be difficult in this "eleventh hour" to change the areas to be returned as they had already been worked out in the reversion agreement, and emphasized the transfer of administrative rights "would have nothing to do with sovereignty claims," a fact which he hoped "would have some calming effect" on demonstrators.[347]

Chow responded by telling the ambassador that the situation was getting out of hand, with threats of violence against government officials, citing the fact that ROC Ambassador to the United States Shen was called a traitor and threatened with bodily harm. The World Chinese Traders Convention in Los Angeles was disrupted by the "Action Committee for the Tiaoyutai," and

Y. S. Sun, Minister of Economic Affairs, and Kao Hsin, head of the Overseas Chinese Affairs Commission, encountered a number of physically aggressive protesters. The leftists, Chow said, were using their version of Chinese patriotism as a weapon against both the GRC and United States, a problem which might flare up into disorders in Taiwan and the United States. "If this minor wound is not healed," Chow argued, "then the broader problem of the propriety of the reversion of Okinawa may be raised" by scholars, the media, and the Legislative Yuan, and "if this problem is disregarded, anti-American and anti-Japanese resentment will be aroused" among Chinese in the United States and in other countries, including continued boycotts of Japanese goods.[348]

McConaughy relayed Chow's message to Washington a couple of days later. The ambassador, while not taking up the merits of the claims of either Japan or Taiwan, nor the "tardiness" of Taiwan's May 31 *demarche*, nevertheless found the idea of deferring the transfer of administrative rights "impressive on practical grounds" in light of the domestic situation in Taiwan and the problems it created for the United States.[349] "The GRC is sustaining severe reverses and disappointments from various quarters and finds itself in a rather beleaguered position," the sympathetic telegram began.[350]

> Some sort of psychological boost to mitigate the series of damaging blows recently suffered is desperately needed. An additional setback now on the Senkaku issue would further undermine GRC prestige in the minds of its national overseas and enable Peking to assume a more plausible pose as the only Chinese government capable of having any impact in defense of Chinese national interests. The likelihood of demonstrations and disorders among Chinese in U.S. and locally on Taiwan as described by GRC Foreign Minister is probably overstated but there may be a basis for anticipation of some disturbances which could put GRC more on defensive.[351]

McConaughy pointed out that the need could be explained on a basis of the undesirability of transferring control before negotiations between the rival claimants had been arranged, and could be bolstered by the undoubted fact that geographically and historically the Japanese relationship to the Senkakus is on a different basis from its relationship to the rest of the islands covered by the draft agreement. The ambassador, aware any changes in the reversion agreement would be problematic for the USG in Japan, argued that the "suggested action is probably the only hope for prevailing on the Japanese to agree to negotiate with the GRC on this issue" and that the Japanese "well know the pressing need at this trying juncture for gestures to bolster GRC morale and prestige."[352]

The telegram was relayed in full by Deputy Secretary of State Irwin who sought the opinions of the Embassy in Tokyo, High Commissioner, and CINCPAC, on June 5.[353] In the meantime, ROC ambassador Shen made the same request to Assistant Secretary Green on June 4.[354]

Shen's calling on Green was specifically done to raise the issue of the Senkakus with the USG again. After acknowledging receipt of the diplomatic note of May 26 setting forth the U.S. position on the status of the Senkakus including the U.S. intention to turn over the administrative rights of the islands to Japan, Shen explained he was aware the United States and Japan had reached a basic understanding on the terms of the reversion agreement and that the USG would soon be submitting it to the Senate for ratification. The reversion of the Senkakus, Shen stated under instructions from Foreign Minister Chow, would present the GRC with a "serious situation."[355] Namely, Shen told Green that the government believed the students were waiting for the signing of the reversion agreement before launching new protests, and feelings were running high in the academic community in Taiwan and abroad, such as in the United States, on the Senkakus issue and viewed it as a test whether the GRC was able to safeguard Chinese rights and interests. "If the GRC failed," Shen emphasized, "scholars would turn to Peking."[356] Appealing on "political, not legal, grounds," Shen asked that the USG, as a "third party" in the dispute, could think of a way to "avoid including the Senkakus for the moment" in the reversion of Okinawa in order to give the GRC "time to work out some solution" with Japan; otherwise, if the Senkakus reverted to Japan with Okinawa the GRC would be "faced with a fait accompli" that would be difficult for the GRC to handle domestically and abroad.[357] In light of the United States having taken over control of the islands on behalf of the Allies after WWII, the USG "has a strong moral obligation," Shen stressed, "to consider the views of the GRC."[358]

Green told Shen that he would consider his remarks, as well as those of Chow to McMonaughy, but pointed out that the USG could not do otherwise than what it has said it would do: the USG "would imperil the reversion agreement if it were now to exempt the Senkakus, inclusion of which has been agreed upon" and "call into question the sincerity of the negotiations."[359] Green advised Shen, as he had done for Chow in his farewell call as well, that rather than asking the USG to reconsider, the GRC should "make its pitch" to Japan, but Shen responded that the GOJ had stated the matter was "non-negotiable" and Shen felt that once the islands were actually turned over to Japan the GOJ would "certainly be even more rigid" in its position.[360] He then asked if the USG, stating "it was in a difficult position vis-à-vis the GRC" would "ask Japan to talk with the GRC" on the Senkaku issue even though reversion negotiations were "essentially completed."[361] Green agreed to consider the suggestion, but pointed out the basic stance of the USG would not change, adding but that "dominant elements of the LDP were sympathetic to the GRC" and thus the "GRC's problem is to demonstrate to Japan that there is something to talk about."[362] Whether Shen knew it or not, but Green in fact was moved by the presentation and facilitated a review of the U.S. stance.

Sneider's response to the U.S. Embassy in Taipei's suggestion to withhold the Senkakus for the time being came on June 7. It was apparent that Sneider and his team were not sympathetic to the GRC position. The telegram,

Sneider noted, "succinctly summed up the problems involved if were to change the U.S. stance on the Senkakus reversion," but "unfortunately, Ambassador Shen lost a real opportunity to impress upon the GOJ Taiwanese views on the Senkakus when he failed to raise the problem with senior foreign office officials during [his] recent visit" to Japan, and sharing that MOFA was "prepared for discussions with Shen if he had raised the Senkakus question."[363]

The Embassy in Taipei was not happy with this response, and prepared a long telegram to the State Department arguing for early U.S. intervention in the dispute in order to bring Japan and Taiwan to the negotiating table. The "recognized channels" to contain this controversy and thus to "remove the U.S. from the dispute" were, in the opinion of the Embassy, Article 22 of the 1951 Allied Peace Treaty with Japan (to which the GRC was not a signatory), and Article 11 of the 1952 Treaty of Peace between the ROC and Japan.[364] Ambassador McConaughy noted that domestic pressure was strong on the GRC to "produce results on the Senkakus" and Foreign Minister Chou was "bearing the brunt of it."[365] The ambassador also expressed a worry about views of the United States and what that meant for the future of GRC–United States relations: "The anti-American feeling generated in April was a new development here which we must make every effort to counter. There is an urgent need to consider this and other ways to remove us from a dispute which basically does not involve us, and which seems to augur greater difficulties for the future unless we can get the GOJ to the conference table where it belongs with the GRC."[366] From McConaughy's perspective, Japan's "refusal" to discuss sovereignty of the Senkakus with the GRC had been the biggest reason for the failure to settle the dispute, and he felt the GOJ was using U.S. assurances to return the Senkakus the following year as a reason not "to show any flexibility."[367] The GRC, on the other hand, preferred in his opinion to discuss only with the USG apparently in part because the GRC did not want to speak directly to Japan as it would enhance Japan's position.

As such, the ambassador asked that the Department authorize the Embassy to suggest privately to Chou that the GRC consider requesting bilateral discussions with the GOJ in the context of the bilateral peace treaty's provisions for settling disputes, and if the GRC were to do so, it would be helpful, McConaughy noted, if the USG could then publicly endorse such GRC–GOJ discussions. The ambassador further suggested that if the GRC had a good reason not to raise the case under its peace treaty with Japan, that the Department consider whether the USG could raise the issue with Japan under Article 22 of the Allied Peace Treaty while the United States still had administrative control over the Senkakus, or at least make a statement that the treaty provides a mechanism for handling the dispute.[368]

Upon receiving the recommendations from the Embassy in Taipei, Robert I. Starr, the legal advisor for the Bureau of East Asian Affairs, produced a five-page memorandum that explored what, if any, legal basis existed for the GRC to raise the Senkakus issue with the GOJ. After analyzing the various related articles in the 1945 Charter of the United Nations, as well as the

Allied Peace Treaty and the GRC–GOJ peace treaty in some detail, Starr concluded that the GRC was "not without legal argument" under its 1952 treaty with Japan or more generally in accordance with the UN charter's principle of peaceful settlement of disputes, to "call upon the GOJ to settle the Senkakus dispute by negotiation or by other pacific means including third party adjudication."[369] With regard to the suggestion that the USG raise the matter with Japan citing Article 22, Starr found that the article was "intended only to provide for settlement of disputes between parties to that Treaty. Since the GRC is not a party to the Treaty, it cannot directly invoke Article 22 vis-à-vis Japan. For these reasons there would appear to be no legal basis for the USG to take the position that the San Francisco Peace Treaty provides a mechanism for dealing with the dispute."[370]

In addition to legal arguments, Starr also provided political and diplomatic advice in the same memorandum. Implying that the perspectives of two other parties in the dispute—Japan and the PRC—were important to consider, Starr closed by first pointing out the importance of the relationship with Japan, which President Nixon called "vital to kind of world we both want" and which Secretary Rogers said in his report, *U.S. Foreign Policy, 1969–1970*, "will be the most important single factor bearing on the success of U.S. policy in East Asia."[371] Starr observed that Japan "obviously attaches great significance" to the impending return of Okinawa, including the Senkakus, and any agreement to negotiate the status of the Senkakus as requested by the GRC might "entail grave political repercussions" for the GOJ, although a willingness "merely to discuss" the matter with the GRC might be less objectionable to the GOJ.[372] Next, Starr hinted at the importance of including the PRC in regional calculations, a full month before the announcement of President Nixon's pending visit to Peking, which was still secret and only known to a few people, although the general tone and direction of U.S. rapprochement with the PRC were becoming clear according to U.S. diplomats at the time:[373]

> Then, too, there is the position of the PRC to consider. The PRC has strongly reasserted its claim to the Taioyu-tai, or Senkakus, and warned Japan not to interfere with China's claim to the islands. If we press the GOJ to negotiate with the ROC, we run the risk of aggravating unnecessarily the state of both the USG's and GOJ's relations with Peking. It is difficult to imagine any conceivable benefit in terms of our relations with the ROC that would justify such a risk, the full consequences of which may not even be calculable at this time.[374]

It was actually during this time that the USG had renewed putting pressure on the GOJ to discuss the Senkakus issue with the GRC, in part due to pressure from the GRC and the belief that this was a way, perhaps the best way, to seek a settlement of the dispute, and in part due to other motivations by U.S. negotiators at the time on a seemingly unrelated issue.

Senkakus for textiles

The issue that became intertwined at this late stage in the final couple of weeks before the signing of the Okinawa Reversion Treaty was the attempt by Ambassador-at-Large for Foreign Economic Development David M. Kennedy to deny the Senkakus to Japan, at the request of Taiwan, in exchange for the latter's cooperation on textile issues—an important and unresolved issue for President Nixon facing re-election in 1972. In a sense, this became a textile issue within the larger textile dispute, or more accurately put, the Senkakus-for-textiles deal that was being sought by Ambassador Kennedy existed within the larger Okinawa-for-textiles deal that Nixon wanted. As such, Kennedy's thorny proposal threatened to further undermine the delicate balance worked at on the Senkakus by the USG that allowed it to extract itself from the problem. While it might have helped Nixon's bid as it would make a larger framework of textile trade-offs possible through Taiwan's desire to see the Senkakus turned over to them, it would have also caused deep and extreme bilateral friction with and unnecessary unhappiness in Japan and have gone against U.S. policy and statements to date. Moreover, it would have fundamentally undermined the U.S. strategic position in the East China Sea as, assuming the United States would be allowed to maintain bases in Okinawa, they would have become unacceptably vulnerable were a third country to control islands close to those bases.

The origin of this Senkakus-for-Taiwan textiles deal is three-fold—the precedent of there being a deal with Japan on its restraining textile exports to the United States parallel to the agreement to return Okinawa (an arrangement that was still being worked out at the time and already causing a great deal of friction between the two countries); the need for Taiwan's acquiescence to make other countries, such as South Korea and Hong Kong, to go along with a larger deal on textiles; and the request by Chiang Kai-shek and his son, Chiang Ching-kuo for U.S. reconsideration of the decision to include the Senkakus in the return of Okinawa to either delay or deny their hand-over to Japan. Kennedy decided to link the latter two issues, and in doing so, get even with Japan, too, for its intransigence on the textile issue and perhaps other issues Kennedy and the White House's economic team had with Japan as they were formulating their "New Economic Policy" vis-à-vis mercantilist Japan, among others in mind.

Kennedy had previously served as Secretary of the Treasury from January 1969 to January 1971, and began his assignment as ambassador-at-large on February 11 at the request of Nixon to stay on as a member of the cabinet. Although basically in favor of free trade, Nixon needed help in light of his election promise in late May 1968 to Senator Strom Thurmond, a former governor of South Carolina, to aid the textile industry. "[This] issue was parochial," Nixon lamented in his memoirs.[375] "Thurmond wanted tariffs against textile imports to protect South Carolina's position in the industry. I reluctantly went along with him on this issue because of political realities, but

I told him that we should try first to get Japan and other countries to agree voluntarily to reduce their exports to the United States before we took tariff route. ... I emerged from this meeting with Thurmond's pledge of support."[376] Initially, Secretary of Commerce Maurice H. Stans had been tasked to try to settle the issue, but he was unsuccessful as were some others.[377] With the White House efforts failing, Wilbur D. Mills, chairman of the House Ways and Means Committee, attempted to broker a deal by urging the Japanese textile manufacturers to limit their exports. They agreed to do so, but the level was seen by Nixon as falling "short of the terms essential to the United States."[378] Thus, Mills' initiative in the spring of 1971 was opposed by the American textile industry and President Nixon.

It was against this background that Kennedy was brought in as ambassador-at-large. Kennedy, according to his biographer, essentially had to work thru not only the bilateral issue with the Japanese, but work out agreements with other countries in the region as well, to include Hong Kong, Korea, and Taiwan, addressing their domestic and economic concerns as well as meeting American expectations. "Patience and tenacity" were necessary to coordinate all of this, as was a "negotiating strategy that would avoid the mistakes of the past."[379] But patience was something the Nixon administration did not have. Shortly before Kennedy's first trip to the region that spring, Peter G. Peterson, the assistant to the president for international economic affairs, wrote, "David, the protectionist measures are building at an alarming rate and we are now afraid if we do not have this wrapped up by mid-June, we could be in real trouble."[380] Peterson was told to support Kennedy, especially in his negotiations with Japan: "The President wants you to play a tough game on textiles and give the Japanese hell for dumping. He does not want you to follow the [Ambassador to Japan Armin H.] Meyer line [of cooperation]. He wants you to hit the Japanese at every chance we can—starting the day after Kennedy leaves."[381]

The "unorthodox" approach Kennedy took was to use "back channel" diplomacy, much like that used by Kissinger, avoiding the bureaucracy, and using CIA communication facilities to coordinate directly with the White House.[382] To do so, Kennedy dealt directly with Peterson, an old friend from banking days,[383] and as a result angering the State Department. But even this system was imperfect, as Kissinger seemed not always in the loop when the textiles-for-Senkakus deal with Taiwan came up and to close the gaps, Kissinger often had to communicate with U. Alexis Johnson who was greatly concerned about Kennedy's effort to be the "President's man" to resolve the textile issue.

Kennedy began his assignment by visiting each country to discuss his work, express his desire to keep the negotiations out of the press and even out of normal diplomatic channels, and request each leader appoint someone at a high level with whom he could work. During his April visit to Taiwan, Chiang Kai-Shek seemed to understand the sensitivities involved, and appointed Sun Yun-suan, the Minister of Economic Affairs since 1969 who had been trained in the United States, to work with Kennedy.[384] Kennedy and his small team returned to Washington upon visiting each country, continued their studies and planning, and then departed for the Far East again on May 31.

The week prior to departing in the early afternoon of May 26, Kennedy's assistant Anthony Jurich met with Peterson. The two of them called Johnson on the phone to discuss the "Okinawa problem" and Johnson agreed to provide further information for them later that day.[385] Kennedy's team was briefed at this point on the Senkakus.

Kennedy's first stop was Taiwan. He spent more than a week there. During that time, Sun announced that an "agreement in principle on certain points" had been worked out, and on June 9, local time, Kennedy held a news conference at the airport where he told the assembled reporters that the two sides had "made very great strides toward solving a number of economic issues, including the textile issue."[386] Kennedy probably was choosing his words carefully as much discussion about the Senkakus had occurred while he was there between him and the White House, as well as with his Taiwanese counterparts, especially Chiang Ching-kuo.

By this point, relations between Taiwan and the United States had been fraying badly as alluded to above. The *New York Times* reported that by the end of April, a "formal correctness has crept into relations ... in place of the warmth that once existed."[387] Chiang lost any liking of or trust he may have had in Nixon or Kissinger. In fact, according to his biographer, "Chiang hated [Nixon] even more than [Joseph W.] Stilwell [Jr.]," the American general who had been a controversial advisor to Chiang during World War II, because Nixon was "naïve about the Communists; he was also disloyal, insincere, and scheming."[388] When Kennedy showed up, following a "cordial discussion" on the textile issue, Chiang spoke about a statement that had been made by the State Department spokesman to the affect that Taiwan's ultimate status awaited final determination, saying it was a "slap in the face" and becoming visibly agitated and upset.[389] U.S. and PRC movements toward opening relations were becoming increasingly apparent as the United States was contemplating inviting the PRC into the General Assembly of the United Nations (but allowing the ROC to retain its seat in the Security Council) and China's invitation to the American ping-pong team to visit China. Chiang, who was also already uncomfortable due to the recently warm and muggy weather and his worsening health, apologized for losing his self-control.[390] Kennedy understood the frustration the Taiwanese felt toward the United States in light of their decline status vis-à-vis China and other issues, such as an oil moratorium on concessions and drilling. He was certainly sympathetic—he later founded the U.S.-Taiwan Business Council in 1976, working closely with Sun in its formation.

Kennedy, in turn, was frustrated with Japan, as were most officials in the Nixon administration. Kennedy, for example, proposed to Washington after arriving in Taiwan in early June that the U.S. government "not sign any Okinawa agreement with the Japanese until the textile negotiations are completed."[391] The scheduled date for the signing, however, was a mere two weeks away, or June 15 (it later became June 17). According to Ernest Johnston and John H. Holdridge of the NSC, the timing Kennedy had in mind was not clear, but Kennedy asked that the president instruct the Embassy in Tokyo, without seeking the State Department's concurrence, that it inform the Japanese government that the United States was "ceasing all discussions with the Japanese on Okinawa" and that after Kennedy met with Prime Minister Sato's older brother, former premier Kishi Nobusuke, to "receive his reaffirmation that we will reach a textile solution" after which "we would then lift the Okinawa suspension."[392] Even the NSC thought this was "too extreme" and instead suggested an "intermediate linkage" which would be relayed via Yamanaka Sadanori, who was visiting Washington, D.C., in early June at the time and who was to meet with Kissinger that evening.[393] The linkage would be done orally, as a request to postpone signing the reversion agreement rather than being done as a unilateral declaration. It is unclear if the message was actually relayed to Yamanaka or not, but the latter did report on his meetings in Washington directly to the prime minister after his return to Tokyo and, according to Sato's diary, Yamanaka "apparently was treated properly by Kissinger there."[394]

It was a couple of days after Yamanaka had met with Kissinger and Johnson that Foreign Minister Chow called in McConaughy and Ambassador Shen called on Assistant Secretary Green about the Senkakus that a pause was initiated to reexamine plans to include the islands among those to be returned.

June 7 was a particularly hectic day. It was made more challenging due to the rushed sense of the Okinawa negotiations to get the agreement signed by the middle of the month, the distances involved (Kennedy being in Taiwan, for example), an apparent unwillingness of Kennedy to share information with anyone other than Peterson, an equal reluctance of the White House to share information with the State Department, media leaks, and the upcoming wedding of the president's daughter, Tricia, that weekend.

Early in the morning, Deputy Undersecretary of State for Political Affairs Johnson called Kissinger mentioning he had heard that Kennedy had sent some cables to Peterson and noting that the Washington Post had printed a story that Kennedy had reached an agreement on Taiwan, with a reference to the Senkaku Islands. Kissinger promised to send the cables to Johnson, noting that he himself found Kennedy's failure to keep him fully informed an "impossible way to do business" and mentioning he was going to "insist that I be sent a copy of everything that goes to Peterson."[395]

A couple of hours later, Kissinger called Johnson and started out abruptly by asking, "About those God damn islands, where do we stand?"[396] Johnson told Kissinger that U.S. policy was "frozen in concrete."[397] Kissinger inquired when U.S. policy had been set, to which Johnson responded that it been established "over a period of several months. I would have to go back on the history of it. The GRC dialogue is 6–7 months. I would have to run it down."[398] Kissinger asked him to do so, and Johnson continued his explanation, "It's frozen in the text of the agreement with Japan. The principle is we received them from Japan and returning them to Japan without prejudice to rights. Just returning them with same rights. No change in rights. They were included in islands in 1945."[399] Kissinger stated he knew the U.S. position already but in fact wanted to know when—"before or after he talked with Chou?"[400] Johnson agreed to check but explained it was difficult to give an exact date because there had been a continuing dialog between the United States and the GRC on it. He added that there was no question with regard to the discussions with the Japanese side and promised him a chronology of bilateral discussions. Kissinger appreciated that offer, telling Johnson that it was "bound to come up with the President."[401]

Johnson eventually gave Kissinger a five-page document entitled "Chronology of Events Relating to Status of the Senkaku Islands," which included statements and American, Japanese, and Taiwanese interactions and movements dating from the Cairo Conference of 1943 through early June 1971,[402] to him later that day, but in the meantime, he called Kissinger in the mid-afternoon. The national security advisor lamented to Johnson that Kennedy was "running amok on these islands," and while qualifying that "I shouldn't be telling you this" that the issue was "now being presented to the President ... as the only thing that can make the textiles go. [Kennedy] has the textiles people lined up."[403] Kissinger then asked Johnson what the legal position was on the islands.

Johnson explained that "in the 1951 treaty with Japan, the territory that we kept out (the Ryukyus) was defined to include these islands."[404] Kissinger asked if it was correct to say that until then the islands had been administered as part of China to which Johnson responded not entirely accurately, "No. You would have to go back to when (sic) Formosa under Japanese rule."[405] Johnson explained he had his staff were working on what position China took at the time of the treaty in 1951—"I want to find out if they made a *reclama* at the time of the treaty or that they signed the treaty at that time."[406] (Here, too, Johnson misspeaks, or he simply forgotten or is downright mistaken, as the ROC never signed the Allied Treaty of Peace with Japan, since it had not been invited, nor had the PRC. Kissinger did not correct him, for he simply tells Johnson, "Find out as quickly as possible ... get the information to my office and they will get it in to me at the meeting."[407]) Kissinger then asked Johnson if altering the status of the Senkakus to placate Taiwan would "blow the whole thing up," namely the Okinawa reversion agreement talks with Japan, or not.[408] Johnson said indeed it would: "There is not the slightest question about this blowing up the Okinawa negotiations with the Japanese."[409] Johnson suggested that the "one thing we can do is get the Japanese (since the Chinese [Taiwanese] have refused to take the initiative in talking to the Japanese) to take the initiative in talking to the Chinese (ROC) and explain our problem."[410] Kissinger asked about the U.S. recommending it go to the International Court of Justice. In response, Johnson stated that the issue "is not ours to say. It is not our territory. We have no sovereignty. It is a territorial dispute under our present administration of Okinawa. We just administer it—it is a Japanese-Chinese [Taiwanese] question."[411]

Johnson called over to the White House a little bit later while Kissinger was in his meeting with the President discussing Taiwan and the Senkakus issue, and reported some of the above answers to U.S. Army Brigadier General Alexander M. Haig, Jr., Kissinger's deputy who had served under MacArthur in Japan during the latter years of the Occupation, who in turn shared them with Kissinger. According to the confidential memo, Johnson relayed four points to Haig for Kissinger—that "Nationalist China" was not a signatory to the 1951 Treaty of Peace, that the Senkakus were included in the 1953 proclamation by the Civil Administration in Okinawa and the ROC at the time did not challenge this delineation and have since admitted this fact, that the State Department was researching the pre-annexation history of the islands, i.e., before Japan's annexation of Formosa (sic), and Johnson's view that the Japanese should be encouraged to take the issue up with Taipei, as Chen did not do so en route to the United States via Japan.[412]

Just after Kissinger talked to Johnson and before he went in to his meeting with Nixon and Peterson, Kissinger's counterpart as the president's assistant for International Economic Affairs, the president called Kissinger. The two of them discussed how to handle the issue. Nixon began by asking Kissinger, "what position are we involved in … does it involve the big thing?"[413] The "big thing" appears, from the context of the Kissinger's response, to be a reference to the opening of relations with the PRC, and thus the reason for the conversation being held over the telephone and not in front of Peterson. Kissinger answered simply, "Blow up negotiations with Japan. Both Chinese prefer it part of Taiway (sic). They figure they could it if they get Taiwan."[414] The President stated, "We have a very important point to make here to try to do something on the textile-thing," to which Kissinger said, "this would be a hell of a price to pay with the Japanese. The [Okinawa Reversion] treaty is to be signed in about a week."[415] Nevertheless, Kissinger told the president that Kennedy thought the USG should raise with Japan the question of the *quid pro quo* over the Senkakus-textile issue with Taiwan.

Both Kissinger and Johnson, for different reasons, were bothered by Kennedy's last-minute actions, raising a possible exchange of the Senkakus for Taiwan's cooperation on textile restraints. Kennedy had written to Johnson and asked "direct questions" about Okinawa. Johnson wrote back but still had not heard anything as of June 5, and nor had Kissinger.[416] Kissinger, speaking with Johnson by phone, said, "I never thought of [Kennedy] as a tiger. He was so meek in Treasury."[417] Johnson expressed his own frustration— "everything he did is told us by the Japanese. It would have been nice to hear it from him."[418] Kissinger joked, "whenever your people weep about me, remind them of what else could happen," and ended by saying when he knew something he would call him.[419]

Kennedy's views on the Senkakus/textile issues had been made known in a telegram he sent from Taipei, where he was negotiating with the Taiwanese on a five-year voluntary restraint agreement for textiles, on the 7th based on a request made by Chiang Ching-kuo during one of their meetings. Peterson, who was on board and was simply "acting as Kennedy's agent" in Kissinger's eyes,[420] summarized Kennedy's telegram and pointed out that Kennedy saw three alternatives to break a serious impasse that had arisen. The third one was to offer concessions to Taiwan. The merits of this alternative, according to Peterson's summary, was that "Ambassador Kennedy feels the impasse can be broken without causing disastrous effects for either our industry or the Taiwan Government. While the [Taiwanese] have stressed the importance of certain military items (F-4's for example) Ambassador Kennedy is convinced that the 'only' way to resolve the issues is to withhold turning the Senkaku Islands over to Japanese administrative control under the Okinawa Reversion Agreement."[421] According to Peterson, Kennedy's argument on the Senkakus was as follows:

This is a major issue in Taiwan with both domestic and international implications. If the U.S. were to maintain administrative control, it would give the GRC a tremendous public boost since they have expressed themselves so forcefully on the issues. Further, it would be a very direct indication of our continued interest in and support for the GRC—and it would be done at Japan's expense, a point that is vital to our ability to proceed effectively with textile negotiations in Hong Kong and Korea and subsequently in Japan. Announcement of such a decision allows the GRC to save face both at home (it takes the Vice Premier off the hook) and abroad. Taiwan could accept the current textile package in face of Hong Kong and Korean pressure. In addition, such an act would, in my opinion, provide a very badly needed shock effect on the Japanese. It would indicate that U.S. acquiescence in all matters requested by the Japanese could no longer be taken for granted. I can fully appreciate the opposition which such a proposal will generate in certain quarters of our government. But I feel that this can and must be done. We accepted stewardship of these Islands after World War II. Neither historically nor geographically are they a part of the Ryukyus Chain containing Okinawa. Consequently, the GRC suffers a great loss of face if we allow Japan to gain administrative control of them. Since possession of the Islands is still in dispute, there is every reason for the United States to maintain administrative control until such time as the dispute is settled. Taiwan feels very strongly that once Japan had administrative control there is absolutely no possibility of their ever relinquishing that control. By no means am I suggesting that we hand the islands over to Taiwan. Rather, I am strongly recommending the wisdom of preserving the status quo rather than allowing Japan to assume administrative control with the great loss of face this entails for Taiwan. I know of no other action sufficiently important or sufficiently dramatic to resolve our textile problems specifically as well as to pave the way for resolution of several general international trade difficulties. The stakes involved are very high which I fully realize. I realize, too, that only the President can make such a decision. Therefore, I urge you in the strongest possible terms to present to him all the potential benefits and ramifications of my recommendations.[422]

Peterson finished his memo by informing the president that Kissinger was looking into the background of the Senkakus dispute and would report to the president at their meeting in the afternoon "on what would be involved in not turning over the Senkaku Islands to Japan at this time."[423] In summary, Peterson was suggesting, based on the exchanges between Taiwan and U.S. officials to date, that the return of the Senkaku Islands to Japan be delayed indefinitely to mollify Taiwan as a price of negotiation on the textiles with Taiwan.

It is unclear when Peterson prepared the memo but it appears to have been delivered by Rose Mary Woods, the president's personal secretary who had been with Nixon since his days as a Congressman in 1951, after lunch, just before 1 p.m.[424] The president reviewed the memo for his meeting with Kissinger and Peterson, which began at 3:26 p.m.[425]

It was Kissinger that had called for the meeting, but the impetus had been Kennedy and his memo. In a memo to the president, requesting the meeting, Kissinger wrote, "Ambassador Kennedy has been approached by both Chiang Kai-Shek and Vice Premier Chiang Ching-Kuo in Taipei about the issue of the Senkaku Islands. Under the present reversion arrangements with Japan, they will revert to Japanese administrative control. This is a delicate issue of the greatest importance to the ROC. I believe it is essential that you meet ... this afternoon to discuss the current status of the Senkakus."[426] They did, and President Nixon decided to continue with the arrangements to revert administrative rights to Japan, but not, it appears, to do any more to openly side with Japan. The desire of the Chiangs, that the return of the Senkakus to Japan be delayed or denied outright, was rejected by the White House.

The next day, Peterson informed Kennedy what took place the evening before. "After a lengthy discussion," he told the ambassador-at-large, who was about to depart Taipei, that the deal has gone too far and too many commitments made to back off now. I showed your wire on this and even reread the portion dealing with its importance. The president was deeply regretful that he could not help on this, but he felt that the decision was simply not possible. The president has instructed me to tell you that he will send a senior military representative in August to review with GRC in "a favorable and forthcoming way" important defense capabilities. I've explained that this makes final negotiations now very difficult but decision is August visit because of need to do this while Congress is out in August.[427]

Kennedy met with Vice Premier Chiang in the morning of the 9th.[428] By the 10th, Chiang had learned of Nixon's decision. He was disgusted, and wrote so in his diary: "[I] heard that the U.S. is returning (territories) back to Japan, in which the Tia Yu Tai are included. (I) feel it is utterly unjust."[429] The next day, the ROC's Ministry of Foreign Affairs issued a long statement (appearing as Appendix 4) re-emphasizing its views, calling on the two governments to recognize its claims, and expressing its "strongest opposition to the impending transfer."[430] The statement had the blessing of President Chiang, as he had reviewed it that morning.[431] An editorial in Taipei the following day described the statement as "just and serious" and added that "all army men and civilians of the ROC fully support the statement and pledge to provide backing for their government in its negotiations with the United States and Japan."[432]

U.S. final push for a GOJ–GRC dialog

Around this time, Secretary Rogers was on the other side of the world, attending the 10th OECD Ministerial Council Meeting being held in Paris. Johnson, who was serving as Acting Secretary, wrote to Rogers to inform him about the status of the situation in a couple of telegrams, both written on June 8th. In the first one, Johnson told Rogers about the meeting the previous day back in Washington explaining, "Henry Kissinger stepped into the breach with material that I supplied him, and last night obtained the President's decision that we would not change our position on the Senkakus [to delay the return of the islands in favor of Taiwan]. However, this points up the heat GRC is bringing to bear on us and in turn in some degree probably reflects the heat that GRC is feeling on a subject that it neglected for so long."[433]

In the second one, Johnson went into greater detail on the background of the Senkakus issue and the situation as seen from Washington: "This has blown up into a major issue with the GRC on which we need Japanese help, and I suggest you discuss with Aichi."[434] Johnson further explained,

> we are inclined to take the GRC concern seriously and are concerned that at the time the Okinawa Reversion Agreement is announced, this issue could provoke serious anti-American and anti-Japanese reaction on Taiwan and in the overseas Chinese community. At a time when the GRC is facing a number of difficult challenges, we feel it is in our mutual interest with Japan to do what can be done to assist the GRC in avoiding such a situation. For example, it might be helpful if prior to announcement of reversion agreement, GOJ would take the initiative in discussing with the GRC possibilities for meeting its problem; alternatively, GOJ might consider making clear it recognizes dispute exists which it believes should be handled through normal diplomatic channels. You might ask Aichi for any ideas he may have, emphasizing value we see in enabling GRC to make showing for its public at least, that reversion agreement does not foreclose all possibility of pursuing its claim. In any event, we and GRC very much need GOJ help on this matter.[435]

Both of these telegrams reached Rogers in Paris. In addition to OECD matters, Rogers was there to meet with Aichi to finalize the arrangements for the Okinawa Reversion Treaty. Ericson had gone to Paris as well to assist Rogers in his meeting with the Japanese foreign minister. Some last minute changes and additions came up, such as the Senkakus issue, and Ericson went over to the "lavish space in the Crillon" where the Japanese delegation was— "a Japanese Foreign Minister and his entourage always travel first class"—to explain them and request Japan's concurrence.[436] Aichi agreed to the change, even though his staff was against it. "I will take responsibility for it," the confident foreign minister, who had met with Sato and the director general of the Prime Minister's Office Hori Shigeru for some final coordination on June 3 on the eve of his departure, responded.[437]

The change in the text was not about the Senkakus, but there was one additional request that Rogers made to Aichi at their meeting. Namely, the secretary of state mentioned it would be "very helpful if the Japanese could fairly promptly initiate discussions" with the GRC on the Senkakus.[438] Aichi, responding in some detail,

> expressed confidence that because of his close relations with the GRC he could assure the Secretary that the matter could be kept under control and would not seriously inconvenience the U.S. He pointed out that the reversion agreement carefully avoided any mention of the Senkakus by name, and that the agreed minute to Article I of the agreement which defines the territories to be returned mentions only longitudes and latitudes. However, recalling that the GOJ had discussed this subject with the GRC immediately following the Nixon/Sato communiqué [of 1969], the Foreign Minister agreed that if it appeared necessary, Japan could do so again. He said the discussion would take the form of Japan informing the GRC of the meaning of what had taken place between the U.S. and Japan. The Secretary commented that we did not think of this point as a condition for the agreement, but did wish to point out that the reversion agreement does not affect the jurisdictional problem one way or another.[439]

Shortly after this, the State Department requested the Tokyo Embassy to immediately follow up, with relaying a "personal message" from Rogers to Aichi that read:

> You will recall our recent discussions on the Senkaku problem. I appreciated your understanding of handling this matter in such a way as will not inconvenience the United States and your offer to discuss this subject with the Republic of China if that appeared necessary. I have given this matter further thought and have concluded that such an approach by your government is indeed both necessary and urgent. The President is most concerned that a situation not arise which, either by provoking serious public criticism in the Republic of China of the agreement we have reached or by subjecting that government to attack, could be harmful to

our mutual interests. I strongly urge, therefore, that you give most serious consideration to discussing this issue with the Republic of China prior to signature of the reversion agreement. In informing the Republic of China of the meaning of what has taken place between our governments, I would hope that you would note your Government's understanding that, in the view of the United States, the inclusion of the Senkakus in the territories defined in Article I of the agreed minute is without prejudice to the claims of either side to those islands. Such a statement, of course, would not in any way affect the legal position of Japan on this issue. Sincerely, William P. Rogers.[440]

The telegram also asked the Embassy to report immediately any comments Aichi made on this request.

In a memorandum to Kissinger dated the same day (June 10), Johnson proposed that once confirmation had been received that the Japanese had in fact discussed the issue with the Taiwanese, "referring to Chiang Ching-kuo's message to the President through Kennedy, we have McConaughy inform Chiang Ching-kuo and take credit for the Japanese move."[441] Johnson also suggested that McConaughy inform Chiang Ching-kuo (as well as the Japanese side) that the State Department spokesman would make the following statement in response to "undoubted questions":

The United States government is aware that a dispute exists between the Governments of the Republic of China and Japan regarding the sovereignty of the Senkaku Islands. The United States believes that a return of administrative rights over those islands to Japan, from which those rights were received, can in no way prejudice the underlying claims of the Republic of China. The United States cannot add to the legal rights Japan possessed before it transferred administration of the islands to the United States, nor can the United States by giving back what it received diminished the rights of the Republic of China.[442]

In the meantime, the Department had been told that Aichi would "do his best with [the] GRC" to fulfill his promise to the secretary.[443] Johnson subsequently wrote to Sneider on the 14th to follow up on Aichi's efforts, and encourage him to do it "as soon as possible and, in any event, before June 17."[444] Johnson further informed Sneider that the State Department spokesman would, "in response to query," make the above statement at its noon briefing on June 17, and that it intended to inform the GRC and GOJ before then.[445] Johnson sought the views of the embassies in both Tokyo and Taipei on the timing, but told them in any case not to take action until instructed.

On June 15, Yoshino told Sneider, who immediately informed the Department, that Aichi, upon his return from Europe to Japan on June 13, met late on June 14 with ROC Ambassador to Japan Peng "to discuss the Senkakus problem in fulfillment of his promise to the Secretary."[446] Specifically, Aichi spoke to Peng about his conversation with Rogers, mentioning "U.S. concerns about the Senkakus problem and the views of the U.S. with respect to these islands as set forth in final para[graph of] Secretary's message."[447] According to the telegram, Aichi also reiterated to Peng that his statement did not affect the legal position of the Japanese government on the Senkakus issue, but "in view of friendly relations between Japan and GRC, the Japanese government intended to treat Senkakus issue with utmost care and play down issue. He urged the ROC to do likewise in interests of strengthening relations between the two countries."[448] For the record Aichi also had also expressed "regret" over the GRC's June 11 statement. Peng informed Aichi that he would report the conversation to his government.

Kennedy, who was in Korea at this time, was informed on the 15th that Aichi and Peng had met to discuss the Senkakus issue and asked if he wanted to tell Chiang Ching-kuo personally of Aichi's approach, or if he wished to have the chargé d'affaires do so. On the 15th as well, Secretary Rogers sent instructions with regard to the contents of the U.S. statement to be made at the State Department press conference on the 17th to both the Embassy in Tokyo ("You should inform the GOJ at anytime on the 16th") and Taipei ("You should inform Foreign Ministry not before 1400 hours June 16 Taipei time" unless Ambassador Kennedy "would personally like to use this information with GRC in order to help his negotiations.").[449]

Earlier on the morning of June 15, the Japanese Cabinet met to discuss the agreement. Foreign Minister Aichi explained its contents, and sought the concurrence of the other Cabinet members. As per the Japanese Cabinet Law (*Naikakuho*), all members of the Cabinet must concur in a decision for it to be official. Two conservative members of the Cabinet—Defense Agency Director General Nakasone and Minister for Administrative Affairs Yamanaka—raised their concerns, according to the posthumously published diary of Prime Minister Sato.[450] In particular, it was Yamanaka, who would become the first minister for Okinawan Affairs the following year, that was most bothered by aspects of the agreement, including the handling of the Senkakus. In his memoirs he wrote,

> I argued that I could not, as a minister in charge, sign my name to a reversion treaty that did not include the Senkaku Islands in it. If I did not sign it, then the treaty would not go into effect. I have no idea what sort of discussions took place between the Japanese and U.S. sides, but Sato, who listened to our discussions, looked troubled. 'Minister Yamanaka,' Sato said, 'is passionate about Okinawa, and I see that he cannot be budged from his position. However, if this is the case, there is no telling then when Okinawa will get returned.' It was as if the prime minister was sending me a lifeboat to rescue me [from my hard-headed position].[451]

Sneider met with Aichi on another matter the next day (16th), but took advantage of the timing to share with him a copy of the statement to be made if asked by the spokesman. In presenting it, Sneider told Aichi that it was necessary to keep the statement secret until issued on the 17th. Aichi read it and "reacted favorably but withheld comment on its specifics."[452] Sneider then proceeded to urge the GOJ to avoid any comments on the U.S. statement that would "further inflame" the Senkakus issue, stressing the "importance, from viewpoint of both GOJ and U.S., to avoid provoking further problems for GRC."[453] Aichi said he understood "this need very fully,"[454] but relations between Japan and Taiwan remained strained despite the close ties between the conservative members of the LDP, including Sato and Finance Minister Fukuda Takeo, soon to be named as foreign minister, and the Kuomintang Party of Chiang Kai-shek. Just before this conversation, for example, on June 15, Ambassador Itagaki called on Chow to protest the June 11 statement and to ask the GRC to keep a lid on the issue.[455] This request did not seem to have its intended effect, as on the 17th, national assemblymen issued a statement denouncing the U.S. and Japanese governments.[456] Indeed, tensions would continue to grow during the summer and into the following year.

Notes

1 John M. Allison, *Ambassador from the Prairie or Allison Wonderland* (Boston, MA: Houghton Mifflin Co., 1973), 157. Article 3, which dealt with the disposition of the Nansei Island chain as well as the Nanpo Islands, of the Treaty of Peace with Japan read: "Japan will concur in any proposal of the United States to the United Nations to place under its trusteeship system, with the United States as the sole administering authority, Nansei Shoto south of 29 degrees north latitude (including the Ryukyu Islands and the Daito Islands), Nanpo Shoto south of Sofu Gan (including the Bonin Islands, Rosario Island and the Volcano Islands) and Parece Vela and Marcus Island. Pending the making of such a proposal and affirmative action thereon, the United States will have the right to exercise all and any powers of administration, legislation and jurisdiction over the territory and inhabitants of these islands, including their territorial waters." Incidentally, Article 2 (b), which the Republic of China stated meant that the Treaty of Peace returned the Senkaku Islands to Taiwan, of the same treaty read: "Japan renounces all right, title and claim to Formosa and the Pescadores."

2 See Eldridge, *The Origins of the Bilateral Okinawa Problem*, 306.

3 See Eldridge, *The Return of the Amami Islands*, and Eldridge, *Iwo Jima to Ogasawara o Meguru Nichibei Kankei*.

4 "Joint Statement of Japanese Prime Minister Sato and U.S. President Johnson, November 15, 1967," *Public Papers of the President: Lyndon B. Johnson, 1967*, 1033–37.

5 Nixon and Sato would meet again a year later on October 24 when Sato, who was in the United States to attend the United Nations General Assembly meeting, traveled down to Washington to meet with Nixon and attend a White House dinner. Some eight issues, including the textile dispute (discussed later), were discussed but at this point it does not look like the Senkakus came up. Nixon reportedly advised Sato that the goal was to accomplish reversion in 1972 but that depended on working out all the essential arrangements to allow the prior approval of the legislatures of both countries. See diary entry for October 24, 1970, *Sato Eisaku Nikki*, Vol. 4, 192, "Memorandum from U. Alexis Johnson for the President on Meeting with Prime Minister Sato of Japan, 4:00 p.m., Saturday,

October 24, October 21, 1970," and "Memorandum from Henry A. Kissinger for the President on Meeting with Japanese Prime Minister Sato, Saturday, October 23, 1970," *Ibid.*

6 "Joint Statement of Japanese Prime Minister Eisaku Sato and U.S. President Richard Nixon, November 21, 1969," *Public Papers of the Presidents: Richard Nixon, 1969,* 953–57.

7 For more on Meyer, see Armin H. Meyer, *Assignment Tokyo: An Ambassador's Journal* (Indianapolis, IN: Bobbs-Merrill Company, Inc., 1974).

8 Aichi died shortly after the return of Okinawa and was unable to pen his memoirs although at least two collections of his writings were published. See Aichi Kiichi Ikoshu Kankokai, ed., *Tenjinmachi Hodan* (Tenjinmachi Dialogue), (Tokyo: Aichi Kiichi Ikoshu Kankokai, 1974), and Nihon Keizai Kenkyukai, ed., *Suteetsuman: Aichi Kiichi Zuisoroku* (Statesman: The Collected Writings of Aichi Kiichi) (Tokyo: Nihon Keizai Kenkyukai, 1979). Meyer dedicated his own memoirs to Aichi's memory.

9 Meyer, *Assignment Tokyo,* 31–32.

10 Meyer, *Assignment Tokyo,* 382.

11 Meyer, *Assignment Tokyo,* 31. Also see Togo Fumihiko, *Nichibei Gaiko Sanju Nen: Anpo, Okinawa to Sono Go* (30 Years of Japan–U.S. Diplomacy: The Security Treaty, Okinawa, and After) (Tokyo: Sekai no Ugokisha, 1982), Okawara Yoshio, *Oraru Hisutorii: Nichibei Gaiko* (Oral History: Japan–U.S. Diplomacy), (Tokyo: The Japan Times, 2006), and Chiba Kazuo, "The Reversion of Okinawa," *Insight Japan,* April 2000, 11–13.

12 Toshijiro Nakajima, "Ending the Post-war Period," *Foreign Service Journal,* Vol. 69, No. 2 (May 1992), 27–29.

13 Author's interview with Yoshino Bunroku, August 29, 2012, Yokohama, Japan.

14 Kuriyama, Takakazu (edited by Nakajima Takuma, Hattori Ryuji, Eto Nahoko), *Gaiko Shogenroku: Okinawa Henkan, Nicchu Kokko Seijoka, Nichibei "Mitsuyaku"* (Diplomatic Testimony: J Okinawa Reversion, Japan–China Normalization of Relations, and the Japan–U.S. "Secret Agreements") (Tokyo: Iwanami Shoten, 2010), 94–95.

15 "Interview with Charles A. Schmitz, July 29, 1993," Association for Diplomatic Studies and Training Foreign Affairs Oral History Project.

16 "Interview with Charles A. Schmitz."

17 Author's interview with Daniel Sneider, December 12, 2012, Stanford, CA (by telephone).

18 "Interview with Charles A. Schmitz."

19 Author's interview with Charles A. Schmitz, March 24, 2009, Washington, DC. Also see Charles A. Schmitz, "Working Out the Details," *Foreign Service Journal,* Vol. 69, No. 2 (May 1992), 24–26.

20 "Interview with Charles A. Schmitz."

21 "Interview with Charles A. Schmitz."

22 "Interview with Charles A. Schmitz."

23 Author's interviews with Richard B. Finn, August, September, November 1997; June 1998, Bethesda, MD.

24 Patricia Sullivan, "Diplomat Richard A. Ericson, Jr. Dies; Korea, Japan Expert," *Washington Post,* December 11, 2005. Also see Don Oberdorfer, *The Two Koreas* (New York: Basic Books, 1997), 54.

25 "Interview with Richard A. Ericson, Jr., March 27, 1995," Association for Diplomatic Studies and Training Foreign Affairs Oral History Project.

26 "Interview with Richard A. Ericson, Jr."

27 "Interview with Richard A. Ericson, Jr."

28 "Interview with Richard A. Ericson, Jr."

29 Author's interview with Howard M. McElroy, July 10, 2012, Warminister, PA (e-mail).
30 "Interview with Richard A. Ericson, Jr."
31 "Interview with Richard A. Ericson, Jr."
32 "Interview with Richard A. Ericson, Jr."
33 "Interview with Richard A. Ericson, Jr."
34 "Interview with Richard A. Ericson, Jr."
35 Kuriyama, *Gaiko Shogenroku*, 92.
36 Author's interview with Yoshino Bunroku, August 29, 2012, Yokohama City, Japan.
37 " Letter from Howard M. McElroy to Charles A. Schmitz, February 27, 1970," Folder: Japan 1970, Box 6, Subject Files of the Office of China Affairs, 1951–75, RG 59.
38 "Telegram 129846 from State Department to Embassy Taipei on Continental Shelf, August 11, 1970," POL 32–36 Senkaku Is, RG 59.
39 "Telegram 135439 from State Department to Embassy Taipei on Senkaku Islands, August 19, 1970," POL 32–36 Senkaku Is, RG 59.
40 "Telegram 6502 from Embassy Tokyo to State Department on Senkaku Islands, August 22, 1970," POL 32–36 Senkaku Is, RG 59. The telegram contained several factual errors, particularly about the dates and Diet discussion.
41 "Telegram 6502."
42 "Telegram 6502."
43 Author's interview with Chiba Kazuo, December 1, 2000, Tokyo, Japan, and Chiba, "The Reversion of Okinawa."
44 "Telegram 6502."
45 "Telegram 6502."
46 "Telegram 6502."
47 "Telegram 6502."
48 Nakasone, later prime minister, was serving as director general of the Defense Agency at this time, in the third Sato Eisaku cabinet, which began on January 14, 1970. See Kitaoka Shinichi, *Jiminto: Seikento no 38 Nen* (The Liberal Democratic Party: 38 Years as the Ruling Party) (Tokyo: Yomiuri Shimbunsha, 1995), 291.
49 For more on him, see Yamano Kokichi, *Okinawa Henkan no Hitorigoto* (The Story of the Reversion of Okinawa) (Tokyo: Gyosei, 1982).
50 "Telegram 6502."
51 "Telegram 6502."
52 "Telegram 6816 from Embassy Tokyo to State Department on Senkaku Islands, September 2, 1970," POL 32–36 Senkaku Is, RG 59.
53 "Telegram 6816."
54 "Telegram 6816."
55 "Telegram 6967 from Embassy Tokyo to State Department on Senkaku Islands, September 4, 1970," POL 32–36 Senkaku Is, RG 59.
56 Interestingly, a memorandum prepared that same day by the U.S. Embassy on the status of reversion negotiations did not seem to identify the Senkakus as a future problem. See "Airgram 902 from Embassy Tokyo to State Department on Okinawa Reversion Negotiations: Status Report after Nine Months, September 2, 1970," Def 4 Japan–U.S, RG 59.
57 "Telegram 147079 from State Department to Embassy Tokyo on Senkaku Islands, September 8, 1970," POL 32–36 Senkaku Is, RG 59.
58 *Ibid.*
59 "Telegram 3913."
60 *Ibid.*
61 "Telegram 7093 from Embassy Tokyo to State Department, September 9, 1970," POL 32–36 Senkaku Is, RG 59.
62 "Telegram 7093."

63 "Telegram 148490 from State Department to Embassy Tokyo on Senkaku Islands, September 10, 1970," POL 32–36 Senkaku Is, RG 59.

64 "Telegram 148490."

65 Although the question was not asked, the State Department had prepared a response if the question, "What is the U.S. position regarding the continental shelf adjacent to the Senkaku Islands?" was asked: "In the event of a dispute over the adjacent continental shelf, this would be a matter for resolution by the parties concerned." See "Telegram 148490."

66 "Telegram 7213 from Embassy Tokyo to State Department on Senkaku Islands, September 11, 1970," POL 32–36 Senkaku Is, RG 59.

67 "Telegram 7213."

68 "Telegram 7213."

69 "Telegram 7213."

70 "Telegram 7213."

71 "Telegram 7213."

72 "Telegram 7213."

73 "Telegram 7213."

74 "Telegram 7213."

75 James C. H. Shen, *The U.S. and Free China: How the U.S. Sold Out Its Ally* (Camarillo, CA: Acropolis Books, 1983).

76 "Telegram 4000 from Embassy Taipei to State Department on Senkaku Islands, September 15, 1970," POL 32–36 Senkaku Is, RG 59.

77 "Telegram 4000." The oral statement read:

"Concerning the legal status of the Tiao-yu-tai Islands (also known as the Senkaku Islands), the Government of the Republic of China wishes to make the following observations:

Prior to its annexation by Japan in 1879, an act which China has never accepted or recognized, the Ryukyus was an independent Kingdom having had a long tributary relationship with China. Since World War II, the islands have been placed under U.S. military occupation. Pursuant to Article III of the Japanese Peace Treaty signed in San Francisco on September 8, 1951, the U.S. excersies all powers over the territory and inhabitants of the islands south of 28 degrees North Latitude and east of a line between 124.40 degrees and 122 degrees East Longitude. The Tiao-yu-tai Islands happen to lie on the border of this area. The Chinese government has hitherto not challenged this arrangement, as it considers the U.S. military presence in the Ryukyus as an important factor in the maintenance of regional security in the Western Pacific.

In the joint communique signed by President Richard M. Nixon and Prime Minister Eisaku Sato on November 21, 1969, it was stated that the U.S. and Japan would immediately enter into consultations regarding specific arrangements with a view to accomplishing the 'reversion' of the Ryukyu Islands to Japan in 1972. The Chinese government has had reservations regarding the proposed disposition of the Ryukyu Islands, because it has all along maintained that the legal status of the Ryukyus should be determined by the principal allied powers concerned through consultations in accordance with the Cairo Declaration and the Potsdam Declaration, and that the people of the Ryukyus should be afforded an opportunity to express their views with regard to their own political future. But out of consideration for its friendly relations with both Japan and the U.S., the Chinese government refrained from making its objection at the time, though it did voice its regret over the failure of the U.S. to follow proper procedure before reaching a decision in this connection.

Recently however, the Japanese government brought up the question of the Tiao-yu-tai Islands. They consist of a group of uninhabited islets only 100 miles or so to the northeast of Taiwan. Fishermen from Taiwan have been visiting these islands every year in large numbers, for fishery and collection of birds eggs as well as to use them as a haven in case of storsm. Both historically and geographically, therefore, the Tiao-yu-tai Islands have had an extremely close relationship with China and particularly with the island province of Taiwan.

The Japanese government's claim is based on two arguments: (1) that an Imperial Edict of 1896 made the Tiao-yu-tai Islands part of the prefecture of Okinawa; and (2) that a Japanese national, named Koga Tatsujiro (*sic*), leased the Tiao-yu-tai Islands from the Japanese government in 1896 for a period of 30 years, that the same Japanese later purchased the islands from the Japanese government in 1930 and that his son, Koga Yoshitsugu (*sic*), is the present owner.

The Chinese government does not find these arguments acceptable. In the first place, when Japan annexed the Ryukyu Islands in 1879, the Tiao-yu-tai Islands were not included. It was not until 1896, one year after Japan had acquired Taiwan 'Together with all islands appertaining or belonging to' Taiwan from China as a result of the Shimonoseki Treaty, that the said imperial edict was issued and the lease granted. The Imperial Edict of 1896, therefore, was only an adminstrative measure on the part of the Japanese government when both Taiwan and the Ryukyus were under its occupation.

Secondly, in the Sino–Japanese peace treaty signed on April 28, 1952, Japan renounced all rights, titles and claims to Taiwan, Penghu (Pescadores) and other islands nearby which appertained or belonged to Taiwan prior to 1895. It is the position of the Chinese government that the 'other islands' included the Tiao-yu-tai Islands.

Moreover, in the Cairo Declaration it is stated that 'Japanse sovereignty shall be limited to the islands of Honshu, Hokkaido, Kyushu, Shikoku' and such minor islands as may be determined by the three principal allied powers, the U.S., China, and the United Kingdom.

As to the lease in 1896 and subsequent purchase in 1930 of the Tiao-yu-tai Islands by the Koga family, they were merely domestic arrangements made by the Japanese government which can not in any way alter the legal status of these islands.

For these above-mentioned reasons, the Chinese government finds itself unable to accept the Japanese claim of sovereignty over the Tiao-yu-tai Islands. It is hoped that the U.S. government will take full notice of the Chinese government's views and position on this question. The Chinese government will keep the U.S. government informed on any further developments as they may arise in the future."

78 "Telegram 3956 from Embassy Taipei to State Department on Senkaku Islands, September 12, 1970," POL 32–36 Senkaku Is, RG 59.

79 "Telegram 150567 from State Department to Embassy Taipei on Senkaku Islands, September 14, 1970," POL 32–36 Senkaku Is, RG 59.

80 "Telegram 152599 from State Department to Embassy Taipei on Senkaku Islands, September 17, 1970," POL 32–36 Senkaku Is, RG 59.

81 "Telegram 152599."

82 "Telegram 4208 from Embassy Taipei to State Department on Senkakus, September 26, 1970," POL 32–36 Senkaku Is, RG 59.

83 "Telegram 7522 from Embassy Tokyo to State Department on Senkakus, September 22, 1970," POL 32–36 Senkaku Is, RG 59.

84 "Telegram 7522." The Taiwan Provincial Garrison Command, which was succeeded by the All-Taiwan Provincial Garrison Command, was established on September 1, 1945. Peng led the command, infamous over the years for suppression and authoritarian rule, from 1947–49.

85 "Telegram 4208."
86 "Telegram 7522."
87 "Telegram 4208."
88 "Telegram 4208." The report was probably not true. At the minimum, it seems to have been a misinterpretation or misunderstanding of the GRI Police's actions, which took place on Uotsuri Jima, and not on any vessel belonging to the Taiwanese.
89 "Telegram 4208."
90 "Telegram 4208."
91 "Telegram 4208."
92 "Telegram 4208."
93 The State Department took up Moser's suggestion that it examine the negotiating record of the 1954 mutual defense treaty with the ROC to see if there was Taiwanese acceptance of Japan's claims. No comment was found in the records of the time, but in part that is because the Senkakus were not disputed then. Moreover, as the State Department noted, because the ROC–United States security treaty did not cover the Senkakus area, it could be interpreted that the GRC had approved of the Senkakus being Japanese.
94 "Telegram 7767 from Embassy Tokyo to State Department, September 30, 1970," POL 32–36 Senkaku Is, RG 59.
95 "Telegram 7767."
96 "Telegram 7767."
97 "Telegram 3995 from AmConsul Hong Kong to State Department on Senkaku Islands, October 2, 1970," Folder 4, Box 20, RG 319, History of USCAR.
98 "Telegram 7767."
99 "Telegram 7767."
100 "Telegram 7767."
101 "Telegram 7767."
102 "Telegram 7767."
103 "Telegram 7767."
104 "Telegram 7767."
105 "Telegram 161340 from State Department to Embassy Taipei on Senkakus, September 30, 1970," POL 32–36 Senkaku Is, RG 59.
106 "Telegram 161340."
107 "Telegram 4377 from Embassy Taipei to State Department on Senkakus, October 8, 1970," POL 32–36 Senkaku Is, RG 59.
108 "Telegram 4377."
109 "Telegram 4377."
110 "Telegram 4377."
111 "Telegram 4377."
112 "Airgram A-341 from Embassy Taipei to State Department on Taiwan Provincial Assembly Resolution on Senkakus, October 29, 1970," POL 32–36 Senkaku Is, RG 59.
113 Itagaki became the Japanese ambassador to the ROC on June 20, 1969. He was succeeded by Uyama Atsushi on March 11, 1972. Uyama had previously served in Tehran as Japan's Ambassador to Iran when Ambassador Meyer was there. Uyama was a "good friend" of Meyer's and "occasional bridge partner" who had counseled Meyer about the important assignment that awaited him in Tokyo, especially the reversion of Okinawa. See Meyer, *Assignment Tokyo*, 7–8.
114 "Telegram 4318 from Embassy Taipei to State Department on Senkaku Islands, October 5, 1970," POL 32–36 Senkaku Is, RG 59.
115 "Telegram 4318."
116 "Telegram 7989 from Embassy Tokyo to State Department on Senkaku Islands, October 6, 1970," POL 32–36 Senkaku Is, RG 59.
117 "Telegram 4377."

118 "Telegram 4377."
119 "Telegram 4377."
120 "Telegram 4377."
121 "Telegram 4377."
122 "Telegram 4377."
123 "Telegram 4377."
124 "Telegram 4377."
125 "Telegram 4377."
126 "Telegram 4377."
127 "Telegram 4377."
128 "Draft cable from Ericson to Tokyo, Taipei, and High Commissioner, Ryukyu Islands, undated," Folder 4, Box 20, RG 319, History of USCAR.
129 "Draft cable from Ericson, undated."
130 "Draft cable from Ericson, undated."
131 "Draft cable from Ericson, undated."
132 "Draft cable from Ericson, undated."
133 "Draft cable from Ericson, undated."
134 Author's interview with William Clark, September 12, 1997, New York City.
135 "Confidential message from High Commissioner, Okinawa, Ryukyu Islands, to Department of Army, undated," Senkaku Retto (Sento Shosho) (Tia Yu Tai) Files, Okinawa Prefectural Archives.
136 "Confidential message from High Commissioner, Okinawa, Ryukyu Islands, to Department of Army, undated."
137 "Confidential message from High Commissioner, Okinawa, Ryukyu Islands, to Department of Army, undated."
138 "Confidential message from High Commissioner, Okinawa, Ryukyu Islands, to Department of Army, undated."
139 "Confidential message from High Commissioner, Okinawa, Ryukyu Islands, to Department of Army, undated."
140 "Confidential message from High Commissioner, Okinawa, Ryukyu Islands, to Department of Army, undated."
141 "Telegram 168794 from State Department to Embassy Tokyo on Senkakus, October 13, 1970," Folder 4, Box 20, RG 319, History of USCAR.
142 "Telegram 168794."
143 Nakajima Takuma, "Kaidai Kuriyama Takakazu to Nichibei-Nicchu Kankei (Introduction: Kuriyama Takakazu and Japan–U.S., Japan–China Relations)," in Kuriyama, *Gaiko Shogenroku*, 2.
144 "Telegram 8347 from Embassy Tokyo to State Department on Senkakus, October 15, 1970," Folder 4, Box 20, RG 319, History of USCAR.
145 "Telegram 8347."
146 "Telegram 8347."
147 "Telegram 8347."
148 "Telegram 8347."
149 "Telegram 8347."
150 "Telegram 4696 from Embassy Taipei to State Department on Continental Shelf and Senkakus, October 30, 1970," POL 19 Ryu Is, RG 59.
151 "Telegram 4696."
152 "Telegram 4696."
153 "Telegram 4696."
154 "Telegram 4696."
155 "Telegram 8684 from Embassy Tokyo to State Department on Senkakus and Continental Shelf, October 26, 1970," Pol 32–36 Senkaku Is, RG 59. The GOJ had also found out the Gulf exploration concession included the Senkakus land areas and areas within the territorial waters of the Senkakus.

156 Nancy Bernkopf Tucker, *Strait Talk: United States–Taiwan Relations and the Crisis with China* (Cambridge, MA: Harvard University Press, 2009), 123.

157 "Telegram 8684."

158 "Telegram 8684."

159 "Telegram 8684."

160 "Telegram 4696." According to a later memorandum of conversation, at some point, following Watanabe's visit to Taiwan, Ambassador Itagaki delivered a note to the GRC on the Senkakus. "The note had proposed a 'truce' and made firm proposals about delineating the continental shelf. It stated categorically that the GOJ would not discuss territorial matters around the Senkakus. Mr. Yoshida, somewhat gleefully, said that the note hinted very obviously that the GOJ did not want a reply, certainly not rapidly. Now, a month later, the GRC has said absolutely nothing more on the subject so the Japanese think that they may have understood their intent. When asked about the recent PRC comment on the continental shelf question, Mr. Yoshida said that precisely because of that, Japan would never, he repeated, never negotiate seriously with the GRC, because of the PRC. He added, saying that this was not a GOJ view, that there was a current theory that the GRC was less interested in the in the economics of the continental shelf and the Senkakus than in successfully negotiating with the GOJ, an act which would involve and thereby commit the GOJ to and with the GRC in this area, and preclude involvement and commitment to the PRC in the area." See "Memorandum of Conversation between Shigenobu Yoshida and L. Desaix Anderson on Senkakus, etc., December 11, 1970," Folder: Japan 1969, Box 6, Subject Files of the Office of China Affairs, 1951–75, RG 59.

161 "Memorandum of Conversation between Shuroku Kuroiwa and Charles T. Sylvester, April 16, 1969, on New Ambassador, etc.," Folder: Japan 1970, Box 6, Subject Files of the Office of China Affairs, 1951–75, RG 59.

162 "Memorandum of Conversation between Kuroiwa and Sylvester."

163 "Telegram 9219 from Embassy Tokyo to State Department on Senkakus, November 14, 1970," POL 32–36 Senkaku Is, RG 59.

164 "Telegram 9219."

165 Frederick Chien, *Qian Fu Huiyi Lu* (Memoirs of Frederick Chien), (Taipei: Tianxiayuanjianchuban Gufenyouxiangongsi [Commonwealth Publishing, Co.], 2005), 138.

166 Chien, *Qian Fu Huiyi Lu*, 138.

167 "Telegram 8128 from Embassy Tokyo to State Department on Okinawa Reversion: General Reversion Agreement-GOJ Counter-Proposal October 8, 1970, October 9, 1970," POL 19 Ryu Is, RG 59.

168 "Telegram 8128."

169 "Telegram 8304 from Embassy Tokyo to State Department on Okinawa Reversion: General Reversion Agreement, October 14, 1970," POL 19 Ryu Is, RG 59.

170 "Telegram 8304."

171 "Telegram 8304."

172 "Telegram 8304."

173 "Telegram 8304."

174 Nevertheless, Nakajima wrote in 1992 that participating in the negotiations was "an unforgettable challenge and, at the same time, [was] my good fortune to have been able to take part in these negotiations." Nakajima, "Ending the Post-war Period," 29.

175 Nakajima Toshijiro (edited by Inoue Masaya, Nakajima Takuma, and Hattori Ryuji), *Gaiko Shogenroku: Nichibei Anpo, Okinawa Henkan, Tenanmon Jiken* (Diplomatic Testimony: Japan–U.S. Security Treaty, the Okinawa Reversion, and the Tiananmen Incident), (Tokyo: Iwanami Shoten, 2012), 243–45.

176 "Telegram 174738 from State Department to Embassy Tokyo on Okinawa Reversion: General Agreement, October 23, 1970," Folder: Basic Documents, Including Communique, Box 9, RG 319.

177 "Telegram 8891 from Embassy Tokyo to State Department on Okinawa Reversion: General Agreement, November 2, 1970," POL 19 Ryu Is, RG 59.

178 Selig S. Harrison, "Red China, Japan Claim Oil Islands," *Washington Post*, December 5, 1970; "Red China Claims Senkaku Island Area," *Japan Times*, December 5, 1970. Shortly after that, an editorial in a pro-KMT newspaper, *Tin Tin Yai Pao*, on December 7 stated that Japan would not have challenged China's territorial sovereignty "had China been united ... Although [it] is not prestigious, the call for national unification in a pro-KMT paper is unusual and interesting," noted David L. Osborn, the Chinese-speaking Consul General in Hong Kong. See "Telegram 5169 from AmConsul Hong Kong to State Department, December 16, 1970," POL 32–36 Senkaku Is, RG 59. Earlier that fall Osborn observed that for a while the PRC might be in a "something of a dilemma" over how to react publicly since the GRC's claims regarding the continental shelf "appear to be an extension of its position that it is the sole legitimate government of China must touch sensitive nerves in Peking ... [It] obviously cannot accept Taipei's right to assert those claims. Thus far, Peking has chosen to meet this problem by remaining silent, but it may decide before long to issue propaganda blasts warning both the GRC and the Japanese away from the area." See "Telegram 3995." The day before, the Consulate had sent a similar analysis as well as the translation of an editorial in the September 21 issue of *Ching Po*. See "Airgram 272 from AmConsul Hong Kong to State Department on Chinese Communist Commentary on Senkaku Islands Issue, October 1, 1970," POL 32–36 Senkaku Is, RG 59.

179 Following the NCNA report on December 4, the Japanese Foreign Ministry spokesmen stated in the afternoon that Japan had been "expecting the PRC to make such a statement, sometime or other, and it is not surprising at all." See "Telegram 9802 from Embassy Tokyo to State Department on Senkakus–PRC Claim, December 4, 1970," POL 32–36 Senkaku Is, RG 59.

180 "Telegram 10171 from Embassy Tokyo to State Department on Okinawa Reversion: General Reversion Agreement, December 16, 1970," Pol 19 Ryu Is, RG 59. The State Department had worked on a "comprehensive study of the complex political, economic, legal, and commercial problems ensuing from conflicting claims to the Chinese continental shelf," an interim report, entitled "Preliminary Discussion of Peking's Most Recent Statements on Latin American Claims to a 200-Mile Territorial Sea, Its Continental Shelf, and the Senkaku Islands, December 11, 1970," which was submitted to Kissinger in mid-December 1970. See "Memorandum for Mr. Henry A. Kissinger on Territorial Seas and Seabeds, December 14, 1970," POL 32–36 Senkaku Is, RG 59. The four-page report noted that "from a foreign policy standpoint, the U.S. is confronted by the totally conflicting claims of the PRC and the GRC, and by the fact the PRC now claims the Senkaku Islands which the U.S. has already declared will go to Japan as part of Okinawa reversion settlement."

181 "Telegram 10171."

182 "Telegram 10171."

183 "Telegram 10171."

184 "Telegram 10171."

185 "Telegram 10171."

186 "Telegram 10171." The author finds the wording here strange and inconsistent with State's position; instead of "along with Ryukyus," the phrase should probably read: "as part of Ryukyus."

187 "Memorandum of Conversation on Review Status of Okinawa Negotiations, February 1, 1971," Folder: Meyer-Aichi Meeting, Box 19, RG 319.

188 "Memorandum of Conversation on Review Status of Okinawa Negotiations, February 1, 1971."
189 "Memorandum of Conversation, February 1, 1971." For the Annex to the Amami reversion agreement, see Eldridge, *The Return of the Amami Islands*, 162, and for the annex to the Ogasawara reversion agreement, see Eldridge, *Iwo Jima to Ogasawara o Meguru Nichibei Kankei*, 452.
190 "Telegram 2280 from Embassy Tokyo to State Department on Okinawa Reversion Negotiations: Inventory of Outstanding Issues, March 15, 1971," Pol 19 Ryu Is, RG 59.
191 "Telegram from EA/J to Embassy Tokyo on Okinawa Reversion: General Agreement, undated" Folder 4, Box 20, History of USCAR, RG 319, National Archives.
192 "Telegram from EA/J to Embassy Tokyo on Okinawa Reversion: General Agreement, undated."
193 "Telegram 61219 from State Department to Embassy Taipei on Senkakus, April 16, 1971," POL 32–36 Senkaku Is, RG 59.
194 "Telegram 3959 from Embassy Tokyo to State Department on Okinawa Reversion: General Agreement—Article 1, April 29, 1971," Folder: Basic Documents Including Communiqué, Box 9, History of the Civil Administration of the Ryukyu Islands, RG 319.
195 "Telegram 3959."
196 "Telegram 079692 from State Department to Embassy Tokyo, May 7, 1971," Folder 4, Box 20, RG 319.
197 Amerikakyoku Hokubei Daikka, "Okinawa Henkan Mondai (Yoshino-Sneider Kaidan), Showa 46.5.6 (Okinawa Reversion Problem (Meeting between Yoshino and Sneider), May 6, 1971)," Chii Kyotei-SOFA no Tekiyo STG-Shisetsu-Kuiki (5), B'.5.1.0.J/U24, H22–011, Gaimusho Gaiko Shiryokan (Diplomatic Record Office, Foreign Ministry), Tokyo, Japan.
198 "Okinawa Henkan Mondai (Yoshino-Sneider Kaidan), Showa 46.5.6."
199 "Telegram 4401 from Embassy Tokyo to State Department on Okinawa Reversion: Draft Agreement—Article 1, May 13, 1971," Folder 4, Box 20, History of USCAR, RG 319.
200 Amerikakyoku Hokubei Daikka, "Okinawa Henkan Mondai (Aichi Daijin-Maiyaa Taishi Kaidan), Showa 46.5.11 (Okinawa Reversion Problem (Meeting between Minister Aichi and Ambassador Meyer), May 6, 1971)," Okinawa Kankei 17, 0600–2010-00029, H22–012, Gaimusho Gaiko Shiryokan (Diplomatic Record Office, Foreign Ministry), Tokyo, Japan.
201 "Telegram 4401."
202 "Telegram 61219."
203 "Telegram 085466 from State Department to Embassy Tokyo on Okinawa Reversion: Article 1, May 17, 1971," Folder: Basic Documents Including Communiqué, Box 9, RG 319.
204 "Telegram 085466."
205 "Telegram 4575 from Embassy Tokyo to State Department, May 18, 1971," Folder 4, Box 20, History of USCAR, RG 319.
206 "Telegram 4575."
207 "Memorandum from Winthrop G. Brown to Ambassador Johnson on Chronology of Events Relating to Status of the Senkaku Islands, June 7, 1971," POL 32–36 Senkaku Is, RG 59.
208 "Taipei Plots Move on Senkaku Issue," *Japan Times*, February 4, 1971.
209 "Telegram 883 from Embassy Taipei to State Department on ROC Claims Senkakus, February 26, 1971," POL 32–36 Senkaku Is, RG 59.
210 "Telegram 883."
211 "Telegram 883."

212 "Telegram 883."
213 "Telegram 883."
214 "Telegram 883."
215 "Telegram 45384 from State Department to Embassy Taipei, March 17, 1971," POL 32–36 Senkaku Is, RG 59.
216 "Telegram 45609 from State Department to Embassy Taipei on GRC Claim to Sovereignty over Senkakus, March 18, 1971," POL 32–36 Senkaku Is, RG 59.
217 "Telegram 45609."
218 "Telegram 45609."
219 "Telegram 45609."
220 "Telegram 45609."
221 "Telegram 45609."
222 "Telegram 45609."
223 "Telegram 45609."
224 "Telegram 45609."
225 "Telegram 1268 from Embassy Taipei to State Department Senkaku Islands: GRC Foreign Vice Minister Shen's Conversation with Ambassador, March 22, 1971," POL 32–36 Senkaku Is, RG 59.
226 "Telegram 1268."
227 "Telegram 1268."
228 "Telegram 1268."
229 "Telegram 1268."
230 "Telegram 1268."
231 "Telegram 1268."
232 "Telegram 1268."
233 "Telegram 1268."
234 "Memorandum for Mr. Henry A. Kissinger on Farewell Call on the President by Ambassador Chow Shu-kai of the Republic of China, April 10, 1971," POL 32–36 Senkaku Is, RG 59.
235 "Memorandum from Brown to Johnson."
236 "Telegram 2666 from Embassy Taipei to State Department on Senkakus and Okinawa Reversion, June 2, 1971," POL 32–36 Senkaku Is, RG 59.
237 Suganuma, *Sovereign Rights*, 226.
238 "Chinese Protest Senkaku Is. Claim at Japanese U.N. Mission," *Japan Times*, February 1, 1971. One of the students at National Taiwan University caught up in the protests, Ma Ying-jeou, later completed his dissertation about the Senkakus issue ("Disputes over Oily Waters: A Case Study of Continental Shelf Problems and Problems and Foreign Oil Investments in the East China Sea and Taiwan Strait") at Harvard University in 1981 where he specialized in the Law of the Sea and international economic law. In 2008, he became president of Taiwan. Interviewed in 1996 for a book about Chiang Kai-shek's son, Ma, who was born in Hong Kong in 1950 and moved to Taiwan the following year, recalled that he joined a group of mainlanders and Taiwanese students who went to the airport to throw eggs at the Japanese ambassador. See Jay Taylor, *The Generalissimo's Son: Chiang Ching-kuo and the Revolutions in China and Taiwan* (Cambridge, MA: Harvard University Press, 2000), 306. An article in a Japanese magazine has Ma, at Harvard University at that time, but that appears to be incorrect. See Wani Yukio, "Fumo na Senkaku Nashonarizumu: Kurihara Ke ga Kakaeru 25 Okuen no 'Fusai' Taiwan-Hong Kong 'Hotsu Undo' to Senkaku Jinushi no Ryodo Bijinesu," *Shukan Kinyobi*, No. 896 (May 25, 2012), translated by John Junkerman, as "Barren Senkaku Nationalism and China-Japan Conflict," *The Asia-Pacific Journal*, Vol. 10, Issue 28, No. 4 (July 9, 2012).
239 "Telegram 1090 from AmConsul Hong Kong to State Department, February 23, 1971," POL 23–28 HK, RG 59.
240 "Telegram 1090."

241 Mok Chiu Yu, "Theater, Migrant Workers and Globalization: The Hong Kong Experience," in Don Adams and Arlene Goldbard, eds., *Community, Culture, and Globalization* (New York: Rockefeller Foundation, 2002), 353–67, (http://arlenegoldbard.com/wp-content/uploads/2007/11/ccg_chapter_20.pdf, accessed August 2012).

242 "Telegram 1090."

243 "Telegram 1090."

244 "Telegram 783 from Embassy Taipei to State Department, February 22, 1971," POL 32–36 Senkaku Is, RG 59.

245 "Telegram 783."

246 "Telegram 783."

247 "Telegram 1337 from Embassy Taipei to State Department on Overseas Scholars on Senkakus: Chang Chun's Reply, March 25, 1971," POL 32–36 Senkaku Is, RG 59.

248 "Telegram 1337."

249 "Telegram 1337."

250 "Telegram 1337."

251 Diary entry for December 7, 1970, Chiang Kai-shek Diary.

252 Diary entry for January 31, 1971, Chiang Kai-shek Diary.

253 "Telegram 1507 from Embassy Taipei to State Department, April 2, 1971," POL 32–36 Senkaku Is, RG 59.

254 "Telegram 1507."

255 "Telegram 1507."

256 "Telegram 1507." An analysis of the December 4 article appears above. With regard to the December 29 commentary in the *People's Daily* warning against oil survey operations along the mainland and in the seabed around Taiwan and the "islands appertaining thereto," an analysis by the Director of Intelligence and Research at the State Department warned that "encounters between Chinese naval vessels and oil company ships involving warnings and harassment could occur, with all the accompanying opportunities for miscalculation, pressures for intervention by the GRC, error, and escalation into more serious incidents. However, the Chinese remain cautious and any physical response will be one that can make their point while keeping the risks of a major confrontation low." See "Intelligence Brief (INBR) 226 from George C. Denney, Jr., to Secretary of State on Communist China: Peking Warns Against Seabed Encroachment, December 29, 1970," POL 32–36 Senkaku Is, RG 59.

257 "Telegram 1507."

258 "Telegram 1507."

259 From Tokyo, Ambassador Meyer chimed in by writing, "We are confident GOJ will continue to hold line on note setting up a meteorological station on Senkakus during period of U.S. administration. Nevertheless, recommend against authorizing GRC to use this information publicly. Should GRC make information public, particularly in manner which would inferentially support its claim to Senkakus, it would likely result in GOJ pressure to construct meteorological station immediately. GOJ already very sensitive about GRC claims to Senkakus. Press is carrying occasional articles supporting GOJ position on this. Should GRC push case very hard publicly, it is quite possible that GOJ resistance would not be limited to Senkaku issue but could affect GOJ position on broader issues such as UN representation." See "Telegram 3054 from Embassy Tokyo to State Department on Senkakus, April 5, 1971," POL 32–36 Senkaku Is, RG 59.

260 "Airgram A-29 from AmConsul Montreal to Department of State on Japan's Claims to Tiao Yu Tai Islands Protested, April 5, 1971," POL 32–36 Senkaku Is, RG 59. The letter from the Chinese Students' Union of Canada read:

Dear Mr. Sato,

This is a letter to express our strong protest against the presumptuous claims of your government over the Tiao Yu Tai Islands. That the Tiao Yu Tai Islands are part of the sovereign territory of China is an indisputable fact based on historical and gerographical (sic) evidences and on international law. We firmly disagree that these islands should be related to the Ryukyu Islands scheduled for reversion to your country in 1972, as unwarrantedly claimed by your government since last summer. In September, 1970, your government incited the use of military personnel to harass our fishermen who have been fishing in that area for year, and to disparage the Nationalist Chinese flag on the islands. These outrageous acts are most intolerable, and have offended the Chinese people. In recent years, the tendency of resurrecting Japanese militarism of forty years ago has become increasingly apparent despite disclaims from your government. The situation is beginning to resemble Japanese militarism of forty years ago. It is our sincere hope that the bloodshed and sacrifices of both our people in the past will prevent a similar tragedy today or in the future. In calling your attention to this, I am speaking on behalf of the Chinese Students' Union of Canada which represents the majority of the Chinese students in Eastern Canada. We seriously urge the Japanese government to reconsider the above mentioned points carefully so as to enhance international justice and not to disappoint all peace-loving people in the world.

Yours truly,

Jimmy Chang Board Chairman, CSUC, Chief Co-ordinator, Special Committee on Tiao Yu Tai Incident, CSUC.

261 Mark Wilson, "Chinese Protest Island Chain," *Montreal Star*, April 5, 1971.

262 "Chinese Students Demonstrate," *Montreal Gazette*, April 5, 1971.

263 "U.S. Cautions Oil Seekers Near China," *Washington Post*, April 10, 1971; "Senkakus Sovereignty Issue Should be Solved in Talks: State Dept. Firms Advised Not to Explore Oil Resources," *Japan Times*, April 11, 1971; Terrence Smith, "Oil Hunt Off China Stirs U.S. Warning: Companies Told They Risk Ships in Dispute Involving Peking, Taiwan, Tokyo," *New York Times*, April 10, 1971.

264 "Draft Guidance to U.S. Oil Companies," Folder: Petroleum March 1971, Box 9, Subject Files of the Office of Republic of China Affairs, 1951–75, RG 59. Interestingly, in a subsequent press conference, State Department spokesman Bray was asked if he considered the guidance to the oil companies a "warning" but he demurred answering directly: "I hesitate only because I can't recall whether it was."

265 "Draft Guidance to U.S. Oil Companies."

266 "Telegram 1627 from Embassy Taipei to State Department, April 10, 1971," Folder: Senkaku Retto (Sento Shosho) (Tia Yu Tai), Okinawa Prefectural Archives.

267 "Telegram 1625 from Embassy Taipei to State Department on Senkakus, April 10, 1971," POL 32–36 Senkaku Is, RG 59.

268 "Telegram 1625."

269 "Telegram 1625."

270 "Telegram 61219."

271 "Telegram 61219."

272 "1,000 Chinese Protest Japan's Islands Claims," *Washington Post*, April 11, 1971.

273 John Sherwood, "Chinese Here Protest Islands Decision," *Sunday Star*, April 11, 1971.

274 "U.S. Chinese Ask Backing on Island," *New York Times*, April 12, 1971.

275 "Telegram 1751 from Embassy Taipei to State Department on Demonstrations over Senkakus, April 16, 1971," POL 32–36 Senkaku Is, RG 59.

276 "Telegram 1752 from Embassy Taipei to State Department on Demonstrations over Senkakus, April 16, 1971," POL 32–36 Senkaku Is, RG 59.

277 "Telegram 1751."
278 "Telegram 1755 from Embassy Taipei to State Department on Demonstrations over Senkakus, April 16, 1971," POL 32–36 Senkaku Is, RG 59.
279 "Telegram 1790 from Embassy Taipei to State Department on Senkakus Demonstrations, April 19, 1971," POL 32–36 Senkaku Is, RG 59.
280 "Telegram 1754 from Embassy Taipei to State Department on Demonstrations over Senkakus, April 16, 1971," POL 32–36 Senkaku Is, RG 59.
281 "Telegram 1754."
282 "Telegram 1754."
283 "Telegram 63601 from State Department to Embassy Taipei on Demonstrations over Senkakus, April 15, 1971," POL 32–36 Senkaku Is, RG 59.
284 "Telegram 63601."
285 "Telegram 63601."
286 "Telegram 1790 from Embassy Taipei to State Department, April 19, 1971," POL 32–36 Senkaku Is, RG 59.
287 "Telegram 1790."
288 "Telegram 1839 from Embassy Taipei to State Department, April 22, 1971," Folder: Senkaku Retto (Sento Shosho) (Tia Yu Tai), Okinawa Prefectural Archives.
289 "Telegram 1839."
290 "Telegram 1839."
291 "Telegram 1790."
292 "Telegram 1790."
293 "Telegram 1790."
294 "Telegram 1840 from Embassy Taipei to State Department on Senkakus Demonstrations, April 21, 1971," POL 32–36 Senkaku Is, RG 59.
295 "Telegram 1868 from Embassy Taipei to State Department on GRC Flag Removed from Senkakus, April 22, 1971," POL 32–36 Senkaku Is, RG 59.
296 "Taiwan Students Continue Protest," *Japan Times*, April 18, 1971, and "Taipei Won't Let Japan Use Senkakus for Weather Station," *Japan Times*, April 22, 1971.
297 For more on the May 24, 1957 riot, see Karl Lott Rankin, *China Assignment* (Seattle, WA: University of Washington Press, 1964), 299–307, and Nancy Bern-kopf Tucker, ed., *China Confidential: American Diplomats and Sino-American Relations, 1945–1996* (New York: Columbia University Press, 2001), 139–41, for example.
298 "Telegram 1814 from Embassy Taipei to USIA, April 20, 1971," Folder 4, Box 20, History of USCAR, RG 319.
299 "Telegram 1814."
300 "Telegram 1814."
301 "Telegram 2593 from AmConsul Hong Kong to State Department on Peking Reports Senkakus Demonstration in U.S., April 26, 1971," POL 23–26 Senkaku Is, RG 59.
302 "Telegram 2593."
303 "Telegram 2593."
304 "Peking Warns Japan Over Senkaku Claims," *Japan Times*, May 3, 1971.
305 Frederick L. Shiels, "Report on the Senkakus Question (Addendum), 22 November 1971, ODCSOPS-IA," Folder 4, Box 20, History of USCAR, RG 319.
306 "Telegram 1869 from Embassy Taipei to State Department, April 22, 1971," Folder 4, Box 20, History of USCAR, RG 319.
307 "Telegram 1869."
308 "Telegram 1869."
309 "Telegram 1869."
310 "Telegram 1869."
311 "Telegram 1869."

312 "Telegram 1869."
313 The Consulate's view of the publication had not improved in the two months since it last reported on it: "[The staff is] always interested in finding a popular cause to espouse." See "Telegram 2284 from AmConsul Hong Kong to State Department on Latest HK Student Demonstration on Senkaku Islands, April 13, 1971," POL 23–28 HK, RG 59.
314 "Telegram 2284 from AmConsul Hong Kong to State Department, April 13, 1971," POL 23–28 HK, RG 59.
315 "Telegram 2284."
316 "Telegram 2284."
317 "Telegram 2284."
318 "Telegram 2284." The U.S. Consulate's report noted, however, that several officers in the Japanese consulate were calm and felt the demonstration "came off as expected." (Ibid.)
319 "Telegram 2284."
320 "Telegram 2284."
321 "Telegram 2426 from AmConsul Hong Kong to State Department, April 19, 1971," POL 23–28 HK, RG 59.
322 "Telegram 2816 from AmConsul Hong Kong to State Department on Student Demonstration Outside Consulate General, May 4, 1971," POL 23–28 HK, RG 59.
323 "Telegram 3160 from AmConsul Hong Kong to State Department on Senkaku Demonstration, May 17, 1971," POL 23–28 HK, RG 59.
324 "An Open Letter to President Nixon and Members of the Congress," *New York Times*, May 23, 1971 (Sunday, p. 7).
325 "An Open Letter to President Nixon and Members of the Congress."
326 "An Open Letter to President Nixon and Members of the Congress."
327 "Telegram 2803 from Embassy Taipei to State Department on Senkakus Dispute, June 9, 1971," POL 32–36 Senkaku Is, RG 59.
328 "Telegram 2803."
329 "Telegram 2803."
330 "Telegram 2200 from Embassy Taipei to HICOMRY, May 10, 1971," Folder 4, Box 20, History of USCAR, RG 319.
331 "Telegram from HICOM Okinawa RYIS to State Department on Senkakus, May 11, 1971," Folder 4, Box 20, History of USCAR, RG 319. The High Commissioner's office had been aware of the University of the Ryukyu survey, described in Chapter 2, and reported its departure from Naha port on March 29. See "Telegram from HICOM Okinawa RYIS to Department of Army on Ryukyu University Survey Team, March 29, 1971," Folder 4, Box 20, History of USCAR, RG 319. The team had originally tried to leave in late September but bad weather and high seas caused them to postpone the trip until October 3. They had to turn around and head back to Ishigaki after just a few hours due to rough seas, and the trip was rescheduled until late March. (See "Telegram from HICOMRY to DA, October 7, 1970," Folder: Message Traffic Concerning the Senkaku Islands, 1971–72, Lampert Files.
332 "Telegram from HICOM Okinawa RYIS to State Department on Senkakus, May 11, 1971."
333 "Telegram 3099 from Embassy Taipei to State Department, June 25, 1971," Folder 4, Box 20, History of USCAR, RG 319.
334 "Telegram 3047 from Embassy Taipei to State Department on Senkakus: Aerial Photography, June 23, 1971," POL 32–36 Senkaku Is, RG 59. Curiously, the State Department had to request comments from the Embassy in Taipei a second time, as it had not responded to the first request. See "Telegram 109963 from State Department to Embassy Taipei on Senkakus: Aerial Photography, June 18,

1971," Ibid., and "Telegram 111408 from State Department to Embassy Taipei on Senkakus: Aerial Photography, June 22, 1971," Ibid.

335 "Telegram 3047."

336 "Telegram from HICOM OKINAWA RYIS to Department of Army on Senkakus: Aerial Photography," Senkaku Retto (Sento Shosho) (Tia Yu Tai) Files, Okinawa Prefectural Archives. The message noted that all photographs were processed through the U.S. Army Ryukyu Islands D/Intelligence before being delivered to the GRI.

337 "Telegram 112340 from State Department to Embassy Taipei on Okinawa Survey, June 23, 1971," POL 32–36 Senkaku Is, RG 59.

338 "Telegram 100858 from State Department to Embassy Taipei on GRC Representations on Reversion of Senkakus to Japan, June 8, 1971," POL 32–36 Senkaku Is, RG 59.

339 "Telegram 61219 from State Department to Embassy Taipei, April 10, 1971," POL 32–36 Senkaku Is, RG 59.

340 "Telegram 61219."

341 "Telegram 61219."

342 "Telegram 92888 from State Department to Embassy Taipei, May 26, 1971," POL 32–36 Senkaku Is, RG 59.

343 It appears in the Taipei Embassy, officials wrote Chou's name with a "u" at the end, while at the National Security Council it was written with a "w."

344 "Telegram 2666."

345 "Telegram 2666."

346 "Telegram 2666."

347 "Telegram 2666."

348 "Telegram 2666."

349 "Telegram 2692 from Embassy Taipei to State Department, June 3, 1971," Folder 4, Box 20, History of USCAR, RG 319.

350 "Telegram 2692."

351 "Telegram 2692."

352 "Telegram 2692."

353 "Telegram 99740 from State Department to Embassy Tokyo on GRC Representations on Reversion of Senkakus to Japan, June 5, 1971," POL 32–36 Senkaku Is, RG 59.

354 "Memorandum from Brown to Johnson."

355 "Telegram 99737 from State Department to Embassy Taipei on GRC Representations on Reversion of Senkakus to Japan, June 5, 1971," POL 32–36 Senkaku Is, RG 59. A subsequent telegram from the State Department to the High Commissioner regarding a GOJ request for a survey by Tokai University in the Senkakus in June and July noted that there apparently was a "genuine uneasiness within the GRC" about the possibility that the Senkakus issue would lead to future protests and growing "dissatisfaction within the Chinese academic community on Taiwan and abroad with the alleged lack of GRC forcefulness in asserting Chinese claim to Senkakus." See "Telegram 100858."

356 "Telegram 99737."

357 "Telegram 99737."

358 "Telegram 99737."

359 "Telegram 99737."

360 "Telegram 99737."

361 "Telegram 99737."

362 "Telegram 99737."

363 "Telegram 5348 from Embassy Tokyo to State Department on GRC Representations on Reversion of Senkakus to Japan, June 7, 1971," POL 32–36 Senkaku Is, RG 59.

364 "Telegram 2803 from Embassy Taipei to State Department on Senkakus Dispute, June 9, 1971," POL 32–36 Senkaku Is, RG 59.

365 "Telegram 2803."

366 "Telegram 2803."

367 "Telegram 2803."

368 Article 22 (Settlement of Disputes) reads: "If in the opinion of any Party to the present Treaty there has arisen a dispute concerning the interpretation or execution of the Treaty, which is not settled by reference to a special claims tribunal or by other agreed means, the dispute shall, at the request of any party thereto, be referred for decision to the International Court of Justice. Japan and those Allied Powers which are not already parties to the Statute of the International Court of Justice will deposit with the Registrar of the Court, at the time of their respective ratifications of the present Treaty, and in conformity with the resolution of the United Nations Security Council, dated 15 October 1946, a general declaration accepting the jurisdiction, without special agreement, of the Court generally in respect to all disputes of the character referred to in this Article."

369 "Memorandum from Robert I. Starr to Thomas P. Shoesmith on the Senkakus Dispute and Article 22 of the 1951 Treaty of Peace with Japan, June 11, 1971," POL 32–36 Senkaku Is, RG 59.

370 "Memorandum from Starr to Shoesmith."

371 "Memorandum from Starr to Shoesmith."

372 "Memorandum from Starr to Shoesmith."

373 See Tucker, ed., *China Confidential*, particularly chapters 3 and 4.

374 "Memorandum from Starr to Shoesmith."

375 Richard M. Nixon, *The Memoirs of Richard M. Nixon* (New York: Grosset and Dunlap, 1978), 305.

376 Nixon, *The Memoirs of Richard M. Nixon*, 305.

377 See Maurice H. Stans, *One of the President's Men: Twenty Years with Eisenhower and Nixon* (Dulles, VA: Brassey's Inc., 1995).

378 Martin Berkeley Hickman, *David M. Kennedy: Banker, Statesman, Churchman* (Provo, UT: Brigham Young University, 1987), 289.

379 Hickman, *David M. Kennedy*, 290–91.

380 "Memorandum from Peter G. Peterson to David M. Kennedy, April 13, 1971," Folder: Negotiations (Far East) 1, Textiles Negotiations (Far East) April-July 1971, White House Staff Files, Staff and Office Files Peter Peterson, Nixon Presidential Materials, National Archives, College Park.

381 "Memorandum from H.R. Haldeman to Pete Peterson, April 23, 1971," Folder: Negotiations (Far East) 1, Textiles Negotiations (Far East) April–July 1971, White House Staff Files, Staff and Office Files Peter Peterson, Nixon Presidential Materials.

382 Hickman, *David M. Kennedy*, 291.

383 Peter G. Peterson, *The Education of An American Dreamer: How a Son of Greek Immigrants Learned His Way From a Nebraska Diner to Washington, Wall Street, and Beyond* (New York: Twelve, 2009), 136.

384 Hickman, *David M. Kennedy*, 292. Sun served as economic minister until 1978 and then as premier from 1978–84. He is credited with having transformed Taiwan from an agricultural country to an economic powerhouse.

385 "TelCon—Wednesday, May 26, 1971–1:00 p.m.," Folder: Chrono—Official—May 1971, Box 72, Records of U. Alexis Johnson, Records of the Department of State, RG 59.

386 I.M. Destler, Haruhiro Fukui, Hideo Sato, *The Textile Wrangle: Conflict in Japanese-American Relations, 1969–1971* (Ithaca, NY: Cornell University Press, 1979), 283–84.

387 "U.S. Ties with Taiwan Lose Warmth," *New York Times*, April 29, 1971. This was echoed in another article a few months later on the eve of the announcement of the Nixon trip to China. See April Klimley, "Taiwan Mistrust Grows as U.S. Courts Peking," *Christian Science Monitor*, July 14, 1971. Of course, some observers wonder if true warmth and friendship ever actually existed. See Tucker, *Strait Talk*. In contrast, CIA station chief Ray S. Cline would argue there were close relationships between officials. See Cline, *Chiang Ching-kuo Remembered*.

388 Jay Taylor, *The Generalissimo: Chiang Kai-shek and the Struggle for Modern China* (Cambridge, MA: Belknap Press, 2011), 561.

389 Taylor, *The Generalissimo*, 561.

390 Taylor, *The Generalissimo*, 561. Also see diary entry for May 23, 1971, Chiang Kai-shek Diary.

391 "Memorandum to Kissinger from Ernest Johnson and John Holdridge on Okinawa Reversion/Textiles Your Meeting at 6pm today with Mr. Yamanaka," Folder: Textiles—Negotiations (Far East) April-July 1971, Peter Peterson Papers, Nixon Presidential Materials.

392 "Memorandum to Kissinger from Ernest Johnson and John Holdridge on Okinawa Reversion/Textiles Your Meeting at 6pm today with Mr. Yamanaka."

393 "Memorandum to Kissinger from Ernest Johnson and John Holdridge on Okinawa Reversion/Textiles Your Meeting at 6pm today with Mr. Yamanaka."

394 Diary entry for June 8, 1971, *Sato Eisaku Nikki*, Vol. 4, 351. Yamanaka communicated with Sato's office through Kusuda Minoru, Sato's personal secretary, while he was in D.C. Kusuda writes in one of his diary entries about being contacted by Okazaki Hisahiko of the Japanese Embassy in Washington on behalf of Yamanaka about receiving instructions for his meetings there. See entry for June 2, 1971 in Kusuda Minoru, *Kusuda Minoru Nikki* (The Kusuda Minoru Diary) (Tokyo Chuo Koronsha, 2001), 596.

395 " Telcon Alexis Johnson/Mr. Kissinger, 8:20 a.m., June 7, 1971."

396 "Telcon Johnson/Kissinger, 10:30 a.m., 6/7/71," Kissinger Office Files, Nixon Presidential Materials. Kissinger and Johnson usually got along. Kissinger joked with the Ushiba Nobuhiko, who succeeded Togo as Japan's ambassador to the United States in the summer of 1970, saying that "you have two ambassadors in Washington. You and Alexis Johnson. I don't know what you do to our people." Like most jokes with Kissinger, there was an element of truth to it at least in his mind.

397 "Telcon Johnson/Kissinger, 10:30 a.m., 6/7/71."

398 "Telcon Johnson/Kissinger, 10:30 a.m., 6/7/71."

399 "Telcon Johnson/Kissinger, 10:30 a.m., 6/7/71."

400 "Telcon Johnson/Kissinger, 10:30 a.m., 6/7/71." It is unclear if Kissinger meant the president or Kennedy when he said "he" in this comment. Afterward, he refers to Nixon so he may have meant the president.

401 "Telcon Johnson/Kissinger, 10:30 a.m., 6/7/71."

402 "Chronology of Events Relating to Status of the Senkaku Islands."

403 "Telcon Alexis Johnson/Mr. Kissinger, 3:05 p.m., June 7, 1971," Kissinger Office Files, Nixon Presidential Materials.

404 "Telcon Alexis Johnson/Mr. Kissinger, 3:05 p.m., June 7, 1971."

405 "Telcon Alexis Johnson/Mr. Kissinger, 3:05 p.m., June 7, 1971."

406 "Telcon Alexis Johnson/Mr. Kissinger, 3:05 p.m., June 7, 1971."

407 "Telcon Alexis Johnson/Mr. Kissinger, 3:05 p.m., June 7, 1971."

408 "Telcon Alexis Johnson/Mr. Kissinger, 3:05 p.m., June 7, 1971."

409 "Telcon Alexis Johnson/Mr. Kissinger, 3:05 p.m., June 7, 1971."

410 "Telcon Alexis Johnson/Mr. Kissinger, 3:05 p.m., June 7, 1971."

411 "Telcon Alexis Johnson/Mr. Kissinger, 3:05 p.m., June 7, 1971." Later that year, an official in the Department of the Army who had been studying the issue for

some time also concluded his report, "the only way out of the quagmire appears to be through outside arbitration, perhaps by an international organization."

412 "Memorandum from Al Haig to Henry Kissinger, June 7, 1971," Kissinger Office Files, Nixon Presidential Materials.

413 "Telcon President/Kissinger, afternoon, 6/7/71," Kissinger Office Files, Nixon Presidential Materials.

414 "Telcon President/Kissinger, afternoon, 6/7/71." "They" likely means the People's Republic of China.

415 "Telcon President/Kissinger, afternoon, 6/7/71."

416 "Telcon Alexis Johnson/Mr. Kissinger, 9:43 a.m., June 5, 1971," Kissinger Office Files, Nixon Presidential Materials.

417 "Telcon Alexis Johnson/Mr. Kissinger, 9:43 a.m., June 5, 1971."

418 "Telcon Alexis Johnson/Mr. Kissinger, 9:43 a.m., June 5, 1971." According to the U.S. Ambassador to Japan, this lack of consultation was Kennedy's style: "[Kennedy's] diplomatic technique was to deal only with the key leaders, to the extent that the secret nature of the meetings allowed. He disliked any sort of publicity. His diplomacy was essentially Theodore Rooseveltian: 'speak softly but carry a big stick.' Often he would simply hibernate in his hotel room, relying on his mere presence to exercise pressure. Meanwhile, as occasion warranted, his key aide [Anthony J. Jurich] would be in communication with the Japanese. Obviously, this type of negotiating was highly unorthodox for old diplomatic hands. My Embassy colleagues, particularly in the economic section, were less than happy, particularly since such details as they did learn were gleaned from Japanese sources. Secretary Kennedy did, however, from time to time give me a general overview of progress made." See Meyer, *Assignment Tokyo*, 290–91.

419 "Telcon Alexis Johnson/Mr. Kissinger, 9:43 a.m., June 5, 1971."

420 "Telcon President/Kissinger, afternoon, 6/7/71." Kissinger later praised Peterson, who "worked out effective coordination that subjected all such economic decisions to our foreign policy strategy," and wrote about his relationship with Peterson in the following way: "I agreed enthusiastically when, at O[ffice of] M[anagement and] B[udget] Director George Shultz's urging, the new post of Assistant to the President for International Economic Affairs was created at the White House—though it technically represented a diminution of my power. Peter Peterson, its first incumbent, and I established a close working relationship reinforced by personal friendship. Peterson, equipped with a subtle and wide-ranging mind, taught me a great deal about international economics; I respected him enormously, and this was another reason why I intervened rarely and only when an overwhelming foreign policy interest seemed involved." Henry Kissinger, *White House Years* (Boston, MA: Little, Brown, and Co., 1979), 840, 951. Others have described the relationship differently, but Peterson seems to have been happy with the relationship, at least according to his memoirs.

421 "Memorandum from the President's Assistant for International Economic Affairs (Peterson) to President Nixon, June 7, 1971," President's Handwriting Files, Box 12, President's Office Files, White House Special Files, Nixon Presidential Materials.

422 "Memorandum from the President's Assistant to President Nixon, June 7, 1971."

423 "Memorandum from the President's Assistant to President Nixon, June 7, 1971."

424 "Tape Subject Log, June 7, 1971, Conversation No. 513–1," Nixon Presidential Materials.

425 "Tape Subject Log, June 7, 1971, Conversation No. 513–1."

426 "Memorandum for the President from Henry A. Kissinger on the Senkaku Island (sic) and Okinawa Reversion, June 7, 1971," Kissinger Office Files, Nixon Presidential Files.

427 "Backchannel Message from the President's Assistant for International Economic Affairs (Peterson) to Ambassador Kennedy, in Taipei, June 8, 1971," Memoranda

for the President, Box 87, President's Office Files, White House Special Files, Nixon Presidential Materials. As of October, Nixon still had not dispatched said mission. (See document 134 for more.) Nixon sent a message to Kennedy, who was in Korea by this point, to express his appreciation for the work Kennedy was doing and perhaps to apologize for not being able to give Kennedy all he wanted in the negotiations with Taiwan. It read, "Pete Peterson has told me of the great work you and your negotiating team are doing under very difficult circumstances. I want you to know of my deep personal appreciation for your efforts. I know the obstacles are formidable, but I have every confidence in you and your associates. We will be doing everything we can possibly do from his (*sic*) end to support your efforts." See "Telegram from the President to Ambassador David M. Kennedy, undated."

428 "Entry for June 9, 1971," Note pad of notes on the trip, Folder 12, David M. Kennedy Collection, L. Tom Perry Special Collections, Brigham University Library, Provo, Utah.

429 Diary entry for Thursday, June 10, 1971, Chiang Kai-shek's Diary.

430 "Transfer of Ryukyus, Tiaoyutais to Japan Protested," Central News Agency International Service in English, June 11, 1971. "Editorial The United States Should Not Sadden Those Near and Dear to Us and Gladden the Enemy," United Daily News, June 12, 1971.

431 Diary entry for June 11, 1971, Chiang Kai-shek Diary.

432 "Editorial The United States Should Not Sadden."

433 "Telegram from U. Alexis Johnson to Rogers, June 8, 1971," U. Alexis Johnson Files; Lot 96 D 695, RG 59.

434 "Telegram from Alexis Johnson to Secretary of State on Okinawa Reversion, June 8, 1971," U. Alexis Johnson Files; Lot 96 D 695, RG 59.

435 "Telegram from Alexis Johnson to Secretary of State on Okinawa Reversion, June 8, 1971."

436 "Interview with Richard A. Ericson, Jr.," 168.

437 "Interview with Richard A. Ericson, Jr.," 168; Diary entry for June 3, 1971, *Sato Eisaku Nikki*, Vol. 4, 348.

438 "Memorandum of Conversation, Okinawa Reversion, Part I of II, June 9, 1971," Folder: Negotiation Status Reports, Box 18, History of the Civil Administration of the Ryukyu Islands, RG 319.

439 "Memorandum of Conversation, Okinawa Reversion, Part I of II, June 9, 1971."

440 "Telegram from Secretary for Ambassador, June 10, 1971." Folder: Textiles—Negotiations (Far East) April-July 1971, Peter Peterson Papers, Nixon Presidential Materials. The message was drafted by Northeast Asia specialist Thomas P. Shoesmith, who since 1967 was serving as the director of the Office of Republic of China Affairs. See "Interview with Thomas P. Shoesmith, December 9, 1991," Association for Diplomatic Studies and Training Foreign Affairs Oral History Project.

441 "Memorandum for Mr. Henry A. Kissinger on the Senkaku Islands, June 10, 1971," Folder: Textiles—Negotiations (Far East) April-July 1971, Peter Peterson Papers, Nixon Presidential Materials.

442 "Telegram 104962 from State Department to Embassy Tokyo on Senkaku Problem, June 14, 1971," POL 32–36 Senkaku Is, RG 59.

443 "Telegram 5981."

444 "Telegram 104962."

445 "Telegram 104962."

446 "Telegram 5721 from Embassy Tokyo to State Department on Senkakus Problem, June 15, 1971," POL 32–36 Senkaku Is, RG 59.

447 "Telegram 5721."

448 "Telegram 5721." Sneider recommended that Taipei and Tokyo be informed on June 16. William N. Morell, Jr., who was serving as the chargé d'affaires at the U.S. Embassy in Taipei, concurred with Sneider's recommendation and in turn urge that they "impress upon both the GRC and GOJ the importance of avoiding leaks before our announcement is made." See "Telegram 2921 from Embassy Taipei to State Department on Senkakus, June 15, 1971," POL 32–36 Senkaku Is, RG 59.

449 "Telegram 106745 from State Department to Embassy Tokyo and Embassy Taipei on Senkaku Islands Issue, June 15, 1971," POL 32–36 Senkaku Is, RG 59.

450 Diary entry for June 15, 1971, *Sato Eisaku Nikki*, Vol. 4, 355.

451 Yamanaka Sadanori, *Kaerimite Kuinashi: Watashino Rirekisho* (I Have No Regrets Looking Back: My Memoirs) (Tokyo: Nihon Keizai Shimbunsha, 2002), 234.

452 "Telegram 5791 from Embassy Tokyo to State Department on Senkaku Islands Issue, June 16, 1971," POL 32–36 Senkaku Is, RG 59.

453 "Telegram 5791."

454 "Telegram 5791."

455 "Telegram 2941."

456 "National Assemblymen Denounce Agreement on Tiaoyutais, June 17, 1971," Folder: Senkaku Retto (Sento Shosho) (Tia Yu Tai) Files, Okinawa Prefectural Archives.

5 The signing and ratification of the Okinawa Reversion Treaty and domestic and regional reactions

With the signing of the Okinawa Reversion Treaty completed on June 17, 1971, done through a simultaneous signing ceremony through satellite hook-up for the first time ever, the next step procedurally would be to seek its ratification in the Japanese Parliament and U.S. Senate while moving forward with the specific reversion arrangements. Criticism of the handling of the Senkakus issue—from all sides—would continue until the actual reversion of Okinawa a year later, however. This chapter explores the ratification process and the domestic and regional reactions to the decision to include the Senkakus in the agreement. Within Japan, criticism was not only directed at Taiwanese and mainland Chinese claims to the islands, but also directed at the United States for taking a neutral, inconsistent, and convenient approach to the symbolic sovereignty issue. Regionally speaking, both Taiwan (ROC) and the People's Republic of China (PRC) increased the frequency and degree of its claims to the Senkakus, in part to challenge those of Japan, but also partly in competition with each other over who legitimately represented the Chinese people.

The signing ceremony and Bray statement

Representative of the advancement of American and Japanese technology, Secretary Rogers had suggested that the reversion treaty should be signed via satellite. As such, the simultaneous proceedings took place in Tokyo at nine p.m. on the 17th, and eight a.m. in Washington (on the same day). With this signing, seven years of occupation, and twenty years of a U.S. administration over Okinawa, would come to an end within a year's time.

The Bray statement, introduced earlier, on the Senkakus was made at the noon press briefing, Washington time. There were several inquiries made to clarify the meaning, including one about the PRC. To a twin-question about the PRC's claims to the Senkakus and the fact that no reference to that claim was mentioned in the press briefing in the statement, the spokesman confirmed that the PRC had made assertions in the past claiming the islands and that the Department's statement made no reference beyond Taiwan and Japan. When pressed if the USG recognized that the PRC might have a legal claim to the islands, Bray sidestepped the question saying, "I am just not going to get any further into this. I am sorry."[1]

Although the Japanese Foreign Ministry was not planning to make any comments on the Bray statement, Foreign Minister Aichi reportedly stated at a press conference for foreign correspondents on the evening of the 18th that with the reversion treaty signed, the "Senkakus were no longer an issue between the U.S. and Japan."[2] He added that Japan "will do what is necessary to prevent ROC claims to Senkakus from irritating the friendly relations between the ROC, Japan, and the U.S."[3] However, Aichi's subsequent comment, probably in reference to the Bray statement, that "there has been no change in Japanese sovereignty over the Senkakus," meant in fact problems would necessarily continue with the ROC, and later with the PRC.

Within Japan, the reactions were positive: newspapers reported on the front pages of the evening editions the Bray statement, focusing on the part that return to Japan of administrative rights over the Senkakus would not prejudice ROC's claims to sovereignty. There was no editorial reaction, however, in the morning papers on the 19th.[4] In contrast, there were front-page stories in the Taipei press in the afternoon of the 18th and morning of the 19th, as well as editorial comments in the largest-circulation dailies. Most of the editorials praised the student demonstrations against the return of the Senkakus to Japan to date as well as those discussed below.[5]

Local attempts to bring attention to the Senkakus issue

One problem—or a foreshadowing of things to come—happened a mere two weeks after the signing of the reversion agreement. Two ROC ships, DD-1 and Patrol Transport PF-4 No. 31, patrolled near the Senkakus for several hours on the afternoon of June 29.[6] The ships were carrying 800 officers and cadets en route to Taiwan from Chinhae, South Korea, on a training cruise. In the area, they saw two Japanese fishing boats, but there was no clash or interaction apparently. The U.S. Embassy in Taipei described the "patrol" as more of a "deviation" from the route normally taken as a "gesture presumably for the benefit of students here and elsewhere as well as for international community."[7] Although the articles about the patrol in the local newspapers emphasized that the islands were Taiwanese and that this was the first cruise conducted by ROC warships since the United States transferred the Senkakus to Japan, the Embassy was surprised that there were not more stories about it. Subsequently, Admiral Soong Chang-chih, the Commander-in-Chief of the ROC Navy from 1970–76, told U.S. Embassy officials that he authorized the deviation of the route at the request of the commander of the ships on the midshipmen's course to enable them to go by the Senkakus, but he instructed them that in no case were the ships to approach closer than six nautical miles to the islands.[8]

Some six weeks before this incident happened in mid-May, the CIA warned in a memorandum produced by the Office of National Estimates it "cannot rule out the possibility that Taipei, in seeking to salvage a losing game, might put a military presence on the Senkakus after they revert to Japan in mid-1972. Indeed, Taipei seems more likely to move in this direction than Peking."[9] Fortunately, the possibility suggested in the memorandum, declassified in 2007, did not eventually happen, but the naval movements in late June 1971 certainly were of interest to observers. In later years, it was the activities of the PRC, as it increasingly conducted maritime incursions by fishing boats, survey vessels, submarines, and surface ships over the years that have caused observers (and Japanese officials especially) to wonder if it intends to land a force or otherwise occupy or surround the islands.

On the eve of the signing ceremony, officials from both Japan and the United States were nervous about anything upsetting the arrangements. While any comments would indeed inflame the situation, passions had already long since been ignited in Taiwan over the reversion treaty, however, with large-scale demonstrations planned for the 17th and protest parades scheduled to go to the U.S. and Japanese embassies in Taipei.[10]

Some of the first reports the U.S. Embassy in Taipei received about the likelihood of demonstrations was from Hsu Chi-tung, the dean of overseas Chinese Students, Overseas Chinese Affairs Commission, who told a local employee at the Embassy on June 15 that students at both National Taiwan University and Taiwan Normal University were "agitating" about the Senkakus.[11] Hsu said he would be visiting the schools later to find out more about the students' plans. In addition to Hsu's reporting, a Taiwanese scholar told Richard L. Walker, a visiting professor of Asian studies at NTU known for his strong anti-Communist views, that there might be trouble from the students on June 17, information which Walker apparently shared with the Embassy.

By the 16th, the Embassy was certain, based on several reports, that there would be student-led demonstrations on the 17th, the day of the simultaneous signing of the reversion agreement in Tokyo and D.C. The sources varied, as did their understandings of the types and participants, their numbers, and plans. Embassy officers visited the campuses of NTU and TNU to get a sense of the atmospherics where they saw posters produced by the "Protect the Taioyutai Movement." MOFA's Chien called the Embassy to inform it that the GRC expected between 300 and 400 students to participate and that a couple of student representatives would wish to meet with the deputy chief of mission to present their protest letter. Morell called back later and spoke with Vice Minister Tsai to discuss the demonstrations and ask MOFA's assurances that every effort would be made by the GRC to protect the Embassy and other U.S. government facilities. Tsai told him that coordination was being done, and that MOFA had also contacted the universities to ask them to persuade the students to "calm down."[12]

It appears their entreaties did not work out. According to news reports, as many as 1000 students protested in Taipei on the 17th against the reversion agreement, which they called "Another Munich under the direction of imperialism in Asia," marching in front of the U.S. Embassy.[13] As mentioned above, editorials tended to endorse the students' activities.

Protests in Hong Kong the same day were not as large as those in Taiwan, in contrast. About thirty protestors showed up on the U.S. Consulate's grounds to demonstrate against the U.S. decision to revert the Senkakus, having visited the Japanese Consulate before that where they reportedly handed over a protest letter.[14] The protestors dispersed peacefully after an hour due to the heavy rains caused by Typhoon Freda.

The protestors did not stay peaceful in subsequent demonstrations, however. In early July, a series of small demonstrations on July 4 and 6 grew to a larger one in the evening of July 7, with some 3000 people in the immediate area (although not all were protestors) of Victoria Park where the protests were held. The demonstration turned violent with several cars stoned and burned. Six protestors were injured and twenty-one arrested. That date was the anniversary of the 1937 Marco Polo Bridge Incident, which is often considered the start of the Second Sino-Japanese War. Victoria Park was chosen as the venue of the protests, advertised for a month prior, by the Hong Kong Police Commissioner in order to get the protestors out of the downtown area and away from the U.S. and Japanese consulates. Permission for the demonstration was not given, however, by the Urban Council but the organizers went ahead with it. Although three organizations were involved in organizing the demonstration, including the HK Federation of Students and the *70's Bi-Weekly* Magazine, and a new group from the Chong Kin Experimental College, the trouble began likely as a result of "young thugs" who took advantage of the breakdown in public order.[15] Interestingly, observers of the protests noticed that in addition to the traditional messages of "protect the Tiaoyutai Islands" and "anti-imperialism," there were also messages of opposition to Taiwanese independence and "two Chinas."

Protests in Hong Kong continued during the summer. At a "Protect the Tiaoyutai" demonstration on August 13 in Victoria Park, which was attended by 1,000 according to organizers, a Japanese flag was ripped, although police had warned the protestors against it.[16] A U.S. Consulate report put the number of demonstrators at 5,000, or five times more.[17] Another clash between police and protesters was likely but the police accepted the last minute application, and although the demonstration was peaceful, a small group of radicals burned a Japanese naval flag. Another rally took place at Hong Kong University on August 23 attended by some 500, at which a "Japanese rising sun symbol" was also torn up.[18]

Ratification of the Okinawa Reversion Agreement

It was amid this environment, and intensive lobbying by supporters in the United States of the ROC's position, that the next step in the process of returning Okinawa—ratification—was to have the Diet in Japan and Senate in the United States deliberate on the treaty. That summer, however, was a time of major reevaluations and shifts of U.S. foreign and economic policies, particularly as they related to Japan. Known as the "Nixon Shocks"—the July 15, 1971 announcement of President Nixon's impending visit to China and the announcement one month later on August 15 of the so-called "New Economic Policy," which removed the U.S. dollar from the gold standard (thus causing the 360 yen to one dollar exchange rate used since 1949 to change dramatically) while charging a ten percent surcharge on imports—impacted Japan tremendously not because these changes weren't necessary or even expected at some point but because they were so abrupt and done without consultation. The deliberations in the U.S. Senate and Japanese Parliament took place following those summer readjustments.

State Department officials were very much aware that the Senkakus issue would come up in the Senate deliberations on the Okinawa Reversion Treaty that fall. During the summer, McElroy prepared a large briefing book of potential questions that might be asked. Five related to the Senkakus including: "What is the status of the Senkaku Islands?" and "What is the basis for including the Senkaku Islands under Article 3 of the Peace Treaty?"[19] This list of them was developed over the summer, with a total of eight questions on Article 1, with more than half directly related to the Senkakus.[20] In September, Under Secretary for Political Affairs Johnson hammered out a division of labor between senior officials as witnesses in support of the treaty agreement, with Johnson himself serving as an expert witness on the provisions that involved Article 3 and the reversion of administrative rights over the islands.[21] This was a most appropriate assignment for him, as he had been closely involved in these issues for many of the previous twenty-seven years.[22]

Secretary Rogers was asked about the Senkakus in testimony on October 27 before the Foreign Relations Committee, and responding to a question by Chairman J. William Fulbright, explained that the USG was relinquishing administration over the Senkakus to Japan but that act would not affect the underlying claims to sovereignty of the various claimants.[23]

A couple of days later on the morning of October 29, public witnesses were invited to testify about the treaty. Several of those speaking had strong views on the Senkakus, and all essentially opposed the inclusion of the islands in the reversion agreement. New York State University Physicist and Nobel Laureate Chen Ning Yang, a naturalized U.S. citizen of Chinese descent, was particularly critical arguing that the continuance of the Navy's gunnery ranges as facilities and areas under the reversion agreement was "a contradiction of public U.S. position of neutrality in Senkaku dispute … [and] has potential for dragging the U.S. government into the territorial dispute between Japan and China."[24] Yang, who had been a university student and graduate student in Kunming during the Sino–Japanese War (1937–45), urged the Senate to "in some way make explicit U.S. government's neutrality on issue and prohibit 'U.S. Navy-Japan (*sic*) alliance to establish de facto recognition of Japanese sovereignty over Senkakus."[25] Robert Morris, a lawyer, testified on behalf of Grace Hsu, who claimed ownership to the Senkakus on the basis of an "alleged grant" from the Empress Dowager,[26] and John H. Fincher, a research fellow at Harvard University's East Asian Research Center and former Foreign Service Officer, read a paper noting that the islands were an issue "on which all Chinese seem to agree," and wondered aloud (although somewhat missing the mark as neither Taiwan nor China made claims against the islands until the early 1970s), "if someone had done this work in the early fifties—Taipei, Tokyo, or Washington in particular—I very much doubt if there would be such a thing as the Tiao Yu Tai controversy."[27]

Despite these and other critical voices, the Foreign Relations Committee recommended unanimously on November 2, 1971, that the Senate accord its advice and consent to the ratification of the Okinawa Reversion Treaty. Senate Majority Leader Michael J. Mansfield, who would later serve as U.S. ambassador to Japan from 1977 to 1989, had immediately scheduled a vote for November 4,[28] but the Senate Armed Services Committee had interposed by calling hearings on November 3 and then after being briefed by State Department and Defense Department officials, recessed them until November 8, requesting that a high-level JCS representative appear to testify.[29] On November 5, a preliminary briefing was given to General Westmoreland by the Joint Staff and Army action officers, in order to prepare him for his appearance on the 8th, to be attended by Lieutenant General Lampert and Vice Admiral Walter L. Curtis, and on November 10, the Senate ratified the treaty by a roll-call vote of eighty-four to six.[30]

Within Japan, in order to consider the Okinawa Reversion Treaty and the supplementary budget, a special session of the Japanese Diet was convened on October 16, 1971, and a special committee on the Okinawa Reversion Agreement (*Okinawa Henkan Kyotei Tokubetsu Iinkai*) was subsequently established on October 29 within the Lower House to deliberate on the treaty.[31] In the meantime, the LDP had agreed, in a "major concession" to the opposition parties, to divide the reversion package into four pieces for consideration by four separate committees of the Lower House, "an arrangement [that] will undoubtedly benefit the Opposition (by providing greater opportunities for disrupting legislative action on the Reversion Treaty)."[32] Chief Cabinet Secretary Hori Shigeru remembered expending a lot of energy on the ratification process.[33]

The Senkakus issue was raised by Nishime Junji, a Lower House LDP member originally from Yonaguni Island. Nishime, who had unsuccessfully challenged his former teacher (Yara Chobyo) in the 1968 contest for the chief executive's position, belonged to the faction of Tanaka Kakuei, who was then serving as the Minister of Trade and Industry, and was elected in the November 1970 special elections held to choose a total of seven representatives from Okinawa to be in the national parliament. Nishime, a graduate of Tokyo University who had served in the Foreign Ministry before returning to Okinawa and beginning his own newspaper, the Okinawa Herald (*Okinawa Herarudo*), before entering politics, stated, "There are some in other countries who are taking a different view of the ownership over the Senkaku Islands. In international law, and historically, I believe there is no doubt that the islands belong to our country. Therefore, I want the government to ensure that the Senkaku Islands do not become a source for dispute, and I would like to ask what the government's views are on this matter."[34]

Foreign Minister Fukuda Takeo, who had succeeded Aichi in the summer following the July 5 cabinet reshuffle and who viewed domestically in Japan and by some officials in the United States as a "hawk," answered that indeed the Senkakus were included in the treaty despite what other countries in the region might say. His views on the Senkakus would become strong and more pronounced over the coming months.

Fukuda, a rival of Tanaka, had been chosen to serve as foreign minister in part because he was seen as a strong candidate for prime minister and it was necessary for him to learn about diplomacy in contrast to his experience to date in economic and financial affairs, having been a bureaucrat in the Ministry of Finance prior to becoming a politician in 1952.[35] Although he was well known for his pro-Taiwan stance, he would approve the signing of the Treaty of Peace and Friendship between Japan and the PRC on August 12, 1978 (a few months after the clashes over the incursion of a large number of fishing vessels from China in April that year).

The Lower House voted 285 to 73 in favor of the treaty a couple of weeks later on November 24. The treaty was immediately sent for consideration to the Upper House, which would have thirty days to act upon it.[36] The status of the Senkaku Islands was of course not the only issue deliberated on in the "Okinawa Diet," and indeed, some of the political parties had not even formulated their official views on the territorial dispute. The next section examines the positions of the political parties which were announced between February and March 1972 on the eve of reversion.

Japan's political parties' positions and the editorials of Major Dailies on the Senkakus

While government representatives had made comments on the Senkakus issue and some individuals had attempted to raise awareness, the political parties themselves appear to have been slow in formulating their positions on the very apparent territorial dispute. This may have been because Japanese political leaders and their staffs were confident in the international legal position of Japan and had not anticipated the dispute becoming so intense.

All of the political parties, including those on the Left, argued that the Senkakus were a part of Japan. While all appealed for dialog to resolve the dispute, the center-left parties particularly stressed the need to discuss the issue of the continental shelf with their neighbors on the basis of international law.

The ruling Liberal Democratic Party, or LDP, was the first to make its party position public, which it did on March 28, 1972. Its Executive Council (*Somukai*), then headed by Nakasone Yasuhiro (who had just finished serving as the director general of the Defense Agency), decided that day that the party should officially establish its view on the Senkaku Islands. Based on that decision, the Foreign Affairs Research Commission of the Policy Affairs Research Council (*Seimu Chosakai Gaiko Chosakai*), chaired by former foreign minister Aiichi Kiichi, announced the same day a five-paragraph statement entitled "Regarding the Territorial Rights Over the Senkaku Islands (*Senkaku Shoto no Ryoyuken ni tsuite*)."[37] It began by stating that the party, which had more than 300 seats in the Lower House and 131 in the Upper House, "recognizes it is extremely clear (*kiwamete meiryo*) that the territorial rights over the Senkaku Islands belong to Japan, in light of the historical facts and international law," and after introducing the history of Japan's administration of the islands and challenging the claims of Taiwan and China to them, the statement ended with the following paragraph: "Our Party maintains a basic diplomatic stand for the promotion of friendship and amity with China. Our Party hopes, however, that the Chinese side will recognize and understand Japan's justifiable position concerning the present case."[38]

The Japan Communist Party (*Nihon Kyosanto*), with twenty-four seats in the parliament (fourteen in the Lower House and ten in the Upper House), followed suit on March 30. Viewing the Senkaku Islands as part of Japan, the statement, "The Japan Communist Party's View Concerning the Senkaku Islands Problem," was presented by Standing Presidium (*Chuo Iinkai Kanbukai*) Member Nishizawa Tomio, who served at one point as the international bureau director of the JCP newspaper, *Akahata* (Red Flag). The statement, which also called for the closure of U.S. training ranges on Kobi Sho and Sekibi Sho, appeared in the party's organ the next day, March 31, 1972, in full.[39]

It wasn't for another two weeks before the largest opposition party at the time, the Socialist Party of Japan, announced its position and appealed for the dispute to be conducted in the spirit of international law. It seems the JSP, with its 156 seats (ninety Lower House and sixty-six Upper House) in the Diet and close ties to the PRC, had more difficulty formulating its position and did not release it until April 13.[40] The view, which said the islands belonged to Japan, but that a peaceful solution should be found among the three nations involved in the rights to underwater resources, should be found through the establishment of diplomatic relations between Japan and the PRC.

The Democratic Socialist Party (*Minshu Shakaito*), or DSP, and Clean Government Party (*Komeito*), or CGP, were slower in announcing their official positions, but party representatives had stated their views previously to the effect that the Senkaku Islands were Japanese.

The CGP, which had officially come into being in 1964 and was closely affiliated with the new religious group *Soka Gakkai*, had a total of sixty-nine members in parliament (forty-seven in the Lower House, and twenty-two in the Upper House). Its chairman since 1967, Takeiri Yoshikatsu, who was supportive of restoring relations with China, asserted that nevertheless the Senkaku Islands were Japanese territory as "a matter of course."[41]

With regard to the DSP, which had broken with the Socialist Party in 1960 and had thirty-one seats in the Lower House and thirteen in the Upper

House, its chairman Kasuga Ikko had just headed a mission to China and exchanged opinions there. This relatively small party represented a middle ground between the Socialists and the LDP and would eventually merge with other parties and individuals who broke away from the LDP in the early to mid-1990s.

It was not only the political parties in Japan who rallied around the government on the issue of the Senkakus, but the mainstream media as well.

The newspapers published their positions in the form of editorials (*shasetu*) in the winter and spring of 1972 prior to the reversion of Okinawa. The Ministry of Foreign Affairs Office of Domestic Public Affairs (*Kokunai Kohoka*) retained copies of major stories and editorials about stories relating to Japan's practice of foreign affairs as well as copies of editorials in the press. Six editorials on the Senkakus representing the most authoritative position of each of the six main newspapers were saved and included in a file prepared on April 20, 1972 by the above office. While there were differences in the nuances and the points emphasized, they were generally similar in argument. Their common themes can be summarized as follows: (1) there is no doubt the Senkakus belong to Japan; (2) in order to resolve the territorial problem, it is necessary to calmly try to convince the other parties and to seek a peaceful resolution; (3) the issue of the continental shelf is a problem separate from ownership of the Senkakus and actually involves many complicated problems, and thus there is no choice but to talk about it with the Chinese side.[42]

The *Tokyo Shimbun*, first begun in 1884, introduced a long editorial on February 20 (1972) analyzing the respective claims, and ending with the argument that "[the government] needs to show a resolute attitude at home and abroad at this juncture, so as not to make this a 'second Takeshima' (*Daini no Takeshima*). We venture to arouse its attention (*aete chui o kanki suru*)."[43]

The next newspaper that had an editorial on the Senkakus was the *Nihon Keizai Shimbun*, seen as the Japanese equivalent of the *Wall Street Journal*, which used the entirety of its editorial space to discuss the various issues, including both sovereignty and development of the seabed resources, relating to the Senkakus. Its March 5 editorial, "Senkaku Shoto no Nihon Ryoyuken Shucho wa Tozen (Japan's Insistence on Its Right to Ownership Over Senkaku Islands is Natural)," was seven paragraphs long, and noted the dilemma Japan (and perhaps China) faced with restoring diplomatic relations while dealing with the Senkakus issue:

> Even though there may be no doubt about our country's justifiable territorial rights over the Senkaku Islands, full consideration is needed to say, in light of the political background for the bringing-up of this problem, that is, the pressing nature of the problem of restoration of Japan-China diplomatic relations, which is the biggest pending issue in our diplomacy, and the new situation after the Sino–U.S. summit talks. It will be unfortunate if Japan and China should fall into confrontation and dispute prior to restoration of diplomatic relations, over the territorial

problem. The Chinese side, too, must be having its say. However, it will be troublesome if the Japanese and Chinese peoples' desire for early restoration of diplomatic relations should cool off due to the territorial problem. The matter should be coped with calmly, strictly on the basis of objective facts.[44]

The next newspaper to take up the issue was the *Sankei Shimbun*, considered the most conservative of the main newspapers. Established in 1933, it and its companion monthly journal, *Seiron* (The Correct Argument), founded in 1973, have been in the forefront of promoting Japan's position in the Senkakus issue and being very critical of China's actions. On March 7, the *Sankei Shimbun*, a former political reporter of whose had been serving as Prime Minister Sato's personal secretary[45] since March 1967, published "Senkaku Retto Waga Kuni no Ryoyuken wa Meihaku (Our Country's Rights to Ownership over Senkaku Islands Clear)," a seven-paragraph editorial "supporting the Government's attitude, that is, its assertion that 'it is clear that the Senkaku Islands are territory of our country'."[46] Importantly, while it was critical of the Chinese description of the reversion of Okinawa as a "fraud," the *Sankei Shimbun* did not take an extreme or uncompromising attitude on the Senkakus issue. In discussing the difference between territorial rights and development of natural resources in the area, it called for dialog:

> It is natural for the Chinese side to be nervous about these moves. In the international situation which is moving from tension to peace, we must not fan the "kindling coal" running counter to the trend. We should strictly distinguish the assertion for the rights to ownership over the Senkaku Islands from the development of the sea-bed resources. We should take a resolute attitude toward the former, while regarding latter, we should listen to the Chinese assertions and take the way to joint development.[47]

The center-left *Mainichi Shimbun*, founded in 1872, was the next major newspaper to publish its editorial on the Senkaku Islands. The March 9 editorial, which was seven paragraphs in length, doubted whether negotiations would succeed, as long as the PRC and ROC insisted the Senkakus were Chinese. Noting the "extremely complicated" international environment, it called on the government to

> tackle the problem prudently and perseveringly. In the past, a dispute occurred between Japan and the ROK over the rights to ownership over Takeshima Island in the Japan Sea belonging to Shimane Prefecture. The two sides would not yield an inch, insisting that the Island is territory inherently belonging to their own countries, respectively, and the problem was left pending in the Japan-ROK Treaty. Virtually, however, the Island remains occupied by the ROK side. Regarding the Senkaku Islands, the mistake of Takeshima Island may possibly be repeated, if the matter is

not properly handled. In order not to repeat such a failure, the Government needs to take appropriate measures, such as appealing to international public opinion.[48]

The next day, the conservative *Yomiuri Shimbun* introduced its editorial stance on the Senkakus issue. Founded in 1874, the *Yomiuri* also believed Japan's rights to the islands were "clear (*meikaku*)," and having "hitherto maintained that there is no room for doubt both legally and actually about the point that the Senkaku Islands ought to be reverted to Japan under the sovereignty of our country as a part of 'Okinawa' at the time of realization of the reversion of Okinawa on May 15[,] we wish to clarify our total support for this once again at this time when the objective grounds for insisting on the legitimacy thereof have been shown."[49] After noting the various claims of China and Taiwan, as well as the dynamics of the territorial issue and problem of sea-bed development, as well as the normalization of relations with China, the eight-paragraph editorial entitled, "Shasetsu Wagakuni no 'Senkaku' Ryoyuken wa Meikaku (Editorial: Our Country's Rights to Ownership over 'Senkaku Islands' Clear)" warned that "if the Chinese side insists on it, we may not be able to avert the problem [that there are competing claims to the Senkaku Islands]."[50] While stressing the difference in territorial rights versus the continental shelf problem, it also encouraged that "development of sea-bed oil fields around the Islands, which has come into the limelight recently, should be settled through talks with the Chinese side."[51]

It was not for another ten days before the position of the *Asahi Shimbun* became clear at this juncture. According to international law scholar Okuhara Toshio, at one point the *Asahi Shimbun*, which tends to publish vague editorials lacking consistency and actionable insights, published one to the effect that Japan's claims to the Senkakus were weak, and that the islands belonged to China. He immediately wrote to them, providing the historical documents to disprove *Asahi*'s assertions, to which the newspaper revised its stance.[52]

In any case, the leftist *Asahi Shimbun*, founded in 1879, in its editorial of March 10 similarly separated the issues of territorial rights and sea-bed development, and while calling on China to "hold talks rationally in accordance with the principle of the Convention on the Continental Shelf," argued that "the Senkaku Islands cannot be said to have belonged to another country, either historically or geographically."[53] The twelve-paragraph editorial, which included a long historical analysis, probably done with the materials provided by Professor Okuhara, added that "the problem of the rights to ownership over the Senkaku Islands should not become a barrier blocking the way to normalization of Japan-China diplomatic relations, which is the biggest diplomatic task."[54]

It should be noted that these examples were not the first instances that the above newspapers introduced the Senkakus issue in their editorials. The *Mainichi*, for example, took up the Senkakus in mid-April 1971, and again in early December.[55] The *Yomiuri* similarly had discussed the Senkakus in early September 1970, especially the issue of their development.[56]

One observer, writing about this period, noted how rare it was in postwar Japan for there to be agreement on a foreign policy issue between the government, all the political parties, and the mainstream media. "There was a unity on the issue of the Senkakus. It was a truly rare consensus in foreign policy."[57] Indeed, within the GOJ, there were many who were happy to see the media and political parties supporting the government's position on the Senkaku issue. Wada Tsutomu, the spokesman for the Ministry of Foreign Affairs, told Sneider "privately" that it was the "first issue in long time on which media have strongly supported government position," and another unidentified Foreign Ministry official noted that the Senkakus issue had also "brought a temporary semblance of unity to a fragmented LDP."[58] The same thing, however, could probably be said of groups in the two Chinas, as well, as we saw in the previous chapter.

Interestingly, not everyone in Japan agreed with the government's stand. While they were a minority, it is necessary to introduce the views and motivations of two groups who were publicly known at the time to oppose the reversion of the Senkakus, for the sake of the historical record.

Domestic opponents to the GOJ's claim on Senkakus

Despite the bipartisan support shown by the political parties and the pro-government position taken by the media, there were still at least a couple of Japanese groups who opposed their government's claim to the Senkakus. The first one that announced its stance was the Association for the Promotion of International Trade, Japan (*Nihon Kokusai Boeki Sokushin Kyokai*), founded in September 1954. JAPIT, as the pro-China trade group is known today, was chaired at the time by former Prime Minister Ishibashi Tanzan, who was known for his pro-China views but had been unable to normalize relations with the PRC since he had to resign due to illness in February 1957 after only two months in office. Nevertheless, Ishibashi visited the PRC as a private citizen in August 1959 and eventually met with Chou En-lai where they had fairly substantive talks. The following year, trade with the PRC was opened, in part due to his efforts. Ishibashi was considered a "dove" within the LDP and having lost in the 30th Lower House elections held in November 1963 retired from politics shortly after that. He remained active in education and other matters of national policy. On March 7, 1972, JAPIT held its annual meeting and adopted a policy and program to "oppose the plot to purloin the Senkaku Islands," based on the view that if the territorial dispute worsened, it would affect the normalization of relations between Japan and the PRC.[59]

The other group that was known to oppose including the Senkakus in the Okinawa reversion agreement in Japan was one comprised of ninety-five "men of culture (*bunkajin*)" who reportedly signed a statement that said, "The Senkaku Islands were seized by Japan in the Sino-Japanese War, and historically, they are obviously territory inherently belonging to China. We cannot approve the Japanese imperialist aggression and affirm the history of aggression."[60] The group, led in part by Ishida Ikuo, an activist writer who was once a member of the Communist Party until he was kicked out in 1961, decided to name the group the "Association for Blocking Japanese Imperialist Seizure of the Senkaku Islands (*Nittei no Senkaku Retto Ryakudatsu Boshi no Kai*)."[61] One of the members of the group was Inoue Kiyoshi, a Marxist historian at Kyoto University (*Kyoto Daigaku*) well known for his criticism of the Emperor system, who had already written a couple of articles to date supporting the PRC's claims to the Senkakus and whose views and imprecise use of documents were strongly challenged by international legal scholar Okuhara.[62] Inoue's articles were republished in PRC journals, such as the *Peking Review*, and newspapers, and the former Japan Communist Party member and Maoist later received an honorary doctorate from the Chinese Academy of Social Sciences in 1997.[63]

It is important to note that in the case of both groups, they were less interested in the Senkakus than they were in Japan's relations with China. Avoiding a dispute over the Senkakus by surrendering its claims was a way, in their mind, for Japan to have better relations with the PRC.[64]

Continued tensions and U.S. involvement

One of the key triggers for the increased attention of the political parties, media, and Japanese government around this time was not only the pending reversion of Okinawa but also a series of incidents in mid-February (1972) by Taiwan that escalated the situation. In doing so, it also drew the United States into the dispute again. This section introduces events following the signing of the Okinawa Reversion Treaty and looks at efforts to further draw the USG into the dispute.

On June 19, a couple of days after the signing of the reversion treaty, Foreign Minister Chou called in Ambassador Itagaki to propose negotiations on the status of the Senkakus. Itagaki asked what the GRC was requesting, and Chou answered that either "negotiations" or "discussions" were acceptable to it.[65] A week later on June 25, Itagaki met again with Chow, having gotten instructions from Tokyo. Itagaki made the following points, which were included in a statement he handed to Chow:

> Status of Senkakus determined by Article 3 of the San Francisco Treaty.
> If the GRC willing to recognize Japan's territorial sovereignty over the Senkakus, GOJ willing to discuss related issues in an effort to maintain cordial relations. However, GOJ realizes this position may be considered inconceivable by GRC.
> Japan is concerned that
> A great harm will occur for both parties if nationals of the respective countries become inflamed and engage in mutual recriminations, and
> That Peking will take opportunity presented by this issue to disrupt friendly GOJ-GRC relations for its own purposes.

Japan advises that both parties from attacking each other's position, and take measures to prevent untoward incidents from occurring as a result of Senkakus dispute. Should any incident occur, the two sides should consult on how to cope with it.[66]

Chow read the statement, and replied "mildly" according to a Japanese official who reported the meeting to the U.S. Embassy, stating that he interpreted the Japanese statement as "not totally excluding the possibility of talks forever."[67] The Japanese official, Yoshida, mentioned that in taking this position on the Senkakus, the Japanese side had to consider that opening the question of sovereignty also opened the question of which "authority" to deal with in China and which was the "real" Chinese government.[68] He assumed that the next step for the GRC was to approach the USG to apply pressure on Japan.

In the meantime, both Chou and Itagaki told Ambassador McConaughy in separate conversations on June 22 that Chang Chun, the old friend of Chiang Kai-shek who served as secretary-general and advisor to the president, would be discussing the Senkakus during an upcoming visit to Korea where they both would be to attend the inauguration ceremonies of Park Chung-hee in July and might also get into the question of offshore oil. Chou said the talks, tentatively scheduled around July 12,[69] Chang would have in Japan would be "reconnaissance" to lay the groundwork for discussions he hoped to have with Foreign Minister Aichi in Manila in the middle of July, and that he hoped the dispute with Japan over the Senkakus could be kept less visible in the future since the mutual criticism has been unhelpful to both sides.[70] While the Taiwanese "obviously remain unhappy" over reversion over Senkakus to Japan, they did seem pleased with Rogers' efforts to get the GOJ to take the initiative to discuss the issue with the GRC.

Sometime after this, Chiang Ching-kuo met with Ambassador McConaughy and expressed his appreciation for the U.S. initiative to ask the GOJ to discuss the Senkakus issues with Taiwan, but noted at the same time that his government was "shock[ed] to find that the Japanese not prepared to discuss the sovereignty question."[71] He expressed his hope that the USG could convince the Japanese to "abandon their evasive posture."[72]

Legal Advisor Starr urged that the State Department be "extremely cautious" about getting anymore involved in this matter, explaining that the USG has already made it clear to both the GRC and GOJ that it believes a dispute exists between them over the Senkaku Islands, and that the USG should be prepared to tell the GRC that the U.S. position was made quite clear to both parties and it continued to adhere to that position.[73]

That is what the State Department did. In a July 21 telegram, it told the Embassy in Taipei that it did not believe it would be "useful" to make any further American approach to the GOJ beyond that which was already being made by Secretary Rogers to Foreign Minister Aichi to persuade him to discuss the Senkakus with the GRC, and let the ambassador know he could so inform Chiang Ching-kuo at any appropriate occasion if he believed a response were necessary.[74]

It seems that little happened during that time as several months later Foreign Minister Chow raised the issue of the Senkakus again in December 1971 with Kissinger and Rogers, asking that the USG "hold back" the Senkakus, perhaps by "retaining the area for U.S. target practice for a certain period."[75] He renewed this request on February 7, requesting Ambassador McConaughy and the USG to "find some way of preventing at least ... [the] complete reversion" of the Senkaku Islands.[76] Chow argued that if the islands were in fact returned to Japan, there would be an outcry by overseas Chinese, which would then be reflected among the students in Taiwan, who would take out their anger on American and Japanese embassies and would be "most embarrassing especially during national assembly session, elections, and cabinet reorganization."[77] McConaughy, writing to Washington, felt "reasonably certain" that Chow knew there was little chance the USG would reverse its decision on the Senkakus and believed he was "undoubtedly acting on instructions from higher level" in order to establish for the record that the GRC had repeatedly stated its position and asked the United States to change its decision.

The ambassador, aware that sentiment ran high on the issue and that the GRC would have "a fairly difficult time" managing popular reactions, told Chow that he would refer the matter to the Department of State but emphasized that he doubted the USG would reverse its decision as the islands were within the area specified for return and that the sovereignty issue was a matter between the ROC and Japan.[78] Chow challenged this argument, pointing out that the long USG "continued to have a responsibility stemming from a long trusteeship (*sic*)" of the islands, that the USG was reserving other areas for military use, and that the GRC's direct negotiations with Japan on the matter "would have no real prospect of success after the islands reverted to Japanese control."[79] Deputy Chief of Mission Oscar Vance Armstrong, who was also in attendance, responded that any attempt to change the reversion treaty arrangements after they had been approved in both the Senate and Diet would be a "highly adverse development" in United States–Japan relations and would "surely boomerang" against Taiwan as well in terms of Japanese public opinion.[80] It is unlikely Chow, who said he was "bracing for a storm," was truly satisfied with their response.[81]

The storm that Chow was referring to seems to have come later that week. On February 11, the international edition of the KMT's Central Daily News reported that the Executive Yuan had "officially decided" that the Senkakus fell within the Ilan County administrative district in northwestern Taiwan and that officials in the district were planning to send a mission to the Senkakus. While the international edition of the party's newspaper was not distributed locally, it was picked up in Okinawa and Japan, for example.[82] Moreover, an earlier story in the *China Times* had stated that the Ministry of Education was revising its textbooks to include the Senkakus within Ilan County.

The earlier story, which was picked up and reported in the February 15 edition of the *Ryukyu Shimpo*, in turn caused the Chief Executive Yara to tell reporters in response to their questions that he would request the GOJ and USG to take "appropriate countermeasures."[83] The High Commissioner was clearly bothered by this—"if the story is correct," he told the Embassy in Taipei, "[I would] appreciate Embassy efforts to dissuade ROC from such ill-advised action."[84] Taiwan's action would later trigger a resolution a few weeks later by the Legislature of the Government of the Ryukyu Islands in early March.

Through its own investigations, the Foreign Ministry found out that the GRC had indeed decided to incorporate the Senkakus into Ilan County. Late the evening of the 17th, Yoshida Kenzo of the Japanese Foreign Ministry's Asia Bureau (*Ajia Kyoku*) called in New Nai-sheng, minister of the Taiwanese Embassy in Tokyo, to issue a *demarche*, or diplomatic protest, about the actions being taken by the Executive Yuan to include the Ilan District Office landing officials on the islands. Yoshida reiterated the GOJ's position on the Senkakus, requested confirmation about the accuracy of the story, and stated that "complications would be created" if it were true.[85]

The next day, Foreign Minister Fukuda informed Prime Minister Sato of the results of their investigation and apprised him of the actions the Foreign Ministry was taking after their regularly scheduled Cabinet meeting that morning.[86] That same day, a Japanese official based in Okinawa who was part of the GOJ Prepcom Element, Naha, called on William Clark, Jr., who had succeeded Richard E. Snyder as the director of the USCAR Liaison Department in 1969, to inform USCAR of the GOJ *demarche* and to request USCAR's assistance should any ROC citizens attempt to land on the Senkakus. Clark received the request with comment but pointed out that the "Senkakus will remain U.S. responsibility until reversion and U.S. will act in accordance with that responsibility."[87] This interaction formed the basis for Yoshino to tell the Diet's Special Committee on Okinawa and Northern Territories and Foreign Relations Research Council of the LDP that the GOJ had requested the High Commissioner to "oust" any ROC survey team sent to the Senkakus.[88]

Shortly after the Japanese government protested the above stories, and the High Commissioner requested the Embassy to apply pressure on the GRC, Armstrong, and the political counselor, William W. Thomas, raised the same question with Chien, who made the following points which he explained had also been relayed to the Japanese chargé: (1) story in question was a local story from Ilan; (2) the ROC claims sovereignty over the Senkakus; (3) the ROC realizes that Japan also claims the Senkakus but that reversion to Japan is scheduled; (4) since there is a conflict over sovereignty and the two governments enjoy friendly relations, the matter is one best solved through amicable diplomatic negotiations; and (5) in line with friendly relations with Japan, the GRC hopes that neither side will play up this incident.[89] The American diplomats did not appear satisfied with the response and followed up by emphasizing that any GRC attempt to survey the Senkakus or establish an administrative office or "even talk of such moves" could only have "unfortunate consequences."[90] "Off the record," Chien replied the issue of the Senkakus was so sensitive that no one in the GRC was willing to deny the story, but he acknowledged this sort of gesturing was "provocative" and "clearly implied" no action will follow.[91]

In reporting the conversation, the Taipei Embassy stated it was "quite certain" that the GRC did not intend to send a survey team to the Senkakus or make an administrative office there but it was "slightly less certain" that the GRC "fully appreciate[d]" that even talk along these lines in the international press was provocative "although we have made this extremely clear" to the Foreign Office in the past.[92] The telegram concluded with the Embassy's observation: "The GRC is faced with a real dilemma on the Senkakus issue. On the one hand officials are quite aware of realities and want to minimize controversy. On the other hand the issue has become so highly nationalistic that no official relishes the job of acting as a dampener."[93]

In the meantime, the U.S. Embassy in Tokyo expressed its displeasure at MOFA's Yoshida speaking directly with the Taiwanese minister on this issue without previously consulting the U.S. side since the administration of the Senkakus remains "the primary responsibility of a USG until reversion."[94] The embassy officer went on to point out that the USG had already launched the "logical steps" to confirm the accuracy of the reports "thus to lay the basis for any official action necessary," and requested that MOFA bear in mind "priority responsibility" of the U.S. government for the Senkakus until reversion and consult with the USG "before taking any further action respecting Senkakus."[95]

Yoshino subsequently called Sneider to apologize for the GOJ's "precipitate action" and explained that the Senkakus situation is "super-sensitive" to the GOJ since "powerful pro-PRC forces" in Japan would not hesitate to take advantage of any "Taiwan-fomented difficulties on Senkakus to upset delicate balance which GOJ striving at present to maintain in its relations between GRC and PRC."[96] Yoshino confided to Sneider that he had already been "called on the carpet before an LDP committee" on these matters.[97]

The USG worked hard at persuading Japan and Taiwan to avoid a confrontation, and continued to take preventative action in part because it did not want to see tensions escalate among its allies but also because it did not wish to get involved. This stance was particularly clear in the case of the desire of a parliamentary vice minister for defense, Noro Kyoichi, who had expressed a desire to fly over the Senkakus in a U.S. military helicopter prior to reversion to become more familiar with the situation. Noro had been named parliamentary vice minister in July the previous year as part of the third reshuffling of the Sato Cabinet. He argued with regard to the Senkakus that the future continued provision of the ranges there to the United States Navy was evidence that the Senkaku Islands were Japanese territory, and as such a sign should be placed on the islands forbidden the trespassing on the islands without permission after reversion.[98] He directed Counselor Yasuda

Yutaka to begin planning for a trip to the Senkakus on their next visit to Okinawa.[99]

This request was made through Ambassador Takase Jiro, who had been appointed in 1968, and who met with Lieutenant General Lampert on March 11 (1972), to explain that Noro had "personally asked him" to convey "in strictest confidence" the latter's wish to do the overflight.[100] According to Takase, it was the GOJ that had asked Noro to make a "personal survey" of the islands, and that because Noro was aware of the current political and international situations, he intended to keep the overflight secret.[101] He said Noro would do the overflight on the latter's trip to Miyako, and that he wanted to do it in a U.S. military plane (although he did not make a specific request at that time). Takase added that the overflight was to be done in connection with a study being conducted by the Defense Agency of joint use of the gunnery ranges in the Senkakus, and that Noro wanted to be able to "present the image of a vigorous JDA."[102]

The High Commissioner told Takase that Noro's request would be kept in the strictest confidence, but that he would have to refer the matter to Washington before he could give any reply. Political Advisor John F. Knowles immediately informed the Embassy in Tokyo of the request, and noted that while he had no details of the flight plan, etc., per se, it would have to be communicated to the Taiwan Air Defense Command Center (ADCC) because the Senkakus fell within the Taiwan Air Defense Identification Zone (ADIZ), and thus it was accessible to the GRC. Knowles asked the Embassy to authorize him to tell Ambassador Takase that the USG was not able to arrange military air transportation or otherwise facilitate Noro's overflight. If pressed, Knowles proposed to tell Takase that public disclosure of the overflight between then and reversion could not be discounted, and as such, U.S. support for an overflight was likely to further complicate the "international political sensitivity" of the Senkakus problem that Takase himself had referred to.[103]

Noro was subsequently informed about the U.S. position, and was incensed apparently. "There was no problem with providing a military helicopter," Noro wrote in his memoirs, "the problem for the USG then was the destination—the Senkakus. The High Commissioner saying he would 'consult with Washington' was a convenient way of saying 'no.' The United States likely had to consider its relations with China. My observation trip to the Senkakus ended up never happening."[104]

Noro was not the only LDP politician and government official apparently frustrated the United States over its stance on the Senkakus. As we saw in the previous chapter, Yamanaka Sadanori, was quite upset about the issue, and even Foreign Minister Fukuda and Prime Minister Sato vented about it. The United States was seen as not only not siding with Japan—a key, and perhaps *the* key, ally in the region—but its long-standing policies on the Ryukyu Islands were also seen as inconsistent.

Equally upset were Taiwanese officials and politicians, both at the USG and toward the Japanese side. On March 24, Foreign Minister Chow told

McConaughy that the National Assembly was "heatedly discussing" the Senkakus issue in light of the recent public debate in Japan, and would reportedly issue a statement before the adjournment of the session scheduled for the 25th.[105] Chow deplored the "inflammatory statements" by Sato and Fukuda (introduced below), and said that he was going to "make moderation and restraint prevail" in Taiwan but could be successful "only to extent the Japanese practice the same virtues themselves," a prospect he thought did not look "bright" due to the "various contenders for Sato's LDP mantle making strong statements on this subject."[106] Chow said he was going to be meeting with Ambassador Uyama Atsushi (a native of Shimane Prefecture, whose Takeshima Islands had been "stolen", according to U.S. documents by South Korea in the 1950s) to "make a strong but amicable presentation ... to advise the GOJ to damp the issue down" and requested the USG to "reinforce" this advice.[107] "The issue could be explosive," Chow said of the potential for domestic protests in Taiwan, and the "GRC badly needs a quiet period with no new provocations to excite the students."[108] This is particularly true as Japan was at the time Taiwan's chief trading partner.[109]

Chow had another request of the United States in addition to its urging the GOJ to show moderation. Chow asked the USG to prolong its administrative control over the two islands it would be using for target practice, and said he hoped the "GOJ would emphasize its overall success in regaining the Ryukyus and omit or play down the Senkakus" as both governments "had more important matters to deal with in this difficult time and should not be distracted and subjected to strain by such a relatively minor subject as ownership of a few rocks sticking out of the sea."[110]

The USG was certainly interested in the issue being de-escalated, but even its efforts did not completely stop the incidents. In mid-April, the GRI Police patrol vessel *Chitose* conducted a routine patrol of the waters near the Senkakus where they found a Taiwanese fishing vessel in the late afternoon of April 11 near Kita Kojima. The police informed the fishermen they were intruding into Ryukyuan waters and asked them to leave, which they did without incident. After spending the night there, the police traveled to Uotsuri Jima the next morning where it found five Taiwanese vessels between 500 and 1000 meters offshore. The police notified these vessels of their intrusion and they, too, departed without incident. The *Chitose* returned to Ishigaki Port eventually.[111]

The story about the GRI police finding the Taiwanese fishing vessels was introduced in the newspapers on April 13 by Kyodo News Agency.[112] After receiving a report from the High Commissioner in Okinawa, the Embassy in Taipei shared this information with the GRC (Chien), who thanked the Embassy officer and explained they had not heard anything about this and imagined the incident had been inflated by the Japanese press.[113] The Embassy officer said he hoped further incidents could be avoided.

As the date of reversion approached, tensions rose about the possibility of protests and a possible incident on or around May 15. The efforts to avoid one are introduced later.

PRC reactions to the reversion treaty

Peking had not quietly watched the statements by the GOJ claiming sovereignty over the Senkakus at the time of the signing of the reversion treaty or later in the Diet deliberations. Instead, it increasingly rebutted them, and also expressed alarm about Japan's plans to patrol the area.

The PRC's claims had been building for a long time as had its criticism of Japan. Even before the signing of the reversion agreement, the New China News Agency criticized the Japanese government for its attempt to "occupy China's territory of the Tiaoyu (Senkaku) and other islands with the support of U.S. imperialism" through the "Okinawa reversion fraud."[114] It went further to say that "Should Japanese militarism dare to act recklessly, it will be made to pay for its rabid evil things."[115]

A month after the signing ceremony, the NCNA continued its attacks by publishing a speech by the People's Liberation Army Chief of Staff, Huang Yung-shen, on July 16, criticizing "encroachments on China's territory."[116] The Senkakus were not specifically named in the newspaper story but a whole litany of U.S. and Japanese "aggression" in East Asia were mentioned.

A few months later, in early November 1971, a little more than a week after the PRC was admitted to the United Nations at the expense of the ROC, the NCNA published an article praising the student-led demonstrations against what it called the "Okinawa reversion fraud" and criticized the "collusion" of the Japanese government with the United States in "scheming to annex China's sacred territory."[117] These comments seem to have been in response to remarks by Prime Minister Sato and Foreign Minister Fukuda in the Upper House's Budget Committee that the Senkakus unquestionably belonged to Japan.[118]

Another effort on China's part to claim the Senkakus was its pressure on a Japanese mission to the PRC led by Asukata Ichio, mayor of Yokohama City and head of the Japan–China Diplomatic Relations Restoration People's Council (*Nicchu Kokko Kaifuku Kokumin Kaigi*), in late November. The pro-Peking group, which was affiliated with the JSP (which Asukata became chairman of in 1977) and General Council of Japan Trade Unions (*Sohyo*), was strongly pressured to accept China's views that the Senkaku Islands were Chinese but resisted.[119] As a result, according to a press conference Asukata held at Tokyo International Airport upon their return, "In the case of entering into Japan–China Government-to-Government negotiations in the future, I think it will not be possible to side-step this question. However, the Chinese side showed the consideration that restoration of relations on the people's level must not be hampered by this matter."[120] The Japanese Consulate in Hong Kong, which relayed its insights on the Asukata mission, noted that "aside from tiny Maoist groups there are no Japanese political elements that could subscribe to Peking's position on this issue" and thus the PRC "cannot hope to capitalize on it within Japan as it tries to do on issues that divide the Japanese politically."[121]

Subsequently, on December 30, the PRC's Ministry of Foreign Affairs issued a long statement declaring the islands to be China's and declared that the "Chinese people are determined to recover the Tiaoyu and other islands appertaining to Taiwan."[122] This statement appears as Appendix 5.

There was not too much agitation for a couple of months as the PRC got ready to host President Nixon in February. It did re-join the fray on March 3 when An Chih-yuan, the PRC delegate to the United Nations, stated as part of a longer speech critical of Japan and the West in the General Assembly's Committee on Peaceful Uses of the Seabed and Ocean Floor that the Senkakus were an integral part of China as part of his longer speech before the committee in which he noted China's opposition to "big power hegemony" and support of "the just stand of safeguarding state sovereignty."[123] In this connection, An criticized both the United States and Japan when he said:

The Chinese people suffered long from imperialist aggression and oppression. The United States is to this date forcibly occupying China's territory, Taiwan Province, and of late it has colluded with the Japanese reactionaries and used the fraud of "the Reversion of Okinawa" in an attempt to include into Japan's territory the Tiaoyu and other islands—islands appertaining to China's Taiwan Province. Furthermore, the United States has in the past few years collaborated with Japan and colluded with the Chiang Kai-shek clique in making frequent and large-scale "submarine explorations" in China's coastal seas in an attempt to further plunder China's coastal sea-bed resources. These flagrant acts of aggression and plunder cannot but arouse the utmost indignation of the Chinese people. On behalf of the Government of the People's Republic of China, I hereby reiterate: China's Taiwan Province and all the islands appertaining to it, including Tiaoyu Island, Huangwei Island, Chihwei Island, Nanhsiao Island, Peihsiao Island, etc., are part of China's sacred territory. The sea-bed resources of the seas around these islands and of the shallow seas adjacent to other parts of China belong completely to China and it is absolutely impermissible for any foreign aggressor to poke his fingers into them. No one whosoever is allowed to create any pretext to carve off China's territory and plunder the sea resources belonging to China and no one will ever succeed in do so.[124]

Japanese Ambassador Ogiso Moto immediately took to the floor to respond to the Chinese representative's remarks, reiterating Japan's claim to the islands and pointing out that An's remarks would incur the resentment of the Japanese people.[125]

Interestingly, while American diplomats felt the Chinese statement was an attack on the United States, the timing of the comments, coming so short after Nixon's visit to China, were seen by some in Japan as a possible example of collusion between the United States and the PRC on the Senkakus, or at the minimum pressure on the Nixon Administration to acquiesce in the PRC's claims. This concern is an example of the effect the so-called "Nixon Shocks," introduced earlier, had on Japanese psyche and sense of vulnerability.

This concern, importantly, was not without validity. Nixon had become very frustrated with Japan in recent years, mostly due to the long time it took the Sato Administration to reach an agreement on Japan's restraints on textile exports to the United States. But Nixon's concerns had also been growing over his more than two decades of interaction with Japan. As vice president during the Dwight D. Eisenhower Administration (1953–61), Nixon had first visited Japan late 1953 and pushed for Japan to rearm and become a more proactive player in the Western alliance against the Communists. He visited twice again in 1964 and 1967 as a private citizen and lawyer representing clients but also to develop his contacts, learn more about Japan following its recovery and during its period of high economic growth, and perhaps push again the above message on a reluctant Japan.[126] Nixon's national security adviser, Kissinger, moreover was not a fan of Japan nor did he even pretend to understand the country. In his memoirs, he writes of Japan, a major U.S. ally and then second-largest economy in the world, as a "string of islands off the coast of China," and admitted that "neither I nor my colleagues possessed a very subtle grasp of Japanese culture and psychology."[127] As a historian of the great powers, the German-born Kissinger preferred to deal with great powers whose moves and national interests were obvious, and seemed to always try to look for the person who was the leader or held the power behind the throne. For this reason it was far easier to deal with China than Japan: "The hardest thing for us to grasp was that the extraordinary Japanese decisions were produced by leaders who prided themselves on their anonymous style. To be sure there were great prime ministers. But they worked unobtrusively, conveying in their bearing that their policies reflected the consensus of a society, not the idiosyncrasy of an individual."[128]

The concern Japan had over the views of Nixon and Kissinger on the Senkaku issues were particularly keen. While the views did not manifest themselves at the time of Okinawa's reversion to Japan, they were seen in early 1974 when at a meeting at the State Department, Kissinger, then serving as secretary of State, was being briefed by Deputy Assistant Secretary of State for East Asian Affairs Arthur W. Hummel, Jr., about the PRC's role in the Paracel Islands and Spratly Islands dispute. Kissinger suddenly asked if the United States "[could] steer them towards the Senkaku Islands?"[129] Hummel, who was born in China and later studied and worked in Beijing before being interned by the Japanese after the attacks on Pearl Harbor, escaping, and joining Chinese Nationalist Forces until the end of the war, was uncertain of what Kissinger was saying, and asked who "them" was. Kissinger responded, "the PRC," to which Hummel, who had joined the Foreign Service in 1950, questioned if the secretary of State really thought "we want to do that?" Kissinger argued that "it would teach religion to the Japanese." Hummel, who later became the U.S. ambassador to China from 1981 to 1985 during which time he negotiated an arms pact with Taiwan, agreed that "we have to teach religion to the Japanese," but wondered if "it [was] worth that price." To this point, Kissinger simply responded, "No, no."[130]

It is unclear if Kissinger, highly concerned about China's perceptions of the Nixon Administration at this juncture during the Watergate crisis paralyzing Washington, D.C., was serious or not, or if he was just testing the waters with his staff.[131] Japan, which had long feared America's sudden rapprochement with China without prior consultation with it—a concern known as the "Asakai Nightmare" after one of Japan's ambassadors to the United States, Asakai Koichiro (1957–63)—seems to have continued to live in a similar nightmare with regard to the United States and the Senkakus issue, never confident that the United States would truly take Japan's side in the dispute. If they did not know of Kissinger's comments at the time, Japanese officials probably still sensed them somehow.[132]

That same day, March 3, the PRC had also singled out Prime Minister Sato for an attack, calling him "and his ilk ... the reactionary chieftains of Japan—and asserting that Japan coveted Taiwan."[133] The article attacking Japan's longest serving premier (Sato came into office in November 1964) and published in the Chinese Communist Party journal *Jinmin Jih Pao* was believed to be written by a high government and Communist Party official.

On instructions from the Foreign Ministry, Ogiso called on John R. Stevenson, the legal adviser of the Department of State and United States Representative on the same committee, and Deputy Assistant Secretary of State for International Organizational Affairs Martin F. Herz, who had been serving in that capacity since 1970 and had previously worked at the U.S. Embassy in Tokyo as first secretary from 1957 to 1959.[134] Ogiso wanted to know if the U.S. representative intended to reply to the PRC "intervention" and if so to ask that Japan be informed in advance of a proposed U.S. reply.[135] Ogiso explained that if the United States did not reply to the PRC remarks about the reversion of Okinawa, it might be interpreted that the USG tacitly agreed with the PRC statement.

In fact, earlier in the day, the U.S. delegation had met with Iguchi Takeo, the son of a former Japanese Ambassador to the United States (1954–56), Iguchi Sadao, and a diplomat in his own right specializing in international law, and explained that the USG was not planning on any further reply to the PRC remarks other than a brief statement it made on March 3 in response to the PRC rejecting PRC accusations and stating the U.S. actions were consistent with international law. Stevenson told Ogiso that he did not think a further reply was necessary as it would open the committee discussion to "further polemics on territorial questions unrelated to its work."[136] If the PRC raised the issue again, Stevenson added, the USG would reply in more detail. In the meantime, he gave Ogiso a copy of that statement, suggesting that Ogiso forward it to Tokyo. Ogiso agreed to do so, and stated his personal view that indeed, it would not be necessary for the USG to make any further reply to the PRC at that time.

Nevertheless, the PRC launched another verbal attack on Japan and the United States at the Seabed Committee. Iguchi visited the U.S. delegation to learn if and how it intended to respond. Iguchi was dismayed to learn that the U.S. representative, Christopher H. Phillips, a former Army captain, newspaper reporter, bank vice president, and chamber of commerce executive-turned-diplomat, intended to use the previously cleared statement: "In connection with the Senkakus, we take no position on the merits of the various claims made by the Republic of China, Japan, and the PRC, nor are we in a position to make any recommendation as to how they might be resolved other than by negotiation between the parties concerned or by third party adjudication."[137] Iguchi urged that the U.S. side not use the text as it would "be taken as flatly contradicting the Japanese position" that the Senkaku Islands were Japanese and that the matter was not subject to negotiation.[138] Iguchi said he would relay the language to Tokyo, and an understanding was reached that the U.S. side would only make a general statement "deploring the introduction of such matters" in the committee meeting, as there was "no necessity for getting into specifics on Senkakus."[139]

A written response by Japan would not follow for a couple of months. At the end of May, the Foreign Ministry instructed its permanent representative to the United Nations, Nakagawa Toru, to send letters to UN Secretary General Kurt Waldheim and U.S. Delegate George H. W. Bush, who was serving as the chairman of the Security Council, that the Senkaku Islands "are Japanese territory, and China's assertions, claiming them to belong to China cannot be accepted."[140]

In the meantime, on March 30, the Xinhua (New China) News Agency denounced Japan's claims (re-emphasized in a March 8 statement below) saying that the "incorporation" of the islands in 1895 by Japan was done while the Ching Dynasty was weak, that the U.S. administration over Okinawa was "unilaterally declared" and that the transfer of administrative rights to Japan was "illicit" and the reversion itself a "fraud."[141] It also added that any efforts by the GOJ to patrol the waters around the islands or to raise the Japanese flag there would be opposed by the people of China "and Japan."[142] The comment did not, however, say direct counteraction would be taken by the PRC to patrols.

The next time China appears to publicly have weighed in on the issue was not until after Okinawa's reversion in mid-May.

The GOJ Statement of March 8, 1972

In light of the most recent moves by the GRC and PRC to push their claims, namely the GRC ordinance in February to include the Senkakus within Ilan County of Taiwan Province and the PRC remarks at the above United Nations General Assembly's Committee on Peaceful Uses of the Seabed and Ocean Floor Committee in early March, the GOJ decided to publicly present its position that the Senkakus were part of Japan, and did so in a Diet committee meeting by "arrang[ing] for the matter to be raised … thus presenting it with the opportunity to place its position formally on Diet record and to release an official" statement.[143] It was a "sympathetic question," Sato Yoshiyasu of the First North American Affairs Division later confessed to U.S. Embassy officials.[144]

On the morning of March 8, Foreign Minister Fukuda attended a meeting of the House of Representative's Special Committee on Okinawa and Northern Territories. There Kokuba Kosho, a Lower House member of Fukuda's faction elected with Nishime and several others from Okinawa in November 1970,[145] asked the foreign minister about the status of the Senkaku Islands. Fukuda responded that the Senkakus were "Japanese territory without a doubt (itten no utagai mo nai wagakuni no ryodo de aru)."[146] As the basis for this statement, Fukuda cited: (1) a January 1895 Cabinet decision incorporating the Senkakus into Japan; (2) the fact that Senkakus were not included as part of Taiwan when Japan took over Taiwan from China as part of the Treaty of Shimonoseki in May 1895; (3) the fact that the Senkakus were not included in the territories renounced under Article 2 under the San Francisco Peace Treaty[147] but instead included in the areas to be administered by the United States under Article 3 and which were to be returned to Japan; (4) the fact that China did not protest the treatment of the Senkakus under the San Francisco Treaty; and (5) the fact that it was only after oil resources were discovered in the East China Sea that the ROC and PRC began to press their claims to the Senkakus. Fukuda, describing the statements of the GRC and PRC as "obscure (*fumeiryo*) and unbelievable (*shingai*)," he said the Foreign Ministry would publish its official view in a statement. The Japanese version in fact was released that day, with the English version (see Appendix 6) coming out on March 23.[148]

Later that day, Director General of the Foreign Ministry Information Bureau Wada released the official statement setting forth the arguments introduced by Fukuda and adding that there was no valid basis for the Chinese claims. Wada also made available various documents for the press to examine that lent doubt about the validity of ROC and PRC claims. The documents introduced included Communist and Nationalist Chinese maps on which the Senkakus were included as Japanese territory. Specifically, the following maps were introduced: (1) a map published in 1965 by the ROC National Defense Research Institute and Chinese Geographical Research Institute entitled "World Map Series, Vol. 1, East Asian Countries"; (2) a map in Volume 4 of an official ROC Middle School Geography Textbook published in January 1970; and (3) a map issued by the Map Publishing Society in Peking in November 1958.

Specifically, prior to 1969, Taiwan had also long demonstrated its understanding that the Senkaku Islands were in fact a part of Japan, showing the islands to be within Japan's jurisdiction and using Japanese names for the islands. For example, on September 3, 1959, the ROC Post Office issued a stamp that did not include the Senkaku Islands on it, and in October 1965, a book of maps jointly published by the above National Defense Studies Institute and Chinese Geological Institute used the Japanese name with the Senkaku

中華民国59年 1 月初版国民中学地理教科書（1970年）

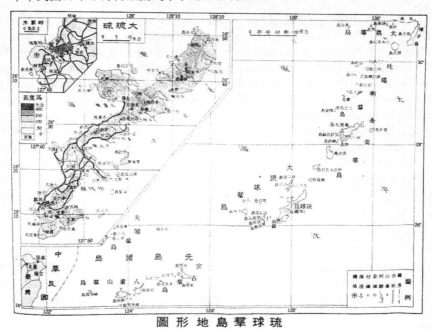

圖 形 地 島 羣 球 琉

Figure 5.1 ROC School Textbook Map

Islands, with the Japanese pronunciation of the islands written out in the English alphabet written next to the islands.[149] Again, in November 1965, the Taiwanese provincial government (*Taiwansho Seifu*) published a volume on local autonomy showing that the northern limit of Taiwan was at Pengchia Yu (otherwise known as Agincourt), 150 kilometers closer to Taiwan than the Senkaku Islands. Similarly, in the October 1968 *Chuka Minkoku Nenkan* (Annual of the Republic of China), the northern limit of Taiwan is written at Pengchia Hsu/Yu and the eastern limit being Mienhua Yu. Moreover, in 1970, the ROC National Middle School geography textbooks included the Senkaku Islands as part of the Ryukyu Islands, and they were written out in the English alphabet using the Japanese pronunciation.[150] The GRC began recalling the textbooks in 1970, but it was apparently too late by then.

Perhaps stung by the strong evidence against the claims by Taiwan (as well as China), the GRC sent Sha Hsueh-chun, a professor at Taiwan Normal University, to the United States in late April to conduct research at the Library of Congress to support Taiwan's claims.[151]

There are other items and documents, as well as behavior, which cast doubt on Taiwanese and Chinese claims to the Senkakus. For example, in the January 8, 1953, edition of the *Renmin Ribao* (People's Daily), a newspaper established in June 1948 that serves as an organ of the Central Committee of the Chinese Communist Party, used the Japanese name for the islands and described the Ryukyu Islands as comprising the Senkaku Islands as well.[152] The headline of the story read: "Struggle of the people of the Ryukyu Islands against U.S. Occupation," and clearly spelled out the "Senkaku Shoto" in the list of smaller island groups within the Ryukyu Islands. In addition, in a map published by the PRC government-sponsored map publisher in November 1958, mentioned above, the Senkaku Islands were shown as part of Japan.[153] In addition, in December 2012, an official ten-page document, prepared on May 15, 1950 by the PRC, that described the Senkakus as part of Japan and not contesting the claim, was discovered in Beijing's Foreign Ministry archives and published by Jiji News Agency.[154]

International law scholar Okuhara Toshio, who was writing in the early 1970s, argued these facts not only make the respective positions of China and Taiwan inconsistent, but they also were in violation of the principle of *estoppel* in international law.[155] Namely, through *estoppel*, a government is not allowed to deny or assert anything to the contrary of what which has been established as the truth by its own deeds, acts, or representations. The official publication of the above maps and publications meant government endorsement, and thus reflected the position of the governments. They would be unable to go back on that, which the GRC and PRC both tried to do nevertheless after 1970 when the two countries began to challenge Japan's claims on the islands.

As discussed in Chapter 1, one of the clearest examples of Chinese (i.e., both PRC and ROC) recognition of Senkakus being part of Japan occurred in 1920 when a letter of appreciation from the Chinese Consul General based in Nagasaki dated May 20 was received by Koga Zenji and two others for aiding thirty-one shipwrecked fishermen in the Senkakus the year before. The letter clearly identified the islands as being part of "Yaeyama County, Okinawa Prefecture, Empire of Japan." Although this letter garnered attention at the time of its delivery, it became publicly known (again) in 1971 when Senkaku Islands Study Group introduced it in the first of its two large studies. It has become common knowledge since then, although both Taiwan and China seem to avoid alluding to the document.

In the spring of 1972, the Ministry of Foreign Affairs prepared a thirty-six page booklet in Japanese entitled *Senkaku Shoto ni Tsuite* (About the Senkaku Islands) which discussed the history of the islands and the Japanese position, as well as including various documents and historical records.[156] Curiously, however, the color brochure was done only in Japanese and not in English, which would have helped Japan's public diplomacy case worldwide.[157]

But this did not mean the GOJ had stopped promoting its view that the Senkaku Islands were Japanese or that it no longer felt the USG should be supporting it. After exchanging ratification documents on March 15 at the Prime Minister's Residence, attended by Foreign Minister Fukuda, Ambassador Meyer, and observed by Sato, Aichi, Yamanaka, and Tokai Motosaburo, minister for Home Affairs (*Jichisho*), among others,[158] a new offensive seems to have been begun on March 21 when Fukuda told a press conference after a regularly scheduled Cabinet meeting that morning that the government would ask the United States to support its claims to the Senkakus on the occasion of the reversion of Okinawa in the form of some "testimony" indicating it understood "Japan's assertions."[159]

Just before that, on March 17, Okawara Yoshio, who was serving as minister at the Japanese Embassy in Washington, D.C., went to the State Department where he was given a copy of the press guidance, dated March 13, that the department intended to use to respond to press inquiries. It was described as "an update and minor elaboration of guidance" originally used on April 9, 1971.[160] This guidance was very likely forwarded to the Foreign Ministry headquarters in Tokyo, which was unhappy with it, and had Ambassador Ushiba Nobuhiko, who had been serving as the Japanese ambassador to the United States since the summer of 1970, re-engage.

That same day (March 17) and again on March 23, Ambassador Ushiba officially informed the Department of the GOJ's unhappiness with the public position of neutrality being taken by the USG, and pointed out the inconsistency, at least in Japanese eyes, of this public stance.[161]

In the meantime, Ambassador Meyer called on Prime Minister Sato on March 21 to bid farewell, as Meyer was leaving Tokyo after three years as the U.S. ambassador to Japan.[162] During their discussion, Sato, according to Meyer's summary of the meeting, raised the issue of the Senkakus, expressing the hope that the USG would make clear that the Senkaku Islands were Japanese territory. Sato noted that so long as Taiwan had been the only other claimant, the problem "might have been manageable via direct negotiations" but the PRC's strongly voicing claims "increased complications tremendously."[163] It is unclear if Meyer expected a matter such as this to come up during his outcall, but he was prepared to respond: "I set forth to Sato the clear USG position that in returning geographically defined areas via Okinawa reversion agreement, we merely are returning custody to authorities administering them when we took them over, but without prejudice to underlying claims to sovereignty that others might have. Clearly the USG has no desire to get in middle of disputants."[164] Sato replied that the USG position was "logical" and "clear" but Meyer sensed, correctly, the prime minister might have wished otherwise.[165]

It is unclear why Sato chose to raise it at this point. It might have been because Meyer was leaving after three years in Tokyo and the prime minister wanted to make sure that Japan's message was heard in Washington. It might as well have been due to criticism of the government's handling of the issue, both outside of the LDP and within it as well, as well as criticism of the U.S. government's neutral policy. Sato's hold on power was rapidly decreasing, and within the LDP a battle had been emerging over who would succeed him. Sato was leaning toward supporting Fukuda, but Tanaka had been rapidly gaining influence (and would eventually win the party presidency in early July and become prime minister shortly after that).

Regardless of the reason, the various pressures on USG officials seemed to be a coordinated effort between the Foreign Ministry and the Prime Minister's office.

In the morning of the 22nd, during a meeting of the Upper House's Special Committee on Okinawa and the Northern Territories Problem, the counterpart to the Lower House's, Kawamura Seiichi of the JSP asked the foreign minister about the U.S. position on the Senkakus. Fukuda expressed his frustration over the ambiguous U.S. stance, saying he was very "dissatisfied" with what he believed was an "evasive attitude."[166] Fukuda even stated he would register a "stern protest" with the USG if it continued its neutral stance.[167]

That evening, Ambassador Meyer "hit" Fukuda on the Senkakus issue, expressing the U.S. position on it.[168] The Embassy, in relaying this to the State Department, added its own analysis to why Fukuda was behaving as he was:

> Fukuda's unpredictable responses on the Senkakus issue might well be result of his anxiety regarding succession to prime minister and his consequent determination to establish himself as firm spokesman for Japanese position on Senkakus and as one not afraid to challenge USG. In Senkakus issue, Fukuda can be reasonably certain to be able to attract almost universal backing in Japan for energetic advancement of GOJ territorial position. Political water had already been tested for Fukuda by issue of FonOff legal position on Senkakus last week, which received wide acclaim in Japan.[169]

There were others who were watching Fukuda as well. Around this time, National Security Advisor Kissinger was planning to visit Japan, nominally to attend a closed session of the Advisory Council on Japan–United States Economic Relations to exchange opinions on bilateral relations, but the real reason was to meet and get a feel for some of the people being considered to succeed Sato as prime minister.[170] One of those being considered, and the one viewed likely to succeed him, was Fukuda.

Columbia University Professor and future National Security Advisor (to President James E. Carter) Zbigniew Brzezinski wrote to Kissinger in April to give him some advice prior to his scheduled departure to Japan (later postponed to June). Brzezinski was not a Japan specialist, but he had just returned from a six-months' fact-finding research trip to Japan where he worked on the book, *The Fragile Blossom*, about Japan, published in 1972.[171] He proffered some very good advice on Japanese politics and society, and added the following about the Senkakus: "The Japanese will press you *very hard* on the Senkaku Islands, and you should not underestimate the potential here for an emotionally anti-U.S. reaction unless we somehow indicate that Japan has a legitimate claim. What if the Chinese (either ones) send their forces to plant the flag there after May 15!?"[172]

Kissinger had been given some other advice, too. A twelve-page memo, entitled "Japan Adjusts to an Era of Multipolarity in Asia," was prepared for him and his staff by Michael H. Armacost, a former professor at Pomona

College who had been working in government since 1969. At the time, he was serving on the State Department's Policy Planning and Coordination Staff, and saw that among the briefing items requested from State for Kissinger's trip to Japan, there wasn't "any general paper assessing the broad thrust of Japanese diplomacy."[173]

Some of the points Armacost raised in it focused on Foreign Minister Fukuda's remarks about the Senkakus and the motivations behind them. One reason, according to the future ambassador to Japan (1989–93), for Fukuda's comments was to strengthen Japan's position vis-à-vis the PRC while the latter delayed improving relations with the Sato government. "By raising the Senkaku Islands claims in a highly public fashion," Armacost wrote, "Mr. Fukuda may be seeking to galvanize nationalist sentiment against China on a territorial issue in order to [put a] brake [on] the accommodationist sentiment in Japan on the China question and thus fortify public support for a tough bargaining position vis-à-vis China for an extended period."[174]

A second reason had to do with Fukuda's own personal and political motivations, to which Armacost issued a warning:

> We may find that Mr. Fukuda's reputation as a staunch friend of the United States is not an unmitigated asset to us. Should he succeed to the Prime Ministership, he may well find his support fragile, and he may frequently feel compelled to enhance his position by mobilizing nationalist sentiment—not least against the US. His recent statements on the Senkakus issue suggest that he is not at all averse to utilizing public pronouncements to mobilize nationalist reactions against the Chinese and the U.S. simultaneously.[175]

Armacost admitted these and other comments in his paper might be "unduly somber" and that they "should not cause one to overlook the vast array of common interests and collaborative enterprises that will continue to mark our dealings with Japan."[176] At the same time, he stressed, his paper "reinforce[d] the point that there is no cause for complacency, and that our relationship could unravel with perhaps unanticipated swiftness if we are not extremely careful."[177] It is uncertain if Armacost's views were his alone or were widely shared within the State Department, but the Embassy had been continuing to monitor the opinions of GOJ officials as well as encourage them to tone them down.

Sneider, for example, followed up on Meyer's meeting with Fukuda on March 22 by meeting with Yoshino the next day.[178] But the interaction with Fukuda and Yoshino seemed to do little in toning down the Foreign Ministry's remarks. According to an American newsman who attended a weekly briefing by the MOFA spokesman (and who told a U.S. Embassy official about it), Wada was "harshly critical" of the U.S. position on the Senkakus in the off-the-record portion.[179]

That same day (23rd), MOFA released the English version of the statement introduced two weeks previously to its press club. The U.S. Embassy immediately transmitted the statement to the State Department.[180] It also commented on the GOJ's actions stating that it may be "designed to establish territorial issue of Senkakus as an obstacle in normalizing relations between Japan and mainland China and give the LDP popular rationale for going slow in approaches to the PRC."[181]

Shortly after noon that same day, Sato spoke to reporters about his disappointment over the U.S. position on the Senkakus. "[It] is not clear. It is not good," he reportedly said, but refused to answer whether he asked Ambassador Meyer to convey any message to President Nixon on the Senkakus.[182] It is unclear if the above motivation was Sato's as well, or if he, knowing his days were numbered as prime minister, was more willing to speak his mind on issues, such as about the Senkakus.

On the same day in Washington, Ushiba called on Assistant Secretary Marshall Green to discuss the GOJ's position on the Senkaku Islands and to issue a *demarche* on the wording of the State Department's new press guidance. Green explained that the new guidance had not yet been used, and as a result of the interaction, Green agreed with a request by Ushiba that in responding to future press inquiries concerning the U.S. position on the Senkakus the State Department essentially follow the line taken in the April 9 (1971) guidance.[183] Ushiba went on to express his hope that the USG would support Japan's claims, and that while the GOJ understood the U.S. position, asked that the U.S. spokesperson avoided statements that would undermine the Japanese position. Ushiba in particular objected to the mentioning of the "existence of dispute or conflicting claims to sovereignty" over the Senkakus, as the GOJ official position is that there is "no legal basis for any claims to sovereignty over Senkakus by any other country than Japan," and thus to it, no dispute existed (a position it continues today).[184]

Green reiterated that the guidance had not yet been used, nor had the State Department received inquiries from the press about the Navy bombing ranges. Ushiba, looking at the guidance, told Green the GOJ thought the USG was being "inconsistent" when it says that the retention of the ranges did not imply support for the GOJ's position and that it was "quite naturally" interpreted by the Japanese in this manner.[185] "Japanese are therefore perplexed," Ushiba, who was close to the Fukuda faction, continued, "when the USG insists it takes no position on this issue. This and other recent developments in U.S–Japan relations have resulted in the feeling in Japan that the 'U.S. suddenly is very cold to Japan'."[186] Green shared a belief in the importance of coordinating with Japan all statements concerning the Senkakus, but expressed concerns over the "obvious dangers" in press stories quoting MOFA officials to the effect that the GOJ felt that U.S. retention of gunnery ranges was indicative of U.S. support of the GOJ position.[187] Ushiba said he understood the U.S. position and agreed that the "less said about all aspects of Senkakus problem the better for both U.S. and Japan."[188] Whether Green was told about it or not ahead of time upon departing from their meeting, Ushiba immediately informed the press afterwards of his visit to the State Department, telling them that Green had reiterated the fact that the USG maintained a neutral stand on the question of ownership.[189]

The next day, reporters asked the State Department spokesman about Foreign Minister Fukuda's comments regarding the U.S. position on the Senkakus. An exchange followed that "depart[ed] slightly from press guidance" according to a telegram from the Department to the Embassy in Tokyo afterwards:

QUESTION: The Japanese foreign minister on Tuesday expressed misgivings about the American position on the Senkakus. Two questions: could you tell us what the American position is, and has there been any discussion between this government and Japan on sovereignty of those islands?

ANSWER: Well, it seems to me that this matter was discussed at some length as part of a range of issues of this kind last April, and you might want to look at the transcript there to refresh your memory. The essence of our position in this matter is that in the event that a situation should arise in which there are conflicting claims, those claims, in effect, predate our connection with the Ryukyus and should be settled by the parties concerned.

Q: Are you taking the position, then, that sovereignty over Senkakus is a matter of international consideration, the position taken regarding Taiwan some time ago?

A: (Aside), as I recall. Let me leave it that we acquired administrative rights to the Senkakus under the peace treaty. We are returning administrative rights to the Government of Japan as part of the Okinawa reversion.

Q: But I'm talking about sovereignty.

A: That is as far as I intend to express myself on this subject.

Q: We have no position, then, on sovereignty?

A: I have said that our position with respect to claims in conflict should be settled by those concerned—which seems to me to express a position.[190]

In the future, the Embassy was urged to "adhere closely to" the press guidance to avoid the type of exchange as above.[191]

Back in Tokyo, officials at the Foreign Ministry showed a "strong repulsion (*tsuyoi hanpatsu*)" to Spokesman Bray's replies to the press, and told contacts in the media that it had previously made a "stern representation" to the USG to "carefully refrain" from making statements that would be "injurious" to Japan's position.[192] They also expressed their views that it was "illogical" for the USG to take a neutral position in light of the fact that it had been exercising administrative rights over the Senkakus for two decades under Article 3 of the Treaty of Peace, and that it would continue using the ranges on the two islands after reversion.[193]

Opposition parties got into the act of criticizing U.S. policy as well. Mori Motojiro, an Upper House member from the JSP who had once served as a secretary to Prime Minister Katayama Tetsu, in questions to Fukuda in the House of Councilors Foreign Affairs Committee, said the USG was making "uncalled-for comments" and suggested to the foreign minister that he go to the United States and tell the USG "not to make unnecessary statements."[194]

The U.S. Embassy in Tokyo, watching the quick escalation of the war of words between Japan and its neighbors, and the criticism Japan was flinging at the United States for its neutrality policy, told the Foreign Ministry at the end of March "at several levels ... that the time has come to cool it."[195] At the same time, it asked the head of the Asian Regional Policy Division, Kiuchi Akitane, to "take soundings" of all the Foreign Ministry bureaus involved in the Senkakus Issue, which he did having spoken with Asian Bureau Director General Yoshida Kenzo, China Desk officer Hashimoto Hiroshi, UN Affairs Director General Kagei Umeo, American Affairs Deputy Director General Tachibana, and Legal Affairs Division Kumagai.[196] Kiuchi, who expressed regret that some of the "off-the-record remarks during the past week had been rather intemperate," gave the Embassy his "frank personal assessment" of the views within the Foreign Ministry.[197] Kiuchi described the consensus as follows:

> After long discussions with the USG on the issue, beginning during the Okinawa reversion negotiations, the Foreign Office recognizes that two sides must simply agree to disagree. The Foreign Office understands it would be difficult for the USG to change its position. Most recent Department guidance is slightly more helpful from the GOJ point of view, particularly since phrase "in even situation should arise" has replaced language which suggested that sovereignty is already in question. Naturally, the GOJ would have wished for even greater change. Be that as it may, FonOff is definitely not desirous of escalating differences with the USG. The Foreign Office and GOJ will therefore attempt to dampen issue though uncontrollable events in the Diet or at the UN may require further public statements.[198]

The conversation concluded with Kiuchi telling the Embassy officials that the GOJ did not expect the Senkakus issue would have a significant effect on GOJ relations with the PRC (in the end it did not prevent normalizing relations in 1972 or even the signing of a peace treaty in 1978). It is uncertain if the Embassy believed this to be the case, as it cited a story in the *Tokyo Shimbun* that the Japanese government was studying the PRC stance and gathering evidence to refute the PRC's claims. In any case, the Embassy felt that the Foreign Ministry was "genuinely committed to moving the issue off the front pages," but noted that "territorial issue had struck a responsive chord among the Japanese public and any future challenges will once again evoke a strong reaction."[199] In a separate telegram, the Embassy reported to the State Department that it felt the people it relayed this message to in the Foreign Ministry were "responsive" and that they hoped to report "some progress" early the following week.[200] They—and perhaps MOFA, or at least Kiuchi—would be disappointed, however, as the PRC quickly chimed in again, criticizing Japan.

In the meantime, the State Department told the Embassy in Taipei in a priority telegram at the end of March that it could inform the GRC that the USG had "impressed" upon the GOJ the necessity of playing down publicity over this sensitive issue if it felt advisable to make further representations.[201] It should also, it advised, inform the GRC that all the islands in the Senkakus group would be returned to Japan under the terms of the reversion treaty and that the U.S. position on the Senkakus remained unchanged.

As part of the finalization of the reversion arrangements, there were a couple of issues involving the Senkakus that still needed to be worked out.

The air defense identification zone and training ranges in the Senkakus

Another matter that required a decision relating to the Senkakus and the reversion of Okinawa that was being worked out in the spring of 1972 concerned the division of defense responsibilities between Japan and the United States and in particular what responsibilities Japan would be assuming. The so-called Kubo-Curtis Agreement, otherwise known as the Okinawa Defense Agreement, signed on June 29, 1971, facilitated these arrangements, including for air defense matters.[202]

One of the arrangements worked out was for the establishment of a new Air Defense Identification Zone, which is an area created to prevent the violation of a country's territorial air space by aircraft of an unidentified nationality, for Okinawa. An ADIZ is separate from a country's territorial limits, and a violation of the ADIZ usually triggers a scramble or other type of response from the country impacted. In the case of Japan at the time, the Air Self-Defense Force would scramble using F104J "Starfighter" interceptor fighters originally acquired from the United States.[203]

Discussions on the issue of the ADIZ began in earnest in the spring of 1971, and became public knowledge at least as early as June 1971.[204] It would take a year before interim arrangements—incomplete from the Japanese perspective (as the demarcation line between the Japan and Taiwan ADIZs met above Yonaguni Island, the southernmost island in the Ryukyu chain)—were worked out.[205]

During the course of discussions on the defense of Okinawa in March 1971, Japanese officials from the Joint Staff Office raised with their U.S. counterparts "the undesirable feature of the ADIZ line (coincident with 120–00 degrees East Longitude) bisecting" Yonaguni Island, noting that it was "significant that the island's only airfield is within the Taiwan ADIZ."[206] These JSO members asked the U.S. side to take action to relocate the ADIZ offshore to the west before the GOJ assumed administrative control of the Ryukyus. The U.S. side attempted to allay their fears by mentioning that the "existing arrangement [had] been entirely satisfactory" but the GOJ apparently "wished to preclude a confrontation with the GRC" on the issue, particularly in light of the Senkakus problem.[207]

In the meantime, CINCPAC received the March 11 request by telegram, and early the following week responded that it was hesitant to automatically support Japan's request. While it acknowledged that Japan's desire to have the ADIZ line relocated to the west prior to reversion was "understandable" and noted the physical adjustment of the line was "relatively simple," it recommended that a careful assessment of the proposal be done in light of "the sensitivities resulting from Okinawa reversion and the sovereignty disputes over the Senkakus."[208] CINCPAC asked it be provided a coordinated response by the U.S. Embassy in Taipei and the Commander of the United States Taiwan Defense Command (COMUSTDC).

That response came the following week, on March 21. The U.S. Embassy in Taipei indicated that there would likely be "strong resistance" from the GRC to moving the ADIZ westward, and advised that the present line be maintained until after the reversion of Okinawa "at which time the issue could be settled between the GOJ and GRC."[209]

While recognizing the sensitivity of the GRC to the issue, CINCPAC, however, was not satisfied with the above response. "If left unresolved," CINCPAC wrote, "this ADIZ issue would be one additional irritant in GOJ–GRC relations resulting from Okinawa reversion and could contribute to reduced regional cooperation," and commented that it was in the U.S. interest to try to remedy the situation under terms that were agreeable to both the GOJ and GRC prior to Okinawa's reversion.[210] On the issue of moving the line westward, CINCPAC suggested an alternative proposal that could be made through the "normal defense organization used for coordinating ADIZ procedures" to the GRC:

> This alternative would adjust the existing ADIZ only in the region of Yonaguni Island by providing for an arc to the west around the island not larger that (sic) that necessary to encompass what will become GOJ sovereign airspace following reversion. This would remove the irritant to the GOJ of having sovereign airspace partially controlled by the GRC while localizing the ADIZ adjustment to an area in which the GRC has no legal basis for sovereign claims.[211]

CINCPAC noted that Washington's approval should be obtained before raising such an idea with the GRC in light of the sensitivities of the issue. However, before any further movement was seen, the Japanese side withdrew its request due to the "sensitivity" of the issue.[212] Ironically or perhaps presciently, this would be the formula that the Japanese Ministry of Defense, the successor to the Japan Defense Agency, itself would pursue forty years later.[213]

In the meantime, in the spring of 1972, the JDA finalized its plans for the ADIZ, which it was inheriting from the U.S. military with some self-imposed changes. Out of consideration not to provoke China, a 23,000-square kilometer area in the northwestern part of the existing ADIZ, which was being covered by the U.S. Fifth Air Force and was close to the mainland of China, was excluded from the new ADIZ, which was finalized in early May 1972 and covered an area of 834,000 square kilometers.[214] In addition, Esaki Masumi, who had been serving as director general of the Defense Agency, had announced that the GOJ was not planning on mobilizing troops for the defense of the Senkakus, likely out of consideration for Taiwan and China.[215]

Nevertheless, the JDA decided to include the Senkakus in the new area in line with the GOJ's view that the Senkakus were Japanese territory. According to a newspaper story at the time, JDA officials feared that "elimination of the islands [from the ADIZ] would give rise to misunderstandings about the Japanese claim to them."[216] This new policy was announced on April 12 by Kubo Takuya, director general of the Defense Bureau (*Boeikyoku*), in a Lower House Cabinet Committee (*Naikaku Iinkai*) meeting in response to a question by Kato Yozo of the LDP.[217]

The ADIZ went into effect on May 15, the date of Okinawa's reversion to Japan, and the U.S. Fifth Air Force, headquartered at Yokota Air Base and which would still be in charge of interceptive operations against airplanes of unknown nationality until the end of 1972 as per the above agreement, was to operate in line with the Japanese decision.

It must be noted, however, that the U.S. side was reluctant to include the Senkakus in any common defense plan. This view became particularly clear in early September 1971. While there was a need for Japan and the U.S. military to discuss an expanded picture called the Coordinated Joint Outline Emergency Plan (CJOEP), CINCPAC, as the headquarters of the senior operational commander in the Pacific, believed "it would appear inappropriate for the U.S. to consider inclusion for any reference to the Senkakus in the CJOEP" because "by permitting the inclusion of the defense of the Senkakus in the CJOEP, the U.S. would be giving tacit recognition and support to the GOJ claim of sovereignty."[218] CINCPAC, of course, pointed out the USG could not prohibit the Joint Staff Office, its counterpart in Japan, from developing a unilateral Japanese defense plan for the Senkakus, it did not want "such plans ... to be a part of any combined/coordinated U.S.–GOJ defense planning effort."[219] While the USG later came to admit that the United States–Japan security treaty in fact covered the Senkaku Islands, it suggests the U.S. side was extremely cautious about conducting any planning on the defense of the Senkakus.

The creation of the new ADIZ received much attention in Japan. Despite the consideration shown to China, the Japan Socialist Party, for example, criticized the new ADIZ as having the potential to provoke China. Kawasaki Kanji, the chairman of the party's International Affairs Bureau and a representative from Kagoshima Prefecture, told a press conference that the Defense Agency's decision was "unwise at the present time as ownership of the islands was being disputed by Japan, Taiwan, and China" and because of the fact that the development of oil resources in the area had become an international issue.[220] Of course, this position is somewhat curious, in light of the Socialist

Party's previously announced position that it believed the Senkakus to be a part of Japan, but the party not only desired closer relations with China but also still had not come to recognize the Self-Defense Force, which was charged with the responsibility of defending Japanese territory including the Senkakus.

The USG was concerned with one other issue—how the GOJ and the Japanese media were portraying the planned continued use of the air-to-ground training ranges on Sekibi Sho and Kobi Sho following the reversion of Okinawa. As early as May 1971, reporters had learned of the U.S. intention to continue to utilize the islands. On May 11, an unidentified Foreign Ministry official leaked that the U.S. Navy intended to use the ranges after reversion.[221] Speculating, the Japanese media were "bending over backwards," perhaps with the blessing of MOFA officials, to note that while the U.S. position was not to become involved in the Senkakus sovereignty dispute, the request for retention of the ranges meant "implicit U.S. support of the GOJ claim to the Senkakus," and in any case might "add some support to the GOJ position."[222] One example of this type of reporting was the story by the conservative *Sankei Shimbun* which noted that "The U.S. side is trying to take an outsider's attitude toward the Senkaku Islands problem, because of its consideration for Sino–U.S. relations. However, the United States will have to obtain approval of the sovereign country, Japan, on its use of the firing grounds after reversion. The Government says that this has provided another hopeful endorsement to the ownership over the Senkaku Islands."[223]

These stories triggered questions the same day in Washington to the State Department spokesman about the Senkakus' ranges.[224] Press guidance was drawn up for answering any questions based on input from the U.S. Embassy in Tokyo and the related offices within the State Department. In addition to explaining that the U.S. Navy had ranges on Kobi Sho and Sekibi Sho, which were used infrequently for training purposes, in the Senkakus, the spokesman was authorized to answer, "if pressed," that the USG was "discussing with the GOJ the possibility of continued U.S. use of these practice sites after reversion."[225] He was also authorized to explain on background that "these ranges are included in a list of sites which the U.S. has submitted to Japan for Joint Committee designation as facilities and areas under the Status of Forces Agreement upon reversion. We do not consider this matter is related to question of sovereignty over Senkakus."[226]

As reversion approached the following year, GOJ officials interpreted the continued use as U.S. endorsement of its claims, something U.S. officials were very concerned about. In light of this, the USG eventually decided toward the end of the 1970s to discontinue use of the training ranges there, although they are still leased to the USG under the SOFA.

Concern over protests on May 15

On April 29, some two weeks before the reversion of Okinawa, the GRC and KMT held a high-level meeting about possible student demonstrations over the Senkakus issue. In particular, according to Chien Foo, otherwise known as Frederick Chien, the Director of North American Affairs Bureau of the Ministry of Foreign Affairs who attended the meeting, GRC intelligence services and KMT Secretary General Chang Pao-shu were "seriously concerned about the possibility of disturbances."[227] Others who attended said there was no evidence of student interest in the Senkakus question "like that of last year."[228]

Nevertheless, the Japanese Embassy in Taipei was concerned enough about a report that a group from Taiwan might attempt a landing on May 15 that Minister Ito Hiromichi called on Chien to inquire about it on May 1.[229] He also told Chien about a possible landing by Japanese rightist extremists as well.[230]

Ito's information was based on reports from Japanese police about rightist groups in both mainland Japan as well as in Okinawa. This same information was shared with Ambassador Takase in Okinawa, who in turn told the High Commissioner and his political advisor, John F. Knowles, about it during lunch on April 28. Takase asked Lampert if he would give "his personal attention" to this matter and have the GRI Police make the necessary preparations to prevent "some move" to land on the islands.[231] A specific need, Takase noted, was to prevent any persons with such a plan from hiring a boat. Takase added that the GOJ wished to keep the situation of the Senkakus quiet until reversion and asked for the High Commissioner's cooperation. Lampert replied that through the USCAR Public Safety Department, the U.S. side would have confidential discussions with the GRI police to reduce the possibility of anyone landing on the Senkaku Island.

The USCAR Public Safety Department subsequently requested the GRI Police to take all possible actions to preclude any right-wing inspired incidents in the Senkakus prior to reversion. The police were maintaining close surveillance of a two-man advance party that was then in Okinawa, and were also coordinating with the National Police Agency, or NPA, to monitor the entire situation. The GRI Police planned to take into protective custody, a telegram reported, anyone attempting to land on the Senkakus in the pre-reversion period, and to conduct a precautionary sweep of the area even if no landing plan for the Senkakus was detected.

The concerns expressed by the GOJ were in turn provided to the U.S. Embassy in Taipei. Upon receiving it, the Embassy wrote to the High Commissioner to suggest that the information be shared with the GRC, as the Embassy believed that if it was able to inform the GRC of the precautionary measures being taken in Okinawa and Japan, the chance of any unauthorized trips by Taiwanese vessels to the Senkakus prior to reversion might be "substantially reduced."[232] Ambassador McConaughy asked permission to inform the GRC, which the High Commissioner gave the following day with the recommendation that the Embassy request the GRC not to make public the attempts by Japanese rightists to land on the Senkakus as this might encourage similar attempts by private groups of Chinese nationalists.[233]

Embassy officers met with Chien in early May informing him that it had classified information that Japanese rightists possibly might try to land on the

Figure 5.2 Okinawa Reversion Agreement Signing Ceremony

Senkakus prior to reversion, and that the GRI police would continue to patrol the area closely including a sweep of the islands on May 14. The Embassy explained that it wanted to avoid publicity which could be played up by press in Tokyo and Taipei.[234] Chien expressed his appreciation for the information, mentioning that he had already been told by Ito, and said he understood the reasons for avoiding publicity.

The effectuation of the reversion of Okinawa took place on May 15, with Lieutenant General Lampert having departed Okinawa the day before to pay his respects to Prime Minister Sato in Tokyo. The Embassy in Taipei was happy to report at the end of the day that no demonstrations had occurred at either the U.S. or Japanese embassies in the city to protest the Okinawa Reversion Agreement's going into effect. U.S. Embassy officials attributed this calming of the situation to several factors: extra police protection of embassy, which was "very evident"; "firm and concerted opposition" to demonstrations; and a proactive GRC public position on Ryukyu and Senkaku reversion issue.[235] Overall, as the U.S. Embassy informed the State Department, the GRC had "thus far successfully channeled sentiment opposed to Ryukyu and Senkaku reversion into modest press protest."[236] The GRC had released a statement on May 9, both for the record as well as a way to demonstrate to its public, especially the students, and the world that it was unhappy and was taking action.[237]

The students were still disappointed. At *Taita*, the nickname for National Taiwan University, students organized a demonstration on May 14. Most of the banners were supportive of the government's efforts, perhaps taking into account the pleas of the foreign minister and Chien to be more understanding of the government's efforts, but the banners nevertheless called for "action not words" by the GRC and attacked Japanese and American "imperialism."[238] Interestingly, the press did not report the demonstration in their May 15 editions and gave only "secondary, inside-page treatment" to Okinawa's reversion, although their editorials declared the U.S. transfer of the Ryukyus to Japan violated the Cairo and Potsdam declarations and the transfer of administrative rights over the Tiaoyutai Islands would greatly impair U.S.–ROC friendship.[239] University and KMT administrators working to dissuade the students, and heavy rain that day, helped to keep the protest smaller than it might have been, but, according to the Embassy's report, the "large crowd of students who were willing to brave heavy rain for several hours convincingly registered their frustration and belief that they should express openly their opposition to what they regard as infringement on Chinese sovereignty."[240]

In Hong Kong, on the other hand, the protests were larger and more unwieldy. The protests were led by students, which had broken into two groups. After requests for permission to hold the demonstration on May 13 in downtown Hong Kong were denied by the government there, the Hong Kong Federation of Students split from their usually more radical allies, the *70's Bi-Weekly Group*, which had accepted a suggestion by the Hong Kong Government to conduct the demonstration at a large park away from the central part of the city, and continued with their plans to stage the demonstration downtown. In the end, the respective rallies by two groups ended up merging.[241]

Unlike previous demonstrations, which had taken an increasingly pro-Peking line, the organizers of the downtown rally, according to a report by U.S. Consul General Osborn, made it clear that the protest against the reversion of Okinawa and the Senkakus would take a neutral position toward the issue of the two Chinas and instead focus on calls for the "Protection of the Tiaoyutai" and denouncing U.S. imperialism.[242] According to Osborn, the "legal demonstration" by the radical group, which took place simultaneously, had attracted about 200 people making speeches and singing, but who were later encouraged to march downtown and join the other demonstrators.[243] As the police had apparently been instructed not to interfere, the downtown demonstration grew to about 1000 people, who then, carrying banners and singing songs, headed to the Japanese and U.S. consulates. At the Japanese consulate they delivered the protest but at the U.S. consulate, they destroyed the petition and dispersed peacefully after being told by the Marine guard that the building was closed on Saturdays.[244]

Editorials in the Hong Kong media, both right and left, were critical of the Okinawa and Senkakus reversion, but did not comment on the demonstrations themselves other than to complement the police for avoiding a violent confrontation.

In Washington, D.C., about 1000 (according to organizers) Chinese students from Hong Kong and Taiwan participated in a rally on the mall between the

Lincoln Memorial and the State Department and then marched to the Japanese Embassy on Massachusetts Avenue.[245] The protest made the State Department's intelligence memorandum, alerting government officials of anti-war and other demonstrations the day before, likely due in part to a request by the group (formerly known as the Tiao Yu Tia Committee but then known as the Committee for the Peaceful Unification of China) to meet with a State Department official to submit a letter.[246] State Department officials examined the contents and tone of letters to Prime Minister Sato and the GRC, and other notes related to the rally and concluded that pro-PRC forces had taken over the movement: "Language underlined here indicates who now calls the shots."[247]

No matter where the demonstrations were held and no matter who they were directed against, the fact is that the involvement of Japan, Taiwan, and the United States (either as a site of the demonstrations or a target of the protests), not to mention China, Hong Kong, and among activists of Chinese descent around the world, showed symbolically that the United States was very much intertwined with the Senkakus issue.

Notes

1 "Telegram 108253 from State Department to Embassy Taipei, June 17, 1971," Pol 32–36 Senkaku Is, RG 59. The Embassy had asked for a special telegraphic transmission of the text, questions, and answers to arrive as quickly as possible for its interaction with the GRC and Taiwan-based media. See "Telegram 2946 from Embassy Taipei to State Department," Pol 32–36 Senkaku Is, RG 59.

2 "Telegram 5953 from Embassy Tokyo to State Department on Japanese Reaction to Department Statement on Senkakus, June 19, 1971," POL 32–36 Senkaku Is, RG 59.

3 "Telegram 5953."

4 "Telegram 5953."

5 "Telegram 3012 from Embassy Taipei to USIA, June 21, 1971," POL 32–36 Senkaku Is, RG 59.

6 "Telegram 3255 from Embassy Taipei to State Department on ROC Naval Patrol of Senkakus, July 5, 1971," POL 32–36 Senkaku Is, RG 59.

7 "Telegram 3255."

8 "Telegram 3280 from Embassy Taipei to State Department on ROC Naval Patrol of Senkakus, July 7, 1971," POL 32–36 Senkaku Is, RG 59.

9 Office of National Estimates, Central Intelligence Agency, "Political Implications of the Senkaku Islands Dispute, May 19, 1971." This memorandum, as well as the Directorate of Intelligence-produced Intelligence Report (CIA/BGI GR-71–79), "The Senkaku Islands Dispute: Oil Under Troubled Waters?" written in May 1971 and focusing on the historic, legal, and geographic aspects of the Senkakus issue, were submitted together to the Director of Central Intelligence Richard M. Helms on May 19, 1971.

10 "Telegram 2941 from Embassy Taipei to State Department on Demonstrations over Senkakus Reversion, June 16, 1971," POL 32–36 Senkaku Is, RG 59.

11 "Telegram 2922 from Embassy Taipei to State Department on Senkakus Reversion, June 15, 1971," POL 32–36 Senkaku Is, RG 59.

12 "Telegram 2941."

13 Photo caption *Japan Times*, June 19, 1971. For some of the coverage in Japan at this time, see "Taipei Opposes Senkaku Return," *Japan Times*, June 18, 1971, and "Taiwan Repeats Claim," *Japan Times*, June 19, 1971.

14 "Telegram 4033 from AmConsul Hong Kong to State Department on Senkaku Island Demonstration, June 18, 1971," POL 32–38 HK, RG 59.

15 "Telegram 4562 from AmConsul Hong Kong to State Department on Senkaku Demonstration Erupts in Violence, June 8, 1971," POL 32–38 HK, RG 59. Twenty-one protesters, mostly students, appeared in a "packed" courtroom on September 6, with several in the audience wearing yellow and black bands with "Protect Tiaoyutai Islands" written on them. See "Anti-Japan Rioters Appear in Court," *Japan Times*, September 8, 1971.

16 "Japan Flag Ripped at H.K. Protest," *Japan Times*, August 24, 1971.

17 "Airgram 257 from AmConsul Hong Kong to State Department on Hong Kong Student Demonstrations on Senkaku Islands, September 9, 1971," POL 32–36 Senkaku Is, RG 59.

18 "Aigram 257."

19 "Okinawa Reversion Congressional Preparation," attachment to "Memorandum from Howard M. McElroy to DOD/ISA, et al., on Okinawa Reversion, July 13, 1971," Folder: DA Messages, Memos, State Cables, Box 3, History of the Civil Administration of the Ryukyu Islands, Records of the Army Staff, RG 319.

20 "Senate Hearings Okinawa Reversion, undated," Folder: Questions/Answers Index: Senate Hearings on Okinawa Reversion, Box 26, RG 319.

21 "Memorandum from Under Secretary for Political Affairs Johnson to Secretary of State on Principal Witness Statements at Senate Hearings on Okinawa Reversion, September 22, 1971," Folder: Chrono—Official—Sept. '71, Box 72, Records of U. Alexis Johnson, RG 59.

22 For more on his career, see U. Alexis Johnson, *The Right Hand of Power: The Memoirs of an American Diplomat* (Englewood Cliffs, NJ: Prentice-Hall, 1984).

23 See "Senkaku Retto Kankei Shogen (Testimony Relating to the Senkaku Islands)," in Nanpo Doho Engokai, ed., *Okinawa Fukki no Kiroku* (Records About the Return of Okinawa) (Tokyo: Nanpo Doho Engokai, 1972), 650.

24 "Telegram 198739 from State Department to Embassy Tokyo, October 30, 1971," Folder: Reversion—Congressional Relations, Box 10, RG 319.

25 "Telegram 198739."

26 Few people knew what to make of the claim by Mrs. Grace Hsu, made through a lawyer, that the Empress Dowager had bequested to Hsu's grandfather, Sheng Hsuan-huai, the Senkakus in 1894. About five months after the Okinawa Reversion Treaty deliberations, Thomas, the political counselor at the U.S. Embassy in Taipei, wrote to his predecessor, Moser, who had since returned to Washington, D.C., to head the ROC desk in the State Department, informing him that Hsu was trying to convince the GRC of the "authenticity of her claim through Chiang Yan-shih, among others." See "Letter from William W. Thomas, Jr., to Leo Moser, March 27, 1972," Folder: PET Senkaku Islands 1972, Box 14, Subject Files of the Office of China Affairs, 1951–75, RG 59. However, Thomas pointed out, Chien, who is "something of an expert on late Ching documents," thought "something is fishy about it but wouldn't say what." (Ibid.) Her goal, according to Thomas, was to delay the transfer of the Senkakus to Japan until the sovereignty and ownership claims are settled. It is unclear whatever happened with her efforts, although she had intended to follow up with the Senators Hiram L. Fong (of Hawaii), Peter H. Dominick (of Colorado), and Senator Barry M. Goldwater (of Arizona) after she secured the GRC's support.

27 "Telegram 198739."

28 Author's interview with Michael J. Mansfield, March 27, 2001, Washington, D.C. For more on Mansfield and the ratification of the Okinawa Reversion Treaty, see Don Oberdorfer, *Senator Mansfield: The Extraordinary Life of a Great American Statesman and Diplomat* (Washington, DC: Smithsonian Books, 2003).

29 Meyer, *Assignment Tokyo*, 57. Also see "Weekly Okinawa Summary for Week Ended 5 Nov 1971, November 8, 1971," Togo-Sneider Consultations (Reversion), Box 18, History of the Civil Administration of the Ryukyu Islands, RG 319. Senate Majority Leader Michael J. Mansfield had immediately scheduled a vote for November 4, but the Senate Armed Services Committee had interposed by calling hearings on November 3 and then after being briefed by State Department and Defense Department officials, recessed them until November 8, requesting that a high level JCS representative appear to testify.

30 Meyer, *Assignment Tokyo*, 57. Also see "Weekly Okinawa Summary for Week Ended 12 Nov 1971, November 12, 1971," Togo-Sneider Consultations (Reversion), Box 18, History of the Civil Administration of the Ryukyu Islands, RG 319.

31 "Weekly Okinawa Summary for Week Ended 22 October 1971, October 22, 1971," Togo-Sneider Consultations (Reversion), Box 18, RG 319.

32 "Weekly Okinawa Summary for Week Ended 5 Nov 1971." That same day, the GRI Legislature had also chimed in, passing a resolution urging ratification of the reversion treaty by the Diet. The session was boycotted by the opposition parties, but the resolution passed through the unanimous support of the Okinawa Liberal Democratic Party.

33 Hori Shigeru, *Sengo Seiji no Oboegaki* (A Memorandum on Postwar Politics), (Tokyo: Mainichi Shimbunsha, 1975).

34 Diet questions. For more on Nishime, see Ryukyu Shimposha, ed., *Sengo Seiji o Ikite: Nishime Junji Nikki* (Living Postwar Politics: The Diary of Nishime Junji) (Naha: Ryukyu Shimposha, 1998).

35 Author's interview with Fukuda Yasuo, November 10, 2011, Tokyo, Japan. According to his Yasuo, his father was also chosen because of his close relationship to the Emperor which would be important for the latter's trip to Europe via Anchorage, Alaska, that October (1971).

36 "Weekly Okinawa Summary for Week Ended 27 November 1971, November 26, 1971," Togo-Sneider Consultations (Reversion), Box 18, RG 319.

37 "Jiminto Kenkai (3 Gatsu 28 Nichi, Jiminto Seimu Chosakai Gaiko Chosakai Happyo), Senkaku Shoto no Ryoyuken ni Tsuite (Position of LDP, March 28, LDP Foreign Affairs Research Commission of the Policy Affairs Research Council, On the Territorial Rights over the Senkaku Islands)," in Joho Bunkakyoku Kokunai Kohoka, "Senkaku Shoto Mondai ni Kansuru Kakuto no Kenkai to Shinbun Roncho ni Tsuite (On the Opinions of the Parties and Newspapers on the Senkaku Islands Problem), April 20, 1972," *Nansei Shoto Kizoku Mondai, Dai 6 kan*, A'.6.1.1.3, Diplomatic Records Office of the Ministry of Foreign Affairs.

38 "Jiminto Kenkai."

39 The JCP's position was published in its party newspaper, *Akahata* (Red Flag), on March 31, 1972. Also see "JCP Believes Senkaku Islands Belong to Japan," *Japan Times*, March 31, 1972.

40 "Senkakus Belong to Japan: JSP," *Japan Times*, April 14, 1972. In late March, Secretary General Ishibashi Masashi stated his belief that the islands were indeed a part of Japanese territory. See "JSP Leader Says Senkakus Japanese," *Japan Times*, March 26, 1972. In early June 1972, Sasaki Kozo, who served as chairman of the JSP from 1965–67, announced he was planning to visit the PRC as early as the middle of the month and would propose a joint survey between Japan and China on the Senkakus question, but the party leadership was "at a loss, fearing such a proposal [would] contradict the Party's official view" that the islands were Japanese. See "Kozo Sasaki (JSP) to Visit China; To Propose Joint Survey of the 'Senkaku Islands'? His Denial of Party View Causes Internal Trouble," *Yomiuri*, June 9, 1972.

41 "JSP and JCP Formulate Party Views on 'Senkaku Islands'; 'Senkaku Islands are Japanese Territory'; Komei and DSP Also of Same View," *Nihon Keizai Shimbun*, March 31, 1972.

42 Ozaki, Shigeyoshi, "Senkaku Shoto no Kizoku ni Tsuite, Jo (Territorial Sovereignty of the Senkaku Islands, No. 1)," *Referensu* (Reference), No. 259 (August 1972), 47.

43 "Shasetsu: Senkaku Retto wa Nihon no Ryodo (Editorial: Senkaku Islands Are Japanese Territory)," *Tokyo Shimbun*, February 20, 1972.

44 "Shasetsu: Senkaku Shoto no Nihon Ryoyuken Shucho wa Tozen (Editorial: Japan's Insistence on Its Right to Ownership Over Senkaku Islands is Natural)," *Nihon Keizai Shimbun*, March 5, 1972.

45 The reporter was Kusuda Minoru, who recorded his experiences in a published diary and two memoirs. The practice of a political reporter becoming an aide or secretary to a prime minister in Japan was a fairly common practice then. Author's interview with Kusuda Minoru, October 1, 1999, and July 31, 2000, Tokyo, Japan.

46 "Shasetsu: Senkaku Retto Wagakuni no Ryoyuken wa Meihaku (Editorial: Our Country's Rights to Ownership over Senkaku Islands Clear)," *Sankei Shimbun*, March 7, 1972.

47 "Senkaku Retto Wagakuni no Ryoyuken wa Meihaku."

48 "Shasetsu: Senkaku Retto no Ryoyuken wa Meikaku (Editorial: Rights to Ownership over Senkaku Islands Clear)," *Mainichi Shimbun*, March 9, 1972.

49 "Shasetsu: Wagakuni no 'Senkaku' Ryoyuken wa Meikaku (Editorial: Our Country's Rights to Ownership over 'Senkaku Islands' Clear)," *Yomiuri Shimbun*, March 10, 1972.

50 "Shasetsu: Wagakuni no 'Senkaku' Ryoyuken."

51 "Shasetsu: Wagakuni no 'Senkaku' Ryoyuken."

52 Author's interview with Okuhara Toshio, June 21, 2011, Nagareyama City, Chiba Prefecture, Japan.

53 "Shasetsu: Senkaku Retto to Wagakuni no Ryoyuken (Editorial: Senkaku Islands and Our Country's Rights to Ownership)," *Asahi Shimbun*, March 20, 1972.

54 "Shasetsu: Senkaku Retto to Wagakuni."

55 "Editorial: Senkaku Islands Problem beyond Dispute," *Mainichi Shimbun*, April 14, 1971, and "Editorial: Senkaku Islands are Part of Okinawa," *Mainichi Shimbun*, December 6, 1970.

56 "Column: Senkaku Islands to Produce Big Effect on Okinawa Economy after Reversion," *Yomiuri Shimbun*, September 8, 1970.

57 Ozaki, "Senkaku Shoto no Kizoku ni Tsuite, Jo."

58 "Telegram 3077 from Embassy Tokyo to Secretary of State on Senkakus Dispute, March 27, 1972," Folder: Message Traffic Concerning the Senkaku Islands, 1971–72, Box 11, Lampert Papers.

59 "Trade Group Favors China's Claim to Senkaku Islands," *Mainichi Shimbun*, March 7, 1972.

60 "Senkaku Islands Belong to China: Statement by Men of Culture," *Mainichi Shimbun*, April 18, 1972.

61 "Senkaku Islands Belong to China: Statement by Men of Culture."

62 See for example, Okuhara Toshio, "Senkaku Retto Mondai to Inoue Kiyoshi Ronbun (The Senkaku Islands Problem and the Writings by Inoue Kiyoshi)," *Ajia Rebyuu*, No. 13 (Spring 1973), 88–92, and Okuhara Toshio, "Ugokanu Senkaku Retto no Ryoyuken: Inoue Kiyoshi Ronbun no 'Rekishiteki Kyoko' o Abaku (The Unmoving Issue of the Ownership of the …)," *Nihon Oyobi Nihonjin*, Spring 1973, 65–75. Interestingly, even a member of the Board of Governors of JAPIT, Takahashi Shogoro, while believing in the importance of good relations with the PRC, disagreed with some of Inoue's historical analysis with regard to the Senkakus. See Chapter 9, "Inoue Kiyoshi Kyoju to Hissha no Kenkai no Soi (The Difference in Viewpoints with Professor Inoue Kiyoshi)," in Takahashi, *Senkaku Retto Nooto*, 208–11. The conclusions did not change, however, in their minds—that the Senkakus were not Japanese territory.

63 Kiyoshi Inoue, "The Tiaoyu Islands (Senkaku Islands) and Other Islands Are China's Territory," *Peking Review*, No. 19 (May 12, 1972), 18–22. The editor of the *Peking Review*, in introducing the article and noting that it was a translation of an article Inoue did in a Japanese monthly, *Nicchu Bunka Koryu* (Japan–China Cultural Exchange), published by the Japan China Cultural Exchange Association (*Nihon Chugoku Bunka Koryu Kyokai*, established in Tokyo in 1956), wrote, "In it the writer cites numerous historical facts to prove that the Tiaoyu and other islands are the sacred territory of the People's Republic of China." (Ibid., 18.) For the Japanese version, see Inoue Kiyoshi, "Tiaoyu Retto (Senkaku Retto) nado wa Chugokuryo de Aru (The Tiaoyu (Senkaku and Other) Islands are Chinese Territory)," *Nicchu Bunka Koryu*, No. 177 (February 1972), 1–8. In addition to the article being published in the *Peking Review*, it was also published by NCNA on May 4, which caught the attention of the U.S. Consulate in Hong Kong, whose job it was in part to monitor PRC publications with its large staff of translators. Chinese linguist and Foreign Service Officer Osborn noted that the PRC has "no doubt been hard put to find support for their Senkaku claim from elements within Japan and NCNA articles on this subject had been vague and fuzzy in their portrayals of the Japanese public's attitude. This is the first clear-cut expression of Japanese support that NCNA has featured (although Hong Kong communist publications [such as *Meiho*] have previously referred to it) and the Chinese doubtlessly want to capitalize on it to the maximum." See "Telegram 3073 from American Consul Hong Kong to Secretary of State on PRC-Japan: Senkaku Islands, May 5, 1972," POL 32–36 Senkaku Is, RG 59.

64 Around the same time, the vice chairman of the Federation of Economic Organizations (*Keidanren*), Horikoshi Teizo, spoke at a press conference prior to his leaving for Taiwan to attend Chiang Kai-shek's inauguration and the 2nd Standing Committee of the Japan-Republic of China Cooperation Committee (*Nikka Kyoryoku Iinkai*), established in 1957. Horikoshi, who served in this capacity from 1968 to 1974, told reporters his "personal views" that "Taiwan's territorial rights over the Senkakus should be recognized," and provided some reasons for it, but also admitted that "no one within the Government and business circles ... supports his position." See "Taiwan's Territorial Rights over Senkaku Islands Should be Recognized; Oil Imports from Islands to Settle Our Excess Exports; Keidanren Vice Chairman Horikoshi," *Mainichi Shimbun*, May 20, 1972. Prime Minister Sato's brother, former prime minister Kishi Nobusuke, was to attend the meeting in Taiwan. See "Japan to Propose Joint Development of Senkaku Islands at Japan-ROC Cooperation Committee Meeting," *Mainichi Shimbun*, May 17, 1972.

65 "Telegram 3192 from Embassy Taipei to State Department on Japanese Position on Senkakus, June 30, 1971," POL 32–36 Senkaku Is, RG 59.

66 "Telegram 3192."

67 "Telegram 3192."

68 "Telegram 3192."

69 The actual meeting took place on July 13. According to a subsequent report provided by China Division Deputy Chief Watanabe, the Senkakus issue did not come up in either meeting. See "Telegram 6880 from Embassy Tokyo to State Department on Senkakus, July 15, 1971," POL 32–36 Senkaku Is, RG 59.

70 "Telegram 3069 from Embassy Taipei to State Department on Chang Chun Visit to Tokyo, June 23, 1971," POL 32–36 Senkaku Is, RG 59.

71 "Memorandum from Robert I. Starr to Thomas P. Shoesmith on the Senkakus Dispute, July 19, 1971," POL 32–36 Senkaku Is, RG 59.

72 "Telegram 3388," cited in "Memorandum from Starr to Shoesmith."

73 "Telegram 3388," cited in "Memorandum from Starr to Shoesmith."

74 "Telegram 132116 from State Department to Embassy Taipei on U.S. Approach to GOJ re Senkakus, July 21, 1971," POL 32–36 Senkaku Is, RG 59.
75 "Telegram 0629 from Embassy Taipei to State Department on Renewal GRC Request that U.S. Retain Administration of Senkakus, February 8, 1972," POL 32–36 Senkaku Is, RG 59.
76 "Telegram 0629."
77 "Telegram 0629."
78 "Telegram 0629."
79 "Telegram 0629."
80 "Telegram 0629."
81 "Telegram 0629."
82 "Telegram from HICOMRY to Embassy Taipei on Senkaku Islands, February 16, 1972," Folder 4, Box 20, History of USCAR, RG 319; "Telegram 0826 from Embassy Taipei to American Consular Unit Naha, February 19, 1972," Folder 4, Box 20, RG 319.
83 "Telegram from HICOMRY to Embassy Taipei on Senkaku Islands, February 16, 1972."
84 "Telegram from HICOMRY to Embassy Taipei on Senkaku Islands, February 16, 1972."
85 "Telegram 1716 from Embassy Tokyo to State Department, February 18, 1972," Folder 4, Box 20, RG 319.
86 "Japan Protests Taiwan's Decision to Incorporate Senkakus," *Kyodo*, February 18, 1972.
87 "Telegram from HICOM Okinawa RYIS to State Department on Senkakus, February 19, 1972," Folder 4, Box 20, RG 319.
88 "Telegram from HICOM Okinawa RYIS to State Department, February 19, 1972."
89 "Telegram 0826."
90 "Telegram 0826."
91 "Telegram 0826."
92 "Telegram 0826."
93 "Telegram 0826."
94 "Telegram 1716 from Embassy Tokyo to Secretary of State, April 18, 1972," Folder 4, Box 20, History of USCAR, RG 319.
95 "Telegram 1716."
96 "Telegram 1716."
97 "Telegram 1716."
98 Noro Kyoichi, *Akasaka Kyuchome Nanbanchi: Boei Seimu Jikan no Memo* (9–7 Akasaka: Memos of the Parliamentary Vice Minister of Defense), (Tokyo: Nagata Shobo, 1972), 137.
99 Noro, *Akasaka Kyuchome*, 137.
100 "Telegram from HICOM Okinawa RYIS/HCRI to DA//DUSA (IA), DAMO-IAR, DAIO// on JDA Vice Minister Requests Senkakus Overflight, March 15, 1972," Folder: Message Traffic Concerning the Senkaku Islands, 1971–72, Box 11, Lampert Papers. Drafted by John F. Knowles, who sat in meeting. "Author's interview with John F. Knowles, March 26, 2001, Alexandria, Virginia."
101 "Telegram from HICOM Okinawa RYIS/HCRI to DA//DUSA (IA), DAMO-IAR, DAIO// on JDA Vice Minister Requests Senkakus Overflight, March 15, 1972."
102 "Telegram from HICOM Okinawa RYIS/HCRI to DA//DUSA (IA), DAMO-IAR, DAIO// on JDA Vice Minister Requests Senkakus Overflight, March 15, 1972."
103 "Telegram from HICOM Okinawa RYIS/HCRI to DA//DUSA (IA), DAMO-IAR, DAIO// on JDA Vice Minister Requests Senkakus Overflight, March 15, 1972." Also see "Telegram from HICOM Okinawa RYIS/HCRI to DA//DUSA (IA),

DAMO-IAR, DAIO// on Senkakus Overflight by Japanese Parliamentary Vice Minister Noro, March 245, 1972," Folder 4, Box 20, RG 319.

104 Noro, *Akasaka Kyuchome*, 136–37.

105 "Telegram 1506 from Embassy Taipei to State Department on Tension over Senkakus Question: Conversation of FonMin with Ambassador, March 24, 1972," POL 32–36 Senkaku Is, RG 59.

106 "Telegram 1506."

107 "Telegram 1506."

108 "Telegram 1506."

109 "Taipei Plots Move on Senkaku Issue," *Japan Times*, February 4, 1971.

110 "Telegram 1506."

111 "Telegram from HICOMRY to Embassy Taipei on Senkakus, April 18, 1972," Folder 4, Box 20, RG 319.

112 "Taiwan Boats Told to Leave Senkakus," *Japan Times*, April 15, 1972.

113 "Telegram 1921 from Embassy Taipei to HICOMRY on Japanese SC Letter on Senkakus, April 19, 1972," POL 19 Ryu Is, RG 59.

114 "Peking Raps Japan on Senkaku Issue," *Japan Times*, June 11, 1971.

115 "Peking Raps Japan."

116 "Telegram 4741 from Hong Kong Consulate to State Department on State Department on PRC Asserts Claim to Spratley and Paracel Islands, July 17, 1971," POL 32–36 Senkaku Is, RG 59.

117 "Telegram 7965 from Hong Kong Consulate to State Department on Senkaku Islands in PRC-Japan Relations, November 29, 1971," Folder 4, Box 20, RG 319.

118 "Statements by Sato, Fukuda Hit by China; 'Bid' to Occupy Taiwan," *Japan Times*, November 7, 1971.

119 "Telegram 7965," and "Yokohama Mayor Says Senkakus 'Vital Issue'," *Japan Times*, November 25, 1971.

120 "The Senkaku Islands Question Cannot be Evaded; Condition for the Restoration of Diplomatic Relations; Statement by Asukata on Returning from China," *Yomiuri Shimbun*, November 24, 1971.

121 "Telegram 7965." The U.S. Embassy was also told that Asukata's comments were "too fuzzy" to tell if there was any flexibility in the PRC position on the Senkakus but the Japanese foreign ministry believed that the PRC had been "refrain[ing] from categorical announcements concerning sovereignty over the Senkakus ... in recent weeks." "Telegram 11734 from Embassy Tokyo to State Department on Senkaku Islands Question in PRC-Japan Relations, November 24, 1971," Folder; POL 32–36 Senkaku Is, RG 59.

122 "Foreign Ministry Statement on Tiaoyu, Other Islands," New China News Agency, December 30, 1971.

123 "Telegram 031754Z from US Mission US UN NY to State Department on PRC Attack on US at Seabeds Committee, March 3, 1972," Folder: Senkaku Retto (Senkaku Shosho) (Tia Yu Tai), Okinawa Prefectural Archives.

124 "Telegram 031754Z."

125 "Japan Repeats Claim Over Senkaku Islands," *Japan Times*, March 5, 1972.

126 Richard M. Nixon, *The Memoirs of Richard M. Nixon* (New York: Grosset and Dunlap, 1978).

127 Henry Kissinger, *White House Years* (Boston, MA: Little, Brown, and Company, 1979), 321, 324.

128 Kissinger, *White House Years*, 324.

129 "Minutes of the Secretary of State's Staff Meeting, Washington, January 31, 1974, 3:08 p.m.," Transcripts of Secretary of State Kissinger's Staff Meetings, 1973–77, E5177, box 2, RG 59, National Archives, College Park, cited in *Foreign Relations of the United States, 1969–1976, Volume E-12, Documents on East and Southeast Asia, 1973–1976,* Document 327. All quotes in this paragraph are from this document.

130 This episode apparently was not the first time Hummel disagreed with Kissinger on an issue. In his oral history, Hummel was asked about working with Kissinger: "I learned to like Henry Kissinger, even though he treated us all abominably ... At times Henry would just go wild over some issue or another ... You [were] always on a kind of knife edge. I found the fact that Henry now likes to pretend that I was the only one who ever talked back to him rather silly. He would say this when he would visit me in Beijing and would address the whole staff at the Embassy. This is not true. He would say that I was mean to him, which is, of course, is ludicrous. However, it is true that when the two of us were together ... in his office, and I objected to something that he was about to do, I would shout back at him. I would say, Henry, I'll do it if you want me to, but I want you to listen. Please listen, and then you make your final decision. I really would talk like that—but never before an outside audience." See "Oral History Interview with Ambassador Arthur W. Hummel, Jr., April 13, 1994," Foreign Affairs Oral History Project, Association for Diplomatic Studies and Training. Interestingly, Kissinger, in a roundtable discussion at the Center for Strategic and International Studies in early October 2012, was extremely vague on the U.S. role in the reversion of the Senkakus. See "Kissinger Cites Deng Deal," *Japan Times*, October 5, 2012. In a speech the year before on the occasion of donating his papers to Yale, Kissinger said that "all the key choices are 51 to 49, and it takes moral and intellectual strength [to pick a course]." (See Zoe Gorman, "Kissinger Visits Yale to Donate Papers," *Yale Daily News*, August 31, 2011.) Unfortunately, Kissinger seems to have viewed the Senkakus issue in the same way, when it was clearly not a 51–49 problem, but more like a 99–1 situation. President Reagan's son, in a biography of sorts about his father, was particularly critical of Kissinger's misunderstanding of issues and lack of a moral compass in the context of the Soviet Union, both in the 1970s as well as on the eve of the collapse of the Berlin Wall when he offered his services to President George H. W. Bush and Secretary of State James A. Baker, III, to propose a *modus vivendi* with the Soviet Union in Eastern Europe. "To their credit, Reagan and Bush rejected Kissinger's offer. Had they adopted Kissinger's plan, the Berlin Wall might still be standing today." (See Michael Reagan, *The New Reagan Revolution: How Ronald Reagan's Principles Can Restore America's Greatness* [New York: St. Martin's Press, 2010], 42.) The same can be said of the Senkakus—as a result of the unwillingness to commit in favor of Japan the territorial dispute between Japan, Taiwan, and China continues today as do the rising tensions in the region.

131 William Burr, *The Kissinger Transcripts: The Top-Secret Talks with Beijing and Moscow* (New York: The New Press, 1998), 265.

132 Kissinger's interest in China, his relationship with Chinese leaders, and his interest in preserving the legacy of the image of his diplomatic "achievements" with China came at the twin expenses of Taiwan and Japan and would color his subsequent views on the balance of power in the region. An op-ed following the heightened tensions between China and Taiwan, and China and the United States in March 1996 no doubt was of interest to Japanese officials, in which he wrote, "America's relations with Japan remain a source of concern in China even as the alliance with Japan must continue as a key element of American foreign policy." See Henry Kissinger, "Let's Cooperate with China," *Washington Post*, July 6, 1997.

133 "Peking, in Attack on Sato, Says Japan Covets Taiwan," *New York Times*, March 4, 1972.

134 For more on the work of the committee in the context of the larger Law of the Sea, see John R. Stevenson and Bernard H. Oxman, "The Preparations for the Law of the Sea Conference," *The American Journal of International Law*, Vol. 68, No. 1 (January 1974), 1–32.

135 "Telegram 833 from US Mission US UN New York to State Department on LOS, Japanese Concern regarding US Reply to PRC Intervention in Seabed Committee on 3 March, March 8, 1972," Folder 4, Box 20, RG 319.
136 "Telegram 833."
137 "Telegram 907 from US Mission US UN New York to State Department on LOS, Senkaku Islands," POL 32–36 Senkaku Is, RG 59.
138 "Telegram 907."
139 "Telegram 907." Iguchi subsequently requested the remainder of the State Department's "contingency guidance," which was given to him after Phillips checked with the department: "Press Guidance: PRC Charges in Seabed Committee (if asked). Question: What is the USG reaction to the attack by the PRC delegation in the UN Seabed Committee? Answer: The U.S. Delegate, John Stevenson, replied at the time, rejecting the accusations of aggression and imperialism and stressing because of the vital importance of the committee's tasks US intention to avoid polemics. As Mr. Stevenson pointed out, the U.S. record is good in seeking to learn the interests of other countries and reconciling those interests with our own. Far from acting unilaterally, the United States has consistently emphasized that the only answer must be an internationally agreed one. On the question of exploitation of resources in the area, we have noted in the past that sovereign rights to the resources of large portions on the continental shelf in the Yellow and East China Seas and the Taiwan Strait are in complicated dispute between the ROC, the Republic of Korea, and Japan. In addition, the PRC has asserted a claim to a large and imprecisely defined area of the shelf and it is possible that the North Koreans may consider themselves to have a claim. The USG cannot take any position on these claims since we are not directly involved. We recognize that a complicated pattern of overlapping claim exists but we take no position on their merits. In view of the conflicting claims, the Department has advised the appropriate companies of the dangers of operation in these areas and of the desire of the USG to avoid any incident which might place American lives and property in jeopardy or create tensions in the area. We have informed the companies that, under the circumstances, we consider it inadvisable for them to undertake operations in the disputed areas. Question: What about the PRC charge with respect to emplacement of nuclear weapons on the seabeds? Answer: We reject this charge. The U.S. played a leading role in the negotiations of a treaty specifically banning the emplacement of nuclear weapons on the seabeds. The U.S. Senate has recently given its advice and consent to U.S. ratification. In the light of the concern voiced by the PRC representative the PRC may also wish to accede to the treaty."
140 "Senkaku Islands are Japanese Territory; To Send Letter to U.N. in Next Few Days," *Yomiuri Shimbun*, May 29, 1972.
141 "Telegram 2187 from Hong Kong Consulate to State Department on PRC-Japan: Senkaku Dispute, March 31, 1972," Folder 4, Box 20, RG 319, History of USCAR. "Sato Government Fabricates Basis to Annex Tiaoyu Islands," *NCNA International Service*, March 30, 1972.
142 "Telegram 2187."
143 "Telegram 2453 from Embassy Tokyo to State Department on Senkaku Islands, March 9, 1972," Folder 4, Box 20, RG 319.
144 "Telegram 2453."
145 For more on Kokuba and his views, see Kokuba Kosho, *Yogawari no Saijiki: Kokusei Sanka Kara no 12 Nen* (A Record of Changing Times: 12 Years Since Participating in National Politics), (Tokyo: Daiyamondosha, 1983).
146 Fukuda's comments in the Diet's special committee can be found at http://kokkai.ndl. go.jp/cgi-bin/KENSAKU/swk_list.cgi?SESSION=26227&SAVED_RID=1&mode= 1&dtotal=1&dmy=27630 (accessed September 2012).

147 Article 2 (b), stated: "Japan renounces all right, title and claim to Formosa and the Pescadores."

148 "Telegram 3001 from Embassy Tokyo to State Department on Senkakus," POL 32–36 Senkaku Is, RG 59.

149 Okuhara, "Senkaku Retto no Ryoyuken," 238–39.

150 Okuhara, "Senkaku Retto no Ryoyuken," 239.

151 See "Expert Sent to U.S. For Senkakus Data," *Japan Times*, April 22, 1972.

152 Okuhara Toshio, "Senkaku Retto no Ryoyuken (The Territorial Rights to the Senkaku Islands)," in Kasaya Susumu, ed. *Gendai no Horitsu Mondai: Toki no Ho o Saguru* (Modern Legal Problems: Exploring Then Laws), (Tokyo: Hogaku Shoin, 1979), 238.

153 Okuhara, "Senkaku Retto no Ryoyuken," 238.

154 "China 1950 Paper Says Senkakus are Japan's," *Japan Times*, December 29, 2012.

155 Okuhara, "Senkaku Retto no Ryoyuken," 239.

156 Kokunai Kohoka, Joho Bunkakyoku, Gaimusho, ed., *Senkaku Shoto ni Tsuite* (About the Senkaku Islands), (Tokyo: Gaimusho, 1972).

157 Decades later, the GOJ finally corrected this situation by including more information in English on its Foreign Ministry website, www.mofa.go.jp/region/asia-paci/ senkaku/senkaku.html (accessed September 2012). However, Japan appears very worried that China's spending power and influence is growing, which affects public perceptions of the dispute in a way unrelated to the actual facts of the dispute. "Senkaku Islands Dispute With China Playing Out as a PR Battle," *Japan Times*, October 9, 2012; "China Outdoing Japan in Swaying Global Opinion," *Daily Yomiuri*, October 9, 2012. Also see Joshua Kurlantzick, *Charm Offensive: How China's Soft Power is Transforming the World* (New Haven, CT: Yale University Press, 2008).

158 Diary entry for March 15, 1972, *Sato Eisaku Nikki*, Vol. 5, 63–64. The ceremony and small reception lasted about 30 minutes. Celebrating with Okinawan *awamori*, Sato noted in his diary that just "two months remained before the reversion of Okinawa."

159 "Foreign Minister Fukuda on Claims to Islands," *Kyodo News*, March 21, 1972. Also see, "to Seek U.S. Government's Testimony: Foreign Minister on 'Senkaku Islands'," *Asahi Shimbun*, March 21, 1972 evening edition. Fukuda suggested such a statement be done at the same time the United States gave its assurance on the exclusion of nuclear weapons. Whether this mentioned as a formal statement was being prepared already for the latter issue, or if this were a hint to the United States that in order to be able to reintroduce nuclear weapons as per the secret agreement that had been worked out in November 1969 it should work with Japan on the Senkakus, remains unclear.

160 "Telegram 051240 from State Department to Tokyo Embassy on Senkakus Dispute, March 25, 1972," POL 32–36 Senkaku Is, RG 59.

161 "The Senkaku Islands, June 1972," and "Issues and Talking Points, August 1972,"

162 Meyer departed Tokyo on March 27. He did not have a next assignment to go to but he was subsequently tasked by Secretary Rogers in the fall to help chair the newly created Cabinet Committee to Combat Terrorism, an interagency body established on September 25 to deal with international terrorism. As a Middle East expert, Meyer became the special assistant to the secretary of state and coordinator for combating terrorism. See Meyer, *Quiet Diplomacy*, 186–87.

163 "Telegram 2882 from Embassy Tokyo to State Department on Sato and Senkakus, March 22, 1972," Folder 4, Box 20, RG 319.

164 "Telegram 2882."

165 "Telegram 2882." Sato's diary notes the meeting with Meyer but does not go into detail. See diary entry for March 21, 1972, *Sato Eisaku Nikki*, Vol. 5, 68.

166 Diet testimony; "U.S. Attitude Toward Question of Title To Senkaku Islands Evasive; Stern Protest If It Maintains Neutrality; Foreign Minister Makes Stiff

Statement," *Tokyo Shimbun*, March 23, 1972. These comments help explain Fukuda's remarks the day before at the 2nd Subcommittee of the Lower House Budget Committee (*Yosan Iinkai Daini Bunkakai*) that seemed to contradict the Foreign Ministry's desire to get the U.S. government to support the GOJ position. In that committee on the morning of the 22nd, Fukuda was asked by a JSP representative, Narazaki Yanosuke about U.S. views on the issue. Fukuda, seemingly frustrated with the U.S. "neutrality" position, stated (seemingly in contradiction to his earlier comments to the press) that there was no need to ask the U.S. government its views as the Senkakus were definitely Japanese territory. See "The Senkaku Islands Are Definitely Japanese Territory; No Need to Seek U.S. Views: Foreign Minister Fukuda's Statement," *Mainichi Shimbun*, March 22, 1972.

167 "U.S. Attitude Ambiguous; Denounced by Foreign Minister on Senkaku Islands, March 23, 1972," *Nihon Keizai Shimbun*, March 23, 1972; "U.S. View on Islets Attacked by Japan," *New York Times*, March 23, 1972; "Senkaku Islands," *Washington Post*, March 23, 1972. Also see "This Week's News," *Far Eastern Economic Review*, April 1, 1972. In light of the stories by the *Times* and *Post*, U. S. officials prepared a one paragraph statement of its position, perhaps to be used as public affairs guidance: "The United States Civil Administration of the Ryukyu Islands now administers the Senkaku Island group as part of its administration. The Reversion Treaty makes it clear that the administrative rights in the Senkakus will be returned to Japan along with administrative rights in the rest of the Ryukyus. The United States is aware that a dispute exists between Japan and the Chinese regarding the sovereignty of the Senkakus; but the United States believes that return of administrative rights over these islands to Japan, from which those rights were received, in no way can prejudice the underlying claims of the Republic of China. The United States cannot add to the legal rights Japan possessed before it transferred administration of the islands to the United States, nor can the United States by giving back what it received, diminish the rights of the Republic of China or the People's Republic of China. The United States has taken no position regarding the conflicting claims to sovereignty over the Senkakus." See "USG Position, undated," in Folder: Senkaku Islands Dispute Press Coverage, 1972–81, Okinawa Prefectural Archives.

168 "Telegram 3000 from Embassy Tokyo to State Department on Senkakus, March 23, 1972," POL 32–36 Senkaku Is, RG 59.

169 "Telegram 3000." The author interviewed Fukuda's son, former prime minister Fukuda Yasuo, regarding his father's stance on the Senkakus issue. Somewhat surprisingly, his son did not seem aware of his father's strong statements at the time. (Author's interview with Fukuda Yasuo, November 10, 2011, Tokyo, Japan.)

170 Alexander M. Haig, Jr., Kissinger's deputy and since promoted to Major General, informed the State Department on March 28 that the unofficial visit was set to go from April 15 to 18, with Ron Zeigler, the press secretary to President Nixon, to make the informal announcement at the afternoon press briefing on Wednesday, March 29. Eventually, however, Kissinger's trip got postponed to mid-June. "Memorandum from Alexander M. Haig, Jr., to Theodore L. Eliot, Jr., on Dr. Kissinger's Unofficial Visit to Japan, March 28, 1972," Kissinger Office Files, Nixon Presidential Files.

171 Zbigniew Brzezinski, *The Fragile Blossom: Crisis and Change in Japan* (New York: Harper and Row, 1972). In an interview with the author, Brzezinski did not recall his views at the time of how he evaluated the Nixon administration's handling of the Senkakus issue and the reversion of Okinawa, but with regard to how and why he included a discussion of the Senkakus in his letter to Kissinger, he explained, "My basic source of information regarding the views which I expressed in my letter to him was derived from my many encounters in Tokyo in the course of my protracted stay there during 1971–72. In the course of that visit I met with

many Japanese officials and I was impressed, as my letter shows, by their sense of unease. Moreover, some of them (e.g., Nakasone) were quite outspoken. That led me then to share my impressions with Henry in the hope that he could somewhat mitigate their unease." Author's interview (by e-mail) with Zbigniew Brzezinski, April 5, 2012, Washington, D.C. (The author would like to thank Diane Reed, Dr. Brzezinski's assistant, for arranging the interview.) With regard to the Senkakus, Brzezinski presciently wrote in *The Fragile Blossom*: "Japan will thus soon have to confront some very difficult choices. The Taiwan issue is likely to become an especially painful one. Many Japanese leaders have close ties with Taiwan, either through economic links or personal connections with the Taipei leadership or because of national sympathy for Taiwan. Indeed, the Taiwanese nationalist movement has been tacitly supported by the Japanese. Many Japanese, one suspects, would like to see a Taiwanese Taiwan, which could quietly become a Japanese security protectorate and an extension of the Japanese economy. The discovery of oil in the Chinese Nationalist-claimed islands of Senkaku (off Okinawa) heightens the potential importance of a separate Taiwan, for a reunited China would be in a stronger position to press Chinese claims. Strong emotions and high interests are thus involved in the question of Taiwan, and they will continue to complicate the Japanese desire to establish closer links also with Peking." (See *The Fragile Blossom*, 87.) Prime Minister Sato immediately read the translation of Brzezinski's book, which was published as *Hiyowa na Hana Nihon* in January 1972 by Simul. As he did not have to go to the Diet that day, Sato read the seventy pages in his first sitting on March 4. "It is supposed to have some dramatic prophecies in it," he wrote in his diary. See diary entry for March 4, 1972, *Sato Eisaku Nikki*, Vol. 5, 57.

172 "Letter from Zbigniew Brzezinski to Dr. Henry Kissinger, April 11, 1972," Kissinger Office Files, Nixon Presidential Files. By chance, Brzezinski's name had come up within the staff the day before he wrote this letter. Peter W. Rodman, a junior assistant to Kissinger who had been brought on to the staff at the age of twenty-five, wrote a note to Kissinger critical of his decision to postpone his trip to Japan—"a cancellation without obvious and immediate reason only affronts the Japanese and proves [we are distracted by Vietnam]"—and notes that "we will be attacked for this at home. The George Balls, Zbigniew Brzezinskis, William Bundys, and Morton Halperins of this world have made a career since July 15 of lamenting our mistreatment of our Japanese ally. The Democrats will be ready and eager to exploit this hole in our foreign policy record. I make this point not because I swallow liberal pap but because the importance of dealing honorably with our allies is something I learned from you." See "Memorandum from Peter W. Rodman to Henry A. Kissinger on Canceling the Japan Trip, April 10, 1972," Kissinger Office Files, Nixon Presidential Files. Winston Lord, who served on the NSC's planning council staff, wrote in the corner, "agree—WL."

173 "Memorandum from Mike Armacost to Winston Lord, May 3, 1972, with attachment, 'Japan Adjusts to an Era of Multipolarity in Asia, April 21, 1972'," Kissinger Office Files, Nixon Presidential Files. It is unclear if this memo was shared with Kissinger. (Author's interview with Dr. Michael H. Armacost, March 19, 2012.) However, Lord, special assistant to Kissinger on the National Security Council, was preparing a binder of talking points for him which may have incorporated some of Armacost's thinking in it as Lord was not a Japan specialist and Armacost was slightly more familiar with the country. John H. Holdridge, a Foreign Service Officer and China specialist on the staff of the National Security Council who handled Northeast Asia, recommended earlier in the spring that most of the background papers could be prepared by the CIA but requested permission to "draw State into helping draft some papers in order to avoid flak otherwise over the alleged lack of Japanese expertise on your staff. What goes into

your book, of course, would not necessarily include everything from State." ("Memorandum from John H. Holdridge for Mr. Kissinger, March 29, 1972," Kissinger Office Files, Nixon Presidential Files.) For more on him, see John H. Holdridge, *Crossing the Divide: An Insider's Account of the Normalization of U.S.-China Relations* (New York: Rowman and Littlefield, 1997), and "Interview with John H. Holdridge, December 14, 1989," Association for Diplomatic Studies and Training Foreign Affairs Oral History Project. One of the topics Holdridge, who had replaced Sneider on the National Security Council in early July 1969, had listed was the Senkaku Islands. Eventually, it appears that the State Department was asked to prepare only two papers, "Japan-Soviet Relations" and "Japanese Policy toward the PRC." ("Memorandum from Department of State Secretariat Staff to NSC Secretariat on Briefing Papers for Mr. Kissinger's Trip to Japan, April 6, 1972," Kissinger Office Files, Nixon Presidential Files.) In any case, a background paper and set of talking points entitled "The Senkaku Islands" was prepared for the June trip, probably by the National Security Council.

174 "Japan Adjusts to an Era of Multipolarity in Asia, April 21, 1972."
175 "Japan Adjusts to an Era of Multipolarity in Asia, April 21, 1972."
176 "Japan Adjusts to an Era of Multipolarity in Asia, April 21, 1972."
177 "Japan Adjusts to an Era of Multipolarity in Asia, April 21, 1972."
178 "Telegram 3000."
179 "Telegram 3000."
180 "Telegram 3001 from Embassy Tokyo to Secretary of State on Senkakus, March 23, 1972," Folder: Senkaku Islands Dispute Press Coverage, 1972–81, Okinawa Prefectural Archives.
181 "Telegram 3000."
182 "Sato, Fukuda on U.S. Attitude to Senkakus," *Kyodo News*, March 23, 1972; "Dissatisfaction Expressed to U.S.; Prime Minister Sato on Title to Senkaku Islands," *Mainichi Shimbun*, March 24, 1972.
183 "Telegram 051240."
184 "Telegram 051240." Japan's maintenance of this position has been criticized and is one reason that observers argue it has difficulty bringing the case before the ICJ. One former Foreign Ministry official, and the son of Togo Fumihiko, who appeared in Chapter 4, Togo Kazuhiko, who has written on the issue of territorial disputes, has called for the government to change its position. See Takao Yamada, "Pursuing a Strategic Compromise to a Difficult Territorial Issue," *Mainichi*, October 1, 2012. A story shortly after that suggested the GOJ was considering just that. "Japan May 'Acknowledge' China's Claim to Islets to Calm Tension," *Japan Times*, October 10, 2012.
185 "Telegram 051240."
186 "Telegram 051240."
187 "Telegram 051240."
188 "Telegram 051240."
189 "Envoy Visits Green for Senkaku Talks," *Japan Times*, March 26, 1972.
190 "Telegram 272106Z from Secretary of State to Embassy Tokyo on Senkaku Dispute, March 27, 1972," Folder 4, Box 20, RG 319.
191 "Telegram 272106Z." The press guidance "as of 3/25/72," read: "Q: What is the U.S. position on the recognition of the Senkaku Islands? Is it Japanese, part of the Ryukyus, belongs to China, or what? A: The U.S. has consistently maintained that in the even a situation arises where there are conflicting claims in this area, any such claims would predate our connection with the Ryukyus and should be settled by the parties themselves. Now, the background of this is that under Article III of the Treaty of Peace with Japan, the U.S. acquired administrative rights over—with apologies for the pronunciation—Nansei Shoto, including the

Ryukyus south of 29 degrees north latitude. The term 'Nansei Shoto' was understood to include the Senkaku Islands, which were under Japanese administration at the end of World War II, and which were not otherwise specifically referred to in the Treaty. Under the provisions of the Okinawa Reversion Treaty, the United States will return to Japan on May 15, 1972 the administrative rights to Nansei Shoto which it acquired under the Treaty of Peace with Japan. The U.S. exercises full authority over these islands and will continue to do so until reversion. Q: Does the U.S. intend to retain U.S. Navy gunnery ranges after reversion of the Senkakus to Japan? A: These ranges are included in a list of sites which the U.S. will retain after reversion as designated in the Okinawa Reversion Treaty. We do not feel that the designation of these ranges in any way affects our basic position on the Senkakus issue as previously described." See "Press Guidance as of 3/25/72," Folder: Senkaku Islands Dispute Press Coverage, 1972–81, Okinawa Prefectural Archives.

192 "Foreign Ministry Irritated by U.S. State Department's 'Non-Intervention Statement,' on Senkaku Islands Question," *Mainichi Shimbun*, March 25, 1972 evening edition. This may have been a reference to two recent interactions (March 17 and 23) that reportedly happened with the Foreign Ministry. According to a briefing paper on the Senkakus prepared by John H. Holdridge of the National Security Council, the Japanese Foreign Ministry officially informed the State Department of its "unhappiness with the public position of neutrality being taken" by the USG and pointed out the "inconsistency, at least in Japanese eyes, of this public stance" with the U.S. request to retain gunnery ranges on Kobi Sho and Sekibi Sho. Japan also indicated it "understands why the U.S. felt it must remain uninvolved in this dispute," a briefing paper on the Senkakus prepared by John H. Holdridge of the National Security Council notes, "but requested in any future public statements we avoid using words or phrases which will in any way undercut the Japanese position or influence Japanese public opinion against the U.S." "The Senkaku Islands, undated (Spring 1972)," Kissinger Office Files, Nixon Presidential Files.

193 "Foreign Ministry Irritated."

194 "JSP Diet Member Mori Sharply Criticizes U.S. Attitude over Senkaku Islands Questions," Nihon *Keizai Shimbun*, March 24, 1972.

195 "Telegram 3077."

196 "Telegram 3124 from Embassy Tokyo to State Department on Senkakus Dispute, March 27, 1972," POL 32–36 Senkaku Is, RG 59.

197 "Telegram 3124."

198 "Telegram 3124."

199 "Telegram 3124."

200 "Telegram 3077."

201 "Telegram 053707 from State Department to Embassy Taipei on Senkakus Dispute, March 29, 1972," POL 32–36 Senkaku Is, RG 59.

202 For more on the agreement, which was signed by Kubo Takuya, Chief, Defense Bureau, Japan Defense Agency and Walter L. Curtis, Jr., Chief Military Representative, U.S. Embassy to Japan (Lieutenant General), see Akikazu Yamaguchi, "Briefing Memorandum: Local Defense Obligations after the Reversion of Okinawa," *The National Institute for Defense Studies News*, No. 151 (February 2011), 1–6.

203 According to an article in mid-April 1972, 18 F104J's were scheduled to be available for scrambles. See "JDA to Include Senkaku Islands in Japan's Air Identification Zone," *Mainichi Shimbun*, April 12, 1972 evening edition.

204 For example, the evening edition of an *Asahi Shimbun* of June 21 reported on the "expansion" of the ADIZ, but in which direction was not specifically mentioned. The Asahi noted that those promoting the expansion of the ADIZ were located in the Air Staff Office (*Koku Jieitai Kubaku*), but that there were other cautious

voices, afraid that discussions on the ADIZ would be "considered to be pouring oil onto a fire of the dispute." See "JDA to Study Expansion of ADIZ Following Reversion of Okinawa: Prudent in Handling Senkaku Islands," *Asahi Shimbun*, evening edition June 21, 1971 (unofficial translation), Folder: Senkaku Retto (Sento Shosho) (Tia Yu Tai), Okinawa Prefectural Archives.

205 On June 25, 2010, following unsuccessful requests for discussions with Taiwan, Japan unilaterally extended its ADIZ westward by two nautical miles to include Yonaguni, a move that was in turn protested by Taiwan. This decision was reportedly in part related to the increased attention the GOJ placed on the defense of the Southwestern Islands and in preparation for the future stationing of Ground Self-Defense Forces on Yonaguni Island. The Japan Ministry of Defense (upgraded from the Japan Defense Agency in January 2007) released a statement the day before the change went into effect, saying that "the decision was taken in order to put at ease the feelings of the people of Okinawa and Yonaguni Island." See Ministry of Defense, "Yonaguni Jima Joku no Boku Shikibetsuken no Minaoshi ni Tsuite (On the Review of the ADIZ Above Yonaguni Island), June 24, 2010," at www.mod.go.jp/j/press/news/2010/06/24a.html (accessed August 2012). For more on this issue, see L.C. Russell Hsiao, "In a Fortnight: Taiwan-Japan Rift over ADIZ," *China Brief: A Journal of Analysis and Information* (Jamestown Foundation), Vol. X, Issue 12 (June 11, 2010), 1–2, and Shih Hsiu-chuan, "Japan Extends ADIZ into Taiwan Space," *Taipei Times*, June 26, 2010.

206 "Telegram 2202 from Embassy Tokyo to CINCPAC on Okinawa/Taiwan ADIZ Boundary Line, March 11, 1971," Folder 4, Box 20, RG 319.

207 "Telegram 2202."

208 "Telegram 151846Z from CINCPAC to COMUSTDC on Okinawa/Taiwan ADIZ Boundary Line, March 15, 1971," Folder 4, Box 20, RG 319.

209 "Telegram 1285."

210 "Telegram 042104Z from CINCPAC to JCS on Okinawa/Taiwan ADIZ Boundary Line, April 4, 1971," Folder 4, Box 20, RG 319.

211 "Telegram 042104Z."

212 "Telegram 100300Z from JCS to CINCPAC on Okinawa/Taiwan ADIZ Boundary Line, April 10, 1971," Folder 4, Box 20, RG 319.

213 See footnote 66 above.

214 Said another way, the original ADIZ for Okinawa, established by the U.S. military, was 857,000 square kilometers, and the new one established by Japan was 834,000. Under the U.S. system, the closest point to the Chinese mainland was 84 km, and to the Chinese Chushan Islands, a mere 36 km. Under the Japanese system that excluded the 23,000 square kilometer zone, the closest point to the mainland was 135 km, and to the islands, 99 km. Curiously, the new ADIZ went over the middle of Yonaguni Island, Japanese territory, and would not be revised until almost forty years later. "Defense Agency Maps Okinawa ADIZ Limits," *Japan Times*, May 4, 1972. Also see "JDA Decides ADIZ in Okinawa, Senkaku Islands to be Included Entirely Section Close to China Cut Out," *Tokyo Shimbun*, May 4, 1972.

215 "JDA to Include Senkaku Islands."

216 "Senkakus Included in Air Defense Zone, But Area near China Excluded," *Asahi Evening News*, May 4, 1972.

217 "JDA to Include Senkaku Islands."

218 "Telegram 030402Z from CINCPAC to COMUSJAPAN on Okinawa Defense Planning, September 3, 1971," Folder 4, Box 20, RG 319.

219 "Telegram P030402Z."

220 "JSP Opposes ADIZ Formula," *Daily Yomiuri*, May 5, 1972.

221 "U.S. Firing Grounds on Senkaku Islands; Endorsement to Japanese Ownership?" *Sankei Shimbun*, May 12, 1971 (translation).

222 "Telegram 4345 from Embassy Tokyo to State Department on Senkakus-Japanese Press Reports Re U.S. Gunnery Ranges, May 12, 1971," POL 32–36 Senkaku Is, RG 59.

223 "U.S. Firing Grounds on Senkaku Islands."

224 "Telegram 2247 from Embassy Taipei to State Department on Artillery Testing Site on the Senkakus, May 12, 1971," POL 32–36 Senkaku Is, RG 59.

225 "Telegram 87994 from State Department to Embassy Taipei on Artillery Testing Site on the Senkakus, May 19, 1971," POL 32–36 Senkaku Is, RG 59.

226 "Telegram 87994."

227 "Telegram 2203 from Embassy Taipei to HICOMRY, May 4, 1972," Folder 4, Box 20, History of USCAR, RG 319.

228 "Telegram 2203."

229 According to an undated memorandum from the summer, fishermen from Suao, Taiwan, landed on the Senkakus in late March 1972 and brought back several hundred shearwater squabs or albatrosses which were sold in markets in Taipei. See "8. Senkakus," Folder: PET Senkaku Islands 1972, Box 14, Subject Files of the Office of China Affairs, 1951–75, RG 59.

230 Kobayashi Ken, the fifty-two year old leader of the Tokyo-based Patriotic Youth League (*Aikoku Seinen Renmei*), landed on Uotsuri on May 15 and hoisted a Japanese flag. See "Japan Rightist Claims Island," *Washington Post*, May 18, 1972. Maritime Safety Agency officials in Okinawa had spotted him and made the announcement. It is unclear if he were arrested or not. Currently, Japanese citizens are banned by their own government from landing on the islands. Ishigaki City Nakayama laments the inability to visit the islands that fall under his city's administration. See Nakayama, *Senkaku Shoto no Futsugo na Shinjitsu*, 62–63.

231 "Telegram from HICOMRY to DUSA, April 30, 1972," Folder 4, Box 20, History of USCAR, RG 319.

232 "Telegram 2125 from Embassy Taipei to HICOMRY on Senkakus, May 1, 1972," Folder 4, Box 20, History of USCAR, RG 319.

233 "Telegram HICOMRY to Embassy Taipei on Senkakus, May 2, 1972," Folder 4, Box 20, History of USCAR, RG 319.

234 "Telegram 2203."

235 "Telegram 2394 from Embassy Taipei to State Department on Ryukyu Reversion, May 15, 1972," POL 19 Ryu Is, RG 59.

236 "Telegram 2394."

237 "'Reversion is Regrettable': Taiwan Unhappy with Terms," *Morning Star*, May 10, 1972.

238 "Telegram 2394."

239 "Telegram 2396 from Embassy Taipei to State Department on IOR/Media Reaction, May 16, 1972," POL 19 Ryu Is, RG 59.

240 "Telegram 2394."

241 "Reversion Protest in Hong Kong," *Pacific Stars and Stripes*, May 15, 1972.

242 "Telegram 3241 from Hong Kong Consulate to State Department on Senkaku Islands Protest Marks Okinawa Reversion, May 16, 1972," POL 19 Ryu Is, RG 59.

243 "Telegram 3241."

244 On Sunday, May 16, while the consulate was still closed, "64 generally docile and disciplined Chinese teenagers" who were "outnumbered by onlooking newsmen, Hong Kong police and spectators," demonstrated on Consulate General grounds over the Senkaku Islands. ("Telegram 3160 from Hong Kong Consulate to State Department, May 16, 1972," POL 33 Senkaku Is, RG 59.) At least one banner declared that "Both Tiao Yu Tai and Hong Kong are Chinese Territories," and U.S. and Japanese imperialism were denounced. Demonstrators asked but were denied permission to burn a Japanese flag, but proceeded to trample and tear a small, homemade flag depicting a rising sun. These were not the first protests that

year. Earlier, members of the Protection of the Taio Yu Tai Action Committee had staged two "poorly attended" demonstrations on January 28 and 29. (See "Airgram 34 from Hong Kong Consulate to State Department on Senkaku Islands Demonstration at Congen, February 3, 1972," POL 33 Senkaku Is, RG 59.) The dates were chosen for two reasons: to commemorate the Japanese attack on Shanghai in 1932 as well as the launching of the Senkaku movement in the United States in 1971. ("Telegram 663 from Hong Kong Consulate to State Department on Senkaku Demonstration at Congen Called for January 28, January 28, 1972," POL 32–36 Senkaku Is, RG 59.) Osborn noticed that "ideological differences which have divided the local Senkaku Movement were also evident among those who took part in the demonstration ... The demonstrations received negative coverage in the English and right-wing Chinese press and only brief mention in the leftist papers." (Airgram 34.) Curiously, Osborn added in the same airgram, "neither group [of Senkaku demonstrators], however, will be able to arouse support among the general public as the Senkakus have become largely a dead issue." (Airgram 34.) As the post reversion history shows, he was very much mistaken in this regard.

245 "Chinese Protest Return of Islands to Japan," *Pacific Stars and Stripes*, May 15, 1972.
246 "Memorandum from Chief, Protective Intelligence Branch to Acting Chief, Division of Investigations on Special Protective Intelligence Project: Anti-War and Protest Activity at Washington, D.C.—May 13, 1972," Folder: PET Senkaku Islands 1972, Box 14, Subject Files of the Office of China Affairs, 1951–75, RG 59.
247 "Routing and Record Sheet by F. Babcock to Dennis Harder on Tiao Yu Tai 13 May 1972 Demonstration in Washington, D.C., May 11, 1972," Folder: PET Senkaku Islands 1972, Box 14, Subject Files of the Office of China Affairs, 1951–75, RG 59.

Conclusion

Ambassador to Japan Armin H. Meyer would later write about this time and dynamics: "[our] position, carefully reflected in the documentation, was that as custodians we were merely returning administrative power [over the Senkaku Islands] to Japan without prejudice to historic claims. This neat position endeared us to none of the three disputants, but it assured our non-involvement in a controversy which is likely to continue for years."[1]

While it is true that we have not been as involved as we were in the 1969–72 period, I am not sure if I can so easily agree with Ambassador Meyer's comment that "it assured our non-involvement." Our interests in peace and stability in the region, and between Japan, China, and Taiwan, are too high to be non-involved.

Indeed, in what has become known as the "Armitage doctrine," the United States has more or less confirmed to Japan over the past decade that the United States–Japan Security Treaty applies to Senkaku Islands as well, and the United States and Japan are finally making the first steps toward greater amphibious interoperability, a capability that would be necessary for landing on and/or retaking those islands. This position—that Article 5 of the bilateral security treaty does indeed apply to the Senkakus—apparently was reaffirmed in light of the deep uncertainty Japan sensed in the defense commitments of the United States in the latter half of the 1990s in the wake of tensions in the Taiwan Strait, confusion in the policies of the State Department, and the rise of China and its increased naval activity.

However, serious concerns emerge if one examines this position in detail, which requires clarification if not outright correction.

As alluded to above, there are two unavoidable problems with the respective positions of neutrality on the one hand and a security commitment on the other. The biggest one is the question: would the United States be willing to come to blows, in support of Japan as per Article 5 of the *mutual* security treaty,[2] with a third country, such as China, over the Senkakus?

This author wants to believe that the United States would do so, as it is vital not only due to treaty obligations and moral duty, but also to maintain the credibility of the U.S. commitment and thus enhance deterrence for Japan and in the region among America's other allies and friends (not to mention the belief that a seizure of the Senkakus by China would be the first step in the eventual seizure or neutralization of Okinawa as a whole). The Senate's passage in the fall of 2012 of the provisions to the FY 2013 National Defense Authorization Act, discussed in the Introduction, about the Senkakus certainly implies the United States might and that it would likely have the support of the Senate. However, as mentioned in the introduction, writer Nicholas D. Kristof raises a very good point when he questions whether the American public and its elected officials would in the end support a decision to employ U.S. forces to defend islands that the U.S. government does not even recognize Japan as having sovereignty over.

On top of this, Japan has not made adequate efforts to date to develop the defenses in its southwestern islands, despite statements to this effect over the past five years (and indeed forty years), and had been even cutting back on its defense commitments and budget over the past decade until 2012. Furthermore, it has not pursued jointness in its Self-Defense Forces to bring about efficiencies and effectiveness or pursued developing amphibious capabilities anywhere near what is required today. The American people and Congress, correctly, would be highly reluctant, therefore, to support the use of American forces to help defend territory that Japan was not even making a serious effort to protect. (Maltreatment of U.S. personnel in Okinawa and Japan by the media and politicians for ideological, political, or other reasons does not help Japan's case with the American public and Congress in this regard.)

Another thorny problem is the frightening situation if a clash of some sort were to erupt in the Senkakus in which it was unclear what exactly happened or if Japan was in fact attacked or not. History, especially that of Sino–Japanese relations, is replete with examples of manufactured incidents, when the aggressor is unclear, or simple vagueness about what really took place. Through economic, political, and diplomatic influence, a proactive public relations campaign, and cyber warfare, an aggressor could cover its actions and make it appear as if it were the victim, or at the minimum sow the seeds of doubt.

In the case of the Senkakus, China, or even Taiwan, who both claim the islands (something which is not refuted by the United States), could easily create a situation in which Japan was made to look like the aggressor and yet still seize the islands and the waters around them. In this case, if the United States were uncertain as to what had happened, it would not be obligated to help defend Japan as per Article 5. Moreover, if an American administration were sufficiently influenced by China economically and politically and fearful of it militarily, or its officials unaware of the previous position of the USG or simply incompetent, or it was preoccupied with another crisis in another part of the world, the USG might look for an excuse not to be involved. Indeed, it or China could point to the fact that China has claimed the islands over the past forty years, particularly since the USG does not outright reject the PRC's claims. China would not, the argument goes, therefore be invading the sovereign territory of another country—it would be freeing up its own territory. The same is true if a naval clash occurred at sea. Having planted the seed of doubt in the mind of the international community that a territorial dispute exists between it and Japan and that in any clash Japan might be or have been the aggressor, China might be able to convince the world or regional players that Japan was trigger-happy especially if the latter used military force in the East China Sea (even if Japan argued it was only protecting its own territory). Japan may find itself losing the islands in a clash not of its choosing simply in a public relations campaign even if it could win the land or sea battle. The international community would call for a ceasefire, before Japan had a chance to make its case or retake the island. Due to the existing tensions, this sort of incident may not be an "if" question but "when." One cannot forget that in the case of U.S. diplomatic history with East Asia, there have often been two schools of thought—a pro-Japan faction and a pro-China group. We saw this a century ago in the years leading up to World War II, and we may see it again (albeit for different reasons, as China—the number two economic power in the world—is no longer the threatened, weaker of the two, struggling to modernize with the help of American missionaries).

Similarly, China could use a number of scenarios that would make it difficult to dislodge it from the islands. Fishermen, who have often gone to the area, could simply end up staying there after having landed on the island and set up a colony of sorts. It would be difficult to remove a large group of men as seen in part. It would be more difficult if actually these "fishermen" were paramilitary forces. In addition, in a less blatant move, Chinese vessels could claim an emergency—either a mechanical problem or a need to avoid bad weather—and just stay there, or create a situation where there was some sort of maritime or land virtual presence. Furthermore, a shipwreck or other accident where Chinese or other people were stranded on one of the Senkakus could lead to calls for there to be a military operation to "rescue" them. Another scenario involves China coming to help islands in the vicinity, such as Yonaguni, Ishigaki, or Miyako after an earthquake or tsunami and used or landed on one or some of the islands in the meantime for whatever excuse it chose to make. In short, the scenarios that could render "Article 5" meaningless are too numerous to count, and thus Japan and U.S. policy makers cannot rely simply on the position that "Article 5 applies to the Senkakus," because it does not apply to all situations. This is not classified information—just intellectual honesty and common sense.

The above assumes that some intentional action by China was behind a conflict. Perhaps Chinese leaders do not desire it, although previous statements suggest they are not opposed to one and it is very likely that the increased military might China has attained only makes them bolder. On the other hand, even if it is not the case, unintentional results through miscalculation could also happen. The former diplomat and late historian George F. Kennan wrote in another context, "But wars ... do not always arise from acts of outright aggression; they are more apt to proceed, as history shows, from confused situations arising against a background of extreme political tension."[3] Confusion and political tension are indeed ripe in this issue, with occasional incidents at sea and regular sparring by national spokesmen and activists.

One international affairs writer and former national security advisor to the president, Zbigniew Brzezinski, who appears in Chapter 5, noted about the Senkaku Islands in his book, *The Grand Chessboard*: "The historical rivalry for regional pre-eminence between Japan and China confuses this issue with symbolic significance as well."[4] In this situation, the strategic ambiguity that America's neutrality policy represents may only add to the confusion. A clearer policy emphasizing deterrence, recognition of Japan's sovereignty over the Senkakus (and all of Okinawa) once and for all by China, and peaceful joint development by interested parties may be in order.

My own view is that the USG should have sided with Japan at the time of reversion on the issue of the Senkakus in light of its long-held policies shared by most nations with regard to the Ryukyu Islands that Japan had residual sovereignty over them, and that the Senkakus belonged to the Ryukyu Islands group. Although Taiwan was also an ally of the United States at the time (one whose relations were already frayed to breaking point at that point—Chiang, for example, was already calling Nixon a "clown"[5]), its claims were belated and at best weak, compared to those of Japan, as discussed throughout this book. This applies to China's claims as well. Indeed, the timing of the claims clearly showed that they were made in light of the possibility of oil reserves being in the area. The United States not only let down an important ally (Japan) and was inconsistent in its own policies, but also paradoxically helped the rivalry grow by creating an environment in which the seeds of false claims and accusations to grow wild and unchecked. The United States, it could be argued, not only did not contribute to peace in the region by taking an aloof attitude, it actually indirectly contributed to the tension. What it should have done, in this writer's opinion, was to chime in once and for all in 1970, 1971, or 1972, that the Senkakus were Japan's in fact as well as in name. By not doing this and instead by saying that the USG was neutral in the territorial dispute, the United States ended up contributing to an already complicated relationship and eventual tense rivalry.

Cynics might argue that was the U.S. intention in the first place—plant the seeds for further or future tension—in order to ensure that the U.S. military presence would be required for years to come. I have found no evidence of that, and indeed, that theory doesn't match the trend at the time of the Nixon Doctrine to reduce our military presence in the region, relying on allies to handle their immediate defense needs. Instead, I attribute the decision to remove ourselves from the dispute and "hope for the best" as being simply wishful thinking and more probably policy that was poorly thought out and based on short-term thinking.

Said another way, I have often wondered if there were no other ways to handle the situation at the time. Rather than punting the problem and hoping it would be caught (ideally by "our team"), should not the United States have made the call right there in front of everyone like a good referee, physically handing off the Senkakus to Japan, and explaining to the other team or teams that the Senkakus were indeed Japan's and to move on? I would argue it was possible, and that it should have been done, not only for our main ally in the region but also in the interests of long-term peace and stability. A U.S. statement on the Senkakus that removed the inconsistency in the U.S. position by recognizing (again) Japan's sovereignty over the Senkakus would, I believe, have squelched the belated claims by Taiwan and China by removing any hint of legitimacy (which America's neutral stance creates or at least encourages) and adding to deterrence, allowing all three countries to focus their energies on cooperation and development rather than the tense state we still have forty years later that threatens peace and stability in the region. By not doing this, ironically, the United States opens itself to criticism from leftist scholars and others opposed to the U.S. presence in Japan and elsewhere that it cynically promotes tension in the region in order to justify its presence. Similarly, some of the same observers themselves argue that the United States has no intention of defending Japan.

In the meantime, many short-term issues exist as well. Because of the political sensitivity of the Senkakus problem, the United States has hesitated from using the training ranges on the islands for more than thirty years, degrading U.S. capabilities and emboldening countries who wish the U.S.–Japan alliance ill. In addition, because of these political sensitivities, it is likely that Japan has been reluctant to request, and the U.S. hesitance to offer, use of the ranges to the Self-Defense Forces for its training, unilateral or bilateral. In the case of the former, Japan's capabilities are degraded and its credibility as a military power is decreased. Similarly, the credibility of its position on the Senkakus—namely that it has sovereignty over the islands—is reduced when it chooses not to make full use of the islands as it deems fit. Likewise, the interoperability of the United States and Japan is impaired, and thus deterrence weakened. The November 2012 cancellation by the Japanese side of a portion of an exercise to attempt to retake an island held by an enemy force out of concern for China's views will further put Japan behind in its abilities to develop jointness and its amphibious capabilities while China steams ahead with all manners of military procurement and development. This cancellation is the equivalent of keeping a qualified student (Japan) behind one grade while allowing another (China) to graduate.

One colleague, who is Okinawan, international, and well read, and defines himself as "normal—not a pure liberal nor a pure conservative," saw the cancellation of the exercises as making the ability to resolve the Senkakus dispute more difficult. He told me in October 2012 that the easiest way to resolve the Senkakus dispute is for the United States to continue to openly demonstrate its presence and for the two militaries to conduct amphibious exercises.

Another issue that undermines confidence in the Japanese government's ability to administer the islands is the fear, on the one hand, by researchers and fisherman to visit the area, afraid of either pirates or hostile groups. At the same time, the Japanese government has tried to limit those who can actually go to the islands, creating the strange situation by which local government officials and assembly members from Ishigaki City, which administers the islands, cannot go there, nor can other Japanese nationals without facing detention, questioning, and possible criminal charges.[6] Indeed, the central government reportedly has not undertaken an official survey of the islands since the latter half of the 1970s, and even tore down a temporary heliport that the predecessor to the Japan Coast Guard, the Maritime Safety Agency, built in the first half 1980s out of concern for China's views (much the same way it was overly cautious in the 1880s about its actions on the islands).

Zukeran Choho, one of the student participants in the Ryukyu University research trip to the Senkakus in 1953, who later became high school teacher, scientist, and three-term member of the Okinawa Prefecture Assembly (1972–80; 1984–88) representing the Okinawa Social Masses Party (*Okinawa Shakai Taishuto*), a local party established in 1950, as well as heading it at one point, lamented at a reunion with Professor Takara and fellow participants of the 1950s trips about the inability to visit the islands anymore. "We could go there freely," he stated about the pre-reversion period,

> but now we can't. [The GOJ] does not allow anyone to land there. It does not allow anyone to do research there. The government is forbidding it, out of concern about China. It says it does not want to cause any unnecessary trouble. It prevents any landings on the Senkakus. The government is useless. The policy is a mistake. We used to freely visit there prior to reversion. It is important to let everyone know we once used to visit there. A monument recognizing these research trips to the islands should be built.[7]

An older, current member of the Miyako City Assembly has said the same thing. At a January 14, 2012 ceremony commemorating the development of the Senkaku Islands conducted on Ishigaki in front of the Monument to the Development of the Senkaku Islands by Koga Tatsushiro (*Koga Tatsushiro Senkaku Retto Kaitaku Kinenhi*),[8] this assembly member, who has visited the Senkakus in the past with the host of the ceremony, Nakama Hitoshi, an assembly member from Ishigaki City, made a short speech in which he asked rhetorically, "The Government of Japan says there is no problem between it and the Chinese government. If that is true, why is it not possible to visit the islands?"[9] The central government's buying of the islands and nationalizing them in September 2012 was meant primarily to limit unauthorized visits to the islands by activists and nationalists in order to create a more stable environment domestically and regionally out of consideration to China and Taiwan. This cautiousness can and should be viewed as a responsible approach to dealing with a highly emotional issue. At the same time, it can also been seen as irresponsible in the long run if it results in Japan being seen internationally (and bilaterally with the United States) as less-than-truly sovereign over the Senkakus and leads to Japan eventually losing the islands. The GOJ, in other words, not allowing elected officials from the administrating city, prefecture, or nation, is quite strange and only gives credence to sovereignty claims by China and Taiwan, much like what happened in the 1880s and 1890s, when the Meiji government was afraid to push too hard or too fast.

Figure C.1 Senkakus Development Monument (photo by author)

With regard to emotions, the media of all the countries involved have regularly been an unhelpful player in this issue. When they are not seemingly trying to inflame the situation through using menacing headlines or focusing on extremist elements, editors and reporters have all-too-often gotten their facts wrong. One example was a story that included a reference to the removal of the Taiwanese flag from Uotsuri Island in September 1970 by police of the Government of the Ryukyu Islands. A story in a newspaper published nine months later described the incident as follows: "The U.S. Navy tore it down. American administrations at Naha, Okinawa, took the attitude that they had an obligation to defend the Senkakus for Japan and turn them over to Japan eventually."[10] The paragraph was factually wrong, as we saw in earlier chapters. It was also interpretive, and the interpretation itself was even partly mistaken. As a result, a reader would finish the story with a completely different understanding of what had taken place. The news tends to get more sensational as time goes on, ironic in that more information is now known from which to do correct, objective stories. Some journalists just don't let facts get in the way of a good story.

A similar phenomenon is the use of the Internet to discuss territorial disputes, both by groups as well as individuals, to post messages, documents, statements, comments, and videos.[11] In this dispute, Japanese writers, bloggers, video-graphers, and website operators tend to look at the battle as a bilateral one, against Chinese, whereas their Chinese counterparts look at the entire world as the audience, and publish where possible in English. The lack of correct information by Japan loses out to the larger amount of disinformation by China.

Amid incorrect reporting, nationalistic passions, economic interests, and real security concerns, it is unclear and highly unlikely if the territorial dispute will ever be resolved if things are left as they are. The United States had hoped that the two parties—Japan and the ROC—would be able to resolve the issue before the PRC got involved. If that did not work, the U.S. government hoped the International Court of Justice might be able to assist.

Charles Schmitz, who was the key negotiator on the Senkakus and other issues in the treaty, explained in an article published on the twentieth anniversary of the reversion that,

> U.S. negotiators felt stuck and vulnerable to attack from all sides. After much research, internal discussion, and diplomatic argument, [we] developed a legal theory that, we felt, neatly extracted us from the middle of a Japanese-Chinese set-to and was, moreover, nicely defensible. It was a "quit claim." We said, in effect, "We have been the temporary administrators, and now we are going to stop. Whatever it was that we got, we now give up." We took a middle road and hoped that a future International Court of Justice case would back us up.[12]

When I asked a former official in the MOFA treaties division several years ago if he thought the ICJ formula would work, he believed Japan had a very good case. However, Japan seems to have been unwilling to raise the issue, although it has done so recently in the case of its dispute with South Korea over the Takeshima Islands, which South Korea has been controlling since the 1950s (which the U.S. government has viewed as an illegal occupation).

Whatever happens, the Senkakus issue is certainly not going to go away easily, although it very likely would have been a non-issue today had the USG not adopted the neutrality policy it did forty years ago. In this case, it is not the seeds the United States planted, but the weeds it ignored and the ignorance it displayed at the time that have now grown out of control.

While the USG cannot change what it did then, it may want to consider today the recommendation by a reserve colonel in the Marine Corps, lawyer, and former Foreign Service Officer long involved with East Asia, which was also the title of his recent op-ed: "U.S. Must Clearly Back Japan in Islands Dispute with China."[13] In the absence of China (and Taiwan) withdrawing once for all its claims to the Senkakus, a true dialog among the three disputants, or outside adjudication through the International Court of Justice, regional forum, or other third party, this show of resolve by the United States ironically may be the only way to ensure further peace and stability in the region. In this case, deterrence and commitment, not neutrality and strategic ambiguity, will clarify and steady the situation.

Notes

1 Meyer, *Assignment Tokyo*, 49–50.
2 The security treaty is not mutual in the traditional sense, which adds yet another element of doubt to the willingness to fight on behalf of small, outlying, uninhabited islands when Japan does not even pledge to defend the United States.
3 George F. Kennan, *The Nuclear Delusion: Soviet-American Relations in the Atomic Age* (New York: Pantheon Books, 1983), xxvi.
4 Zbigniew Brzezinski, *The Grand Chessboard: American Primacy and Its Geostrategic Imperatives* (New York: Basic Books, 1997), 154.
5 See diary entries in July 1971, Chiang Kai-shek Diary.
6 Nishimuta Yasushi, "Nihonjin ga Joriku Dekinai Nihon no Ryodo to wa (What is the Japanese Territory That Japanese People Are Not Allowed to Land On)?" *Chuo Koron*, Vol. 122, No. 6 (June 2007), 108–19.
7 Senkaku Shoto Bunken Shiryo Hensankai, ed, *Senkaku Kenkyu: Takara Gakujutsu Chosadan Shiryoshu*, 273. Ironically Zukeran's son, Chobin, elected to the Diet in August 2009 from the Democratic Party of Japan (*Minshuto*) but who lost in the December 2012 election, is strongly opposed to the deployment of the SDF to the Southwestern Islands, while schizophrenically calling for protection of the Senkakus.
8 The dignified monument unveiled on January 19, 1996 at Rokuchi Park in the Yashima district of Ishigaki City honoring the efforts of Koga to develop the islands. It was built by the Koga Association (*Zaidan Hojin Koga Kyokai*), a foundation established by Kurihara Kunioki in September 1988 with the inheritance he received from Koga Hanako, in part to promote sports, travel, and recreation in Okinawa Prefecture. Kunioki's mother, Sayoko, served as the initial chair of the nine-person board prior to her passing in 2006. His sister, Yagihashi Hisako succeeded her mother as the second chairperson of the board.
9 I observed these remarks at a private morning ceremony, and then went to an official one in the afternoon at the Central Hall of the Civic Center commemorating the second anniversary of Ishigaki City having named January 14 as "Senkaku Islands Development Day (*Senkaku Shoto Kaitaku no Hi*)." While the mayor of Ishigaki, Nakayama Yoshitaka, attended, Governor of Okinawa Prefecture Nakaima Hirokazu, who has been courting Chinese investment, did not for the second year in a row opening him up to criticism by his fellow conservatives.
10 Henry S. Bradsher, "Two Chinas Share a View: Any Oil is Ours," *Evening Star*, May 17, 1971. The *Evening Star* was a D.C-based paper that published between 1852 and 1981. Bradsher was badly incorrect here, but won national recognition for his reporting on the 1971 Bangladesh Civil War and on China.
11 Eriko Arita, "Symposium Looks at the Disturbing Rise of Online Nationalism," *Japan Times*, November 4, 2012.
12 Schmitz, "Working Out the Details," 24.
13 Newsham, "U.S. Must Clearly Back Japan in Islands Dispute with China."

Appendix 1

Agreement between Japan and the United States of America concerning the Ryukyu Islands and the Daito Islands

Tokyo, Washington
June 17, 1971

Japan and the United States of America

Noting that the Prime Minister of Japan and the President of the United States of America reviewed together on November 19, 20, and 21, 1969 the status of the Ryukyu Islands and the Daito Islands, referred to as "Okinawa" in the Joint Communique between the Prime Minister and the President issued on November 21, 1969, and agreed that the Government of Japan and the Government of the United States of America should enter immediately into consultations regarding the specific arrangements for accomplishing the early reversion of these islands to Japan

Noting that the two Governments have conducted such consultations and have reaffirmed that the reversion of these islands to Japan be carried out on the basis of the said Joint Communique

Considering that the United States of America desires, with respect to the Ryukyu Islands and the Daito Islands, to relinquish in favor of Japan all rights and interests under Article 3 of the Treaty of Peace with Japan signed at the city of San Francisco on September 8, 1951, and thereby to have relinquished all its rights and interests in all territories under the said Article; and

Considering further that Japan is willing to assume full responsibility and authority for the exercise of all powers of administration, legislation and jurisdiction over the territory and inhabitants of the Ryukyu Islands and the Daito Islands

Therefore, have agreed as follows:

Article I

1. With respect to the Ryukyu Islands and the Daito Islands, as defined in paragraph 2 below, the United States of America relinquishes in favor of

Japan all rights and interests under Article 3 of the Treaty of Peace with Japan signed at the city of San Francisco on September 8, 1951, effective as of the date of entry into force of this Agreement. Japan, as of such date, assumes full responsibility and authority for the exercise of all and any powers of administration, legislation, and jurisdiction over the territory and inhabitants of the said islands.

2. For the purpose of this Agreement, the term "the Ryukyu Islands and the Daito Islands" means all the territories and their territorial waters with respect to which the right to exercise all and any powers of administration, legislation and jurisdiction was accorded to the United States of America under Article 3 of the Treaty of Peace with Japan other than those with respect to which such right has already been returned to Japan in accordance with the Agreement concerning the Amami Islands and the Agreement concerning Nanpo Shoto and Other Islands signed between Japan and the United States of America, respectively on December 24, 1953 and April 5, 1968.

Article II

It is confirmed that treaties, conventions and other agreements concluded between Japan and the United States of America, including, but without limitation, the Treaty of Mutual Cooperation and Security between Japan and the United States of America signed at Washington on January 19, 1960 and its related arrangements and the Treaty of Friendship, Commerce and Navigation between Japan and the United States of America signed at Tokyo on April 2, 1953, become applicable to the Ryukyu Islands and the Daito Islands as of the date of entry into force of this Agreement.

Article III

1. Japan will grant the United States of America on the date of entry into force of this Agreement the use of facilities and areas in the Ryukyu Islands and the Daito Islands in accordance with the Treaty of Mutual Cooperation and Security between Japan and the United States of America signed at Washington on January 19, 1960 and its related arrangements.

2. In the application of Article VI of the Treaty of Mutual Cooperation and Security between Japan and the United States of America, regarding Facilities and Areas and the Status of United Sates Armed Forces in Japan signed on January 19, 1960, to the facilities and areas the use of which will be granted in accordance with paragraph 1 above to the United States of America on the date of entry into force of this Agreement, it is understood that the phrase "the condition in which they were at the time they became available to the United States armed forces" in paragraph 1 of the said Article IV refers to the condition in which the facilities and areas first came into the use of the United States armed forces, and that the term

"improvements" in paragraph 2 of the said Article includes those made prior to the date of entry into force of this Agreement.

Article IV

1. Japan waives all claims of Japan and its nationals against the United States of America and its nationals and against the local authorities of the Ryukyu Islands and the Daito Islands, arising from the presence, operations or actions of forces or authorities of the United States of America in these islands, or from the presence, operations or actions of forces or authorities of the United States of America having had any effect upon these islands, prior to the date of entry into force of this Agreement.
2. The waiver in paragraph 1 above does not, however, include claims of Japanese nationals specifically recognized in the laws of the United States of America or the local laws of these islands applicable during the period of United States administration of these islands. The Government of the United States of America is authorized to maintain its duly empowered officials in the Ryukyu Islands and the Daito Islands in order to deal with and settle such claims on and after the date of entry into force of this Agreement in accordance with the procedures to be established in consultation with the Government of Japan.
3. The Government of the United States of America will make ex graita contributions for restoration of lands to the nationals of Japan whose lands in the Ryukyu Islands and the Daito Islands were damaged prior to July 1, 1950, while placed under the use of United States authorities, and were released from their use after June 30, 1961 and before the date of entry into force of this Agreement. Such contributions will be made in an equitable manner in relation to the payments made under High Commissioner Ordinance Number 60 of 1967 to claims for damages done prior to July 1, 1950 to the lands released prior to July 1, 1961.
4. Japan recognizes the validity of all acts and omissions done during the period of United States administration of the Ryukyu Islands and the Daito Islands under or in consequence of directives of the United States or local authorities, or authorized by existing law during that period, and will take no action subjecting United States nationals or the residents of these islands to civil or criminal liability arising out of such acts or omissions.

Article V

1. Japan recognizes the validity of, and will continue in full force and effect, final judgments in civil cases rendered by any court in the Ryukyu Islands and the Daito Islands prior to the date of entry into force of this Agreement, provided that such recognition or continuation would not be contrary to public policy.

2. Without in any way adversely affecting the substantive rights and positions of the litigants concerned, Japan will assume jurisdiction over and continue to judgment and execution any civil cases pending as of the date of entry into force of this Agreement in any court in the Ryukyu Islands and the Daito Islands.
3. Without in any way adversely affecting the substantive rights of the accused or suspect concerned, Japan will assume jurisdiction over, and may continue or institute proceedings with respect to, any criminal cases with which any court in the Ryukyu Islands and the Daito Islands is seized as of the date of entry into force of this Agreement or would have been seized had the proceedings been instituted prior to such date.
4. Japan may continue the execution of any final judgments rendered in criminal cases by any court in the Ryukyu Islands and the Daito Islands.

Article VI

1. The properties of the Ryukyu Electric Power Corporation, the Ryukyu Domestic Water Corporation and the Ryukyu Development Loan Corporation shall be transferred to the Government of Japan on the date of entry into force of this Agreement, and the rights and obligations of the said Corporations shall be assumed by the Government of Japan on that date in conformity with the laws and regulations of Japan.
2. All other properties of the Government of the United States of America, existing in the Ryukyu Islands and the Daito Islands as of the date of entry into force of this Agreement and located outside the facilities and areas provided on that date in accordance with Article III of this Agreement, shall be transferred to the Government of Japan on that date, except for those that are located on the lands returned to the landowners concerned before the date of entry into force of this Agreement and for those the title to which will be retained by the Government of the United States of America after that date with the consent of the Government of Japan.
3. Such lands in the Ryukyu Islands and the Daito Islands reclaimed by the Government of the United States of America and such other reclaimed lands acquired by it in these islands as are held by the Government of the United States of America as of the date of entry into force of this Agreement become the property of the Government of Japan on that date.
4. The United States of America is not obliged to compensate Japan or its nationals for any alteration in made prior to the date of entry into force or this Agreement to the lands upon which the properties transferred to the Government of Japan under paragraphs 1 and 2 above are located.

Article VII

Considering, inter alia, that United States assets are being transferred to the Government of Japan under Article VI of this Agreement, that the

Government of the United States of America is carrying out the return of the Ryukyu Islands and the Daito Islands to Japan in a manner consistent with the policy of the Government of Japan as specified in paragraph 8 of the Joint Communique of November 21, 1969, and that the Government of the United States of America will bear extra costs, particularly in the area of employment after reversion, the Government of Japan will pay to the Government of the United States of America in United States dollars a total amount of three hundred and twenty million United States dollars (U.S. $320,000,000) over a period of five years from the date of entry into force of this Agreement. Of the said amount, the Government of Japan will pay one hundred million United States dollars (U.S. $100,000,000) within one week after and the remainder in four equal annual installments in June of each calendar year subsequent; to the year in which this Agreement enters into force.

Article VIII

The Government of Japan consents to the continued operation by the Government of the United States of America of the Voice of America relay station on Okinawa Island for a period of five years from the date of entry into force of this Agreement in accordance with the arrangements to be concluded between the two Governments. The two Governments shall enter into consultation two years after the date of entry into force of this Agreement on future operation of the Voice of America on Okinawa Island.

Article IX

This Agreement shall be ratified and the instruments of ratification shall be exchanged at Tokyo. This Agreement shall enter into force two months after the date of exchange of the instruments of ratification.

IN WITNESS WHEREOF, the undersigned, being duly authorized by their respective Governments, have signed this Agreement.

DONE at Tokyo and Washington, this seventeenth day of June, 1971, in duplicate in the Japanese and English languages, both equally authentic.

For Japan:

Kiichi Aichi
For the United States of America:
William P. Rogers

Appendix 2

Agreed minutes[1]

The representatives of the Government of Japan and of the Government of the United States of America wish to record the following understanding reached during the negotiations for the Agreement between Japan and the United States of America concerning the Ryukyu Islands and the Daito Islands, signed today:

Regarding Article I:

The territories defined in paragraph 2 of Article I are the territories under the administration of the United States of America under Article 3 of the Treaty of Peace with Japan, and are, as designated under the Civil Administration Proclamation Number 27 of December 25, 1953, all of those islands, islets, atolls, and rocks situated in an area bounded by the straight lines connecting the following coordinates in the listed order:

North Latitude	East Longitude
28 degrees	124 degrees 40 minutes
24 degrees	122 degrees
24 degrees	133 degrees
27 degrees	131 degrees 50 minutes
27 degrees	128 degrees 18 minutes
28 degrees	128 degrees 18 minutes
28 degrees	124 degrees 40 minutes

Notes

1 Embassy of the United States of America, Tokyo, Japan, "Okinawa Reversion Agreement of June 17, 1971, and Related Documents," July 1, 1971.

Appendix 3

Guidance to U.S. oil companies (April 1971)

In view of the disputed national claims to sovereign rights over the natural resources in certain areas of the Yellow and East China Seas and the Taiwan Straits, the Department wishes to advise American firms conducting survey activities in the area that:

1. The People's Republic of China has recently issued several statements, the strongest which appeared in the Peking *People's Daily* on December 29,

   — asserting its claims to wide areas of shallow seas off its coast in opposition to the claims of the Republic of China, Japan, and the Republic of Korea,
   — objecting to surveys of the seabed and subsoil resources of these seas conducted by the three countries with the participation of American firms,
   — claiming the Senkaku and other islands also claimed by the Republic of China and/or Japan,
   — warning that the People's Republic of China will not permit encroachment of its territory and sovereignty by foreign governments, particularly mentioning the United States.

2. The United States Government does not have the authority to determine the national boundaries of the continental shelf of East Asia.
3. This Government is determined not to permit itself to be drawn into the dispute over conflicting claims of the People's Republic of China, the Republic of China, Japan, the Republic of Korea, and the Democratic Republic of Korea or into contention with any of the disputants over the merits of their claims.
4. The United States Government is unable to assess whether the People's Republic of China might take action, including military action, against foreign survey vessels and drilling installations operation in waters claimed by mainland China.

5. The United States Government cannot give American firms any commitment to protect their concessions, operations, vessels, equipment, or personnel, including U.S.-citizen personnel, in a disputed area.
6. The United States Government strongly recommends that American firms suspend all exploration and exploitation activities in areas of the Yellow and East China Seas and the Taiwan Straits subject to two or more claims until the claimants reach agreement regarding the limits or their rights to these areas.

Appendix 4

Statement by the Ministry of Foreign Affairs, Republic of China

June 11, 1971

In the course of recent years, the Government of the Republic of China has never ceased to follow with the deepest concern the question of the status of the Ryukyu Islands and has on repeated occasions sought to bring to the attention of the government of the states concerned its views on the merits of the question and its preoccupations particularly with reference to the related problems of security in the Asian and Pacific area.

Having learned that the United States Government and Japanese Government are going to sign in the immediate future formal instruments for the transfer of the Ryukyu Islands, and together therewith, the Tiaoyutai Islets, over which the Republic of China exercises its territorial sovereignty, the Chinese Government considers it necessary to emphasize once again its position, and make its views known to the world.

First, as regards the Ryukyu Islands. In 1943, principal allied powers, viz., China, the United States and the United Kingdom issued jointly the Cairo Declaration. In 1945 the Potsdam Declaration was issued which provides, inter alia, that the terms of the Cairo Declaration shall be carried out and that Japanese sovereignty shall be limited to the islands of Honshu, Hokkaido, Kyushu, Shikoku and such minor islands as the principal allies may determine. It was older that the future status of the Ryukyu Island was reserved for subsequent determination by the principal allies.

The peace treaty with Japan, signed on September 8, 1951 at San Francisco, was based in substance upon the two above-mentioned declarations.

Article III of this treaty contained explicit provisions concerning the legal status of the Ryukyu Islands and the manner of its future disposition.

The position of the Republic of China has consistently been that the final disposal or the Ryukyu Islands should be determined by the Allied Powers concerned through consultations in accordance with the Cairo Declaration and the Potsdam Declaration. This position has been repeatedly made known to the United States Government. As one of the principal Allied Powers which were at war with Japan, the Republic of China was and is naturally entitled to participate in any such consultations. The Republic of China must express its profound regret that the United States Government without going through the consultations referred to above, hastens to transfer the Ryukyu Islands to Japan.

Secondly, as regards the transfer of the Tiaoyutai Islets the Chinese Government views with some consternation the announcement that the contemplated transfer of the Ryukyu Islands by the United States to Japan will be accompanied by that of the Tiaoyutai Islets.

These islets belong to the Chinese province of Taiwan and thus constitute part of the territory of the Republic of China. They are closely linked to the latter by reason of geographical location, geological structure, historical association, and above all, by reason of the long and continued use which the inhabitants of Taiwan have made of these islets. Bound by the sacred duty to defend its national territory, the Chinese Government will never relinquish any particle of its territorial sovereignty under any circumstances.

Thus, it has continuously informed the United States Government and Japanese Government that in terms of history, geography, usage, and law, the Chinese Government deems that these islets belong, with the slightest doubt, to the territorial sovereignty of China and that they should be returned to the Republic of China upon the completion of the administration by the United States.

The Chinese Government considers it absolutely inadmissible that the administrative rights of these islets should now be transferred by the United States to Japan together with the Ryukyu Islands, and it deems that this transaction between the United States and Japan can in no way affect the claim of sovereignty on the part of the Republic of China over these islets.

For the above reasons, the Chinese Government must express its strongest opposition to the impending transfer. It cherishes, however, the sincerest hope that the states concerned will respect China's sovereignty over these islets and will at once take reasonable and legal steps accordingly, in order to avert serious consequences in the Asian and Pacific area.

Appendix 5

Statement by the Ministry of Foreign Affairs, People's Republic of China

December 30, 1971

In the past few years, the Japanese Sato government, ignoring the historical facts and the strong opposition of the Chinese people has repeatedly claimed that Japan has the so-called "title' to China's territory of the Tiaoyu and other islands, and in conclusion with U.S. imperialism, has engaged in all kinds of activities to invade and annex the above-mentioned islands. Not long ago, the U.S. Congress and the Japanese Diet one after the other approved the agreement on the "reversion" of Okinawa. In this agreement, the governments of the United States and Japan flagrantly included the Tiaoyu and other islands in the "area of reversion." This is a gross encroachment upon China's territorial integrity and sovereignty. The Chinese people will absolutely not tolerate this!

The fraud of the "reversion" of Okinawa to Japan jointly contrived by the U.S. and Japanese governments is a new grave step to strengthen U.S.-Japanese military collusion and to accelerate the revival of Japanese militarism. The Chinese Government and people have consistently supported the Japanese people's valiant struggle to smash the fraud of the "reversion" of Okinawa and for the unconditional and complete recovery of Okinawa, and they are strongly opposed to the U.S. and Japanese reactionaries' making a deal over China's territory of the Tiaoyu and other islands and using this to sow seeds of discord in the friendly relations between the peoples of China and Japan.

The Tiaoyu and other islands have been China's territory since ancient times. Back in the Ming dynasty, these islands were already within China's sea defence areas; they were islands appertaining to China's Taiwan but not to Ryukyu, which is now known as Okinawa. The boundary between China and the Ryukyu in this area lies between Chihwei Island and Kume Island and fishermen from China's Taiwan have all along carried out productive activities on the Tiaoyu and other islands. During the 1894 Sino-Japanese War, the Japanese Government stole these islands and in April 1895 it forced the government of the Ching dynasty to conclude the unequal "Treaty of Shimonoseki" by which "Taiwan, together with all islands appertaining to Taiwan" and the Penghu Islands were ceded. Now the Sato government has gone to the length of making the Japanese invaders' act of aggression of seizing China's territory in the past a ground for claiming that Japan has the so-called "title" to the Tiaoyu and other islands. This is sheer and outright gangster logic.

After World War II, the Japanese Government illicitly handed over to the United States the Tiaoyu and other islands appertaining to Taiwan, and the United States Government unilaterally declared that it enjoyed the so-called "administrative rights" over these islands. This in itself was illegal. On June 28, 1950, shortly after the founding of the People's Republic of China, Foreign Minister Chou En-lai, on behalf of the Chinese Government, strongly condemned U.S. imperialism for sending its Seventh Fleet to commit aggression against Taiwan and the Taiwan Strait, and solemnly declared that the Chinese people were determined to "recover Taiwan and all territories belonging to China." Now the U.S. and Japanese governments have once again made an illicit transfer between themselves of China's Tiaoyu and other islands. This encroachment upon China's territorial integrity and sovereignty cannot but arose the utmost indignation of the Chinese people.

The Ministry of Foreign Affairs of the People's Republic of China hereby solemnly declares: Tiaoyu Island, Huangwei Island, Chihwei Island, Nanhsiao Island, Peihsiao Island, etc., are island appertaining to Taiwan. Like Taiwan, they have been an inalienable part of Chinese territory since ancient times. It is utterly illegal for the U.S. and Japanese governments to include China's Tiaoyu and other islands in the so-called "area of reversion" in the Okinawa "reversion" agreement. Their act cannot in the least alter the sovereignty of the People's Republic of China over her territory of the Tiaoyu and other islands. The Chinese people are determined to liberate Taiwan! The Chinese people are determined to recover the Tiaoyu and other islands appertaining to Taiwan!

Appendix 6

The Japanese Foreign Ministry's view concerning the rights to ownership over the Senkaku Islands

March 8, 1972

In and after 1885, the Government repeatedly conducted field surveys on the Senkaku Islands, and having confirmed with prudence that they were not merely uninhabited islands but also had no traces of control by Ch'ing (Government of China), made a Cabinet decision on January 14, 1895, to the effect that a marker post would be put up on the Islands and, thus, decided to incorporate them formally into our country's territory.

Since then, the Senkaku Islands have consistently, historically, comprised a part of the Nansei Islands which are our country's territory, and they are not included in Taiwan and the Pescadores, the cession of which our country obtained from Ch'ing on the basis of Article 2 of the Shimonoseki Treaty which took effect in May, 1895.

Accordingly, even under the San Francisco Peace Treaty, the Senkaku Islands are not included in the territory our country relinquished on the basis of Article 2 of the Treaty. They are placed under U.S. administration as a part of the Nansei Islands, in accordance with Article 3, and are included in the areas the administration rights over which are to be reverted to our country under the Okinawa Reversion Agreement. The above-mentioned facts clearly indicate, before everything else, the Status of the Senkaku Islands as territory of our country.

Appendix 7

Statement by the Ministry of Foreign Affairs

Republic of China
May 9, 1972

The Government of the Republic of China has always been deeply concerned about the future status of the Liu Chiu Islands (of the Ryukyu Islands) and has on several occasions declared its position on this question.

Now that the Government of the United States of America has decided to transfer the Liu Chiu Islands to Japan on May 15, 1972 and that the said transfer would even include the Tiao-Yu-Tai islets, which are under the sovereignty of the Republic of China, the Government of the Republic of China deems it of particular importance to state once again its position solemnly to the world.

Regarding the Liu Chiu Islands, the Government of the Republic of China has consistently held the view that the matter should be dealt with by the principal allied powers of World War II, including the Republic of China, through joint consultation and in accordance with the principles enunciated in the Cairo and Potsdam declarations. The Government of the Republic of China considers it exceedingly regrettable that the United States should unilaterally transfer the Liu Chiu Islands to Japan without having followed the agreed procedure of consultation.

As far as the Tiao-Yu-Tai Islets are concerned, they constitute part of the territory of the Republic of China. From the standpoints of geographical position, geological structure, historical affinity, continued usage over an extended period of time as well as from the standpoint of law, the claim of the Republic of China to the sovereignty over the territory of the said islets to Japan, together with the Liu Chiu Islands, is therefore, strongly opposed by the Government of the Republic China. The Government of the Republic of China, bound by the sacred duty of preserving its territorial integrity, cannot under any circumstances relinquish its sovereignty over the Tiao-Yu-Tai Islets.

Bibliography

Primary sources

Public archives and personal manuscript collections

L. Tom Perry Special Collections, Brigham University Library, Provo, UT
    David M. Kennedy Collection
Military History Institute, U.S. Army War College, Carlisle, PA
    James B. Lampert Papers
Okinawa Prefectural Archives, Haebaru-cho, Okinawa Prefecture
    Yara Chobyo Nisshi (Diaries of Yara Chobyo)
    Edward Freimuth Papers
    Senkaku Collection
United States National Archives, College Park, MD
    Record Groups 59, 319
    Nixon Presidential Materials

Oral histories

C.O.E. Ooraru Seisaku Kenkyu Purojekuto (COE Oral Policy Research Project),
    Graduate Research Institute for Policy Studies (Tokyo, Japan)
Okawara Yoshio Ooraru Hisutorii (Oral History with Okawara Yoshio)
Yoshino Bunroku Ooraru Hisutorii (Oral History with Yoshino Bunroku)
Foreign Affairs Oral History Project, Association for Diplomatic Studies and Training
    (Arlington, VA)
Heritage Project (Cactus Hills, AZ)
Oral History with Millard Engen

Interviews

Armacost, Michael H. March 19, 2012, Stanford, CA (by e-mail).
Brzezinski, Zbigniew. April 5, 2012, Washington, DC (by e-mail).
Clark, William, Jr. September 12, 1997, New York City, New York.
Deming, Rust M. October 8, 2012, Washington, DC (by e-mail).
Finn, Richard B. August, September, November 1997; June 1998, Bethesda, MD.
Fukuda, Yasuo. November 10, 2011, Nagata-cho, Chiyoda-ku, Tokyo.
Green, Marshall. September 1997; February 1998, Bethesda, MD.
Kiuchi, Akitane. September 19, 2012, Tokyo, Japan (by telephone).

Knowles, John F. March 26, 2001, Alexandria, VA.
Kusuda, Minoru. October 1, 1999, and July 31, 2000, Tokyo, Japan.
Mansfield, Michael J. March 27, 2001, Washington, DC.
McElroy, Howard M. July-August 2012, Warminister, PA (by e-mail).
Nishi, Takayuki. November 1, 2012, Shizuoka City, Japan (by e-mail).
Okuhara, Toshio. June 21, 2011, Nagareyama City, Japan.
Oxnam, Bernard H. August 6, 2012. Miami, FL (by e-mail).
Schmitz, Charles A. March 24, 2009, Washington, DC.
Sneider, Daniel. December 12, 2012, Stanford, CA (by telephone).
Suganuma, Unryu. October 27, 2012, Tokyo, Japan (by e-mail).
Yoshino, Bunroku. August 29, 2012, Yokohama City, Japan.

Documents and official histories

Belcher, Sir Edward. *Narrative of the Voyage of H.M.S. Samarang during the Years, 1843–1846*, Vols 1 & 2, (London: Reeve, Benham, and Reeve, 1848), 315–20.
Documents on United States Policy toward Japan and Ryukyu Islands (hereafter State book), Kashiwashobo, 2006.
Gaimusho Johobunkakyoku. *Senkako Retto ni Tsuite* (Regarding the Senkaku Islands), Tokyo: Gaimusho, 1972.
High Commissioner of the Ryukyu Islands. *Civil Administration of the Ryukyu Islands, Report for Period 1 July 1969 to June 1970*, Vol. XVIII.
High Commissioner of the Ryukyu Islands. *Civil Administration of the Ryukyu Islands, Report for Period 1 July 1970 to June 1971*, Vol. XIX.
Ishigaki Shishi Henshu Iinkai, ed. *Ishigaki Shishi, Minzoku, Jo* (Ishigaki Municipal History, People, Vol. 1), Ishigaki City: Ishigaki Shishi Henshu Iinkai, 1994.
——. "Joint Statement of Japanese Prime Minister Eisaku Sato and U.S. President Richard Nixon, November 21, 1967," *Public Papers of the Presidents: Richard Nixon, 1969*, pp. 953–57.
Kaigunsho Suirokyoku, ed. *Kanei Suiroshi* (Journal of the Waterways of the World), Vol. 1 (March 1884).
Niksch, Larry A. "Senkaku (Diaoyu) Islands Dispute: The U.S. Legal Relationship and Obligations," *CRS Report for Congress*, 96–798F, September 30, 1996.
Manyin, Mark E. "Senkaku (Senkaku Diaoyu/Diaoyutai) Islands Dispute: U.S. Treaty Obligations," *CRS Report for Congress*, 7–5700, September 25, 2012.
Naha Shishi Henshu Iinkai, ed. *Naha Shishi* (History of Naha City), Naha: Naha City Office, 1966.
Nanpo Doho Engokai, ed. *Okinawa Fukki no Kiroku* (Records about the Return of Okinawa), (Tokyo: Nanpo Doho Gengokai, 1972).
National Institute for Defense Studies, ed. *NIDS China Security Report 2011*, Tokyo: National Institute for Defense Studies, 2012.
Okinawaken Bunka Shinkokai, ed. *Okinawa Kensh Bijuaruban 6 Kindai 1: Okinawa to Taiwan* (Visual Version of Okinawa Prefectural History, Vol. 6, Modern 1: Okinawa and Taiwan), (Itoman: Okinawaken Kyoiku Iinkai, 2000).
Ryukyu Ginko Chosabu, ed. *Sengo Okinawa Keizaishi* (The Economic History of Postwar Okinawa), (Naha: Ryukyu Ginko, 1984).
Teruya Eiichi, ed. *Okinawa Gyosei Kiko Hensenshi, Meiji 12 Nen-Showa 59 Nen* (Okinawa Government Organization History, 1879–1984), (Naha: Matsumoto Taipu, 1984).

Memoirs and personal accounts

Aguni, Yasuo. "Ahodori o Motomete (Looking for the Albatross)," *Okinawa Taimusu*, May 20–24, 1963 (5 installments).

Allison, John M. *Ambassador from the Prairie or Allison Wonderland*. Boston, MA: Houghton Mifflin, Co., 1973.

Arasaki, Moriteru, ed. *Okinawa Gendaishi he no Shogen* (Testimony about Modern Okinawan History), Vol. 2, Naha: Okinawa Taimususha, 1982.

Barnett, Robert W. *Wandering Knights: China Legacies, Lived and Recalled*. Armonk, New York: M. E. Sharpe, 1990.

Brzezinski, Zbigniew. *Power and Principle: Memoirs of the National Security Advisor 1977–1981*, New York: Farrar, Straus, and Giroux, 1985.

Buckner, Simon B., Jr., and Joseph W. Stilwell (edited by Nicholas Evan Sarantakes). *Seven Stars: The Okinawa Battle Diaries of Simon Bolivar Buckner, Jr. and Joseph Stillwell*, College Station, TX: Texas A & M University, 2004.

Chiba, Kazuo. "The Reversion of Okinawa," *Insight Japan*, April 2000, 11–13.

Chien, Frederick. *Qian Fu Huiyi Lu* (Memoirs of Frederick Chien), Taipei: Tianxiayuanjianchuban Gufenyouxiangongsi (Commonwealth Publishing, Co.), 2005.

Cline, Ray S. *Chiang Ching-kuo Remembered: The Man and His Political Legacy*, New York: University Press of America, 1989.

Ehrlichman, John. *Witness to Power: The Nixon Years*, New York: Pocket Books, 1982.

Emery, Kenneth O. "Autobiography: Some Early Stages of Marine Geology," *Marine Geology*, Vol. 188, Issues 3–4 (August 2002), 251–91.

Fukuda, Takeo. *Kaiko Kyuju Nen* (Recalling 90 Years), Tokyo: Iwanami Shoten, 1995.

Haig, Alexander M., Jr. *Inner Circles: How America Changed the World, A Memoir*, New York: Warner Books, 1992.

Haldeman, H.R. *The Haldeman Diaries: Inside the Nixon White House*, New York: Berkley Books, 1994.

Higa, Kenji. "'Keikoku Ita' Secchi no Omoide (Recollections on Setting Up the 'Warning Sign')," *Yaeyama Mainichi Shimbun*, August 25, 2009.

——, "Keikoku Ita Secchi no Omoide (Recollections on Setting Up the Warning Signs)," in Senkaku Shoto Bunken Shiryo Hensankai, ed. *Senkaku Kenkyu: Takara Gakujutsu Chosadan Shiryoshu* (Research on the Senkaku Islands: The Papers of the Takara Scientific Investigation Group), Naha: Deetum Rekiosu, 2007, 283–88.

Holdridge, John H. *Crossing the Divide: An Insider's Account of the Normalization of U.S.-China Relations*, New York: Rowman and Littlefield, 1997.

Hori, Shigeru. *Sengo Seiji no Oboegaki* (A Memorandum on Postwar Politics), Tokyo: Mainichi Shimbunsha, 1975.

Inamine, Ichiro. *Sekai o Butai Ni: Inamine Ichiro Kaikoroku* (The World is a Stage: The Memoirs of Inamine Ichiro), Naha: Okinawa Taimusu, 1988.

Ishihara, Shintaro. "Senkaku Shoto to Iu Kokunan (The National Problem That is the Senkaku Islands)," *Bungei Shunju*, Vol. 90, No. 10 (July 2012), 148–56.

Isshiki, Masaharu. *Nani ka no Tame ni Sengoku38 no Kokuhaku* (Why I Did It: Sengoku38's Report), Tokyo: Asahi Shimbun Shuppan, 2011.

Johnson, U. Alexis. *The Right Hand of Power: The Memoirs of an American Diplomat*, Englewood Cliffs, NJ: Prentice-Hall, 1984.

Kaya, Okinori. *Senzen, Sengo 80 Nen* (80 Years of the Prewar and Postwar), Tokyo: Keizai Oraisha, 1976.

Kissinger, Henry. *White House Years*, Boston, MA: Little, Brown, and Company. 1979.

Koga, Hanako. "Kiryu Shonin no Tsuma to Shite: Koga Hanako San ni Kiku (As a Wife of a Meiji Businessman in Okinawa: An Interview with Mrs. Koga Hanako)," in Arasaki Moriteru, ed. *Okinawa Gendaishi e no Shogen, 2* (Testimonies about Modern Okinawan History, 2), Naha: Okinawa Taimusu, 1982, 113–42.

Koga, Zenji. "Mo San, Sato San, Senkaku Shoto wa Watashi no 'Shoyuchi' Desu (Mr. Mao, Mr. Sato: I Own the Senkaku Islands)," *Gendai*, Vol. 6, No. 6 (June 1972), 142–47.

———. "Senkaku Shoto no Aruji wa Watashi (I am the Owner of the Senkaku Islands)," *Nihon Keizai Shimbun*, August 26, 1970.

Kokuba, Kosho. *Yogawari no Saijiki: Kokusei Sanka Kara no 20 Nen* (A Record of Changing Times: 20 Years Since Participating in National Politics), Tokyo: Daiyamondosha, 1983.

Kurihara, Hiroyuki. "Senkaku Shoto 'Baikyaku' no Uchimaku (Behind the Scenes of the 'Purchase' of the Senkaku Islands)," *Shincho*, Vol. 31, No. 6 (June 2012), 22–25.

———. *Senkaku Shoto Urimasu* (Senkaku Islands for Sale), Tokyo: Kosaido Shuppan, 2012.

Kuriyama, Takakazu (edited by Nakajima Takuma, Hattori Ryuji, Eto Nahoko). *Gaiko Shogenroku: Okinawa Henkan, Nicchu Kokko Seijoka, Nichibei "Mitsuyaku"* (Diplomatic Testimony: J Okinawa Reversion, Japan-China Normalization of Relations, and the Japan-U.S. "Secret Agreements"), (Tokyo: Iwanami Shoten, 2010).

———. "Sengo Nihon Gaiko no Kiseki (Postwar Japanese Diplomacy's Achievements)," *Ajia Jiho*, No. 467 (February-June 2011).

Kusuda, Minoru. *Kusuda Minoru Nikki* (The Kusuda Minoru Diary), Tokyo: Chuo Koronsha, 2001.

Kuwae, Choko. *Tochi ga Aru, Ashita ga Aru* (When You Have Land, You Have a Tomorrow), Naha: Okinawa Times, 1991.

Maher, Kevin. *Ketsudan Dekinai Nihon* (The Japan That Can't Decide), Tokyo: Bungei Shunju, 2011.

Makino, Kiyoshi. "Senkaku Retto Kenkyu Kaiso (Remembering the Senkaku Islands Study Group)," in Yoshida Shien Tsuito Bunshu Kanko Iinkai Henshubu, ed., *Kaiso Yoshida Shien* (Remembering Yoshida Shien), Tokyo: Yoshida Shien Tsuito Bunshu Kanko Iinkai, 1990, 244–46.

Meyer, Armin H. *Assignment Tokyo: An Ambassador's Journal.* Indianapolis, IN: Bobbs-Merrill Company, Inc., 1974.

Meyer, Armin H. *Quiet Diplomacy: From Cairo to Tokyo in the Twilight of Imperialism*, New York: iUniverse, Inc., 2003.

Midorima, Sakae. "Senkaku Retto no Gakujutsu Chosa (A Scientific Survey of the Senkaku Islands)," *Nanto Bunka Kenkyusho Shoho*, No. 40 (February 8, 1996), 1.

Miyamatsu, Kyuzo. "Chugoku ga Okinawa o Heigo Suru Hi: Muteiko Heiwa Shugi no Tsuke ni Nayamu Nihon (The Day China Annexes Okinawa: Japan's Dilemma with the Foolishness of Pacificist Non-Resistence)," *Okinawa Yoron*, Vol. 6, No. 2 (Fall 2010), 8–14.

Miyazato, Matsusho. *Fukki Nijugonen no Kaiso* (Reflections on the 25 Years since Reversion), Naha: Okinawa Taimususha, 1998.

Mondale, Walter F. *The Good Fight: A Life in Liberal Politics*, New York: Scribner, 2010.

Mutsu, Munemitsu. *Kenkenroku: A Diplomatic Record of the Sino-Japanese War, 1894–1895.* Princeton, NJ: Princeton University Press, 1982.

Nakajima, Toshijiro. "Ending the Post-war Period," *Foreign Service Journal*, Vol. 69, No. 2 (May 1992), 27–29.

Nakajima, Toshijiro (edited by Inoue Masaya, Nakajima Takuma, and Hattori Ryuji). *Gaiko Shogenroku: Nichibei Anpo, Okinawa Henkan, Tenanmon Jiken* (Diplomatic Testimony: Japan-U.S. Security Treaty, the Okinawa Reversion, and the Tiananmen Incident), (Tokyo: Iwanami Shoten, 2012).

Nakamoto, Masakazu. "Senkaku Shoto ha Nihon no Ryodo: Uotsuri Jima to Seitenhaku Nikki (The Senkaku Islands are Japanese Territory: Uotsuri Island and the Taiwanese Flag)," *Ryukyu Shimpo*, November 6, 2010.

Nakasone, Yasuhiro. *The Making of the New Japan: Reclaiming the Political Mainstream*, Richmond: Curzon, 1999.

Nixon, Richard M. *The Memoirs of Richard M. Nixon*, New York: Grosset and Dunlap, 1978.

Noro, Kyoichi. *Akasaka Kyuchome Nanbanchi: Boei Seimu Jikan no Memo* (9–7 Akasaka: Memos of the Parliamentary Vice Minister of Defense), Tokyo: Nagata Shobo, 1972.

Ohama, Nobumoto. *Henkan Hishi: Watashi no Okinawa Sengoshi* (The Secret History of the Reversion: My Postwar History of Okinawa), Tokyo: Konshu no Nihon, 1971.

Okawara, Yoshio. *Oraru Hisutorii: Nichibei Gaiko* (Oral History: Japan-U.S. Diplomacy), Tokyo: The Japan Times, 2006.

Okuhara, Toshio. "Shuto na Jinzai Katsuyo to Surudoi Senkensei: Senkaku Retto Kenkyukai (Skillful Use of Personnel and Keen Foresight)," in Yoshida Shien Tsuito Bunshu Kanko Iinkai Henshubu, ed., *Kaiso Yoshida Shien* (Remembering Yoshida Shien), Tokyo: Yoshida Shien Tsuito Bunshu Kanko Iinkai, 1990, 242–44.

Omija, Tsunehisa. "Okinawa Kaitei Dai-yuden ha Waga Te no Naka ni Ari (Okinawa's Big Undersea Oil Fields Are in My Hands)," *Gendai*, Vol. 9, No. 3 (March 1975), 358–63.

Ota, Seisaku. *Hiun no Shima Okinawa: Fukki e no Uzu o Otte* (Okinawa, A Tragic Island: Looking for the Uzu in the Reversion), Tokyo: Nihon Kogyo Shimbunsha, 1987.

Ota, Shizuo. "Yaeyama after WWII," in Okinawa: The 50 Years of the Postwar Era Committee, ed., *Okinawa: The 50 Years of the Postwar Era*, (Naha: Okinawa Prefecture, 1995), 436–37.

Peterson, Peter G. *The Education of An American Dreamer: How a Son of Greek Immigrants Learned His Way From a Nebraska Diner to Washington, Wall Street, and Beyond*, New York: Twelve, 2009.

Rankin, Karl L. *China Assignment*, Seattle, WA: University of Washington Press, 1964.

Ryukyu, Shimposha ed. *Sengo Seiji o Ikite: Nishime Junji Nikki* (Living Postwar Politics: The Diaries of Nishime Junji), Naha: Ryukyu Shimposha, 1998.

Sakurai, Tsuyoshi. "Kokueki to ha Nanika: Senkaku Retto ni Yoseta Yoshida Senpai no Jonetsu (What is National Interest: The Passion Our Superior, Mr. Yoshida, Showed toward the Senkaku Islands)," in Yoshida Shien Tsuito Bunshu Kanko Iinkai Henshubu, ed., *Kaiso Yoshida Shien* (Remembering Yoshida Shien), Tokyo: Yoshida Shien Tsuito Bunshu Kanko Iinkai, 1990, 240–42.

——. *Okinawa Sokoku Fukki Monogatari* (The Story of the Reversion of Okinawa to the Homeland), Tokyo: Okurasho Insatsukyoku, 1999.

Sato, Eisaku. *Sato Eisaku Nikki* (The Diaries of Sato Eisaku), Tokyo: Asahi Shimbunsha, 1998.

Schmitz, Charles A. "Working Out the Details," *Foreign Service Journal*, Vol. 69, No. 2 (May 1992), 24–26.

Senkaku Retto Senji Sonan Shibotsu Ireino Kenritsu Jigyo Kiseikai, ed., *Chinmoku no Sakebi: Senkaku Retto Senji Sonan Jiken* (Screaming in Silence: The Senkaku Islands Wartime Shipwreck Incident), (Ishigaki City: Nanzansha, 2006).

Shen, James C.H. *The U.S. and Free China: How the U.S. Sold Out Its Ally*, Camarillo, CA: Acropolis Books, 1983.

Shimoda, Takezo. *Sengo Nihon Gaiko no Shogen: Nihon ha Koshite Saisei Shita* (A Testimony about Postwar Japanese Diplomacy: Japan Was Reborn in This Way), Tokyo: Gyosei Mondai Kenkyusho, 1984.

Stans, Maurice H. *One of the President's Men: Twenty Years with Eisenhower and Nixon*, Dulles, VA: Brassey's Inc., 1995.

Suetsugu, Ichiro. *Onko Soshin: Sengo ni Chosen Kokoro ni Nokoru Hitobito* (Reflecting on the Past, Building for the Future: People I have Known in the Postwar), Tokyo: Bungei Shunju, 2002.

――. *'Sengo' e no Chosen* (Challenging the Postwar), Tokyo: Ooru Shuppan, 1981.

Taira, Ryosho. *Taira Ryosho Kaikoroku: Kakushin Shisei 16 Nen* (The Memoirs Taira Ryosho: 16 Years of Reformist City Administration), Naha: Okinawa Taimususha, 1987.

Takaoka, Daisuke. "Senkaku Retto Shuhen Kaiiki no Gakujutsu Chosa ni Sanka Shite (Participating in the Academic Surveys in the Waters Around the Senkaku Islands)," *Kikan Okinawa*, No. 56 (March 1971), 42–64.

――. "Senkaku Retto Ittai no Shisatsu Hokoku Yoshi (A Summary Report of the Investigation Trip to the Senkaku Islands)," in Fukki Mondai Kenkyukai, ed. *Fukki Mondai Kenkyu*, Vol. 1 (Naha: Fukki Mondai Kenkyukai, 1968), 222–23.

Takase, Tamotsu. *Shuno Gaiko no Uchimaku* (Behind the Scenes of Leaders Diplomacy), Tokyo: Toyo Keizai Shimposha, 1991.

Tazumi, Tomokichiro and Moriguchi Katsu. "Mujinto ha Ikiteiru (The Uninhabited Islands are Alive)," *Ryukyu Shimpo*, May 19–26, 1963 (7 installments).

Tobaru, Yoei. *Yaeyama no Fukki Undoshi* (A History of the Yaeyama Reversion Movement), Ishigaki: Self-published, 1978.

Togo, Fumihiko. *Nichibei Gaiko Sanju Nen: Anpo, Okinawa to Sono Go* (30 Years of Japan-U.S. Diplomacy: The Security Treaty, Okinawa, and After), Tokyo: Sekai no Ugokisha, 1982.

Tokumatsu, Nobuo. "Ishigaki kara Miru Senkaku Mondai to Sono Kaiketsuho wo Kangaeru (The Senkaku Problem as Viewed from Ishigaki and Thinking about the Solution to the Problem)," *Okinawa Yoron*, Vol. 6, No. 2 (Fall 2010), 15–19.

Valeriani, Richard. *Travels with Henry*, New York: Berkley Books, 1979.

Walters, Vernon A. *Silent Missions*, Garden City, NY: Doubleday and Co., 1978.

Yamanaka, Sadanori. *Kaerimite Kuinashi: Watashino Rirekisho* (I Have No Regrets Looking Back: My Memoirs), Tokyo: Nihon Keizai Shimbunsha, 2002.

――. "Taidan Moto Okinawa Kaihatsucho Chokan Yamanaka Sadanori Okinawa o Ooi ni Kataru, 1 (Interview: Former Okinawa Development Agency Minister Yamanaka Sadanori Discusses Okinawa, 1)," *Okinawa Yoron*, No. 1 (November 1990), 50–66.

――. "Taidan Moto Okinawa Kaihatsucho Chokan Yamanaka Sadanori Okinawa o Ooi ni Kataru, 2 (Interview: Former Okinawa Development Agency Minister Yamanaka Sadanori Discusses Okinawa, 2)," *Okinawa Yoron*, No. 2 (March 1991), 58–72.

Yamano, Kokichi. *Okinawa Henkan Hitorigoto* (The Story of the Reversion of Okinawa), Tokyo: Gyosei, 1982.

Yara, Chobyo. *Yara Chobyo Kaikoroku* (The Memoirs of Yara Chobyo), Tokyo: Asahi Shimbunsha, 1977.

Yasukawa, Takeshi. *Wasureenu Omoide to Kore Kara no Nichibei Gaiko: Paaru Haabaa Kara Hanseiki* (Unforgettable Memories and Japan-U.S. Diplomacy from Now On: A Half-Century Since Pearl Harbor), Tokyo: Sekai no Ugokisha, 1991.

Yoshida, Shien. *Chiisana Tataki no Hibi: Okinawa Fukki no Urabanashi* (The Days of Many Small Struggles: Behind the Scenes of the Reversion of Okinawa), Tokyo: Bunkyo Shoji, 1976.

Secondary sources

Akamine, Mamoru. "Daiichiji Senkaku Retto Hozen Undo ni Tsuite (Regarding the First Movement to Preserve the Senkaku Islands)," *Nihon Toyo Bunka Ronshu*, No. 5 (March 1999), 1–26.

——. *Ryukyu Okoku: Higashi Ajia no Koonaasutoon* (The Ryukyu Kingdom: East Asia's Cornerstone), Tokyo: Kodansha, 2004.

Allen, Donald R. "The Legal Status of the Continental Shelf of the East China Sea," *Oregon Law Review*, Vol. 51 (1972), 586–605.

Amano, Tetsuo. "Kuroiwa Hisashi: Okinawa Shizenkai no Gakumonteki Kaitakusha (Kuroiwa Hisashi: The Academic Developer of Okinawa's Natural World)," *Shin Okinawa Bungaku*, No. 37 (December 1977), 83–94.

Arasato, Kinbuku and Oshiro Tatsuyuki. *Kindai Okinawa no Hitobito* (The People of Modern Okinawa), Tokyo: Taiheiyo Shuppansha, 1972.

Asano, Tatsuo. *Senkaku Shoto, Ryukyu, Chugoku: Nicchu Kokusai Kankeishi Bunseki, Shiryo, Bunken* (The Senkaku Islands, the Ryukyus, and China: The International Relations History of Japan and China by Analysis, Documents, and Previous Research), Tokyo: Sanwa Shoseki, 2002.

Austin, Greg. *China's Ocean Frontier: International Law, Military Force, and National Development*, Canberra: Allen and Unwin, 1998.

Babbin, Jed and Edward Timperlake. *Showdown: Why China Wants War with the United States*, Washington, DC: Regenery Publishing, C., 2006.

Blanchard, Jean-Marc F. "The U.S. Role in the Sino-Japanese Dispute over the Diaoyu (Senkaku) Islands, 1945–71," *China Quarterly*, No. 161 (March 2000), 95–123.

Boei Shisutemu Kenkyusho, ed. *Senkaku Shoto ga Abunai* (The Senkaku Islands are in Danger), Tokyo: Naigai Shuppansha, 2010.

Bradley, James. *The Imperial Cruise: A Secret History of Empire and War*, New York: Little, Brown, and Co., 2009.

Brzezinski, Zbigniew. *The Fragile Blossom: Crisis and Change in Japan*, New York: Harper and Row, 1972.

——. *The Grand Chessboard: American Primacy and Its Geostrategic Imperatives*, New York: Basic Books, 1997.

Burr, William. *The Kissinger Transcripts: The Top-Secret Talks with Beijing and Moscow*, New York: The New Press, 1998.

Bush, Richard C. *The Perils of Proximity: China-Japan Security Relations*, Washington, DC: The Brookings Institution, 2010.

Calder, Kent E. *Pacific Defense: Arms, Energy, and America's Future in Asia*, New York: William Morrow and Co., Inc., 1996.

Carpenter, Ted Galen. *America's Coming War with China: A Collision Course Over Taiwan*, New York: Palgrave MacMillan, 2005.

Cheung, Tai Ming, and Charles Smith, "Rocks of Contention," *Far Eastern Economic Review*, November 1, 1990, 19.

Chijiwa, Yasuaki. *Taishitachi no Sengo Nichibei Kankei: Sono Yakuwari o Meguru Hikaku Gaikoron, 1952–2008* (The Ambassadors' Postwar Japan-U.S. Relationship: A Comparative Foreign Policy Study of Their Roles, 1952–2008), Kyoto: Mineruva Shobo, 2012.

Copper, John F. *Taiwan: Nation-State or Province, 4th Edition*, Cambridge, MA: Westview Press, 2003.

——. "The Fishing Islands Controversy," *Asia Quarterly*, 1972–73, 217–27.

Deans, Phil. "Contending Nationalisms and the Diaoyutai/Senkaku Dispute," *Security Dialogue*, Vol. 31, No. 1 (March 2000), 119–31.

Destler, I.M., Haruhiro Fukui, Hideo Sato. *The Textile Wrangle: Conflict in Japanese-American Relations, 1969–1971*, Ithaca, NY: Cornell University Press, 1979.

Downs, Erica Strecker, and Phillip C. Saunders. "Legitimacy and the Limits of Nationalism: China and the Diaoyu Islands," *International Security*, Vol. 23, No. 3 (Winter 1998-/99), 114–46.

Dutton, Peter. "Carving Up the East China Sea," *Naval War College Review*, Vol. 60, No. 2 (Spring 2007), 49–72.

——. "Far Eastern Round-Up: A Summary of Events in Asia, March 22 to 27," *Far Eastern Economic Review*, April 1, 1972, 4.

Eldridge, Robert D. *The Origins of the Bilateral Okinawa Problem: Okinawa in Postwar U.S.-Japan Relations, 1945–1952*, New York: Routledge, 2001.

——. "'Mr. Okinawa': Ohama Nobumoto, the Reversion of Okinawa, and an Inner History of U.S.-Japan Relations," *Doshisha Amerika Kenkyu*, No. 39 (March 2003), 61–80.

——. *The Return of the Amami Islands: The Reversion Movement and U.S.-Japan Relations*, Lanhamm, MD: Lexington, 2007.

——. *Iwo Jima to Ogasawara o Meguru Nichibei Kankei* (Iwo Jima and the Ogasawara Islands in U.S.-Japan Relations), Kagoshima: Nanpo Shinsha, 2008.

——. "Option for Senkakus' Funds," *Japan Times*, November 18, 2012.

Fenby, Jonathan. *Chiang Kai-Shek: China's Generalissimo and the Nation He Lost*, New York: Carroll and Graf Publishers, 2004.

Fravel, M. Taylor. *Strong Borders, Secure Nation: Cooperation and Conflict in China's Territorial Disputes*, Princeton, NJ: Princeton University Press, 2008.

——. "Explaining Stability in the Senkaku (Diaoyu) Islands Dispute," in Gerald Curtis, Ryosei Kokubun, and Wang Jisi, eds., *Getting the Triangle Straight: Managing China-Japan-US Relations*, (Tokyo: Japan Center for International Exchange, 2010), 144–64.

Funabashi, Yoichi. *Alliance Adrift*, New York: Council on Foreign Relations Press, 1999.

Fung, Hu-hsiang. (nd) "Evidence Beyond Dispute: Tiayutai (Diaoyutai) is Chinese Territory!" (statement published on Internet).

Furukawa, Koji. "Bordering Japan: Towards a Comprehensive Perspective," *Journal of Borderlands Studies*, Vol. 26, No. 3 (2011), 297–314

Gibney, Frank. "The View from Japan," *Foreign Affairs*, Vol. 50, No. 10 (October 1971), 97–111.

Glosserman, Brad. "Fade to Gray," in McKinsey and Company, ed. *Reimagining Japan: The Quest for a Future that Works*, San Francisco, CA: Viz Media, 2011, 88–93.

Goddard, W.G. *Formosa: A Study in Chinese History*, London: Macmillan and Co., 1966.

Gorman, Zoe. "Kissinger Visits Yale to Donate Papers," *Yale Daily News*, August 31, 2011.

Gorsline, Donn S. and Rodolfo, Kelvin S. "Rock Stars: Kenneth Orris Emery (1914–98): Pioneer Marine Geologist," *Geological Society of America (GSA) Today*, Volume 13, No. 11 (November 2003), 18–19.

Green, Michael J. "The Forgotten Player," *The National Interest*, No. 60 (Summer 2000), 42–49.

———. *Japan's Reluctant Realism: Foreign Policy Challenges in an Era of Uncertain Power*, New York: Palgrave Macmillan, 2001.

Gries, Peter H. *China's New Nationalism: Pride, Politics, and Diplomacy*, Berkeley, CA: University of California Press, 2004.

Guntharp, Walter A. "United States Foreign Policy and the Reversion of Okinawa to Japan," Unpublished Ph.D. dissertation, George Washington University, 1972.

Hackett, Roger F. *Yamagata Aritomo in the Rise of Modern Japan, 1838–1922*, Cambridge, MA: Harvard University Press, 1971.

Hamagawa, Kyoko. "Senkaku Shoto no Ryoyu o Meguru Ronten: Nicchu Ryokoku no Kenkai o Chushin Ni (The Debate over Ownership of the Senkaku Islands, with a Focus on the Views of Japan and China)," *Chosa to Joho*, No. 565 (February 28, 2007).

Hanafusa, Nagamichi. "Okinawa Kizoku no Enkaku (An Overview of the Sovereignty of Okinawa)," *Kokusaiho Gaiko Zasshi,* Vol. 54, Nos. 1–3 (1955), 3–40.

Hara, Kimie. "Rethinking the 'Cold War' in the Asia-Pacific," *The Pacific Review*, Vol. 12, No. 4 (1999), 515–36.

———. "50 years from San Francisco: Re-examining the Peace Treaty and Japan's Territorial Problems," *Pacific Affairs*, Vol. 73, No. 4 (Fall 2001), 361–82.

———. "The Post-war Japanese Peace Treaties and China's Ocean Frontier Problems," *American Journal of Chinese Studies*, Vol. 11, No. 1 (April 2004), 1–24.

———. *San Furanshisuko Heiwa Joyaku no Moten: Ajia Taihei Chiiki no Reisen to "Sengo Mikaiketsu no Shomondai" o Kangeru* (Blind Spots of the San Francisco Peace Treaty: Re-thinking the Cold War in the Asia-Pacific Region and the "Unresolved Problems" since the Second World War), Hiroshima: Keisuisha, 2005.

———. "Cold War Frontiers in the Asia-Pacific: The Troubling Legacy of the San Francisco Treaty," *The Asia-Pacific Journal: Japan Focus*, 2006.

———. "The San Francisco Peace Treaty and Frontier Problems in the Regional Order in East Asia: A Sixty Year Perspective," *The Asia-Pacific Journal*, Vol. 10, Issue 17, No. 1.

———. *Cold War Frontiers in the Asia-Pacific: Divided Territories in the San Francisco System*, New York: Routledge, 2007.

Harada, Nobuo. *Senkaku Shoto: Sappo Ryukyu Shiroku o Yomu* (Senkaku Shoto: Reading the Records of the Ryukyu Tributary State), Ginowan, Okinawa: Gajumaru Shorin, 2006.

Harrison, Selig S. *China, Oil, and Asia: Conflict Ahead?* New York: Columbia University Press, 1977.

Harrison, Selig S., ed. *Seabed Petroleum in Northeast Asia: Conflict or Cooperation?* Washington, DC: Woodrow Wilson International Center for Scholars, 2005.

Hartzell, Richard W. "Understanding the San Francisco Peace Treaty's Disposition of Formosa and the Pescadores," *Harvard Asia Quarterly*, Fall 2004, 1–12.

Hickey, Dennis Van Vranken. *The Armies of East Asia: China, Taiwan, Japan, and the Koreas*, Boulder, CO: Lynne Rienner Publishers, 2001.

Hickman, Martin B. *David M. Kennedy: Banker, Statesman, Churchman*, Provo, UT: Brigham Young University, 1987.

Hirao, Koji. *Kaiyo Kaihatsu Sangyo* (Ocean Development Industry), Tokyo: Toyo Keizai Shinposha, 1970.

Hiyajo, Yasuharu. "Higashi Shinakai Tairikudana no Kyokai Kakutei: 'Nicchu Chukansen' Fukin no Kaitei Shigen Kaihatsu ni Kanren Shite (Delineating the Continental Shelf in the East China Sea and the Development of Nearby Seabed Resources)," *Okinawa Hogaku*, No. 35 (2006), 199–237.

Hoshino, Michihei. "Shigen (Resources)," *Asahi Shimbun*, February 14, 1971.

Hsiao, Russell. L.C. "In a Fortnight: Taiwan-Japan Rift over ADIZ," *China Brief: A Journal of Analysis and Information* (Jamestown Foundation), Vol. X, Issue 12 (June 11, 2010), 1–2.

Hsiung, James. *China and Japan At Odds: Deciphering the Perpetual Conflict*, Tokyo: Palgrave Macmillan, 2007.

Huth, Paul K. *Standing Your Ground: Territorial Disputes and International Conflict*, Ann Arbor, MI: University of Michigan, 1996.

Inabuchi, Shozo. "Senkaku Retto Meguru Senjin Arasoi: Hondo Fukki Mokuzen ni Shite, Taiwan, Chukyo, Kankoku mo Nanori (The Competition over the Senkaku Islands: Taiwan, China, and Korea are Throwing Their Names in the Hat on the Eve of Reversion to Japan)," *Zaikai*, February 15, 1971, 86–90.

Inoue, Kiyoshi. "Tiaoyu Retto (Senkaku Retto) nado wa Chugokuryo de Aru (The Tiaoyu (Senkaku and Other) Islands are Chinese Territory)," *Nicchu Bunka Koryu*, No. 177 (February 1972), 1–8.

——. "Tiaoyu Retto (Senkaku Retto nado) no Rekishi to Kizoku Mondai (The History and Problem of the Ownership of the Daioyu (Senkaku and Other) Islands)," *Rekishigaku Kenkyu*, No. 381 (February 1972), 1–8.

——. "Tiaoyu Retto (Senkaku Rettoto) no Rekishi to Sono Ryoyuken (Sairon) (The History and Problem of the Ownership of the Daioyu (Senkaku and Other) Islands, A Reexamination)," *Chugoku Kenkyu Geppo,* No. 292 (June 1972), 1–47.

——. *"Senkaku" Retto: Tiaoyu Shoto no Shiteki Kaimei* (The "Senkaku" Islands: A Historical Clarification of the Diaoyu Islands), Tokyo: Gendai Hyoronsha, 1972.

——. "The Tiaoyu Islands (Senkaku Islands) and Other Islands Are Chinas Territory," *Peking Review*, No. 19 (May 12, 1972), 18–22.

Inoue, Masaya. *Nicchu Kokko Seijoka no Seijishi* (The Political History of the Normalizationalization of Relations between Japan and China), Nagoya: Nagoya University Press, 2010.

Inoue, Kazuhiko. *Senkaku Buryoku Shototsu: Nicchu Moshi Takawabu* (Japan, China, and a Military Conflict in the Senkakus), Tokyo: Asuka Shinsha, 2012.

Ishihara, Shintaro. "Opinionu Amerika e no Fumie, 'Senkaku' (Opinion Force the U.S. to Take a Loyalty Test on the 'Senkakus'), *Sankei Shimbun*, November 5, 1996.

——. "Watashino Suki na Nihonjin: Kaya Okinori Kyoki na Riarisuto, Zenhen (Japanese People That I Like: Kaya Okinori, A Major Realist, Part 1)," *Puresidento*, No. 673 (June 30, 2008), 136–39.

Ishimine, Ashin. "Senkaku Retto Kaiyo Chosa Hokoku (A Report of the Maritime Survey of the Senkaku Islands)," *Ryuki Jiho*, No. 7 (May 30, 1963), 28–36.

Jahana, Atsushi. "Senkaku Shinpan Saizensen o Yuku (Going to the Frontlines of the Illegal Incursions on the Senkaku Islands)," *Joho to Shiryo*, No. 25 (June 1978), 44–57.

Ji, Guoxing. "The Diaoyudao (Senkaku) Disputes and Prospects for Settlement," *The Korean Journal of Defense Analysis*, Vol. 6, No. 2 (Winter 1994), 285–311.

Johnson, Chalmers. "How China and Japan See Each Other," *Foreign Affairs*, Vol. 50, No. 3 (July 1972), 711–21.

Kaneko, Hidetoshi. "Taiwan Kaikyo to Senkaku Oki no Nicchu Shototsu Jiken (The Japan-Chinese Crash Incident in the Taiwan Strait-Senkaku Waters)," *Ajia Jiho*, No. 463 (January-February 2011), 23–42.

Kaneshima, Kiyoshi. "Senkaku Retto no Suishitsu (Chemical Survey of Waters in the Senkaku Islands)," *Kogyo Yosui*, No. 128 (1969), 42–45.

Kendall, James R. "Deterrence by Presence to Effective Response: Japan's Shift Southward," *Orbis*, Vol. 54, No. 4 (Fall 2010), 603–14.

Kerr, George H. *Okinawa: The History of an Island People*, Boston, MA: Tuttle Publishing, 1958.

——. *Formosa Betrayed*, New York: Houghton Mifflin, 1965.

——. *Formosa: Licensed Revolution and the Home Rule Movement, 1895–1945*, Honolulu, HI: University of Hawaii Press, 1974.

Kim, Young Il. "Prospective Oil Fields on the Continental Shelf in Eastern Asia and Some Associated Political Problems," *Proceedings of the Association of American Geographers*, Vol. 3 (1971), 93–96.

Kissinger, Henry. *On China*, New York: The Penguin Press, 2011.

Kitaoka, Shinichi. "Koga Tatsushiro Shi no Eiyo (Mr. Koga Tatsushiro's Honoro)," *Okinawa Mainichi Shimbun*, December 25, 1909.

——. *Jiminto: Seikento no 38 Nen* (The Liberal Democratic Party: 38 Years as the Ruling Party), Tokyo: Yomiuri Shimbunsha, 1995.

Ko, Jishin. *Sho Kaiseki to Nihon: Tomo to Teki no Hazama de* (Chiang Kai-shek and Japan: Between Friend and Enemy), Tokyo: Takeda Random House Japan, 2011.

Kojima, Tomoyuki. "Nicchu Tairitsu o Arawani Shita Senkaku Shoto Mondai (The Senkaku Islands Problem that Highlighted the Japanese-Sino Tensions)," *Sekai*, No. 628 (November 1996), 257–61.

Kristof, Ladis K.D. "The Nature of Frontiers and Boundaries," *Annals of the Association of American Geographers*, Vol. 49, No. 3 (September 1959), 269–82.

Kristof, Nicholas D. "Look Out for the Diaoyu Islands," *Wall Street Journal* "On the Ground" blog entry, September 10, 2010 (http://kristof.blogs.nytimes.com/tag/senkaku-islands/).

Kristof, Nicholas D. "My Father's Gift to Me," *New York Times*, June 19, 2010.

Kristof, Nicholas D. and WuDunn, Sheryl. *Thunder from the East: Portrait of a Rising Asia*, New York: Alfred A. Knopf, 2000.

Kurlantzick, Joshua. *Charm Offensive: How China's Soft Power is Transforming the World*, New Haven, CT: Yale University Press, 2008.

Kuroiwa, Hisashi. "Senkaku Retto Tanken Kiji (An Article about Exploring the Senkaku Islands)," *Chigaku Zasshi*, Vol. 12, No. 9 (August 1900), 476–83.

——. "Senkaku Retto Tanken Kiji (An Article about Exploring the Senkaku Islands)," *Chigaku Zasshi*, Vol. 12, No. 10 (September 1900), 528–43.

——. "Raleigh Rock," *Chigaku Zasshi*, Vol. 12, No. 10 (September 1900), 560–61.

LaLonde, Suzanne. *Determining Boundaries in a Conflicted World: The Role of Uti Possidetis*, Montreal: McGill-Queen's University Press, 2002.

Lee, Peter. "High Stakes Gamble as Japan, China and the U.S. Spar in the East and South China Seas," *The Asia-Pacific Journal*, Vol. 1, No. 43 (October 25, 2010).

Lee, Seokwoo. "Territorial Disputes Among Japan, China and Taiwan concerning the Senkaku Islands," Study in series edited by Shelagh Furness and Clive Schofield, International Boundaries Research Unit, Department of Geography, University of Durham, United Kingdom, 2002.

Li, Victor H. "China and Off-Shore Oil: The Taio-yu Tai Dispute," *Stanford Journal of International Studies*, Vol. 10 (Spring 1975), 142–62.

Lohmeyer, Martin. "The Diaoyu / Senkaku Islands Dispute Questions of Sovereignty and Suggestions for Resolving the Dispute," Unpublished master's thesis, Faculty of Law, University of Canterbury, New Zealand, 2008.

Ma, Ying-jeou. "Disputes over Oily Waters: A Case Study of Continental Shelf Problems and Problems and Foreign Oil Investments in the East China Sea and Taiwan Strait," Unpublished doctoral dissertation, Harvard University, 1981.

MacMillan, Margaret. *Nixon and Mao: The Week that Changed the World*, New York: Random House, 2007.

Magosaki, Ukeru. *Nihon no Kokkyo Mondai: Senkaku, Takeshima, Hoppo Ryodo* (Japan's Borders Problem), Tokyo: Chikuma Shinsho, 2011.

Makino, Kiyoshi. "Igunkuba Jima Shoshi (A Short History of the Senkaku Islands)," *Kikan Okinawa*, No. 56 (March 1971), 65–78.

——. *Shin Yaeyama Rekishi* (A New History of Yaeyama), Kumamoto: Shirono Insatsusho, 1972.

——. *Tonoshiroson no Rekishi to Minzoku* (The History and People of Tonoshiro Village), Kumamoto: Shirono Insastsusho, 1975.

Makise, Tsuneji. *Okinawa Sandai Senkyo: 1970 Nen Mondai to Okinawa* (The Three Big Elections in Okinawa: The 1970 Problem and Okinawa), Tokyo: Rodo Junposha, 1969.

Manthorpe, Jonathan. *Forbidden Nation: A History of Taiwan*, New York: Palgrave MacMillan, 2005.

Marcot, Neal A. "The Japanese Foreign Policymaking Process: A Case Study—Okinawa Reversion," Unpublished Ph.D. dissertation, Georgetown University, 1981.

Martin, Richard G. "The Okinawa Factor in U.S.-Japan Post World War II Relations," Unpublished Ph.D. dissertation, University of George, 1982.

Matsui, Yoshiro. "International Law of Territorial Acquisition and the Dispute over the Senkaku (Diaoyu) Islands," *Japanese Annual of International Law*, No. 40 (1997), 3–31.

Matsuda, Yoshitaka. *Taiwan Sokai: 'Ryukyu Nanmin' no Ichinen Juikkagetsu* (Evacuation to Taiwan: The One Year and Eleven Months of the 'Ryukyu Refugees'), Ishigaki City: Nanzansha, 2010.

Matsumoto, Kenichi. "Chugoku ni Nani ga Okotte Iru no Ka? Senkaku Mondai ga Rotei Shita Mono (What is Happening in China? What the Senkakus Problem has Exposed)," *Gaiko*, No. 4 (December 2010), 25–33.

McCormack, Gavan. "Small Islands, Big Problem: Senkaku/Diaoyu and the Weight of History and Geography in China-Japan Relations," *The Asia-Pacific Journal*, Vol. 9, No. 1 (January 3, 2011).

McCune, Shannon. "The Senkaku Islands," *Ryukyu Islands Project: Research and Information Papers*, No. 11 (January 30, 1972).

——. *The Ryukyu Islands*, Harrisburg, PA: Stockpole Books, 1975.

Megumi, Ryunosuke. *Dare mo Katarenakatta Okinawa no Shinjitsu: Shin Okinawa Nooto* (Facts about Okinawa No One Has Spoken About: New Okinawa Notes), Tokyo: Wac, 2011.

Megumi, Tadahisa. *Senkaku Shoto, Uotsuri Jima Shashinshu Shiryoshu* (A Collection of Photographs and Documents about Uotsuri Jima in the Senkaku Islands), Naha: Senkaku Shoto Boei Kyokai, 1996.

Midorima, Sakae. "Senkaku Retto no Rekishi to Hoteki Chii, 1 (The History and Legal Status of the Senkaku Islands, Part 1)," *Okinawa Hogaku*, No. 5 (1977), 17–60.

——. "Senkaku Retto no Rekishi to Hoteki Chii, 2 (The History and Legal Status of the Senkaku Islands, Part 2)," *Okinawa Hogaku*, No. 6 (1978), 27–67.

——"Senkaku Retto no Rekishi to Hori (The History and Legal Status of the Senkaku Islands)," *Joho to Shiryo*, No. 24 (May 1978), 28–35.

——. "Senkaku Retto Shuhen Kaiiki no Kaihatsu to Hori (The Development and Legal Status of the Sea Areas around the Senkaku Islands)," *Okinawa Hogaku*, No. 8 (1980), 23–83.

——. "200 Kairi Gyogyo Suiki (Two-hundred Nautical Miles Fishing Area)," *Okinawa Hogaku*, No. 10 (1982), 97–137.

——. "Okinawa Henkan Koshoshi (A History of the Reversion of Okinawa)," *Nanto Bunka*, No. 5 (1983), 1–26.

——. *Senkaku Retto* (Senkaku Islands), Naha: Hirugisha, 1984.

——. "Haitateki Keizai Suiiki Gainen (The Exclusive Economic Zone Concept)," *Okinawa Hogaku*, No. 12 (1984), 71–113.

——. *Kaiyo Kaiiki Kaihatsu to Kokusaiho* (The Development of Sea Areas and International Law), Tokyo: Kindai Bungeisha, pubdate>1995.

——. "Kaiyoho no Rekishi to Tenbo: Wagakuni o Meguru Konnichiteki Mondai (The History of Maritime Law and its Future Prospects: Today's Problems Surrounding Our Country)," *Okinawa Hogaku*, No. 30 (2001), 151–81.

Miyajima, Mikinosuke. "Okinawa Kenka Mujinjima Tankendan (A Discussion about the Uninhabited Islands under Okinawa Prefecture's Control)," *Chigaku Zasshi*, Vol. 12, No. 10 (October 1900), 585–96.

——. "Kobisho (Kuba Island), 1" *Chigaku Zasshi*, Vol. 12, No. 11 (November 1900), 647–52.

——. "Kobisho (Kuba Island), 2" *Chigaku Zasshi*, Vol. 12, No. 12 (December 1900), 689–700.

——. "Kobisho (Kuba Island), 3" *Chigaku Zasshi*, Vol. 13, No. 1 (January 1901), 12–18.

——. "Kobisho (Kuba Island), 4" *Chigaku Zasshi*, Vol. 13, No. 2 (February 1902), 79–93.

Miyazaki, Masahiro. *Chugoku ga Takuramu Taiwan Okinawa Shinko to Nihon Shihai* (China's Plot to Invade Taiwan and Okinawa and to Control Japan), Tokyo: KK Besutoseraazu, 2008.

Mochidome, Soichiro. "Maritime Delimitation: The Historical Development of States' Territorial Jurisdictions and Its Legal Effect in the Asian Seas," *The Transactions of the Asiatic Society of Japan*, Fifth Series, Vol. 3 (2011), 133–41.

Momose, Takashi, and Ito, Takashi. *Shiryo Kensho: Nihon no Ryodo* (Examining the Documents on Japan's Territory), Tokyo: Kawade Shobo Shinsha, 2010.

Muller, Christian. "Senkaku or Tiao Yu Tai?" *Swiss Review of World Affairs*, Vol. 24, No. 11 (February 1975), 7–10.

Murata, Tadayoshi. *Senkaku Retto Uotsuri Jima Mondai o Do Miru Ka: Tamesareru 21 Seiki ni Ikiru Wareware no Eichi* (How Should the Senkaku Islands and Uotsuri Island Problem be Viewed? Testing Our Knowledge in the 21st Century), Kawaguchi, Saitama: Nihon Kyohosha, 2004.

Nakama, Hitoshi. *Kiki Semaru Senkaku Shoto no Genjo* (The Dangerous Situation Today Facing the Senkaku Islands), Tokyo: Adobansu Kikaku, 2002.

Nakamura, Hideki. *Senkaku Shoto Oki Kaisen: Jieitai wa Chugokugun to Kono Yo ni Tatakau* (The Sea Battle Off the Senkaku Islands: This is How the Self-Defense Forces Will Fight the Chinese Military), Tokyo: Kojinsha, 2011.

Nakanomyo, Masaaki. *Senkaku, Takeshima, Hoppo Yonto: Gekido Suru Nihon Shuhen no Umi* (The Senkaku Islands, Takeshima, and the Four Northern Islands: The Rapidly Changing Seas Around Japan), Tokyo: Nanundo, 2011.

Nakayama, Yoshitaka. *Chugoku ga Mimi o Fusagu: Senkaku Shoto no Futsugo na Shinjitsu* (The Inconvenient Truth about the Senkaku Islands that China Does Not Want to Hear), Tokyo: Wani Bukkusu, 2012.

———. "Namidakai Senkaku Retto o Yuku (Going to the Senkaku Islands, with Their High Waves)," *Mainichi Gurafu*, Vol. 23, No. 46 (October 25, 1970), 3–22.

Nanpo, Doho E. ed. "Tokushu Senkaku Retto (Special Issue for Senkaku Islands)," *Kikan Okinawa* (Quarterly Okinawa), No. 56 (March 1971).

———, "Tokushu Senkaku Retto Dainishu (Second Special Issue for Senkaku Islands)," *Kikan Okinawa* (Quarterly Okinawa), No. 63 (December 1972).

Newsham, Grant F. "U.S. Must Clearly Back Japan in Islands Dispute with China," *Christian Science Monitor*, October 25, 2012.

———"Nicchukan ni Arata na Nanmon: 'Senkaku Retto' no Zenyo (A New Problem in Japan-China Relations: 'The Senkaku Islands' in Full)," *Toyo Keizai*, July 26, 1971, 42–45.

Niiro, Yoshima. "Senkaku Retto no Shokusei (Vegetation of the Senkaku Islands)," *Ryukyu Daigaku Bunrigakubu Kiyo* (Bulletin of the Arts and Science Division of the University of the Ryukyus), No. 7 (May 1964), 71–93.

Niksch, Larry A. "Senkaku (Diaouyu) Island Dispute: The U.S. Legal Relationship and Obligations," *PACNET*, No. 45, Pacific Forum CSIS, November 8, 1996.

Nishi, Takayuki. "The Diaoyu/Senkaku Islands: A Japanese Scholar Responds," *Wall Street Journal* "On the Ground" blog entry, October 4, 2012 (http://kristof.blogs. nytimes.com/2012/10/04/the-diaoyusenkaku-islands-a-japanese-scholar-responds/).

Nishimuta, Yasushi. "Nihonjin ga Joriku Dekinai Nihon no Ryodo to ha (What is the Japanese Territory That Japanese People Are Not Allowed to Land On)?" *Chuo Koron*, Vol. 122, No. 6 (June 2007), 108–19.

Nishio, Kanji. and Naoto, Aoki. *Senkaku Senso: Beichu Hasami Uchi ni Atta Nihon* (The Senkaku War: Japan Caught in the Crossfire), Tokyo Shodensha Shinsho, 2010.

Oishi, Eiji. *Senkaku Soshitsu* (Losing the Senkakus), Tokyo: Chuo Koron Shinsha, 2012

Okinawa Daihyaka Jiten Kanko Jimukyoku, ed. *Okinawa Daihyakka Jiten Jokan* (Okinawa Encyclopedia, Vol. 1), Naha: Okinawa Times, 1983.

Okuhara, Toshio. "Senkaku Retto (The Senkaku Islands)," *Okinawa Taimusu*, September 2–9, 1970.

———. "Senkaku Retto no Hoteki Chii (The Legal Status of the Senkaku Islands)," *Kikan Okinawa*, No. 52 (March 1970), 1–12.

———. "Senkaku Retto: Rekishi to Seiji no Aida (The Senkaku Islands, Between History and Politics)," *Nihon Oyobi Nihonjin,* January 1970, 54–63.

———. "Senkaku Retto: Sono Hoteki Chii (The Senkaku Islands: Their Legal Status)," *Okinawa Taimusu*, September 2–9, 1970.

———. "Senkaku Retto no Ryoyuken to 'Meiho' Ronbun (Ownership of the Senkaku Islands and the "Ming Pao" Article)," *Chugoku*, No. 91 (June 1971), 38–48.

——. "Senkaku Retto Ryoyuken no Hori: Nichi-Chu-Tai no Shucho no Konkyo to Tairitsuten (The Legal Status of the Ownership of the Senkaku Islands: The Respective Positions and Points of Contention between Japan, China, and Taiwan)," *Nihon Oyobi Nihonjin*, Spring 1972, 98–105.

——. "Senkaku Retto Ryoyu no Enkaku to Ronkyo (An Overview of the Basis of the Territorial Rights over the Senkaku Islands)," *Nihon Seiji Bunka Kenkyusho Seiji Shiryo*, No. 103 (1972).

——. "Senkaku Retto to Ryoyuken Mondai (The Senkaku Islands and the Territorial Problem)," *Sandei Okinawa*, 1–54 (July 8, 1972-August 4, 1973).

——. "Senkaku Retto to Ryodoken Kizoku Mondai (The Senkaku Islands and the Problem of Territorial Ownership)," *Asahi Ajia Rebyuu*, No. 10 (Summer 1972), 18–25.

——. "Senkaku Retto Mondai to Inoue Kiyoshi Ronbun (The Senkaku Islands Problem and the Writings by Inoue Kiyoshi)," *Ajia Rebyuu*, No. 13 (Spring 1973), 88–92.

——. "Ugokanu Senkaku Retto no Ryoyuken: Inoue Kiyoshi Ronbun no 'Rekishiteki Kyoko' o Abaku (The Unmoving Issue of the Ownership of the Senkaku Islands: Clarifying the Historical Falsehoods in the Article by Inoue Kiyoshi)," *Nihon Oyobi Nihonjin*, No. 13 (Spring 1973), 65–75.

——. "Senkaku Retto no Ryodo Hennyu Keii (The Details of the Senkaku Islands Becoming a Part of Japan)," *Seikei Gakkaishi*, No. 4 (February 1975), 7–47.

——. "Senkaku Retto Ryoyuken no Konkyo (The Basis for the Territorial Rights to the Senkaku Islands)," *Chuo Koron*, Vol. 93, No. 7 (July 1978), 66–76.

——. "Senkaku Retto no Ryoyuken (The Territorial Rights to the Senkaku Islands)," in Kasaya Susumu, ed. *Gendai no Horitsu Mondai: Toki no Ho o Saguru* (Modern Legal Problems: Exploring Then Laws), Tokyo: Hogaku Shoin, 1979.

——. "Senkaku Retto to Nihon Ryoyuken (The Senkaku Islands and Japan's Territorial Rights: A Historical Look at the [Islands'] Becoming a Part of Japan)," *Sekai to Nihon*, No. 234 (April 15, 1979), 9–56.

Okuma, Shinji. "Zappo Taiwan no Hokuto ni Isuru Koritto (Various News: The Small Isolated Islands Located to the Northeast of Taiwan)," *Chigaku Zasshi*, Vol. 11, No. 10 (October 1900), 722–23.

Omija, Koju. *Senkaku Yuden no Kaihatsu to Shinso: Sono Futatsu no Sokumen* (The Development of the Senkaku Oil Fields and the Truth: Those Two Aspects), Self-published report, May 15, 1970.

——. *Shuisho: Senkaku Yuden ni Tsuite no Shinso o Akkirakani Shi, Shikisha no Minasama no Gorikai to Gokyoryoku o Uttaeru* (), Self-published report, July 1970.

Oshiro, Masataka ed. *Kuroiwa Hisashi Sensei Kensho Kinenshi* (Commemoration Publication of the Unveiling of Mr. Kuroiwa Hisashi's Statue), Nago: Kuroiwa Hisashi Sensei Koseki Kenshokai, 1969.

Ota, Masakatsu. *Nichibei "Kakumitsuyaku" no Zenyo* (Everything About the Japan-U.S. Secret Nuclear Agreements), Tokyo: Chikuma Sensho, 2011.

Ozaki, Shigeyoshi, "Senkaku Shoto no Kizoku ni Tsuite, Jo (Territorial Sovereignty of the Senkaku Islands, No. 1)," *Referensu* (Reference), No. 259 (August 1972), 30–48.

——, "Senkaku Shoto no Kizoku ni Tsuite, Jo (Territorial Sovereignty of the Senkaku Islands, No. 2)," *Referensu* (Reference), No. 261 (October 1972), 28–60.

——, "Senkaku Shoto no Kizoku ni Tsuite, Jo (Territorial Sovereignty of the Senkaku Islands, No. 3)," *Referensu* (Reference), No. 262 (November 1972), 58–67.

——, "Senkaku Shoto no Kizoku ni Tsuite, Jo (Territorial Sovereignty of the Senkaku Islands, No. 4)," *Referensu* (Reference), No. 263 (December 1972), 152–73.

Paal, Douglas H. "China and the East Asian Security Environment: Complementarity and Competition," in Ezra F. Vogel, ed. *Living with China: U.S.-China Relations in the Twenty-first Century*, New York: W. W. Norton and Company, 1997.

Pace, Vincent A. "The U.S.-Japan Security Alliance and the PRC: The Abandonment-Entrapment Dynamic, the Balance of Threat and National Identity in the Trilateral Relationship," Enosinian Honors Senior Thesis Program, Elliott School of International Affairs, George Washington University, May 3, 2003.

Paine, S.C.M. *The Sino-Japanese War of 1894–1895: Perceptions, Power, and Primacy*, Cambridge: Cambridge University Press, 2003.

Park, Choon-Ho. "Professor Niino's Report on Submarine Geology near Senkaku Islands," *Japan Petroleum Weekly*, September 29, 1969, 2.

——. "Continental Shelf Issues in the Yellow Sea and East China Sea," *Law of the Sea Institute, University of Rhode Island Occasional Paper No. 15* (1972).

——. "Oil Under Troubled Waters: The Northeast Asia Sea-Bed Oil Controversy," *Harvard International Law Journal*, Vol. 14, No. 2 (Spring 1993), 212–60.

Ramos-Mrosovsky, Carlos. "International Law's Unhelpful Role in the Senkaku Islands," *University of Pennsylvania Journal of International Law*, Vol. 29, No. 4 (2008), 903–46.

Reagan, Michael. *The New Reagan Revolution: How Ronald Reagan's Principles Can Restore America's Greatness*, New York: St. Martin's Press, 2010.

Richardson, Michael. "Ryukyu Gunto ni Okeru Kogashi no Koseki (Mr. Koga's Accomplishments in the Ryukyu Islands)," *Okinawa Mainichi Shimbun*, January 1–9, 1910.

——. "Will Intimidation Win China the Yellow Sea?" *Japan Times*, August 26, 2010.

Sado, Akihiro. "Nihon no Boei Taisei ha Ryodo Yuji ni Kino Suru Ka (Will Japan's Defense Establishment Be Able to Respond in a Territorial Crisis?)," *Chuo Koron*, Vol. 127, No. 15 (November 2012), 118–26.

Sakaiya, Taichi. *The Knowledge-Value Revolution or a History of the Future*, Tokyo: Kodansha International, 1991.

Sanger, David E. "What Went Wrong—and How Japan Can Get it Right," in McKinsey and Company, ed. *Reimagining Japan: The Quest for a Future that Works*, San Francisco, CA: Viz Media, 2011, 74–81.

Sarantakes, Nicholas E. *Keystone: The American Occupation of Okinawa and U.S.-Japan Relations*, College Station, TX: Texas A & M University, 2001.

Sasajima, Masahiko. "Senkaku Joriku Jiken ni Miru Chugoku Nashonarizumu Seiji no Shuho" (The Method of Chinese Nationalist Politics as Seen in the Landing on the Senkakus Incident), *Chuo Koron*, Vol. 119, No. 6 (June 2004), 100–107.

Sasamori, Gisuke. *Nanto Tanken* (Southern Islands Exploration), Hirosaki: private publisher, 1894.

Seigal, Albert. "Senkaku Retto: 'Sekaiteki Daiyuden' o Meguru Nichi-Kan-Tai-Chu-Bei (Senkaku Islands: 'The World's Largest Oil Field' and Japan, Korea, Taiwan, China, and the U.S.)," *Toyo Keizai*, September 5, 1970.

——. "Senkaku Retto no Kaitei Daiyuden o Nerau Nichiryubeitai (The Large Seabed Oil Reserves near the Senkaku Islands Sought by Japan, Okinawa, the U.S., and Taiwan)," *Shukan Asahi*? 1971, 135–38.

——. "United States Policy toward Okinawa, 1945–52: A Study in Organizational Interaction in Policy-making," Unpublishied Ph.D. dissertation, West Virginia University, 1978.

Senkaku Shoto Boei Kyokai, ed. *Senkaku Shoto Uotsuri Jima: Shashin-Shiryohen* (Uotsuri Jima, Senkaku Islands: Collection of Photos and Documents), Naha: Senkaku Shoto Boei Kyokai, 1996.

Senkaku Shoto Bunken Shiryo Hensankai, ed. "Senkaku Shoto Mondai Shiryoshu (Collection of Documents Relating to the Senkaku Islands Problem)," *Asahi Ajia Rebyuu*, Vol. 3, No. 2 (1972), 41–42.

——. *Senkaku Kenkyu: Takara Gakujutsu Chosadan Shiryoshu* (Research on the Senkaku Islands: The Papers of the Takara Scientific Investigation Group), Naha: Deetum Rekiosu, 2007.

Serita, Kentaro. *Nihon no Ryodo* (Japan's Territory), Tokyo: Chuo Koron Shinsha, 2002.

Shapiro, Robert J. *Futurecast: How Superpowers, Populations, and Globalization Will Change the Way You Live and Work*, New York: St. Martin's Press, 2008.

Shaw, Han-yi. "The Diaoyutai/Senkaku Islands Dispute: Its History and Analysis of the Ownership Claims of the P.R.C., R.O.C., and Japan," *Occasional Papers/Reprint Series in Contemporary Asian Studies*, University of Maryland School of Law, March 1999.

Shaw, Han-yi. "The Inconvenient Truth behind the Diaoyu/Senkaku Islands," on Nicholas D. Kristof blog, *On the Ground*. Available at: http://kristof.blogs.nytimes.com/2012/09/19/the-inconvenient-truth-behind-the-diaoyusenkaku-islands/

Shimada, Yoichi. "Senkaku to Nichibei Kankei (Senkakus and Japan-U.S. Relations)," *Shin Nihongaku*, No. 19 (Winter 2011), 11–15.

Shinzato, Keiichi. "Senkaku Retto no Yuden Kaihatsu ni Tsuite (On the Development of the Oil Fields in the Senkaku Islands)," self-published pamphlet, September 1970.

Shu, Kenei. "Senkaku Mondai ga Utsusu Chugoku no Ronri to Honne (The Logic and Truth Behind China's Position as Seen in the Senkaku Problem)," *Gaiko*, No. 4 (December 2010), 53–61.

Stevenson, John R., and Oxman, Bernard H. "The Preparations for the Law of the Sea Conference," *The American Journal of International Law*, Vol. 68, No. 1 (January 1974), 1–32.

Su, Steven W. "The Tiaoyu Islands and Their Possible Effect on the Maritime Boundary Delimitation between China and Japan," *Chinese Journal of International Law*, 1997

Suganuma, Unryu. *Sovereign Rights and Territorial Space in Sino-Japanese Relations: Irredentism and the Diaoyu/Senkaku Islands*, Honolulu, HI: University of Hawaii Press, 2000.

Taira, Koji. "The China-Japan Clash Over the Diaoyu/Senkaku Islands," *The Ryukyuanist*, Spring 2004.

Taiwan Law Society and Taiwan Institute of International Law, *Proceedings of the International Law Conference on the Dispute over Diaoyu/Senkaku Islands*, April 1997.

Takahashi, Shogoro. "Iwayuru Senkaku Retto wa Nihon no Mono Ka (Are the Senkaku Islands Japan's?)," *Asahi Ajia Rebyuu*, No. 10 (Summer 1972), 26–31.

——. *Senkaku Retto Nooto* (Notes on the Senkaku Islands), Tokyo: Seinen Shuppansha, 1979.

Takara, Tatsuo. "Senkaku Retto no Dobutsuso ni Tsuite (Fauna of the Senkaku Islands, Ryukyus)," *Ryukyu Daigaku Nogakubu Gakujutsu Hokoku*, No. 1 (April 1954), 57–74.

Takara, Tetsuo. "Senkaku no Ahodori o Saguru (Looking for the Albatross on the Senkaku Islands)," *Minami to Kita*, No. 26 (March 1964).

——. "Senkaku Retto no Umidori ni Tsuite (Sea-fowls of the Senkaku Islands, Ryukyus)," *Ryukyu Daigaku Nogakubu Gakujutsu Hokoku*, No. 16 (October 1969), 1–12.

Tamogami, Toshi ed. *Tamogami Toshio no Jieitai Vs. Chugokugun: Jieitai ha Chugo-kugun to Ko Tataku* (Tamogami Toshi's Discussion of the Self-Defense Forces Versus the Chinese Military: This is How the SDF Would Fight the Chinese Military), Tokyo: Takarajimasha, 2012.

Tanaka, Sakai. "Rekindling China-Japan Conflict: The Senkaku/Diaoyutai Islands Clash," *The Asia-Pacific Journal*, Vol. 39, No. 3 (September 27, 2010).

Tawada, Shinjun. "Senkaku Retto no Shokubutsuso ni Tsuite (Flora of the Senkaku Islands, Ryukyus)," *Ryukyu Daigaku Nogakubu Gakujutsu Hokoku*, No. 1 (April 1954), 75–89.

Taylor, Jay. *The Generalissimo's Son: Chiang Ching-kuo and the Revolutions in China and Taiwan*, Cambridge, MA: Harvard University Press, 2000.

——. *The Generalissimo: Chiang Kai-shek and the Struggle for Modern China*, Cambridge, MA: Belknap Press, 2011.

Teng, S.Y., and Fairbank, John K. "On the Ch'ng Tributary System," *Harvard Journal for Asiatic Studies*, Vol. 6, No. 2 (June 1941), 506–10.

Teruya, Kenkichi. "Senkaku Shoto no Rekishiteki Keika to Genjo (The Historical Path of the Senkaku Islands and the Situation Today)," in Shimojo Masao, et al., eds. *Shitte Imasuka, Nihon no Shima* (Do You Know Japan's Islands?), Tokyo: Jiyu Kokuminsha, 2002, 43–70.

Tobaru, Yoei. *Sengo no Yaeyama Rekishi* (The History of Postwar Yaeyama), Ishigaki: Tobaru Yoei, 1986.

Tokyo Foundation. "Japan's Security Strategy toward China: Integration, Balancing, and Deterrence in the Era of Power Shift," *The Tokyo Foundation Policy Proposal*, October 2011.

Toyama, Masaki. *Seiji no Butaiura: Okinawa Sengoshi, Seito Seijihen* (Behind the Scenes in Politics: Political Parties and Politics in Postwar Okinawa History), Ginowan: Okinawa Aki Shobo, 1987.

Toyoshita, Narahiko. "'Senkaku Mondai' to Anpo Joyaku (The Senkakus Issue and the Japan-U.S. Security Treaty)," *Sekai*, No. 812 (January 2011), 37–48.

Tucker, Nancy Bernkopf ed. *China Confidential: American Diplomats and Sino-American Relations, 1945–1996* (New York: Columbia University Press, 2001).

Tucker, Nancy Bernkopf. *Strait Talk: United States-Taiwan Relations and the Crisis with China*, Cambridge, MA: Harvard University Press, 2009.

Ueji, Tatsunori. *Senkaku Retto to Takeshima: Chugoku, Kankoku to no Ryodo Mondai* (The Senkakus and Takeshima: Territorial Problems with China and Korea), Tokyo: Kyoikusha, 1978.

Valencia, Mark J. "Foreign Military Activities in Asian EEZs: Conflict Ahead?" *NBR Special Report #27* (May 2011).

——. "The East China Sea Dispute: Context, Claims, Issues, and Possible Solutions," *Asian Perspective*, Vol. 31, No. 1 (2007), 127–67.

Vogel, Ezra F. ed. *Living with China: U.S.-China Relations in the Twenty-first Century*, New York: W. W. Norton and Company, 1997.

Wada, Haruki. "Resolving the China-Japan Conflict Over the Senkaku/Diaoyu Islands," *The Asia-Pacific Journal*, Vol 43, No. 3 (October 25, 2010).

Wani, Yukio. "Fumo na Senkaku Nashonarizumu: Kurihara Ke ga Daeru 25 Okuen no 'Fusai' Taiwan-Hong Kong 'Hotsu Undo' to Senkaku Jinushi no Ryodo Bijinesu," *Shukan Kinyobi*, No. 896 (May 25, 2012), translated by John Junkerman as "Barren Senkaku Nationalism and China-Japan Conflict," *The Asia-Pacific Journal*, Vol. 10, Issue 28, No. 4 (July 9, 2012).

Watanabe, Toshio. "Chugoku to Do Mukiau Ka (How to Face China)," *Ajia Jiho*, No. 476 (May 2012), 74–86.

Welfield, John. *An Empire in Eclipse: Japan in the Postwar American Alliance System*, London: The Athlone Press, 1988.

Winchester, Simon. *Pacific Rising: The Emergence of a New World Culture*, New York: Prentice Hall Press, 1991.

Yamada, Yoshihiko. *Nihon no Kokkyo* (Japan's Borders), Tokyo: Shinchosha, 2005.

Yamaguchi, Akikazu. "Briefing Memorandum: Local Defense Obligations after the Reversion of Okinawa," *The National Institute for Defense Studies News*, No. 151 (February 2011), 1–6.

Yamamoto, Tsuyoshi. "Senkaku no Nicchu Kindaishi (Modern Japanese-Sino History Surrounding the Senkaku Islands)," *Sekai*, No. 629 (December 1996), 257–62.

Yamamoto, Koichi. *Nihonjin ga Ikenai "Nihon Ryodo": Hoppo Ryodo, Takeshima, Senkaku Shoto, Minami Tori Jima, Okino Tori Jima Jorikuki* ("Japanese Territory" that Japanese Can Not Go To: Accounts of Landing on the Northern Territories, Takeshima, Senkaku Islands, Minami Tori Jima and Okino Tori Jima), Tokyo: Shogakukan, 2007.

Yamazaki, Minoru. "Ningen Kaya Okinori: Chugoku Mondai ni Tsuite (Kaya Okinori, the Person: His Views on the China Problem)," *Karento*, Vol. 145, No. 12 (December 2002), 68–72.

Yokoyama, Matajiro. "Zatsuroku Nanto Tsushin (Various Records: Correspondence over the Southern Islands)," *Chigaku Zasshi*, Vol. 12, No. 4 (April 1900), 221–24.

Yoshiwara, Shigeyasu. "Ryukyu Mujinto no Chiri (The Geography of the Uninhabited Islands of the Ryukyus)," *Chigaku Zasshi*, Vol. 12, No. 8 (August 1900), 528–43.

Yoshihara, Toshi, and Holmes, James R. *Red Star over the Pacific: China's Rise and the Challenge to U.S. Maritime Strategy*. Annapolis: Naval Institute Press, 2010.

Yu, Peter Kien-hong. "Solving and Resolving the East China Sea Dispute: Beijing's Options," *The Korean Journal of Defense Analysis*, Vol. 17, No. 3 (Winter 2005), 105–27.

Zukeyama, Shigeru. *Okinawa Henkan Kyotei no Kenkyu: Genso no "Kakunuki-Hondonami" Henkanron* A Study of the Okinawa Reversion Agreement: The Myth of the "Without Nuclear Weapons-On Par with the Mainland" Reversion, Tokyo: Chobunsha, 1982.

Index

Socialist Party of Japan (JSP) 257, 285–86
Soong Chang-chih 251
South Korea 314
sovereignty over the Senkaku Islands 3–6, 9–11, 56, 86, 121, 165–67, 170, 172, 176–82, 187–88, 193–99, 215, 251, 254, 264, 280, 286, 310–12; *see also* "residual sovereignty"
Stans, Maurice H. 218
Starr, Robert I. 215–16, 263
Stevenson, John R. 272
Stilwell, Joseph W. Jr. 53, 219
student demonstrations 197–200, 203–9, 214, 251–53, 269, 286–90
Suematsu Kencho 33
Suganuma Unryu 14–15, 36
Sun Yun-suan 212–13, 218
Sunagawa Keisho 140, 143–44
Suzuki, George E. 73–74
Sylvester, Charles T. 184

Taira Ryosho 115, 145–46
Taira Shigeharu 72–73, 75–76
Taiwan Strait crisis (1954–55) 61
Takada Toshisada 53
Takahashi Shogoro 14, 108, 122
Takaoka Daisuke 68, 72, 116–17, 141–44
Takara Gakujutsu 64–67, 116
Takase Jiro 267, 287
Takeiri Yoshikatsu 257
Takeuchi Yukio 7
Tamamura Yakichi 125
Tanaka Kakuei 255, 277
Tang Wu 77–78
Tawada Shinjun 66–67
temporary shelter, Chinese request for 86–87
textile issues 217–25, 271
Thomas, William P. 208, 210
Thomas, William W. 128, 265
Thurmond, Strom 217–18
Timperlake, Edward 11
Tkacik, John J. Jr. 9

Tobaru Yoei 136–39
Togo Fumihiko 161, 164, 170, 177
Tokano Satoko 171
Tokonami Tokuji 116–17
Tokyo Shimbun 258
Tsai Wei-Ping 178, 183, 252

uninhabited islands 181
Union Carbide 130–31
Uotsuri Island 5
Ushiba Nobuhiko 161, 277, 280–81
Uyama Atsushi 268

Wada Tsutomu 261, 274, 279
Waldheim, Kurt 273
Walker, Richard L. 252
Watanabe Koji 182–83
weather station on the Senkakus, proposals for 91–95, 188, 193
Wei Tao-ming 173, 193–94, 198
Westmoreland, William 255
Woods, Rose Mary 224
Wu Po-Chen 118

Xinhua news agency *see* New China News Agency

Yamagata Aritomo 31–33
Yamanaka Sadanori 168, 220, 228, 267
Yamano Kokichi 75, 168
Yang, Chen Ning 254
Yang Hsi-kun 199–201
Yara Chobyo 255
Yara Chokei 74, 126–27, 139–43, 146–47
Yasuda Yutaka 266–67
Yomiuri Shimbun 260
Yoshida Kenzo 263–66
Yoshida Shien 116–17, 142–45
Yoshida Shigenobu 193–94
Yoshino Bunroku 161, 165, 191, 227
Yoshino Kozen 58, 94

Zukeran Choho 312